American Education

The Task and the Teacher

Second Edition

American Education

The Task and the Teacher

Second Edition

John H. Johansen
Northern Illinois University

Harold W. Collins
Northern Illinois University

James A. Johnson
Northern Illinois University

WM. C. BROWN COMPANY PUBLISHERS

Dubuque, Iowa

75; 103, *upper right;* 377, *middle;* 378	Courtesy of Ampex Company, Elk Grove Village, Illinois.
418	Caudill Rowlett Scott, Houston, Texas (CRS) Cox Elementary, Guilford, Conn. Wald and Zigas, Consulting Engineers. CRS Photo.
2; 154; 209; 225; 323; 327; 341; 349; 370, *upper*	Courtesy of Community Educational Television for South Central Pennsylvania.
208; 266; 328; 416	Courtesy of DeKalb Daily Chronicle, DeKalb, Illinois.
39, *upper;* 46; 72, *upper right;* 102; 109; 248; 250, *upper and lower;* 252; 253; 254; 326; 368	Courtesy of DeKalb High School, DeKalb, Illinois.
330	Courtesy of DeKalb Journal, DeKalb, Illinois.
76; 373 *lower right and left*	Courtesy of Eastman Kodak Company
13, *upper left and right;* 14; 15, *left and upper and lower right;* 16; 72, *upper left;* 268; 269; 272; 274; 276; 278; 279; 280; 282; 284	Courtesy of History of Education Research Center, Northern Illinois University, DeKalb, Illinois.
182; 186	Courtesy of Illinois Education Association. Photos by Charli.
425	Joliet Community College, Joliet, Illinois. CRS photo.
74; 345; 351	PS219, Paul Klapper School, Satellite Building, Flushing, New York. Photos by John Bintliff.
7; 65, *upper;* 312; 370, *lower left;* 371, *upper left and right;* 372; 374; 375; 376; 377, *upper right;* 481	Courtesy of Minnesota Mining and Manufacturing Co. (3M) New York, New York. 3M Company Photo.
249; 251	Courtesy of Naperville Central High School, Naperville, Illinois.
10; 80; 106, *upper;* 108; 200; 215; 216; 240; 298; 312; 367; 343	National Education Association. Joe di Dio.
32; 35; 36; 38; 44; 45; 68; 71; 79; 81; 83; 94; 95; 97; 98; 106; 255; 318; 325; 373, *upper left and right;* 390; 391; 392; 401; 480	Courtesy of Northern Illinois University, DeKalb, Illinois.
424	Quincy Vocational-Technical School, Quincy, Mass. Kenneth F. Perry & Associates, Associate Architects. Photo by John Bintliff.
9; 65, *upper right;* 377, *lower;* 378	Courtesy of RCA, Camden, New Jersey.
116	Rohn Engh, photographer.
92	Simmons Junior High School, Aurora, Illinois.
24; 170; 403; 485	Courtesy of Triton College, Northlake, Illinois.
422	Winona Senior High School, Winona, Minnesota. Eckert and Carlson, Associate Architects. CRS photo.

To Our Children

Contents

List of Figures

Preface

This textbook seeks to introduce the reader to teaching as a career. It is relevant to introductory undergraduate education courses and is particularly pertinent for students who might be considering entering teaching and other allied educational careers, both professional and paraprofessional. Special emphasis is given to the importance, development, roles, opportunities, rewards, and frustrations of teaching. The concepts and functions of teacher organizations are also discussed.

American Education: The Task and the Teacher presents an overview of the past roles of education, and the expectations and beliefs that both society and individuals hold for it today. It considers the American educational enterprise in terms of its problems, possibilities, and potentialities. Discussions of patterns of school organization, elements of control, and the basics of school financing are included. The characteristics of learners and the curricula provided for the many different kinds of learners are considered in the light of emerging and innovative methods of instruction, including the use of recent technological advances and multimedia resources. The history of educational thought, practice, and persistent issues is treated as it relates to the contemporary scene.

Illustrative materials, pictorial and graphic, are used along with quotations and examples to assist the reader in identifying with the content. While clarity and brevity were considered to be of prime importance, bibliographic information is provided to enable the reader to pursue his interests in greater depth. Discussion questions and suggested learning activities are presented with each chapter. Included with each chapter is a brief and pertinent article selected to enhance the concepts discussed within that chapter. The articles provide a specific point of view and provide the basis for a provocative discussion.

This edition represents a thorough revision of the book, retaining its clarity and brevity, yet updating useful information. An increased emphasis is placed on the interrelationships among American education, individuals, a pluralistic society and its problems, and the teaching profession.

xx   Valuable contributions to this edition were made by the suggestions of the many users of the previous edition, the opinions of colleagues and students, and the evaluations of experienced reviewers. Appreciation is expressed to the many authors and publishers who granted permission for the use of their materials in the book. Special recognition is given to Nita Collins for her efforts in preparing the manuscript.

Becoming a Teacher

There is probably no better place to begin a book entitled *American Education— the Task and the Teacher* than with a discussion of the importance of teaching and the value of education. How one becomes a teacher, what a teacher does, and the various careers available in the field of education will be discussed. Together these areas tell the contemporary story of the teaching profession. This story is one of both sacrifice and reward. Sacrifice, because one must work long and hard to complete a teacher education program and to become a certified teacher. After becoming a teacher, there is the further sacrifice of having to devote long, difficult hours to one's profession. In a sense, a teacher actually sacrifices a part of himself to his students and to the profession. By the same token, while teaching requires sacrifice from the educator, it also rewards him handsomely. The financial rewards of the teaching profession (discussed in section II) have improved in recent years to the point where educators can now look forward to a life of financial security. Yet another reward that teachers receive from their profession is the knowledge that they are making an extremely valuable contribution

2   to our society—helping to produce the enlightened citizenry essential to our democratic way of life. But perhaps the greatest reward of all is the feeling that one gets from giving to and receiving from our country's youth.

Perhaps the greatest reward of teaching is the knowledge that one is making a lasting contribution to American youth.

chapter 1
The Importance of Teaching as a Career

goals

- Explores the role the teacher plays in the American society.

- Explains why education represents an excellent national investment.

- Presents data on the size of the American educational establishment.

- Provides a glimpse of some great teachers of the past.

- Points out the important role the teacher plays in contemporary America.

The Increasing Importance of the Teacher in Today's Society

Contemporary teachers are in a position to make an even greater contribution to society than were their historical counterparts. This is true mainly because education is much more important today than it has been in the past. Whereas in the past a young person could earn a good living and have a productive career with relatively little formal education, the vast majority of today's youth simply must acquire an extensive educational background to become successful, productive,

4 self-fulfilling citizens. This means that the work of the teacher has become more crucial and important in our society.

Many authorities even feel that education is the only long-range solution to many of our major social problems such as poverty, race relations, delinquency and crime.

Figures 1.1 and 1.2 provide some insight into the value of education in these areas. Figure 1.1 shows the education level of inmates in correctional institutions. The data in this figure point out that prison inmates have significantly less formal education than the general nonprison population. For instance, while 8.4 percent of the U.S. population had four or more years of college education, only 1.1 percent of the prisoners have received that much education. Likewise, while six percent of the U.S. population were limited to four or less years of schooling, 14.4 percent of the prison inmates were so limited. Thirty-four percent of the U.S. population received eight or less years of education while 54.7 percent of the inmates were in that category. These data suggest that education may be a factor in crime prevention. In fact, there are those who go so far as to suggest that a dollar spent on education will likely save a dollar on our nation's crime-fighting bill. While it is impossible to document such an assertion, logic plus data such as that presented in Figure 1.1 suggest that education does indeed have crime prevention value.

> *Teachers everywhere have as important a role to play as politicians and diplomats . . . . One of the most important tasks of the teacher, as I understand it, is to bring to clear consciousness the common ideals for which men should live. These common ideals have a force which unites.*
>
> U Thant

Figure 1.2 suggests another example of the value of education. This figure shows the education level of persons admitted to public mental hospitals. Figure 1.2 indicates that for all age groups there is an inverse relationship between amount of schooling and the rate of admissions to public mental hospitals.

Years of school completed	Percent of population aged 25–64	
	U.S. population	Inmates
Elementary 0–4 years	6.0	14.4
5–8 years	28.0	40.3
High School 1–3 years	20.7	27.6
4 years	27.5	12.4
College 1–3 years	9.4	4.2
4 years or more	8.4	1.1
Total	100.0	100.0

Figure 1.1 Education Level of Inmates in Correctional Institutions.

Source: President's Commission on Law Enforcement and Administration of Justice, *Task Force Report: Corrections* (Washington, D.C.: U.S. Government Printing Office, 1967).

Highest grade completed	Age group (Rate per 100,000 population)		
	25–34	35–44	45–64
All entrants	270.0	345.2	291.1
0–7 years grade school	603.9	691.5	451.2
Completed grade school	589.7	535.0	350.6
Some high school	529.4	530.1	315.6
Completed high school	183.2	250.3	256.1
College	131.8	150.5	135.4

Figure 1.2 Admissions to Public Mental Hospitals by Education Level.

Source: U.S. Department of Health, Education, and Welfare, National Clearinghouse for Mental Health Information, "Admission Rates by Highest Grade of School Completed, State and County Mental Hospitals, 1969," Statistical Note 34 (Rockville, Md.: National Institute of Mental Health, 1970).

Put another way, the greater the amount of education, the lower the rate of admissions to mental hospitals. While it is difficult to document a cause and effect relationship between these two variables, it seems plausible that education contributes to the mental health of our nation.

Education as a National Investment

Education is one of the best economic investments that our nation can make. This fact is substantiated by the information presented in Figure 1.3. As this figure shows, the average person completing less than eight years of formal education earns $225,102 during his lifetime, whereas the average lifetime income for people completing five or more years of college is $592,696. If one takes into account the additional taxes that the college graduate pays during his lifetime, then the money spent on his education becomes an excellent national investment.

This positive relationship between education and national development can also be seen in other statistics and in other countries.

Educational level of men	Lifetime income
Total U.S.	$364,653
Elementary, less than 8 years ...	225,102
8 years ...	270,470
High school, 1–3 years	305,231
4 years	357,166
College, 1–3 years	414,578
4 years	554,859
5 years or more.....	592,696

Figure 1.3 Lifetime Income by Education Level.

Source: U.S. Department of Commerce, Bureau of the Census, "Annual Mean Income, Lifetime Income, and Educational Attainment of Men in the United States, for Selected Years 1956 to 1968," Current Population Reports, series P–60, no. 74 (Washington, D.C.: U.S. Government Printing Office, 1970).

For instance, the United States is a relatively new nation with only approximately five percent of the world population, but also owns approximately one-half of the wealth in the entire world and is recognized as a leader among nations in nearly all facets of life— scientifically, culturally, militarily, diplomatically, and educationally.

Almost without exception, the nations

6 which have emphasized education (such as Denmark, England, Japan, United States, and more recently Russia) have developed thriving economies with relatively healthy gross national products and high standards of living. Conversely, those countries which have not emphasized education (such as most South American and African countries) have not developed well economically even though many of these countries have great natural resources. One can conclude that education is indeed a good national investment—one which pays handsome returns in the forms of a higher standard of living, more productivity, higher scientific achievement, as well as lowering some national expenses such as crime fighting and providing mental health care.

> *A good teacher is first of all a good human being—someone who in personality, character, and attitudes exercises a wholesome and inspiring influence on young people.*
>
> Norman Cousins

This is not to imply that education in the United States or any other country is perfect, nor that education has been very successful in solving some of our most persistent and perplexing problems such as hunger, poor health, human and international relations. In fact, there are those who claim that education has little impact on solving many of our social problems. Christopher Jencks, for example, claims that research that he and his colleagues have conducted suggests that schools do not contribute significantly to adult equality in America and therefore, if we want economic equality in our society, we will have

to get it by changing our economic institutions rather than by changing our schools.[1]

Much of the remainder of this book enumerates and analyzes these difficult social problems in an effort to help the reader understand the implications they hold for the task of the teacher.

> *If you become a teacher, by your pupils you'll be taught.*
>
> Anna

The Enormity of the Task

Teaching is by far the largest of all the professions. As of the 1970–71 school year, approximately 59.2 million Americans (about one-third of our total population) were enrolled in various kinds of schools. Figure 1.4 shows a breakdown of these enrollments.

Level of instruction	Fall 1970
Kindergarten through grade 8	36,800,000
public schools	(32,600,000)
private schools	(4,200,000)
Grades 9–12	14,800,000
public schools	(13,400,000)
private schools	(1,400,000)
Higher education	7,600,000
public schools	(5,600,000)
private schools	(2,000,000)
Grand total	59,200,000

Figure 1.4 Enrollment in Educational Institutions in the United States—1970.

Source: U.S. Office of Education, *Statistics of Public Schools, Fall 1970* (Washington, D.C.: U.S. Government Printing Office, 1971).

1. Christopher Jencks, et al., *Inequality: A Reassessment of the Effect of Family and Schooling in America* (New York: Basic Books, Inc., Publishers).

Figure 1.5 further shows the enrollment in public schools at each grade level. These two figures help to point out the enormity of the task of educating the nation's youth.

Grade	Number of students
Preprimary	2,557,000
1st	3,810,000
2nd	3,651,000
3rd	3,665,000
4th	3,677,000
5th	3,636,000
10th	3,455,000
11th	3,129,000
12th	2,774,000

Figure 1.5 Enrollment in Public Schools at Each Grade Level—1970.

Source: U.S. Office of Education, *Statistics of Public Schools, Fall 1970* (Washington, D.C.: U.S. Government Printing Office, 1971).

There are approximately 2,600,000 full-time teachers in the United States whose function it is to accomplish this task.

> *A teacher affects eternity; he can never tell where his influence stops.*
> Henry Adams

Testimonials for Teaching

Perhaps the best single indication of the high regard that people generally have for teachers and for the importance of the teaching profession can be found in comments that individual citizens make about this subject. A number of such testimonials can be found in an excellent book entitled *Why Teach?* which was edited by Professor D. Louise

A teacher is a highly educated, well-prepared professional who is respected in the American society.

Sharp. Several of these comments about the teaching profession are reproduced here.

Mrs. Alice K. Leopold, who served as Assistant to the Secretary of Labor for Women's Affairs during President Eisenhower's

8 administration, had this to say about the importance of teaching:

———— ◆ ◆ ————

Everyone who works at a job he likes and does well contributes to the well-being of all of us. But some jobs are indispensable to our very survival. Teaching, like nursing, is one of these.

Unless our children learn how to read, write, and calculate they cannot live without contant help from others. Unless they learn how to develop their talents and overcome their handicaps, they cannot work effectively and harmoniously with others for the common good. Unless they learn from the preceding generation the heritage of the past, they cannot add to our progress.

Teachers share with parents and religious leaders the main responsibility for this large educational task. They accept the lion's share of the responsibility for seeing that young people acquire the knowledge, skills, attitudes, and habits they will need as adults. Although all teachers are alike in this responsibility, there is infinite variety in the personality and background each brings to her task. This variety enriches our children, offering countless opportunities to each child for challenge and stimulation along the lines of his particular abilities and interests.[2]

———— ◆ ◆ ————

Mary Ellen Chase—teacher and award-winning author—has the following to say about teachers and teaching.

———— ◆ ◆ ————

I have always been more than a little suspicious of those who go into the teaching pro-

2. D. Louise Sharp, *Why Teach?* p. 129. From *Why Teach?* edited by D. Louise Sharp. Copyright © 1957 by Holt, Rinehart and Winston, Inc. Reprinted by permission of Holt, Rinehart and Winston, Inc.

fession from missionary zeal, or even of those who remain in it for the same insufficient, if not dangerous reason. In my experience, lofty purposes alone do not often make good teachers. Teaching is, without doubt, a serious business; but overseriousness in a teacher is fatal. It is excitement in teaching, the sheer fun of it, the sharing of knowledge and enthusiasm, the opportunity to go on learning, which make teaching, at its best, not only the highest of the arts, in my opinion, but the most exhilarating of occupations.

The increasing prestige of the teaching profession is due not only to the increasing importance of education in our society, but also to the increasing competence of teachers.

Importance of Teaching

As a matter of sober fact and as all honest, first-class teachers will acknowledge, the histrionic qualities of the teachers are of more value than the mere didactic, however noble their aim. For in the best teachers lies always something of the actor, of that creative gift of so entering into one's subject that the subject, whatever it is, is reborn, reclothed, reenacted.

I am also skeptical as to the value of that patience, without which the teacher is presumably doomed to failure. When I look back upon the few really great teachers I have known, it is their sublime impatience which is most memorable; impatience with mediocre or sloppy work; with laziness, lack of taste or of moral sense; righteous rage against apathy and dullness. To me, patience per se in the teacher is a perilous virtue, prophetic of little except indifference both in himself and in his students.

> *He who governs well, leads the ignorant; he who teaches well, trains them to govern themselves in justice, mercy, and peace.*
>
> Alexander G. Ruthven

I began to teach not because I felt in any sense a vocation or calling, but merely because at the time it seemed the most sensible, perhaps even selfish, thing to do in order to continue to enjoy my love of books and to earn a necessary and respectable living. It just happened to suit me admirably. I have never known a dull moment in nearly fifty years at it, whether in a Maine country school where I began my work, in public and private high schools, in classes in adult education, or in college. I have taught or, more accurately, studied with, Maine coast children, midwestern and western high school students, taxi drivers, plumbers, streetcar conductors,

Each teacher must utilize his or her own personality and particular talents to develop a challenging and stimulating school program for each student.

housewives, and Smith College girls. I am extremely doubtful of any so-called "good" which I may have given them, but entirely certain that they have given me the best life anyone could have.

My advice to those who are now considering teaching, in these days when the young ponder more about their callings than

10 they did in my youth, is similar to that given by someone or other about marriage: "Don't go into it unless you can't help yourself!"[3]

———— •·• ————

Yet another famous author, Norman Cousins, gives the following testimonial about the importance of teaching.

———— •·• ————

A good teacher is first of all a good human being—someone who in personality, charac-

3. Ibid., pp. 25–26.

ter, and attitudes exercises a wholesome and inspiring influence on young people. I underline the word "inspiring" because I believe that of all the many qualities that go into the making of a good teacher, the ability to inspire is perhaps paramount. The names that come to mind in any discussion of great American teachers—names such as Horace Mann, Mark Hopkins, Charles Eliot, John Dewey—are the names of inspired teachers.

By inspiration I have in mind the quality of teaching that somehow strikes a spark deep inside the student, raising his level of awareness in life, enlarging rather than satisfying his natural curiosity, opening up a sense of

A good deal of a teacher's time is devoted to getting to know each student as an individual.

individual capacity and responsibility, holding up before the student an ideal worth pursuing and realizing as a person. The factual content of education may fall away from the individual over the years, or it may become obsolete; what is not lost, however, is the deep influence of a great and inspiring teacher, someone whose general approach to knowledge and life serves as a practical guide for the individual in the world beyond the school.

Obviously, inspiration is a quality not easily come by, whether with respect to teaching or any other branch of public service. Nor is it easy to devise means for measuring a teacher's ability to inspire. But the importance of this intangible quality is so great that it

should be recognized in principle as the prime essential of a good teacher.[4]

Lastly, Rabbi Morris Silverman, who, among other things, has received much acclaim for his work in the field of civil rights, has the following to say about the importance of teaching:

Who does not recall the influence of dedicated teachers upon his life? My love of good music can be traced back nearly half a century

4. Ibid., pp. 30–31.

A teacher influences hundreds of lives and has an opportunity to help children become good citizens, earn good livings, and live full, rich lives.

12 to the principal of a public school in Brockton, Massachusetts. I remember him vividly, a colorful personality, bearded, riding to school on his bicycle. I can still hear his pitch pipe as he taught our class once a week and explained classical music.

I can still quote hundreds of lines of poetry because of a high school teacher in Utica, New York, who made English literature a fascinating subject. My present interest in a projected history of the local Jewish community goes back to the inspiration and guidance of a college instructor at Ohio State University who was later called to teach at Harvard. All can recall similar experiences.

I come from a people who stressed learning as a cardinal principle, education as a lifelong process, and that accords the greatest honor and respect to teachers and scholars. The very title "Rabbi" means "my teacher." "The guardians of a city are not its military but its consecrated teachers." This is one of the many sayings in our ancient literature that emphasizes the position of teachers.

Although preaching is a form of teaching, I find among my varied activities that the most rewarding, stimulating, and satisfying is the actual teaching of two classes—one of teenagers, the other adults.

The genius of Sir Isaac Newton would have been lost to the world were it not for a teacher by the name of Mr. Stokes who recognized the talent in the student and persuaded his mother to let him continue his education.

The teaching profession offers a great opportunity for influencing the lives of hundreds of people and of guiding them not only to earn a living; but to live a good life.[5]

Great Teachers of the Past

One of the reasons that teaching is now a respected profession and that contempo-

5. Ibid., pp. 197–98.

rary educators occupy a prestigious place in our society is that there have been many great teachers in the past. All of us can recall teachers that we have had who were influential in the shaping of our lives.

History is replete with educators who have made great contributions to mankind. Space permits mentioning only a few at this time.

Socrates (470–399 B.C.) is often mentioned as one of the world's first truly great teachers. This man, who lived in the Greek city-state of Athens, devoted his life to teaching the students who followed him wherever he went. His main method of teaching consisted of asking leading questions which helped the student to discover the answer for himself. In fact, this technique has been so closely identified with Socrates that it has come to be known as the "Socratic Method" of teaching. Socrates was eventually put to death for inciting the people against the government in his relentless search for truth. His dedication to teaching, knowledge, and truth inspired many of his students to become renowned educators in their own right. Plato became one of Socrates' most famous students.

> *The very spring and root of honesty and virtue lie in good education.*
>
> Plutarch

Another famous teacher of his day was Quintilian (A.D. 35–95), a Roman educator. Quintilian, also a prolific educational writer, exhibited a perceptive understanding of students far in advance of his time when he wrote:

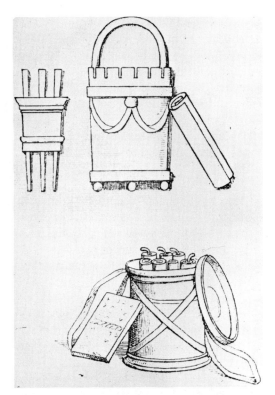

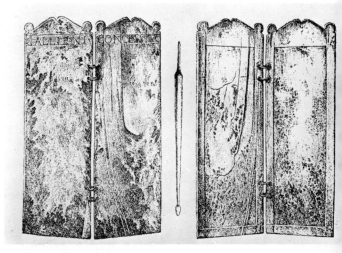

Dipticha, or Roman wax tablet with stylus—found on the Esquiline Hill, Rome, and preserved in the local museum. The tablets were covered with wax and were used for accounting or in schools by writing on the wax with the stylus. The name on the upper end of the left illustration, Galleri Concessi, shows its owner to have been a man of some importance.

Relics of a Roman school from a wall painting now found in a museum at Naples. The left-hand case contains three styli for writing; the upper right is a capsa containing rolls or books. Leaning against it is a book. At the bottom a capsa is open showing the scrolls. Leaning against it on the left is a writing tablet.

I am by no means in favor of whipping boys, though I know it to be a general practice. In the first place, whipping is unseemly, and if you suppose the boys to be somewhat grown up, it is an affront in the highest degree. In the next place, if a boy's ability is so poor as to be proof against reproach he will, like a worthless slave, become insensible to blows. Lastly, if a teacher is assiduous and careful, there is no need to use force. I shall observe further that while a boy is under the rod he experiences pain and fear. The shame of this experience dejects and discourages many pupils, makes them shun being seen, and may even weary them of their lives.

One of the most famous teachers of the Dark Ages was an Englishman by the name of Alcuin. Alcuin became Charlemagne's educational advisor and established the Palace School at Frankland which Charlemagne himself frequently attended.

There were many famous educators during the Renaissance and Reformation periods, including Erasmus (1466–1536), Me-

The lower schoolroom of Eton College founded in 1440. The wood from which these benches were made, as well as the wainscoting and timbers in the room, was taken from the wrecked vessels of the Spanish Armada. This was one of the means by which patriotic ideals were instilled in the English boys.

lanchthon (1497–1560), Ignatius of Loyola (1491–1556), Jean Baptiste de la Salle (1651–1719) and Johann Amos Comenius (1592–1670). Comenius authored a great number of textbooks. Comenius's textbooks were some of the very first to contain pictures. Comenius was also among the first to recommend that a series of schools should be established. Concerning this point he wrote, "There should be a maternal school in each family; an elementary school in each district; a gymnasium in each city; an academy in each kingdom, or even in each considerable province."[6]

There were a countless number of great educators during the eighteenth and nine-

teenth centuries. Some of the famous American educators from this period, such as Benjamin Franklin, Horace Mann, Henry Barnard, and Samuel Hall, are discussed in more detail elsewhere in this book. There were also a number of famous European educators during this time whose work greatly influenced American education. These included, among others, Jean Jacques Rousseau (1712–1778), Johann Friedrich Herbart (1776–1841), Friedrich Froebel (1782–1852), and Johann Heinrich Pestalozzi (1746–1827). Of these, Pestalozzi, a Swiss educator, stands out as one who gained a great deal of fame as the founder of two schools—one at Burgdorf (1800–1804) and another at Yverdun (1805–1825).

It was at these schools that Pestalozzi put into practice his educational beliefs that children should be treated with love, respect, understanding, and patience (a belief that was in contradiction to the prevailing, religiously inspired view that children were born full of sin and inherently bad). Pestalozzi reflected his beliefs when he wrote:

———— • ————

I was convinced that my heart would change the condition of my children just as promptly as the sun of spring would reanimate the earth benumbed by the winter. . . . It was necessary that my children should observe, from dawn to evening, at every moment of the day, upon my brow and on my lips, that my affections were fixed on them, that their happiness was my happiness, and that their pleasures were my pleasures. . . .

I was everything to my children. I was alone with them from morning till night. . . . Their hands were in my hands. Their eyes were fixed on my eyes.[7]

———— • ————

6. G. Compayre, *History of Pedagogy,* trans. W. H. Payne (Boston: D. C. Heath and Co., 1885), p. 128.

7. Ibid., p. 425.

The direction in which education starts a man will determine his future life.
Plato

Pestalozzi also believed that teachers should use objects and games to help students learn. In fact, he developed a series of teaching materials which were very advanced for their time. A number of American educators visited Pestalozzi's schools and brought many of his ideas back to the United States where they were put into practice.

The number of Americans who have earned a reputation as outstanding educators is great indeed. In fact, to list them

Pestalozzi's first teaching experience was at Stans in 1798. There he took charge of a group of children orphaned by one of the massacres of the French Revolution. There were no teaching aids so Pestalozzi taught by using objects. This illustration is from an early 19th century woodcut.

The library of the University of Leyden in the sixteenth century. By this time, the library had become an important part of the university. The books are chained to the shelves so they could not be stolen—an indication of their scarcity and value. Leyden was founded in 1575, and for over a century was the center of advanced thought and instruction.

Pestalozzi eventually moved to Yverdun where, at this castle, he conducted an experimental school for twenty years. Educators came from all around the world to visit and study the teaching methods and materials he developed here.

	Cornix cornicatur, á á	A a
	The Crow crieth.	
	Agnus balat, *b é é é*	B b
	The Lamb blaiteth.	
	Cicáda ftridet, *ci ci*	C c
	The Grafhopper chirpeth.	
	Upupa dicit, *du du*	D d
	The Whooppoo faith.	
	Infans ejulat, *é é é*	E e
	The Infant crieth.	
	Ventus flat, *fi fi*	F f
	The Wind bloweth.	
	Anfer gingrit, *ga ga*	G g
	The Goofe gagleth.	
	Os halat, *háh háh*	H h
	The mouth breatheth out.	
	Mus mintrit, *í í í*	I i
	The Moufe chirpeth.	
	Anas tetrinnit, *kha kha*	K k
	The Duck quaketh.	
	Lupus ululat, *lu ulu*	L l
	The Wolf howleth.	
	Urfus murmurat, *mum mum*	M m
	The Bear grumbleth.	
	B 2	*Felis*

A page from the early edition of one of Comenius's books, *Orbis Pictus,* published in 1657. Comenius's textbooks were among the first to use pictures. On this page, the idea was to have the child learn the sound of each letter in the alphabet through some sound in nature with which he was familiar. Hence, the illustration of the wind, the goose, the cricket, etc.

would be an impossible task. Perhaps it will suffice to say that educators such as Horace Mann, Henry Barnard, Samuel Hall, Cyrus Pierce, John Griscom, Noah Webster, Edward Sheldon, David Camp, William Phelps, Charles and Frank McMurry, Francis Parker, John Dewey, George Counts and many, many others far too numerous to mention, have made very significant contributions to our society through their various educational works. Many contemporary educators are also among our leading statesmen, scientists, artists, civil rights leaders, Nobel prize winners, civic leaders, authors, researchers, and philosophers. In fact, many educators can be found in all of the most important walks of life in our American society.

> *The future of America is written on school blackboards and in student notebooks. The quality of thought in our classrooms today will determine the quality of our lives a generation hence.*
>
> Lyndon B. Johnson

In conclusion, it is hoped that this brief chapter has pointed out that teaching is a worthy profession, is highly regarded by Americans, and is one of the most important and potentially rewarding careers in our society. A teacher has an excellent opportunity to live a rewarding and socially significant life—an opportunity not equally afforded by many other careers.

> *A world whose schools are unreformed is an unreformed world.*
>
> H. G. Wells

Point of View

This chapter has attempted to set the stage for the rest of the book by discussing the importance and role of public education in the United States. Not everyone agrees about what the role of education is or should be. For instance, some believe that education should only reflect and be responsible to our society's values and needs. Others believe that our schools should change and mold our society. The following article entitled "The

Role of Public Education" represents one point of view. This selection has been authored by one of the most respected educators in America—Dr. Robert Maynard Hutchins. Dr. Hutchins is past president of the University of Chicago and currently chairman of the Center for the Study of Democratic Institutions. Dr. Hutchins is well known as a critic of contemporary American education. It is from this perspective that he discusses the role of public education. This selection should provide the reader with challenging ideas about the role of public education in the United States.

The Role of Public Education

Robert Maynard Hutchins

The Constitution of the United States contemplates government by discussion, with all citizens participating in it. The members of a political community do not have to agree with one another—the First Amendment, which deals with freedom of speech, assumes that Americans will not—but they do need to understand one another. The aim is twofold, unity and diversity, an aim we see reflected in John Stuart Mill's argument for public education in his essay, *On Liberty.*

If this is the ideal, what part does public education have to play in it? Those who have been leading the antischool campaign have ignored this question. Yet it is, after all, *the* question. It cannot be answered by saying that we should have no schools at all or that we should let our children go or that we should

Robert Maynard Hutchins, "The Role of Public Education," *Today's Education,* November-December 1973, pp. 80–83. Used by permission.

encourage them to pursue their own interests or that we should have schools they could drop into and out of as they pleased or that the schools should be turned over to parents or private businesses, for such decisions would promote cultural, social, and economic segregation and the kind of individualism Tocqueville saw as a danger to every democracy.

The doctrine of every man for himself, or every nation for itself, loses its charm in an interdependent world. This doctrine has to give way before the idea of a world community. We have to understand and rely on our common humanity if we are to survive in any condition worthy to be called human. Everything else sinks into triviality in comparison with this task. To consider most of the topics of current education discussion is irrelevant to the real issue we face. So is the great antischool campaign, except that if it succeeds, we shall be deprived of the one institution that could most effectively assist in drawing out our common humanity.

Democracy is the best form of government precisely because it calls upon the citizen to be self-governing and to take his part in the self-governing political community. This is the answer to the individual/community dilemma. The individual cannot become a human being without the democratic political community; and the democratic political community cannot be maintained without independent citizens who are qualified to govern themselves and others through the democratic political community.

The primary aim of the educational system in a democratic country conscious of the impending world community is to draw out the common humanity of those committed to its charge. This requires careful avoidance of that which may be immediately interesting

18   but which is transitory, or that which is thought to have some practical value under the circumstances of the time but which is likely to be valueless if the circumstances change.

The most elementary truth about education is the one most often disregarded: It takes time. The educator must therefore remember that unless he wants to be a custodian or a sitter or a playmate, he must ask himself whether what he and his pupils are doing will have any relevance 10 years from now. It does not seem an adequate reply that they were having fun, any more than it would be to say they were learning a trade. Nor would it be much more adequate to say they were learning what their parents wanted. The community includes parents but is not confined to them. Taxes for the support of schools are paid by bachelors, spinsters, childless couples, and the elderly on the theory that the whole community is interested in and benefits from its schools.

The first object of any school must be to equip the student with the tools of learning. "Communication skills," which is the contemporary jargon for reading, writing, figuring, speaking, and listening, appear to have permanent relevance. These arts are important in any society at any time. They are more important in a democratic society than in any other, because the citizens of a democratic society have to understand one another. They are indispensable in a world community: They are arts shared by people everywhere. Without them the individual is deprived and the community is too. Learning these arts cannot be left to the choices of children or parents.

The second object of any school—and this is vital to a democratic community—should be to open new worlds to the young.

Whatever the charms of the neighborhood school, whatever the pleasures of touring one's native city, whatever the allure of the present, emphasis upon the immediate environment and its current condition must narrow the mind and prevent understanding of the wider national or world community and any real comprehension of the present. Hence, those who would center education on the interests of children and on their surroundings are working contrary to the demands contemporary society is making upon any educational system.

The third object of any education institution must be to get the young to understand their cultural heritage. This, too, is in the interest of the individual and the community. Comprehension of the cultural heritage is the means by which the bonds uniting the community are strengthened. The public school is the only agency that can be entrusted with this obligation.

Within the limits set by the Constitution and by the necessity of allocating resources in the most economical way, school districts, schools, and classes should be as small as possible. Even if, according to the Coleman Report, such changes would not materially affect the achievement of children, they would facilitate variety and experimentation, and they would make schools less formidable to those who must attend.

Ways must be found to break the lockstep, the system by which all pupils proceed at the same pace through the same curriculum for the same number of years. The disadvantages of small schools can be overcome by building them in clusters, each with somewhat different courses and methods and permitting students to avail themselves of anything offered in any one. This is an extension of the idea of dual enrollment or shared time, which now exists everywhere, and which allows students in one school to take advantage of what is taught in another, even if one is private and the other public.

Variety in the methods and curriculum is one way of breaking the lockstep. Another is allowing the student to proceed at his own rate of speed. Under the present system the slow learner is eventually thrown into despair because he cannot keep up, and the fast learner is in the same condition because he has "nothing to do." If we are to have a graded curriculum, we can overcome some of the handicaps it imposes by substituting examinations for time spent and encouraging the student to present himself for them whenever in his opinion he is ready to take them.

It is self-evident that if a course of study is designed to provide the minimum requisites for democratic citizenship, nobody can be permitted to fail. If, then, the basic curriculum is revised as proposed above, so that it is limited to studies essential to the exercise of citizenship, it follows that grades would be eliminated and with them the invidious distinction between winners and losers. We have reason to believe that everybody is educable. The rate and method of education may vary; the aim of basic education is the same with all individuals, and the obligation of the public schools is to achieve it with all. On this principle, if there is failure, it is the failure of the school, not of the pupil.

I take for granted the adoption or adaption of many of those reforms about which so much noise has been made of late. The critics of the schools have performed a public service in calling attention to shortcomings that can be repaired by keeping them in mind and working on them. Interest, for example, can be restored to schooling without coming to the indefensible conclusion that whatever is

not immediately interesting to children should be omitted from their education.

About some other matters, the elementary and secondary schools can do little or nothing. They cannot do much to change parental attitudes, though they should certainly try by keeping in touch with the families of pupils. They can do nothing about the socioeconomic status or the slum environment of the children in their charge. The present efforts in preschool education have a trifling effect in improving the conditions of the earliest years in the lives of slum children. The schools can do nothing about the high taxes that infuriate their no-nonsense, hard-headed critics. They can see to it that money is not wasted, but the definition of waste depends upon an understanding of the purpose of the activity and the best methods of accomplishing it.

The purpose of the activity is the crucial question. The purpose of the public schools is not accomplished by having them free, universal, and compulsory. They may do many things for the young: They may amuse them, comfort them, look after their health, and keep them off the streets. But they are not public schools unless they start their pupils toward an understanding of what it means to be a self-governing citizen of a self-governing political community.

The conclusion of Christopher Jencks's book, *Inequality,* is that schools should be pleasant places for children. Because one child's pleasure is another child's poison, schools should vary according to the preferences children display. Why the power of the state should be invoked to compel children to enjoy themselves remains obscure. If a child and his parents agree that he has a better time at home than he has at school, why should he not stay home? If he and his parents have no

20 interest in education, and if the community has no interest in having him educated, why not simply give up education?

This is in effect what Carl Bereiter advocates in an article in the *Harvard Educational Review,* called, in all seriousness, "Schools Without Education." I can understand him only as proposing the abandonment of all institutions he calls educational.

To Mr. Bereiter education is "the deliberate development of human personality, the making of citizens. . . . Schools cannot cease to be places where intellectual growth and personality development go on, but they can cease to be places where an effort is made to direct or shape these processes. . . . Parents typically educate, and it's my contention . . . that they are the only ones who have a clear-cut right to educate."

If parents are the only ones who have a clear-cut right to educate, the interest of the community in education or in "the making of citizens" is at best unclear, Bereiter, like Jencks, favors voucher plans that would enable parents to decide how tax dollars would be spent on their children.

He proposes to retain schools, apparently compulsory, for two purposes: child care and training in reading, writing, and arithmetic. If parents have the only clear-cut right to educate their children, one would think they have the only clear-cut right to determine what care their children had outside the home or indeed whether they needed any at all. If compulsory education is unjustifiable, compulsory child care seems less so.

If parents are for any reason not interested in having the child learn to read, write, and calculate, why should the state assert the right to "train" him to do so? Reading, writing, and arithmetic are the essential tools of education. They have other uses, but a parent unconcerned about education might feel that he did not want his child to waste much time acquiring them. If education is the exclusive territory of the parent, his conclusion on reading, writing, and arithmetic should have great weight.

Since reading and writing, if not arithmetic, are certain to have an educational effect, depending on what is read and written in learning to read and write, training in these activities comes dangerously close to the process that parents, and parents only, have a right to direct.

Mr. Bereiter says, "The need for training arises from the incompleteness of normal experience." This is precisely the way the need for education arises. To intimate that the normal experience of a slum child does not teach him arithmetic, whereas it does "make a citizen" out of him is to display a lamentable ignorance of the facts of life. Consider the implications of Bereiter's recommendation that after training is completed, we should "then simply provide enough resources in the environment that the child can put the skills to use if he feels inclined."

The conclusions of Jencks and Bereiter are based on the proposition that schools make no difference. The logical result would be to abolish them or at least any compulsion to attend them. This would also be the result of the opposite argument, advanced by Joel H. Spring: that schools make too much difference. In his book, *Education and the Rise of the Corporate State,* the community is the villain. It uses the schools as an "instrument of social control," to fit the young into the established social, economic, and political structure. The power of the school is enormous, and it must be broken in order to achieve democracy, which means "freedom to choose one's own goals and the opportunity to develop one's own life-style."

Whereas Jencks and Bereiter ignore the community and make light of schools as ineffective, Spring thinks of the community as the modern Medusa and finds the schools all too effective in her service. He cannot stand "socialization." Neither can I, chiefly because I do not know what it means. When it appears, as it often does, to be synonymous with Carl Bereiter's definition of the purpose of education—making citizens—it seems sensible enough.

According to Spring: "The solution is not to change the goals and directions of socialization and social control. This is impossible. As long as the public schools take responsibility for the socialization of the child, social adaptation to the institution becomes inevitable. . . . The only possible solution is to end the power of the schools." If "socialization" as Spring uses the word can be equated with "education" as Bereiter uses it, then the way to end the power of the schools is to restrict their educational efforts along the lines Jencks and Bereiter propose. This means the community would have no interest in what went on in the schools.

The novel definition of democracy put forward by Spring—freedom to choose one's own goals and the opportunity to develop one's own life-style—leads to the conclusion, by what it omits as much as by what it contains, that there can be no such thing as a democratic community anyway. A community of any kind must impose some limits on the freedom to choose one's own goals and develop one's own life-style. Those who talk about a community at all, even those who

refer to it in the most high-minded, disinterested, and (it seems to me) reasonable way, play a consistently fiendish role in Spring's book.

There is no easy way by which a political community can make itself better. It seems doubtful that it can do so by leaving education, "the making of citizens," to chance. The whims of children are unreliable guides and the vagaries of parents not much better. There is some evidence that compulsory schooling came to existence to rescue children from their families, and neglect and exploitation by parents are visible in every American city.

How, then, do we change the status quo? If I understand the authors discussed here, they hold we can do nothing about it through educational institutions. Jencks and Bereiter believe these institutions can make no difference. Spring says they can do nothing but sustain the existing order. What would happen if the schools or compulsory attendance at them were abolished and "the making of citizens" were left to parents? The status quo would be maintained—or would deteriorate.

This must be so because those who had the power would start with all the advantages, and their children would end with them. The restraints now placed on snobbishness and exclusivity, on prejudice, would disappear and any idea of the common good would vanish into thin air.

But perhaps there is nothing in that idea or in the idea of community, anyway. Since there is no space for argument, I shall have to content myself for the moment with the assertion that man has never been able to live without the community and that, if he is to live well, he must try to make the community as good as it can possibly be.

The American political community is

22 based on the notion of the continuous engagement of all the people in dialogue about their common concerns. I am aware of the obstacles that make this dialogue an ideal rather than a reality. I am also aware that an educational system operates within severe limitations. It cannot proclaim a revolution and survive.

But to proclaim rededication to basic American principles, to announce a commitment to prepare the rising generation for that dialogue which it should carry on, to enunciate the reasons why the rising generation should be prepared, and to work out the methods by which it could be is within the scope—and I hope the competence—of American educators.

American citizens have an awful responsibility: They have to try to understand the world. Of course the public schools cannot provide this understanding. But statistics showing the dubious results of our present efforts will not convince me that it is impossible to formulate an educational program that will make a difference in the degree of understanding the citizen achieves.

————◆•◆————

QUESTIONS FOR DISCUSSION

1. What is your reaction to the "point of view" article by Robert Maynard Hutchins?
2. To what degree, if any, do you believe education to be a good national investment?
3. How much prestige do you believe contemporary teachers have in the eyes of the general public? What evidence do you have to support your answer?
4. You and three others (not teachers) are playing bridge. One of the others asks you, "I understand that Sally Jones is a student in one of your classes. She strikes me as being a rather dull girl. Do you know what her I.Q. is?" What would you say?
5. What do you see as the advantages and disadvantages of teaching as a career?

SUPPLEMENTARY LEARNING ACTIVITIES

1. Interview an elementary or secondary school teacher to discuss how he/she feels about teaching as a career.
2. Have each member of your class write a brief description of the characteristics of the best teacher they ever had. Compare these qualities listed by the class members.
3. Make a list of the most important questions that you have in your mind as you consider a career in teaching.
4. Attempt to locate in the library some additional material dealing with the value of education as a national investment. Read this material and compare it to your own beliefs on this topic.
5. Invite a member of another profession (medicine, law, engineering, etc.) to speak to your class on the subject of the importance of teaching.

SELECTED REFERENCES

Alexander, William M. *Are You a Good Teacher?* New York: Holt, Rinehart and Winston, Inc., 1959.

Boyer, William H. "Education for Survival." *Phi Delta Kappan* 52 (January 1971): 258–62.

Darling, Charles M., III. *Prospectives for the 70's and 80's.* New York: National Industrial Conference Board, Inc., 1970.

Fantini, Mario D. "Schools for the 70's: Institutional Reform." *Today's Education* 59 (April 1970): 43–44, 60–62.

Goodlad, John I. "The Future of Learning: Into the 21st Century." *Bulletin* 24 (March 1971): 1, 4–5. Washington, D.C.: American Association of Colleges for Teacher Education, 1971.

Haskew, Laurence D., and Jonathon C. McLendon. *This Is Teaching*. rev. ed. Chicago: Scott, Foresman and Company, 1962.

Lindsey, Margaret, ed. *New Horizons for the Teaching Profession*. National Commission on Teacher Education and Professional Standards, National Education Association. Washington, D.C.: National Education Association Publications, 1961.

Mason, Ward S. "The Beginning Teacher: Status and Career Orientations." U.S. Office of Education, circular 644, 1961. Washington, D.C.: U.S. Government Printing Office, 1961.

Michael-Smith, Harold. "It Takes Self-Understanding," *NEA Journal* 49(1960): 37–40.

National Education Association, Department of Classroom Teachers. *Classroom Teachers Speak on Teaching as a Profession*. Washington, D.C.: National Education Association Publications, 1960.

Peterson, Houston, ed. *Great Teachers*. New York: Random House, Inc. Vintage Books, 1946.

Polley, Ira. "What's Right with American Education?" *Phi Delta Kappan* 51 (September 1969): 13–15.

Ragan, William B. *Teaching America's Children*. New York: Holt, Rinehart and Winston, Inc., 1961.

Richey, Robert W. *Planning for Teaching*. 3rd ed. New York: McGraw-Hill Book Company, 1963.

Shane, Harold G., and Owen N. Nelson. "What Will the Schools Become?" *Phi Delta Kappan* 52 (June 1971): 596–98.

Sharp, D. Louise. *Why Teach?* New York: Henry Holt & Co., 1957.

Stinnett, T. M. "Reordering Goals and Roles: An Introduction." In *Unfinished Business of the Teaching Profession in the 1970's*, pp. 1–7. Bloomington, Ind.: Phi Delta Kappa, 1971.

Thomas, Lawrence G., et al. *Perspective on Teaching*. Englewood Cliffs, N.J.: Prentice-Hall, Inc., 1961.

Toffler, Alvin. *Future Shock*. New York: Random House, Inc., 1970.

Wasson, Margaret. "Teaching Is Exciting." Washington: Association for Childhood Education International, bulletin no. 88, 1951.

"What Is a Well Educated Man?" *NEA Journal* 51(1962): 22–25.

Who's a Good Teacher? American Association of School Administrators. Washington, D.C.: National Education Association Publications, 1961.

chapter 2

Teacher Education Today

goals

- Identifies the personal qualifications desired for teaching.

- Points out why people become teachers, in hope of providing a yard-stick against which a college student may measure his/her own motives for entering the teaching profession.

- Describes typical contemporary programs for training teachers.

- Explores one of the newer innovative approaches to teacher preparation—competency-based teacher education (CBTE).

- Explains current teacher certification requirements.

- Discusses teacher certification reciprocity among states.

- Provides the reader with a glimpse of what it is like to be a teacher.

My warmest congratulations go out to each of you for the decision you have made to follow a teaching career.

Today—as never before—we rest our hopes for America on the teachers of America. We know that our future is being forged in the

26 *classrooms and campuses of our nation. We see the wisdom of an uncompromising commitment to educational excellence and expansion.*

So you have chosen well. And America will be richer for your dedication to a task that holds the promise of a better tomorrow.

I wish you Godspeed as our nation's custodians of opportunity for the children who will inherit the precious heritage we share.[1]

Lyndon B. Johnson

Yesterday's Teachers

The teacher in America has historically been ridiculed by his fellow citizens. In the past, a teacher has often been depicted as an untalented, poor undesirable who could make a living no other way. Examples of this characterization include the following:

———•———

Built like a scarecrow, a gangling, pinheaded, flat-topped oaf. But what would anyone expect? He was just a teacher.

(Washington Irving's Ichabod Crane)

A ridiculous figure, his bald head covered with an ill-fitting wig . . . a man who had aspired to be a doctor but who had been forced by poverty to be nothing more than a schoolmaster.

(Mark Twain's description of "Old Dobbins")

Their teacher was a gaunt, red-faced spinster, with fierce, glaring eyes.

(A teacher in Thomas Wolfe's *Look Homeward, Angel*)

1. ASCUS, *Teaching Opportunities for You* (Hershey, Penn.: Association for School and University Staffing, 1968), p. 3.

Those who can, do: those who can't, teach.

(Attributed to George Bernard Shaw)

———•———

One can understand why teachers were viewed this way by briefly examining the history of teacher education. We might first postulate that teaching may well be one of the world's oldest tasks. Certainly early man spent much time instructing his young in the intricacies of hunting and gathering food, knowledge of the world as he knew it, and the secret rituals of early social life. But it was not until the development of symbolic language that formal education took place outside the structure of the family in what might be called schools. These first schools probably came into existence about 2000 B.C. The teachers in these first schools were probably religious men whose aim it was to pass on religious values and attitudes.

While schools have existed for approximately 4,000 years, specific efforts to train teachers are less than 300 years old. One of the early training schools was established in 1685 by Jean Baptiste de la Salle (1651–1719) at Rheims, France.[2] The first known teacher-training school in the United States was that established in 1823 by Samuel Hall at Concord, Vermont. Despite these early, humble efforts to train teachers, it may be said that until the twentieth century, most teachers had very little, if any, specific training for the work they did.

Teacher Certification

One of the main reasons that teachers have historically commanded little respect

2. G. Compayre, *History of Pedagogy*, trans. W. H. Payne (Boston: D. C. Heath and Co., 1885), p. 261.

and prestige is that until quite recently, there were no standards governing the preparation of teachers. Anyone could be a teacher simply by declaring himself so. It was not until quite recently that states passed teacher certification laws governing the training of teachers.

An excellent account of the history of teacher certification in the United States is the following:

———•-•———

Since there was very little in the way of teacher education in the colonial days—at least as we think of it today—there was little in the way of certification. Each community solved its educational needs in its own way. In areas where church influence was strong, a teaching license—if required at all— stressed moral character, religious zeal, and conformity to church doctrine. The first loyalty oath was demanded by the governor of New Jersey, in a proclamation requiring teachers to swear they would not engage in subversive activities against the British Crown. This was also required in other colonies and quite often was more important than anything else in the license. In general, however, the basic requirement of a colonial teacher was the ability to keep order in the classroom; not too much attention was given the question of whether or not he knew anything at all about the Three R's. There was mobility of teachers in those days, too. A teacher dismissed by one community as drunk, disorderly, dishonest and immoral, or maybe just plain ignorant, had only to hike to the next community to get another job.

Changes in teacher certification were slow to come after America won its independence (although the loyalty oath to the British Crown was followed by one to the United States). Gradually there came a movement toward state supervision of pub-

lic schools, a movement that began when the states began bearing part of the cost, but it was not until after the Civil War that the authority to issue a certificate began to move slowly from local and county authorities to the states. Really, not until the early 1900's did this shift get underway in earnest. State certificates were issued on the basis of written examinations, usually without regard to the prospective teacher's own education. Even after the turn of the twentieth century the typical examination did not require education beyond the tenth grade, and it was not until 1907 that Indiana became the first state to require a high-school diploma as a condition for all teachers' certificates.

The explosive expansion of American education after 1910 brought new rules and regulations in certification. Before 1900, most states issued a blanket certificate that was good for any subject at any grade level. Only six of the states required a different certificate for elementary- and secondary-school teaching. Gradually there was a move toward special certificates for special teaching assignments. The standards were tightened and graduation from college became more important, even though it was some time before courses in professional education were required.

World War I reversed the trend toward insistence on better teachers and better education. A survey by the National Education Association in 1918 showed that half of the teaching force of 600,000 persons had no special professional education, and 100,000 of the total had less than two years of education beyond the eighth grade. In 1921 there were thirty states which had no definite scholarship requirements for a certificate, but by 1926 this number had dropped to fifteen.

With the Depression and general unemployment of the 1930's, there came a surplus of teachers and a continuing rise in mini-

28 mum standards. It was during this period that the first major demands were made for a five-year college program for teachers. Even so, it is shocking to realize that as recently as 1931 nearly half the states would issue a certificate to a high-school graduate. These graduates—and many of them from poor high schools at that—were given teaching jobs in elementary schools and it is impossible to calculate the damage they were able to do.

Whatever improvements were made during the Depression were virtually wiped out by the effects of World War II. Teachers flocked to war industries and the number of students enrolled in teacher education programs dropped off. A teacher shortage developed. . . . Because somebody had to be in the classroom, emergency or substandard certificates became the order of the day. At the height of the teacher shortage it was estimated that as many as 140,000 teachers held emergency certificates. By 1948 the number was about 101,000 and by 1959 it was 95,700.

But during these postwar years the total number of teachers increased tremendously and there is hope in the fact that while one out of ten teachers held an emergency certificate in the 1949–50 school year, by 1958–59 the ratio had dropped to one out of thirteen. It should be pointed out again that there is no precise or universal definition of an "emergency certificate"; some are better than others, and some are even better than a few standard certificates.

Any history of teacher certification in this country has to be a chronicle of chaos. The situation is better now than ever before, but there is still considerable room for improvement.[3]

———— • ————

3. G. K. Hodenfield and T. M. Stinnett, *The Education of Teachers* (Englewood Cliffs, N.J.: Prentice-Hall, Inc., 1961), pp. 101–3. Used with permission.

Men have sought and still seek an elixir of youth. I've found it as a teacher of junior high school science. Teaching has made it possible for me to enjoy the fun, excitement, wonder, humor, intensity, and sensitivity of youth while enjoying the benefits of mature adulthood (whatever these may be).
Christopher R. Vagts

Current certification requirements differ considerably from state to state. Nearly all states require at least a bachelor's degree for permanent certification at the elementary or secondary level. Most states also require a sequence of special courses in psychology and education, plus a series of supervised clinical experiences (such as observation, participation, microteaching, student teaching, simulation, and internship) as well as extensive study in the subject matter to be taught. A secondary school teacher needs a major in whatever subject he wishes to teach (such as English, history, mathematics, biology, chemistry, business education, industrial education, home economics, physical education, art, or music). An elementary school teacher needs a major in elementary education, which typically includes a study of the materials and methods for teaching language arts, science, social studies, mathematics, art, music, etc. —all of the areas included in the elementary school curriculum.

A summary of the minimum requirements for the lowest regular teaching certificate for each state is presented in Figure 2.1. Of course, the specific certification requirements for each state are much more elaborate and detailed than the brief summary data presented in Figure 2.1.

As one can see in Figure 2.1, teacher

Getting to know your advisor and other college instructors and having an opportunity to work individually with them is a valuable part of the formal teacher education program.

certification is very complex. Furthermore, certification requirements differ from state to state. Space does not permit the inclusion of the complete certification requirements for each state; however, abbreviated examples of the 1969 certification requirements in a sampling of other states are as follows:

1. To be an elementary school teacher in the state of Washington, one must obtain a "Classroom Teaching Certificate." This certificate is based upon a broad state pattern adopted by the State Board of Education effective July 10, 1961. The pattern provides for: Provisional Certificate valid for three years, two years of teaching experience following preservice education, and a fifth year of teacher education at the graduate level prior to issuance of a standard certificate. Content pattern for the preservice program of four years: thirty-five percent undergraduate study in broad education in liberal arts and sciences, thirty-five percent in fields or areas of learning applicable to public schools, twenty percent in professional education,

State	Elementary School			Secondary School		
	Degree or Number of Semester Hours Required	Professional Education Required, Semester Hours (Total)	Directed Teaching Required, Semester Hours (Included in Column 3)	Degree or Number of Semester Hours Required	Professional Education Required, Semester Hours (Total)	Directed Teaching Required, Semester Hours (Included in Column 6)
1	2	3	4	5	6	7
Alabama	B	27	6	B	21	6
Alaska	B	24	C	B	18	C
Arizona	5[a]	24	6	5[a]	22	6
Arkansas	B	18	6	B	18	6
California	B[b]	AC[b]	AC[b]	B[b]	AC[b]	AC[b]
Colorado	B	AC	AC	B	AC	AC
Connecticut	B	30	6	B	18	6
Delaware	B	30	6	B	18	6
District	B[c]	15	C	5[c]	15	C
Florida	B	20	6	B	20	6
Georgia	B	18	6	B	18	6
Hawaii	B	18	AC[d]	B	18	AC[d]
Idaho	B	24	6	B	20	6
Illinois	B	16	5	B	16	5
Indiana	B	27	8	B	18	6
Iowa	B	20	5	B	20	5
Kansas	B	24	5	B	20	5
Kentucky	B	24	8[e]	B	17	8[e]
Louisiana	B	24	4	B	18	4
Maine	B	30	6	B	18	6
Maryland	B	26	8	B	18	6
Massachusetts	B[f]	18	2	B[f]	12	2
Michigan	B	20	5[g]	B	20	5[g]
Minnesota	B	30	6	B	18	4
Mississippi	B	36	6	B	18	6
Missouri	B	18	5	B	18	5
Montana	B	AC	AC	B	16	AC
Nebraska	60[h]	8	3	B	AC	AC
Nevada	B[i]	18[j]	6	B	20	6
New Hampshire	B	30	6	B	18	6
New Jersey	B	30	6[k]	B	21	6[k]
New Mexico	B	24	6	B	18	6
New York	B	24	C[l]	B	12	C[l]
North Carolina	B	24	6	B	18	6
North Dakota	B	16	3	B	16	3
Ohio	B	28	6	B	17	6
Oklahoma	B	21[m]	6	B	21[m]	6
Oregon	B	20	—[n]	B[c]	14	—[n]
Pennsylvania	B	AC	6–12[p]	B	AC	6–12[p]
Puerto Rico	68[q]	53[q]	6[q]	B[q]	29[q]	5[q]
Rhode Island	B	30	6	B	18	6
South Carolina	B	21	6	B	18	6
South Dakota	60[r]	15	3	B	20	6

Figure 2.1 Minimum Certification Requirements for Lowest Regular Teaching Certificates for Each State.

Source: T. M. Stinnett, *A Manual on Certification Requirements for School Personnel in the United States* (Washington D.C.: National Commission on Teacher Education and Professional Standards, 1970). Used with permission.

Tennessee	B	24	4	B	24	4
Texas	B	18	6	B	18	6
Utah	B	26	8	B	21	8
Vermont	90	18	6	B	18	6
Virginia	B	18	6	B	15	6
Washington	B[s]	AC	AC	B[s]	AC	AC
West Virginia	B	20	6	B	20	6
Wisconsin	64[t]	26	5	B	18	5
Wyoming	B	23	C	B	20	C

LEGEND: — means not reported. AC means approved curriculum; B means a bachelor's degree of specified preparation; 5 means a bachelor's degree plus a fifth year of appropriate preparation, not necessarily completion of the master's degree; C means a course.

* Professional requirements listed are the basic requirements for degree or lowest regular certificates. Some variations from the professional requirements as stated in this table may be found in the requirements for specific certificates listed for the respective states.

[a] Standard certificates: master's degree or 30 semester hours (s.h.) of graduate credit. Temporary certificates: bachelor's degree and completion of an approved program; valid for five years only.

[b] Under the approved-program approach for elementary and secondary teacher certification, California will accept the number of semester hours for the major, minor, professional education, directed teaching, and general education as required by the preparing institution for the completion of its approved teacher education curriculum. However, professional education is not acceptable for a credential major or minor. Four years of preparation (bachelor's degree) is the minimum requirement for initial elementary or secondary certification; a fifth year is required for the permanent certificate.

[c] Bachelor's degree for elementary and junior high school; master's degree for senior and vocational high.

[d] Not included in Columns 3 and 6.

[e] A teacher who has taught successfully for four or more years is required to take only 4 s.h. of practice teaching or a seminar of 4. A teacher who has had two years of successful experience may take a seminar dealing with professional problems instead of the 8 s.h. in practice teaching.

[f] Completion of the bachelor's degree or graduation from an approved four-year normal school.

[g] Total of 8 s.h. of laboratory experience, 5 of which must be student teaching.

[h] Provisional teaching certificates are issued for specifically endorsed grades, subjects, fields, and areas in designated classes of school districts upon evidence of partial completion of an approved teacher education program, generally at least 60 s.h., including specified amounts of general and professional education. Effective September 1, 1972, elementary teachers in accredited schools must hold a certificate based on degree preparation.

[i] A temporary certificate will be issued on completion of 96 hours in a program leading to the bachelor's degree.

[j] For a five-year nonrenewable certificate. Must establish eligibility for regular five-year certificate, the requirement for which is 30 s.h.

[k] The practice-teaching requirement is 150 clock hours, 90 of which must be in actual classroom teaching.

[l] One-year of paid full-time satisfactory teaching experience on the level for which certification is sought may be accepted in lieu of college supervised student teaching, but only when such experience carries recommendation of the employing school district administrator.

[m] For the standard certificate; for the temporary certificate the requirement is 12 s.h.

[n] Required, but there is no specific hours requirement.

[o] Provisional certificate only; for standard certification, a fifth year must be completed within five years after provisional certification.

[p] Minimum 6, maximum 12.

[q] Puerto Rico did not report for 1970. Requirements shown are carried over from the 1967 edition.

[r] All teachers in independent school districts must have a certificate based on a bachelor's degree. The 60-hour certificate has very limited validity. It will seldom be used after July 1, 1970; none will be issued after July 1, 1972.

[s] Provisional certificate only; for standard certification, a fifth year must be completed within six years after provisional certification.

[t] Bachelor's degree must be completed within seven years. Apparently issued only to graduates of two- or three-year programs in state or county colleges. Will not be issued after 1971–72. Effective with the 1972–73 school year, the bachelor's degree will be the minimum requirement for initial certification.

A future teacher learns much about child development by working with individual students.

Future teachers should capitalize upon every opportunity to work with children whether it be in regular classrooms, recreation programs, social welfare agencies, or church activities.

ten percent in electives. Provisional Certificate may be renewed once on successful experience and 8 semester hours earned during period covered by certificate.

2. To be an elementary school teacher in Florida requires a bachelor's degree from an accredited institution of higher learning. Academic requirements—General Preparation 45 semester hours: Communication Arts 6–12; Human Adjustment 6–12; Biological and Physical Science (may include Math) 6–12; Social Studies 6–12; Humanities and Applied Arts 6–12. Professional Requirements 20: Foundations of Education (Psychological and Sociological) 6; Teaching in the Elementary and/or Secondary School—at least 3 at elementary level—6; Methods of Teaching Reading 2; Observation and Practice Teaching or an approved internship program, 6, or three years teaching experience, or 3 hours in observation and practice teaching plus two years of teaching experience. Specialization in each of the following elementary subjects 21: Materials; Science or Nature Study; Social Studies or Geography; Health and/or Physical Education; Art; Music; Arithmetic 6 hours or three years of teaching experience in the past five years.

3. The requirements for teaching secondary school (grades 6–12) in Illinois (excluding Chicago) are as follows: Possession of a bachelor's degree. General education requirements 42: Language Arts 8; Science and/or Mathematics 6; Social Studies (including a course in American History and/or Government) 6; Humanities 6; Health and Physical Education 3; Additional work in above fields and/or Psychology (except Educational Psychology) to total 42. Professional Requirements 16: Educational

Psychology (including Human Growth and Development) 2; Methods and Technology (Secondary) 2; History and/or Philosophy of Education 2; Student teaching in grades 6–12, 5; Electives to total 16. Specialization requirements: single major 32 or 3 minor areas of 16–18–20–24 each, 48–72: Electives 0–30. Total Hours 120.[4]

It must be kept in mind that certification requirements change frequently as states pass new certification laws. Because these laws change frequently and vary from state to state, the only sure way of obtaining the current certification requirements for a particular state is by contacting the state office of education, usually located in the capital city of that state.

In recent years there has been some effort made to develop reciprocity agreements between states so that a teacher certified in one state could be automatically certified in another state. One reciprocity plan that has gained some support involves the automatic certification of any graduate of an NCATE (National Council for Accreditation of Teacher Education) accredited teacher education program, regardless of which state that program may be located in. In other words, if a person graduates from a college in Florida that has been accredited by NCATE, other states would automatically certify that person as a teacher. Figure 2.2 shows those states that, as of 1970, granted at least some degree of reciprocity based on NCATE accreditation. As the map indicates, twenty-eight states had entered into such an agreement as of that time. These included Alabama, Arizona, Colorado,

4. Philip C. Wells, Verl M. Short, and Howard D. Sims, *U.S. Teacher Certification Map* (105 Thornbrook Road, DeKalb, Ill. 1969).

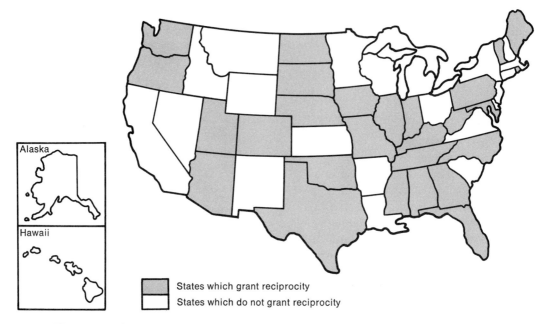

Figure 2.2 States Granting Certification Reciprocity Based on NCATE Accreditation.

Source: National Council for Accreditation of Teacher Education (Washington, D.C., 1970).

Delaware, Florida, Georgia, Illinois, Indiana, Iowa, Kentucky, Maine, Maryland, Mississippi, Missouri, Nebraska, North Carolina, North Dakota, Oklahoma, Oregon, Pennsylvania, Rhode Island, South Dakota, Tennessee, Texas, Utah, Vermont, Washington, and West Virginia. This reciprocity may differ from state to state, so interested persons should contact each specific state for details.

Yet another type of certification reciprocity is that developed by various groups of states on a regional basis. An example of such regional reciprocity is that known as the Interstate Reciprocity Project which was initiated by New York. Approximately twenty-five states have thus far entered into this particular regional reciprocity project.

Other regional accreditation reciprocity agreements may involve only two or three neighboring states. Since the specific details regarding reciprocity agreements vary from state to state, teachers interested in becoming certified in any particular state should check with that state for current details regarding certification requirements and reciprocity agreements.

Teacher Education Programs Today

State certification laws specify the minimum legal requirements for becoming a teacher in each state. As one might expect, the formal teacher education programs found in

Nor am I less persuaded, that you will agree with me in opinion, that there is nothing which can better deserve your patronage than the promotion of science and literature. Knowledge is in every country the surest basis of public happiness. In one, in which the measures of government receive their impression so immediately from the sense of the community, as in ours, it is proportionably essential. To the security of a free constitution it contributes in various ways; by convincing those who are intrusted with the public administration, that every valuable end of government is best answered by the enlightened confidence of the people; and by teaching the people themselves to know, and to value their own rights; to discern and provide against invasions of them; to distinguish between oppression and the necessary exercise of lawful authority, between burthens proceeding from a disregard to their convenience and those resulting from the inevitable exigencies of society; to discriminate the spirit of liberty from that of licentiousness, cherishing the first, avoiding the last, and uniting a speedy but temperate vigilance against encroachments, with an inviolable respect to the laws.

President George Washington

Future teachers must also become familiar with and proficient in using all of the tools of teaching.

colleges and universities are designed to meet at least the minimum certification requirements in the respective states. In fact, most teacher education programs provide more than the minimum certification requirements in their efforts to prepare teachers.

The young person deciding to enter the teaching profession today has a broad field of choices as to the specific program which he may wish to pursue. He must decide what age range of students and what subject or subjects he wishes to teach. This wide choice of educational careers is examined in considerable detail later in this book.

The specific educational career that a student selects determines the nature of the training to be undertaken. The future elementary teacher, for instance, is schooled in a broad variety of subjects because many subjects are taught in each elementary class-

College students preparing for educational careers also take courses dealing with various aspects of teaching such as educational psychology, foundations of education, and teaching methods. Closed circuit television is often used in such courses to facilitate the study of learners and of teaching.

room. Mathematics, science, grammar, phonics, spelling, geography, history—are all part and parcel of the elementary teacher's preparation. In addition, the prospective elementary teacher delves deeply into the psychology of the developing child. He must know what to expect from the child at each stage of growth and how to identify that which might be atypical in the individual child, so that problems might be identified early and unusual capabilities might be developed.

The specific courses required for a major in elementary education differ from college to college; however, Figure 2.3 shows the requirements listed in the catalog of a midwestern university and are rather typical of those found throughout the country.

The person who chooses to teach junior or senior high school undergoes a somewhat similar program of training. The primary difference is that at this level the training concentrates less on breadth of subject matter preparation and more on depth. For example, if one wishes to become an English teacher,

Major in Elementary Education (with the degree Bachelor of Science in Education)

This is a comprehensive major for those who plan to teach in the kindergarten and grades 1–8.

Required of all majors*
Professional Education courses:

Educ. 275	Human Development & Learning (Prerequisite: Psych. 102 Introduction to Psychology—3)	(6)
Educ. 375	Elementary School Curriculum & Instruction	(10)
Educ. 476	Seminar in Elementary Education	(4)
Educ. 477	Problems of the Beginning Teacher (Elementary)	(2)
Educ. 478	Tests & Measurements (Elementary)	(2)
Educ. 496	Student Teaching (Elementary)	(7)
	and one additional course to be approved by adviser	
	Group total	(34)

Related courses in other departments:

Art 383	Teaching Art in Elementary Schools	(3)
Math 402	Teaching Practices in Arithmetic	(3)
Music 209	Fundamentals, Principles & Practices in Elementary Music	(4)
PE-W 302	Elementary School Physical Education	(2)
	Group total	(12)

Additional requirements: A 15-hour area of concentration in a
field outside Education .... (15)

Total for major .... (61)

* An outdoor education experience is required for three days during the junior block and five days during the senior block Education courses. The student will be required to stay overnight and assume his share of the responsibility for additional costs which may be incurred as a result of this off-campus assignment.

Figure 2.3 A Typical Elementary Teacher Education Program.

he will make an extensive study of that subject in his college program. He, too, undertakes considerable study in the psychology of the adolescent, learning perhaps most importantly that he is teaching *children* subject matter, rather than teaching *subject matter* to children. This distinction is essential.

While programs vary considerably from college to college, Figure 2.4 shows the requirements listed in the catalog of a midwestern university for a program leading to certification as a junior high school teacher. This program is typical of other programs found throughout the country.

This same university lists the requirements shown in Figure 2.5 for a major in secondary education.

For the young person who feels himself capable of extreme patience and dedication, there is yet another field, special education.

38

Major in Junior High School Education (to meet secondary school certification requirements with the degree Bachelor of Science in Education).

Students wishing to specialize in teaching at the junior high school level may choose one of the several subject matter patterns which may be incorporated into the following program. A student may wish to elect a particular major and minor combination such as English-History or Mathematics-Science. This program is intended to meet the needs of junior high schools whose curricula are organized in terms of such a dual approach. Students in this program shall have advisers in each subject area involved.

  Required of all majors:
1. **University General Education requirements.**
2. **A major and a minor.** Each student's program must be approved by the Junior High School advisers in the major and minor departments.
3. **Professional Education Courses:**

Educ. 302	Human Development & Learning (Secondary)	**(6)**
Educ. 486	Foundations & Evaluation of Secondary Education	**(5)**
Educ. 495	Student Teaching (Secondary)	**(7)**
Method Course(s) in the subject matter Major & Minor Areas		**(2, 2)**
	Group total	**(22)**

Figure 2.4   A Typical Junior High School Teacher Education Program.

Near the end of the teacher education program the future teacher participates in student teaching. During this time he gradually assumes the role of a teacher under the close supervision of a regular teacher. The student teacher is often videotaped so he can see himself in action and improve his performance.

There are many challenges for the student teacher, one of which is being able to work effectively with a large group of students.

Student teachers soon discover that students learn best by having an opportunity to actively participate in the classroom activity.

40

Major in Secondary Education (with the degree Bachelor of Science in Education)

Students preparing to teach in the high school should have two teaching areas (two majors, or a major and a minor). In addition to meeting "General Education Requirements" these students must take the following sequence of courses:

Professional Education Requirements—20–25 Semester Hours

Educ. 302	Human Development and Learning (Secondary) .... (6)	

Human Growth and Development—Birth Through Adolescence
Educational Psychology
Guidance Function of the Teacher

Educ. 486* Foundations and Evaluation of Secondary Education .... (5)
History and Philosophy of Education
Curriculum Patterns and Construction
Organization and Administration in Secondary Education
Educational Measurement: basic statistics, construction of
teacher-made tests, and other evaluative techniques and
instruments.

Educ. 495* Student Teaching .... (7)**
Nine weeks full-time student teaching routinely taken in the
same semester as Education 486.

A course or courses in the Methods of Teaching a particular secondary school subject, offered by the respective subject-matter department (2–7), is required of students preparing to teach in the secondary school. In the event the special methods course for their major is not offered, they may substitute Education 424 Methods and Materials in the Secondary School.

---

* Nine-week courses are blocked together or alternate.
** Required of majors in some of these fields, such as Art, Home Economics, Industrial Arts, Music, or Physical Education, Education 493 Student Teaching (Elementary, Special Subjects) (1–3).

Figure 2.5 A Typical Senior High School Teacher Education Program.

It is the special education teacher who undertakes to educate the handicapped—those unable for reasons of physical or mental shortcomings to participate in a normal classroom environment. The special education teacher may have the most rewarding job of all, but it is equally true that working with special education students can be very frustrating. Becoming a special education teacher requires a very specialized form of training. Sign language, braille, lip reading, the natures and limitations of the various forms of physical

and mental disability—all are within the purview of special education. Careers in special education are discussed more fully in chapter four.

If one wishes to teach at a junior or community college or university, he must obtain advanced degrees (at least a master's, but often also a doctor's degree). Most master's degrees require a total of five or six years of study (including the bachelor's degree) while most doctor's degrees require a total of approximately eight years of study (including the bachelor's and master's degrees). Of course, these advanced degrees must be in the subject that one wishes to teach at the college or university level.

In addition to teaching there are a host of other careers in the education field available at the elementary, secondary, and higher education level. These are discussed in chapter four.

Competency-based Teacher Education

In recent years, a new approach to teacher education, known as competency-based teacher education (CBTE) has come into being. This approach to teacher education represents an attempt to emphasize helping future teachers learn and refine the skills or competencies that one must possess to be an effective teacher. While this has always been one of the goals of traditional teacher education programs, CBTE represents an attempt to put extreme emphasis on the specific teaching skills that are deemed essential.

If a teacher-preparing institution decided to plan and implement a competency-based teacher education program, it might begin by clearly stating what they thought were the essential competencies a teacher should possess. Of course, this is a very difficult task for many reasons. For one thing, teaching is an extremely complex task which is very difficult, if not impossible, to accurately describe. Unfortunately, research has not yet (and some people feel probably never will) objectively determine what constitutes "good" teaching. Be that as it may, CBTE requires that somehow, one must begin by determining the essential teacher competencies.

Once the competencies are determined, the college must design a series of learning experiences that will provide the student with an opportunity to acquire each particular competency. As soon as students can demonstrate a competency, they move on to another. CBTE puts an emphasis on learning teaching skills and competencies rather than the accumulation of course credits to graduate and become a certified teacher.

Even though CBTE is still in its early stages of development, some state departments of education are already moving toward competency-based teacher certification wherein people would presumably receive a teaching certificate by demonstrating that they possess the necessary competencies and could in fact teach—rather than by completing certain college courses and degrees. It is unclear as of yet, however, just what long-range effect the CBTE movement will have on American teacher education. Additional information about CBTE is presented in the "point of view" article at the end of this chapter.

Personal Qualifications Needed for Teaching

No matter what choice the individual may make as to the age level of students and/or the subject matter he wishes to teach, certain personal qualifications are essential for all teachers.

One attempt to describe the personal qualities of an effective teacher is that presented in Figure 2.6. This figure lists, conversely, the ineffective behaviors of teachers. Dr. David G. Ryans has compiled the information presented in Figure 2.6 through many years of studying the characteristics of teachers.

Obviously, no one person can hope to possess all of these traits to a liberal degree;

Effective teacher behaviors	Ineffective teacher behaviors
Is alert, appears enthusiastic	Is apathetic, dull; appears bored
Appears interested in students and classroom activities	Appears uninterested in pupils and classroom activities
Is cheerful, optimistic	Is depressed, pessimistic; appears unhappy
Is self-controlled, not easily upset	Loses temper easily, is easily upset
Likes fun, has a sense of humor	Is overly serious, too occupied for humor
Recognizes and admits own mistakes	Is unaware of, or fails to admit, own mistakes
Is fair, impartial, and objective in treatment of students	Is unfair or partial in dealing with students
Is patient	Is impatient
Shows understanding and sympathy in working with students	Is short with students, uses sarcastic remarks or in other ways shows lack of sympathy with students
Is friendly and courteous in relations with students	Is aloof and removed in relations with students
Helps students with personal as well as educational problems	Seems unaware of students' personal needs and problems
Commends effort and gives praise for work well done	Does not commend students; is disapproving, hypercritical
Accepts students' efforts as sincere	Is suspicious of students' motives
Anticipates reactions of others in social situations	Does not anticipate reactions of others in social situations
Encourages students to try to do their best	Makes no effort to encourage students to try to do their best
Classroom procedure is planned and well organized	Procedure is without plan, disorganized
Classroom procedure is flexible within overall plan	Shows extreme rigidity of procedure, inability to depart from plan
Anticipates individual needs	Fails to provide for individual differences and needs of students
Stimulates students through interesting and original materials and techniques	Uninteresting materials and teaching techniques used
Gives clear, practical demonstrations and explanations	Demonstrations and explanations are not clear and are poorly conducted
Is clear and thorough in giving directions	Directions are incomplete, vague
Encourages students to work through their own problems and evaluate their accomplishments	Fails to give students opportunity to work out their own problems or evaluate their own work
Disciplines in quiet, dignified, and positive manner	Reprimands at length, ridicules, resorts to cruel or meaningless forms of correction
Gives help willingly	Fails to give help or gives it grudgingly
Foresees and attempts to resolve potential difficulties	Is unable to foresee and resolve potential difficulties

Figure 2.6 Effective and Ineffective Teacher Characteristics

Source: David G. Ryans, *Characteristics of Teachers* (Washington, D.C.: American Council on Education, 1960), p. 82.

however, unless one possesses a fair number of these qualities he probably should not pursue a career in the teaching profession.

A very creative and insightful discussion of the qualities necessary to be an effective teacher appeared in *Today's Education*. This essay, authored by Richard Calisch and entitled "So You Want to Be a Real Teacher?" states:

———•———

Over the years, literally thousands of young people have neglected to write and ask my advice as to whether they were making a mistake in preparing to be teachers. By now, hundreds and hundreds of them (many no longer quite so young, of course) are moving about in the world of the classroom. With more brashness than modesty, I have finally decided to speak out to them, and to all teachers and would-be teachers everywhere. Although I'd run for cover if anyone started deciding just how qualified I am to be a career teacher, I'm prepared to list what I think those qualifications ought to be. Many people will undoubtedly disagree with one or several items on my list, but here goes, anyway.

In the first place, if you're not a brainy, top-level, creative student, consider doing something else. Good teaching is done by good students, by people who themselves are compulsive about learning. It takes intelligence; it takes the ability to read and to write well.

Good teaching takes the kind of person who wants to know just about all there is to know about his subject and who tops everything off with a strong desire to help his students acquire knowledge. You can't be content to keep just a few pages ahead of them. You must really know the field, whether it be mathematics or physical education, literature or cooking. (This calls for even greater emphasis on subject matter courses

in college.) You need to be an expert, a specialist, a scholar, a consistent learner, in order to be a teacher. Teaching is, after all, primarily an intellectual art.

Being an intelligent specialist isn't enough, however. You must also have a wide range of adult knowledge and interests. It goes without saying that a teacher of any subject should be well-versed in the literature, music, art, and history of his world, as well as alert to the newest of the new. He should be hip to the world around his eyes and ears —knowledgeable about the latest cars, movies, fashions, books. You may not be able to answer all your students' questions or participate in all their discussions, but at least you should know the terms they use. A teacher who can't rap with the guys on their ground isn't going to educate them on his.

But—and this is important—never forget that you are there to bring young people up the educational ladder, not to bring yourself down.

A teacher must understand students' likes and dislikes, hopes and fears, but at the same time, he must teach as an adult. Sometimes it takes courage to tell a youngster he is wrong; but when he *is,* pretending he *is not* is a grave sin, in my mind. I guess what I am saying here is that I wholeheartedly endorse the client concept of education, in which the teacher has the obligation to know his subject and much more besides; in which the student comes to the teacher as a client to absorb what he can, to learn what the teacher has to teach.

Your responsibility is to make your teaching relevant to your students, but you must not succumb to the pressure to tell them only what they want to hear because that way is easier.

Treating children childishly produces childish grown-ups. To avoid doing this, you must use all of the intelligence, knowledge,

A special education student teacher discovers that teaching is an exciting, stimulating experience—an opportunity to put into practice all that she has learned in her teacher education program.

A teacher must be adaptable.

and expertise that you possess. You must be in command, and this takes that added combination of confidence, wit, maturity, and strength of character. If you lack these attributes or are satisfied with your present attainment of them, there is another occupation for you.

I have stressed the teacher's need to have knowledge and intelligence. Hand in hand with these attributes go two others: creativity and imagination. A teacher needs to be an idea person. You must be able to make use of any idea, from any source, and turn it to a thought-producing teaching technique.

When Georgy asks, "Why?" when Suzy says, "What for?" when Mary says, "Are you kidding?" you've got to be able to come up with answers, and they aren't always in the book. Answering a question, such as "What good is this ever going to do me?" from a

belligerent, bored, boorish troublemaker is going to take creativity and imagination, as well as a conviction on your part that whatever it is *will* do him some good. This conviction can arise only if you yourself are an expert in whatever field you teach.

In summary, a teacher, first and foremost, must be intelligent, knowledgeable, creative, and imaginative. I know that's not the standard definition, but if Mr. Binet doesn't complain, I won't knock his test. Score yourself one point each for intelligence, expertise in your subject matter, creativity, and imagination. If you don't have four points now, quit here.

My next bit of advice will seem strange, but take it anyway. Sometime when you're feeling up to par, find a quiet, secluded room with no books, no TV, no transistor radio, no cokes, no tasty snacks. Go in, sit down, and stay for an hour. Ask a friend to let you

46 know when the time is up. If the hour seems like a year or if you fall asleep, forget about teaching.

If your inner resources are not enough to keep you interested in yourself for one class period, imagine how you will affect your students. Your subject matter is only subject matter until you add the vital ingredient to it—you. And if your *you* isn't enough to make that hour of solitude pleasant and interesting, it is going to be hell for the 30 or so squirming students who have just straggled in after an hour's ordeal with some other dull pedagogue.

That hour you spend alone in the empty room may be the most eye-opening hour of your life. You'll find out whether someone could possibly spend 60 minutes in your company without going out of his mind from simple boredom.

If you've read this far and still think you want to teach, test your weirdo quotient. Every good teacher has in him the confidence

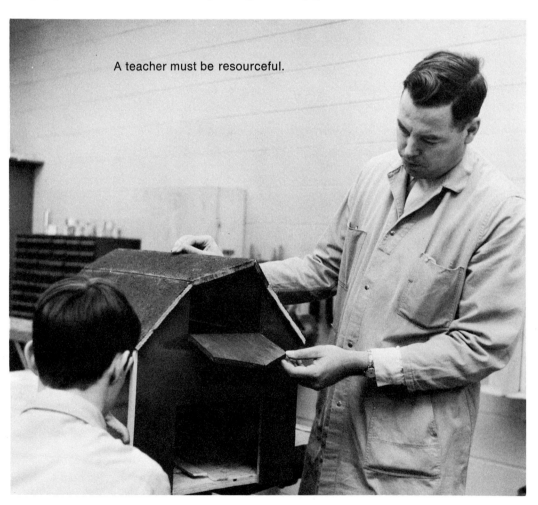

A teacher must be resourceful.

and self-reliance to be a weirdo. From Socrates to "Sock it to me!" the memorable lessons have been taught by showmen who knew the value of a vivid performance. The classroom is a stage and the teacher is the player: hero, villain, clown, and the whole supporting cast of the greatest long-run, hit show ever to play off Broadway or on. And it's a show whose script changes daily, without notice, and usually without consultation with the cast.

In every good classroom personality, there is some of P. T. Barnum, John Barrymore, Ringo Starr, and Houdini. Are you afraid to stand up and sing with a wastebasket over your head, to demonstrate the various qualities of sound? Can you be King Richard bawling "A horse! A horse! My kingdom for a horse!" or act out photosynthesis, playing all parts yourself?

Think back to your own teachers. From which did you learn the most? Certainly not from the sit-behind-the-desk mumblers who read their lectures from neatly typed notes. Teaching involves a great deal of showmanship and salesmanship, and the great teaching personalities are those that are not afraid to be different, unusual, or what the current jargon styles "weirdo." Classroom spontaneity and showmanship take confidence and a degree of cool that the average person doesn't possess; but, then, a teacher isn't an average person.

Have you ever tried to talk a dyed-in-the-wool Democrat into voting for a Republican, or a vegetarian into eating meat, or a Card fan into cheering for the Cubs? How did it come out? Probably it produced a humdinger of an argument—one with sparks, flames, daggers, and music played by the brasses. Or else the person you were talking to just turned you off, wouldn't even listen.

Those two responses to persuasion are most typical, because people just don't like to have their cherished beliefs challenged they can. Yet teaching involves challenging and will protect them from attack in any way the sacred beliefs of the student and asking him, forcing him if necessary, to examine them.

Each student brings to the classroom a whole complex of his own folk beliefs about those aspects of life of which he is ignorant. Typically, his attitude will be that if he has never heard of it, it either isn't true or is unimportant. He will cling to his preconceptions like the proverbial drowning man to the proverbial log. Your job is to push him off the log and see that he stays afloat. Don't expect him to be overjoyed about it. Don't expect him to love you for it. If he learns from you, if he matures and gains confidence under your direction, then you have achieved success. If you also want love, get married.

I tell my pupils that if I can't send them home muttering darkly at least once a week, I've failed. And I mean that. An exasperated student will think, ask, read, search for answers—and that is education. Even though he may come up with answers that disagree with your beliefs, you have done your job as a teacher if he has arrived at those answers through intelligent thought.

What students need is some answers and a lot of needling questions. So I agree with Socrates that a teacher must try to be the most irritating person for miles around. (You can expect hemlock as your reward.)

Most books I've read about teaching indicate that the prime requisite for a teacher is a "love of children." Hogwash! That bit of misinformation has probably steered more softhearted and softheaded Mr. Peeperses and Miss Brookses into our art than any other deception ever practiced on the mind of man. What you must love is the vision of the well-informed, responsible adult you can help the child become.

48   Your job as a teacher is to help the child realize who he is, what his potential is, what his strengths are. You can help him learn to love himself—or the man he soon will be. With that kind of understanding self-love, the student doesn't need any of your sentimentality. What he needs is your brains, and enabling him to profit from them calls for decisive firmness. "I must be cruel only to be kind," say Hamlet and many a good teacher. Discipline and firm guidance are often called meanness by those subjected to them, but in my experience they are the kind of loving care most likely to produce intelligent, knowledgeable, perceptive adults who can do a better job of coping with the problems of the world than did those who taught them.

The fact that real teaching is an art is too often pooh-poohed. Some critics place teaching in the same category as baby-sitting; and far too many people enter the field because it seems like an easy way to earn a fair living. Girls may look on it as a pleasant way of biding their time until they capture husbands.

But the kind of teacher I have been talking about is a dedicated person who plans to stay in teaching despite its drawbacks. He looks upon his work with individual children as an art to which he brings his talent, his craftsmanship, his experience, learning, intelligence, and that indefinable something called inspiration.

I hope, prospective teachers, that as you take an honest, searching look at yourselves you can sense that you have the potential for being this kind of teacher.[5]

———•—•———

5. Richard Calisch, "So You Want to Be a Real Teacher," *Today's Education,* November 1969, pp. 49–51. Used with permission.

One of the characteristics that is vital for the teacher needs emphasizing—the desire to be a continuing scholar. Most school boards require that a teacher continue his academic work past the bachelor's degree at a certain rate in order for advancement, and in some cases to retain his position. The required number of courses within a specific time period varies with the level at which the teacher is employed and from school district to school district. Some high schools, for instance, require that the master's degree be earned within six years after the beginning of employment. But many teachers pursue graduate work at a rate far beyond the minimum required. These people may be attempting to qualify for a position such as school administrator, but many are seeking to improve their skills as teachers. They realize that becoming a teacher is a lifelong process—one never to be fully realized. Teaching is a process that is constantly dynamic, never reaching consummation. Changes in the weather, the moods of students, moods of the teacher himself, the changing body of knowledge which he seeks to impart—all are variables from day to day and even hour to hour. The teacher must seek to gain knowledge even more ardently than he seeks to impart it.

Why People Become Teachers

Further insight into some of the personality traits that teachers should possess can be gleaned from a research study which asked a large number of teachers to state the main reason they selected teaching as a career. The results of this study are shown in Figure 2.7. As this figure indicates, the main reason listed by the 2,316 teachers participating in this

Consideration in Choosing Teaching as Career	All Reporting	Men	Women	Elementary	Secondary	Secondary Men	Secondary Women
Number of teachers reporting	2,316	723	1,593	1,218	1,098	600	498
Desire to work with young people	34.4%	33.2%	34.9%	39.1%	29.1%	32.3%	25.3%
Opportunity for rendering important service	27.6	24.6	28.9	31.7	23.0	23.0	23.1
Interest in a subject-matter field ...	13.6	18.9	11.1	4.7	23.4	21.2	26.1
A tradition in my family ..	6.4	2.9	8.0	7.5	5.3	3.2	7.8
Example set by a favorite teacher	6.0	5.3	6.3	5.4	6.6	5.8	7.4
Job security	5.8	7.7	5.0	5.6	6.1	7.7	4.2
Financial rewards	1.6	0.6	2.1	1.9	1.3	0.7	2.0
Easiest preparation program in college	1.1	1.8	0.8	1.2	0.9	1.0	0.8
Unsuccessful in another line of work	0.4	1.0	0.1	0.1	0.7	1.2	0.2
Stop-gap until marriage ..	0.3	...	0.4	0.3	0.3	...	0.6
Other reason	2.9	4.0	2.4	2.5	3.3	4.0	2.4
	100.0%	100.0%	100.0%	100.0%	100.0%	100.0%	99.9%

Figure 2.7 Why Teachers Become Teachers.

Source: National Education Association, Research Division, *The American Public School Teacher,* research report 1967–R4 (Washington, D.C.: National Education Association Publications, 1967), p. 59. Used by permission.

study for entering the teaching profession was a desire to work with young people. The second most frequently listed reason was "opportunity for rendering important service." These two qualities, a desire to work with young people and an interest in rendering service, are perhaps the two very most important traits for a person to possess before entering a teaching career.

The person who is considering becoming a teacher must seriously examine his own personal qualifications for this kind of work. If you are considering entering the teaching profession you might consider—with your parents, teachers, counselors, or fellow students—some of the following points:

■ Do you have the personal qualifications necessary to become a successful teacher?
■ Do you really want to devote your life to working with students?
■ What age group of students do you wish to work with?
■ What subjects do you wish to teach?
■ Do you wish to be a master teacher, a paraprofessional, or some other kind of specialist such as a media specialist, supervisor, or administrator?
■ Should you attempt to obtain experience as a teacher aide as part of your training for a career as a teacher?
■ How can you obtain the best possible preparation for teaching?

50   This chapter has attempted to briefly introduce some of the important concepts related to the subject of teacher certification, the nature of teacher education programs today, and personal qualifications needed for teaching—all vital topics for one contemplating a career in teaching. It is hoped that this brief discussion will stimulate the reader to explore further these important topics.

Point of View

An attempt has been made in this chapter to highlight both traditional and innovative teacher education programs. The truth of the matter is that there have been relatively few truly innovative changes in teacher education during the past several decades. Performance-based teacher education (PBTE) could become one of the more radical recent departures from traditional teacher education if it becomes widely adopted and if it is carried to its logical conclusion.

Because of this, and of the newer ideas in teacher education, the topic of performance-based teacher education has probably generated more interest than any other. Performance-based teacher education (PBTE) —or competency-based teacher education (CBTE), as it is sometimes called—is examined in the following selection authored by Dr. Margaret Lindsey. Dr. Lindsey, a nationally known authority on teacher education, is a professor of education at Teachers College, Columbia University. She has devoted her professional career to teachers' education and has earned the respect of colleagues throughout the nation. An innovator herself, she is eminently qualified to critique the performance-based teacher education movement.

Performance-based Teacher Education: Examination of a Slogan

Margaret Lindsey

In American education, slogans have played a prominent role in both discourse and practice. *Performance-based teacher education* (PBTE), a popular slogan on the current scene, is already serving as both stimulant and irritant. Like other slogans preceding it, this one neither clarifies meanings, explains theory, nor signifies programmatic consequences. The words themselves, individually and collectively, do not carry precise meaning, as evidenced by the polarity of interpretations brought to *performance* and the variation in degree of inclusiveness ascribed to the term *teacher education*. Neither does the slogan imply any set of principles that might make up a theory, nor does it indicate the scope and sequence of a teacher education program.

However, as Scheffler has suggested, educational slogans "make no claim to facilitating communication or to reflecting meaning." Slogans are to be "repeated warmly and reassuringly, rather than pondered gravely. . . . They provide rallying symbols of the key ideas and attitudes of an educational movement. They both express and foster community of spirit, attracting new adherents and providing reassurance and strength to veterans."[1]

Margaret Lindsey, "Performance-based Teacher Education: Examination of a Slogan," *Journal of Teacher Education,* Fall 1973, pp. 180–86. Used by permission.
1. Israel Scheffler. *The Language of Education* (Springfield, Ill.: Charles C. Thomas, 1960), p. 36.

Performance-based teacher education is doing exactly what Scheffler said such slogans can do. Key ideas in a whole range of propositions intended to reform not only the education of teachers but also education in general are now attached to the words *performance-based teacher education*. Advocates convene to promote the goodness of the ideas; individuals and groups labor to make the ideas operative at local levels; former adversaries join together in praise of the potential they believe inherent in PBTE. A warm, friendly, and good feeling that something worthwhile is on the horizon pervades the atmosphere; a growing chorus claims that educational opportunity for all people will be vastly improved if teachers are educated to perform in desirable ways; and more and more persons are committed to achieving performance-based teacher education.

Performance-based Teacher Education as an Assertion

Individuals who originate slogans select and put together in sequence symbols they assume will communicate their message. In selecting and sequencing the symbols, they read into the slogan their own special connotations and interpretations. In Scheffler's words, With the passage of time, however, slogans are often increasingly interpreted more literally both by adherents and by critics of the movement they represent. They are taken more and more as literal doctrines or arguments, rather than merely as rallying symbols. When this happens in a given case, it becomes important to evaluate the slogan both as a straight-forward assertion and as a symbol of a practical social movement.[2]

2. Ibid., p. 37.

This has happened to PBTE. The need to examine the slogan is urgent. Both antagonists and protagonists bring to performance-based teacher education their own meanings and practical interpretations. Some persons immediately reject the idea because they interpret it as antithetical to their philosophical commitments. Too often those committed to the idea cannot even arrive at a stage of program planning because of barriers resulting from opposing interpretations of words like *performance* or *teacher education*. Sometimes credit or discredit is assigned to the slogan solely on the basis of the ease or difficulty with which persons reach decisions in designing program components. When advocates get below the surface and consider alternatives in designing specific experiences, preparing materials of instruction, or making definitive explanatory statements, they frequently discover that they are talking about very different things while using the same slogan words. Confusion is rampant.

In everyday discourse about education, slogans tend to encompass topical words which must bear tremendous responsibility for messages sent and received. It is very difficult to engage in productive dialogue with one's peers when the meanings each discussant brings to topical words are diverse and confused.

Increasingly, meanings surrounding the slogan *performance-based teacher education* become clouded as more persons deepen their personal and professional identification with it. Some become involved in research and development. Others engage in various kinds of implementation. Out of these efforts new knowledge is produced, individual interpretations of the slogan are refined, and the urge to persuade others to adopt singular interpretations grows.

52 It is everyone's privilege to stipulate definitions to clarify his position. However, communication is made more difficult when terms become idiosyncratic with private meanings. A search for more precision in meanings brought to PBTE is not a game undertaken for the fun of it; rather it is a task the achievement of which is essential to productive dialogue.

A step-by-step examination of the expression *performance-based teacher education* reveals several points of confusion. The word *teacher* is used by some to mean classroom teachers in elementary and secondary schools and by others to encompass all professional practitioners in formalized school settings. Still others use the term in its generic sense, meaning anyone whose behavior is designed to induce change in another (e.g., parent, minister, news analyst, advertiser). While a definition of *teacher* may be stipulated anywhere along a continuum of increasing inclusiveness, in this article a teacher is considered to be a classroom practitioner working with children or youth.

Some extend the meaning of PBTE to include the education of professional personnel in addition to teachers. While performance-based education is surely as appropriate for the preparation of other educational personnel as for teachers, it is confusing to use the term *teacher education* in this connection. The earlier definition of *teacher* at once limits the definition of *teacher education*.

Teacher education needs further definition however. *Teacher education* is used by some to refer exclusively to student teaching in the traditional preservice programs. Others use it to mean the entire collegiate program provided as initial preparation of teachers (e.g., traditional components of general education, subject matter specialization, and pro-

fessional education). Still others employ the term to mean continuing cycles of diagnosis, treatment, and assessment of needs and interests of persons from initial preparation for teaching through a career of practice. Here again, a continuum of increasing comprehensiveness is illustrated.

There is little justification for saying teacher education if we mean student teaching or any other single aspect of teacher education. When *teacher education* is used hereafter without qualification, it means the total initial and continuing education of teachers. It is possible, however, without sacrificing the concept of continuity in the education of teachers, to isolate a part of the total program. When the initial stage of teacher education is the referent, the qualifier *preservice* is useful. The second and major section of this article is limited to preservice teacher education.

Performance, another word in the expression under discussion, actually is a neutral term meaning an act. The mounting evidence of the failure of the school to meet the needs of some children and youth in the American society, particularly those in depressed urban areas, has led to intense public and professional interest in what teachers *do* in the classroom. It is believed that *performance,* defined as observable behavior, makes a difference in the lives of pupils.

This very concern makes it doubtful that anyone involved in the education of teachers is interested solely in neutral acts or performances. All strive to help teachers behave in ways believed to contribute to desired ends. Many are aware that knowledge relevant to a teaching act is essential to high quality performance. Many are concerned that teachers and those evaluating them employ adequate criteria in determining the quality of action. Furthermore, it is widely recognized that performance in the classroom does not represent the complete professionalism expected of a teacher. As a professional person a teacher is responsible for rational decision making in the classroom and for systematic inquiry into conditions and practices leading to improved decision making in planning for teaching and classroom performance. He is responsible for possession and use of knowledge and for the discovery and certification of knowledge in his own practice.

Although *performance* is quite inadequate for expressing ideas contained in the preceding paragraph, many solve the problem by stretching the meaning of the word to cover some or all of them. If challenged, they may protest that words can mean whatever we wish. They ignore the fact that they have thus rendered a word completely useless in communication, for without specification of the inclusiveness with which *performance* is used, no one can know the conceptual load it is meant to carry.

The solution preferred by a growing number of educators is to move to a revised expression, *competency-based teacher education* (CBTE). While competencies deemed important must be spelled out, the word is not neutral. It connotes valued abilities, including the ability to perform in desired ways. It allows focused dialogue on a broad spectrum of competencies to be developed and displayed that match the complexity of the teacher's role. In the remainder of this article competency-based teacher education is used as a "symbol of a practical social movement."

Competency-based Teacher Education as a Practical Movement

In the preceding section the slogan *performance-based teacher education* was exam-ined for its adequacy as a straightforward assertion. It was proposed that more adequate language is *competency-based teacher education,* with *competency* defined to include performance, knowledge, and values and with *teacher education* defined as total (initial and continuing) education of classroom teachers. In this remaining section of the article CBTE will be examined as a practical movement limited to consideration of preservice teacher education.

The process of designing a competency-based program of initial teacher education requires specifying in advance expected outcomes in terms of competencies to be demonstrated by graduates of the program, developing learning opportunities and environments expected to facilitate students' progress toward specified outcomes, and constructing and using evaluating procedures and instruments directly relevant to the stated competencies. In a well designed program, the result of these steps is a system where feedback channels are busy conveying evidence on the functioning and effect of the system.

This process of curriculum development is not novel at any level of education, and a good deal of curriculum designing has always proceeded from this conceptual base. Nevertheless, the present movement toward CBTE has made an explicit demand for precision in each step of the process, a demand that has been seldom satisfactorily met in past program planning. Furthermore, the present movement has made an explicit requirement that the process and content of all steps be made public, particularly for the students in the program. Public display of both the criteria and the evidence used in making judgments was viewed almost as heresy by some teacher educators only a few years ago.

Certain conditions have become so

54 widely associated with competency-based preservice teacher education that without them a program is judged as lacking. Illustrative of such conditions are student-centeredness, individualization, self-instruction, and field-centeredness. The notion that such conditions ought to prevail in all preservice programs is surely not new. What is novel in the competency-based movement is the serious commitment of many teacher educators to make such conditions operative and to perceive them as obligatory and central rather than as frills.

One of the first observations about CBTE as a practical movement is that affirmative action in both research and development and in program implementation is unprecedented in amount and quality. Contemporary efforts to design and implement competency-based teacher education are increasingly producing new knowledge as well as competent professional practitioners for elementary and secondary schools. Attention is called to the cruciality of school, university, and state department cooperation in competency-based programs and to some aspects of that cooperation already apparent in the movement.

School, University, and State Education Department Cooperation

Planning, conducting, and evaluating a competency-based program of initial teacher education cannot proceed successfully without involvement of persons from the schools, the universities, and state departments of education. The degree and nature of involvement may vary, but some involvement is essential at every stage in the process.

Universities have long held decision-making power in preservice programs. They are chartered by state education departments to grant credits and degrees. They have specially prepared staffs devoting full time to research, development, and instruction in the initial preparation of teachers. These staffs have broad experience in many different schools and school systems and are disinterested parties in local school politics. There is no reason to take this power away from universities and place it elsewhere. In fact, teacher education would suffer irreparable loss if the expertise of the universities were to be discarded. There are abundant reasons, however, for making arrangements to share this power with others.

Because initial certification of teachers is inevitably tied to preparatory programs and because the legal authority of state departments of education represents the public interest, such representatives should share in arriving at major decisions regarding competencies to be developed. Without involvement in cooperative planning, teacher education divisions in state departments of education are left with no role except to mandate and to enforce certification and program requirements. If the experienced judgment of state officials can be combined with that of other interested parties, superior decisions can be made. Moreover, if state officials are on the firing line in efforts to implement requirements, they are likely to be more cautious in mandating drastic modifications in standards and procedures prior to essential research and development.

The arguments for including representatives of the schools in a competency-based program of initial teacher education are compelling. Since teacher education students are expected to demonstrate their competence in real situations (the schools), they should have a role—along with university and state department personnel—in the definition of competencies needed, in determining in what ways and under what conditions students might acquire and demonstrate competencies, and in collecting and analyzing data on student achievement.

Because their experience is current and their contact with pupils, parents, and community is intimate, school personnel are convinced that they possess knowledge critical to the preparation of teachers. Their observation of recent entrants into practice often leads them to conclude that present programs are inadequate, that higher education personnel planning and conducting programs are far removed from reality, and that the contribution they themselves could make would greatly improve the competence of novices as they join professional ranks.

An important characteristic of a profession is that it controls its own destiny, including the selection, preparation, and admission of persons into practice. Therefore, practitioners already in the schools are not demanding token involvement, but significant power in decision-making bodies, especially in those groups making major decisions about initial and continuing education of teachers.

In CBTE program planning and operation, insufficient effort has been devoted to cooperation among the schools, universities, and state departments of education. Residual predispositions and attitudes regarding hierarchical status and authority too often limit honest partnership in program development and implementation.

Some teacher educators in higher education institutions openly argue for maintaining power in the universities. They seem to believe that they have a monopoly in valid conceptualizations of competencies required of teachers. These persons reveal an astonishing

lack of confidence in school personnel. Commonly, they doubt the competence of graduates of their own preservice programs, thus, unwittingly casting aspersions on their own preparation of those graduates. Often the arguments they present rest more on political considerations.

As they join in deliberations with school and university groups, state department personnel also may exercise their power in political rather than professional ways. They diminish their leadership in program development when they neglect attention to professional-intellectual dimensions.

Clearly if programs are to be cooperatively planned, conducted, and evaluated—and if they are to be field centered—this aspect of CBTE as a practical movement needs considerably more development in theory and practice. Particularly the political dimension needs more attention. The input of ideas and practices by classroom teachers and other local and state personnel is too central to adequate conceptualization of a competency-based program to risk losing such input because of failures in the process of cooperation.

The quality and consequences of involvement of personnel from schools, universities, and state education departments in cooperative designing, conducting, and assessing of CBTE programs is likely to be affected in positive directions by the degree of intellectual and professional expertise each person involved brings to the decisions and actions of which he is a part. Collaborative engagement in a CBTE program by these personnel requires new concepts of management (e.g., time, personnel, and money), deliberate training of participants as well as development of a capacity to live with role ambiguities and uncertainties. All parties will need to develop

56 the knowledge, skills, and attitudes requisite for successful collaboration. Additional observations can be made by briefly examining the three major steps in designing CBTE programs: identifying competencies, designing instruction, and evaluating programs.

Identifying Competencies

There are three main observations that can be made about this first critical step in the process of CBTE program development. They are (a) sources employed in the process of identifying and validating competencies, (b) the scope and nature of competencies identified, and (c) the question of essential or minimal competencies required in teaching.

Fundamentally, the identification of teaching competencies requires a conception of the nature and goals of education in a particular setting and the roles of teachers in that setting. A conception of teacher roles may be developed from available bodies of knowledge, overlaid with personal and social values and attitudes, and drawn heavily from reported empirical evidence about practice. Using the same bodies of knowledge, personal values, and empirical data, it is possible to make substantial translations from educational goals to ideal teacher roles, to competencies essential in performing those roles, to behaviors that make up competencies, and thus to develop a set of theoretically-derived competencies. Because translations made in such a process require intellectual leaps over important gaps in knowledge, theoretically-derived statements of competencies need to be subjected continuously to further analysis and to tests of validity and practicality in the real world.

Another approach to identifying competencies involves departing from many descriptions of teacher behavior; subjecting those descriptions to analysis, synthesis, and evaluation; and finally abstracting sets of behaviors that make up teaching competencies. The danger of this approach is in atomizing the complex act of teaching and arriving at statements of preferred performances rather than competencies (as earlier defined in this article). If the anticipated outcome of a teacher education program is a practitioner who may be considered *professional* in the best sense of the word, then that program should be based on a range of relevant knowledge, values, and attitudes and not restricted to performance. To put it another way, if the competent teacher is expected to know and to feel and to do, the bases for program planning should be derived from more than descriptions of teacher behavior in interaction with pupils in classrooms.

Whatever approach or combination of approaches is employed in arriving at competencies to serve as the basis for planning a CBTE program, a critical question needs to be asked: What knowledge or body of concepts is essential in making the decisions required in the exercise of the competence? Considerably more attention needs to be given to those disciplines which help in understanding and interpreting individual and group behavior—which contribute principles and methods fundamental to rational decision making in teaching. Failure to draw upon bodies of knowledge and methods in such disciplines as sociology, anthropology, psychology, and philosophy when identifying competencies may result in lists of behaviors limited to the craftsmanship of teaching rather than the full range of competencies expected of the professional teacher.

An interesting and significant requirement in a CBTE program is that competencies be identified but that the selection of competencies be left to the program planners. If the list of competencies identified is limited to those in the cognitive domain and neglects those competencies in the affective domain, the fault rests with persons who identified the competencies, not with the concept of CBTE.

A frequently observed constraint during the process of identifying competencies is found in the weight attached to assessment and evaluation of demonstrated behavior. Whether or not instruments and techniques are available to assess and measure a competency in teacher behavior is not a legitimate basis on which to accept or reject a competency when designing programs. If a set of behaviors is viewed as desirable on the basis of reason and observation, it should be included in program planning. Deliberate effort should be made during the entire process of designing, conducting, and evaluating a CBTE program to build ways of validating the competency and of assessing the degree of its presence in teacher behavior.

Whether or not there are competencies that should be required of teachers is a question currently begging for direct attention. Unfortunately, there is so little agreement about goals of education and about means of achieving such goals, it is impossible to arrive at essential or generic competencies fundamental to teaching. Lack of such agreement on fundamental competencies makes it difficult to establish teaching as a profession requiring unique competence. This lack also presents difficulties for mobile teachers when competency-based preparation for teaching in one state may be quite unsatisfactory in another state.

Identification and validation of fundamental competencies in teaching would require a great expenditure of time on the part of experts with adequate financial support. Efforts along this line by a reputable group could contribute enormously to advancing both pre- and in-service CBTE.

Certain additional observations can be made regarding the identification of competencies as one phase in examining CBTE as a practical movement. Some lists of competencies contain such detail that they number in the hundreds. A great danger here is that a desirable wholeness in education may become lost in a mass of unrelated bits and pieces. Dangers also lurk in the interpretations participating personnel make of such lists and the implications they draw from them. For example, they are seen as being unreal for any single person to achieve; they are viewed as rigid, inflexible, and prescriptive; and they are interpreted as denying personal style in teaching. It may be profitable to try a forced-choice strategy and require program planners to arrive at a more reasonable number of important competencies stated at a relatively high level of abstraction. Efforts could then be made to develop a wide range of alternative behaviors relevant to each competency. Such constellation could be open-ended for input by creative students and teachers from their personal style and experience in diverse settings.

It is sometimes argued that a teacher may be so intent on a specific behavior modification that he is unaware of or insensitive to everything else. If this is true, then program planners must build competencies into the system essential to observation, perception, and examination of one's own practice. Particular emphasis should be placed on monitoring the relation of parts to the whole so that teacher education students may learn to maintain unity, integrity, and continuity in educational programs. Of strategic importance are competencies essential to keeping the entire system open to new corrective data.

This phase of planning is perhaps the most critical because all other stages in plan-

58 ning, conducting, and evaluating a CBTE program rest squarely on the foundation of the competencies identified. It is, of course, a public statement of a basic point of view and commitment on educational goals and how teachers may facilitate pupils' achievement of those goals.

Designing Instruction

When a competency has been identified, alternative behaviors relevant to it defined, and the competency validated to the extent possible, the fundamental question of instruction must be confronted. For the teacher educator, as for all teachers, that question has four parts: (a) What is the present status of the student with respect to the competency as an expected outcome? (b) What conditions will facilitate the student's progress toward achievement of the competency? (c) What interventions by the teacher educator will generate those conditions? (d) How can the achievement of the competency be determined?

The first and last questions in that list are questions of assessment and evaluation, but they are also important in designing instruction. It is folly to design instructional strategies for a given student and to subject him to those strategies without reference to what he already knows and can do. An instructional system that does not attend to final assessment of competence is a closed system and is weakened by lack of feedback. To allow either thing to happen is to waste human and physical resources at the risk of boredom and eventual rejection by the student.

Presumably, teacher educators make rational decisions about conditions to be fostered in the learning environment of prospective teachers. Each decision that is made

deliberately is a prediction of relationships between conditions and students' progression toward an expected outcome. Likewise, when a teacher educator decides to intervene in the environment of a student, by whatever means, to create a specified condition, he is making an assumption of relationship between his intervention and the resultant condition.

Adequate evidence is not now available to validate many of the predictions and assumptions on which teacher educators depend in designing instruction. Where evidence is available, it should be used. When adequate evidence is unavailable, it is incumbent upon teacher educators to produce needed knowledge systematically. Continuing investigation into components of an instructional system and feedback into its various parts is required in all open systems. This feature promises to hasten the day when decisions can be based on more firm predictions. The need for teacher educators to increase their attention to systematic inquiry into the knowledge base for their instructional decisions cannot be overemphasized.

In part, designing instruction is creating, selecting, and using materials of instruction. In the rush to implement competency-based programs, many instructional modules have been produced without benefit of required expertise or field testing. Such haste has contributed largely to the low quality of some products among the plethora of materials flooding the market. These instructional materials seem to follow a single pattern in design, make use of a few of the same strategies over and over, and fail to present to the student a range of approaches to achieve a skill or acquire a concept.

So much designing of the instructional materials has been done within traditional courses that teacher educators continue business as usual under the guise of CBTE. The materials market has been overloaded with instructional modules and protocols on those behaviors easily defined, taught, observed, and measured. It has been undersupplied with materials to help with instruction in connection with more complex competencies.

Earlier it was stated as an assumption that teacher educators make deliberate decisions in the various stages of designing their instruction. If this is true, teacher educators require certain competencies which have implications for their initial and continuing preparation for work. Wherever teacher educators function, it must be assumed that the context in which they work, the ideas relevant to their work, and the persons and programs involved will change. Because this is as true for them as it is for elementary and secondary school teachers, teacher educators also must be responsible for continuing a process of diagnosing, treating, and evaluating their own professional practice.

After long avoidance of the problem of initial and continuing education of teacher educators, it is now essential that competencies needed by teacher educators be identified and validated; that instructional activities designed to prepare them be relevant to those competencies; and that assessment of their achievement be based on the criteria built into the definition of required competencies.

Competency-based programs demand that teacher educators assume new and different roles and responsibilities where special preparation is needed. Furthermore, as a wider group of persons, especially those in the elementary and secondary schools, assume teacher education roles, they need special preparation for acquiring the necessary competencies.

This brief examination of designing instruction as a phase of CBTE has resulted in some pride in accomplishment but in considerable concern and some disappointment. If competency-based teacher education has merit, its benefits should be accessible to teacher educators and to those in graduate professional schools who prepare them.

Evaluating Programs

Evaluating a CBTE program is a large task encompassing many and diverse activities. Only a few of the most pervasive and critical questions about program evaluation can be considered and commented upon here.

First, it seems important to ask: What is being evaluated when the program is the object of evaluation? Is it the program design as a plan for initial preparation of teachers? Is it the design in operation as prospective teachers are prepared? Or is it the consequences or effect of the program on those who go through it? All three aspects—the plan, the operation, and the consequences—need to be evaluated if program evaluation is to be complete. Findings in evaluating any one aspect should be fed back to other aspects as appropriate.[3]

It is foolish to ask about the consequences of a program unless some evidence exists that program features believed to be active were in fact active. For example, it is pointless to ask how effective the program was in producing teachers with creative individual styles if nothing in the program was geared to that outcome. It is unfair to ascribe failure to a program because graduates are

3. Arthur J. Lewis and Alice Miel. *Supervision for Improved Instruction* (Belmont, Ca.: Wadsworth Publishing Company, Inc., 1972), pp. 85–109.

60 unable to manage a classroom if the program did not provide any opportunity for training students to manage a real classroom. To put it another way, if consequences of some sort are the dependent variable, it is critical to have adequate data on the independent variable (program or program component) before drawing conclusions about possible relationships between them.

A concern of interest to the public as well as to teacher educators relates to the point just made. Are graduates of a CBTE program actually competent as teachers (more so than others) and does their competence relate positively to pupil progress (more so than others)? The second part of that question should have been answered in program planning when competencies were being identified and validated, since the most dependable validation of a competency is evidence of its relation to pupil progress.

The first part of the question, however, is critical since it addresses one of the most serious problems in the CBTE movement. What shall be the primary criterion for determining the extent to which a graduate of the program demonstrates the expected competencies? Is the chief criterion teacher behavior, the conditions created by teacher behavior, or pupil progress? Rather than argue fruitlessly for any single criterion, it seems more intelligent to agree that there are five major points in a long process of teacher education where evaluation is appropriate: (a) the plan, (b) the operation, (c) the consequences in terms of teacher behavior, (d) the consequences in terms of conditions created by teacher behavior, and (e) consequences in terms of pupil progress. Only a broad and continuing program of evaluation of data gathered all along the line can answer the question of the value of competency-based teacher education.

Conclusion

Performance-based teacher education is a slogan with the advantages and disadvantages of that form of communication. It has caught the attention of many teacher educators and has led to worthwhile modifications in programs. However, the concept of performance is a limiting one. It should be replaced by the concept of competency. It is *competence* that professional educators are expected to possess and demonstrate, including performance and the knowledge, attitudes, and values relevant to performance. With the broader concept of competence carried in the slogan and with both the public and educators generally responding favorably, constructive reform in teacher education can be expected to proceed with increasing success.

———◆•◆———

QUESTIONS FOR DISCUSSION

1. What personal qualifications do you believe a teacher should possess?
2. What are the teacher certification requirements in your state?
3. Try to recall the best teacher that you have ever had. What age level and subject(s) did he/she teach? What qualities did this teacher possess? What made him/her such a good teacher?
4. What is your reaction to the CBTE "point of view" article by Dr. Margaret Lindsey?
5. What steps do you believe a teacher should take after beginning teaching to keep up on his subject matter and on the latest teaching techniques?

SUPPLEMENTARY LEARNING ACTIVITIES

1. Conduct an informal poll of teachers to see what qualities they believe one should possess before entering a teacher education program.
2. Write to several state departments of education and inquire about the certification laws of each state.
3. Write to the National Council for the Accreditation of Teacher Education and request information about their standards, procedures, and list of accredited institutions.
4. Arrange a field trip to visit a nearby school. While there, try to visit with a variety of school personnel, talk with students, and observe different aspects of the school operation.
5. Arrange a panel discussion on the general topic "Becoming a Teacher." Invite a college teacher, high school teacher, elementary school teacher, student teacher, and school administrator to participate on the panel.

SELECTED REFERENCES

AACTE, "Performance Based Teacher Education: An Annotated Bibliography." Series no. 7, ERIC Clearinghouse on Teacher Education, 1972.

Alexander, William M. *Are You a Good Teacher?* New York: Holt, Rinehart and Winston, Inc., 1959.

American Association of School Administrators, Department of Classroom Teachers, and National School Boards Association. *Who's a Good Teacher?* Washington, D.C.: National Education Association Publications, 1961.

Armstrong, W. Earl, and T. M. Stinnett. *A Manual on Certification Requirements for School Personnel in the United States.* National Commission on Teacher Education and Professional Standards, National Education Association. Washington, D.C.: National Education Association Publications, 1971.

Biddle, Bruce J., and William J. Ellena, eds. *Contemporary Research on Teacher Effectiveness.* New York: Holt, Rinehart and Winston, Inc., 1964.

Bruce, William F., and A. John Holden, Jr. *The Teacher's Personal Development.* New York: Holt, Rinehart and Winston, Inc., 1957.

Highet, Gilbert. *The Art of Teaching.* New York: Alfred A. Knopf, Inc., 1950.

Hughes, Marie. "What Is Teaching? One Viewpoint." *Educational Leadership* 19(1962):251–59.

McGrath, Earl J. "The Ideal Education for the Professional Man." In *Education for the Profession,* ed. Nelson B. Henry, pp. 281–301. The Sixty-first Yearbook of the National Society for the Study of Education, Part II. Chicago: University of Chicago Press, 1962.

Mason, Ward S. "The Beginning Teacher: Status and Career Orientations." U.S. Office of Education circular 644, 1961. Washington, D.C.: U.S. Government Printing Office, 1961.

Massey, Harold W., and Edwin E. Vineyard. *The Profession of Teaching.* New York: Odyssey Press, 1961.

Michael-Smith, Harold. "It Takes Self-Understanding." *NEA Journal* 49(1960): 37–40.

62 National Education Association. *Teaching Career Fact Book*. Washington, D.C.: National Education Association Publications, 1966.

————. "Who's a Good Teacher?" Washington, D.C.: National Education Association Publications, 1961.

Ragan, William B. *Teaching America's Children*. New York: Holt, Rinehart and Winston, Inc., 1961 (chapter 2).

Turner, Richard L., and Nicholas A. Fattu. "Skill in Teaching, Assessed on the Criterion of Problem Solving." Bulletin of the School of Education. Bloomington, Ind.: Indiana University Press, May 1961.

Van Til, William. *The Making of a Modern Educator*. Indianapolis: The Bobbs-Merrill Co., Inc., 1961.

Wiles, Kimball. *Teaching for Better Schools*. Englewood Cliffs, N.J.: Prentice-Hall, Inc., 1959.

Wynn, Richard. *Careers in Education*. New York: McGraw-Hill Book Company, Inc., 1960.

chapter 3
The Role of the Teacher

goals

- Describes the day-by-day work of the teacher.

- Identifies the various roles that a teacher plays in the educational establishment.

- Contrasts the work of the contemporary educator with that of his historical counterpart.

- Illustrates that teachers are better prepared and increasingly competent as professional educators.

- Introduces the concept that the most effective learning takes place when the teacher serves as a "learning facilitator" rather than a "dispenser of knowledge."

- Articulates the importance of the "planning" that a teacher must do if effective learning is to take place.

- Describes the diagnostic and evaluation functions that an educator must fulfill.

- Explains the concept that the effective contemporary educator must be a "student of teaching."

64   It has already been mentioned in the opening remarks of this section of the book that a teacher must be willing to sacrifice many long and hard hours of work to his profession. This fact was born out in a recent study completed by the Research Division of the National Education Association in which a large number of teachers were asked how

> *Education is a painful, continual and difficult work to be done by kindness, by watching, by warning, by precept, and by praise, but above all—by example.*
>
> John Ruskin

they spend their working week. The results of this study are shown in Figure 3.1. This figure shows that the average teacher in this study devoted a total of approximately 48 hours per week to his job as a teacher. Of this total time, he spends 29.8 hours actually working with pupils; 6.8 hours performing other duties (such as planning, faculty meetings, clerical work, and preparing teaching materials) during the school day; and 10.8 hours doing

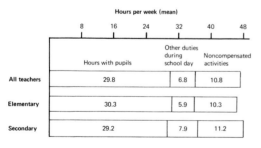

Figure 3.1 The Teacher's Working Week.

Source: National Education Association, Research Division, *The American Public School Teacher,* research report 1967–R4 (Washington, D.C.: National Education Association Publications, 1967) p. 27. Used with permission.

school-related work outside of the school day (such as correcting papers, writing reports, scoring tests, preparing lesson plans, and attending professional meetings). It is obvious that teaching requires many long hours of hard work—and is not a job that would appeal to "clock watchers."

A teacher wears many hats in the course of a school day, a school week, and a school year. For example, he must be a lesson planner, purveyor of knowledge, motivator, disciplinarian, counselor, confidant, mediator, curriculum planner, worker for his professional organization, human relations expert, and record keeper. Truly, a teacher must have a multitude of talents and be competent in many different roles if he is to be successful. In this chapter we will examine some of the more specific tasks included in the role of the teacher.

Keeping School

One of the tasks that has historically consumed much of a teacher's time is that traditionally called "keeping school." School keeping involves such "chores" as ordering supplies, keeping the classroom tidy and clean (even though most schools now hire competent custodians to do all the major cleaning, a teacher still has a good deal of minor house cleaning chores to perform), keeping attendance records, checking books in and out, collecting lunch money, putting up bulletin boards and displays of various sorts, and filling out forms and reports that the school may require. While school-keeping chores such as these are important and must be done, they have historically consumed too much of a teacher's valuable time—time that could be better spent working with students. Fortunately, in recent years schools have found

Teaching is a demanding task requiring many long hours of planning.

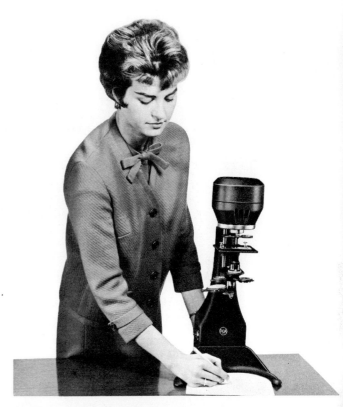

Today's teacher devotes many hours to the preparation of teaching materials.

ways to relieve the teacher of many of these chores. Many schools have developed simplified methods of record keeping which require very little time on the part of the teachers. Also, some schools now employ "paraprofessional" help to do these school-keeping chores, thereby freeing the teacher to spend more time working with students. A discussion of the important role and function of these paraprofessionals will be provided in chapter four.

Planning

One of the most important roles that a teacher plays is that of "planner." A teacher is given a great deal of freedom and autonomy in planning what will take place in his or her classroom. This is as it should be, because today's teacher is a highly trained, competent professional who is the best qualified to determine what each student needs in his classroom. In some instances, a teacher will be given a broad planning document such as a curriculum guide that may originate at the state, county, or school district level. Such documents, however, are only general guidelines and each individual teacher must still plan the specific day-to-day program. An increasing amount of the planning task is being done cooperatively by groups of teachers, in

66

An increasing amount of educational planning is being done by groups or teams of teachers.

One must learn by doing the thing; for though you think you know it you have no certainty, until you try.

Sophocles

conjunction with team teaching or in summer efforts to prepare various types of units and other curricular materials. More and more, school districts are realizing the value that can accrue from hiring teachers during the summer to do such cooperative planning.

The success of a school program for a given student will be dependent, in a large amount, upon the quality of planning that went into that student's program. By the same token, the success of the educational program of an entire school system will be determined by the planning that goes into that program.

The same thing is true, incidentally, for the entire American educational system—its success is largely dependent upon the quality of the planning that goes into it.

There are a number of different levels of planning that a teacher must do. These levels are shown in Figure 3.2. As this figure shows, a teacher begins with a very general long-range yearly lesson plan for each subject that he teaches. This yearly lesson plan must be very flexible so that changes can be made in the plan during the year as the need arises. Figure 3.2 further shows that a teacher must also make semester plans (or quarter plans, depending upon how the school year may be divided). Like the yearly plan, these semester plans must be very general and very flexible. One of the many values of long-range plans (such as those a teacher makes for an entire school year or for a semester) is that they

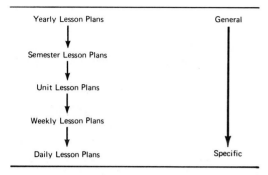

Yearly Lesson Plans   General

Semester Lesson Plans

Unit Lesson Plans

Weekly Lesson Plans

Daily Lesson Plans   Specific

Figure 3.2   Levels of Lesson Planning.

permit the teacher to gather more and better instructional materials (some of which may be difficult to obtain) by the time they are needed. Long-range planning also permits a teacher to think through what he really wants the students to learn over a long period of time.

Perhaps the single most important and valuable type of planning that a teacher does is what is commonly known as the unit lesson plan. The unit plan is one that is done for a rather discrete segment of the year's work in a given subject. Units can vary greatly in size; however, most of them range between a week and a month in length. Units can also vary greatly in scope, depending upon the grade level and subject. Examples of typical units are: finger painting in first grade art, the American Indian in third grade social studies, poetry in fifth grade English, the digestive system in seventh grade science, squares and square roots in tenth grade mathematics, forms of mental illness in twelfth grade psychology, or the role of the teacher in a college introduction to teaching course.

A unit may be defined as an organization of learning activities and experiences around a central theme, developed cooperatively by a group of pupils under a teacher's leadership.

The essential features implied by this definition are that (1) learning takes place through many types of experiences rather than through a single activity such as reading and reciting; (2) the activities are unified around a central theme, problem, or purpose; (3) the unit provides opportunities for socialization of pupils by means of cooperative group planning; and (4) the role of the teacher is that of a leader rather than a taskmaster.

There are a variety of different approaches that a teacher can take in planning a unit. For instance, a teacher can plan what is essentially a "subject matter unit." A subject matter unit is a selection of subject matter materials, and of educative experiences centering upon subject matter materials, which are arranged around a central core found within the subject matter itself. The core may be a generalization, a concept, a topic, or a theme. The unit is to be studied by pupils for the purpose of achieving learning outcomes derivable from experiences with subject matter.

Or a teacher may plan what is essentially an "experience unit." This is a series of educative experiences organized around a pupil purpose, problem, or need, utilizing socially useful subject matter and materials, resulting in the achievement of the purpose and in the achievement of learning outcomes inherent in the process.

In reality all units use both experience and subject matter. The difference is primarily one of emphasis. It should be understood that in actual practice the terminology used is not the important consideration. What is important is that the teacher must be concerned with providing rich and varied learning experiences for each student.

Yet a third type of unit plan is that commonly referred to as a "resource unit." A

68 resource unit is not ordinarily planned as a single teaching unit. It is usually developed by a committee of teachers with little or no pupil assistance. Hence, it becomes a "resource *of* units." Frequently they are not developed with any particular group of children in mind; in fact, the materials may be used in several grades; they cover broad areas of content and always contain more information and many more suggestions than could be used with any one class. A resource unit on conservation might include materials to be used in teaching several units on recreation, public health, lumbering, fishing, mining, and flood control.

In preparing a unit plan, it is recommended that a teacher:

a. State clearly the purposes (*objectives* or *goals,* as they are often called) in teaching the unit. In other words, what changes does the teacher want to make in the child in terms of knowledge, skills, habits, attitudes, and appreciations? These stated purposes of the unit should be expressed in "behavioral" terms, or, in other words, in terms of student behavior that will be exhibited when the purposes of the unit have been accomplished. When stated this way, a teacher can measure the success of the unit.

b. Look up references on the subject, read them, and write a content outline of the material, listing references.

c. List the materials to be used in the unit. This will include such items as pictures, slides, movies, models, and construction materials.

d. List the ways the teacher will lead the children into the unit of work; these are called *possible approaches.*

e. List the activities that will help the children attain the purposes or outcomes of the unit.

f. List the ways which the teacher will use in the evaluation of the unit. If a written test is considered, at least a rough draft of the test should be included in the unit.

Many schools ask teachers to make very brief weekly lesson plans so that if in the event a regular teacher becomes ill, a substitute teacher would have an idea of what was

Part of the task of preparing a unit plan is locating and developing the teaching resources to be used in the unit.

planned each day for each class. These weekly lesson plans are usually extremely brief and are frequently written on special forms prepared for this purpose.

The most specific planning that a teacher does is that done for a specific lesson on a specific day. Daily lesson planning is relatively simple providing the teacher has already made adequate unit lesson plans. Excellent unit plans will have permitted the teacher to gather all of the necessary learning resources ahead of time and to have thought through clearly the general objectives for the unit. The final detail and specific objectives necessary in a daily lesson plan flow naturally and quite easily out of a well-done unit lesson plan. The lesson plan is designed simply as a means to good instruction. It has no magic value in and of itself and cannot be justified simply as an elaborate masterpiece. The lesson plan is simply a means to an end— a device to help the teacher be well prepared to teach.

Lesson plans may take numerous forms. There is no one best way to prepare lesson plans; however, most teachers find it desirable to follow some structured format and to

do much of this planning on paper. One lesson plan format that has been found useful by many educators is that found in Figure 3.3. This format can serve for all the levels of planning that a teacher must do, whether they be yearly plans, semester plans, unit plans, weekly plans, or daily plans. As Figure 3.3 shows, the first task that a teacher has in planning is that of determining the objectives of the plan involved. Objectives become the road map of the lesson—they indicate the purposes of the lesson and the desired learning outcomes for the students. As has already been suggested, educational objectives should always be stated in terms of student behavior that can be measured. This is necessary so that after the lesson is completed, the teacher can determine whether or not each student has achieved the desired outcomes. Objectives thus stated are frequently called *behavioral objectives*.

Figure 3.3 also shows that in planning a lesson, a teacher must determine what materials will be needed for the lesson. As will be indicated in chapter fourteen, a wealth of instruction materials is now available to educators. A teacher must not only be familiar

69

A. Objectives (Stated in behavioral terms that can be measured):
B. Materials Needed:
C. Procedure:
    1. Teacher Activity
    2. Student Activity
D. Provisions for Measuring Extent to Which Stated Objectives Were Achieved:

Figure 3.3 A Suggested Lesson Plan Format.

No nation can remain free which does not recognize the importance of education. Our public schools are the backbone of American life and character. We must recognize their importance and stand firmly against any groups which oppose popular education.

Liberty can never flourish in any nation where there is no popular education.

Samuel M. Lindsay

70 with these teaching materials but must also know which is the most effective material to use in a given situation.

Figure 3.3 further indicates that a teacher must thoroughly plan the procedure for each lesson. To effectively do this, he must have a thorough understanding of the nature of the learner—a topic discussed in chapter twelve. He must also be familiar with a wide variety of teaching techniques.

Lastly, Figure 3.3 shows that a teacher must make provisions for measuring the extent to which the stated objectives for each lesson are achieved. This provides the teacher with a measure of the overall success of the lesson and also helps him to determine which students have learned the contents of the lesson and which students need additional instruction.

One last important point concerning the planning role of a teacher deals with the need to individualize the learning experiences for each student insofar as it is humanly possible to do so. Unfortunately, since a typical elementary school teacher has between 20 and 30 students and a typical secondary teacher may have as many as 150 students each day, it is simply not humanly possible for a teacher to make a specific lesson plan for each student. At best, a teacher can hope to modify a single lesson plan to fit the individual needs of each specific student. There is an indication that some of the newer innovations in education, such as individually prescribed instruction, modular scheduling, computer-assisted instruction, independent study, team teaching, and a differentiated teaching staff—all of which are discussed in some detail elsewhere in this book—will make it possible for teachers to do a much better job of tailoring an educational program for each individual student.

Helping Students to Learn

Historically, the role of the teacher has been viewed mainly as that of a "dispenser of knowledge." Today's teacher can better be characterized as one who "helps students to learn." This new "helping" role of the contemporary teacher is exemplified by a teacher assisting a group of students as they plan a small group project; circulating in a science laboratory giving help to individual students; listening to an individual student who has a reading problem read aloud; or counseling with a student who has a personal problem. The following factors have helped to bring about this new relationship that the teacher has with the learner:

I have never let my schooling interfere with my education.

Mark Twain

- Whereas a colonial school teacher had very few tools to use, except a few poorly written textbooks and his own knowledge of the subject matter he was attempting to teach, the contemporary educator has a wealth of teaching aids at his disposal. These instructional devices now make it possible for a teacher to help students learn much more efficiently and effectively than was possible when teachers had to "dispense" whatever knowledge the students were to learn.

- An increased understanding of the learning process has also helped educators to assume their present "helping" relationship with learners. Since the turn of the century, thanks to the pioneering efforts of the child study movement and the con-

Effective lesson planning incorporates a maximum amount of active student participation in the learning process.

tinued refinement of the discipline of educational psychology, an ever-increasing knowledge of the manner in which learning takes place has been made available to teachers. One of the tasks of the teacher is to mold this knowledge of the learning act into excellent learning experiences for each of his students. The colonial schoolmaster had very little knowledge of the learning act at his disposal and consequently cannot be blamed for his ignorance of the fact that students tend to quickly forget rotely

Historically, students have generally been treated badly in schools. A variety of frightening and ingenious punishments have been devised by teachers in the past. This illustration of a German school during the late 19th century shows examples of punishment then employed. These included the hanging of various marks of disapproval around the offender's neck, wearing of a dunce cap, hanging of a boy in a basket to the ceiling, tying a boy to a stationary ring, and frequent whippings.

Early lesson planning allows sufficient time for the development of a variety of teaching materials. This student is putting audiotapes on a dial access retrieval system which allows individual students to listen to prerecorded learning materials by using headphones and simply dialing the lesson they wish to hear.

memorized facts, learn best from firsthand experiences rather than being lectured to, and learn more quickly and permanently that which they are highly motivated to learn—all of which are examples of important principles of learning that have grown from an increased understanding of the learning processes, those processes which guide the work of contemporary educators.

■ Another factor that has contributed to the view that teachers should help students learn rather than dispense knowledge has been the changes that have taken place in educational philosophy down through the ages. There was a time, for instance, when children were viewed by the church, most parents, and most teachers to be basically bad and full of original sin which somehow must be beaten from them. And "beat," literally, many schoolmasters did, in their misguided efforts to teach and discipline their students. Fortunately, most contemporary educators agree with Jean Jacques Rousseau (1712–1778)—the great French philosopher who deserves at least part of the credit for bringing about this change in the way youth are viewed—that children are born basically good and become bad only in the hands of man. This

change in the philosophical view of the nature of a child has had a profound influence on the relationship between teacher and student.

■ Another change that has contributed to the idea that teachers should help children learn rather than dispense knowledge has been the gradual infusion and acceptance of the concept of democracy into many education philosophies. Most American educators strongly believe that the relationship between a teacher and students should be a democratic one; that is, one in which students have a voice and are respected as individuals. Students who participate in such a classroom are likely to enjoy school more, learn more, and be-

A teacher participates in a small group discussion with members of a creative writing class.

A contemporary teacher's role can best be characterized as "helping students learn" rather than "dispensing knowledge."

come better citizens in our democratic society.

Evaluation, as contrasted with measurement, embraces a wider range of technique and evidence.

Paul L. Dressel
Lewis B. Mayhew

Evaluating

In addition to school keeping, planning, and helping students to learn, a teacher must also be an evaluator. For it is through a well-planned program of evaluation that a teacher is able to determine the abilities and achievements of each student. This knowledge is essential for the teacher to plan an appropriate program for each student. In his role as an "evaluator" the teacher is continually assessing each student's abilities, interests, accomplishments, and needs. To help him gather data to accomplish evaluation, an educator employs standardized tests, teacher-made tests, and subjective observations.

76   A standardized test is one which has been constructed using carefully prescribed techniques; and one for which norms have been established. There are literally hundreds of commercially prepared standardized tests available for teachers to use. These tests are available to measure different dimensions of student aptitude, achievement, and interest. Most school districts now have rather well developed standardized testing programs which supply the teacher with a wide variety of data to use in his role as an evaluator.

Teacher-made tests, as the name implies, are those which the teacher himself constructs. These tests are usually designed to measure student achievement in the various subjects. Constructing good teacher-made tests is a time-consuming task and requires a thorough knowledge of the principles of test construction on the part of the teacher.

In addition to the data obtained from standardized tests and teacher-made tests, a teacher can obtain useful evaluation information by simply observing students. The skilled educator can learn a good deal about a student's abilities, achievements, interests, and needs through careful observation.

A record of the evaluative data accumulated on each student is usually kept by a school district. It becomes part of a record called a "cumulative record" and contains standardized test scores, grades, health information, and other background information about the student. A sample cumulative record card for a pupil is shown in Figure 3.4.

Reporting

A role of the teacher that is closely connected with evaluating is that of "reporting."

Examples of the vast array of technical aids now available for use in schools.

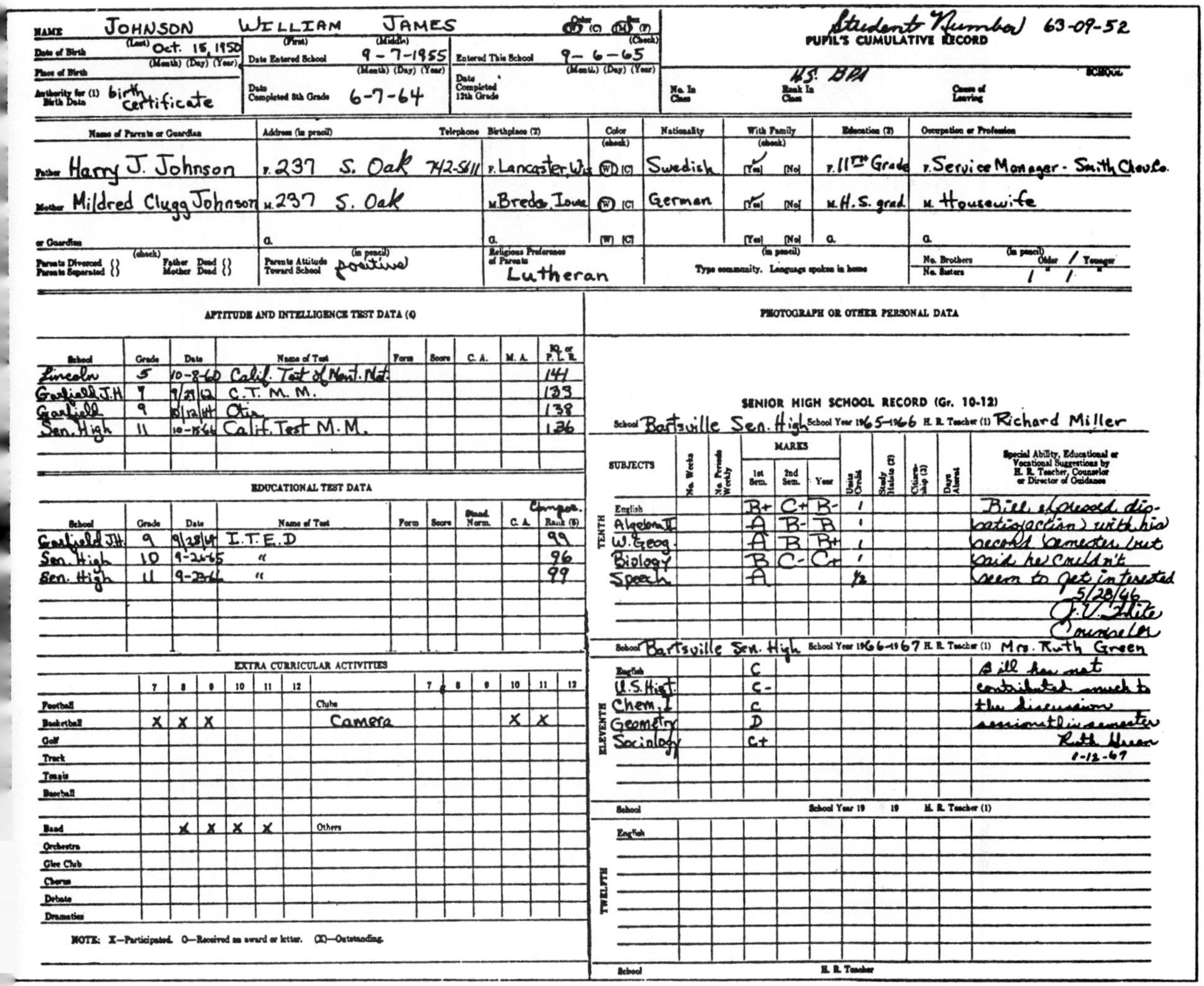

Student Number 63-09-52
PUPIL'S CUMULATIVE RECORD

NAME JOHNSON (Last) WILLIAM (First) JAMES (Middle) Color (C) (M) (F) (Check)
Date of Birth Oct. 15, 1950 (Month) (Day) (Year) — Date Entered School 9-7-1955 (Month) (Day) (Year) — Entered This School 9-6-65 (Month) (Day) (Year)
Place of Birth — SCHOOL H.S. BPH
Authority for (1) Birth Data birth certificate — Date Completed 8th Grade 6-7-64 — Date Completed 12th Grade — No. in Class — Rank in Class — Cause of Leaving

Name of Parents or Guardian	Address (in pencil)	Telephone	Birthplace (2)	Color (check)	Nationality	With Family (check)	Education (2)	Occupation or Profession
Father Harry J. Johnson	F. 237 S. Oak	742-5611	F. Lancaster Wis	(W) (C)	Swedish	Yes [No]	F. 11th Grade	F. Service Manager - Smith Chev. Co.
Mother Mildred Clugg Johnson	M. 237 S. Oak		M. Breda Iowa	(W) (C)	German	Yes [No]	M. H.S. grad.	M. Housewife
or Guardian	G.		G.	(W) (C)		[Yes] [No]	G.	G.

Parents Divorced {} Parents Separated {} (check) Father Dead {} Mother Dead {} — Parents Attitude Toward School (in pencil) positive — Religious Preference of Parents Lutheran — Type community. Language spoken in home (in pencil) — No. Brothers Older 1 Younger — No. Sisters 1 1

APTITUDE AND INTELLIGENCE TEST DATA (4)

School	Grade	Date	Name of Test	Form	Score	C. A.	M. A.	I.Q. or P. L. R.
Lincoln	5	10-8-60	Calif. Test of Ment. Mat.					141
Garfield J.H.	7	9/21/62	C.T.M.M.					133
Garfield	9	10/12/64	Otis					138
Sen. High	11	10-15-66	Calif. Test M.M.					136

EDUCATIONAL TEST DATA

School	Grade	Date	Name of Test	Form	Score	Stand. Norm.	C. A.	Compos. Rank (5)
Garfield J.H.	9	9/28/64	I.T.E.D					99
Sen. High	10	9-26-65	"					96
Sen. High	11	9-26-66	"					99

EXTRA CURRICULAR ACTIVITIES

	7	8	9	10	11	12		7	8	9	10	11	12
Football							Clubs						
Basketball	X	X	X				Camera				X	X	
Golf													
Track													
Tennis													
Baseball													
Band		X	X	X	X		Others						
Orchestra													
Glee Club													
Chorus													
Debate													
Dramatics													

NOTE: X—Participated. O—Received an award or letter. (X)—Outstanding.

PHOTOGRAPH OR OTHER PERSONAL DATA

SENIOR HIGH SCHOOL RECORD (Gr. 10-12)

School Bartsville Sen. High — School Year 1965-1966 — H. R. Teacher (1) Richard Miller

	SUBJECTS	No. Weeks	No. Periods Weekly	1st Sem.	2nd Sem.	Year	Units Credit	Study Habits (3)	Citizenship (3)	Days Absent	Special Ability, Educational or Vocational Suggestions by H. R. Teacher, Counselor or Director of Guidance
TENTH	English			B+	C+	B-	1				Bill expressed dissatisfaction with his second semester, but said he couldn't seem to get interested 5/28/66 J. V. White Counselor
	Algebra II			A	B-	B	1				
	W. Geog.			A	B	B+	1				
	Biology			B	C-	C+	1				
	Speech			A			½				

School Bartsville Sen. High — School Year 1966-1967 — H. R. Teacher (1) Mrs. Ruth Green

	SUBJECTS	No. Weeks	No. Periods Weekly	1st Sem.	2nd Sem.	Year	Units Credit	Study Habits (3)	Citizenship (3)	Days Absent	Remarks
ELEVENTH	English			C							Bill has not contributed much to the discussion sessions this semester Ruth Green 1-12-67
	U.S. Hist.			C-							
	Chem. I			C							
	Geometry			D							
	Sociology			C+							

School — School Year 19 19 — H. R. Teacher (1)

TWELFTH — English

School — H. R. Teacher

Figure 3.4 A Sample Cumulative Record.

Reporting basically involves communicating to the parents about their child's progress in school. This is usually accomplished in two ways: in writing, on one of the many different forms that have been created by schools for this purpose, and in person, during a conference.

There are a great variety of forms used by various schools in their efforts to report to parents. In fact, most schools create their

STUDENT *Sue Stone*   ENGLISH *III*

ADVISOR *Mrs. Anderson*   TEACHER *Mrs. Anderson*

EVALUATION

	Quarters	Superior	Above average	School average	Below average	Decidedly below average
EFFORT	1				✓	
	2				✓	
	3					✓
	4					✓
ACHIEVEMENT	1	✓				
	2	✓				
	3		✓			
	4		✓			

ANALYSIS OF EVALUATION

QUARTERS	Strength 1	2	3	4	Weakness 1	2	3	4
Conduct					✓	✓	✓	✓
Work habits in class					✓	✓	✓	✓
Homework					✓	✓	✓	✓
Skills								
Oral activities	✓	✓						
Reading	✓	✓						
Written work	✓	✓	✓					
Content	✓	✓						
Mechanics	✓	✓						
Punctuation	✓	✓	✓					
Grammar	✓	✓						
Spelling	✓	✓						
Penmanship	✓	✓	✓	✓				

Figure 3.5   A Sample Report Card.

own report card forms. An example of such a form is shown in Figure 3.5.

The role of "reporter" requires that a teacher possess not only a thorough knowledge of the progress of each student, but also the communication and human relations skills necessary to effectively pass this information along to parents.

A teacher must possess good human relations skills to develop the type of relationship with pupils that is essential for the development of good learning experiences.

One of the very most important general tasks of a teacher is that of understanding and getting along with the many different people with which he must deal. He must possess good human relations skills and, in a sense, must be a public relations expert. The teacher who is not able to successfully fulfill this role is destined to failure.

There are many different groups of people with whom the teacher must relate. Obviously, the group that the teacher spends the most time with is the students. It may seem redundant to suggest that a teacher must be able to understand and get along with students; however, there are a number of teachers who do have difficulty in these areas. For instance, the teacher who continually has discipline problems in his classroom quite likely does not understand students and obviously can't get along very well with them.

Parents constitute another group which a teacher must understand and get along with. Most parents are extremely interested in, and in many instances rather emotional about, their child's progress in school. Furthermore, it is difficult for many parents to be objective about their child's success and/or behavior in school. It requires a good deal of understanding and human relations skill on the part of the teacher, for instance, to tell a mother and father that their child has been behaving badly and/or is not achieving academically.

Lastly, a teacher must understand and get along with his colleagues—fellow teachers, supervisors, and administrators. This is more true today than it has ever been before due to the fact that education is now a very complex undertaking and teachers often work in teams, do joint planning, have the help of specialists

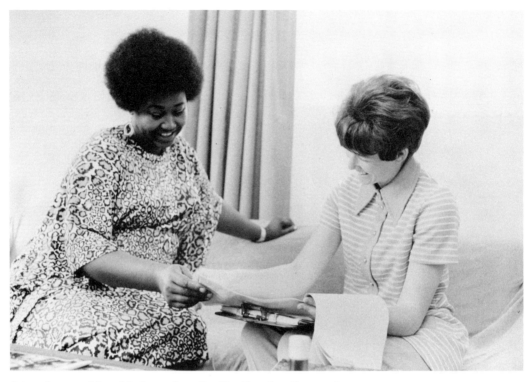

A teacher must be able to work well with other faculty members.

and paraprofessionals, and generally work more closely together than has traditionally been the case (the one-room country school teacher had no colleagues, for instance). Some teachers understand and get along with students but find it difficult to relate to their colleagues. The teacher who finds himself in this situation is doomed to failure just as surely as the one who cannot relate to students.

In order to understand people a teacher must develop insight into human motivations, needs, fears, hopes, weaknesses, prejudices, and desires. A teacher's ability to get along with people is largely dependent upon his own personality, attitudes, and values, as well as the extent to which he basically likes and respects people in spite of the fact that they may be different and may possess weaknesses. The person who is considering entering the teaching profession should carefully assess his human relations skills and decide whether or not his personality, attitudes, and values will enable him to get along effectively with the many people with whom he will have to deal as a teacher.

Keeping Up to Date

American education, both the task and the teacher, are rapidly changing. Teachers

Attending a variety of different kinds of conventions, conferences, and other professional meetings is one way that educators keep up to date.

82 must not only keep pace with these changes, but must actually bring some of them about through devising improved teaching methods, developing educational innovations, and helping to expand the body of knowledge within their disciplines. This means that a teacher must keep up to date on all aspects of his work —advances in knowledge in the subject matter, improved teaching techniques (including discovering some of his own), changes in our social system, changes in our youth, and changes on the national and international political scene. Then too, a teacher must keep up on research findings in education and put into practice those findings that are of use to his particular work. In fact, a teacher in order to be most effective must become a student of teaching, constantly studying and experimenting with learning and constantly improving his work as an educator.

This means that a teacher must spend a good deal of time reading professional literature; must attend professional conventions, conferences, and workshops; take an active part in in-service training programs; go back to a college or university and take graduate courses and possibly work on an advanced degree; and in general seek out ways of keeping up to date.

In conclusion, the role of the contemporary teacher is a many-faceted one. This

A teacher must also be able to relate effectively to parents.

One of the ways that teachers can keep up to date in their subject matter specialty is by enrolling in graduate courses, workshops, or institutes dealing with their specialty.

Education is an admirable thing, but it is well to remember from time to time that nothing that is worth knowing can be taught.

Oscar Wilde

chapter has mentioned but a few of the major tasks that a successful teacher must be capable of performing. Perhaps the most important concept presented in this chapter is the fact that today's teacher is no longer

84 merely a dispenser of knowledge, but rather helps arrange learning experiences for the student—in a real sense, he is a colearner with the students. Students learn—teachers assist them.

Point of View

The role of the teacher outlined in this chapter is very complex indeed. It has been suggested that the successful teacher must be extremely dedicated, willing to work long and hard hours, and be a bit of a custodian. On top of this he must be very dedicated to helping students, able to wisely plan a learning program for each student, and be able to motivate each student. The teacher must furthermore be capable of assessing student progress and designing remedial learning experiences where required. The teacher must be a "human relations expert" capable of understanding, communicating with, and getting along well with a wide variety of people—students, parents, voters, colleagues, administrators, etc. Above all, the teacher must keep up with the knowledge explosion and constantly improve his teaching skill—in a sense, be a continuing "student of teaching."

The following article by Joseph Giusti and James Hogg is an excellent analysis of the role of the teacher. These authors contend that the teacher must manage three major variables—(a) the students with whom he exercises his teaching skills, (b) the objectives he hopes to achieve with the students, and (c) the instructional methods he uses to reach the objectives. This concept is very much compatible with the concepts just presented in this chapter. This selection serves as an excellent conclusion to this chapter dealing with the role of the teacher.

---•◆•---

Management in Instruction

Joseph Giusti and James Hogg

The act of teaching is performed solely for the purpose of helping students learn. Unless learning is facilitated by the teacher's activities, the art of pedagogy is merely an idle exercise which squanders the time and talents of students. Since direct responsibility for the outcome of each classroom experience rests with the teacher, making learning easier is a primary goal for educators.

As in all encounters involving human relationships, the process of teaching and learning involves many significant variables. Frequently, as this research has substantiated, the teacher loses sight of, or is completely unaware of, the need to manage these variables so that they work with him rather than against him in the promotion of learning.

If teachers are to create conditions in the classroom which facilitate rather than impede learning, there needs to be developed through careful examination of the teaching-learning process, a general frame of reference about instructing which recognizes the complexity of the variables involved in a way that lends itself to some practical method of operation. The main problem here, then, is to develop such a framework. As the teacher works from this base to improve his professional techniques, he would be able to take advantage of situations which provide opportunity for learning. As analytic skill develops, appropriate strategies would be used in lieu of rigid, standardized procedures which often prevent rather than encourage cognitive

Joseph Giusti and James Hogg, "Management in Instruction," *Journal of Teacher Education,* Spring 1973, pp. 41–43. Used by permission.

growth. Denton's research supports this concept when he suggests that "in some classrooms, one will find teachers who encourage —and participate in—imagination, spontaneity, and play, who live openly with students to the extent that a sense of community develops, and who recognize that individual appropriation of subject matter to one's own life and meanings is as important as correct responses on a standardized test!"[1]

In order to investigate this teaching-learning concept three major variables which provide the teacher a working basis for effective analysis are recognized: (a) the students with whom he exercises his skills, (b) the objectives he hopes to achieve with the students, and (c) the method he uses to reach the objectives. Figure 1 diagrams the study model.

Careful examination of the foregoing variables reveals their closely interrelated status and the difficulty to plan for improving excellence in teaching without considering them collectively. It should be noted that the variable of "method" is directly affected by the teacher's personal style and the peculiarities of the subject area. Much instruction appears to operate on the assumption that there is no relationship among the aim of the teacher, the method he uses, and the students he instructs. A more intelligent approach to the problem should make the teacher aware of the fact that to achieve certain objectives for certain students requires a very careful selection of a particular method from the wide range of resources which are part of the professional equipment of an educator.

Certain methods of operation work with one phase of a subject and not with another, with one group of students and not another.

The personality of one teacher may make it unwise for him to use a method which a colleague practices with great success. Awareness of this, however, should serve as a guard and should not become a defense mechanism which prohibits experimentation with strategies different from the one previously used— as sometimes happens. Chaffee agrees that since no single technique is always ideal, it appears that for optimum student achievement instruction should be tailored to the situations at hand.[2]

As the study focuses on each variable, the situation alone is found to be a significant and frequent factor in affecting the approach to any given lesson. Some students resent the lack of opportunity to discuss debatable issues in class. Others sit with pencils poised to write what is being offered on the issues and resent attempts by other members of the class to debate them. One class may be well prepared for the day's topic; in another some review of concepts pertinent to the day's topic may be essential before progress can be made. Nor can the teacher divorce his own ideas from the total process. Each class is but a sample of all students and may vary considerably from the norm which is representative of the teacher's stereotype of a "class."

Teacher's Objectives

It is essential that the teacher have a clear picture of what he is trying to accomplish not only in the course but in each class meeting. To be realistic, attention must be given to changes in students which will result from the course. All learning involves some change in behavior. It is necessary for

1. D. E. Denton, "The Classroom and Consciousness I, II, III," *School and Society,* 100 (January 1972), p. 11.

2. John Chaffee, Jr., and Patricia Wagner, "Teachers Do Make a Difference," *American Education,* 6 (May 1970), p. 24.

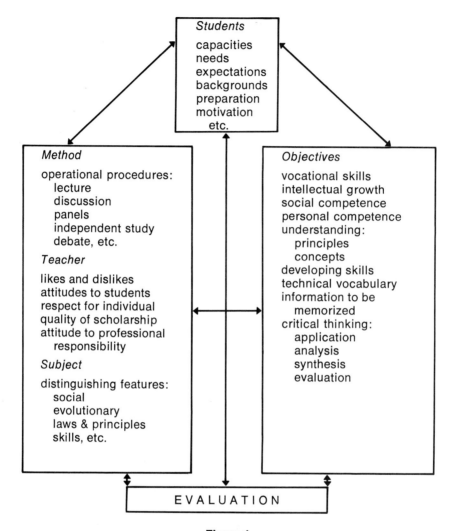

Figure 1

objectives to be seen in terms of student behavior after the course is completed, since
learning must account for the transfer of skills
from classroom experiences to life situations.[3]

3. D. Cecil Clark and Robert J. Wilson, "Behavioral
Objectives: Suggestions for Some New Priorities,"
The Journal of Teacher Education, 22 (Fall 1971),
p. 325.

However, day-to-day instruction frequently
suffers from a lack of clearly defined objectives. No doubt all teachers feel they are performing optimally, but it is often difficult for
the students or for an observer to see clearly
what specific objectives are desired for the
students.

Students, parents, and society in general

expect that certain changes will occur in the student as a result of his education. Due to confusion about specific instruction outcomes, it is difficult, if not impossible, for the interested parties to determine the value of proposed changes. In fact, some critics claim that educators purposely deceive students. Nevertheless, even though many course syllabi are vague about the changes they hope for in student performance, most departments do have available upon request a statement of objectives for which teachers are expected to strive. These objectives are usually prepared by faculty committees and adopted by the collective department members as an official guidance statement. Although a majority of the statements of objectives concentrate on intellectual and vocational goals, one-third to one-half relate to the personal, social, and emotional competence of the student, indicating the value placed by educators on the student's total development.

A teacher who disagrees radically with the statement of objectives needs to seek clarification from administrators and from colleagues before proceeding on the basis of his own preference. Too often the teacher ignores the statement of objectives and sets his goal as simply instructing in his subject. The narrow goal lacks specificity and leads simply to going over the subject in the physical presence of the students. It can be speculated at this point that this method of operation would not change even if the students were not present.

Provision for Individual Differences

As important as the objectives of the course are, the key to successful instruction is provision for individual differences. If the teacher proposes to bring about changes in students it is essential that he know what each is like. He cannot operate on the assumption that everyone in his classes conforms to a general stereotype of a "student." Unfortunately, the institutional framework in which the teacher meets his students has contributed to a concept of mass students. But each student is a unique personality with special drives and abilities, and if instruction is to be performed at a high level of professional skill, it is in adapting learning experiences to the needs of individual students wherein a teacher capitalizes on the interaction between genetic potential and school environment.[4]

Due to the interrelatedness of student, objective, and method, as can be seen from the diagram in Figure 1, these variables must be treated collectively whenever any attempt to improve instruction is made. For example, to develop new objectives for use with methods that were successful with different goals and under previous class conditions is to invite disappointment if not disaster. Each group of students presents varying conditions which call for some special adjustment in one or more of the major variables to maximize learning. The teacher with a professional, analytical viewpoint will be aware of this and will move to make whatever changes are indicated.

The interaction of these variables occurs within certain limits of freedom. The nature of the classroom, the time of day, the impending examination, access to needed equipment, and many other factors can limit the actions of the teacher and his students. Also, the field trip, lab, or in-service experience may not be possible because of limitations imposed by

4. For further discussion on this subject see: Harold W. Bernard, *Psychology of Learning and Teaching* (New York: McGraw-Hill Book Company, 1972), p. 25.

88 budget. In a multiple-section course, a common examination for all sections usually limits the initiative of the teacher. It is noted that consideration of limitations which prohibit innovation comes easily. Sometimes these obstructions to change are real; sometimes they are given as excuses for not using more effective techniques. And too, teachers voice the fact that other responsibilities limit time for interest in individual students and for varying procedures to meet individual needs. But, it must be recognized that better conditions for learning will result only if provision for improving instruction is given high priority on the list of "musts."

Perhaps the most common mistake found is made in planning for classroom work when the teacher assumes that the three variables are relatively simple to define. As judged by classroom performance most objectives are simply defined as having students learn a sufficient amount of the knowledge presented to secure a passing grade, with small regard to thinking which could enable students to use what they have learned in class. Researchers have long pointed out the wastefulness of this approach. One concludes that "by and large, merits of mastering specific content and specific techniques are considered to be quite limited. This kind of knowledge is described as static, 'dead end.' Its mastery does not produce new ideas, does not lure the mind onward."[5]

It is regrettable that in many instances little or no provision is being made for range of ability, preparation for present studies, motivation, individual needs, and background diversity. As far as the professional aspects of teaching are concerned, the system resists

5. Hilda Taba, *Curriculum Development: Theory and Practice* (New York: Harcourt, Brace and World, Inc., 1962), p. 175.

change. In a rapidly changing world onlookers may well ask if this is an occupational hazard, a human fallacy, or a demonstration of a low level of aspiration set by the teaching profession.

Although evaluation is a variable in its own right, it begins in objective planning, runs throughout the instructional process, and is weighted in some measurement of learning. (Figure 1) While this variable is somewhat less direct than the other three, it is a factor which limits freedom of choice among the others. Whatever the teacher believes about his total specific objectives, the possibility of getting students to reach them will be affected by what they have come to know about the nature of the topics and ideas covered in whatever kind of achievement measure the teacher uses for the course. Objectives for which no evaluation is possible become unrealistic goals. An examination which is much beyond the level of the students can only result in frustration for both teacher and student. One which calls for independent thinking, while the method of instruction stresses acceptance and memorization, cannot be expected to measure fairly learning resulting from the course of study. It is repeatedly verified that only when students and objectives are carefully analyzed and teacher methods are judiciously applied to fit the circumstances called for by this analysis, can effective evaluation be structured and implemented.

QUESTIONS FOR DISCUSSION

1. How did the role of the teacher in colonial America differ from that of contemporary educators?
2. In what ways might "school-keeping" chores be minimized so that teachers might spend more time working with students?

Microteaching (teaching short lessons to small groups of students) is one technique that teachers can use to improve their teaching methods. These microlessons are usually videotaped. Here a group of teachers view and discuss the playback of a videotaped microlesson in an effort to learn more about the teaching process and to improve their teaching.

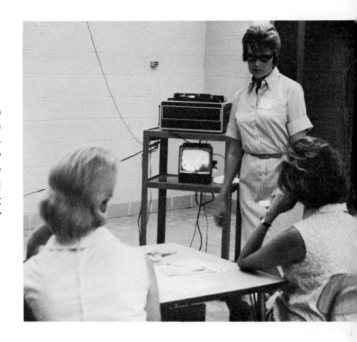

3. What is your reaction to the "point of view" article by Giusti and Hogg?
4. What factors have helped to bring about the idea that teachers, rather than dispensing knowledge, should help students to learn?
5. What qualities must a teacher possess in order to have good human relations skills?

SUPPLEMENTARY LEARNING ACTIVITIES

1. Plan a hypothetical lesson using the suggestions presented in this chapter.
2. Analyze the pupil's cumulative record presented in Figure 3.4. What does this record tell you about William James Johnson?
3. Interview a teacher concerning his or her role as an educator.
4. Study the report card in Figure 3.5. What does it tell you about Sue Stone? How

could this type of report card form be improved?
5. Role-play several situations in which a teacher displays poor human relations skills. Also role-play some situations in which a teacher exhibits good human relations skills.

SELECTED REFERENCES

Abraham, Willard. *A Handbook for the New Teacher*. New York: Holt, Rinehart and Winston, Inc., 1960.

Adams, Beatrice. "The Magic Ingredient." *NEA Journal* 47(1958):571.

American Association of School Administrators. "The High School in a Changing World." In *NEA Yearbook, 1958.* Washington, D.C.: National Education Association Publications, 1958.

90 Clark, D. Cecil, and Robert J. Wilson. "Behavioral Objectives: Suggestions for Some New Priorities," *The Journal of Teacher Education* 22(Fall 1971):325.

Deuel, Leo, ed. *The Teacher's Treasure Chest*. Englewood Cliffs, N.J.: Prentice-Hall, Inc., 1956.

Eckel, Howard. "How Can We Get Quality Teaching?" *The School Executive* 77(1958):19–21.

Evans, Eva Knox. *So You're Going to Teach*. New York: Hinds, Hayden & Eldridge, 1948.

Filbin, Robert L., and Stefan Vogel. *So You're Going to be a Teacher*. Great Neck, N.Y.: Barron's Educational Series Inc., 1962.

Highet, Gilbert. *The Art of Teaching*. New York: Alfred P. Knopf, Inc., 1950.

Holman, Mary V. *How It Feels to Be a Teacher*. New York: Teachers College Press, 1950.

Jersild, Arthur T. *When Teachers Face Themselves*. 2nd ed. New York: Teachers College Press, 1957.

Lambert, Sam M. "Angry Young Men in Teaching." *NEA Journal* 52(1963): 17–20.

Leonard, George B., Jr. "What Is a Teacher?" *Look,* February 21, 1956, pp. 29–39.

Mayer, Martin. "The Trouble with Textbooks." *Harper Magazine,* July 1962, pp. 65–71.

Peters, Herman J., et al. *Introduction to Teaching*. New York: Macmillan Company, 1963.

Russell, William F. "Should You Be a Teacher?" *Career Opportunities*. New York: New York Life Insurance Co., 1958.

Snow, Robert H. "Anxieties and Discontents in Teaching." *Phi Delta Kappan* 44(1963):318–321.

Stroh, M. Margaret. *Find Your Own Frontier*. Austin, Tex.: Delta Kappa Gamma, 1948.

Wilson, Charles H. *A Teacher Is a Person*. New York: Holt, Rinehart and Winston, Inc., 1956.

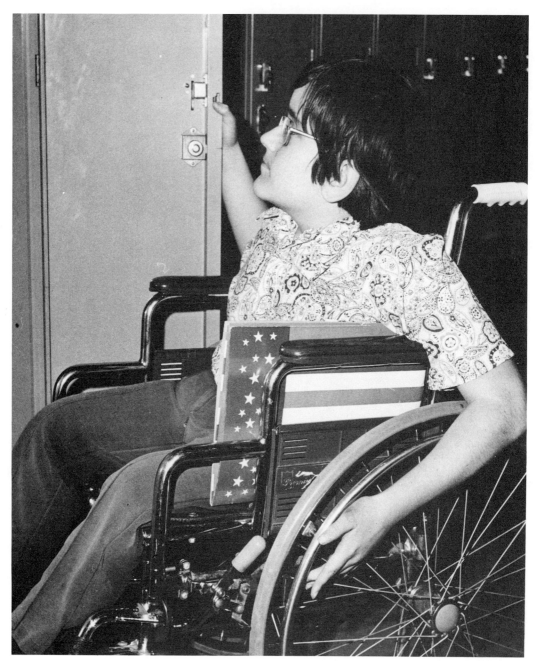

A great deal of specialized equipment is now available for use with handicapped students.

chapter 4

Other Careers in Education

goals

- Lists and describes a variety of nonteaching but education-related careers.

- Discusses in some detail the work of the special education teacher.

- Presents some of the training requirements of adult and continuing education teachers.

- Explains the work of an early childhood teacher.

- Outlines the training requirements for a number of the more common teaching-related jobs.

- Highlights the work of educational specialists such as the school counselor, media specialist, school social worker, librarian, supervisor, and administrator.

- Generalizes about the training requirements and educational role of paraprofessionals and teacher aides.

- Explains the concept of a differentiated teaching staff.

94   The previous chapter dealt with various aspects of the training and qualifications of the regular classroom teacher. There are, of course, a number of other important related careers that are available to those who are considering a career in American education. This chapter will explore some of these alternatives.

Special Education

Over the past several decades, an increasing number of students with special learning problems of various sorts have been provided with special educational programs by the American public school system. Chapter three pointed out that the special education teacher must possess great patience and dedication to be effective working with students who have special learning problems.

It is sometimes difficult for a school to distinguish between students with special learning problems and the so-called normal student. In fact, in a real sense all students have special learning problems of one sort or another. However, in most school systems the special education student is defined as "one who deviates intellectually, physically, socially, or emotionally so markedly from what is considered to be normal growth and development that he cannot receive maximum benefit from a regular school program and requires a special class or supplementary instruction and services."[1]

There are four different broad categories of special education students. Those include the intellectually handicapped, the physically

With proper help, facilities, and equipment, special education students can participate in nearly all of the learning activities that normal students take part in.

handicapped, the emotionally handicapped, and the multihandicapped.

The intellectually handicapped student is essentially one whose native intelligence is sufficiently lower than the average student as to require a special class or supplementary instruction and services. Intellectually handicapped children can be roughly classified as "trainable" (having I.Q.'s ranging roughly from twenty-five to fifty), and the "educable" (having I.Q.'s ranging roughly from fifty to

1. William M. Cruickshank and G. Orville Johnson, *Education of Exceptional Children and Youth,* pp. 3–4.

eighty). Students with I.Q.'s in the eighty to ninety-five range are often referred to as "slow learners." One must keep in mind, however, that the I.Q. scores obtained from even the best intelligence tests available today are still only rough estimates of a student's native intelligence. In fact, some authorities feel that most intelligence tests really reflect a student's environmental exposure to learning opportunities more than his native intelligence, and therefore should not be used at all to classify students.

It is estimated that .3 percent of the school population fall into the trainable category. The schools can hope only to train students in this category to take care of their own immediate personal needs (dressing, eating, using the bathroom, personal hygiene, how to

> *I have indeed two great measures at heart, without which no republic can maintain itself in strength. 1. That of general education, to enable every man to judge for himself what will secure or endanger his freedom. 2. To divide every county into hundreds, of such size that all the children of each will be within reach of a central school in it.*
>
> Thomas Jefferson

get along with others, etc.). Trainables require care and supervision throughout their life. The school's objective with trainable students is to help make their lives as comfortable and useful as possible.

It is estimated that approximately 3 percent of the student population falls into the "educable" category. Some schools place these students in special classes and other schools attempt to provide these educable

mentally retarded students with supplemental help while leaving them in the regular classes with other so-called normal students. The typical educable student, with special help, can learn to be a productive, self-sufficient adult. The school's objective for these students is to provide them with this special educational help.

It is estimated that roughly 15 percent of the school population falls into the "slow learner" category (I.Q.'s roughly from eighty to ninety-five). Nearly all school systems

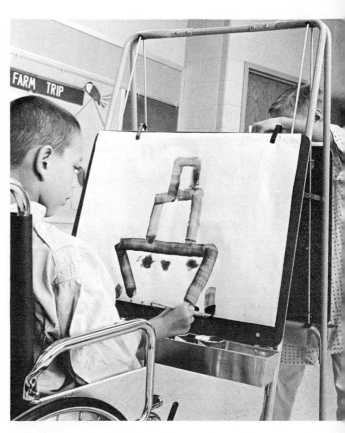

An effective special education teacher must possess a good deal of understanding and patience.

96 allow the slow learners to remain in the regular classroom. Unfortunately, most schools do not supply the slow learner with much special help other than that which the regular teacher is able to provide.

The physically handicapped student, as the name implies, is one who has a physical disability extensive enough to require a special class or supplementary instruction and services. Special education students in this category may be blind, partially sighted, deaf, hard of hearing, may have speech defects such as stuttering or that caused by a cleft palate, or may have had any one of a number of crippling diseases such as cerebral palsy or poliomyelitis. Children with some forms of brain damage also fall into this category.

The emotionally handicapped student is one who is so socially maladjusted or emotionally disturbed that he requires a special class or supplemental instruction and services. Estimates of the number of students in the United States that fall into this category range all the way from one to four million. It is often difficult to identify the emotionally handicapped student due to the fact that all children from time to time exhibit neurotic behavior. Unfortunately, many emotionally disturbed children go undetected, especially those who are quite shy and withdrawn, and never receive the special help they so badly need.

> *No man can reveal to you aught but that which already lies half asleep in the dawning of your knowledge. . . . If he is indeed wise he does not bid you enter the house of his wisdom, but rather leads you to the threshold of your own mind.*
>
> Kahlil Gibran

The multihandicapped child is, as the name implies, one who has a combination of the handicaps just discussed. For instance, it is quite common to find children who are

> *Education is leading human souls to what is best, and no crime can destroy, no enemy can alienate, no despotism can enslave. At home a friend, abroad an introduction, in solitude a solace, and in society an ornament. It chastens vice, it guides virtue, it gives at once grace and government to genius. Without it, what is man? A splendid slave, a reasoning savage.*
>
> Joseph Addison

both mentally retarded and physically handicapped. It is also rather common to find children who, due to their mental retardation, also have rather severe emotional problems. This problem is frequently caused, at least in part, by normal students making fun of the slow learner.

Figure 4.1 shows the enrollment of exceptional children in special education classrooms throughout the United States as of 1970–71.

As this figure points out, there are a considerable number of special education students in the United States.

Becoming qualified to work in any one of these many special education areas requires a great deal of special training in addition to regular teacher training. Not all colleges and universities offer training in special education and, therefore, people contemplating entering such a training program must seek out a college or university that offers specialized training in special education. Each state has its own certification

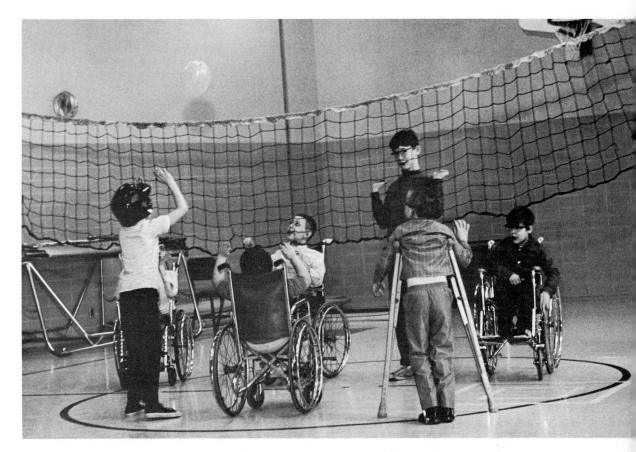

Our schools have the responsibility of providing a good education for each child in our society.

requirements for becoming a special education teacher. A bachelor's degree with a major in special education is the most common requirement; however, the specific requirements for each state can be obtained by writing to the state superintendent of schools in the capital city of each respective state.

To reshape reality by means of ideas is the business of man, his proper earthly task; and nothing can be impossible to a will confident of itself and of its aim.
Frederich Paulsen

Area of Exceptionality	1970–71		
	Total Enrollment	Local Public Schools	Public and Private Residential Schools
Total	3,158,000	2,982,000	176,000
Deaf and hard of hearing	78,000	50,000	28,000
Visually handicapped	24,000	16,000	8,000
Speech impaired	1,237,000	1,237,000	—
Crippled and special health problems	269,000	269,000	—
Emotionally and socially maladjusted	113,000	42,000	71,000
Mentally retarded	830,000	761,000	69,000
Other handicapped conditions	126,000	126,000	—
Gifted	481,000	481,000	—

Figure 4.1 Enrollment of Exceptional Children in Special Education Programs

Source: Kenneth A. Simon and W. Vance Grant, *Digest of Educational Statistics, 1972*, U.S. Office of Education (Washington, D.C.: U.S. Government Printing Office, 1973).

Special education programs are growing rapidly and there is currently a great demand for well-qualified teachers to staff these programs.

Early Childhood Education

A relatively new and rapidly developing teaching field is that in the area of early childhood education. Early childhood education deals with children up to the age at which they enter formal elementary school—usually the age at which they enter kindergarten or first grade.

Figure 4.2 shows that early childhood education is the first of many levels of education in the United States. Many authorities maintain that by the time a child begins regular elementary school at the age of five or six, he has already developed the attitudes and skills that will later determine his success or failure in school and in adult life. For this reason, the advocates of early childhood education believe it is important to provide enrichment experiences for the very young—in a sense, to provide a rich early childhood upon which the future formal education can be built.

Qualifications for teaching in early child-

Early Childhood Education

Elementary Education

Middle School Education

Secondary Education

Higher Education

Adult and Continuing Education

Figure 4.2 Levels of Education

hood educational programs are not yet well developed or defined in most states. This is due in part to the fact that this is a very new and still developing educational area. It is also due to the fact that many agencies are involved in early childhood education efforts. For instance, many private nursery schools,

church day-care centers, federally funded agencies (such as Head Start, Migrant Worker Child Projects, etc.), private kindergartens, as well as public and private school systems are involved in varying degrees with early childhood education programs. In some states there are no certification requirements for people teaching in early childhood education. An increasing number of states, however, are developing certification and/or licensing standards for such teachers. Since these requirements vary greatly, it is suggested that people interested in knowing the specific requirements for early childhood education teachers in any particular state should write directly to that state for current information on the topic.

Adult and Continuing Education

Another rapidly growing educational field in America is that dealing with adult and continuing education. Figure 4.3 shows some

1808	College extension classes started at Yale
1839	Ohio passes law providing for evening schools
1883	Correspondence University opened at Ithaca, New York
1914	Smith-Lever Act providing federal funds for agricultural work enacted
1925	Free adult education first provided by law
1926	American Association for Adult Education founded
1933	Adult education provided on mass basis through WPA and TVA
1952	First *Adult Education Journal* published
1961	White House Conference on Aging
1962	Legislation passed establishing Manpower Developing and Training Act
1965	Federal Administration on Aging established
1970	Congress legislates secondary education for adults through Basic Education Act

Figure 4.3 Historical Highlights of Adult and Continuing Education

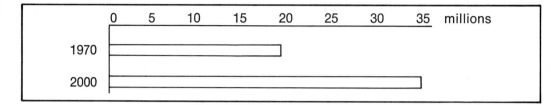

Figure 4.4 Projected Growth in Number of Americans Over Age Sixty-five

Source: U.S. Office of Education.

of the historical highlights of the development of this area of education.

Today there are approximately 204 million people in the United States. Of these, only approximately 59 million (or about thirty percent) are involved in formal education (as reported in Figure 1.4). The remaining 145 million people (approximately 7 out of 10 Americans) are not full-time students but do have educational interests and needs. As an example, many young adults need practical job training to obtain employment. For that matter, many older adults need retraining for new jobs. Also, adults of all ages desire various forms of continuing education as a means of learning more about hobbies and different personal interests that have nothing to do with employment. Our senior citizens have an increasing interest in continuing education during retirement years. Figure 4.4 shows that there will be a dramatic increase in the number of Americans over sixty-five years of age in the near future.

Many agencies are attempting to meet this growing demand for adult and continuing education. For instance, most secondary schools now offer various evening courses for adults. Almost all community colleges offer a wide range of evening courses. Figure 4.5 shows the 1969 adult enrollment in various

Type of Institution	Total
Total	13,150,000
Public or private school	277,000
College or university, part-time	252,000
Job training	275,000
Correspondence courses	80,000
Community organizations	134,000
Tutor or private instructor	58,000
Other	103,000

Figure 4.5 Participants in Adult Education in the United States, 1969.

Source: U.S. Office of Education, "Participation in Adult Education, Initial Report, May 1969" (Washington, D.C.: U.S. Government Printing Office, 1969).

types of institutions. There are, in fact, many more than the 13.15 million people shown in this figure taking part in adult and continuing education in the United States because many such programs do not report their activity to the U.S. Office of Education.

The qualifications for teachers in adult and continuing education programs vary with the specific program. Many programs require only that the teacher have a practical working knowledge of the subject being taught. An example of such a situation might be an adult sewing class offered by a local YWCA or church. Other adult education programs may require specific training and even certification of the teacher. It is, in fact, impossible to generalize about the requirements for teaching in adult and continuing education programs throughout the United States. A person interested in such a teaching career must seek specific information about training requirements and possible certification from appropriate authorities in each state.

Counseling

A school counselor spends most of his time working in a one-to-one relationship with individual students. These students may need vocational or college information, help in selecting elective courses, someone to talk with concerning a girl or boy friend, help with peer or parental conflict, or assistance with any one of a variety of different kinds of emotional and psychological problems. A school counselor does not, however, attempt to provide therapy for students with severe problems, but rather refers such cases to appro-

priate specialists such as a clinical psychologist or psychiatrist. The long-term goal of a counselor is not to solve problems for the students, but rather to help students solve their own problems. To do this a counselor must himself: be well adjusted, have a good understanding of human psychology, be familiar with and proficient in using a wide variety of counseling techniques, highly respect the dignity and worth of individual students, and possess a sincere desire to understand and help his fellowman.

In most states, to be certified as a counselor requires that a person have some teaching experience and possess a master's degree with a major in school counseling. There are some states, however, that do not require prior teaching experience to be certified as a school counselor.

School Social Worker

An educational career closely related to that of a school counselor is that of a school

The school social worker visits the homes of students in an effort to help parents maximize the learning experiences of their children.

social worker, the distinction being that a social worker goes out into the community and into the home to work with students and parents. For instance, if a school counselor, in working with an individual student, suspects that the student's problem may be caused by conditions in the home, he may refer the case to the school social worker. The social worker will then call at the home and may work closely with members of the family in an attempt to bring about a solution to the problem.

Of course, not all schools have a school social worker on the staff. In some school systems this function is carried on by a school counselor and in other schools the teacher does whatever work in the home with parents that needs to be done. An increasing number of school systems, however, are finding it advantageous to have a school social worker on the staff who is specifically trained to do this kind of work.

A school social worker typically possesses a master's degree with a major in school social work.

Media Specialists

Chapter fourteen discusses the general topic of instructional resources that are now available for use by teachers. More and more school systems are now employing specialists who have been trained in media and whose sole job it is to help teachers create and utilize a wide variety of different kinds of media in their teaching. These media specialists must, of course, be familiar with all of the different kinds of audiovisual equipment available for use in schools. Such equipment includes, for example, movie projectors, film strip projectors, 35-mm slide projectors, opaque projec-

tors, overhead projectors, audiotape recorders, videotape recorders, record players, overhead transparency makers, photocopy machines, cameras—the list gets longer each year as more and more such hardware is developed and made available for use in schools.

The media specialist, in some schools, also does minor repair work on audiovisual equipment; however, the main function of the media specialist so far as media hardware is concerned is to advise the school system on what hardware to buy and help teachers use such equipment.

The school counselor is a valuable member of the educational staff—helping individuals or small groups of students with a wide variety of problems.

A media specialist should have had prior teaching experience and have a master's degree with a major in educational media.

Educational Administration and Supervision

There are many different kinds of specific educational administration careers that one may pursue. These include, for example: general superintendent (in charge of an entire school system), assistant superintendent (assisting the general superintendent with the operation of part of the school operation, such as curriculum, personnel, business, elementary education, or secondary education), principal (in charge of a single elementary or secondary school building), and assistant principal (assisting the principal with specific parts of the operation of a single school building). The size and philosophy of each school district determines the number and type of administrative positions that school district will have.

Many school systems also employ a number of different kinds of supervisors. Whereas an administrator typically has a certain amount of "authority" over the area in which he administers, a school supervisor frequently does not actually have authority over teachers. Rather, a supervisor plays more of a "consultant" role. For example, an elementary music supervisor would help the regular elementary teachers do a better job of teaching music. She might do this by occasionally teaching the music class in each of the elementary classrooms and/or by helping the regular classroom teacher do a better job of teaching her own music lessons. Common supervisory positions are those in elementary music, elementary art, ele-

The educational media specialist must be familiar with all of the educational hardware now available for use in the schools.

An important function of the media specialist is that of helping teachers develop and prepare teaching materials.

104 mentary physical education, elementary reading, and some schools even have supervisors who have broad responsibility supervising one subject, such as science, for instance, in all grades starting at kindergarten and continuing through the twelfth grade. In many of the larger junior and senior high schools, department heads will have supervisory responsibility for their respective departments.

It is difficult to generalize about administrative and supervisory positions in American schools because the number and nature of such positions vary a great deal from school to school. However, there are a considerable number of such positions existing in the American public school system. To pursue a

> *Small boy scowling over report card to Dad: "Naturally I seem stupid to my teacher; she's a college graduate."*
> Dallas Morning News

career in educational administration and/or supervision one must obtain a good deal of successful teaching experience and at least a master's degree which is related to that kind of work.

Librarians

A school librarian is, in one sense, really a teacher whose classroom is the library. Some people erroneously think of a school librarian as one who only takes care of books and periodicals. Much to the contrary, a good librarian can be one of the very most effective teachers in an entire school. One of the major goals of American public education is to help each student become capable of learning on his own without the help of the classroom teacher. The library contains many of the resources necessary for independent study and the task of the librarian is to help each student learn how to use these resources. To do this effectively, a librarian must not only be able to order, classify, catalog, and shelve books, but also must be able to work effectively with individuals and groups of students.

Almost all of the junior and senior high schools in this country have libraries and, therefore, librarians. It has been only recently that elementary schools have begun to have libraries in many schools. The library has been expanded into "learning resource centers" where a wide range of learning materials such as books, periodicals, learning machines, programmed self-teaching materials, film strips, single concept films,

> *I love to teach as a painter loves to paint, as a musician loves to play, as a singer loves to sing, as a strong man rejoices to run a race. Teaching is an art—an art so great and so difficult to master that a man or a woman can spend a long life at it, without realizing much more than his limitations and mistakes, and his distance from the ideal.*
> William Lyon Phelps

records, audiotapes, and dial access materials are made available for students to use. Schools of the future are destined to put a greater emphasis on learning centers and with this emphasis will come an increased demand for well-trained librarians and directors of learning centers.

Paraprofessionals

One of the newer educational careers is that known as a paraprofessional (also often called a teacher aide). A paraprofessional assists the regular classroom teacher, or in some cases a number of teachers, with many aspects of teaching that have traditionally taken up much valuable time of the teacher.

> *The direction in which education starts a man will determine his future life.*
>
> Plato

The following is a partial list of the kinds of duties typically performed by a paraprofessional:

Tutorial activities
—help children in their search for materials such as charts, pictures, and articles
—help children organize games and sports
—play with children and help them to use toys and playthings, and assist in supervising at recess
—assist teachers in the use of equipment such as projectors, viewers, and tape recorders
—help teachers with emotionally upset children by giving them personal attention
—serve as laboratory assistants
—help the teacher in reading and evaluating pupil work
—assist the teacher with children who have learning difficulties in reading and number work
—help the teacher with problem cases by working with the child outside of the class in activities he is interested in
—assist with instructional activities in art, music, on field trips.

Clerical activities
—help the teacher with files of materials such as pictures, stories, and articles

—help with making and preparing materials of instruction, and type and duplicate instructional materials
—help teachers with examinations and records.

Housekeeping activities
—keep order in cafeteria and hallways
—help in the library
—help in class with the distribution of materials
—supervise clean-up activities.[2]

As one can see from this list of activities, a paraprofessional is an important member of the teaching team.

The qualifications necessary for becoming a paraprofessional vary greatly from state to state and from school district to school district. Most states do not yet issue certificates for paraprofessionals. However, there seems to be a trend in this direction—which means that the qualifications are determined by each local school district. Some school districts hire mothers of school age children—regardless of how much formal education they may have had—to assist elementary teachers. This practice has been particularly popular and successful in inner-city schools. Other school districts require a minimum of two years of college for paraprofessional work. A small but increasing number of junior colleges and community colleges are developing specific two-year training programs for paraprofessionals.

One can glean from the following comments of a third grade teacher the importance of a paraprofessional in today's school:

2. B. Othanel Smith, et al., "The Role of Teacher Aides," *Teachers for the Real World* (Washington, D.C.: American Association of Colleges for Teacher Education, 1969), p. 35. Used with permission.

The library or learning resource center is one of the most essential parts of a contemporary school. A good librarian can be one of the most effective teachers on a school staff.

A supervisor's main task is that of helping each teacher become a more effective educator. Here, a supervisor helps a beginning teacher analyze a videotape of a lesson she has just taught.

Click, click, click, click! The sound echoes in an empty hallway. It probably means nothing to the average American citizen, but to three third-grade teachers at Douglas School in Freeport it is the welcome sound of our teacher's aide tripping gaily down the hall.

"Good morning," she calls in a cheery voice; and we know immediately that it is a good morning, for at last we have someone to help us with the numerous tasks that confront us each day—tasks that are necessary and demanding, yet the kind that can be done by a non-professional.

We teachers are busy, so she checks her folder which contains the day's schedule and an outline of the work that is to be done. She checks papers and workbooks (objective tests only), records grades, and calls attention to children who are having difficulties that will require special help from the teacher. She gives vocabulary and arithmetic flash card drills, which are necessary for some children. This she can do as efficiently as a teacher. Her listening ear is welcomed by children who need an audience plus a little help while reading a library book or a story from a reader. She cares for the room library and assists in selection of books.

The aide "listens in" on small-group planning. She makes master copies of ditto work and arranges material for free-time activities. She weighs and measures children and records the information on the health cards. She folds and puts on book covers (nearly 500 of them), makes numerous trips to the office, picks up mail, prepares supplies for art and science, cleans up after a painting session, orders films that we want to use from the central office, gets all audio-visual equipment, and sees that everything is ready to do.

Bulletin boards are wonderful teaching aids, but in the primary grades the teacher is largely responsible for preparing them and putting them up. Now we give our helper the ideas and materials and our bulletin boards take shape as if by magic!

But the days are never long enough to accomplish all we have set out to do, and our minds are still full of valuable ways to use an aide. A teacher's aide must contribute to the achievement of goals which teachers see to be those of the school program, and this we feel she has done. Elementary education, particularly at the primary level, is committed to the development of children educationally, emotionally, and physically. This commitment is one that is almost impossible for a teacher to fulfill to the best of her ability when there are innumerable routine tasks to be accomplished in addition to teaching an average of 35 children. When a teacher is relieved of some of these duties there is more time for careful planning, more time for individualized instruction, and more time for guidance. A full-time teacher's aide would mean that at least a teacher could become a full-time teacher. Wouldn't that be wonderful?

Click, click, click, click! For three teachers at Douglas School that is music to our ears. We hear a cheery "Good morning" and we know that every morning is a good morning because a teacher's aide has come to our rescue.[3]

Closely associated with the development of the paraprofessional position is the concept of "differential teaching staff." This concept involves the idea that our schools should be staffed with a wide variety of different types of educators, each of whom would play a slightly different role in the education process. Such a differential staff, for example, might include the following categories of personnel:

3. Vera E. Johansen, "A is for Aide," *Illinois Education,* December 1968, p. 149. Used by permission.

108

Many schools select, as paraprofessionals and teacher aides, mothers who have school age children. The paraprofessional is becoming an increasingly important member of the teaching team.

> *What can only be taught by the rod and with blows will not lead to much good; they will not remain pious longer than the rod is behind them.*
>
> Martin Luther

■ *Teacher Aide.* This might be a person who could not certify for standard or provisional credentials; a person who is willing to devote only a part-time effort to education; a person unable to decide upon education as a career; or a person using education as a background for another field.

■ *Assistant Teacher.* This might be a person who is provisionally qualified or minimally qualified for a standard certificate; a person who views teaching as a means of second income, exerting minimal time and effort; a person who is merely "exploring" before trying to move elsewhere in education, or a person who is using teaching as a transition position before moving into another endeavor, such as business, marriage, the military, etc.

■ *Regular Teacher.* This might be a beginner with a master's degree along with a great deal of preparation beyond certification requirements; a person of several years of

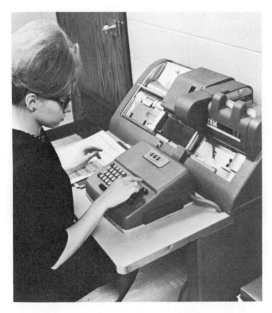

Other schools employ people who have a minimum of two years of college to perform a wide variety of paraprofessional tasks.

otherwise successful experience, who does not wish to exert much more than a "40-hour week" in teaching, or who is an adequate teacher of several years of experience who does not exert real effort to improve.

■ *Senior Teacher.* This may be a person with a few years of highly successful experience who is well beyond certification requirements and exerts "extra effort" beyond regular school hours and days, or a good teacher who has taught dozens of years and operated as a "professional" in all respects.

■ *Master Teacher.* This might be a teacher with several outstanding years of teaching and service to the profession, who continually makes outstanding or unique contributions to some phase of education, or a teacher who puts to good use an outstand-

ing degree of expertise gained from experiences of preparation.[4]

109

———•—•———

While educational staff differentiation schemes such as this are not yet widely used in school systems, they are becoming more common and will undoubtedly become even more so in the future as schools search for more effective ways to utilize staff.

In conclusion, this chapter has attempted to briefly discuss some of the careers, other than classroom teaching, that exist in American public education. All of these different kinds of educational careers are essential in the American educational task. A career in any one of these educational careers can be rewarding and enable a person to make a significant contribution to the education of American youth.

> *Knowledge is power.*
>
> Francis Bacon

Point of View

This chapter has attempted to point out that there are many specializations within teaching as well as a wide variety of non-teaching jobs that are in one way or another closely related to teaching. This chapter has also attempted to briefly highlight the training requirements for some of the more common of these teaching-related jobs.

4. Wade N. Patterson, "Teacher-Ranking: A Step Toward Professionalism," *Educational Forum,* January 1969, p. 172. Used by permission. Also permission of Kappa Delta Pi, an Honor Society in Education, owners of the copyright.

110   One of the specialized teaching areas that has come into the forefront in recent years is that dealing with the teaching of very young children. This area is usually referred to as "early childhood education" but is also sometimes called "preprimary education" or "nursery education."

Early childhood education has received a considerable amount of attention in recent years on the American education scene. This attention is due in part to a belief that the experiences a child has during his or her very early years will determine, in large part, future success in school and in adult life. The following article, authored by Jenny W. Klein of the U.S. Department of Health, Education, and Welfare, explains a new emphasis on, and hope for, early childhood education on the part of the U.S. Office of Education.

———————◆◆———————

Toward Competency in Child Care

Jenny W. Klein

Sound child development and early childhood education are assuming increasing importance in the United States. The significance of the early years is well established, and the value of good programs for preschool children is agreed upon by representatives of many disciplines.

With the advent of such programs as Head Start and Title I, and the rising demand for preschool nursery and day care services, both the availability and the quality of such services have become matters of growing national concern.

Jenny W. Klein, "Toward Competency in Child Care," *Educational Leadership,* October 1973, pp. 45–48. Used by permission.

The question of whether or not we should have preschool and day care programs seems to have been largely answered by the increase in such programs all over the country. Since 1960, the number of licensed day care facilities has tripled and the number of children in other preschool programs has doubled. It is anticipated that by 1980 the number of preschool children in the United States will increase by three million, to reach an all-time high of 28 million. Kindergarten and nursery school enrollment is likely to reach 6.3 million by that date.

The issue this nation must face is how to provide quality programs for our children. Quality programs must facilitate and support the child's potential for growth and development and meet the wide range of emotional, intellectual, social, and physical needs of preschool children. The nation must find an answer to Edward Zigler's question in the fall of 1971, when he headed HEW's Office of Child Development: "Are we going to provide the children of this nation with developmental child care, or are we merely going to provide them with babysitting?"

Those who work with children know that the key element in any program for young children is the staff—the adults who teach, supervise, and relate to the children both individually and in groups. This is true of early childhood programs in day care centers, Head Start centers, or public school settings. The best facilities, materials, and curricula, and the best intentions of program sponsors, cannot guarantee quality child care or educational programs unless those who deal directly with the children are competent, knowledgeable, and dedicated.

However, up to now, large numbers of individuals who bear primary responsibility for the development and education of children in child care programs have had insufficient preparation for the vital and complex task that they have undertaken.

Responding to the personnel needs for child care programs, the Office of Child Development began in 1970 to plan for a new program. The plan was based on the assumption that numbers alone would offer no solution.

Thus responding positively to the dual challenges of increasing the supply of competent staff members for early childhood programs and at the same time enhancing the quality of child care services, the Office of Child Development created a new concept for training professional staff in the field of child care—that of the Child Development Associate (CDA).

It is hoped that the CDA program will provide this nation with a cadre of well-trained, competent, professional men and women who will be responsible for the daily activities of groups of preschool children in center-based programs. It is assumed that CDA's will not work in isolation, but will work in settings with differentiated staffing patterns, in close contact with more trained and experienced staff members. CDA's will be child care specialists working with and responsible for groups of children. They will not have direct responsibility for the extended activities of the total program, but they should have the assistance of a paraprofessional aide or staff helper. Eventually each CDA should hold a nationally recognized credential certifying professional competency.

The basic purpose of the program is to promote a system of training and credentialing for individuals working with preschool children and for those planning to enter the field.

The specific goals of the program are to:

- Upgrade the quality of programs for children and provide them with maximum opportunity for growth and development
- Increase the supply of competent child care personnel
- Develop innovative and flexible competency-based training programs with heavy emphasis on center-based field training
- Establish the Child Development Associate as a recognized and vital resource within the field of human service occupations
- Encourage and provide opportunities for training for staff members (including paraprofessionals) seeking to become CDA's
- Establish a competency-based assessment and credentialing system to grant professional recognition to the CDA.

The key feature of the project is that, unlike the traditional approach to professional training, the credential of the CDA will not be based solely on courses taken, academic credits earned, or degrees awarded (although credits and degrees will have their place in the training programs). Credentials for the CDA will be based upon careful evaluation of each candidate's demonstrated competency to assume primary responsibility for the education and development of a group of young children.

The CDA project is made up of several components or parts. First, the CDA competencies, which basically describe what a CDA should be and do, will be the foundation for the development of training and assessment techniques. Second, training programs will develop innovative training methods to help trainees in the acquisition of the

112 competencies. Third, an assessment system will assure that CDA's are indeed competent child care staff members. Fourth, a credentialing system will assure that CDA's present a recognized and accepted professional group holding a credential that is nationally negotiable.

Competencies

Competencies were developed by a task force of educators and child development specialists, in cooperation with the Office of Child Development.[1] These competencies are presently being reviewed by the CDA Consortium, a nonprofit corporation composed of organizations and individuals concerned with quality care for preschool children. (The Consortium was funded by OCD and is responsible for developing a prototype system for assessing and credentialing of the CDA.)

The competencies fall into six broad areas and require that the CDA have the knowledge and skill to:

- Set up and maintain a safe and healthy learning environment
- Advance physical and intellectual competence
- Build positive self-concept and individual strength
- Organize and sustain the positive functioning of children and adults in a group in a learning environment
- Bring about optimal coordination of home and center child-rearing practices and expectations
- Carry out supplementary responsibilities related to the children's programs.

1. Major credit should go to Dr. Barbara Biber, Bank Street College, New York.

Within each of these categories there are numerous specific skills or competencies which each CDA must acquire. The competencies are stated broadly so that they can be used by local programs as a framework for training and program development reflecting particular local needs and preferences. These competencies are based on the assumption that broad guidelines can be formulated without violating the divergent educational views or cultural and ethnic backgrounds of various child care groups.

Training

In the spring of 1973, the Office of Child Development funded 13 pilot training programs to prepare trainees to acquire the competencies mentioned and, hopefully, to become CDA's. Each program is somewhat unique in its organizational pattern and approach to training. However, all training programs provide:

- Training geared toward acquisition of the CDA competencies
- Academic and field work as a set of coordinated experiences
- A minimum of 50 percent field training
- Individualized training geared to the strength and weakness of each trainee
- Flexible scheduling which will allow each trainee to complete the training within a range of time necessary for his acquisition of competencies
- Willingness to work closely with the CDA Consortium.

Thus, training is based on innovative approaches to teaching and learning and differs from traditional teacher training.

Central to CDA training is a careful integration of theoretical preparation in child development and early childhood education with practical, on-the-job experience. At least half of each trainee's time will be spent working with young children in situations in which appropriate staff models and regular feedback promote acquisition of CDA competencies. These settings may be in Head Start programs, nursery schools, day care centers, university laboratory schools, other child development programs, or a combination of several programs—settings in which the CDA candidate is currently employed or may be employed when training is completed.

The integration of field and academic training varies among institutions. Some programs provide some academic work every day, while others have set aside specific days of the week or several one-week "mini-mesters" for theoretical work. Some programs introduce competencies through academic experience and expect acquisition through field experience. Others reverse or combine the process.

Training programs include both urban and rural communities, and different ethnic, racial, and bilingual programs. Training institutions comprise a broad mix of organizations such as universities, junior and/or community colleges, Head Start programs, private training organizations, and consortia. In most instances several groups are cooperating to provide CDA training.

It is expected that the CDA project will legitimatize field training for child care staff, and will provide whatever additional training is necessary to bring many experienced workers up to a level of competency that warrants the CDA credential. By emphasizing demonstrated competencies rather than length of training or accumulation of course credits, the CDA program will give recognition to workers in the field who are fully or partially

qualified but may not have formal preparation.[2]

Assessment and Credentialing

Assessment and credentialing techniques will be developed by the CDA Consortium. The Consortium is made up of national organizations which are directly involved in or have primary interest in early education and child care. It was formed in June 1972, and received a grant from the Office of Child Development to initiate its activities. At present, over 30 organizations have joined the Consortium. A 16-member board of directors has policy-making responsibility, and a full-time professional staff carries out the complex task of this newly formed organization.

With the help of consultants and subcontractors, the Consortium will develop assessment and credentialing systems. Training programs and the Consortium will work cooperatively to ensure that training and assessment are part of a unified system for the preparation and credentialing of CDA's. It is also expected that both trainers and the Consortium will cooperate in facilitating acceptance of the Child Development Associate as a qualified professional in the field.[3]

The CDA project is an all-out effort to provide the nation with an adequate number of professional workers competent to guide

2. For additional information on the training aspect of the Child Development Associate project, write to: Dr. Jenny W. Klein, Director of Education Services, Program Improvement and Innovation, Office of Child Development, P.O. Box 1182, Washington, D.C. 20013.

3. For additional information on assessment and credentialing of the CDA, write to: Dr. C. Ray Williams, Executive Director, CDA Consortium, 7315 Wisconsin Avenue, N.W., Suite 601E, Washington, D.C. 20014.

114 the growth and development of preschool children in a variety of settings. Hopefully, it will also facilitate the improvement and expansion of child care services throughout the country. The task to be done is difficult, but can be accomplished by the cooperation of all those concerned with the education and care of young children.

———————◆•◆———————

QUESTIONS FOR DISCUSSION

1. What do you believe the function and the role of a superintendent should be in a public school system today? A principal?
2. What do you believe would be some of the characteristics of a successful school administrator?
3. Discuss the advantages and disadvantages of putting exceptional children into special classes as opposed to attempting to provide for their special needs while leaving them in the regular classroom.
4. Discuss the advantages and disadvantages of some of the different types of careers in American public education.
5. What are your views concerning the role of counselors in our educational system? What qualities do you believe a counselor should possess?

SUPPLEMENTARY LEARNING ACTIVITIES

1. Invite a public school administrator to your class to discuss his or her work.
2. Visit a relatively large school and interview the various types of educational personnel you find there.
3. Describe what you believe would be an ideal staff (in terms of number and types of positions) for an elementary school; a junior high school; a senior high school.

4. Select one of the educational careers discussed in this chapter and make arrangements to spend one full day following in the footsteps of someone now serving in that career.
5. Make arrangements for a school librarian or learning center director to discuss his or her work with your class.

SELECTED REFERENCES

Association for Supervision and Curriculum Development. *Leadership for Improving Instruction.* Washington, D.C.: National Education Association Publications, 1960.

Bricker, W. A., and D. D. Bricker. "A Program for Language Training for the Severely Language Handicapped Child." *Exceptional Children* 37(1971):101–111.

Bullock, L. M., and R. J. Whelan. "Competencies Needed by Teachers of the Emotionally Disturbed and Socially Maladjusted: A Comparison." *Exceptional Children* 37(1971):485–89.

"The Business Official." *Overview* 2(1961):43–46.

Calvert, D.; R. Reddell; U. Jacobs; and S. Baltzer. "Experiences with Pre-School Deaf-Blind Children." *Exceptional Children* 38(1972):415–21.

"Children with Problems: What Does the Social Worker Do?" *NEA Journal* 51(1962):55–57.

Cruickshank, William M., and G. Orville Johnson, eds. *Education of Exceptional Children and Youth.* 2nd ed. Englewood Cliffs, N.J.: Prentice-Hall, Inc., 1967.

Deno, E. "Special Education as Developmental Capital." *Exceptional Children* 37(1970):229–37.

Eiserer, Paul E. *The School Psychologist.* Washington, D.C.: The Center for Applied Research in Education, Inc., 1963.

Goldman, Samuel. *The School Principal.* New York: The Center for Applied Research in Education, Inc., 1966.

Green, John A. *Fields of Teaching and Educational Services.* New York: Harper & Row, Publishers, 1966.

Griffiths, Daniel E. *The School Superintendent.* New York: The Center for Applied Research in Education, Inc., 1966.

Heiny, R. W. "Special Education: History." In *The Encyclopedia of Education.* New York: Macmillan Company and The Free Press, 1971.

————. "Field Teachers: An Introduction to an Alternative to Schools." *Peabody Journal of Education* 49(1972):83–84.

Heiny, R. W., and J. Cunningham. "Field Teaching: A Social History." *Peabody Journal of Education* 49(1972):97–103.

Hildreth, Gertrude H. *Introduction to the Gifted.* New York: McGraw-Hill Book Company, 1966.

Johnson, G. Orville. *Education for the Slow Learners.* Englewood Cliffs, N.J.: Prentice-Hall, Inc., 1963.

Johnson, Wendell, and Dorothy Moeller, eds. *Speech Handicapped School Children.* 3rd ed. New York: Harper & Row, Publishers, 1967.

"Lay Readers of English Papers." *School and Society* 90(1962):102.

Lilly, S. "Special Education: A Tempest in a Teapot." *Exceptional Children* 37(1970):43–48.

————. "A Training Based Model for Special Education." *Exceptional Children* 37(1971):745–49.

National Education Association, National Commission on Teacher Education and Professional Standards. *Auxiliary School Personnel.* Washington, D.C.: National Education Association Publications, 1967.

National Education Association. *Teaching Career Fact Book.* Washington, D.C.: National Education Association Publications, 1966.

Riessman, Frank. *The Culturally Deprived Child.* New York: Harper & Row, Publishers, 1962.

Roeber, Edward C. *The School Counselor.* Washington, D.C.: The Center for Applied Research in Education, Inc., 1963.

Shadick, R. G. "School Librarian: A Key to Curriculum Development." *Elementary School Journal* 62(1962):298–303.

Turney, D. T. "Secretarial Help for Classroom Teachers." *Education Digest* 28(1962):24–26.

U.S. Office of Education. *Employment Outlook for Teachers.* Washington, D.C.: U.S. Government Printing Office, 1967.

Zirbes, Laura. *Spurs to Creative Teaching.* New York: G. P. Putnam's Sons, 1959.

the Teaching Profession

This section is devoted to professional aspects of the teacher's life. Chapter five, the first chapter in this section, deals with a topic that should be of prime interest to the college student who is contemplating entering a teacher education program—namely, employment prospects for the new teacher. This chapter presents a good deal of information about the current teacher supply and demand picture—a picture which has changed rather dramatically over the past decade, from a drastic shortage of teachers in the 1950s and early 1960s to an oversupply in the late 1960s and the 1970s. Some are predicting a growing oversupply of teachers while others are predicting another teacher shortage as early as the mid-1980s. The data and assumptions with which these predictions are being made —birthrate trends, enrollment statistics and projections, and teacher production data—are presented and discussed in this timely chapter.

The current abundant supply of teachers brings with it several searching concerns in the minds of prospective teachers. It is reasonable to wonder whether the risk of preparing for a career which appears to be a crowded field so far as employment is concerned is worth tak-

118 ing. Most people give some attention to economic aspects when seeking a career. Considerable salary data from various sectors of the United States is provided in chapter six for examination in relation to such economic concerns. Most people desire to consider rewards other than economic ones, as well as the problems, associated with a career choice. Discussions of the rewards of teaching usually convey a "Pollyannish" connotation. Chapter six presents a discussion of the *rewards and frustrations* of teaching as related to both social and personal views of this vocation.

Most communities are aware of the relatively recent thrust of teacher militancy upon the schools. Teacher strikes, or threats of them, have aroused emotions within the teaching profession and within the entire educational community. Teacher organizations are commonly viewed as unions by the lay public. In the larger school systems, teachers are pressured to belong to the teacher organization which represents them to the board of education. Chapter seven provides considerable information about membership, organizational structure, and the objectives of both major teacher organizations, the American Federation of Teachers (AFT) and the National Education Association (NEA). In addition, selected activities and merger trends at the national, state, and local levels are reviewed.

chapter 5
Employment Prospects for New Teachers

goals

● Presents the current teacher supply and demand picture in the United States.

● Analyzes the relatively recent history of teacher production in America.

● Reports on birthrate trends.

● Formulates a picture of enrollment trends in elementary, secondary, and higher education.

● Documents the fact that there is no longer a teacher shortage in the United States.

● Notes that graduates of teacher education programs are no longer automatically assured of finding a teaching position.

● Hypothesizes about the causes of the current oversupply of teachers.

● Predicts, using logical assumptions, what the future employment prospects for new teachers will be.

● Suggests some of the important aspects of seeking and obtaining a teaching position.

120 "My how times change—seems like only yesterday there was a big shortage of teachers." This, or some similar statement, has been uttered countless times during the past few years as an oversupply of teachers has developed throughout the United States. The current oversupply of teachers has great implications for the student entering a teacher education program who must compete for a teaching position after graduation. This chapter will present basic information about teacher supply and demand in the hope that it will allow the reader to analyze the employment prospects for new teachers.

Record Teacher Production

During the 1950s and 1960s, when there were dramatic increases in the numbers of elementary and secondary school children, there were also dramatic increases in teacher production. Figure 5.1 shows the annual production of education degrees in the United States from 1958–59 up to the present and projected through 1978–79.

As this figure shows, there are approximately 125,000 new education degrees awarded each year.

Yet another indication of the large teacher production in the United States is the information presented in Figure 5.2. As shown in this figure, 21 percent of all bachelor's degrees, 38.5 percent of all master's degrees, and 19.9 percent of all doctor's degrees awarded in 1970–71 were in the field of education.

The story told by Figures 5.1 and 5.2 is one of American colleges and universities turning out large numbers of new teachers to meet the demands of an expanding population as well as expanding school programs. While

Year	Education Degrees
1958–59	69,515
1959–60	71,145
1960–61	74,028
1961–62	78,153
1962–63	82,627
1963–64	90,813
1964–65	95,667
1965–66	94,294
1966–67	95,859
1967–68	107,778
1968–69	120,900
1969–70	119,580
1970–71	120,450
1971–72	120,700
1972–73	122,740
Projected	
1973–74	124,390
1974–75	126,550
1975–76	127,630
1976–77	128,260
1977–78	128,340
1978–79	126,890

Figure 5.1 Education Degrees Awarded in the United States.

Source: Kenneth A. Simon and W. Vance Grant, *Digest of Educational Statistics*, 1972, U.S. Office of Education (Washington, D.C.: U.S. Government Printing Office, 1973).

this large teacher production was excellent during a time of teacher shortage, it has, along with the leveling off of school enrollments, which we will now examine, led to an oversupply of teachers.

Declining Birthrates

School enrollment is, of course, influenced by birthrates. Figure 5.3 shows the number of live births in the United States from 1961 to 1971.

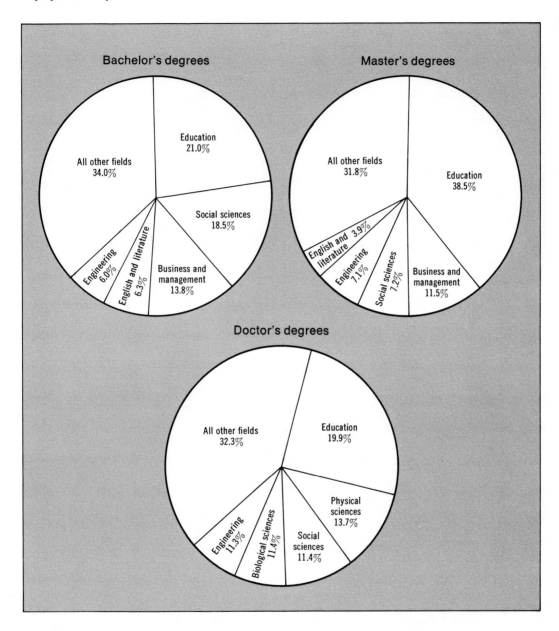

Figure 5.2 Bachelor's, Master's, and Doctor's Degrees, by Major Field of Study: United States, 1970–71.

Source: U.S. Office of Education, *Earned Degrees Conferred, 1970–71* (Washington, D.C.: U.S. Government Printing Office, 1971).

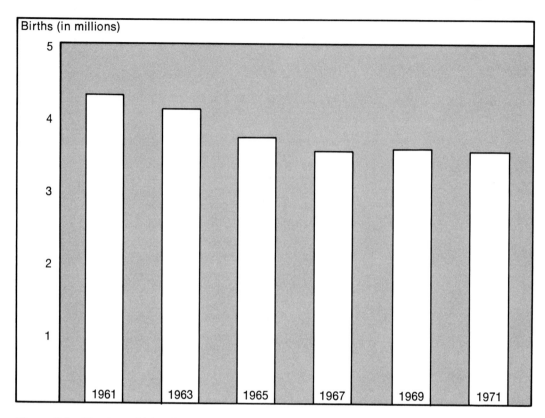

Births (in millions)

Figure 5.3   Number of Live Births: United States, 1961 to 1971

Source: U.S. Public Health Service, National Center for Health Statistics.

This information, from the National Center for Health Statistics, indicates that the number of live births in the United States peaked in 1961 at an all-time high of 4.3 million. Live births then fell to 3.6 million in 1971. Preliminary data reveals that there were only 3.5 million children born in 1972—the smallest number since 1946. Furthermore, the National Center for Educational Statistics estimates that, due largely to improved birth control methods, the birthrate will continue to decline in the next decade.

Figure 5.4 shows the history of the birthrate per 1,000 population in relationship to the death rate. The combination of a slower birthrate coupled with a lower death rate has many implications for the employment prospects for new teachers. The most obvious of these is that a lower birthrate ultimately means fewer teaching jobs. On the other hand, as people live longer, the brighter become the prospects of more adult and continuing education teaching jobs.

Rate per
1,000
population

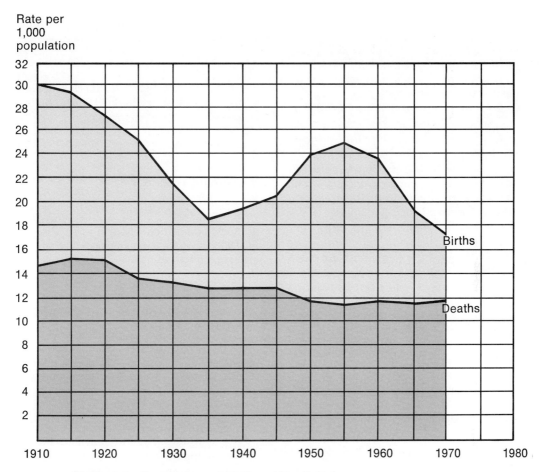

Figure 5.4 Comparison of Birth and Death Rates

Source: Data from "Statistical Abstract of the United States," U.S. Department of Commerce,
Bureau of the Census (Washington, D.C.: U.S. Government Printing Office, 1971), pp. 50 and 55.

> *It is an opinion which I have long entertained, on which every day's experience and observation tends to confirm, that however free our political institutions may be in the commencement, liberty cannot long be preserved unless the society in every district, in all its members, possesses that portion of useful knowledge which is necessary to qualify them to discharge with credit and effect, those great duties of citizens on which free Government rests. The responsibility of public servants, however well provided for by the Constitution, becomes vain and useless if the people in general are not competent judges, in the course of the administration, of all the questions which it involves. If it was wise, manly and patriotic in us to establish a free Government, it is equally incumbent on us to attend to the necessary means of its preservation.*
>
> James Monroe

The implications for school of the declining birthrate are forcefully brought out in Figure 5.5, which shows both the numbers of children three to five years old in the United States and the numbers of these children enrolled in preprimary educational programs. This figure shows that while the overall population of children in the three to five age group was decreasing from 12,496,000 in 1964 to 10,166,000 in 1972, the enrollment in preprimary programs was increasing from 3,187,000 to 4,231,000. Both of these factors have served to increase substantially the percent of that age group enrolled in school—from 25.5 percent to 41.6 percent. This helps to explain why, despite the lowering birth-rates, employment prospects for preprimary teachers have remained relatively good.

> *I had, out of my sixty teachers, a scant half dozen who couldn't have been supplanted by phonographs.*
>
> Don Herrold

Enrollment Trends

More than 3 million American youth graduated from high school in 1972. The class of 1973 is expected to exceed 3.1 million, which will be the largest ever. The size of these classes reflects the high birthrate of the 1950s as well as lower dropout rates. About 78 percent of our American youth now finish high school. About 48 percent of them (or about 62 percent of our high school graduates) enter some type of higher education institution. About 25 percent of our youth now earn a bachelor's degree, 8 percent earn a master's degree, and between 1 and 2 percent go on to earn a doctor's degree.

These and other enrollment trends are shown in Figure 5.6. As this figure shows, enrollment in elementary schools reached a peak in 1971 and is now declining. The U.S. Office of Education projects that elementary school enrollment will continue to decline until about 1976 and then begin to increase. Secondary school enrollments are still on the rise and will continue to increase until about 1976, when they will begin to decline. Enrollment in higher education is increasing and will likely continue to do so until at least 1981. Needless to say, these projected enrollments have great implications for the employment prospects of new teachers.

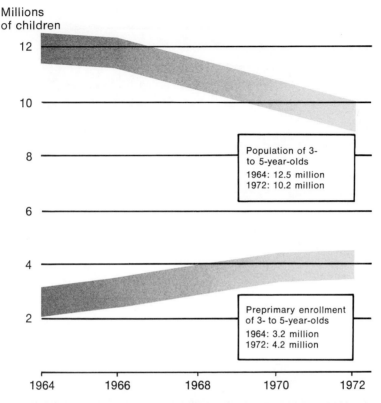

Millions
of children

Population of 3-
to 5-year-olds
1964: 12.5 million
1972: 10.2 million

Preprimary enrollment
of 3- to 5-year-olds
1964: 3.2 million
1972: 4.2 million

Figure 5.5 Population of Children Three to Five Years Old and Enrollment in Preprimary Programs: United States, 1964 to 1972.

Source: U.S. Office of Education, "Preprimary Enrollment, October 1972."

In addition to future enrollments, several other factors will affect the demand for teachers. One of these factors, which has been discussed earlier in this chapter, is the number of new teachers entering the market. Class size or pupil-teacher ratio will also influence teacher demand. In 1959 the pupil-teacher ratio for public elementary schools was 28.7 students per teacher. In 1973 this ratio had been lowered to 24 students per teacher. Similar statistics for public secondary schools were 21.5 in 1959 and 20 in 1973. While the pupil-teacher ratio tends to be somewhat higher in nonpublic elementary and secondary schools, the ratio in these schools, too, has decreased in the past decade. Obviously, the lower the pupil-teacher ratio, the more teachers must be hired. If the pupil-teacher ratio continues its downward trend in the next decade, employment prospects for the new teacher will be brighter. If this ratio levels off or rises, of course, fewer teachers will be employed.

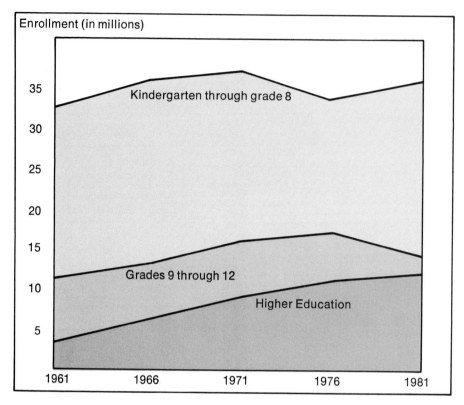

Figure 5.6 Enrollment in United States Educational Institutions, by Level, with Projections to 1981.

Source: U.S. Office of Education, *Projections of Educational Statistics to 1980–81* and unpublished data.

Taxpayer attitude, also, influences teacher demand. Insofar as our citizenry is willing to pay higher taxes to support education, more teachers can be hired. Some authorities have even suggested that the current oversupply of teachers is not really that, but is rather an "underemployment of teachers" brought about by the taxpayers' unwillingness to pay higher taxes to support education. Most educators feel that we need more teachers than the schools can now afford to hire.

Yet another of the many factors that influence teacher demand is our national economy. When the economy is poor, more housewives who are teachers return to the classroom to supplement the family income.

Also, when the economy is poor there are fewer higher paying nonteaching jobs to attract teachers out of the classroom. Conversely, when the economy is thriving, housewives are less likely to resume teaching careers and teachers are more likely to leave teaching for higher paying jobs elsewhere in the economy. This means that there will tend to be more teachers competing for teaching positions when the economy is poor and fewer teachers seeking teaching jobs when the economy is good.

Countless other factors influence the demand for teachers in various ways and to different extents; however, the two main factors that will determine the future employment prospects for new teachers will be the number of new teachers produced and the number of students enrolled in our schools.

No Longer a Shortage

The conditions discussed thus far in this chapter—record teacher production, declining birthrates, enrollment trends, taxpayer attitude—have combined to produce a relatively large and perhaps even growing oversupply of teachers in the United States. Figure 5.7 shows the estimated demand for public elementary and secondary teachers from 1964 to 1979 throughout the United States. Figure 5.8 shows the corresponding data for nonpublic elementary and secondary schools. The U.S. Office of Education explains the information contained in these two figures as follows:

———— • ————

The total demand for public elementary and secondary school teachers (not employed in the public schools the previous year) includes those needed to allow for increased enrollment, additional staff required for lowering pupil-teacher ratios, and those needed for replacement of teachers leaving the profession (turnover). During the period fall 1965 to fall 1969, the cumulative demand for additional public school teachers (including returnees to the profession) was 1,080,793. During the period 1970 through 1974, on the basis of trend alone, it would total 806,000 and from 1975 through 1979, 770,000. Allowance for the expected impact of ESEA, however, will increase these totals to 888,000 and 842,000, respectively. This means that 1.7 million new teachers or returnees to the profession are expected to be employed by the public schools during the next 10 years, 1970 through 1979.

The projected demand for additional public school teachers is shown in Figure 5.7. The number of teachers necessary to take care of enrollment increases and pupil-teacher ratio changes was computed for each year as the difference between the total employed for the current year and the total employed for the previous year. The number for turnover was based on the assumption that 8 percent of the total classroom teachers will leave the profession temporarily or permanently each year. Projection A includes the increases in classroom teachers under the operation of ESEA (Elementary, Secondary Education Act of 1965 will provide relatively large sums of money for education).

The future demand for additional nonpublic school teachers is expected to change only slightly from the recent past. About 40,000 new nonpublic school teachers or returnees to the profession were employed during fall 1965 through fall 1969. This number is expected to be 44,000 in 1970 through 1974 and 50,000 in the 1975 through 1979 period. Approximately 94,000 additional nonpublic school teachers will be employed during the next 10 years, 1970 through 1979.

Year (fall) (1)	Total teacher demand (2)	Demand for additional certificated teachers			
		Total (3)	For enrollment increase (4)	For pupil-teacher ratio changes (5)	For teacher turnover (6)
A. Includes Effect of Elementary and Secondary Education Act of 1965					
ACTUAL[1]					
1964	1,648,184	......	......	......	......
1965	1,710,319	193,990	28,832	33,303	131,855
1966	1,789,238	215,745	37,811	41,108	136,826
1967	1,855,189	209,090	43,180	22,771	143,139
1968	1,936,331	229,557	51,285	29,857	148,415
1969	2,013,836	232,411	34,944	42,561	154,906
1965–69	......	1,080,793	196,052	169,600	715,141
PROJECTED[2]					
1970	2,050,000	197,000	20,000	16,000	161,000
1971	2,065,000	179,000	11,000	5,000	164,000
1972	2,073,000	173,000	3,000	5,000	165,000
1973	2,080,000	172,000	–3,000	10,000	165,000
1974	2,080,000	167,000	......	1,000	166,000
1970–74	......	888,000	31,000	37,000	821,000
1975	2,079,000	165,000	–7,000	5,000	166,000
1976	2,080,000	168,000	–4,000	6,000	166,000
1977	2,082,000	168,000	–3,000	5,000	166,000
1978	2,086,000	170,000	–2,000	6,000	167,000
1979	2,089,000	171,000	1,000	2,000	167,000
1975–79	......	842,000	–15,000	24,000	832,000
B. Excludes Effect of Elementary and Secondary Education Act of 1965					
ESTIMATED[3]					
1965	1,680,000	164,000	29,000	3,000	132,000
1966	1,720,000	174,000	36,000	4,000	134,000
1967	1,764,000	182,000	37,000	7,000	138,000
1968	1,817,000	194,000	49,000	4,000	141,000
1969	1,847,000	176,000	31,000	....	145,000
1965–69	......	890,000	182,000	18,000	690,000

Turnover will account for nearly all of this demand.

The projected demand for additional nonpublic elementary and secondary school teachers is shown in Figure 5.8. The number for taking care of enrollment increases and pupil-teacher ratio changes were computed in the same manner as for public schools, and the number for turnover is based on the assumption that 4 percent (one-half the public school rate) of the nonpublic school teachers will leave the profession permanently or temporarily each year. This lower rate (4 percent) was assumed because large numbers of nonpublic school teachers belong to religious orders, where the turnover is presumably small.

Year (fall) (1)	Total teacher demand (2)	Demand for additional certificated teachers			
		Total (3)	For enrollment increase (4)	For pupil-teacher ratio changes (5)	For teacher turnover (6)
		PROJECTED[4]			
1970	1,870,000	171,000	19,000	4,000	148,000
1971	1,885,000	166,000	12,000	4,000	150,000
1972	1,893,000	159,000	4,000	4,000	151,000
1973	1,900,000	158,000	−1,000	8,000	151,000
1974	1,900,000	152,000	−3,000	3,000	152,000
1970–74	......	806,000	31,000	23,000	752,000
1975	1,899,000	150,000	−5,000	3,000	152,000
1976	1,900,000	153,000	−2,000	3,000	152,000
1977	1,902,000	153,000	−2,000	3,000	152,000
1978	1,906,000	158,000	1,000	5,000	152,000
1979	1,909,000	156,000	......	4,000	152,000
1975–79	......	770,000	−8,000	18,000	760,000

1. Includes full-time and part-time classroom teachers (in 1969, 99 percent of teachers in the public schools were full-time). Does not include teachers in independent nurseries and kindergartens, residential schools for exceptional children, sub-collegiate departments of institutions of higher education, Federal schools for Indians, schools on Federal installations, and other schools not in the regular school system.

2. The projection of classroom teachers in public schools, including the effect of the Elementary and Secondary Education Act of 1965 (ESEA), assumes an additional increase in classroom teachers of 180,000 each year over the number projected under the 1959–64 trend assumptions. This increase is based on 1969 experience as well as on the amount of funds made available by provisions of ESEA.

3. Estimated, using the 1959–64 trend.

4. The projection, excluding the effect of ESEA, of demand for teachers in the public schools in addition to those retained from the previous year was based on the following assumptions: (1) For enrollment increase, the number of additional teachers needed will be the difference between the projected number that must be employed in a given year to maintain the 1959–64 trend in the pupil-teacher ratio and the similarly projected number in the previous year; and (2) for teacher turnover, the number of additional teachers needed to replace those leaving the profession either temporarily or permanently will be 8 percent of the total employed in the previous year. The 8 percent separation rate is based on the Office of Education study "Teacher Turnover in Public Elementary and Secondary Schools, 1959–60."

The projected demand makes no allowance for replacement of teachers who hold substandard certificates (about 5 percent of employed teachers).

Figure 5.7 Estimated Demand for Classroom Teachers in Regular Public Elementary and Secondary Day Schools: United States, Fall 1964 through 1979.

Sources: U.S. Office of Education, "Statistics of Public Schools," Fall 1964 through 1969, and "Enrollment, Teachers, and Schoolhousing," 1959 through 1963.

NOTE: Data are for 50 States and the District of Columbia for all years. Because of rounding, detail may not add to totals.

Section B of Figure 5.7 excludes the effect of the Elementary and Secondary Education Act of 1965 and shows what teacher demand would have been and is likely to be if funding for this act should be withdrawn. These two figures contain a wealth of information and should be of considerable interest and value to future teachers.

Year (fall) (1)	Total teacher demand (2)	Demand for additional certificated teachers			
		Total (3)	For enrollment increase (4)	For pupil-teacher ratio changes (5)	For teacher turnover (6)
1964	234,000	......	......	......	......
1965	240,000	15,000	1,000	5,000	9,000
1966	243,000	14,000	2,000	2,000	10,000
1967	232,000	−1,000	−13,000	2,000	10,000
1968	225,000	2,000	−9,000	2,000	9,000
1969	227,000	10,000	−3,000	4,000	9,000
1965–69	......	40,000	−22,000	15,000	47,000
PROJECTED[1]					
1970	225,000	8,000	−3,000	2,000	9.000
1971	224,000	8,000	−3,000	2,000	9,000
1972	222,000	7,000	−4,000	2,000	9,000
1973	224,000	10,000	......	2,000	9,000
1974	225,000	11,000	......	2,000	9,000
1970–74	......	44,000	−10,000	10,000	45,000
1975	226,000	10,000	......	1,000	9,000
1976	228,000	10,000	......	1,000	9,000
1977	229,000	10,000	......	1,000	9,000
1978	230,000	10,000	......	1,000	9,000
1979	231,000	10,000	......	1,000	9,000
1975–79	......	50,000	......	5,000	45,000

1. The projection of demand for teachers in the nonpublic schools in addition to those retained from the previous year was based on the following assumptions: (1) For enrollment increase, the number of additional teachers needed will be the difference between the projected number that must be employed in a given year to maintain the 1959–68 trend in pupil-teacher ratios and the similarly projected number in the previous year; and (2) for teacher turnover, the number of additional teachers needed to replace those leaving the nonpublic schools either temporarily or permanently is assumed to be 4 percent of the total employed in the previous year.

Figure 5.8 Estimated Demand for Classroom Teachers in Regular Nonpublic Elementary and Secondary Day Schools: United States, Fall 1964 through 1979.

Sources: U.S. Office of Education, prepublication data from "Statistics of Nonpublic Elementary and Secondary Schools, 1968–69," "Statistics of Nonpublic Elementary and Secondary Schools, 1965–66," "Statistics of Nonpublic Elementary Schools, 1961–62," and "Statistics of Nonpublic Secondary Schools, 1960–61."

NOTE: Data are for 50 States and the District of Columbia for all years. Because of rounding, detail may not add to totals.

> *Whom, then, do I call educated . . . ? First, those who manage well the circumstances which they encounter day by day, and who possess a judgment which is accurate in meeting occasions as they arise and rarely misses the expedient course of action; next, those who are decent and honourable in their intercourse with all with whom they associate, tolerating easily and good-naturedly what is unpleasant or offensive in others and being themselves as agreeable and reasonable to their associates as it is possible to be; furthermore, those who hold their pleasures always under control and are not unduly overcome by their misfortunes, bearing up under them bravely and in a manner worthy of our common nature; finally, and most important of all, those who are not spoiled by successes and do not desert their true selves and become arrogant, but hold their ground steadfastly as intelligent men, not rejoicing in the good things which have come to them through chance rather than in those which through their own nature and intelligence are theirs from their birth. Those who have a character which is in accord, not with one of these things, but with all of them— these, I contend, are wise and complete men, possessed of all the virtues.*
>
> *These then are the views which I hold regarding educated men.*
>
> Isocrates

Figure 5.9 shows yet another dimension of the current teacher supply and demand picture. This figure, prepared by the National Education Association, shows both the supply of and demand for beginning teachers in each teaching field. It can be readily seen that in most fields, the 1972 supply of teachers was greater than the demand. In fact, the oversupply in some fields was considerable. For instance, if one uses the conservative demand for about 44,000 elementary teachers this leaves a surplus of about 60,000 since 102,852 new elementary teachers were prepared in that year. Put another way, we may have graduated nearly sixty percent more elementary teachers than were needed in that year. In fact, only two teaching areas—trade, industrial and technical; and mathematics—were listed as having an actual teacher shortage by the NEA. Two other areas—industrial arts and sciences—were shown to have a relatively low supply of teachers. All other areas, to varying degrees, produced more teachers than were needed in 1970. This, essentially, has been the case since the late 1960s in the United States.

The fact that more teachers have been produced than needed each year for a number of years, of course, means there is a growing oversupply of teachers. This will continue to be the case until such time that fewer teachers are produced than hired each year. One can only estimate, using a number of assumptions, when this may happen. For instance, there are some indications that enrollment in teacher education programs throughout the country may be starting to decline. In fact, the law of supply and demand suggests that this should indeed happen since there is a considerable oversupply of teachers. Insofar as this trend materializes, and depending upon the degree of enrollment decline in teacher education programs, there could even conceivably be another shortage of teachers in the next decade.

Another factor that could lead to a brighter employment prospect for beginning teachers is earlier teacher retirement. Since

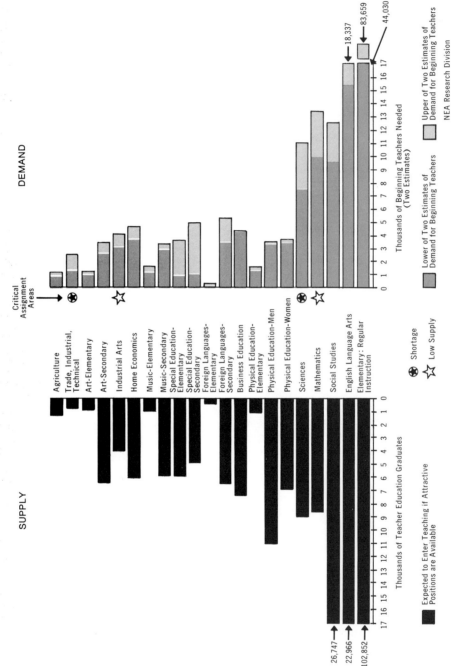

Figure 5.9 Supply and Demand for Beginning Teachers, by Teaching Field, 1972.

Source: "Teacher Supply and Demand in Public Schools," research report 1972, National Education Association, Research Division, Washington, 1972.

there seems to be a trend toward earlier retirement in all fields of work, it is not inconceivable that a similar trend may occur in the teaching profession. If, for example, states would pass legislation making it possible for teachers to retire with full retirement benefits at age fifty-five, the demand for new teachers would sharply increase.

Compulsory early childhood education would be yet another factor that could create many new teaching jobs. As was pointed out earlier in this chapter, many early childhood educational opportunities are now provided on an optional basis. If states decide to mandate compulsory early childhood education programs, schools will need to hire a great number of teachers to staff these programs.

> *I consider knowledge to be the soul of a republic, and as the weak and the wicked are generally in alliance, as much care should be taken to diminish the number of the former as of the latter. Education is the way to do this, and nothing should be left undone to afford all ranks of people the means of obtaining a proper degree of it at a cheap and easy rate.*
>
> John Jay

The message in the current teacher supply and demand picture for students considering a career in teaching is this—there is, at this juncture, no guarantee of a teaching job. On the other hand, teaching is going to continue to be one of the nation's largest enterprises, and those teacher education graduates with good credentials who are willing to accept teaching positions where they occur are going to continue to get jobs.

133

The teaching areas in which there will likely be the best employment opportunities include industrial arts and other related trade and technical areas, mathematics, and sciences (as pointed out in Figure 5.9) as well as early childhood education, special education, adult education, and higher education.

One can glean from Figure 5.10 an indication of the employment opportunities in special education. This figure also shows estimates of the number of elementary and secondary school children affected by each of the different types of handicaps. Figure 5.10 clearly points out that there is a shortage of qualified teachers and specialists in the area of special education. Unfortunately, it is unlikely that schools will have sufficient money to hire as many of these special education teachers as are needed.

Area of Handicapped	Estimated Children of Elementary and Secondary School Age	Number of Additional Teachers and Specialists Needed
Speech Handicapped	1,833,230	12,733
Emotionally Disturbed	1,047,560	121,791
Mental Retardation	1,204,694	58,406
Specific Learning Disabilities	523,780	22,564
Hard of Hearing	261,890	12,100
Crippled and Other Health Disorders	261,890	5,674
Visually Handicapped	52,378	2,877
Deaf	39,283	823
TOTAL	5,224,705	236,968

Figure 5.10 Manpower Needs to Educate the Handicapped.

Source: Council for Exceptional Children, National Education Association.

134

The various types of adult and continuing education programs are rather thoroughly discussed in chapters four and fifteen. The demand for teachers in these various adult and continuing education programs is likely to remain quite good.

So are employment prospects likely to remain relatively good in higher education. The total of full-time and part-time jobs in all higher education institutions increased from 281,506 in 1959–60 to approximately 578,000 in 1969–70 and is expected by the U.S. Office of Education to be about 801,000 in 1979–80. The bulk of these additional positions will likely be in community colleges and trade schools.

Obtaining a Position

For those who are nearing the successful completion of a formal teacher education program, obtaining a teaching position becomes an important task. The following discussion, entitled "Selecting the First Teaching Position," contains excellent suggestions about this important task.

———•—•———

You have a big question to answer—where do I want to start this exciting career? The mind whirls and dreams of making your own money, owning your own car, being master of your own destiny push out all else and the exciting possibilities of taking a position in far-off places further stir the imagination. Hawaii, California, New England, Alaska, English-speaking schools in the Far East, Europe, Central or South America—all are real and exciting possibilities. The opportunities are so great for the new teacher of today that you can truly say, "The world's my oyster which I with 'learning' will open."

Stop a moment, though, before your thoughts go too far afield. The first basic decision you must make which definitely affects how you go about selecting a teaching position is determined by looking inward. Considering you—yourself—honestly, dispassionately, objectively, you ask yourself the question, "Am I looking for a position where there is the greatest need for help, where I can do the greatest good for society, where my abilities will be challenged to the utmost by difficult situations or am I looking for a position which will be most beneficial to me—gives me the greatest opportunity to travel, pays the highest salary, contains the pleasantest environment, commands the strongest resources, and includes the most stylish and compatible faculty? Your choice is a very personal one and to be happy and successful in your first professional experience it must be fought through with yourself honestly and dispassionately for the good of your own mental health and the goodness of society. Dedicated, superior teachers are needed desperately in the slums, ghettos, in poverty-stricken outlying areas and in developing countries—but what we don't need is more frustrated, unhappy and inept teachers who may do more harm than good. Nor do we need the "do-gooder" who is impervious and unconscious to the real problem.

You must face yourself honestly in regard to this question and not feel guilty for the direction you choose. There are many legitimate reasons why you should not seek out trouble in your first experience. One important consideration is that in the safe sanctity of the suburb you may find opportunity to gain needed experience before facing more difficult teaching experiences.

Now that you have faced the more personal and philosophical question of how far you are ready to go in helping society, the next step of decision-making is simpler in terms of establishing an objective list of pros and cons.

Selecting implies choosing, making comparisons, evaluating and carefully arriving at a final decision. While you can make this next phase of the selection process quite simple and mechanical, it does take time. You should not relegate it to a last-minute activity during your senior year. The task is too crucial. Do not think you are just choosing a job for one year but rather you are beginning a career.

To keep the choice of the first teaching position from becoming a near-perfunctory one, you might ask significant questions such as the following:

What do I look for in the school system with which I wish to be associated?

How important are working conditions?

What are the opportunities for professional growth?

What are the positions for orientation and induction of new teachers?

Can I make a contribution to this school and community?

Is recognition given to staff achievement and contributions?

How will I be evaluated?

Many of the answers to questions like these can be secured by early and persistent investigation of numerous and various sources of information available to you. Talk with teachers already employed in school systems in which you are interested. Talk with your college and university instructors and the people in the placement bureaus about the local schools or schools in another state. Even more valuable would be visits to these schools during semester breaks. These visits would permit you to see and appraise first-hand the physical facilities, variety of instructional materials and methods, and also sense the climate of the school and community.

If you are interested in teaching in another state, you could secure additional information about the schools and communities by writing to the state departments of education, the superintendents of the various school systems or to the chambers of commerce. State educational associations and state departments of education very often publish comparative fact sheets about the schools of their states which would assist you in analyzing a school system. Most school systems publish brochures, pamphlets or handbooks containing information on the school program, salary schedules and prerequisites, teaching

136 and special services staff, policies pertaining to supervision and tenure, opportunities for professional growth, professional associations, and the history of the community. Some schools publish separate and special materials for new teachers which include very detailed orientation information on daily teaching schedule, classroom discipline, policies regarding homework, procedures for fire drills, location and distribution of instructional materials and resources, samples of forms for reporting pupil progress, checklists of duties and suggested teaching plans for the first few days of school.

A critical examination of all the information you receive through informal discussions or printed materials will enable you to eliminate from future consideration those teaching situations which are least promising or attractive to you. The personal visits that you make to schools and communities recommended by teachers in service or by college staff will reveal whether you can adjust to the situation, and, more important, be stimulated to grow as a member of the profession. Analysis of the content of the printed materials you receive can also help you in selecting the most promising teaching situation. These materials often contain statements about "meeting the needs of pupils of varying interests and abilities," or "providing for the gifted, the mentally retarded and the emotionally disturbed." Are there supportive statements regarding special services personnel, flexibility in the educational program and descriptions of special programs? Take a careful look at the sample report card or reporting form which the school system uses in communicating to parents the growth of the progress of the child. Many educators agree that the pupil reporting forms reflect the operating philosophy of the school, the curriculum and the organizational pattern. Does the report form set forth a list of subject matter areas and a letter or numerical grade for each area? Can this type

of reporting be reconciled with statements about "full partnership in evaluating each child's growth," "attainment and uniqueness of each child" or "learning is personal, unique, unstandardized"? Examine the statements concerning supervision and evaluation of probationary teachers. Who is involved in evaluation? Are written records kept? Are these records available to you? What new media or procedures are being used for appraising performance? What support, cooperation and assistance will be given during your beginning years of service? Those school systems which you feel are presenting the most positive or desirable practices in these areas should be included on the list of school systems to which you would apply for your first teaching position.

The personnel in the placement office in your college or university can give you much help in obtaining a teaching position. There are many forms to be completed and records to be filed. Great care should be given to the preparation of these materials. You will also need to write a letter of application. It, too, should be carefully written. Specific suggestions about the form and content of these letters are usually presented by the college director or coordinator of student teaching. Sample letters may be found in publications such as student teacher handbooks or professional texts dealing with the student teaching program. Your letter should include a statement regarding arrangements for an interview.

For most students the interview experience is a strained one. They often report that they were tense, nervous and uncomfortable. However, if you devoted the necessary time and thought in visiting and inquiring about many schools, and applied only in selected schools, your interview should be an exhilarating experience. The background of information that you will already have about the school system will not only allow you to ask pertinent and meaningful questions but will also facilitate communicating your own dedication to teaching and your sincere interest in the particular teaching position. It will also permit you to respond to questions with confidence and clarity, and serve you well in decisions you will have to make.

The decision regarding the particular position to accept is often a troublesome one, especially when accompanied by a deadline date for acceptance. However, your preliminary research should make your decision an easy one. Since you have applied only in selected systems, any offer should be immediately desirable to you.

When you have signed the contract, you should inform your college placement office that you have accepted a position. It is also in good taste to notify at least the school systems which interviewed you and include some expression of gratitude or appreciation for any consideration they may have given to your application.[1]

————— • • —————

In summary, this chapter has endeavored to provide the reader with a wealth of information about future employment prospects for new teachers. Hopefully, this information will help the reader decide if these prospects are bright enough to warrant pursuing a career in education.

Point of View

An attempt has been made in this chapter to analyze the current teacher supply and demand picture in the United States. Topics such as birthrate trends, teacher production, and school enrollment projections have also

1. William H. Roe and Rose M. Verdi, "Selecting the First Teaching Position," *Teaching Opportunities for You.* Assn. for School, College and University Staffing, 1969, pp. 19–20. Used by permission.

been discussed in an effort to help the reader understand the employment prospects for new teachers.

Predicting the future is, of course, a very difficult if not totally impossible task. While one can, as has been attempted in this chapter, analyze different variables and apply logic to a prediction, all predictions must be based on assumptions. If the assumptions do not prove to be accurate, the predictions will be wrong. It therefore behooves the reader to critically analyze the data and assumptions set forth in this chapter and arrive as his or her own conclusions about the employment prospects for beginning teachers. In so doing, the reader will quickly realize that there are many opinions on this topic.

The following article represents a synthesis of many estimates of the extent of the teacher oversupply. One of the most interesting things pointed out in this article is that the "experts" do not agree about the future oversupply of teachers. One thing, however, is clear: all the experts do predict an oversupply of teachers, at least for the next decade.

————— • • —————

Predictions for Extra Teachers by End of Decade Range from 412,000 (PDK) to 1,700,000 (HEW)

Betty Levitov

The first characteristic of data about the "teacher surplus" is that the experts disagree

Betty Levitov, "Predictions for Extra Teachers by End of Decade Range from 412,000 (PDK) to 1,700,000 (HEW)," Study Commission, University of Nebraska (Lincoln: University of Nebraska Press, 1973), pp. 33–34.

138 (or appear to). Predictions range from expecting 412,000 extra teachers by 1979 to a 1,700,000 possible surplus by 1980. The figure most often used by data gatherers is a surplus of about 100,000 per year.

A National Education Association (NEA) report (*Teacher Supply and Demand in Public Schools, 1972*) shows that about 320,000 persons probably completed their degrees for entry into the teaching profession in the 1972–73 school year—36.1 percent of the total of students in undergraduate education (p. 9).

NEA: 65,000 to 115,000

The NEA estimates that only about 85 percent of the persons educated as elementary teachers and 70 percent of those educated as secondary teachers would actually take teaching jobs, even when jobs are plentiful in "shortage" times. This means that a total of about 110,000 elementary and 135,000 secondary (245,000 new teachers) would be considered likely to want to enter the field. In the NEA view, the probable need for the 1972–73 school year was about 50,000 new elementary teachers and 80,000 new secondary teachers (these were minimum estimates: maximum estimates were for 90,000 new elementary teachers and 90,000 new secondary). Thus, the surplus of new people educated to be teachers for the 1972–73 year would appear to be between 65,000 (using maximum need figures) and 115,000 persons (using minimum need figures). The NEA has estimated the overall surplus for 1972–73 at 100,000 persons, and a preliminary report from NEA for the 1973–74 school year shows a probable surplus of 125,000 teacher education graduates.

Syracuse: 110,000 to 150,000

Similarly, a Syracuse Education Policy Research Center publication estimates a possible annual demand of 145,000 teachers and a possible annual job-seeking group of from 240,000 to 320,000 people between 1970 and 1980—a possible surplus of 110,000 to 150,000 would-be teachers per year. However, the Research Center posits that the student response to counselling and to the law of supply and demand will not allow such extreme surpluses to build up. Syracuse sees the issue as one of teacher recruitment: "Will the surplus be used 'to attract better teachers' or to allow colleges of education to continue to be 'homes for less capable students who float'?" It also seems probable, according to the Syracuse center, that some new programs —early childhood, adult education, peripheral educational activities and remedial programs for the high schools' 20 percent who drop out —could absorb some of the possible surplus, but not all of it.

NCES: 800,000 by 1981

Furthermore, "Projections of Education Statistics to 1981–82," from the National Center for Education Statistics, suggests that whereas in the four-year period from 1967 to 1971 the schools employed somewhat more than a million new teachers, in the period from 1972 to 1976, they will employ somewhat fewer than 800,000 new ones, and in the period from 1977 to 1981, they will employ about 950,000 new teachers (about 1.8 million in the eight-year period). The National Center estimates that about 2.1 million new teachers will be graduated in the same eight-year period. If those wanting to return to teaching after leaving the field (60,000 per year in NEA estimates or a total of 480,000 over the eight-year period) are counted, there could be a surplus of about 800,000 by 1981, using NCES projections.

Others: 412,000 to 1,700,000 by 1980

The Education Professions: 1971–72 (HEW) and the Study Commission's Information Committee (Evelyn Zerfoss and Leo Shapiro, *Supply and Demand of Teachers and Teaching,* using Department of Labor predictions) estimate the surplus at one million to 1.7 million by 1980. In contrast, a Phi Delta Kappa Educational Foundation publication predicts the surplus may be 412,000 by 1979.

These forecasts are difficult to believe in the light of recent events. It is hard to believe that people would be dumb enough to make themselves part of a million-person surplus at any time. Furthermore, institutions of higher education are being mandated by planning commissions to "counsel people out" of teaching as a career, and an NEA survey of teacher education percentages suggests that things *are* changing some. In 124 institutions surveyed, it appeared that teacher education graduates would drop from 35 percent of bachelor's degrees in 1972 to 30 percent in 1974 and to under 25 percent in 1975. It is not clear whether these apparent "fall-offs" will continue as poorer students at many institutions float into teacher education in their junior or senior years (see the Folger, Astin, Bayer study, *Human Resources and Higher Education,* pp. 103–14 and pp. 200–16).

Surplus Partly Illusory

Even if the figures on number of student candidates for teaching do not fall as fast as the NEA and the state planning commissions expect, the large surplus which remains is partly an illusory one. It is clear that we are not piling up 100,000 angry unemployed would-be teachers per year. The number of people who graduate with an "education degree" and then report being unable to get a job is about 10 percent of the 200,000 to 250,000 who graduate annually. With these figures, the actual surplus may be more like 100,000 by 1980, rather than 100,000 annually. Even the NEA predicts that the ratio of education graduates seeking jobs to jobs available will decline from 2:1 to 1½:1 by 1976.

The most interesting group may be neither the 50 percent of teacher education graduates who get jobs nor the 10 percent who graduate and can't get them, but that vague other 40 percent—those who go into other jobs (6.5 percent); those who go on to graduate or other schools (5 percent); and, most of all, that 20 percent (plus) who just seem to get lost (persons receiving teacher education degrees, but concerning whom the universities have no information as to employment, future plans, or whatever). It appears likely that many of the people who make up the "teacher surplus" but who don't really try to go into teaching immediately are either:

A. Flexible people who want to "try out" various roles in life before trying to teach;

B. People who regard their teaching certificates as insurance policies (women who may wish to teach later, but who marry immediately after graduating and begin to raise a family, and people who have other first-choice careers but plan to teach if it becomes necessary later).

Youth and Careers in Education (published by the National Center for Information on Careers in Education for the Bureau of Education Personnel Development) suggests that many young people regard education as a second-choice career—part of a system which is a little too cold (pp. 8–10), a little too anti-intellectual, and a little too lacking in prestige to be a career of first choice. Martin Haberman has described the personality type who seeks teaching as a career as too often associated with what he calls the "anomalous vocational student," as opposed to the intellectually-oriented student. This "anomalous vocational student" sees little value in college as general education or preparation for a specific occupation, but sees it as a "hurdle to be surmounted in an uninteresting, weary struggle toward a higher place in the world."

The more serious questions of the teacher surplus may not be the graduating of large numbers of dissatisfied persons who cannot find employment. It may be a matter of social priority as to who should "occupy spaces" in colleges and how colleges should be used to serve public needs. For example, to what extent is public need served by educating those who do not have a sense of teaching as a vocation or who see college as a hurdle in a struggle for place? The question is unanswered.

Shortages in Some Areas

The reform of education may require a clear conceptualization not only of where shortages or low supply areas exist, but also of what the existence of these areas tells one about the rest of teacher education. NEA's 1972 low supply areas included high-intellectual-skills areas (mathematics, natural and physical sciences, special education) and "field" areas (trade—industrial, vocational, and technical—and industrial arts, distributive education) associated with specific occupations. More recent Study Commission correspondence with state information gatherers indicates a shortage in rural areas in a few states. Looking more broadly, by any reasonable criterion, adequate numbers of bilingual teachers are lacking. The U.S. Commission on Civil Rights has documented that fewer than three percent of the Mexican-American student population is being reached by bilingual programs, and similarly dismal figures have been provided for Indian, Puerto Rican and other populations which do not use English as a first language (the Kotz study of manpower for National Planning Associates and the NCES figures also point to a shortage of bilingual teachers). However, the "shortage" here is different from that for other areas in that its existence will depend on removal or transfer of non-bilingual teachers.

Ironically, while many students do not choose teaching because they are uncertain about the possibilities of "bringing about constructive social change" through teaching (*Youth and Careers in Education,* p. 5), the "social-service" areas of education are often those with the largest shortages. (Education's image may be improved somewhat in this regard with the recent changing of several large teacher training institutions to "college of community and human development" or "college of education and social services.")

QUESTIONS FOR DISCUSSION

1. In your estimation, what factors have led to the current oversupply of teachers?
2. What do you think will happen to the birth-

rate in the United States between now and the year 2000?

3. What do you believe the supply and demand picture for teachers will look like in 1980?

4. Many hiring officials put a good deal of emphasis on the personal interview when hiring new teachers. How do you feel a candidate should act during an interview to make a favorable impression?

5. If you were a hiring official, what would you look for when hiring a new teacher?

SUPPLEMENTARY LEARNING ACTIVITIES

1. Analyze various statistics such as birthrates, teacher production, school districts' voting trends, school enrollments, etc., and then make your own predictions about further teacher supply and demand.

2. Visit a variety of different schools—nursery, elementary, middle, secondary, trade, and/or community college. Try to arrange informal discussions with teachers and administrators during your visit.

3. Make a list and/or discuss the advantages and disadvantages of different types of teaching careers.

4. Invite a school administrator to your class to discuss what he looks for when hiring new teachers.

5. Role-play, with a classmate, a situation in which a school superintendent is interviewing a candidate for a teaching position.

SELECTED REFERENCES

American Association of Colleges for Teacher Education. *Teachers for the Real World*. Washington, D.C.: American Association of Colleges for Teacher Education, 1969.

Elam, Stanley, ed. *Improving Teacher Education in the United States*. Bloomington, Ind.: Phi Delta Kappa, 1967.

Hughes, Marie M. "What Teachers Do and the Way They Do It." *NEA Journal* 53 (September 1964):11–13.

Lambert, Sam M. "Angry Young Men in Teaching." *NEA Journal* 52 (February 1963):17–20.

Mood, Alexander M. *The Future of Higher Education*. New York: McGraw-Hill Book Company, 1973.

National Education Association, National Commission on Teacher Education and Professional Standards. *The Teacher and His Staff*. Washington, D.C.: National Education Association Publications, 1969.

National Education Association. "Teacher Supply and Demand in Public Schools. 1971." Washington, D.C.: Research Report 1971, National Education Association Publications, 1971.

———. "Teacher Supply and Demand in the Public Schools, 1972." Washington, D.C.: Research Report 1972, National Education Association Publications, 1972.

Pedersen, K. George. *The Itinerant Schoolmaster: A Socio-Economic Analysis of Teacher Turnover*. Chicago: Midwest Administration Center, 1973.

Peter, Laurence J., "The Peter Principle: We're All Incompetent," *Phi Delta Kappan* 48 (March 1967):339–41.

Phi Delta Kappa. *Improving Teacher Education in the United States*. Bloomington, Ind.: Phi Delta Kappa, 1967.

Reisert, John E. "Migrating Educator? What About Your Teaching Credentials?" *Phi*

142 *Delta Kappan* 47(March 1966):372–74.

Rettig, Solomon, and Benjamin Pasamanick. "Status and Job Satisfaction of Public School Teachers." *School and Society* 87(March 14, 1959):113–16.

Robb, Felix. *Teachers: The Need and the Task*. Washington, D.C.: American Association of Colleges for Teacher Education, 1968.

Shipman, Helen, and Elizabeth Foley. *Any Teacher Can . . . : A Systematic Approach to Behavior Management and Positive Teaching*. Chicago: Loyola University Press, 1973.

Stinnett, T. M., ed. *The Teacher Dropout*. Ithaca, N.Y.: F. E. Peacock Publishers, Inc., 1970.

Stinnett, T. M., and Albert J. Huggett. *Professional Problems of Teachers*. 2nd ed. New York: Macmillan Company, 1968.

Study Commission. "Report of Teacher Supply and Demand." Andrews Hall, University of Nebraska, December, 1973.

chapter 6

Rewards and Frustrations of Teaching

goals

- Describes the rewards and frustrations of teaching in terms of both personal and monetary areas.

- Explains attitudes of the public toward education by the systematic grouping of social and personal beliefs.

- Compiles salary data related to teaching positions throughout the United States for various levels.

- Tells of the human relation functions and the responsibility of the specialists in the teaching profession.

- Integrates many of the facets of the rewards and frustrations of teaching.

There are various economic, as well as intangible, rewards and problems associated with any vocation. Historically, the teaching profession has been somewhat "Pollyannaish" in that disproportionate worth has been ascribed to the intangible rewards of teaching, i.e., community status and rapport among teachers, as opposed to such tangible rewards as salary and fringe benefits. One of the factors identified with the rise of teacher mili-

143

144 tancy through strong organizations is the demand by teachers that increased attention be given to the economic rewards of teaching. The most attractive professions are those which provide challenges to problems and a proportionate balance of tangible and intangible rewards to the professional who satisfactorily meets those challenges. Teaching as a vocation is presently an attractive profession and has the potential of becoming increasingly more attractive.

Teachers' Salaries

Salary is the prime economic aspect of teaching. A major reason for the post–World War II teacher shortage was that both private business and government jobs provided higher salaries. While the salary gap has narrowed, teaching has not as yet caught up to all the private business and government agencies. Figure 6.1 compares teachers' salaries with wage and salary workers, manufacturing employees, and civilian employees of the federal government. Teachers' salaries permanently surpassed wage and salary workers in 1954 and manufacturing employees in 1967. Teachers' salaries had not caught up with government civilian employees at the end of 1971.

In comparing starting salaries of teachers to private industry, teachers' salaries still fall significantly behind for both men and women. Figure 6.2 for men and Figure 6.3 for women show that in 1972–73, both men and women were behind the starting salaries of all other bachelor degree starting employees. The widest gap for starting male teachers was the $3,251 a year less than starting male engineers with similar bachelor's degrees earned. Figure 6.3 shows the widest gap between starting female teachers and private industry was with the starting salaries of engineering-technical research females who began earning over $3,203 a year more than the teachers. It is obvious that a gap remains between beginning teachers' salaries and beginning salaries offered by other fields of endeavor. However, tabled comparisons of this kind do not show that teacher salaries are usually for nine months whereas the other salaries are for twelve months. A potential for increased teacher salaries lies in the expansion of summer teaching opportunities which would permit teachers to earn from their profession on a twelve-month basis.

Teachers' salaries differ from city to city and from state to state. In comparing minimum teachers' salaries in twelve of the largest cities in the United States at the end of 1973, the range, shown in Figure 6.4, was from $7,100 (Houston) to $9,571 (Chicago) at the bachelor degree–no experience level. Maximum salaries at this level ranged from $10,300 (Houston) to $15,250 (Chicago).

Since the compilation of the data given in Figure 6.4 for the 1972–73 school year, new contracts have been negotiated with each showing additional gains in the starting salary for first-year teachers. Figure 6.5 lists the minimum salaries for beginning teachers with the bachelor degree for the same cities as of February 1, 1974. The Chicago Teachers' Union became the first American Federation of Teachers (AFT) affiliate to negotiate a $10,000 a year salary for starting teachers with a bachelor's degree. The $10,000 salary was a goal set in 1966 by the AFT for unionized teachers across the country. At that time, new teachers in Chicago were paid $5,500 a year.

The National Education Association (NEA) affiliates in Jericho, New York and Jersey City, New Jersey still boast the highest

Calendar Year Basis

Calendar year	Average annual earnings				Index: Teachers = 100.0			
	Public-school teachers	Wage and salary workers—all industries	Employees in manufacturing	Civilian employees of federal government	Public-school teachers	Wage and salary workers—all industries	Employees in manufacturing	Civilian employees of federal government
1	2	3	4	5	6	7	8	9
1950	$2,823	$3,008	$3,300	$3,503	100.0	106.6	116.9	124.1
1951	3,123	3,231	3,606	3,777	100.0	103.5	115.5	120.9
1952	3,357	3,414	3,828	4,034	100.0	101.7	114.0	120.2
1953	3,519	3,587	4,049	4,226	100.0	101.9	115.1	120.1
1954	3,746	3,670	4,116	4,320	100.0	98.0	109.9	115.3
1955	3,907	3,847	4,351	4,595	100.0	98.5	111.4	117.6
1956	4,116	4,036	4,584	4,808	100.0	98.1	111.4	116.8
1957	4,350	4,205	4,781	4,971	100.0	96.7	109.9	114.3
1958	4,646	4,346	4,939	5,514	100.0	93.5	106.3	118.7
1959	4,863	4,558	5,215	5,682	100.0	93.7	107.2	116.8
1960	5,088	4,707	5,342	5,946	100.0	92.5	105.0	116.9
1961	5,355	4,843	5,509	6,285	100.0	90.4	102.9	117.4
1962	5,587	5,065	5,730	6,450	100.0	90.7	102.6	115.4
1963	5,820	5,243	5,920	6,792	100.0	90.1	101.7	116.7
1964	6,062	5,503	6,196	7,267	100.0	90.8	102.2	119.9
1965	6,292	5,710	6,389	7,614	100.0	90.8	101.5	121.0
1966	6,600	5,967	6,643	7,841	100.0	90.4	100.7	118.8
1967	7,028	6,230	6,880	7,985	100.0	88.6	97.9	113.6
1968	7,599	6,657	7,347	8,746	100.0	87.6	96.7	115.1
1969	8,180	7,098	7,775	9,424	100.0	86.8	95.0	115.2
1970	8,846	7,571	8,155	10,519	100.0	85.6	92.2	118.9
1971	9,414	8,061	8,638	11,503	100.0	85.6	91.8	122.2

Figure 6.1 Average Annual Earnings of Public School Teachers and Certain Other Occupational Groups, 1950 to 1971.

Sources: Column 2 calculated on calendar-year basis by NEA Research. Columns 3, 4, and 5 from U.S. Department of Commerce, Office of Business Economics. Figures for 1950 through 1955 from *U.S. Income and Output*, a supplement to the *Survey of Current Business*, 1959, Table VI-15, p. 213. Figures for 1956 through 1969 from *Survey of Current Business*, various issues. Indexes in columns 6 through 9 computed by NEA Research Division, *Economic Status of the Teaching Profession, 1972–73*, research report 1973–R3 (Washington, D.C.: National Education Association Publications, 1973), p. 49. Used by permission.

NOTE: It was not until 1967 that average earnings of teachers passed earnings of employees in manufacturing, most of whom are nonprofessional workers. Civilian employees of the federal government have had higher average earnings than teachers at least since 1950.

Position or subject field	Average starting salaries									Percent change, 1973–74 over 1972–73
	1964–65	1966–67	1967–68	1968–69	1969–70	1970–71	1971–72	1972–73	1973–74	
1	2	3	4	5	6	7	8	9	10	11
Beginning teachers with bachelor's degree	$4,707	$5,144	$5,523	$5,941	$6,383	$ 6,850	$ 7,061	$ 7,357	...	...
Male college graduates with bachelor's degree										
Engineering	7,356	8,112	8,772	9,312	9,960	10,476	10,500	10,608	$10,860	2.4
Accounting	6,444	7,128	7,776	8,424	9,396	10,080	10,260	10,476	10,824	3.3
Sales—Marketing	6,072	6,744	7,044	7,620	8,088	8,580	8,736	9,408	9,648	2.6
Business Administration	5,880	6,576	7,140	7,560	8,100	8,124	8,424	8,448	8,664	2.6
Liberal Arts	5,712	6,432	6,780	7,368	7,980	8,184	8,292	8,424	8,688	3.1
Production management	6,564	7,176	7,584	7,980	8,736	9,048	9,792	9,720	9,792	0.1
Chemistry	6,972	7,500	8,064	8,520	9,276	9,708	9,720	9,972	10,116	1.4
Physics	7,200	7,740	8,448	8,916	9,348	10,080	9,636	10,344	10,560	2.1
Mathematics—Statistics	6,636	7,260	7,944	8,412	8,952	9,468	9,192	9,288	9,552	2.8
Economics—Finance	6,276	6,732	7,416	7,800	8,304	8,880	9,216	9,324	9,480	1.7
Other fields	6,360	7,044	7,644	7,656	8,796	9,264	8,580	9,552	9,696	1.5
Total—all fields (weighted average)	$6,535	$7,243	$7,836	$8,395	$8,985	$ 9,361	$ 9,534	$ 9,648	$10,016	3.8

Figure 6.2 Average Starting Salaries: Teachers versus Private Industry (Men).

Sources: NEA research report 1973–R3, *Economic Status of the Teaching Profession, 1972–73*, p. 74; and annual reports from Frank S. Endicott, Director of Placement Emeritus, Northwestern University.

NOTE: Salaries are based on offers made to graduates by approximately 200 companies located throughout the United States. Salaries for 1973–74 are based on offers made in November 1972 to men who graduated in June 1973.

Position or subject field	Average starting salaries									Percent change, 1973–74 over 1972–73
	1964–65	1966–67	1967–68	1968–69	1969–70	1970–71	1971–72	1972–73	1973–74	
1	2	3	4	5	6	7	8	9	10	11
Beginning teachers with bachelor's degree	$4,707	$5,144	$5,523	$5,941	$6,383	$6,850	$7,061	$7,357	...	...
Women college graduates with bachelor's degree										
Mathematics—Statistics	6,108	6,324	7,104	7,776	8,484	8,952	9,312	9,516	...	...
General business	4,848	5,520	6,000	6,840	7,104	8,184	8,016	8,280	8,748	5.7
Chemistry and sciences	6,060	...	...	8,496	9,000	9,456	9,960	9,816	9,960	1.5
Accounting	5,664	6,768	6,984	7,716	8,304	8,952	9,516	10,224	10,404	1.8
Home Economics	5,112	5,664	6,276	6,660	7,056	7,380	7,932	ND	ND	...
Engineering—Technical research	7,224	7,260	8,208	8,280	9,672	10,128	10,608	10,560	10,968	3.9
Economics—Finance	5,448	6,000	6,636	6,984	7,224	8,400	8,400	ND	ND	...
Liberal Arts	4,620	...	...	6,264	6,900	7,572	8,256	8,112	8,580	5.8

Figure 6.3 Average Starting Salaries: Teachers versus Private Industry (Women).

Sources: NEA research report 1973–R3, *Economic Status of the Teaching Profession, 1972–73*, p. 74; and annual reports from Frank S. Endicott, Director of Placement Emeritus, Northwestern University.

NOTE: Salaries for women are based largely on information concerning direct hires of women by many of the same companies as the men.

City	Bachelor's Degree			Master's Degree		
	Min.	Max.	Years to Reach Max.	Min.	Max.	Years to Reach Max.
Chicago	$9,571	$15,254	14	$10,645	$17,170	14
Detroit	9,032	14,198	10	9,908	16,255	10
Los Angeles	7,590	11,010	10	9,160	13,270	10
San Francisco	7,760	13,285	13	8,825	14,405	13
Milwaukee	8,300	13,210	11	8,654	13,857	12
New York	9,500	14,850	7	11,250	16,600	7
Philadelphia	8,900	15,075	10	9,200	16,258	10
Baltimore	7,750	12,500	13	8,250	13,200	13
Boston	8,459	14,359	8	9,159	15,259	8
Cleveland	7,450	12,675	13	7,950	14,850	13
St. Louis	7,200	12,600	15	7,920	13,320	15
Houston	7,100	10,300	11	7,720	11,750	13

Figure 6.4 What Teachers Earn in Twelve Large Cities (1972–73).

Source: Adapted from *Economic Status of the Teaching Profession, 1972–73*, research report 1973–R3, p. 28. National Education Association.

City	Starting Salary
Chicago	$10,000
New York	9,600
Los Angeles	8,170
Philadelphia	9,256
Detroit	9,032
Houston	7,200
Cleveland	7,823
St. Louis	8,000
Milwaukee	8,900
San Francisco	8,625
Boston	8,459

Figure 6.5 Minimum Salary with a Bachelor's Degree (1974).

Source: Adapted from *Economic Status of the Teaching Profession, 1972–73*, research report 1973–R3, p. 28. National Education Association.

starting salaries for beginning teachers with a bachelor's degree. Those salaries are $10,168 and $10,100 respectively.

The average annual salaries for both beginning and experienced teachers on a state by state basis vary greatly. Figure 6.6 illustrates the difference by states in salary levels. For the 1971–72 school year, Mississippi at $6,741 and Arkansas at $7,092 had the two lowest annual average salaries, while Alaska at $14,584 and New York at $12,810 had the two highest annual average salaries.

Fringe Benefits for Teachers

In addition to examining the salary provisions, beginning teachers would be wise to investigate the nature of the fringe benefit program in the district where they are seeking employment. Districts vary greatly in this regard with fringe benefits often worth considerable amounts. Fringe benefits accrue to teachers in the forms of paid insurance pre-

Figure 6.6

State	School year								Percent change, 1972–73 over 1971–72
	1962–63	1964–65	1966–67	1968–69	1969–70	1970–71	1971–72	1972–73[a]	
1	2	3	4	5	6	7	8	9	10
50 states and D.C.	$5,921	$6,465	$7,129	$8,272	$9,047	$9,698	$10,213	$10,643	4.2
Alabama	4,100	4,870	5,800	6,159	6,954	7,525	7,887	8,262	4.8
Alaska	7,517	8,450	9,392	10,887	10,993	14,025	14,584	15,176	4.1
Arizona	6,400	6,850	7,430	8,465	8,975	9,550	10,200	10,863	6.5
Arkansas	3,773	4,360	5,113	6,244	6,461	6,715	7,092	7,613	7.3
California	7,400	8,300	9,000	10,138	10,950	11,650	12,330	12,700	3.0
Colorado	5,750	6,340	6,824	7,523	8,105	9,152	9,744	10,280	5.5
Connecticut	6,757	7,286	7,959	8,900	9,597	10,600	10,800	11,200	3.7
Delaware	6,450	7,191	7,804	8,678	9,387	10,157	10,902	11,100	1.8
Florida	5,647	6,177	7,085	8,511	8,785	9,230	9,435	9,740	3.2
Georgia	4,707	5,200	6,075	7,200	7,520	8,010	8,252	8,644	4.8
Hawaii	6,070	6,244	7,910	8,300	9,600	10,475	10,500	10,900	3.8
Idaho	4,925	5,354	6,012	6,581	7,081	7,393	7,621	8,058	5.7
Illinois	6,535	6,881	7,525	9,100	9,789	10,500	10,961	11,564	5.5
Indiana	6,219	6,783	7,663	8,704	9,239	9,914	10,287	10,300	0.1
Iowa	5,312	5,859	6,531	8,075	8,779	9,395	9,933	10,564	6.4
Kansas	5,238	5,707	6,270	7,217	7,811	8,248	8,580	8,839	3.0
Kentucky	4,531	4,935	5,680	6,824	7,325	7,623	7,648	8,150	6.6
Louisiana	5,250	6,026	6,598	7,104	7,264	8,570	9,047	9,388	3.8
Maine	4,853	5,336	5,950	7,288	8,059	8,650	9,051	9,277	2.5
Maryland	6,439	6,980	7,547	9,269	9,885	10,670	11,128	11,787	5.9
Massachusetts	6,200	7,160	7,550	8,709	9,347	10,244	10,844	11,200	3.3
Michigan	6,444	6,972	7,650	9,492	10,125	11,408	12,092	12,400	2.5
Minnesota	5,975	6,601	7,050	8,100	9,250	10,300	10,800	11,115	2.9
Mississippi	3,674	4,249	4,707	5,910	5,959	6,202	6,741	7,145	6.0
Missouri	5,413	5,773	6,307	7,390	8,064	8,492	8,934	9,329	4.4
Montana	5,250	5,750	6,300	7,255	7,875	8,437	8,514	8,908	4.6
Nebraska	4,880	5,150	5,800	7,077	7,633	8,400	8,746	9,080	3.8
Nevada	6,215	7,161	7,786	8,733	9,615	9,990	10,600	11,472	8.2
New Hampshire	5,093	5,545	6,207	7,268	8,016	8,650	8,704	9,313	7.0
New Jersey	6,510	6,933	7,647	8,775	9,650	10,560	11,220	11,750	4.7

Figure 6.6 (continued)

State	School year								Percent change, 1972–73 over 1971–72 [a]
	1962–63	1964–65	1966–67	1968–69	1969–70	1970–71	1971–72	1972–73 [a]	
1	2	3	4	5	6	7	8	9	10
New Mexico	5,947	6,395	6,740	7,609	8,125	8,400	8,512	8,600	1.0
New York	7,200	8,000	8,500	9,500	11,240	11,730	12,810	13,450	5.0
North Carolina ...	5,049	5,230	5,869	7,053	7,762	7,948	8,819	9,314	5.6
North Dakota	4,425	5,043	5,515	6,524	6,840	7,489	7,848	8,362	6.5
Ohio	5,950	6,176	6,782	7,913	8,594	9,040	9,161	9,800	7.0
Oklahoma	5,257	5,312	6,103	6,739	7,257	7,690	7,900	8,200	3.8
Oregon	6,205	6,622	7,274	8,589	9,200	9,416	9,857	9,949	0.9
Pennsylvania	5,840	6,420	7,181	8,223	8,899	9,639	10,411	11,000	5.7
Rhode Island	6,140	6,550	6,975	8,178	9,030	9,587	10,262	10,800	5.2
South Carolina ...	4,231	4,540	5,421	6,108	7,069	7,300	7,660	8,310	8.5
South Dakota	4,320	4,735	5,000	6,200	7,200	7,561	7,800	8,034	3.0
Tennessee	4,329	4,941	5,755	6,621	7,187	7,695	8,154	8,450	3.6
Texas	5,470	5,611	6,075	6,853	7,598	8,423	8,755	9,029	3.1
Utah	5,350	6,188	6,780	7,377	8,049	8,465	8,850	8,990	1.6
Vermont	5,000	5,529	6,200	7,545	8,225	8,603	8,959	9,110	1.7
Virginia	5,032	5,570	6,342	7,576	8,364	8,892	9,417	9,842	4.5
Washington	6,360	6,808	7,597	8,861	9,792	10,427	10,673	11,100	4.0
West Virginia	4,946	4,804	5,917	6,820	7,954	7,980	8,425	8,505	0.9
Wisconsin	5,940	6,357	6,954	8,345	9,150	9,850	10,400	10,812	4.0
Wyoming	5,840	6,135	6,635	7,827	8,496	9,037	9,611	9,900	3.0

a. Estimated by NEA Research.

Figure 6.6 Average Annual Salaries of Instructional Staff by State, Selected School Years, 1962–63 Through 1972–73.

Source: NEA research report 1973–R3, *Economic Status of the Teaching Profession, 1972–73*, p. 28. Used by permission.

Provision	Enrollment Stratum					
	1, 2 and 3— 25,000 or More	4— 12,000- 24,999	5— 6,000- 11,999	Total— 1 through 5	6— 3,000- 5,999	7— 1,200- 2,999
1. Hospital and Surgical Ins.						
A. Amount of premium paid by board—						
Single policy—						
None	11.2	14.3	18.8	16.5	17.6	18.7
Part	34.1	21.3	23.1	24.2	23.1	22.9
Full	41.3	46.9	42.3	43.5	45.1	42.0
No data	13.4	17.5	15.7	15.9	14.3	16.4
Total	100.0	100.0	99.9	100.1	100.1	100.0
Number of systems reporting	179	343	718	1,240	273	262
Family policy—						
None	32.4	33.2	33.1	33.1	32.2	35.1
Part	35.8	30.6	28.6	30.2	30.4	28.6
Full	19.0	18.7	22.7	21.0	23.1	19.8
No data	12.8	17.5	15.6	15.7	14.3	16.4
Total	100.0	100.0	100.0	100.0	100.0	99.9
Number of systems reporting	179	343	718	1,240	273	262
2. Group Life Insurance						
A. Amount of premium paid by board—						
None	35.4	44.4	50.6	46.7	59.3	61.5
Part	16.3	12.0	10.2	11.6	8.8	7.3
Full	34.8	26.0	22.8	25.4	17.6	14.5
No data	13.5	17.5	16.4	16.3	14.3	16.8
Total	100.0	99.0	100.0	100.0	100.0	100.1
Number of systems reporting	178	342	718	1,238	273	262

Figure 6.7 Summary of Insurance Provisions Reported for Teachers, 1972–73.

Source: National Education Association, Research Division, *Salary Schedules and Fringe Benefits for Teachers, 1972–73*, research report 1973–R3 (Washington, D.C.: National Education Association Publications, 1973). Used by permission.

				Enrollment Stratum		
Provision	1, 2 and 3— 25,000 or More	4— 12,000– 24,999	5— 6,000– 11,999	Total— 1 through 5	6— 3,000– 5,999	7— 1,200– 2,999
1. Sick Leave						
A. No. of days granted per school year						
4 or fewer	...	...	.1	.1	...	.4
5–9	8.9	11.7	11.3	11.0	11.0	10.7
10–14	66.5	56.3	55.0	57.0	50.9	51.9
15–19	10.1	14.0	16.2	14.7	20.9	18.7
20–24	1.7	1.2	.6	.9	1.1	.4
25 or more	...	1.2	.7	.7	...	...
Varies	...	.6	.6	.5	...	.4
None or no data reported	12.8	15.2	15.6	15.1	16.1	17.6
Total	100.0	100.2	100.1	100.0	100.0	100.1
Number of systems reporting	179	343	718	1,240	273	262
Mean	11	11	11	11	11	11
Median	10	10	10	10	10	10
Low	5	5	4	4	5	3
High	20	90	90	90	21	20
B. Maximum accumulation						
None	1.7	1.7	2.1	1.9	2.9	1.9
1–49	2.8	5.2	6.0	5.3	6.2	8.8
50–99	12.3	9.0	13.4	12.0	14.7	21.0
100–149	16.8	11.7	10.9	11.9	9.5	19.5
150–199	14.0	14.6	15.7	15.2	18.7	13.0
200 or more but not unlimited	5.6	2.9	1.9	2.7	1.8	...
Unlimited accumulation	33.5	39.7	34.4	35.7	31.5	18.7
No data reported	13.4	15.2	15.6	15.2	14.7	17.2
Total	100.0	100.0	100.0	99.9	100.0	100.1
Number of systems reporting	179	343	718	1,240	273	262
2. Emergency or personal leave						
A. No. of days granted per school year						
None	2.8	2.0	4.2	3.4	4.8	5.0
1	3.9	7.6	5.1	5.6	8.1	11.2
2	32.0	31.6	28.5	29.9	32.1	29.6
3	21.9	17.3	19.3	19.1	17.7	16.2
4	.6	1.5	1.7	1.5	1.5	1.9
5	8.4	4.7	5.1	5.5	7.0	6.9
6–9	9.6	14.6	10.6	11.6	7.7	5.8
10 days	3.9	1.2	.8	1.4	1.1	.4

Provision	1, 2 and 3— 25,000 or More	4— 12,000— 24,999	5— 6,000— 11,999	Enrollment Stratum Total— 1 through 5	6— 3,000— 5,999	7— 1,200— 2,999
11 or more days	1.1	1.2	1.1	1.1	.4	.4
No data reported	15.7	18.4	23.6	21.0	19.6	22.7
Total	99.9	100.1	100.0	100.1	100.0	100.1
Number of systems reporting	178	342	709	1,229	271	260
B. Charged to sick leave						
Yes	34.1	30.3	25.2	27.9	21.2	19.1
No	48.0	49.3	47.6	48.1	54.6	54.2
No data	17.9	20.4	27.2	24.0	24.2	26.7
Total	100.0	100.0	100.0	100.0	100.0	100.0
Number of systems reporting	179	343	718	1,240	273	262
3. Sabbatical leave:						
A. Maximum time granted						
None	22.6	29.2	30.1	28.8	32.0	48.8
1 semester	2.3	.9	.7	1.0	1.5	1.5
2 semesters	57.6	50.7	47.4	49.8	49.4	30.4
1 full year	6.8	5.6	5.1	5.5	1.5	2.7
Other	...	.3	...	.1	...	...
No data	10.7	13.3	16.6	14.8	15.6	16.5
Total	100.0	100.0	99.9	100.0	100.0	99.9
Number of systems reporting	177	339	704	1,220	269	260
B. Amount of salary paid by board while on sabbatical leave						
None	1.6	2.1	8.1	5.5	14.6	16.2
Less than one-half	2.4	1.7	1.7	1.8	.5	1.5
One-half	65.4	55.8	45.7	51.5	38.4	41.2
More than one-half but less than full	8.7	11.6	8.7	9.5	9.2	2.9
Full salary	3.1	3.0	6.7	5.1	7.0	2.9
Other	3.1	2.6	4.4	3.7	3.8	1.5
No data	15.7	23.2	24.7	22.9	26.5	33.8
Total	100.0	100.0	100.0	100.0	100.0	100.0
Number of systems reporting	127	233	481	841	185	136

Figure 6.8 Summary of Leave Provisions Reported for Teachers, 1972–73.

Source: National Education Association, Salary Schedules and Fringe Benefits for Teachers, 1972–73, Research Report 1973–R2, pp. 30–31. Copyright © 1973 by National Education Association. All rights reserved.

154 miums, sick leave, emergency or personal leave, and sabbatical leave. Figure 6.7 presents a summary of insurance provisions reported for teachers in 1972–73 to the National Education Association Research Division. Figure 6.8 presents a summary of leave provisions reported for teachers.

Intangible Rewards of Teaching

Whatever the tangible problems and rewards, certain intangibles of teaching as a vocation are very much worth considering. Generally speaking, being a teacher in a community carries with it reasonably high community status which is important to most professionals. Since teachers are highly motivated and well educated, various job satisfactions come about from working with such persons. Teachers benefit from assorted intangibles associated with working with youth. A kind of pride is generated within a teacher from feelings that he is contributing to the future of his nation through helping to educate the young. Only in the United States has universality of educational opportunity come to be a part of the national tradition.

All the intangibles of teaching are not so positively idealistic. Teachers are often hard pressed to produce evidence of their accomplishments. The accomplishments of teachers are not readily given to visual assessment. Therefore, teaching is accompanied by a kind of personal mental anxiety brought on by the lack of knowledge that what you are doing as a teacher is productive. Because of this aspect of teaching, the ego gratification afforded teachers through their job is at a minimum.

The intangible rewards of teaching are difficult to measure.

Thus, the rewards and problems of teaching are both tangible and intangible. Certainly, there are times when an individual teacher might feel that the problems and frustrations of teaching outweigh the rewards. However, the overall attractiveness of the teaching profession steadily improves. Tangible rewards are increasing while tangible problems are being solved. The intangible rewards continue to provide teachers with drives for professional improvement. Teaching as a vocation offers most to those who enter the profession well prepared in their chosen area of specialty. Further, prospective teachers who orient their preparation toward those specific areas of teacher shortage can be assured of finding excellent opportunities throughout the United States.

Problems of Teaching

Teachers' problems are varied. In the spring of 1968 the NEA Research Division conducted a survey among a nationwide sample of public school classroom teachers. The questionnaire listed seventeen areas of potential teacher problems and asked respondents to indicate if each one had been a major or minor problem or not a problem in their schools the past year. Results of the survey as reported in the *NEA Research Bulletin,* December 1968, are as follows:

Inadequate teaching conditions and insufficient compensation are the biggest problems for the greatest number of teachers. Insufficient time for rest and preparation, large classes, and insufficient clerical help top the list of items teachers rate as "major problems." Inadequate salary and inadequate fringe benefits follow closely.

The five top-ranking aspects of teaching conditions and compensation were considered major problems by more than 25 percent of the respondents. In addition, about 40 percent rated them minor problems, placing the total number of teachers who have problems in these areas in the range of 65 to 75 percent.

	Major problems	*Minor problems*
Insufficient time for rest and preparation in school day	37.6%	36.4%
Large class size	34.7	37.3
Insufficient clerical help	30.5	38.3
Inadequate salary	29.7	42.3
Inadequate fringe benefits	26.9	40.1

Less widespread are problems occurring in other areas, for the most part more specialized aspects of school activity. With one exception (ineffective faculty meetings), more than half the respondents rated the following areas either major or minor problems:

	Major problems	*Minor problems*
Inadequate assistance from specialized teachers, e.g., remedial reading, speech therapy	24.5%	34.0%
Lack of public support for schools	22.7	38.5
Ineffective grouping of students into classes	22.1	41.7
Ineffective faculty meetings	20.1	29.0
Inadequate instructional materials	18.7	40.7
Ineffective testing and guidance program	18.5	33.8
Inadequate consultative assistance with instructional problems	17.3	38.9

Lowest on the list of major problems were:

	Major problems	Minor problems
Ineffective administration	17.2%	28.7%
Classroom management and discipline	15.2	45.3
Ineffective local teachers association	14.4	30.5
Lack of opportunity for professional growth	11.8	30.4
Negative attitude of colleagues toward teaching	8.6	35.0

Among these, classroom management and discipline are a special case. Although not a major problem for many teachers, the large percentage of those who rate it a minor problem brings the total percentage of teachers who consider this a problem to over 60 percent. Less than 50 percent found the other items in this group either major or minor problems.

Teacher problems vary with different types of communities. Class size and discipline are major problems for a greater proportion of urban than of suburban or rural teachers. The major problem for rural teachers, as opposed to urban or suburban teachers, is inadequate assistance from specialized teachers. Rural and urban teachers, in contrast to those in suburban communities, share complaints about the inadequacy of salaries and fringe benefits, the ineffectiveness of student grouping and testing and guidance programs, and lack of public support, as major problems.

	Major Problems		
	Urban	Suburban	Rural
Large class size	40.4%	33.4%	30.6%
Classroom management and discipline	23.3	10.8	12.1
Inadequate assistance from specialized teachers ...	22.5	21.0	30.3
Inadequate salary	34.9	24.5	30.3
Inadequate fringe benefits	27.7	22.3	31.3
Ineffective grouping of students into classes	24.3	18.2	24.2
Lack of public support for schools	27.8	17.4	23.7
Ineffective testing and guidance program	21.1	14.2	20.8

When figures for major and minor problems are considered together, additional community differences appear. The problem of clerical help is most widespread among urban teachers; least among rural teachers. Inadequacy of instructional materials is a problem which rural teachers share with urban teachers, while lack of opportunity for professional growth is a more extensive problem among teachers in rural than in urban or suburban areas.

	Major and Minor Problems		
	Urban	Suburban	Rural
Insufficient clerical help	74.9%	68.4%	63.0%
Inadequate instructional materials	62.3	55.0	61.5
Lack of opportunity for professional growth	41.2	37.7	48.3

An earlier study (March 1967) by the NEA Research Division dealt with employment status. In this study, the respondents cited the major reasons for changing location of employment as shown in Figure 6.9.

Teaching is not without problems. Certain problems that teachers associate with teaching are also cited as major reasons for teachers changing employment from school to school. The problems of teaching also provide the challenges. Teaching as a vocation will become more attractive as school boards, administrators, and teachers assist each other in solving problems.

Frustrations of Teaching

The word "frustrate" implies a depriving of effect or a rendering worthless of efforts directed to some end. Teachers may often feel frustrated in their work. Much of this frustration comes about from the very nature of teaching. Many teachers enter the profession filled with a high degree of idealism, anxious to be doing such a socially important job. Such idealism would probably hold up strongly if each of the teacher's classes consisted of one, or at most, a very small number of pupils. However, the problem of large class size and other problems previously cited take an immediate effect. It becomes quite easy for a teacher to feel her best-meant efforts are rendered worthless and are not related to some desirable end.

Teaching is accompanied by a frustrating kind of lonesomeness also. When faced with problems in the classroom, it seems logical that a teacher would seek assistance from peer professionals. More often than not, such assistance is not meaningful to his or her teaching situation; often outside assistance is not available at all. Frustration results.

Major reason for change	Percent of teachers who transferred to teach in a different school				
	Elementary	Secondary	Men	Women	Total
Higher salary	20.0%	23.2%	40.0%	11.6%	22.1%
Improved working conditions	9.0	20.3	20.0	11.6	14.7
Personal reasons	11.9	15.9	8.0	17.4	14.0
Husband's work changed location	20.9	2.9	0.0	18.6	11.8
Undesirable community situation	9.0	2.9	4.0	7.0	5.9
Position eliminated	10.4	1.4	4.0	7.0	5.9
Marriage	4.5	5.8	0.0	8.1	5.1
Disagreed with school policies, administration, etc.	0.0	8.7	6.0	3.5	4.4
Termination of contract	1.5	4.3	4.0	2.3	2.9
Other	11.9	14.4	14.0	12.8	13.2
Total	100.0%	99.8%	100.0%	99.9%	100.0%
Number of persons	67	69	50	86	136

Figure 6.9 Major Reasons for Changing Location of Employment Reported by Teachers Transferring to Teach in Other Schools.

Source: *NEA Research Bulletin* 46 (December 1968): 120. Used by permission.

Evaluation of teaching effectiveness does not usually exist. Building administrators, department chairmen, and teaching colleagues are reluctant to attempt to evaluate teacher effectiveness, since the criteria for evaluation are nebulous. Consequently, a teacher has little feedback regarding effectiveness and is, therefore, frustrated by this vague aspect of teaching. Most of us like to know when we are effective in our work. Jobs are less frustrating to us when we are able to know that our work is effective. The outcomes of a teacher's efforts are for the most part unknown. For those who take the frustrations as continuing challenges of the profession, the frustrations often become the driving forces for improvement in teacher behavior. For those whose personality disposition requires a constant reinforcement that their work is effective, the frustrations are cause enough for leaving the teaching profession.

To provide the reader with a bit of personal insight regarding the frustration dimension of teaching, a few teachers were asked to comment about their personal frustrations experienced as teachers. Some of their remarks are as follows:

———— • ————

I have experienced overwhelming frustration and failure in teaching and have experienced remarkable success. I have also noticed that what chafes one teacher is some other teacher's particular joyful challenge. From these observations there is a suggestion that if one is genuine in his interest in teaching and comprehends his subject there is a place he can serve educational needs with little frustration and much satisfaction. The implication of this suggestion requires realistic assessment by the teacher of himself and of the educational situation of his school.

Suburban Elementary School Teacher

My biggest frustration lies within myself. I cannot blame administrators, school boards, or anyone. This inability to reach children comes from within.

I was probably trained the way my own teachers were trained. The teacher was the authority and the students accepted and conformed. My first two classes were like this. I considered them good students because they did everything I told them to do. I felt that I was a good teacher and they were good "learners." I didn't worry too much about the two or three who weren't falling in line. I considered their borderline I.Q.'s and attributed it to this. I never considered it could be my fault.

I found that each year my two or three problem children were increasing in numbers. I found my classes generally not so accepting or conforming. I found [them] disinterested in what I was teaching and displaying an "I don't care attitude." My solution—tighten up on discipline and use threats of failure. None of this was successful. I finally began to question myself. With so many students not achieving could it be the teacher? It took me a long time to realize that perhaps it was.

Inner-City Elementary School Teacher

Like all other work, teaching has its minor annoyances: clerical work such as taking the roll, filling out reports, completing rating sheets, etc.; housekeeping duties such as hall duty, lunchroom and playground supervision, cleaning transparencies and equipment; and routine classroom work such as dittoing student work sheets, grading objective-type tests, checking daily homework papers, etc. Very few schools have sub-professional help to alleviate the teacher of these time-consuming duties so that he can spend his time teaching —the activity for which he was hired and trained to do.

Many who have not had teaching experience view teaching as a thirty-hour work week. Such is far from true. What they fail to realize is that although actual teacher-student contact time may in some cases be thirty hours, the time spent in deciding upon the best method to present a certain concept or the way to handle a specific student learning or discipline deviation problem requires many, many more hours. It is these outside-of-school hours that very much affect and are so important to the effectiveness and efficiency of the teacher during the teacher-student contact time.

As a teacher you probably associate with and have more friends among teachers than any other group of people. As a group, they are usually quite stimulating, for they are interested in the world, its events, its people, and its cultural offerings. Teachers are now far more worldly realistic in thought, and allowed to live their own lives outside of the yester-year's rigid glass fish bowl—in short, they are human beings while still being the determiners of future society.

High School Mathematics Teacher

Public Attitudes Toward Education

While much of the rewards and frustrations of teaching can be examined under the lens of the teacher's world of work, public attitudes toward education can provide other kinds of considerations. The Fifth Annual Gallup Poll of Public Attitudes Toward Education surveyed 1,627 adults in every area of the country and in all types of communities.[1] At the same time, a separate survey of professional educators (teachers, principals, assistant principals, administrators, superintendents) was conducted. When the respondents were asked to name the most important prob-

1. George H. Gallup, "Fifth Annual Gallup Poll of Public Education," pp. 38–51.

lems confronting the public schools, the following list of problems in order of mention for 1973 was formulated:

■ Lack of discipline
■ Integration/segregation problems
■ Lack of proper financial support
■ Difficulty of getting "good" teachers
■ Use of drugs
■ Size of school/classes
■ Poor curriculum
■ Parents' lack of interest
■ Lack of proper facilities
■ School board policies.

When professional educators were asked the same question, their replies in general agreed with the public's, with a few notable differences.

When the respondents were asked to tell what they thought was right with the schools, the following list in order of mention for 1973 was formulated:

■ The curriculum
■ The teachers
■ School facilities
■ Extracurricular activities
■ Up-to-date teaching methods
■ Absence of racial conflicts
■ Good administration.

Professional educators named the good points about the public schools in about this same order.

When the respondents were asked in what ways the schools are now better, they replied, in order of mention, as follows:

■ Wider variety of subjects offered
■ Better facilities/equipment

160

- Better qualified teachers
- Up-to-date teaching methods
- Less structured teaching
- Equal opportunities for all
- Special help available
- Educational system is better (general).

Those who answered that education is worse today gave these reasons, in order of mention:

- Less discipline
- Educational requirements are lower
- Lack of student interest
- Lack of interest by teachers
- Too many irrelevant subjects offered
- Lack of qualified teachers
- Larger school, classes too large
- Too many educational experiments
- Poor student/teacher relationships
- Educational system is worse (general).

School Human Relations Specialist

A new kind of position which could be of great importance for teachers in their day-to-day endeavors is the human relations specialist. Some schools have recognized the need for a staff member to help everyone to see the need for, and to practice, effective human relations. Figure 6.10 defines the scope of the human relations specialist job from survey responses of such specialists.

Obviously, a thorough analysis of the rewards, frustrations, and problems associated with teaching must be made from a multi-dimensional view. As with most jobs, the definition of the scope of teaching comes from both internal and external considerations. Furthermore, as with most jobs, teaching is both rewarding and problematical. Beginning teachers are urged to actively consider all the aspects of this particular choice of livelihood prior to signing their first contracts.

Point of View

"Our society is an organizational society. We are born in organizations, and most of us spend much of our lives working for organizations."[2] In view of this fact of life, most of us seek information about the organizational work which we are considering. Prospective teachers, and practicing teachers as well, might lose sight of the presence of a reward side of teaching when attention seems most often focused on the frustrating aspects. There obviously must be associated with the work of teachers rewards of all kinds which attract and hold highly competent persons in the vocation. Certainly the monetary rewards are important considerations. In addition, there are personal and professional rewards and frustrations which ought to be examined by prospective teachers.

While oftentimes not getting the attention deserved, there are programs devoted to increasing the feelings aspect of working with pupils. For example, an experimental program of the Atlanta public school system, funded by Title III of the Elementary and Secondary Education Act, strives to provide a success environment for the pupils by utilizing the positive reinforcement concept whenever students exhibit desired behavior. This concept, and this approach, does not necessarily represent harmonious philosophical agreement. Some educators would vehemently argue against material incentives as a part of pedagogy. Nonetheless, the Atlanta teachers work-

2. Amitai Etzioni, *Modern Organizations* (Englewood Cliffs, N.J.: Prentice-Hall Inc., 1964), p. 1.

Human relations functions	Percent of human relations specialists reporting degree of responsibility			
	Has primary responsibility for	**Shares responsibility for**	**Serves as consultant on**	**Has no responsibility for**
Liaison with community service groups on human relations matters	65	25	9	10
Staff in-service activities in the area of human relations	55	29	14	2
Liaison with student organizations on human relations matters	53	29	13	5
Reviewing policies affecting human relations	40	42	14	4
Student human relations program	38	34	19	9
Public relations on human relations problems and activities	37	45	14	4
Pupil personnel problems of a racial nature	29	47	20	4
Receiving and processing community complaints	26	57	12	5
Liaison with, and/or consultative services to, school and area citizens' advisory councils	23	44	30	3
Planning to achieve racial and cultural balance in schools	20	45	25	10
Liaison with social and welfare agencies	12	44	25	19
Developmental and evaluation of inter-cultural materials and teaching units ..	11	46	36	7
Liaison with local law enforcement agencies	7	29	29	35
Recruiting members of minority groups for professional positions	5	36	39	20
Development and evaluation of programs for the culturally deprived ..	5	35	44	16
Adult basic education program	2	6	24	68

Figure 6.10 Duties and Responsibilities of Human Relations Specialists, 108 Local School Systems Enrolling 12,000 or More, 1970–71.

Source: *NEA Research Bulletin* 50 (March 1972): 13. Copyright © National Education Association. All rights reserved.

162 ing in the new success environment which they have worked to develop are satisfied that the technique is effective for their pupils and enhances their work as teachers. Anne Sapp illustrates some of the highlights of the Atlanta program in the following article.

———————◆◆————————

Succeeding with Success Environment

Anne C. Sapp

Two years ago Beth Brown decided to quit teaching. It wasn't that she didn't like to teach or that she didn't consider herself a good teacher. Quite the contrary, in fact. What's more she had the natural endowments to be an outstanding teacher. Attractive, with a warm, friendly smile and a calm controlled manner, she really was the "adult friend" that every parent would like his child to have for a teacher and that most education professors encourage their students to be.

Let Ms. Brown tell how she came by the decision to quit teaching: "I just couldn't take it any more. I had worked in an inner-city school in Atlanta for four years. I had really tried. In every class I had *good* children, who wanted to learn in spite of all the stuff they had to put up with in the neighborhood. But it took so much time to deal with the angry children who didn't want to be in class and who fought the whole idea of the classroom that the good children never got the kind of attention they deserved. I just couldn't face those good children anymore."

Anne C. Sapp, "Succeeding with Success Environment," *American Education,* November 1973, pp. 5–10.

Frances Arnold has been teaching in Atlanta's inner-city schools a lot longer than Beth Brown—17 years to be more specific. The children in her classroom caught on quickly that "when you get in Miss Arnold's room, you just don't fool around." Frances Arnold started teaching under somewhat less than ideal conditions: She had 42 children on the second shift of double sessions and a principal who demanded quiet, orderly classes. "I knew if I was going to please my principal I *had* to have quiet in that room. I had all those little children and I *had* to have order. And I could get it. I was bigger. My voice was so much stronger, I could frighten them into doing things my way. And if I had to swat a child once in awhile, I just had to. Of course, my classroom wasn't happy. It was always *my* system, *my* way. But I always had good discipline."

Frances Arnold and Beth Brown had different teaching styles, but both were dealing with the established fact that inner-city children are turned off by school. Consequently, their academic achievements are pretty scanty; they are chronically absent, disruptive in the classroom, and likely to drop out.

Explanations for the failure of the inner-city classroom are legion. Perhaps the most popular as measured by frequency points the finger at the home and neighborhood environment. The reasoning goes something like this: The pressures of dealing with the inner-city environment are so intense that parents do not have time to prepare their children for school; therefore, the children enter school poorly equipped to handle the information presented, and as a result they attach little significance to school activities. One crushing implication of this explanation would have improvement in academic performance completely dependent on making radical changes in the neighborhood.

Other critics assign the blame to the structural organization of the school and the middle-class format of the classroom. They argue that in the typical classroom environment, the teacher rarely praises children for being good but inevitably pounces on them when they're bad. When disruptive behavior and failure are the primary means to gain the teacher's attention, many children all too often intentionally misbehave and thus invite failure, only to respond later to the resulting feelings of inadequacy with either apathy or violent aggression. As one Atlanta principal expresses it: "The kids are happy and excited and busy when they enter school. But somehow a lot of negative stuff gets put on them— 'Don't do that,' 'Sit down,' 'Be quiet.' School gets to be a kind of drag. And too many children react in extreme ways. They become passive and apathetic, or wild and boisterous. And they lose either way."

The attempts to understand inner-city school failure, to explain it, go on and on. And so do projected solutions, ranging from making radical social changes to revamping the structure of the entire educational system —for example, creating open classrooms where children will not be stifled. But there's never enough money, or support, or the reforms don't go far enough, and in the meantime, teachers like Beth Brown and Frances Arnold either quit or get locked into teaching styles that won't allow them to do their best work. And the children they teach fall further and further behind the national norms, more and more turned off by school.

However, Beth Brown ultimately decided not to quit teaching after all. In fact she refused the opportunity to be transferred to a suburban school. And Frances Arnold's class-room has turned into one of the most relaxed classrooms at the Wesley Avenue School. What's more, the majority of the children they teach are now reading at or above grade level and, when last tested, their I.Q. scores were slightly above the national average. The explanation for this encouraging turn of events is remarkably free of differing opinion. Practically everyone concerned attributes the change to Project Success Environment.

Project Success Environment, an experimental program of the Atlanta Public School System, is founded by ESEA Title III and involves 51 classes at five schools. Boyd McCandless, consultant to the project and professor of psychology at nearby Emory University, recalls the project's inception. "About four years ago Marion Thompson, who is now project director of Success Environment, and I were in the Central Cities area of Atlanta running an after-school program for inner-city children—remedial reading, tutorials, that kind of thing. In one year we had a turnover of 110 percent. We realized we couldn't possibly accomplish our goals in that kind of unstable situation. Yet, there had to be some way to glue down those children. We decided to revamp our approach.

The Central Cities program operated on the premise that the educational system was as it should be and that something was wrong with the students. This, of course, was an easy assumption as we were working with the failures. In rethinking our approach, however, we started with the assumption that something was wrong with the system itself. This led to an examination of classroom practice with the idea that by changing the system we could reach the children in the most logical place—right there in the classroom.

"I put Marion in touch with Howard Rollins, a young associate professor of psy-

164 chology at Emory University, and together, in a remarkable collaboration between practical and theoretical educators, we came up with a new approach to the classroom. Our premise was that every child is a worthwhile human being, and we tried to create a classroom in which children are treated like human beings who are esteemed and valued."

Project Director Marion Thompson had spent 14 years as an elementary school principal, many of them working with disadvantaged children in Appalachia as well as the inner city. So he approached the project with a keen awareness of the classroom teacher's need to feel secure and in control, which is to say the need for classroom structure. Furthermore, he was aware that any school attended by disadvantaged children is planned according to expectations—what the children expect from school (a punitive environment), what the teachers expect from the students (not much), and what the students expect from themselves (less than that expected by the teachers).

From Thompson's double awareness sprung the technique used in Success Environment. The project itself is really a tightly organized system involving three components: a positive reinforcement apparatus, an engineered classroom, and a modified curriculum. The technique enables the classroom teacher to create an environment where children consistently experience success and approval, where, as Thompson puts it, "Instead of failure leading to failure, success leads to success. We want to take these children off a treadmill to nowhere and get them on a pathway to fulfillment."

All Project Success teachers provide positive reinforcement—a tangible reward coupled with verbal praise—whenever students exhibit desired behavior. In the elementary schools, students earn checkmarks on Success cards. In the middle school, they earn tickets. Filled-in cards and accumulated tickets may then be exchanged for specific rewards during "trading time," a period set aside for this purpose.

Putting the reinforcement system into operation requires a radical change in teaching attitude. If a teacher adheres to traditional teaching techniques—giving attention to wrong answers and disruptive behavior—the Success technique doesn't have a chance. Mrs. Arnold recalls that "the biggest problem with the Success technique was me, changing my attitude. I felt that it was wrong to reward children for doing what they were *supposed* to do; they should do it without a reward. The children's attitude was easy to change."

Project Success begins at the beginning, with the teacher and the teacher's attitudes. In a three-week workshop held before school opens, the project staff trains teacher volunteers for the program in both the philosophy underlying the reinforcement system and the ways of administering reinforcement. To be effective, reinforcement must be administered consistently, in specific ways.

Each Success teacher observes three basic rules. First, *reinforcement must be immediate.* To reward a child on Tuesday for being a "good girl" or a "good boy" on Monday simply isn't effective. Second, *reinforcement must be accompanied by descriptive praise.* A Project Success teacher would never say, "I'm giving you a checkmark, Jimmy, because you've been so good today." Instead, the teacher would say, "Thank you for raising your hand, Jimmy. You've earned a checkmark for that." Descriptive praise accomplishes two things: It identifies the precise behavior being rewarded (a student can only repeat a behavior if he knows exactly what it is), and it tells a student that the reward is the result of his own actions, that he has coped with his environment. Third, and most important, *only desirable behavior receives attention.* Old habits of disrupting the class to gain the teacher's attention cannot be allowed to succeed. The Project Success teacher uses the technique of "ignore and praise" to insure that they don't.

The "ignore and praise" technique is crucial to a Success class; it insures that the children receive attention only for desirable behavior. Unless disruptive behavior is dangerous to others or so persistent that the teacher can find nothing positive to reward, it is ignored. Instead of punishing the offender, the teacher focuses on a nearby student who is exhibiting exemplary behavior and rewards that child. The children usually get the message in a hurry.

Experienced teachers frequently have a hard time accepting this technique. Once they do, however, they staunchly stand by it. Says one teacher, "If you can just grit your teeth and say, 'I don't care if Johnny *is* swinging from the light fixture, I will *not* pay attention to him,' he will eventually come down. And the good thing is that he won't get up there anymore. It really works if you can conquer that urge to shout and scold."

On the day the Success technique is introduced into the class, the children receive positive reinforcement as soon as they enter the classroom. The teacher greets the children at the door and presents each of them with a piece of candy—a reward just for coming to school—and either a Success card or a ticket. As soon as class begins, the teacher introduces the students to the basic framework for positive reinforcement—the classroom rules. Some teachers, like Beth Brown, formulate the rules before the students enter the

class. Others, like Frances Arnold, allow the students to participate in deciding on the rules in the class. No matter how they are arrived at, all the classroom rules meet three criteria: They must be brief and specific; they must be stated positively; and there must be no less than three and no more than five of them.

Typical rules might be, "Have necessary tools for work," "Raise your hand to speak," or "work hard." Once the rules are agreed on, they are posted prominently on the walls. From that point on, each child knows he can succeed simply by following the rules. As one teacher expresses it, "The rules define for you and for your students exactly what your—and their—responsibilities are. And since the rules are their rules, they *know* what they are supposed to do and when they're not doing it. You don't have to fuss at them about being bad."

Experience has shown that after four to six weeks, conduct in a project classroom generally stabilizes so that disruptive behavior there is much less than in regular classrooms. "The children come to feel that they can *participate*," says a project teacher. "They develop a closeness with one another and come to believe that the teacher can be their friend. You can see the changes in their expressions."

As the children's behavior changes, the rewards change too. At first the students trade in their cards and tickets for tangible rewards like toy watches, toy jewelry, comic books, and model cars because these are items they respond to immediately. But, because these rewards can get expensive, other kinds of rewards are generally substituted for them. These are the activity reinforcers, some of which—feeding the animals, watering the plants, or erasing the boards—are built into the regular routine of every classroom.

And the project has created some reinforcers of its own. A student, for example, may exchange a card for the privilege of leading the class to lunch or to music or to physical education for a week. Of course, in doing so the student also earns the responsibility of keeping order in the line. One of the most popular of these rewards is being a "mini-teacher," a reward available only to students who have demonstrated mastery of a particular subject. A mini-teacher can grade papers, write questions or instructions on the blackboard, and explain problems to the other children. Mrs. Arnold points out that this allows the child to feel important and competent—"not like when I was in school and the teacher had to do all the talking."

One problem with activity reinforcers is that no one classroom has enough of them to go around. The project has met this condition by establishing an activity room for Success students. Stocked with a variety of games and equipment especially attractive to students, the activity room opens as the tangible rewards are phased out, and students can trade for 30 minutes of time playing with soccer or football games, working puzzles, or building with blocks. Once this room is opened, time spent in it becomes the basic reward supporting the reinforcement system.

For the teacher, Success Environment pays off when class conduct has stabilized and the activity reinforcers have been phased in. At this point the engineered classroom and the modified curriculum become especially important. As Beth Brown puts it, "The project helps set a pattern for the class so that the teacher can get down to academics. Academics have always been important to me, and it's a real joy to be able to *teach*. Once a teacher gets things organized through

using the Success technique, it's even possible to work with students almost completely on an individual basis."

In reinforcing academic behavior, the Project Success teacher observes three basic rules, all requiring some modification of curriculum. First, *each child must experience success.* To assure that each child does, the teacher regularly assigns simple tasks that any child can do, for example, copying a simple design or naming pictures of common objects—firetruck, train, dog, swing—as a way of building success into the daily classroom routine. Further, only academic *success* is emphasized, never failure. Project teachers, for example, never "X" incorrect answers; they check correct answers.

Second, *each child must receive work at his own level—work he can do.* At the start of school, project teachers administer diagnostic tests to determine each child's level of achievement. The class is then divided into three groups based on reading ability, and the teacher selects from both the standard curriculum and the programed materials available to all project classes those materials which will enable each child to receive work he can perform successfully.

Finally, *each child's work must be evaluated frequently and reinforced immediately.* To make this possible, the teachers subdivide the curriculum into units that can be completed in 20 to 30 minute periods and evaluated immediately. Among other things, they have designed skill sheets which quickly test comprehension and provide possibilities for immediate reinforcement.

Clearly there's no way to reinforce success immediately in a classroom where 25 children are all doing the same thing at the same time. So Project Success has modified the classroom to make consistent grouping feasible. It has so engineered the classroom that the desks typically are placed in a U, with each of the three reading groups having a clearly defined area. This part of the room is the mastery center, where students do seat work and the teacher provides direct instruction. Placed at intervals around the walls are interest stations, special areas containing high-interest-level materials which, though selected to foster specific skills, require little teacher supervision. In most cases the classes are broken into periods allowing the student 30 minutes with the teacher, 30 minutes doing seat work, and 30 minutes at various assigned interest stations, thus facilitating the individual instruction so important to the Success technique.

Data thus far collected by the project staff confirm the benefits of the Success technique. Project classes are less disruptive and more work-oriented than regular classes, and conduct isn't the only thing that benefits. Project classes have made significantly greater gains in I.Q. scores than comparison classes. Further, they have gained twice as many months in reading and almost that much in math.

Whatever the data show, however, the real benefits of the program can be measured in happier children and in teacher comments such as, "The Success technique helps me be a person in the classroom and gives me a way to let the children be people," or in a project principal's observation, "The project has given me a new way of looking at an instructional program. Now I focus on what matters —the children's response."

Perhaps the most enthusiastic response of all comes from Frances Arnold, "I don't get tired or tense anymore. I can teach till the bell rings and then teach on. No matter what happens, I'll never go back to my old way."

—————•◦•—————

QUESTIONS FOR DISCUSSION

1. Do the generally lower salaries for beginning teachers compared to beginning salaries for other jobs seem unreasonable to you? Do you feel teachers should be employed on full-year (twelve-month) contracts?

2. How would you respond to the following statement? "The most effective teachers are committed teachers."

3. What are some possible reasons for the differences in teachers' salaries from city to city and from state to state?

4. What do you consider to be the three most important problems related to inadequate teaching conditions? Why?

5. To what extent should teachers adjust their methodology to satisfy community desires? How can teachers help educate communities toward accepting newer procedures?

SUPPLEMENTARY LEARNING ACTIVITIES

1. Let each class member report the qualities of the best teacher he has had. Formulate a list of qualities most common of "excellent teachers."

2. Conduct interviews with teachers who have a varied length of experience for the purpose of discussing the tangible and intangible rewards and problems of teaching. Formulate a summary of the interview findings.

3. Conduct interviews with individuals of varied length of experience in other vocations for the purpose of discussing the

168   tangible and intangible rewards and problems of their jobs. Formulate a summary of the interview findings.

4. Interview two or three members of a local school board to obtain their views on the rewards and problems of teaching in their school district. Summarize the findings.

5. What are two or three ways in which school law affects teaching as a profession?

SELECTED REFERENCES

Allen, Paul M., et al. *Teacher Self-Appraisal: A Way of Looking over Your Own Shoulder.* Worthington, Ohio: Charles A. Jones Publishing Company, 1970.

Barrilleaux, Louis E. "Accountability Through Performance Objectives." *NASSP Bulletin* 56(May 1972):103–10.

Day, James F. *Teacher Retirement in the United States.* North Quincy, Mass.: Christopher Publishing House, 1971.

Donovan, John C. "Implications of Manpower Training." *Phi Delta Kappan* 46(1965):366–69.

Gallup, George H. "Fifth Annual Gallup Poll of Public Education." *Phi Delta Kappan* (September 1972):38–51.

Haskew, Laurence D., and Jonathon C. McLendon. *This Is Teaching.* 3rd ed. Glenview, Ill.: Scott, Foresman and Company, 1968.

Herman, Jerry J. *Developing an Effective School Staff Evaluation Program.* West Nyack, N. Y.: Parker Publishing Company, 1973.

Kirsch, Michael G. "The Telephone: An Unexploited Resource." *Phi Delta Kappan* 54(April 1973):556–57.

Lieberman, Myron. "Teacher Strikes: Acceptable Strategy?" *Phi Delta Kappan* 46(1965):237–40.

Lieberman, Myron, and Michael H. Moskow. *Collective Negotiations for Teachers: An Approach to School Administration.* Chicago: Rand McNally & Company, 1966.

Michaels, Patricia. "Teaching and Rebellion at Union Springs." *Phi Delta Kappan* 52(January 1971):262–66.

NEA Research Bulletin 47(March 1969).

——— 50(March 1972).

"Public Funds and Parochial School Pupils." *NEA Research Bulletin* 45(1967):43–46.

Simmons, James C. "Advanced Degrees: Does It Pay to Get One?" *Education Forum* 37(November 1972):25–29.

Sobol, Thomas. "The Broader Meaning of Articulation." *Phi Delta Kappan* 53(September 1971):25–29.

Sterling, Philip. *The Real Teachers.* New York: Random House, Inc., 1972.

Stinnett, T. M.; Jack H. Kleinmann; and Martha L. Ware. *Professional Negotiation in Public Education.* New York: Macmillan Company, 1966.

Teacher Supply and Demand in Public Schools, 1972. Washington, D.C.: Research Report 1972–R8, National Education Association, 1972.

U.S. Office of Education. *Education 65: A Report to the Profession.* Washington, D.C.: U.S. Government Printing Office, 1966.

chapter 7
Teacher Organizations

goals

- Outlines the functions of teacher organizations through the use of graphs, charts, and current publications.

- Focuses the objectives conflict between the American Federation of Teachers (AFT) and the National Education Association (NEA) into a perspective.

- Presents the data and sequences the events that point in the direction of a merger of AFT and NEA.

- Translates the emotions and issues of teacher strikes into understandable teacher concerns.

- Integrates the social, parental, and professional views of school into a cohesive unit of study.

During the process of socialization we strive to identify ourselves as acceptable members of groups in our social milieu. Most of us want to "belong" and, in order to belong, we often do what others expect of us. Sometimes we do not do what we would personally like to do, but that which will win for us the approval and acceptance of others. As a member of a

172 group, one has a sense of belonging that is further enhanced by conforming to group norms.

Membership in teacher organizations may also be considered as an important determinant of social success, and even physical survival in certain situations. Organizations are prized by some members in terms of what the organization can do for them. Often the pressures of special interest groups, such as teacher organizations, have a significant influence on the operations of school government. In this way teacher organizations are effective agents in dealing with teacher concerns.

Teachers are solicited for membership in numerous and varied types of organizations. The most popular types of organizations are those which bring members of an occupational group together for the advancement of their mutual purposes. The two major teacher organizations are the American Federation of Teachers, a union affiliated with the American Federation of Labor–Congress of Industrial Organizations, and the National Education Association, a nonunion group which claims to be the professional organization. Speaking in terms of sociological stratification that affects the specialized lower echelon employees in a large-scale industry, Fred M. Smith suggests the following for teachers:

————•—•————

Teachers in smaller areas work under conditions and live in a social milieu similar to professionals and develop attitudes similar to professionals. Working conditions and social milieu of the metropolitan teacher are similar to those of lower level employees of mass industry.

Therefore, teacher unions will be perceived by metropolitan teachers as the best means of attaining those things which are important to them, and teachers not in metropolitan centers will perceive the professional association as the best means of attaining those things which are important to them.[1]

————•—•————

The largest teacher organization in the United States is the National Education Association with over one million members located in large metropolitan schools, suburban schools, and rural schools. The second largest teacher organization is the American Federation of Teachers, with most of its 375,000 membership found in the large metropolitan schools.

National Education Association (NEA)

The NEA was originally founded in 1857 as the National Teachers Association. In 1870 a merger was affected with the National Association of School Superintendents and the American Normal School Association to form the National Education Association (NEA). The two purposes stated in the charter are "to elevate the character and advance the interests of the profession of teaching and to promote the cause of education in the United States."

The Association is governed by the annual Representative Assembly composed of over 8,275 delegates from affiliated state and local associations. This body develops policy resolutions which are interpreted by the Board of Directors, of which each state has one member for every 20,000 NEA members,

1. Fred M. Smith, "The Teachers' Union vs. the Professional Associations," *School and Society,* pp. 439–40.

and the Executive Committee, made up of the officers and four elected members.

Tied into the Association are a number of departments. While a part of the parent NEA, these department associations often represent the major organizational affiliation for the teachers. These department associations are self-governing groups within the profession, some serving general interests, such as the Association of Classroom Teachers (ACT), others representing separate disciplines, such as the Department of Art Education. Created by the Representative Assembly and financed by the Association, a number of national commissions also develop their own programs. Typical of these are the National Commission on Professional Rights and Responsibilities (PR&R) and the National Commission on Teacher Education and Professional Standards (TEPS). The Association also organizes a number of standing committees which are charged with developing specific programs in such areas as citizenship and ethics. The organization chart of the NEA, as outlined in Figure 7.1, shows the various departments, institutions, divisions, commissions, committees, and councils within the NEA.

The income of the Association is derived almost entirely from membership dues with a small amount returning from the sale of publications. In 1967–68 budgeted expenditures totaled $11.25 million.

Headed by the Executive Secretary, who is chosen by the Executive Committee, a staff of approximately 600 individuals serves in the NEA Center (1201 Sixteenth St. N.W., Washington, D.C. 20036) and in eleven regional offices. The staff is organized into divisions whose directors serve under a cabinet of one deputy, two associates, and six assistant executive secretaries. Employees of the departments housed in the NEA Center bring the total staff to more than 1,000 individuals.

The Association is an affiliate of the World Confederation of Organizations of the Teaching Profession (WCOTP) which includes national teacher organizations in practically every country of the free world.

A pamphlet published by the National Education Association entitled *Your Future in a Great Profession* lists a few close-up looks at professional cooperation at work on three levels—local, state, and national—as follows:

———— • • ————

Each year . . .

The NEA produces several half-hour films designed to acquaint Americans with the problems, purposes, and progress of education in this country . . .

The state associations cooperate in planning the films and arrange bookings for them on TV stations throughout the state . . .

The local associations promote and publicize the TV film programs and often arrange for supplementary showings to PTA, civic, business, and other community groups . . .

Continuously . . .

The NEA represents you and the nation's teachers before Congress and Federal Agencies . . .

The state association represents you and the teachers of your state before the State Legislature and State Department of Education . . .

The local association represents you before the School Board and often before other local legislative bodies . . .

Cooperatively . . .

The local, the state, and the NEA conduct instructional and professional welfare workshops, institutes, conferences, conventions,

GOVERNANCE ORGANIZATION

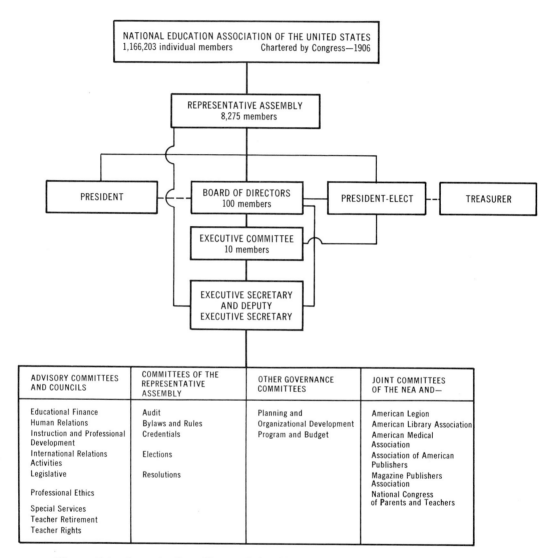

Figure 7.1 Organization Chart of the National Education Association of the United States.

Source: National Education Association. NEA Handbook for Local, State, and National Associations, Washington, D.C. 1973. By permission.

exhibits, and demonstrations—local, state-wide, or on a regional or national scale . . . and publish the world's outstanding professional journals, newsletters, instructional materials, and classroom aids . . .

———•———

The NEA, in the same publication, suggests that the organizational benefits are not automatic. Things which the members need to do at the local, state, and national level are:

———•———

LOCALLY

Meet your faculty representative at once. He is your faculty's professional leader and will introduce you to professional members and friends. He will help you, or secure help for you, during those hectic first weeks of school. . . . He is your source of information about your professional associations.

Read the newsletters published by your local association and become familiar with events and issues which concern you.

Attend meetings. Meet your fellow teachers who serve as association officers and chairmen. Become acquainted with your professional co-workers who volunteer to work for you. Conscientiously use your influence and vote.

Learn about the activities of committees and meet the committee members who are working voluntarily to improve your salary, and gain other welfare benefits for you.

Volunteer to work in your local education association in some capacity. Take full advantage of your local association's services, savings, and social events.

STATEWISE

Read your state journals. Inform yourself about educational and professional affairs in your state. They concern you.

Learn about special state association services such as insurance programs and others. Plan to make full use of them.

Attend state institutes, conferences, conventions, and workshops.

Plan to meet association officers and leaders who serve and represent you on the state level.

Keep informed about, and do your part to support, state legislative campaigns.

NATIONALLY

Read *Today's Education*—mailed to members monthly. Take full advantage of its professional articles, classroom aids, guides to publications, instructional tools, and many other special features. Read, also, the NEA Reporter which will keep you up-to-date on NEA accomplishments and plans.

Secure a copy of NEA's Publications Catalog, arranged by subject matter and available to members on request. NEA is the world's largest publisher of professional materials. Obtain and use them to meet your needs.

Write the NEA for information or resources that will help you to meet your classroom needs, improve your relations with parents, help you function well in local association activities, or guide you in your advanced studies.

Plan to spend a day at the NEA Center when you visit Washington, D.C. At the NEA Center you will meet staff employees who work for you on the national level: produce your publications, represent you before Congress; maintain contacts with the press and with national lay organizations; provide many kinds of information and service.

Plan to attend an NEA Convention, held annually during the summer in some large city. At NEA conventions about 20,000 members of your profession and visitors from every state and many foreign countries meet, exchange ideas, share experiences, and learn. Some 7,000 delegates from local and state

176 affiliated associations vote to determine NEA's program of activities for the coming year.

Take full advantage of NEA materials to help you to participate effectively in NEA-originated events such as American Education Week.

Learn to use NEA's many special services, such as NEA's field representatives; NEA's salary and negotiation consultants; NEA's consultants in instruction; NEA's research in all areas of educational practice and teacher welfare; NEA's publications and aids with such classroom problems as discipline and the use of TV and teaching machines; NEA's regional instructional conferences in basic and in special subject matter areas.

Avail yourself of savings and advantages made possible by NEA, such as NEA's Life Insurance programs; NEA Accidental Death program; NEA tours—U.S. and foreign—some with opportunities to earn college credits enroute; NEA-secured deductions on your federal income taxes for your advanced-educational expenses; quantity discounts for NEA's professional publications.

———•———

American Federation of Teachers (AFT)

The American Federation of Teachers is not a new organization. It was organized on April 15, 1916, affiliated with the American Federation of Labor May 9, 1916, and has grown in membership and influence every year since. While the AFT is the largest teachers' union in the United States, the general membership of 375,000 as of August 1, 1973 is small compared to the one million members of the NEA. However, the AFT functions as the dominant teachers' organization in some of our largest cities.

In the fall of 1961, an election was held among New York City teachers to elect an agent to bargain with the Board of Education. In the election, the United Federation of Teachers (AFL-CIO) defeated the Teacher's Bargaining Organization which was supported by the National Education Association. This election has been referred to as the opening skirmish of what has grown to be a noisy battle for the loyalties of American teachers.[2] The New York election is cited as a major factor in the rise of the AFT to a position of national prominence.

A pamphlet entitled *Questions and Answers about AFT* published by the AFT provides information regarding organizational structure and affiliation with organized labor. The American Federation of Teachers comprises more than 650 local unions of teachers in the United States, the Canal Zone, Guam, and in Armed Forces Overseas Dependents Schools. State federations of teachers exist in a majority of the states, and are active in legislative and organizational work. The national headquarters of the AFT is located at 1012 14th St. N.W., Washington D.C. 20005. The president, secretary-treasurer, and administrative and office staffs, from here, supply organizational, membership, and other aid to local unions and members as requested.

The general offices include those of the president, secretary-treasurer, administrative staff, and the following departments: financial, organizational, legal, research, publications, public relations and publicity, civil rights, state federations, colleges and universities, membership, and mailing.

The annual convention functions as the

2. Stanley Elam, "Who's Ahead and Why: The NEA-AFT Rivalry," *Phi Delta Kappan*, September 1964, p. 12.

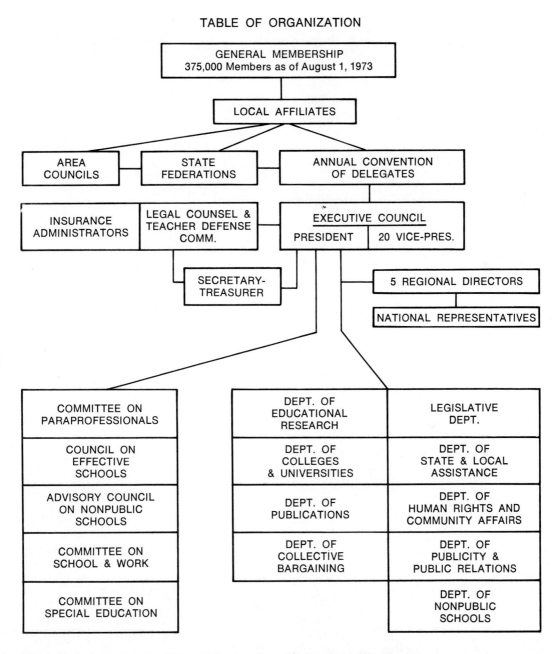

TABLE OF ORGANIZATION

Figure 7.2 Organization Chart of the American Federation of Teachers.

Source: American Federation of Teachers Washington, D.C. Used with permission.

178 AFT's governing body. Delegates to this convention are elected by local union members. Each affiliated local is entitled to one delegate for 25 or fewer members and one delegate for each 100 additional members.

The interim governing and administrative body is the Executive Council of 20 vice-presidents, and the president, who is a full-time officer. The president and vice-presidents are subject to election every two years. Vice-presidents, who are assigned to specific geographical areas, serve without remuneration (see Figure 7.2).

Organized labor was a major instrumentality in establishing our system of free public schools, and has actively backed every practical public school improvement at local, state, and national levels. The objectives of the American Federation of Teachers coincide with labor philosophy on the importance of public education.

Labor affiliation gives the AFT and its members the support of the more than 14 million members of unions in the AFL-CIO. Local and state teachers' federations can rely on the support of state and local central labor bodies. AFT local unions have often won better salaries and other benefits for teachers with the aid and support of local labor trades and labor councils, after teachers' organizations outside the labor movement failed to accomplish these objectives.

Labor affiliation does not impose any obligations on union teachers which would deter them from the best professional service they can render and the highest professional ethics they can command. Labor affiliation, by emphasizing the dignity of the teaching profession, makes it easier for teachers to act, on the job, as the professionals they are. Figure 7.3 outlines the relationship of American Federation of Teachers to the American Federa-

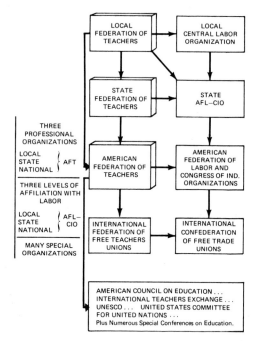

Figure 7.3 Relationship of American Federation of Teachers to AFL-CIO.

Source: American Federation of Teachers, Washington, D.C. Used by permission.

tion of Labor—Congress of Industrial Organizations.

Membership in the AFT includes principals, supervisors, department heads, and teachers, but does not permit superintendents to join on the grounds that superintendents represent the interests of the employer. As with the NEA, a Student Federation of Teachers may be chartered in any college or university under the auspices of the parent AFT.

The AFT boasts that John Dewey held Membership Card Number 1 in the American

Federation of Teachers. Dr. Dewey, who died in 1952 at the age of 93, was professor of philosophy at Teachers College, Columbia University. In an address by Dr. Dewey, published in the *American Teacher,* publication of the AFT, January, 1928, he said:

————•————

The very existence of teachers' unions does a great deal more than protect and aid those who are members of it; and that, by the way, is one reason the teachers' union is not larger. It is because there are so many teachers outside of it who rely and depend upon the protection and support which the existence and the activities of the union give them, that they are willing to shelter behind the organization without coming forward and taking an active part in it.

And if there are teachers . . . who are not members of the union, I should like to beg them to surrender the, shall I call it, cowardly position, and come forward and actively unite themselves with those who are doing this great and important work for the profession and teaching.

————•————

Total membership in the AFT at the time of Dr. Dewey's address (1928) was approximately 5,000. The steady rise in membership had reached approximately 60,000 at the time of the 1961 New York City teacher election won by the United Federation of Teachers supported by the AFL-CIO labor union. From May 1, 1968 to August 1, 1973 the membership in the teachers' unions affiliated with AFL-CIO rose to 375,000 which represented a gain of approximately 212,000 during a five-year span. Much of the recent gains in membership reported by the AFT may be attributed to mergers of the AFT and NEA in places such as Los Angeles and New York. While the rivalry for membership continues strongly between the NEA and the AFT the total membership of the two organizations combined represents only slightly over fifty percent of all teachers. Therefore, many teachers elect to join local teacher groups or do not join any teacher organizations.

NEA versus AFT

During the past decade the tactics and behaviors of the AFT have greatly influenced the tactics and behaviors of the NEA and vice versa. While the two organizations have differences, such differences are becoming less and less obvious. Figure 7.4 illustrates that so far as stated objectives of the AFT and the NEA are concerned, the two organizations are not in basic conflict. In view of the general similarities of purposes which continue to evolve, considerable speculation also evolves regarding the possible merger of the AFT and NEA to form a singular, more representative organization for all teachers in the United States. David Selden was elected president of the AFT in August 1968 on a "merger" platform. On October 4, 1968 the AFT extended an invitation to the NEA to enter into discussions of merger. On October 11, 1968 the NEA Executive Committee declined the AFT invitation to discuss merger prospects.

After nearly five years of informal discussion both the NEA and the AFT confirmed future merger considerations. In June 1973, the NEA's annual Representative Assembly reversed its opposition to merger talks and voted to authorize discussions for the fall of 1973, despite its coolness to ties with the AFL-CIO. The AFT quickly followed suit.

AFT Objectives	NEA Objectives
1. To bring associations of teachers into relations of mutual assistance and cooperation.	1. Educational opportunity for every individual to develop his full potential for responsible and useful citizenship and for intellectual and spiritual growth.
2. To obtain for them all the rights to which they are entitled.	2. Balanced educational programs to provide for the varied needs and talents of individual students and for the strength and progress of the nation.
3. To raise the standard of the teaching profession by securing the conditions essential to the best professional service.	3. The services of a professionally prepared and competent educator in every professional position.
4. To promote such a democratization of the schools as will enable them better to equip their pupils to take their places in the industrial, social and political life of the community.	4. School plant, equipment, and instructional materials appropriate to the educational needs of all learners.
5. To promote the welfare of the childhood of the nation by providing progressively better educational opportunities for all.	5. Effective organization, controls, administration, and financial support of public education in every state.
	6. A local-state-federal partnership in the financial support of public education with control of education residing in the states.
	7. Public understanding and appreciation of the vital role of education in our American democracy.
	8. Understanding and support of the teacher's right to participate fully in public affairs.
	9. Fair standards of professional welfare for teachers.
	10. Professional associations that evoke the active participation of all educators in working toward the highest goals for education.

Figure 7.4 AFT and NEA Objectives.

Sources: *Constitution of the American Federation of Teachers,* Article II. In *NEA Handbook,* "The Platform of the National Education Association" (Washington, D.C.: National Education Association Publications, 1961), pp. 50–53.

At the AFT convention in Washington, D.C. in August 1973, delegates voted to support merger talks aimed at bringing members of the AFT and NEA into one organization affiliated with the labor movement. Seemingly, the major deterrent to the prospects of merger is the issue of affiliation with the labor movement. Nonetheless, the first day of discussions on merger between top Federation and Education Association officers was concluded in

Washington, D.C. on October 2, 1973 with agreement on procedural rules for future meetings. AFT President David Selden and NEA President Helen Wise issued a joint press conference statement on October 3, 1973 confirming that talks were held under authorizations from the preceding conventions of the two organizations.

On February 1, 1970 teachers in the Los Angeles school district merged their two rival professional organizations (NEA and AFT) into a single teachers' group. The new teachers' unit, to be called United Teachers–Los Angeles, was approved on a 8,999–5,042 vote by members of the Association of Classroom Teachers, and members of local 121, AFL-CIO. The merger is the first ever of major urban locals of the rival National Education Association and the American Federation of Teachers. The only other merger occurred in October 1969, in Flint, Michigan, where 1,800 teachers joined together. The Los Angeles merger is regarded as a major breakthrough and may be the harbinger of a single national teachers' group. Since the Los Angeles merger, mergers have also occurred at the state or local level in New York State, New Orleans, and Gibralter, Michigan. The most recent merge vote occurred in November 1973 in Dade County (Miami), Florida, where teacher unity discussions began in November 1972 among state affiliates of the AFT and NEA. While the negotiations did not bring about a statewide merger, they did produce a favorable climate for further discussions in Dade County and other parts of Florida. In July 1973 both organizations in Dade County agreed to enter into joint activities to resolve problems. Negotiations were held, and in August 1973, representatives of the two groups—the national and state AFT and the Florida Education Association—signed an agreement spelling out general conditions and a timetable for merger.

National, State, and Local Affiliation

In the early years of the sixties decade, the NEA was viewed philosophically and operationally as the national organization which served as an umbrella under which the state and local associations were sheltered. Each of the three levels of affiliation could remain as autonomous as desired by their respective memberships. Individual teachers could pay membership dues for local membership only, for both state and local membership, or for national, state, and local membership. This mutually autonomous organizational structure and membership dues arrangement was espoused as a desirable feature in membership recruitment announcements by the NEA and state affiliates. During the mid-sixties teacher militancy increased sharply lending to the concept of teacher power. Concomitant with the expansion of teacher power was a new need for unification of the three levels of affiliation. Local associations sought increased support from state associations, and state associations sought increased national unity. The need for unity across state and local levels of membership to build teacher power prompted an alteration in the NEA point of view regarding the independent organizational and dues structures. The later years of the sixties found the NEA espousing the desirability of a unified dues approach in which members would pay a single membership fee to cover all three levels of association affiliation. Several state associations have taken direct unification steps by amending their bylaws so that their dues include membership fees for both the state and

Teacher strikes are increasing.

national associations. The National Education Association has taken indirect steps toward unified membership by requiring both state and national association membership as criteria for eligibility for various fringe benefit programs, such as insurance programs, which are NEA sponsored. The AFT has always had a single dues arrangement whereby AFT members were automatically members at the local, state, and national levels.

Yearly dues paid by the classroom teacher vary from approximately fifty ($50.00) dollars to one hundred ($100.00) dollars for membership at the national, state, and local levels. Most of the state affiliates of the NEA have utilized a sliding dues scale whereby the lowest paid teachers pay the least membership dues for state affiliation. The 1969–70 dues for NEA membership exclusive of state and local dues was $15.00. Local association dues are set by the local group with a set minimum fee for each member (typically $2.00) paid to the state association for affiliation. Under the NEA unified dues approach, a teacher in a given association would pay set yearly dues which would cover national, state, and local costs. As indicated earlier, the AFT has always had a unified dues arrangement.

The Local Association and Teacher Power

Teacher power is manifested at the local school district level by the use of a local organization to press for negotiations. Since the local school district is the quasi-municipal governing agency, the decisions of the local board of education are the decisions which directly affect the teachers. Thus, the most powerful voice for teachers to use regarding the decision-making process which affects them is the collective voice of a strong teacher association. The state Education Associations and the state Federations of Teachers provide organizational assistance to the local teacher groups ranging from formalized procedural information, printed materials, and consultant services to legal services. Generally, the local teacher organizations in the rural and small town school districts are affiliated exclusively with the state affiliate of the National Education Association. The National Education Association also has considerable strength through suburban and large city local chapters. The strength of the American Federation of Teachers is mostly associated with local affiliates in suburban and large city schools. In a few districts, strong local teacher associations exist independent of affiliation with either the NEA or the AFT.

The primary objective of a local association, whatever the state affiliation, is to vie for direct negotiation rights with the local board of education. In many school districts, two or more local organizations exist, each competing to become the sole negotiations agent for the district. Both the NEA and AFT recognize that a single negotiating agent gives maximum power to the local teachers. In school districts which have more than one strong local teacher association, elections are usually held to determine which organization will be the negotiations agency to meet with the local board of education.

After the negotiation process has been affirmed, the local teacher associations exercise their teacher power through the kinds of matters which they negotiate with the local boards. In addition to salary, negotiation items range to include curriculum matters, textbooks, teacher assignments, class size, in-service training, student teaching programs, faculty participation in the retention and selection of personnel, academic freedom, and fringe benefits.

Teacher Strikes

Teacher strikes occur when negotiations between a local teachers' organization and the local board of education do not produce acceptable resolutions to the teachers' demands. The use of the strike by teachers became the vehicle of teacher power in the later part of the sixties decade. A summary of teacher strikes for the 1967–68 school year stated that a total of 114 work stop-

184 pages (strikes) occurred, which was considered a "veritable explosion in teacher strikes."[3] These 114 strikes accounted for over one-third of the number of teacher strikes since 1940.

An overview of teacher militancy around the nation covering the same period (1967–68) follows:

———◆•◆———

The equinoctial storms of teacher militancy raged from Florida, where 25,000 teachers left their classrooms for three weeks, to New Mexico, where a one-week strike by teachers in the capital threatened to spread across the state; from Pittsburgh, where high schools were closed by teachers demanding an election as a prelude to negotiations, to San Francisco, where a jurisdictional dispute closed schools for a day. A strike was barely averted in Oakland, California. In St. Paul, Minnesota, an impasse was reached when the teachers' association charged the board with "bad faith bargaining." Oklahoma teachers staged a one-day walkout and voted to maintain a sanctions alert. The Colorado Education Association voted sanctions in the form of notifying colleges and universities nationwide that unsatisfactory educational conditions exist in that state. Many other warning notes have been sounded, like the advice South Dakota teachers were given by their association to sign contracts for only one semester of 1968–69.

The targets of most spring strikes were not local school boards, even where the walkouts were limited to a single city, but state legislatures. The Florida and New Mexico protests were aimed at pressuring the governors and legislatures of those states to approve substantially increased support programs for the schools. The AFT-inspired

3. "Teacher Strikes in Perspective," *NEA Research Bulletin,* December 1968, p. 113.

strikes in Pittsburgh and San Francisco were intended to prod the legislatures of California and Pennsylvania into passing new negotiation legislation more favorable to the union.

Nearly every stoppage ended with sufficient gains that teachers could call the effort successful, even though the success was in no case complete. Florida teachers did get a revenue bill, but a smaller one than they had demanded. In some Florida counties school boards took teacher resignations at face value and refused to rehire in some cases. And the AFT stepped in with a state-wide recruiting campaign, hoping to capitalize on teacher unhappiness with results of the walkout. The Pittsburgh walkout won a negotiation election in which neither the union nor the association won a majority, but no negotiations will follow unless the legislature passes a law authorizing it. Since then the Pennsylvania State Teachers Association has voted to apply state-wide sanctions and to censure the governor. The strike called by the AFT in San Francisco did result in an election, but the AFT lost the election and there is no evidence yet that the desired changes in the Winton Act will be forthcoming. In both cities union leaders figure they cannot lose. This time they have won the right to an election; next time they expect to win the election. The New Mexico militancy led to appointment of a task force that has recommended convening a special session of the legislature, a move rejected earlier by the governor.

What lies behind the militancy? Are conditions in the affected states really substandard, or have the strikes resulted more from inter-organizational rivalry and jurisdictional disputes than from an accurate perception of genuine grievances?

If five selected criteria of state-wide educational performance are applied to the nine states cited for March work stoppages, four of these states fall below the national mean in four of the five measures. In these four states

—Colorado, Florida, Oklahoma, and South Dakota—the case for educational delinquency by the state seems pretty clear. In the other states the picture is less clear, though the specific deficiency attacked by the strikers may be very real.

The five criteria selected for comparison are:

- Average salaries of all teachers in public schools, 1967–68.
- Percent increase in instructional staff salaries, 1957–58 to 1967–68.
- Percent of revenue for public schools from state government, 1967–68.
- Per capita state expenditures for all education, 1966.
- Current expenditures for public elementary and secondary education per pupil in ADA, 1967–68.

South Dakota falls below the national norm in all five measures, ranking 49, 33, 48, 34, and 33.

On only one measure do all nine states rank below the national average, the percent of increase in salaries during the past decade. This suggests the positive relationship between failure to maintain relative salary gains and presence of teacher militancy. In no other category did more than five states fall below the median, though six of the nine were beneath the mean in average salaries paid this year. The influence of salary in motivating militancy is apparent, even where other factors are present. Obviously, other conditions than low salaries must be present before militancy becomes operative. Nine of the ten lowest states in average salaries paid are *not* among those states experiencing strikes. It may be significant that all but one of the nine states in which there were strikes (Florida) have a higher percentage of men in the teaching force than the national average.

Only one of the nine states experiencing

a significant spring teacher strike (California) currently has a negotiations law, and in that state the major goal of the strike was to achieve revision of that law.

The fact that teacher discontent seems to center chiefly in the cities reflects not only the well-known axiom that urban dwellers are politically more active than their rural colleagues; even more, it mirrors the genuine crisis of the city schools. The teacher strikes are storm signals to state and federal officials that the cities need more attention—which means more money.

As usual, observers see a variety of possible patterns emerging from the wave of strikes. Some see the decline of the NEA, which has accepted the strike tactic recently and reluctantly, and the further strengthening of the union, for whom the strike is a natural weapon. Some analysts predict a wave of state-wide teacher strikes, while others proclaim that the lesson of Florida is that a state-wide walkout jeopardizes the positions of the teachers in the most vulnerable spots. A better tactic, they say, is pressure applied on state authorities by strikes in key urban areas where the strike is most likely to succeed.[4]

Teacher strikes continue to be used by teacher organizations as a means of applying pressure to obtain favorable resolution of yearly demands. During September 1973, more than 25,000 AFT members alone were on the picket lines in more than twenty communities in Illinois, Michigan, Massachusetts, New York State, and Rhode Island. By the third week of September, some settlements had been reached, but in several districts in Michigan and New York State the prognosis was for long, bitter walkouts.

Thousands of NEA teachers also were on strike throughout the country. However,

4. D.W.R., "Teacher Militancy Around the Nation," *Phi Delta Kappan,* June 1968, p. 554. Used with permission.

Parents' concerns for the problems of the schools are often the same as the teachers' concerns.

an NEA research memo indicated that strike idleness during the 1971–72 school year declined sharply from 1970–71 suggesting further that the 181 strikes in 1969–70 may have represented a peak.[5] Figure 7.5 shows the number of strikes and the estimated number of strike participants. The estimate of par-

ticipants is based on the greatest number of teachers not reporting for work at any one time during a strike. Strike participation does not necessarily indicate the size of a school system, nor whether the strike was statewide or for a single school building within a school system.

Teachers Jailed for Striking

In various communities, school officials ask for court orders which require teachers to return to work, keeping the schools open. When such court orders are not obeyed the result is the arrest and jailing of teachers continuing strike activities. During the Yorktown, New York strike in September 1973, twenty-two of the striking teachers spent most of one day in the county jail as penalty for defying a court order to return to work. Six of the strike's leaders were sentenced to thirty days in jail and fined $250 each, while the remaining sixteen teachers received sentences of fifteen days and fines of $250. State officials said this was the first time rank and file teachers had been sent to jail. All of the sentences have been stayed, pending appeal. In addition, the local teacher organization (AFT-NEA) was fined $1,000 a day for each day of the strike under New York's Taylor Law. The Harrison Association of Teachers (AFT-NEA), ended its month long strike on October 8, 1973 after around-the-clock negotiations with the board of education.

Fringe Benefits and Support Programs

The NEA and the AFT differ in degree in their approaches to specific benefits or programs, but in general terms each organi-

5. *NEA Research Memo 1972–18,* National Education Association (Washington, D.C.: National Education Association Publications, October 1972).

Type of organization, month, and state	Number of strikes, work stoppages, and interruptions of service	Estimated number of personnel involved	Estimated number of man-days involved*
1	2	3	4
TYPE OF ORGANIZATION			
Professional association	76	28,642	184,145
Teacher union	13	4,710	63,935
MONTH			
August	19	4,851	48,907
September	30	13,810	74,208
October	8	2,054	13,873
November	8	2,705	12,114
December	4	1,185	5,700
January	7	4,739	35,227
February	2	453	453
March	3	218	218
April	3	2,274	42,936
May	5	1,063	14,444
STATE			
California	1	227	4,767
Connecticut	3	1,985	7,780
Illinois	11	2,878	19,957
Indiana	1	1,800	39,600
Massachusetts	1	534	534
Michigan	9	6,504	33,596
New Jersey	2	1,460	13,880
New York	14	5,892	35,031
Ohio	10	2,226	3,744
Pennsylvania	30	8,705	84,523
Rhode Island	3	474	2,034
Tennessee	1	64	576
Washington	2	508	1,108
Wisconsin	1	95	950
TOTAL	89	33,352	248,080

* Based on instructional days of full-time teachers during regular school year. Teacher report-in days, holidays, weekends, and vacation days are excluded.

Figure 7.5 Teacher Strikes, Work Stoppages, and Interruptions of Service, by Type of Organization, by Month, and by State, 1971–72 School Year.

Source: Published and unpublished information collected by the Bureau of Labor Statistics, U.S. Department of Labor, and NEA Research. By permission.

zation strives to offer similar benefits to its members. Figure 7.6 illustrates the kinds of fringe benefits and support programs which are mutual concerns of both organizations.

Affiliate publications come to the members of the teacher associations. These usually consist of national journals and state journals, newsletters, handbooks, research studies, and various booklets and reports.

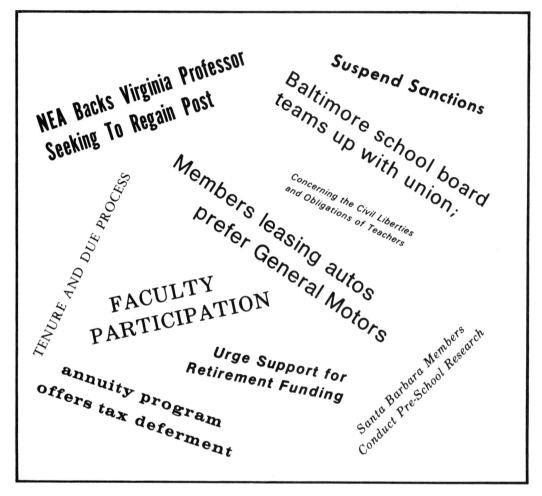

Figure 7.6 Mutual Concerns of the AFT and the NEA.

The benefits of research services come to members in the form of reports such as salary studies, estimates of school statistics, negotiations information, summaries of court decisions, leaves of absence, and fringe benefit programs which exist.

Each of the parent associations have legislative committees at both the state and national levels. These legislative committees work on improving certification standards and improving the laws which relate to teaching.

Teacher welfare is an area of prime importance to the parent associations. Many kinds of programs which focus on advancing and protecting the welfare of members are sponsored by the parent organizations. The NEA and her state affiliates have considerably outdistanced the AFT in this area. Consequently, many teachers have been members of both organizations simultaneously in order to be eligible for teacher welfare-oriented programs. The AFT is steadily increasing research services, publications, printed materials, insurance programs, and consultant services for their members. Among the state educational association teacher welfare programs are included teacher placement services, investment programs, retirement benefits, insurance programs, liability protection, auto leasing programs, and regional service centers. Similar programs are sponsored by the NEA, but to be eligible for their programs the teacher must also belong to the state association. The requirement of state membership is consistent with the unified dues emphasis of the NEA and prevents the teacher from paying only the national dues in order to profit from the nationally sponsored NEA welfare programs.

A Summary View

Myron Lieberman, professor of education, is considered an authority on the growth of teacher power. Lieberman has reviewed the issues that divide the two organizations, the possible advantages of merger, and whether NEA-AFT peace would slow down growth of the collective negotiation movement in an article written for the *Phi Delta Kappan*. The following quote from Professor Lieberman's article expresses his view of the future relationship between the NEA and the AFT.

———•—•———

A merger of the National Education Association and American Federation of Teachers will probably be negotiated in the near future. Such a move will have far-reaching national implications for teacher militancy. Perhaps because very few educators realize how im-

minent merger is, our professional literature is virtually devoid of any consideration of the likely conditions and consequences of merger. Inasmuch as organizational rivalry plays such an important role in teacher militancy, it would be unrealistic to consider the dynamics of teacher militancy without serious attention to the effects of merger upon it. . . .

Without question, the organizational rivalry between the NEA and AFT has been an important stimulus to teacher militancy. At all levels, the two organizations and their state and local affiliates have come under much more pressure to achieve benefits than would be the case if there were only one organization. A representation election almost invariably causes the competing organizations to adopt a more militant stance in order to demonstrate their effectiveness in achieving teacher goals. For the same reason, any failure to press vigorously for teacher objectives becomes a threat to organizational survival. State and national support are poured into local elections and negotiation sessions in order to protect the interests of the state and national affiliates. Thus at the local level organizational rivalry has led to a vastly greater organizational effort to advance teacher objectives. This development is consistent with the experience of competing organizations in other fields.

The crucial importance of the NEA-AFT rivalry in stimulating teacher militancy raises the question of whether the merger of the two organizations will reduce such militancy. Probably, the merger will simultaneously encourage some tendencies toward greater teacher militancy and some toward less militancy; the overall outcome is likely to vary widely from district to district and time to time. . . .[6]

———•—•———

6. Myron Lieberman, "Implications of the Coming NEA-AFT Merger," *Phi Delta Kappan* 50, November, 1968, pp. 139–144. Used by permission.

The philosophical statements of the two major national teacher associations are expressed in the form of the Bill of Teacher Rights (NEA) and the Bill of Rights (AFT). The two statements are included here in their entirety.

———— • ————

Bill of Teacher Rights

National Education Association

Preamble

We, the teachers of the United States of America, aware that a free society is dependent upon the education afforded its citizens, affirm the right to freely pursue truth and knowledge.

As an individual, the teacher is entitled to such fundamental rights as dignity, privacy, and respect.

As a citizen, the teacher is entitled to such basic constitutional rights as freedom of religion, speech, assembly, association and political action, and equal protection of the law.

In order to develop and preserve respect for the worth and dignity of man, to provide a climate in which actions develop as a consequence of rational thought, and to insure intellectual freedom, we further affirm that teachers must be free to contribute fully to an educational environment which secures the freedom to teach and the freedom to learn.

Believing that certain rights of teachers derived from these fundamental freedoms must be universally recognized and respected, we proclaim this Bill of Teacher Rights.

Article I   Rights as a Professional

As a member of the teaching profession, the individual teacher has the right:

Section 1.   To be licensed under professional and ethical standards established, maintained, and enforced by the profession.

Section 2.   To maintain and improve professional competence.

Section 3.   To exercise professional judgment in presenting, interpreting, and criticizing information and ideas, including controversial issues.

Section 4.   To influence effectively the formulation of policies and procedures which affect ones professional services, including curriculum, teaching materials, methods of instruction, and school-community relations.

Section 5.   To exercise professional judgment in the use of teaching methods and materials appropriate to the needs, interests, capacities, and the linguistic and cultural background of each student.

Section 6.   To safeguard information obtained in the course of professional service.

Section 7.   To work in an atmosphere conducive to learning, including the use of reasonable means to preserve the learning environment and to protect the health and safety of students, oneself, and others.

Section 8.   To express publicly views on matters affecting education.

Section 9.   To attend and address a governing body and be afforded access to its minutes when official action may affect ones professional concerns.

Article II   Rights as an Employee

As an employee, the individual teacher has the right:

Section 1. To seek and be fairly considered for any position commensurate with ones qualifications.

Section 2. To retain employment following entrance into the profession in the absence of a showing of just cause for dismissal or non-renewal through fair and impartial proceedings.

Section 3. To be fully informed, in writing, of rules, regulations, terms, and conditions affecting ones employment.

Section 4. To have conditions of employment in which health, security, and property are adequately protected.

Section 5. To influence effectively the development and application of evaluation procedures.

Section 6. To have access to written evaluations, to have documents placed in ones personnel file to rebut derogatory information and to have removed false or unfair material through a clearly defined process.

Section 7. To be free from arbitrary, capricious, or discriminatory actions affecting the terms and conditions of employment.

Section 8. To be advised promptly in writing of the specific reasons for any actions which might affect ones employment.

Section 9. To be afforded due process through the fair and impartial hearing of grievances, including binding arbitration as a means of resolving disputes.

Section 10. To be free from interference to form, join, or assist employee organizations, to negotiate collectively through representatives of ones own choosing, and to engage in other concerted activities for the purpose of professional negotiations or other mutual aid or protection.

Section 11. To withdraw services collectively when reasonable procedures to resolve impasse have been exhausted.

As an individual member of an employee organization, the teacher has the right:

Section 1. To acquire membership in employee organizations based upon reasonable standards equally applied.

Section 2. To have equal opportunity to participate freely in the affairs and governance of the organization.

Section 3. To have freedom of expression, both within and outside the organization.

Section 4. To vote for organization officers, either directly or through delegate bodies, in fair elections.

Section 5. To stand for and hold office subject only to fair qualifications uniformly applied.

Section 6. To be fairly represented by the organization in all matters.

Section 7. To be provided periodic reports of the affairs and conduct of business of the organization.

Section 8. To be provided detailed and accurate financial records, audited and reported at least annually.

Section 9. To be free from arbitrary disciplinary action or threat of such action by the organization.

Section 10. To be afforded due process by the organization in a disciplinary action.[7]

Bill of Rights

American Federation of Teachers

The teacher is entitled to a life of dignity equal to the high standard of service that is justly de-

7. National Education Association, "Bill of Teacher Rights" (Washington, D.C.: National Education Association Publications). Used by permission.

192 manded of that profession. Therefore, we hold these truths to be self-evident:

I

Teachers have the right to think freely and to express themselves openly and without fear. This includes the right to hold views contrary to the majority.

II

They shall be entitled to the free exercise of their religion. No restraint shall be put upon them in the manner, time or place of their worship.

III

They shall have the right to take part in social, civil, and political affairs. They shall have the right, outside the classroom, to participate in political campaigns and to hold office. They may assemble peaceably and may petition any government agency, including their employers, for a redress of grievances. They shall have the same freedom in all things as other citizens.

IV

The right of teachers to live in places of their own choosing, to be free of restraints in their mode of living and the use of their leisure time shall not be abridged.

V

Teaching is a profession, the right to practice which is not subject to the surrender of other human rights. No one shall be deprived of professional status, or the right to practice it, or the practice thereof in any particular position, without due process of law.

VI

The right of teachers to be secure in their jobs, free from political influence or public clamor, shall be established by law. The right to teach after qualification in the manner prescribed by law, is a property right, based upon the inalienable rights of life, liberty, and the pursuit of happiness.

VII

In all cases affecting the teacher's employment or professional status a full hearing by an impartial tribunal shall be afforded with the right to full judicial review. No teacher shall be deprived of employment or professional status but for specific causes established by law having a clear relation to the competence or qualification to teach proved by the weight of the evidence. In all such cases the teacher shall enjoy the right to a speedy and public trial, to be informed of the nature and cause of the accusation; to be confronted with the accusing witnesses, to subpoena witnesses and papers, and the assistance of counsel. No teacher shall be called upon to answer any charge affecting his employment or professional status but upon probable cause, supported by oath or affirmation.

VIII

It shall be the duty of the employer to provide culturally adequate salaries, security in illness and adequate retirement income. The teacher has the right to such a salary as will: a) Afford a family standard of living comparable to that enjoyed by other professional people in the community b) To make possible freely chosen professional study c) Afford the opportunity for leisure and recreation common to our heritage.

IX

No teacher shall be required under penalty of reduction of salary to pursue studies beyond those required to obtain professional status. After serving a reasonable probationary period a teacher shall be entitled to permanent tenure terminable only for just cause. They shall be free as in other professions in the use of their own time. They shall not be required to perform extracurricular work against their will or without added compensation.

X

To equip people for modern life requires the most advanced educational methods. Therefore, the teacher is entitled to good classrooms, adequate teaching materials, teachable class size and administrative protection and assistance in maintaining discipline.

XI

These rights are based upon the proposition that the culture of a people can rise only as its teachers improve. A teaching force accorded the highest possible professional dignity is the surest guarantee that blessings of liberty will be served. Therefore, the possession of these rights impose the challenge to be worthy of their enjoyment.

XII

Since teachers must be free in order to teach freedom, the right to be members of organizations of their own choosing must be guaranteed. In all matters pertaining to their salaries and working conditions they shall be entitled to bargain collectively through representatives of their own choosing. They are entitled to have the schools administered by superintendents, boards or committees which function in a democratic manner.[8]

---

8. American Federation of Teachers, *Bill of Rights* (Washington, D.C.: American Federation of Teachers). Used by permission.

Teacher militancy continues to manifest itself in the form of vote procedures for negotiation representation, negotiated teacher contracts, teacher strikes, teacher involvement in political arenas, and various other activities and events. In some communities teachers have been threatened with dismissal or jail sentences, or both, as a result of their participation in such activities. Among the outcomes of this kind of tense climate are increasing salaries and fringe benefits for teachers, advocacy of stronger teacher organizations by more active membership drives and the merger of competing organizations, and more and more demands by teachers for improved conditions of work.

During the last few years, the objectives of the two largest teacher organizations (AFT and NEA) have drawn closer. *Teacher unions* as a description of teacher organizations is much more acceptable than a decade ago. The teacher organization as an informal group within the structure of a school system is now viewed as a powerful force in most districts.

There are, however, indications that some educators are beginning to again criticize the effect of unionized labor tactics within the schools. In the following article, Gerald Dart, a former school administrator, suggests that as a result of the negotiations process the teachers and the administrators in his school district were set against one another. He also holds that the strike has proved a disastrous failure to those organizations which have used it and that we do not need to keep on with what has become an obvious educational mistake. While strong teacher organization leaders would strongly disagree with this notion, the history of the union movement in the industrial sector suggests that as negotiations

194 procedures mature, the strike is used less and less as a technique for solving management-employee problems. Might the implication be made that the time has arrived when the business of education ought to have reached a maturity level which would preclude the use of divisive tactics for solving problems related to the work of the teacher?

———————◆•◆———————

Educational Negotiations: Downhill All The Way

Gerald E. Dart

I have just left a position as educational administrator where the duties of the position required my being one of the "silent" members of the administrative negotiation team. My sad duty was to attend meetings with my colleagues who were on what is known in our state as the "certificated employees council." It was terribly depressing to watch these teachers—all of them sincere and dedicated people—go through antic and degrading charades at the meetings. To compound the inanity by participation on the other side gave me a deep feeling of guilt. This convinced me that collective bargaining, collective negotiations, "meet and confer," or whatever you may call it is a terrible waste of the competencies of a lot of people in smaller school districts and is a dishonest and demeaning procedure unworthy of use in larger districts.

A mere description of the meetings in which I participated should be conclusive

Gerald E. Dart, "Educational Negotiations: Downhill All The Way," *Educational Leadership,* October 1972, pp. 9–12. By permission.

substantiation of these assertions, but I am afraid that those who are not familiar with the process will think I am making up the account.

I assure you that this is not so. I give this assurance because a good many of my non-educator friends have refused to believe me when I have told them what our teachers and administrators went through in aping a weird model of labor negotiations.

"Silent" Members

In the first place, there was the idea of "silent" members. The teacher team in the district I left consisted of five members of the single organization representing certificated employees. The administrative team consisted of the personnel man, me (representing central office), and whoever else among principals and other administrators cared to attend. By common agreement, one teacher did all the talking for the teacher side and the personnel man did all the talking for our side. The rest of us sat there in silence no matter what we were thinking or what the two speakers said.

Once in a while someone would holler "caucus." This signal meant that one of the silent members wanted to say something. Because neither I nor any other member of the administrative team ever signaled, it was always one of the teachers who wanted to say something. But the teacher did not want to say something where we could hear it. So then came the business of leaving the room. Because leaving the room somehow signified an inferior status for the side which had to leave, we agreed to take turns leaving the room. The teacher side either stayed in the room or went out to "caucus," depending on whose turn it was.

I never did find out what the teachers talked about when they caucused. They never said when we came back together. It was eerie. I know they talked quite spiritedly because I could hear the noise through the walls. Sometimes they would go at it for 30 minutes or more, but when the joint meeting was resumed the speaker for the teacher side went on as though there had been no interruption. Several times our speaker tried to elicit what, if anything, had been discussed in their caucus. The rules seemed to dictate, however, that the teachers do not talk about what they talk about in caucus. I had the idea that the state teachers association, or someone, had told the teachers to keep quiet because you never want to let the other side know if there is any dissension in the ranks.

When we were isolated for the caucus, my personnel man and I (and whoever else was present for our side) sometimes would exchange a few impromptu remarks about the business at hand. But most of the time we talked about the foolishness of the teachers in insisting on those procedures when we all knew each other rather well. And if we were not careful we found ourselves tempted to get back at the teachers for acting the way they did. It certainly did not promote any feeling of common effort in pursuit of answers to problems under discussion.

Then there was the business of when the meetings were held. The administrative side insisted on meeting with the teachers group on school days after school was over. This was done deliberately on the assumption that teachers who have given a great deal to learners all day (as these had) would not be so alert as the administrators. Since the teachers did all the proposing and most of the disposing, they were not apt to carry on as long

at the end of the day. It was felt that the only way to avoid this situation was to release teachers on the team from teaching, and this would have been an open invitation to carry on indefinitely. The school district felt (and I think now justifiably) that releasing teachers to negotiate would be paying them for doing something they were not supposed to do. Additionally, since the meetings could have gone on all day, it would have amounted to paying the administrators for doing something other than what they were employed to do.

However debatable the reasons for the meeting time may have been, setting the time at the end of the day worked. The teacher talker remained reasonably functional by virtue of his participation, but the rest of us quite frequently found our eyelids at half mast. Only a couple of meetings ran past six o'clock and most concluded before five.

There was a disadvantage in the meeting time, however. Because of the reasonable time, we seldom disposed of all the business that had been proposed. This unfinished business was not carried over without addition at the next meeting. At the next meeting, the teachers would invariably bring back the old business and some new business besides. This resulted in a considerable backlog of unfinished items and a good deal of recrimination on the part of all the teachers because they were led to believe the administration was dragging its feet on their proposals.

Only "Demands"

And this brings up the items of business that were taken up at the sessions. The teacher side always had a good many booklets, position papers, reading material of all kinds from their state and regional associations. One of these booklets was *More! Teacher Power at* the Bargaining Table.[1] The following are illustrative bits of counsel from this publication:

Make sure your demands are escalated beyond what you really want, so that you may bargain back to that point. (Don't negotiate with yourself.) Do not bring in your lawyer to counter the county counsel or the school board's lawyer. Plead ignorance; tell the board's lawyer that his opinion is only that, and that he is a biased spokesman pleading a cause. Talk down to the board's lawyer from the standpoint of a professional teacher— "How can a lawyer understand teachers' problems?" Try to keep money items until the latter stages of the bargaining so that you will not be left with little to arouse the membership when you negotiate such non-felt needs as association security and other organization items.[2]

As a result of this kind of advice, the teachers and the administrators in this district talked about a great many items of business that were sheer fabrications. The teachers did not really expect anything from their "demands" and the administrators knew they did not, but the whole business was discussed in solemn tones and polite language. Quite frequently things were discussed which were totally unfeasible or inappropriate to the conditions in the school district, just because someone had proposed them as excess baggage.

The administrative team also had booklets and advice. One book talked about negotiation tactics and explained the following ploys: surprise, fait accompli, innocence, feedback, breakoff, feinting, crazymaking,

smog, me too, you too, chance, limits, artichoke, good guy–bad guy, NATO, participation, statistics, and undermining. A couple of explanations should give the flavor of the kind of low chicanery advocated: "Crazymaking is the tactic of giving the opposing negotiators so many things to choose from that they will become confused and make concessions. In employee negotiations this is an extremely sophisticated device, and if done badly results either in breakoff by the other negotiators or in such confusion that they cling to proposals which you know they don't really want." Or, "NATO is the tactic of No Action—Talk Only. In NATO the negotiator talks and seeks concessions from the other party but holds his concessions. NATO frustrates the opposing negotiator because it maintains the negotiating relationship without giving him propaganda he can use against you." Or, again: "Innocence is the art of expressing ignorance. . . . The first instance in which this tactic is useful is when the district has engaged in some kind of fait accompli. . . . This type of innocence can be called 'trying to look good with your hand in the cookie jar.' "[3]

Actually, these tactics were never used in the district in which I was employed, but they are in a book made available to acquaint the administrators with bargaining. What the book advocates, quite simply, is lying.

Even though the negotiators to whom I am referring did not engage in direct falsifications and deliberate obscurantism, the process was full of dishonesty and deceit. It set the tone for much more that was insincere.

1. Roger P. Kuhn. *More! Teacher Power at the Bargaining Table,* Los Angeles: California Teachers Association, Southern Section, 1969.
2. Ibid., p. 6.

3. Lee Paterson. *The Management Guide to the Winton Act.* Fullerton, California: School Research and Service Corporation, 1971.

As a result of the negotiations process the teachers and the administrators in this district were set against one another. The teacher negotiators went back to their organization's executive board and cast the administrators in the role of villains. When the personnel man reported to the board of education in executive session, he always conveyed the intransigence of the teachers and their lack of candor.

Polarization

With negotiations there was a widening communications gap in the district. The administrators did not talk frankly and honestly to the teachers and the teachers did not talk that way to the administrators. At each school in the district, whenever a teachers meeting was held, the teachers would exclude the principal and hold an "association" meeting after the regular meeting. There was suspicion and mistrust.

And this was all so unnecessary. Each one of the district administrators had been trained in working with children, as had all the teachers. All of the administrators had been teachers and all of them viewed their main responsibility as providing children with a maximum opportunity for growth in a good educational environment—just as the teachers did. The administrators did not view themselves as "managers" and the teachers did not view themselves as "labor." Yet they fell into the tactics of "labor" and "management."

Nothing was accomplished in the negotiations session that could not have been accomplished simply by having everyone get together in a democratic discussion. There were only about 160 teachers and adminis-

trators in the district. When they did get together, they made decisions with a great deal more understanding than they ever got out of negotiations. And all the school board policies and the administrative rules which were developed by negotiation could have been developed either by district meetings or by appropriate committees, probably more rapidly, certainly more cooperatively, and with more good will of a surety.

Of course, the district could have escaped the kind of negotiations it carried on by having the teachers association hire a professional negotiator, with the school board doing the same. Some of the larger districts have done this. It still does not prevent the kind of lying and estrangement that is inherent in the labor model of negotiations which is now so widely accepted by school districts. In fact, it probably worsens the process, because with professional negotiators all communication is secondhand and subject to distortions, deliberate falsification, manipulation for the privately conceived purposes of the negotiators. This has occurred in California, where the largest school district in the state will not admit any teachers to the meetings where their representatives meet with a professional negotiator hired by the school board, and all teachers and administrators know about negotiations only what the representatives of each side want them to hear.

The happenings in other large cities should make it clear that the negotiations process is not working well. The story of the connivings, manipulations, falsehoods, strife, and finally the deep alienation of the public from their schools which have taken place in Philadelphia, New York, and Newark—to mention a few besides Los Angeles—is testimony to the futility of labor negotiations in school affairs. In all these cities, there are deep rifts in teacher organizations. The process has harmed everyone.

I do not think we have to participate in this process of conflict and polarization. I do not believe we have to listen to those people who say we must now accept the labor model in negotiations because we have gone too far to turn back. The strike has proved a disastrous failure to those organizations which have used it. While it may have gained some temporary salary benefits in some cities, it has fractionated teachers in other cities and has turned the general public against any salary increases for teachers. We do not need to keep on with what has become an obvious educational mistake.

It is still possible to solve our common educational problems without the tragicomedy of negotiations. Action research is still valid. What happens with people when they meet together in groups is still a valid argument for continuation of this approach to educational problems. We can still meet together sensibly and in dignity without the kind of hypocritical farce I have described.

The attitude of the British teachers as expressed by Sir Alexander Clegg may be enlightening in this regard: "The schools must establish humane and unselfish relationships in their communities even while outside both sides of industry recriminate against each other with charges and counter-charges, strikes, and lockouts."

QUESTIONS FOR DISCUSSION

1. What is an operational difference between the NEA and AFT?
2. Why are teacher organizations actively engaged in attempting to have state laws passed which sanction the negotiations process?
3. Do you think it is a good idea to have teachers running for political offices? Should teachers be permitted to serve on boards of education?
4. Would a merger of the AFT and the NEA be advantageous or not? Discuss.
5. In what way does teacher militancy do a disservice to the teaching profession? Discuss.

SUPPLEMENTARY LEARNING ACTIVITIES

1. Invite representatives of the state affiliates of the NEA and the AFT to class sessions to discuss their organizations.
2. Interview the officers of a local teacher association regarding their relationships with their board of education.
3. Read and evaluate various collective bargaining agreements.
4. Invite a negotiator for school boards to class to discuss his views regarding the role of teacher organizations and the negotiations process.
5. Invite an elected political figure to a class session to discuss his views regarding the role of teacher organizations.

SELECTED REFERENCES

American Civil Liberties Union. *Academic Freedom, Academic Responsibility, Academic Due Process.* New York: American Civil Liberties Union, 1966.

American Federation of Teachers AFL-CIO. *Constitution of the American Federation of Teachers.* Washington, D.C.: American Federation of Teachers, 1973.

American Teacher. September, October, November 1973.

Bishop, Leslie J. *Collective Negotiation in Curriculum and Instruction: Questions and Answers.* Washington, D.C.: National Education Association Publications, 1967.

Degnan, James. "California's Militant Professors." *Changing Education* (Winter 1967).

Goodlad, John I. *The Future of Learning and Teaching.* Washington, D.C.: National Education Association Publications, 1968.

Henry, David D. *What Priority for Education?* Champaign, Ill.: University of Illinois Press, 1961.

Johnson, James, et al. *Introduction to the Foundations of American Education.* Boston: Allyn & Bacon, Inc., 1973.

Keck, Donald J. "Tenure: Who Needs It?" *Phi Delta Kappan* 54(October 1972): 124–27.

Lieberman, Myron. "Implications of the Coming NEA-AFT Merger." *Phi Delta Kappan* 50(1968):139–44.

———. "Teacher Strikes: Acceptable Strategy?" *Phi Delta Kappan* 46(1965): 237–40.

———. *The Future of Public Education.* Chicago: University of Chicago Press, 1960.

———. "Why Teachers Will Oppose Tenure Laws." *Saturday Review,* March 4, 1972, pp. 55–56.

Morrissey, W. Michael. "Sex(ism) and the School Board Member." *Phi Delta Kappan* 55(October 1973):142–43.

Moskow, Michael. "Recent Legislation Affecting Collective Negotiations for Teachers." *Phi Delta Kappan* 47(1965): 136–41.

National Education Association. *Guidelines for Professional Negotiations.* Office of Professional Development and Welfare, National Education Association. Washington, D.C.: National Education Association Publications, 1965.

———. *NEA Handbook.* Washington, D.C.: National Education Association Publications, 1973.

NEA Research Memo 1972–18. Washington, D.C.: National Education Association Publications, October 1972.

Smith, Allen W. "Have Collective Negotiaions Increased Teachers' Salaries?" *Phi Delta Kappan* 54(December 1972): 268–70.

Smith, Fred M. "The Teacher's Union versus the Professional Associations." *School and Society* 90(December 5, 1962): 439–40.

Stinnett, T. M., Jack H. Kleinmann, and Martha L. Ware. *Professional Negotiation in Public Education.* New York: Macmillan Company, 1966.

Strom, Robert D. *The Inner-City Classroom: Teacher Behavior.* Columbus, Ohio: Charles E. Merrill Publishing Company, 1966.

Tanner, Daniel. *Schools for Youth.* New York: Macmillan Company, 1965.

Zeluck, Stephen. "The UFT Strike: Will It Destroy the AFT?" *Phi Delta Kappan* 50(1969):250–55.

———. NEA Research Memo

the Role of Education in the United States

In this section the authors have chosen to view education in terms of the expectations of societies and individuals. Chapters eight and nine approach the topic from a contemporary viewpoint, while chapter ten examines expectations of education as they have related to our history. Chapter eleven presents both traditional and contemporary beliefs about education.

American society is a reflection of our representative democratic form of government. As such it professes the ideal precepts of a democracy. The basis of these ideals is freedom: freedom of expression, freedom of opportunity, and the freedom of people to determine their own destinies. A high premium is placed on the worth of the individual and his opportunities for education. A major function of education in a democracy is to develop individuals to their fullest capacities so that they in turn may contribute to the achievement of the ideals of a democratic society.

The societal expectations for education

202 are many and varied. Among these expectations two consistent desires can be recognized: the perpetuation of certain knowledge elements of our culture, and the refinement of our actual ways of living to cause them to become more congruent with our ideals. The latter of these goals gives rise to expectations for the schools to be instrumental in resolving some of our social problems.

Individual expectations for education are also many and varied. Every American in his own individual way has ideas of what he wants the schools to do for him and for his children. These expectations are expressed and our school programs reveal these expressions. Individual voices join to form societal choruses to be heard by those who are charged with directing education. While the size and complexities of our society make it increasingly difficult for an individual to be heard, our form of government and our educational systems are committed to the protec-

tion of the right of individuals to be heard.

Historically, expectations for education have changed as our nation has developed. Generally, our educational system has responded to the demands of individuals and to the demands of society. In the future the needs of individuals and of society are not likely to be met by schools that take merely a reflective or responsive posture. The schools must assume a leadership role.

Individuals from all walks of life hold beliefs about education. Philosophers, scholars, professional educators, and lay citizens in either a very formal or informal way function from a set of beliefs about the basic purposes of education, including what should be taught and the methodologies of instruction. These beliefs have had a powerful influence on education and will continue to do so in the future. Chapter eleven provides a brief introduction to the relationship of beliefs, or philosophies, to American education.

chapter 8

Societal Expectations for Education

goals

- Presents a variety of expectations that Americans hold for their schools.

- Explains the nature of culture, subcultures, and the concept of cultural pluralism.

- Discusses values and raises questions about the values that schools should transmit.

- Illustrates the relationship of selected social problems—race relations, poverty, unemployment, crime and violence, and drug abuse— to schools.

- Presents and discusses four commitments in American education: universality, equality, liberation, and excellence.

American society is pluralistic. It contains many diverse groups within the larger group: young and old, liberal and conservative, black and white, atheists and believers, urbanites and farmers, union members and non-union members, haves and have-nots, and many more. Each of these subsocieties has purposes. Their purposes are sometimes

204 in harmony with the majority of the members of the larger American society and sometimes in discord. The purposes of the overall American society, plus those of its subgroups, give rise to societal or group expectations for education.

The American Scene

Many Americans famous in our history have stated their views on the relationship of education to our overall democratic society:

———— • ————

Above all things, I hope the education of the common people will be attended to; convinced that on their good sense we may rely with the most security for the preservation of a due degree of liberty.

Thomas Jefferson

Of all the work that is done or that can be done for our country, the greatest is that of educating the body, the mind, and above all the character, giving spiritual and moral training to those who in a few years are themselves to decide the destinies of the nation.

Theodore Roosevelt

Without popular education, moreover, no government which rests upon popular action can long endure.

Woodrow Wilson

The common school is the greatest discovery ever made by man. It is supereminent in its universality and in the timeliness of the aid it proffers. The common school can train . . .

children in the elements of all good knowledge and of virtue.

Jails and prisons are the complement of schools; so many less you have of the latter, so many more you must have of the former.

Horace Mann

———— • ————

More recently others have said:

———— • ————

The human mind is our fundamental resource. . . . The Federal government's responsibility in this area has been established since the earliest days of the Republic—it is time now to act decisively to fulfill that responsibility for the sixties.

John F. Kennedy

Because our schools help shape the mind and character of our youth, the strength or weakness of our educational system today will go far to determine the strength or weakness of our national wisdom and our national morality tomorrow. That is why it is essential to our nation that we have good schools. And their quality depends on all of us.

Dwight D. Eisenhower

———— • ————

The previous quotations were directed generally to the relationship between education and the survival and welfare of the overall American society. Other Americans not so famous also have thoughts and expectations about what schools should be doing for society. If a person could tune in on their thoughts as he walked the streets and visited in the meeting halls throughout the nation, he would very likely hear some of the following ideas expressed:

———•—•———

Our schools must first of all teach children to be devoted and loyal to their country. Young people have to learn to respect the Constitution and the flag of the best country in the world. Kids got it good in this country and they better appreciate it—they might have to fight for this land someday.

Better help me and my kind get jobs—*good* jobs. You got to have a *good* job that's regular if you're gonna be somebody. And another thing, the schools better quit saying my kids can't learn and begin to teach them. My kids gotta have a chance too, you know.

The best thing the school can do for society is to teach youngsters all the knowledge they can and then help them learn how to think with it. The more a young person knows the better prepared he is to live in this competitive world—and therefore, probably the better able to serve this society and help solve its problems. That makes sense to me—apply brain power, not babble power, and remember we'll always have problems. Kids need good, solid, fundamental college preparatory training. They also need to learn a few more social graces—many of them are crude.

The difference between right and wrong, that's what the schools should teach. All the technical knowledge and cultural appreciation in the world isn't going to help us nearly so much as it could so long as we have killing, stealing, drug addiction, and all that goes with moral decay. In addition to the customary three "r's" we need respect and religion. For this country to survive, children have to learn respect for other people, respect for rule by law and respect for our Creator. Really, I don't see what's so wrong about religion in the public schools—after all, this is a religious

country—and it might help teach about right and wrong. Those who don't want it can ignore it.

Whatever they do in schools it costs too much. Sometimes I wish somebody could really tell me how much kids learn from some of the things they do. It seems to me they're always trying some different way of teaching that costs more money, but the kids don't seem to be any better. I think *we taxpayers* ought to decide what the schools ought to be doing, and then see to it that they do just that. We ought to get some kind of report that tells how many kids learned what and how much it cost.

———•—•———

These statements reflect further the pluralistic nature of American society, and also the many and varied expectations its members have for education. Citizens do recognize the relationship between societies and their schools. The first statement expressed a concern for developing loyalty to the United States along with an appreciation for its history and heritage. Schools were envisioned as playing a major role in causing the young to love their country and to be ready to defend what it stands for from those who would destroy it either from without or from within. Another statement recognized the relationship between education and jobs, and the relationship between jobs and freedom from poverty. Education was seen as a means for men to improve themselves, to loosen their shackles, and to determine their destinies. It was further emphasized that the schools must serve all children from all the classes of society and cause them to learn. The failure of a child to learn in school appeared in the previously quoted statement as a failure of the school to teach the child. It was indicated that

206 schools need to align their teaching to the needs of their constituent society. Still another statement reiterated the relationship between knowledgeable individuals and effective citizenship. Great faith was evidenced in the educated to use rational methods to resolve their social problems. Morality and law and order were the theme of another statement cited, as schools were viewed as having an obligation supplementary to the home in developing the character of its students.

The last statement, in effect, calls for cost-efficiency. It raises questions about the relationship between spending and learning productivity. In a sense it implies that the individual is willing to pay if he knows what learning is being produced. With that information, citizens would know what the school could do best—and perhaps reorder its priorities. It implies that citizens want something to say about priorities. Americans hold many expectations for their schools.

What does the American society expect from its schools? The answers, if itemized, would result in an infinite list. Most of the items on the list, however, could be classified under two major headings: (1) the transmission of culture, and (2) resources for assisting in the resolution of social problems. These two tasks require the mustering of major talents and resources, for both tasks are highly complex. Cultures are diverse, and the social problems of the United States are many and varied.

Transmission of Culture

Culture may be defined as the ways of living that societies have evolved or developed as their members have encountered and interacted with their environment. As such it includes knowledge, beliefs, arts, morals, values, laws, languages, tools, institutions, and ideas. Every individual is cultured—that is, he has a way of living; however, rarely, if ever, would any individual know the complete culture of his society. For example, while most citizens of the United States enjoy and use plumbing facilities they do not have the specialized knowledge of plumbers. Nor do most citizens have a complete knowledge of medicine, yet they benefit from its advanced state in our culture. Individuals learn the culture of their societies from infancy; much of it they gain from imitation and by osmosis. With maturity, individuals consciously or unconsciously choose for their purposes that which they value from the largest culture.

> *Culture is a human production, and man differs from animals because he creates culture, and because he transmits what he has learned and what he has created from one generation to the next.*
>
> Robert J. Havighurst

The United States, because of its multi-ethnic origins, contains many subcultures. Most large cities have neighborhoods which reflect immigrant cultures. These neighborhoods feature the foods, arts, and handicrafts of the ancestoral backgrounds of the inhabitants.

Frequently, the neighborhood residents sponsor festivals featuring facets of their ethnic culture. Cultural elements with a distinct uniqueness also develop in geographic regions of our nation, and in the rural, suburban, and urban demographic groups. From these fertile milieus, which have been accumulating, admixing, and altering for the past three and one-half centuries, Americans seek to identify the uniqueness of their total culture.

Schools in our society have been given the responsibility of transmitting culture. They are expected by the citizenry to accomplish this task. What shall they transmit? While a clear and specific answer to this question cannot be given, history has provided some guidelines.

There is little question that the schools are expected to transmit the knowledge element of culture. Historically in our early colonies this meant to teach the young to read, write, and cipher, using the Bible as the basic textbook. As the colonies grew and became a nation and the westward movement began, knowledge came to include vocational skills necessary for our growth. During these periods the secondary schools came into existence, partly in recognition of the added knowledge necessary to foster the development of our growing nation. Today, one need only look at the curriculum of a modern secondary school to realize that "knowledge" has become an increasingly comprehensive term. It still represents reading, writing, and ciphering; it also represents social studies, biological and physical science, agriculture, home economics, industrial education, languages, business, art, and a multitude of other specialties ranging from automobile body repair to contract bridge.

The "knowledge explosion" has caused many educators to seriously consider what knowledge the school should transmit. It is obvious that in the amount of time customarily dedicated to formal schooling, only a small portion of the total knowledge that man now possesses can be passed on to the student. If one could conceptualize knowledge as being of a material nature, such as books, and then

Learning to read is considered a basic cultural necessity.

try to imagine the size of the mountain it would make, the immensity of the task can be partly realized. Selectivity is necessary as decisions are made regarding which portions of the total knowledge available are to be transmitted by the schools. Americans seem to have said: first of all, let us make certain that each individual is required to learn the knowledge which is necessary for his survival in our society; secondly, let us permit each individual to determine what he wants to learn which will assist him and perhaps incidentally advance our society; and thirdly, let us plan and hope that in the process, skills will be mastered to foster and enhance the development of more knowledge to the betterment of our way of life. So certain parts of the "mountain" are parcelled out to all young people, after which

Citizenship education through social studies.

they can select some more if they so desire, while hopefully and simultaneously the mountain gets larger and larger.

Knowledge transmission, through the American school system, has undoubtedly contributed to the relatively high leadership position of the United States in materialistic manifestations of cultural accomplishments. Our standard of living is closely related to the United States' commitment to knowledge for all citizens through a public education. Level of education is definitely a fourth variable in the economic formula of land, labor, and capital.

A second traditionally accepted responsibility of the schools in terms of cultural transmission is that of citizenship education. The schools are expected to, and do, make

Active involvement in citizenship education.

citizenship education will vary, perhaps from blind indoctrination to the advocacy of laissez-faire behavior, the most common position of the schools has been that of causing mature students to analyze critically and then to participate in improving our system.

Our overall society has prescribed democratic ideals—ideals toward which our society is striving, and which the schools are expected to exemplify, practice, and teach. A democratic society places a high premium on the worth of the individual. In 1960 the President's Commission on National Goals, in reporting on the domestic goals of our society, stated:

The status of the individual must remain our primary concern. All our institutions—political, social, and economic—must further enhance the dignity of the citizen, promote the maximum development of his capabilities, stimulate their responsible exercise, and widen the range of effectiveness of opportunities for individual choice.[1]

Closely related to the importance of the individual is the commitment to equality. On this subject the Commission reported:

Vestiges of religious prejudice, handicaps to women, and, most important, discrimination on the basis of race must be recognized as morally wrong, economically wasteful, and in many respects dangerous. In this decade we must sharply lower these last stubborn barriers.[2]

efforts to cause children to appreciate and understand our system of government. An educated citizenry is not only one that has knowledge, but one that is composed of individuals who will use this knowledge to foster an effective scheme of government, of, by, and for the people. In addition to formal instruction in our schools, youngsters also learn about good citizenship by participating in various forms of student government simulating our local, state, and national systems. Student councils, mock elections, and student government days are examples of these activities. While specific societal expectations for

1. *Goals for Americans,* p. 3.
2. Ibid., pp. 3–4.

210   It is important to note that a major responsibility for achieving the societal goal of equality, particularly in reference to the elimination of racial discrimination, has been placed on the schools. The U.S. Supreme Court in their 1954 *Brown* v. *Board of Education of Topeka* decision marked the beginning of an era of efforts to eliminate racial segregation.

In terms of the democratic process, which is the core of citizenship training, the Commission said, "To preserve and perfect the democratic process in the United States is therefore a primary goal in this as in every decade."[3] In elaboration of this point the Commission continued:

————— • • —————

Democracy gives reality to our striving for equality. It is the expression of individual self-respect; it clears the way for individual initiative, exercise of responsibility, and use of varied talents. It is basic to the peaceful adjustment of differences of opinion.[4]

————— • • —————

In citizenship education, the schools are expected to bring about a congruency between the American ideals and real life circumstances. Some of the dissension apparent in young people today can be attributed to this lack of congruency. Students seem to be saying, "Your actions speak so loudly that I can't hear your words." They have accused the older generations of professing peace and practicing war, espousing equality of opportunity and perpetuating inequality, and advocating participation in political and school

decision making while at the same time castigating those who would dare raise a dissenting voice. Some persons seem to have lost faith in the American system, advocating its destruction, while still others strive to work from within to improve it. Schools today, particularly at the levels of secondary and higher education, in response to student dissent and protest, are changing their traditional ways of participatory student citizenship education.

While American society in general recognizes the necessity of, and subscribes rather unanimously to, the transmission of knowledge and training for citizenship in our schools, the unanimity begins to fragment as subcultural elements are considered. The influence of community subcultures can be observed as local schools decide what they shall teach. The increase of Afro-American studies in many urban schools is indicative of this phenomenon.

Pluralism, Democracy, and Values

As has been indicated, America is a pluralistic society consisting of many different subsocieties. This results not only from our multiethnic origin, but also from our emphasis on the protection and enhancement of individual freedoms, as specified in the United States Constitution and as practiced in our daily life. Thus, the democratic form of government fosters pluralism. Gans has suggested that American democracy needs to be modernized to accommodate itself to pluralism.

————— • • —————

I believe that the time has come to modernize American democracy and adapt it to the needs of a pluralistic society; in short, to create a

3. Ibid., p. 4.
4. Ibid., p. 5.

pluralistic democracy. A pluralistic form of democracy would not do away with majority rule, but would require systems of proposing and disposing which take the needs of minorities into consideration, so that when majority rule has serious negative consequences, outvoted minorities would be able to achieve their most important demands, and not be forced to accept tokenism, or resort to despair or disruption.

Pluralistic democracy would allow the innumerable minorities of which America is made up to live together and share the country's resources more equitably, with full recognition of their various diversities. Legislation and appropriations would be based on the principle of 'live and let live,' with different programs of action for different groups whenever consensus is impossible. Groups of minorities could still coalesce into a majority, but other minorities would be able to choose their own ways of using public power and funds without being punished for it by a majority.[5]

———•———

In the preface to *Cultural Pluralism in Education,* Harry Rivlin addresses himself to the concept of cultural pluralism and its importance and ramifications for education, particularly in dealing with urban school problems.

———•———

The Cuban writer Jesus Castellanos once remarked that it is to be expected that a man should love the region in which he was born, but that that was no reason for hating those who were born elsewhere. Similarly, it is

5. Herbert J. Gans, "We Won't End the Crisis Until We End 'Majority Rule,' " from *More Equality.* Copyright Pantheon Books, 1973. Used by permission.

understandable that a person should respect and love the culture into which he was born and in which he has been brought up, but that is no reason for despising or hating the culture into which other people have been born.

One of the most difficult words for people to understand when they look at various cultures or sub-cultures is *different. Different* means *different*; it does not mean *better than* or *worse than.* This whole-hearted acceptance of one's own culture and of other people's culture is basic to the development of a sense of cultural pluralism that is far more enriching than is the outworn concept of the melting pot.

No child should have to feel that he must reject his parents' culture to be accepted. Indeed, his chances of adjusting successfully to his school, to his community, and to the larger society are enhanced if he is not encumbered by feelings of shame and of inferiority because he was not born into another family and another culture. To speak of any child as "culturally disadvantaged" merely because of his ethnic origin is damaging not only to the child but also to society, for it deprives the nation of the contributions that can be made by each of the many groups that make up our country.

Dewey's famous dictum that what the best and wisest of fathers wants for his child, that the state should want for all its children, has special significance today, for we stress the word *all.* By *all,* we mean *all*—the rich, the poor, the Whites, the Blacks, the Puerto Ricans, the American Indians, the Chicanos, the Chinese, and all the other ethnic groups in the United States.

In any program that aims at dealing with urban school problems and opportunities, pride of race is important but racism is vicious, whether it be expressed in discriminatory actions or in objectionable epithets or comments. As American citizens, especially as American educators working in urban

212 communities, we must make every effort to stamp out racism and its manifestations, for racism is corrosive to all students and damages the learning process.[6]

———— • — • ————

The National Coalition for Cultural Pluralism, a newly formed group, has issued the following statement calling for action to help bring about a truly multicultural society.

———— • — • ————

America has long been a country whose uniqueness and vitality have resulted in large part from its human diversity. However, among all the resources formerly and currently used to insure physical and social progress for this nation, the human resource with its myriad ethnic, cultural, and racial varieties has not been used to its fullest advantage. As a result, the American image that has been delineated by its governmental, corporate, and social structures has not truly reflected the cultural diversity of its people.

There should be no doubt in anyone's mind that America is now engaged in an internal social revolution that will thoroughly test her national policies and attitudes regarding human differences. This revolution manifests itself in many ways, through many movements. Blacks, Spanish Americans, women, college students, elderly people, etc., are all finding themselves victimized by technological and social systems which look upon significant differences among people as unhealthy and inefficient. But, whether the society likes it or not, many individuals and groups will never be able to "melt" into the American "pot." And it is these groups who are now gearing themselves up to be more self-determining

6. Madelon D. Stent, William R. Hazard, and Harry N. Rivlin, *Cultural Pluralism in Education,* p. vii. Copyright 1973 by Fordham University. Reprinted by permission of Prentice-Hall, Inc., Englewood Cliffs, New Jersey.

about their own destinies. For them it is a simple matter of survival in America.

In the future, surviving in America will of necessity be the major concern of every citizen, regardless of his wealth, heritage, race, sex, or age. This has already been made abundantly clear by the developing crisis in ecology. The national concern over pollution, overpopulation, etc., will probably be solved through our technological expertise. But the social crisis facing this country will require a different solution concept, one which will provide unity with diversity where the emphasis is on a shared concern for creating and maintaining a multicultural environment.

The concept of cultural pluralism, therefore, must be the perspective used by the different social groups in their attempt to survive as independent, yet interdependent, segments of this society. Pluralism lifts up the necessary and creative tension between similarity and difference. It strongly endorses standards of variety, authentic options, diverse centers of power, and self-direction.

It is the institutions of our society which provide the supports for some individual and group attitudes, values, and standards which, when applied, are clearly discriminatory against others. It is these same institutions which can reverse many of the current social trends by establishing supports for a culturally pluralistic society—where everyone recognizes that no single set of values and standards is sufficient to inspire the full range of human possibilities.

The creation of a truly multicultural society will not happen automatically. There must be established a plan of action, a leadership, and a cadre of supporters that will effectively implement the concept of cultural pluralism throughout the length and breadth of every community in America. Institutions, groups, and individuals must be actively engaged in working toward at least three goals, which are:

- The elimination of all structural supports for oppressive and racist practices by individuals, groups, and institutions.
- The dispersal of "power" among groups and within institutions on the basis of cultural, social, racial, sexual, and economic parity.
- The establishment and promotion of collaboration as the best mechanism for enabling culturally independent groups to function cooperatively within a multicultural environment.

The accomplishment of these and other goals can be facilitated only through a national effort. Therefore, the emergence of the National Coalition for Cultural Pluralism is an important first step in the right direction. . . .[7]

———•◆•———

The fostering of pluralism encourages the perpetuation and development of many different value systems. What are values? Phenix has recognized two distinct meanings of the term *values:* ". . . a value is anything which a person or persons actually approve, desire, affirm, or expect themselves to obtain, preserve, or assist. According to the second meaning, a value is anything which *ought to be* approved, desired, and so forth, whether or not any given person or persons in fact do adopt these positive attitudes toward it."[8] Schools must be concerned with both definitions—they operate in "what is" and are expected to create "what ought to be," and have some difficulty being certain of the values in either case. The United States Constitution has set forth some values,

7. Ibid., pp. 149–50.
8. Philip O. Phenix, "Values in the Emerging American Civilization," *Teachers' College Record* 61(1960):356.

and a body of case law seeks to define them. What of issues not so clearly defined? What, for example, are the value preferences of different groups of people regarding honesty, cleanliness, manners, loyalty, sexual morality, and punctuality? As one reflects upon this problem it becomes clear that people cherish different viewpoints. Whose viewpoints should be perpetuated? When must individual freedom be sacrificed to the needs of society? Are there absolute values that must be accepted and adhered to by all for the success and vitality of our society? Or, are values relative in nature depending upon circumstances?

Absolutists believe that there are time-honored *truths,* upon which value systems can be based. These truths are generally thought of as being derived from either God or Nature. Relativists believe that—

———•◆•———

1. Moral or ethical rules are invented—not discovered—by man; they are not derived from natural or divine law.
2. As such, they are not necessarily universal or eternal; they may vary widely from culture to culture. This is not the same as "cultural relativism"—which regards any moral value as good if it conforms with the cultural norm in which it exists.
3. Moral or ethical rules can be expected to change over the course of time. What is true in one situation will be false in another because moral truth does not "stay put." However, change is not necessarily or even desirably rapid.
4. Moral rules vary according to the situation, provided we define situation as a "field" of psychological forces whose basic datum is the interaction of a person with his psychological environment. That is, a person interacts with a perceived (not to be confused with physical) environment and out of such interaction forms concepts

214

and principles which guide moral behavior at that time. (The domination of a specific psychological *situation* in governing moral choice is why we use the term "situational ethics".)

5. Like many other kinds of human commitment ethical principles, even though relativistic, may be cherished with great intensity—enough to "die for"—to use a trite but direct expression.[9]

———•—•———

The search for universal values continues while the trend is currently toward relativism. Sorokin has said:

———•—•———

"We live in an age in which no value, from God to private property, is universally accepted. There is no norm, from the Ten Commandments, to contractual rules and those of etiquette, that is universally binding . . . What one person or group affirms, another denies; what one pressure group extols, another vilifies . . . Hence the mental, moral, religious, social, economic and political anarchy that pervades our life and culture. . . ."[10]

———•—•———

Yet, it seems that if we are to survive in a pluralistic society some agreement on major or superordinate values must be reached. Further, these values must then be learned by children of that society. Such a system would certainly not preclude the holding of different values so long as they did not conflict with the overall values.

Havighurst has suggested that the following, which he considers to be values of an urban, industrial, democratic society, and *not* social class values, must be taught by the American schools:

———•—•———

Punctuality, orderliness, conformity to group norms, desire for a work career based on skill and knowledge, desire for a stable family life, inhibition of aggressive impulses, rational approach to a problem situation, enjoyment of study, and desire for freedom of self and others.[11]

———•—•———

The task of the schools in doing their part in educating youth for citizenship in pluralistic urban America is both complex and immense.

The School and Its Relationship to Social Problems

The United States has many unresolved problems both foreign and domestic; problems that affect groups and individuals; problems that individuals expect society to help them solve. In many cases these problems are so complex an individual may feel helpless as he faces them. The days of the American pioneer resolutely and quite individually making his way in his environment are fast fading. Today, man's destiny is strongly interdependent on that of others; his basic necessities of life, such as food, shelter, and clothing, are difficult to create by himself. The American citizen today exists

9. Maurice P. Hunt, "Some Views on Situational Morality," *Phi Delta Kappan* 50(1969):454.

10. Pitirim Sorokin, *The Reconstruction of Humanity* (Boston: Beacon Press, 1948), p. 104.

11. Robert J. Havighurst, "Overcoming Value Differences," *The Inner-City Classroom: Teacher Behaviors,* ed. Robert D. Strom, pp. 47–48 (Columbus, Ohio: Charles E. Merrill Publishing Company, 1966).

in a complicated environmental system over which he as an individual has very little control. Therefore, his individual problems become social problems which require the organized efforts of society to solve. Schools as agencies of society are looked to as one resource for solving these problems. Let us briefly examine some of these problems.

Race Relationships

A rather persistent major social problem throughout history that has received in-

creased attention in the United States the last decade has been that of race relations. In 1954 the United States Supreme Court in *Brown* v. *Board of Education of Topeka* reversed prior decisions supporting the separate but equal doctrine, and said that separate but equal facilities in education were inherently unequal. The Court based its reasoning on the idea that while schools may be equally excellent educationally, with highly qualified staff members and superior facilities, they will differ because of the composition of the student population. This difference, if based on racial segregation, will have an adverse effect upon

Physical integration in the classroom is one beginning step in achieving social integration wherein hopefully members of each group accept and respect members of the other group.

A form of integration in the classroom. School integration has been interpreted as including an integrated faculty, an integrated student body, and a faculty-student combination form of integration.

black students. Since the *Brown* decision, some progress has been made in integrating schools in both the South and the North. School segregation in the North has been most often termed *de facto* segregation. This type of segregation is considered to be of the fact and not "deliberate," resulting primarily from neighborhood residence patterns and neighborhood schools. The *Brown* decision made *de jure* or "deliberate" segregation illegal. The legal status of de facto segregation is still in question. Courts have ruled that attendance center (neighborhood school) lines are illegal if drawn in such a way to promote segregation

(*Taylor* v. *Board of Education in New Rochelle, New York*). They have also ruled that de facto segregation in and of itself is not illegal. The issue becomes further complicated when an entire school population of a district or city becomes predominantly black. In these circumstances, arrangements involving complex legal problems would have to be made to transport students from one school district to another, and in some instances from one state to another. Some plans involving voluntary exchange of students to foster integration have been made. Other programs which attempt to resolve the problem of segregated schools have included bussing, open enrollment, redistricting, creation of educational parks, and consolidation, Bussing plans involve the transportation of students, both white and black, from one school to another in order to bring about racial balance. Theoretically, open enrollment basically permits students to enroll in any school of their choice. Redistricting involves the redrawing of school attendance boundary lines to facilitate racial balance. Consolidation plans are designed to merge smaller school districts into larger ones, and thus permit a more desirable racial balance. Educational parks represent an attempt to group elementary and secondary school facilities in planned locations so that the pupils who attend come from a wide area, thus avoiding segregation that results from neighborhood schools. Recent complication to the resolution of the problem has been a growing tendency for black separatism, in which black leaders have opposed integration as strongly and vociferously as white segregationists have.

Kenneth Clark, a psychologist who provided the NAACP with much of the social scientific data upon which the Supreme Court's decision in *Brown* v. *Board of Education of Topeka* was based, has recently written an article reflecting on that decision and its many ramifications, both direct and subtle. His comments are reproduced here in their entirety.

———— • • ————

The history of civil rights litigation in state and federal courts up to the *Brown* decision of 1954 can be understood in terms of a basic struggle, dating back to the *Dred Scott* decision of 1857, to determine the social and judicial perception of the Negro, to determine how the Negro is to be perceived and treated in relation to the treatment of other human beings within the framework of American democracy.

The underlying problem was that the Negro was regarded as semi-human or in some subtle way as subhuman; and as not only different, but different and inferior. The common denominator of *Dred Scott, Plessy vs. Ferguson,* and almost all related court decisions up to *Brown* was that the Negro in some way was special and inherently unworthy of the rights white American citizens would be expected to have without question and without litigation. Indeed, the fact that the Negro was required to persist in seeking judicial determination of his rights was, in itself, indicative of the basic racist reality of the society of which he was a part.

Therefore, the May 31, 1955, implementing decision of the Supreme Court in *Brown,* which enunciated a policy of guidance to the states for carrying out the *Brown* mandate to desegregate public schools "with all deliberate speed," was a conscious effort to make fundamental social change less disruptive. The court, in seeking to facilitate a rational and orderly transition from a system of segregation to one of nonsegregated schools, asked that such criteria as "local conditions" be considered. It was clear that in this decision the court was stepping outside the limited role of determining the constitutionality of segregation and was assuming the more complex role of establishing guidelines for administrative and social change.

Some observers interpreted this decision —with some justification—as the court's accepting the gradualist approach as means for effective desegregation. In retrospect, the "deliberate speed" formula seems a serious error to many, including Supreme Court Justice Hugo Black, who criticized the court in a 1968 statement. In practice it seems to have led to more rather than to less disruption. Here, court reliance on social science evidence would have been useful, for students of social

218 change have observed that prompt, decisive action on the part of recognized authorities usually results in less anxiety and less resistance in cases where the public is opposed to the action than does a more hesitant and gradual procedure. It is similar to the effect of quickly pulling off adhesive tape—the pain is sharper but briefer, and hence more tolerable.

The essential questions faced by the Supreme Court were not questions of legal precedent, historical in nature, but questions relating to the social consequences of legally imposed segregation. Without such evidence, the court could only speculate about the probable damage caused by the violation of Constitutional rights implicit in segregated education. The social scientists testified concerning the damage inherent in the total pattern of segregation on the human personality. On the basis of their testimony, the court held that separate educational facilities are inherently unequal by virtue of being separate. By providing such evidence, the social scientists made it possible to avoid the need to obtain proof of individual damage, and to avoid assessment of the equality of facilities in each individual school situation. The assumption of inequality could now be made wherever segregation existed.

However, in doing so, the court, which appeared to rely on the findings of social scientists in the 1954 decision, rejected the findings in handing down the 1955 implementation decision. An empirical study of various forms and techniques of desegregation suggested that the gradual approach to desegregation did not increase its chances of success or effectiveness. The findings further suggested that forthright, direct desegregation within the minimum time required for the necessary administrative changes tended to facilitate the progress. Gradualism or any form of ambiguity and equivocation on the part of those with the power of deci-

sion was interpreted by the segregationists as indecision, provided them with the basis for increasing resistance, and gave them time to organize, intensify, and prolong their opposition. The pattern of massive resistance and sporadic, violent opposition to desegregation occurred after the 1955 decision. There is no evidence that a more direct, specific, and concrete implementation decree would have resulted in any more tension, procrastination, or evasion than the seemingly rational, statesmanlike deliberate speed decision of the court. It does not seem likely that the pace of public school desegregation could have been slower.

The results of "all deliberate speed" have been ironic and tragic. In the South, where, admittedly, American racism was most violent, primitive, and deeply rooted, progress could be substantial and still leave a racist society fundamentally untouched. After *Brown,* a number of Southern states developed and tested strategies of resistance to the court decision. Massive resistance of interposition was resorted to in defiance of the court, and the degree of integration in elementary and secondary schools has been minimal. Nevertheless, the South has accepted or initiated more overt changes than the North. In fact, the South can look at the North with a certain ironic condescension in terms of the acceptance of rapid change toward a non-racist society.

The North, for its part, did not think the *Brown* decision applied to its schools. The North had joined earlier in the Negro reaction against Southern resistance to change. Now it became clear that racism was also virulent in the North, all the more insidious for its having been long unrecognized. Even Negroes had not consciously acknowledged the depth of racism inherent in Northern society. And when the North discovered its racism, it tended to provide justification for it. In addition, in the academic community, it began to be clear in the 1960s that apparently sophisticated and compassionate theories used to explain slow Negro student performance might themselves be tainted with racist condescension. Some of the theories of "cultural deprivation," "the disadvantaged," and the like, popular in educational circles and in high governmental spheres until recently and in fact still prevalent, were backed for the most part by inconclusive and fragmentary research and much speculation. The eagerness with which such theories were greeted was itself a subtly racist symptom.

The cultural deprivation theory rejects explanations of inherent racial or biological inferiority, and asserts that the total pattern of racial prejudice, discrimination, and segregation found in a racist society blocks the capacity of school personnel to teach minority group children with the same observable efficiency as that given other children. These children may, therefore, be expected to remain academically retarded no matter how well they are taught. Among the specific barriers emphasized by different writers in varying degrees are: environmentally determined sensory deficiencies; withdrawn or hyperactive behavior; low attention span; peculiar or bizarre language patterns; lack of verbal stimulation; absence of father or stable male figure in the home; and lack of books in the home.

In spite of the fact that these factors have dominated the literature and have been frequently repeated and generally accepted as explanations of the academic retardation of lower status children, they have not been verified as causal factors through any precise and systematic research reported in the published literature. The evidence, or indeed lack of evidence, suggests, therefore, that this concept has gained acceptance through intuition, general impressions, and repetition.

Nevertheless, cultural deprivation theorists have not only provided the public school

educational establishment with a respectable rationalization for maintaining the status quo of educational inefficiency for low status children, but the related technology of this theory —compensatory or educational enrichment programs—appears to provide the basis for inherent contradictions in its premises and assumptions.

An uncritical acceptance of this theory and explanation seems to be contradicted by:

■ the concretely demonstrated psychological fact of the normal curve in the distribution of human intellectual potential, personality characteristics, motivation, and other personal characteristics believed to be related to academic performance;

■ the modifiableness of human beings;

■ the fact that normal human beings who are taught, motivated to learn, expected to learn, and provided with conditions conducive to learning, will learn up to or near the limits of their capacity.

Furthermore, the cultural deprivation theories are clear violations of the law of parsimony, since they seek more complex explanations without determining that simpler explanations are not adequate. Cultural deprivation theories appear to by-pass more direct and specific educational variables such as quality of teaching and supervision, acceptance or rejection of the students by teachers, and educational methods and facilities.

Given the history of educational rejection of Negro children, it would seem obvious to one trained in the methods of science that much more direct variables would have to be held constant and checked out with more precision and more sensitive instruments than the Coleman report [*Equality of Educational Opportunity,* by James Coleman] does before one could resort to the more elaborate, ambiguous, and seemingly uncontrollable catchall variable of cultural

220 deprivation. In this regard it is significant that the literature, while eloquent and repetitive in its expansion of the cultural deprivation hypothesis, is almost totally silent on discussions or research that seek to determine the relationship between subtle or flagrant rejection of a child by his teachers because of race, color, economic status and family income, and the level of his academic performance. These social, psychological, and educational variables seem worthy of a serious attention and research that they have not as yet received.

Theories of cultural deprivation are often regarded as liberal, because they posit environmental inadequacy rather than genetic inferiority, and because they are often used to support demands for integration. The problem with this approach, exemplified by the Coleman report, is that it concludes that the environmentally caused characteristics of white children are the positive component of integrated schools, and that Negro children educationally gain primarily from association with white children.

Further research is necessary to determine whether correlation and causal factors have been confused in this important study. But perhaps most important, it is necessary to study the majority white school as a total unit as compared to the majority Negro school, to determine what happens in the school itself *because* white children are present. Sensitive instruments must be sought to measure teacher and administrative expectations, counseling attitudes, quality of curriculum, and the like, but beyond the assessment of these individual factors it is necessary to evaluate the total pattern of advantage or deprivation.

On the basis of years of observation and research of ghetto education, I would advance the proposition that one would find a significantly high correlation between a pattern of deprivation and ghetto schools, and a pattern

of advantage and white urban and suburban schools. It is not the presence of the white child per se that leads to higher achievement for the Negro child who associates with him in class; it is the quality of the education provided because the white child is there that makes the difference or so I believe the empirical evidence indicates. To argue, without irrefutable proof, that this is not the case is to lend support to a racially defined environmental theory of academic achievement that is no less callous in its consequences than a genetic theory of racial inferiority would be.

Perhaps the most ironic development since the 1954 *Brown* decision, however, has not been the continuation of white racism in the South, nor the acknowledgment of the more subtle white racism of the North, but the emergence and growth of black racism. In 1954, when the *Brown* decision was handed down, desegregation and integration were the priority of the civil rights movement and Negroes generally. Fifteen years later, many militants have proclaimed the death of the civil rights movement and have denied the value of integration itself, and specifically have questioned the significance of the *Brown* decision and the truth of the social science findings on which it rested. One must thus look at the decision and its social science foundation from a new perspective, and inquire whether these charges are justified.

During the period since 1954, black nationalism has experienced a sharp rise in support from young Negro militants and from many whites. This represents in some forms the continuation of the nationalism of the Garvey movement of the 1920s, identifiable in degree by the black nationalism of Malcolm X. In other, and more serious, manifestations it has gained support among Negro students and youth. The seeming common denomination of both is the repudiation of integration and the apparent repudiation of the struggle for desegregation, the rejection of the *Brown* decision, and the implicit rejection of the whole rationale and psychological approach to the meaning of racism. This would logically include a denial of the social science explanation of the inevitability of inferiority in segregated systems, on which the *Brown* decision depended.

Under the guise of assuming a positive identity, black nationalism has adopted an imitation of white racism with its hallowing of race, its attempt to make a virtue out of color, its racist mystique. This rationale argues that the detrimental consequences of a biracial society are neutralized or transformed into positive consequences by virtue of the fact that Negroes themselves are now asserting the value of racism. This argument would give primary weight to voluntarism, that is, that racism would lead to affirmative not negative results if it were voluntarily accepted or sought by the previous victims, as it was voluntarily maintained by the oppressors. The character of racism would depend on the attitude one had toward it; it would have no objective reality of its own.

The paranoia of racism, whether imposed or sought, must rest on insecurity. It is the verification of the psychological interpretation of the negative consequences of segregation. Racism does produce doubts and insecurities in the victims as well as in the perpetrators. It increases hostility and aggression and self-hatred.

The Lorelei quest for identity through racism is based on superstition. Despite the verbal transformation from self-contempt to apparent pride, the conditions of injustice remain. We are asked to obscure them by the rhetorical posturing of pride. In a strikingly similar analogy, it is psychologically obvious that any man who proclaims how irresistible and potent and virile he is must have deep doubts about it. He would clearly be regarded as preoccupied with sexual anxiety. Such self-pretense conceals—or attempts

to conceal—deep, poignant, and tragic insecurity. Given the fact that the realities of racism in America have not changed, that the Negro is still condemned to segregated schools, to segregated and deteriorated residential areas, and to an economic role that is not competitive with the white society, the cult of blackness must be recognized as what it is —a ritualized denial of anguished despair and resentment of the failure of society to meet its promises.

Separatism is an attempt to create verbal realities as substitutes for social, political, and economic realities. It is another and intense symptom of the psychological damage a racist society inflicts on its victims.

A specific indication of the damage of separatism is that the victims internalize racism. Some forms of black separatism involve genuine and deep self-destructive, suicidal dynamics. They reflect the most cruel, barbaric, tragic, dehumanizing consequences of white oppression—the wish of the oppressed to die—and in dying to destroy others in a similar predicament. The white racists who so damage their fellow human beings must be prepared to face the same judgment the Nazis, who sent millions to death camps, must face.

Responding to a button reading "Being Black Is Not Enough," some Negroes have said, "Well, being white has always been enough." But if one looks at the moral decay, the instability, and the unresolved problems of white society, one perceives that being white is not enough, that it is effective only in terms of self-aggrandizement and at the expense of exploitation of those who are not white. Its success depends on victimization, for racism is not only subjective, it also demands an object. Positive racism has the necessary obverse of rejection of all those who do not happen to meet the chosen racial criteria.

So, rather than refute the social science assumptions that led to the *Brown* decision,

222 the present cult of black separatism intensely verifies it. Black separatism can be seen as a "sour-grapes-and-sweet-lemon" reaction against the failure of the society to implement and enforce the findings of *Brown.*

The vocal, well-publicized, well-endowed cult has to be understood for what it is, for otherwise it can be cynically manipulated and used by white racists who are now the often silent allies of the separatists. The rationale of the sophisticated white intellectual who endorses black separatism in his university, his church, his political party, his academic or professional society, while continuing to live in a restricted suburb and continuing to support the institutional relegation of Negroes to inferior status, must be seen by Negroes for what it is: an attempt to handle racial antiviolence, to deal with guilt.

The basic standard for such understanding is that which functioned in the *Brown* decision, namely that racism and segregation are a reflection of superstition, institutionalized untruth, cruelty, and injustice, and that race is irrelevant as a criterion for preference or rejection. The poignant tragedy is that the society is using the victimized groups as the agent for the perpetuation of irreconcilable injustice and racial irrelevance. Any white or black intellectual who denies this must be more comfortable with superstition and rationalization. One cannot deal with the reorganization of society on a nonracial basis by intensifying racist symptoms.

Nor can one build a solid pride on the quicksands of emotion, anger, rage, hatred —no matter how justifiable. Genuine pride —the pride that makes life worth the struggle with some hope of serenity—must come from solid personal achievement from sensitivity and concern and respect for one's fellow man, from compassion and willingness to struggle to give some substance to one's own life by trying to help others live with confidence in the possibility of positives. Pride, like humility, is destroyed by one's insistence that he possesses it.

Racism in any form is dangerous, but particularly, as is now true among many whites and Negroes, when it is intellectually supported. Such supporters often fail to follow the implication of their rhetoric to its logical conclusion: that, if segregation and separatism are desirable and good as a phase and as a means, they are even more to be desired as ends in themselves.

All the implications of the *Brown* decision and all the social science arguments in its support point to the inherent dangers of racism. The latest surge toward self-imposed separatism is the greatest verification of all. I read into the separatist movement among Negroes a more severe symptom than those described in *Brown.* It convinces me even more persuasively that we must redouble our efforts to obliterate racism, whatever its manifestations, wherever it appears.[12]

———————•·•———————

In addition to the *Brown* decision, Title IV of the 1964 Civil Rights Act specifies that racial discrimination must end in all programs receiving federal financial assistance in order to qualify for future aid. This additional legislative aid provided incentive power to bring about further integration. Between 1954 and 1964 integration moved at a very slow pace in the South. Since the passage of the Civil Rights Act of 1964 it has proceeded more rapidly. In 1964, only about one percent of the Negro pupils in the South attended integrated schools; by 1969, the percentage of Negro pupils attend-

12. Kenneth B. Clark, "Fifteen Years of Deliberate Speed," *Saturday Review,* December 20, 1969, pp. 59–61, 70. Copyright Saturday Review, Inc., 1969. Used by permission.

ing integrated schools had risen to approximately twenty percent. It is important to note that in interpreting these percentages an integrated school is considered to be one that Negroes attend in which a majority of the pupils in attendance are white.[13]

A sample of data in 1971 taken from large city districts around the nation revealed that in many instances Negro students still attend schools whose enrollments are predominately minority pupils. Figure 8.1 presents data on the percentages of Negro pupils in schools by degree of segregation.

The Civil Rights Act of 1964 resulted in the Department of Health, Education, and Welfare being charged with the responsibility of enforcing those portions of the Act that pertained to education. Various guidelines and timetables were established. The original guidelines came out in April 1965 and called for integration of all grades by

13. "The Progress of School Desegregation in the South," *U.S. News and World Report,* May 19, 1969, p. 51.

the fall of 1967. They were subsequently revised and the fall of 1969 was established as the deadline for compliance. In the summer of 1969, HEW indicated that there would be a slight easing of desegregation guidelines in the most troublesome districts of the South. This announcement was followed by a flurry of various kinds of announcements and pronouncements. The most significant end product of the activity was that the U.S. Supreme Court on October 29, 1969, ruled that the Constitution no longer allows "all deliberate speed" as a standard for desegregation. The decision called for integration immediately in all school districts, and struck down the Nixon administration's late summer policy decision to delay desegregation in thirty-three Mississippi school districts.

Desegregation thrusts are also being made toward the North. The Justice Department has filed a desegregation suit against the Madison County School District in Illinois. It has also accused the Chicago Board of Education of maintaining and perpetuating

School District	Percent Negro Students in District	Percent Negro Students Attending Schools Which Are Minority Schools		
		0–49.9%	80–100%	100%
Los Angeles, California	24.9	6.8	86.6	7.6
Cleveland, Ohio	57.3	4.6	91.3	35.4
St. Louis, Missouri	67.7	2.1	89.8	47.5
Jefferson City, Kentucky	3.8	85.8	14.2	—
Newark, New Jersey	72.0	2.6	91.3	22.5
Oakland, California	58.1	6.3	73.1	1.6
El Paso, Texas	3.0	70.9	18.5	—
Akron, Ohio	27.8	33.7	40.2	2.9
St. Paul, Minnesota	7.0	68.4	9.6	—
Shawnee Mission, Kansas	.4	91.7	1.9	1.9

Figure 8.1 Negro Pupils in Schools by Degree of Segregation in School, 1971.

Source: Adapted from *Indicators of Educational Outcome, Fall 1972* (Washington, D.C.: U.S. Government Printing Office, 1973), p. 56.

224 faculty segregation. The legal actions in desegregation are presented in greater detail in chapter sixteen.

It should be recognized that race problems in the United States have many causes and that the efforts to promote integration, while concentrated heavily on the schools, cannot be completely resolved by the schools. The resolution of racial issues resides in the attitudes of citizens, both black and white. While these attitudes are formulated under strong influences within the home and within peer group associations of the child, the school can and must continue to be a strong influence on the attitudes developed by the pupils.

Poor People in America

Another domestic social problem which is intimately related to education is that of poverty. While the United States is one of the richest nations on earth in terms of material wealth, some of its people suffer from extreme poverty. The definition of poverty as revised in 1969 ranges from an income of $1,757 for an unrelated individual sixty-five years old to $6,101 for a family of seven or more persons.[14] The average poverty threshold in 1969 for a non-farm family of four headed by a male was $3,745.[15] In 1969, about one out of ten families was poor, compared to one out of five in 1959.[16] As of 1969 there were 24.3 million persons with incomes below the poverty level.[17] Out of approximately 52 million families in the United States in 1970, nearly 3 million of them had incomes of less than $5,000.[18]

There is a far greater percentage of nonwhite people affected by poverty than white people. Approximately 20.1 percent of the nonwhite and 7.5 percent of the white families in our country are now living in poverty.[19] While there is a higher percentage of nonwhite families living in poverty, numerically there are many more impoverished white families.

Many more statistics could be cited to further delineate the problem. Let it suffice to conclude that poverty in America is a very serious problem; that while poverty affects both whites and nonwhites, the problem percentage-wise is much more serious for nonwhites; that it is widely distributed throughout both metropolitan and farm areas; and that with the exception of the suburban area, approximately one of every four children is being reared under conditions of poverty.

How does the poverty problem relate to education? Children of poverty, sometimes inaccurately labeled as "culturally deprived" or "disadvantaged," simply do not possess at the time of entrance into school as many of the skills needed for success in school as those children who have not been impoverished. This is caused by combinations of many factors, among them physical debilitation, lack of intellectual stimulation, different cultural background, negative self-concept, and many more factors related to their environmental background. Further,

14. U.S. Department of Commerce, Bureau of the Census, "24 Million Americans—Poverty in the United States 1969," Current Population Reports, series P–60, no. 76, p. 18.
15. Ibid.
16. Ibid., p. 1.

17. Ibid.
18. U.S. Department of Commerce, Bureau of the Census, "Income in 1970 of Families and Persons in the United States," Current Population Reports, series P–60, no. 80, p. 1.
19. Ibid., p. 22.

and perhaps more significantly, many schools have not developed the kinds of programs necessary to enable these students to succeed. As a result, their poverty background is reinforced by failure in school. Many teachers, either having been of the middle class originally or having become a part of the middle class due to upward social mobility, have difficulty in relating to and therefore teaching impoverished children. The schools then have the task of adjusting their programs, changing their techniques, doing their very best to enable their students to obtain the skills necessary to compete fa-

Substandard housing is a reflection of unemployment and poverty.

226 vorably in our society. The federal government has recognized this task, and is endeavoring to help. Title I, in particular, of the Elementary and Secondary Act of 1965 provides funds to state education agencies specifically for the purpose of improving education programs for the poor. Under Title I, local school districts design programs, ranging from those providing physical necessities such as eyeglasses and shoes to those providing counselors and remedial reading specialists to supplement their existing programs. Funds are allocated on the basis of the number of poor families in a school district. Other federal programs such as Head Start, National Teacher Corps, and Upward Bound were and are aimed at improving the opportunities of the poor.

Jencks and Bane in their controversial essay "The Schools and Equal Opportunity" challenged the assumption that the primary reason poor children cannot escape from poverty is that they do not acquire basic cognitive skills. Among other evidence, they point out the fact that there is almost as much economic inequality among those who score high on standardized tests as there is in the general population. Jencks concludes:

———•———

In America, as elsewhere, the long-term drift over the past 200 years has been toward equality. In America, however, the contribution of public policy to this drift has been slight. As long as egalitarians assume that public policy cannot contribute to equality directly but must proceed by ingenius manipulations of marginal institutions like the schools, this pattern will continue. If we want to move beyond this tradition, we must establish political control over the economic institutions that shape our society. What we will need, in short, is what other countries call socialism. Anything less will end in the same disappointment as the reforms of the 1960's.[20]

———•———

For a complete discussion and rebuttals to Jencks' assertions the interested student might wish to read *Christopher Jencks in Perspective* published by the American Association of School Administrators, or "Perspectives on Inequality," reprint series no. 8, *Harvard Educational Review*.

Unemployment

Closely related to poverty are unemployment and underemployment (that is, individuals working at jobs who are qualified for better jobs). It has been estimated that today there are about 10 million underemployed, 6.5 million of whom work full-time and earn less than the annual poverty wage. Approximately 500,000 of the unemployed are "hardcore" unemployed who lack the basic education necessary to secure and hold a job.[21] Daniel P. Moynihan has expressed the importance of employment quite poignantly:

———•———

The principal measure of progress toward equality will be that of employment. It is the primary source of individual or group identity. In America what you do is what you are: to do nothing is to be nothing; to do little is to be little. The equations are implacable and blunt, and ruthlessly public. . . .

———•———

20. Christopher Jencks and Mary Jo Bane, "The Schools and Equal Opportunity," *Saturday Review,* September 16, 1972, pp. 37–42.
21. *Report of the National Advisory Commission on Civil Disorders,* p. 414.

In relating to the Negro American he continued:

———•—•———

For the Negro American, (employment) is already and will continue to be the master problem. It is the measure of white bona fides. It is the measure of Negro competence, and also of the competence of American society. Most importantly, the linkage between problems of employment and the range of social pathology that afflicts the Negro community is unmistakable. Employment not only controls the present for the Negro American, but in a most profound way, it is creating the future as well.[22]

———•—•———

There is a relationship between unemployment rates and years of school completed. Figure 8.2 illustrates the relationship. While the relationship is not perfect, undoubtedly because of other variables, the positive correlation between increased level of education and reduced unemployment rate is evident.

22. Ibid., p. 252.

Further, with the exception of the elementary level of education, and exclusive of eight years of education completed, the nonwhite rates of unemployment are higher than those for whites. Also, the unemployment rates for women tend to be higher than those for men. Recognizing that relationships are not indicative of "cause and effect," nevertheless, one possible explanation of the data in respect to nonwhites and women could be discrimination.

Do the schools have a societal role to fill in solving the problem of unemployment and underemployment? They certainly do, from basic reading and writing skills to vocational and technical training programs for adults. Efforts are being made in these directions in high schools through day and night programs, technical and trade schools, and community colleges. Further, schools must continue to urge equal opportunity for education and employment in society. Again, though, the schools cannot completely resolve the problem; they can, as one agency of society, however, make a major contribution.

Years of School Completed		Unemployment Rates (Percent of Civilian Labor Force)				
		Total	Men	Women	Nonwhite	White
Total U.S.		5.8	5.5	6.4	8.8	5.5
Elementary	1–4 years*	6.4	6.4	6.6	4.7	7.2
	5–7 years	7.7	8.0	6.9	7.4	7.7
	8 years	6.4	5.9	7.5	9.7	6.1
High School	1–3 years	8.7	8.0	9.8	11.7	8.1
	4 years	5.5	5.0	6.0	8.7	5.1
College	1–3 years	5.6	5.6	5.7	6.5	3.8
	4 years or more	2.3	2.0	2.8		

* Includes no school years completed

Figure 8.2   Unemployment Rates by Years of School Completed, 1971

Source: Adapted from *Indicators of Educational Outcome, Fall 1972* (Washington, D.C.: U.S. Government Printing Office, 1973), p. 33.

228   *Crime and Violence*

A fourth issue, contributed to by problems of race relationships, poverty, and unemployment, is that of crime and violence. In the late 1960s and early 1970s civil disorders increased, ranging from riots in cities to campus takeovers to student protests in high schools, reaching the point where the schools were closed. Does this problem have relevance to education? It most certainly does. Contributory causes of riots in the cities were racial difficulties, poverty, and unemployment. The late President Johnson, in an address to the nation on July 27, 1967, in referring to riots and violence, said:

———— • ————

. . . The only genuine, long-range solution for what has happened lies in an attack—mounted at every level—upon the conditions that breed despair and violence. All of us know what those conditions are: ignorance, discrimination, slums, poverty, disease, not enough jobs. We should attack these conditions—not because we are frightened by conflict, but because we are fired by conscience. We should attack them because there is simply no other way to achieve a decent and orderly society in America. . . .

———— • ————

Schools cannot ignore these issues. They must attack with the peaceful weapons of education to solve them.

The causes of riots and campus violence were researched, and no single cause stood out boldly among the rest. It became apparent, however, that social unrest in society was reflected in its collegiate institutions. Students in the early 1970s were calling for greater degrees of participation in determining their destinies. They wanted a vote, or at least a strong voice, in curriculum decision making and the hiring and firing of faculty. Many colleges and universities placed students on committees to assure them a voice in their education. Further, the doctrine of *loco parentis* was markedly altered. This trend is discussed in further detail in chapter sixteen.

Drug Abuse

Senator Harold E. Hughes, as chairman of the Senate subcommittee on alcoholism and narcotics, in referring to drug abuse said: "The truth is that we have a cancerous problem that has the capability of destroying our society. By and large, we have not begun to awaken to its magnitude."[23]

Data that indicate the magnitude of the problem include:

- Of the 18 million public secondary students, 6 million are taking drugs illegally.
- Twelve to fifteen percent of the public secondary students are taking marijuana and other soft drugs on a regular basis.
- From two percent to three percent of the public secondary students are hooked hopelessly on hard drugs like heroin.
- Nationwide, arrests of persons under eighteen for narcotics violations grew an almost unbelievable 1860% from 1960 to 1968, according to the Federal Bureau of Narcotics Director Ingersoll.[24]

Professor John Eddy has been working and teaching in the area of drug addiction since 1954. His observations are pertinent:

———— • ————

23. National School Public Relations Association, *Drug Crisis,* p. 3.
24. Ibid., pp. 3–4.

Alcohol

The drug that is most widely used among youth as well as adults is alcohol. The nation has over ten million alcoholics, and this number is increasing. The biggest single contributor to road accidents and deaths on the highways is the consumption of alcohol. Over half the vehicle wrecks are related to drinking and driving. It is estimated that the misuse of alcohol cost the nation's economy over fifteen billion dollars in accidents, decreased productivity, and absenteeism in 1973, Alcohol-related deaths by vehicles are over 28,000 per year. The National Institute on Alcohol Abuse reports that their figures show that 85 percent of American youth have alcohol drinking experiences before they reach 18 years of age. School personnel are misguided if they take any comfort in youth being attracted to alcohol rather than to "drugs," however, for alcohol is the most serious drug problem we have.

Smoking Tobacco

Statements that smoking is dangerous to health appear on cigarette packs today, and cigarette commercials are banned on television—still, the rating of smoking tobacco remains high. Lung cancer took over 70,000 persons by death in 1973 with the majority cigarette-related, and a heavy smoker can reduce his life by about sixteen years. However, as with alcohol and other drugs, persons rationalize by saying, "It can't happen to me," or "As long as we are going to die eventually, what does it matter?" Even when a person quits smoking completely, it takes a number of years before his or her lungs heal over and improve. Marijuana, according to surveys, is the third choice of both youth and adults in drug use with alcohol first and tobacco second. However, both alcohol and tobacco are legal drugs whereas marijuana is an illegal drug in this country. Nevertheless,

users of tobacco and marijuana most commonly smoke both of them. Research recently has pointed out that both nicotine in tobacco and marijuana cause lung cancer as the gases get into the body. If marijuana is ever legalized, it will add one more drug to the public market that has proven itself to have adverse affects similar to those of nicotine and alcohol when used in extreme.

Other Drugs

The Second Report of the National Commission on Marijuana and Drug Abuse, published in March, 1973, confirms the suspected trends in drug abuse behavior. Drug use is more widespread among youth than among persons over thirty. Drug abuse is more common in metropolitan than rural areas. Alcohol, usually beer, is the drug most abused among youth. Youth experimenters are increasingly using drugs other than alcohol and tobacco—most young people are in the category of experimenters who try a drug once or twice. The order of preferred use of drugs is alcohol (with beer, wine, and hard liquor representing the order of frequency), tobacco, marijuana, over-the-counter drugs, prescription sedatives, prescription tranquilizers, prescription stimulants, hallucinogens (e.g., LSD), glue or other inhalants, cocaine, and heroin.

It should be pointed out that this study admits to problems concerning validity and reliability. Moreover, the report gives the impression that more is unrevealed about the extent of youth drug abuse than is shown. For example, allusions to "patterns of use," "percentages without raw data," and "conversions" from survey data to "rates of increase" are difficult to assess, as they appear to remove humanistic considerations from the evaluation of the drug problem. Even the commission recognizes that the composites may not be representative of all schools in this country.

Schools As Drug Sources

As embarrassing and as impossible as it may seem to some school personnel—some officials deny it even after a study is made by competent, nonpartisan observers of their schools—many schools are the main distribution centers for drugs. Early in 1973, a team of *Chicago Sun-Times* reporters went into Chicago and suburban elementary and secondary schools (private, parochial, and public) to find out the status of the drug use and abuse problem among students. The findings, published in the *Chicago Sun-Times* on April 29, 1973, were that "Chicago and suburban students can buy dangerous drugs—even heroin—almost as easily as their parents can purchase alcohol . . . and that a youth with a few dollars, a little ingenuity and a knowledge of street talk can get anything he or she wants, often just down the street from his or her school." This newspaper study, in essence, substantiates what other academic surveys, drug experts' best estimates, and other evaluations have been indicating for some time. The generalization to other parts of the nation may be made on the basis of urbanization, the development of the youth culture, and other factors.

In light of the difficulties facing school personnel, the drug problem is not about to be solved immediately or ever with the resources available. However, more can be done by school personnel than has been done in the past. . . .

In the past, as drug education has been carried on in the schools, different states have had different leaders for different facets of it as part of the total school curriculum. With the National Drug Education Training Program funding and training personnel, practices in the states have become more uniform, with local community approaches developing. In each state, there is a drug education coordinator. In Maine, for example, the state's original training program produced forty community teams that now conduct their own local school and community programs. Maine has set as its objective to have one or more drug education teams in each of its 136 school districts. Teen centers with "rap rooms" in storefront locations, churches, and other facilities throughout Maine are providing places for youth to gather with trained drug education personnel as well as parents or guardians. One of the most important ingredients for a successful drug education program is the handling of personnel in-service training—it will either make or break the program.

Not all drug education programs are equally good, nor should all continue without modification or improvement. In fact, some programs may be harming students. For example, in the first intensive study of the relationship between drug education and drug use (reported in the December 3, 1972, *Chicago Tribune* article "Drug Education Is Linked To Use") researchers have found that of 600 junior high school students in Ann Arbor, Michigan, who had received drug education classes increased their experimentation with illegal drugs. By contrast, the control group of 350 junior high school students who did not receive drug education classes did not experiment as much with illegal drugs. This study confirms previous surveys in California and Texas that assert that some drug education programs seem to be encouraging drug use. However, even Richard B. Stuart, who headed the research team, admitted the findings may not be accurate because students exposed to drug education might be more willing to acknowledge their drug experiences than those youths not involved in drug education classes. This same hypothesis is supported by the 1973 work of Horowitz and Sedlacek, as well as by the author's personal experience. Stuart's approach, primarily using a fact-oriented drug education curriculum is inadequate. It is important for the drug educator to recognize many different ways to treat and to rehabilitate drug abusers. Consequently, approaches that work for some persons fail with others.[25]

———•·•———

Drug addiction is certainly a serious problem. Schools must play a role in its reduction. The definition of the most effective role that schools can play is still to be determined. Drug abuse, like most other problems of society, is interrelated with other social problems, and has multiple causes.

While social problems other than race relations—or stated more broadly, intergroup conflict, poverty, unemployment, violence, and drug abuse—exist and are related to the schools, these particular problems stand out as being illustrative of some of the most urgent in this decade. It should be recognized that these problems are those of an urban industrial society and have grown in intensity as people have moved from farms and small towns to cities. The degree of interrelatedness of the social problems, one to another, each and all to the schools, further demonstrates the complexity of devising solutions.

The Role of the School: Transmit—Respond—Lead

What should be the posture of the school in American society? Historically, and into the present, schools have been responsible for the transmission of culture. In this role, as has been indicated, they have assumed a passive and reflective posture. What society deems has been the "good" of the past and is worth

25. John Eddy, *The Teacher and the Drug Scene*. Bloomington, Indiana: The Phi Delta Kappa Foundation, 1973, pp. 11–15. Used by permission.

231

preserving, even if not utilitarian or relevant, was presented to children in school for their use and for posterity. In many schools today, transmission is still the primary goal. However, schools have also added another role, a different posture: that of *responding*. As society changes, and needs are recognized in society that can be fulfilled by the school, the school responds or adjusts to these needs. For example, as computers were developed and operators were needed, the schools began to train the specialists necessary. Much of the schools' reactions to social problems fall into the response posture. As poverty was recognized as a problem, and children came to school hungry, the schools fed them. A third posture is possible, that of *leading*. In this posture the schools would strive to achieve the ideal society as it has been envisioned. In this role, the school acts as an agent of change for society, attempting to mold and shape it to desired ends. While schools did not serve as the initiator, they have been placed in a position of leadership in building an integrated society. It appears that they may be increasingly called upon to take the leadership role. Schools assume all three postures (transmit, respond, lead) in their various responsibilities. The blend of these postures changes as societal expectations change.

Commitments in Education: Universality—Equality— Liberation—Excellence

Four definite commitments have been in evidence in the development of education in the United States. These four, universality, equality, liberation, and excellence, are most intimately related to our society and culture. *Universality* refers to the basic idea

232   that every child should have a good common school education. Our forefathers recognized the importance of education to the survival of the concept of democratic living, and as states were formed, they placed in their constitutions the provision for a free common school education. This provision was most often accompanied by specific legislation requiring compulsory school attendance through a specified age. The age requirements varied, but ordinarily they were set to make certain that the child received an elementary education through approximately the eighth grade. This commitment for all practical purposes has been achieved and it has contributed greatly to the strength of our nation. Today, there is strong evidence of a commitment to universality in education beyond the common school; proportionately more and more students attend secondary schools, community colleges, colleges, universities, and various continuing education programs. Secondary education became legal (in a sense) in the famous *Kalamazoo Case* in 1872 when the Supreme Court of Michigan recognized the right of a community to tax itself for secondary schools. Communities now tax themselves directly for community colleges. America has done reasonably well in accomplishing its commitment to a common school education for all.

In terms of *equality* we have espoused equal opportunity. While legal strides have been made, realistically assessed, the goal has not been achieved. It is still quite apparent, for example, that the wealth of a local area has much to do with opportunity. States have tried to eliminate these disparaging differences with state aid formulas designed to equalize at least a minimum amount of expenditure per child for education. Differences in wealth among the states further compound

the national problem. As has been mentioned earlier, the residential living patterns also compound the issue, as the poor live with the poor, blacks with other blacks, and middle class persons with other middle class persons. Segregated education by race, and by criteria other than race (by social class, for example), deprives all youth of the richness of our culture and of the knowledge that they need, knowledge which can be gained by interaction with others. Social interaction which can be accomplished in schools seems necessary to help solve some of our major social problems. As a nation, we have much distance to travel before our commitment to equality has been met.

Liberation, closely related to equality, refers to the opportunity for individuals in our society to better themselves. While this requires individual motivation, it also requires a society that not only permits but encourages and facilitates personal advancement. Education is seen as a great liberator; the skills learned in school can help an individual to rise above his environment. The second generation of a family should, if we are meeting this commitment, do better than the first. This kind of development should continue. There is no question that it has for many people; but for others, such as those in many minority groups, or those in poverty, society has slowed down, blocked, and even trapped their progress. The situations of many of the poor have been perpetuated by our society, perhaps unconsciously; but nevertheless, it has happened. Education can provide the opportunity for liberation. We must, however, examine our educational system to make certain that it is providing opportunities rather than inhibiting them. To accomplish equality, changes will have to be made in much that is done in education. Herein lies an opportunity for schools to play the leadership role; they can in fact help change and mold society. They must, however, convince those who finance the schools, the American citizens, of the worthiness of their cause and their suggested solutions.

Excellence adds another dimension. In addition to providing basic education and basic opportunity for all, our future strength lies in using our human resources so that each individual can develop his unique talents to the fullest. At this task, to which we are committed, we have barely begun. To accomplish this excellence our instructional procedures must be modified; we need to do a better job of tailoring in order to suit our students. Again, herein lies a chance for schools to lead, to utilize their resources to the fullest and to gain more resources.

Point of View

A major emphasis in chapter eight dealt with the concept of a pluralistic society. Our larger society is made up of subgroups who have different values and different goals. As schools pursue their missions it is not unusual for subgroups to be in conflict. These conflicts must be resolved in some fashion for society to function. The article "Conflict: Make It Work for You" describes a technique used to train people to help them deal with conflict. The position is taken that conflict can be functional.

The subgroups in the illustration in the article include not only subgroups of the larger society, but subgroups of the school community; that is, teachers, principals, parents, paraprofessionals, and board members. Each of these subgroups professes to its values, and also possesses power. While the

concept of power was not discussed directly in chapter eight, power is a strong factor in our society and comes into play in the resolution of conflict. In many instances, power through domination results in a temporary solution to intergroup conflict.

The schools are expected to play a role in solving societal problems. As such they become, in some instances, the arena for debate. Occasionally they actually become a battleground.

Those who work in schools need to know how to deal with conflict. Brenton describes a technique, both emotional and rational in nature, that appears to be successful to some extent for the participants. The situations described in the article, while simulated, are *real*—that is, they have happened. The article is particularly relevant to urban heterogeneous situations. Needless to say, however, it is a very unusual area that is free from conflict. America is pluralistic; its cities, states, and communities are pluralistic. Its schools are pluralistic. Ways to resolve intergroup conflict are welcome; ways to help individuals deal with conflict are also welcome.

————————◆•◆————————

Conflict
Make It Work for You

Myron Brenton

The great majority of citizens from all corners of the United States would most likely agree with the thesis that conflict is bad, dysfunctional to society—and conversely, that

Myron Brenton, "Conflict: Make It Work for You," *American Education* 9 (January-February 1973): 30–32.

234 peace and harmony are good and the proper state of things. It is, to be sure, a comfortable and comforting national notion and to dispute it would be considered rudely un-American— like carping on the dietary imperfections of Mom's apple pie. And yet, last summer on the Southern Connecticut State College campus at New Haven, in a workshop called, "Dynamics of Intergroup Conflict," this red, white, and blue notion itself was tagged as "dysfunctional."

"Only in the cemetery is there a situation truly without conflict. In all life there's continuous conflict, and under certain conditions the conflict process can work for you." Thus spoke Benjamin N. Levy, director of the college's Center for Urban Studies and the man behind the summer workshop idea. Ever since 1969, with grants from the Commission on Aid to Higher Education, Levy has been demonstrating that conflict can be used creatively. His annual workshop, now part of the college's urban studies program, is in effect a stage on which are acted group conflict exercises that illustrate how conflict can change racial and other social attitudes, how it can bring on effective interaction between hostile groups, and how it can promote societal change.

About a third of some 50 participants in the intergroup conflict workshop are students from the urban studies program. Another third are professionally engaged in some aspect of education—teachers, guidance counselors, administrators. The remainder are workers from community agencies, which accounts for the presence of nuns, nurses, policemen, and other professionals most likely to become involved in group conflict situations.

Since the program emphasizes to some degree white-black relationships within the context of intergroup hostility, whites and blacks are both represented; participants sometimes discover how, in actual group conflict situations in which they had been involved, they were part of the problem rather than the solution. They see how easy it is for them to reflect the social prejudices of the larger community. They are shown how they too can succumb to the subtleties of those irrational forces of intergroup hostility that they felt could grip only those who are less sophisticated and not professionally trained. Armed with this knowledge, they learn how to sensitize themselves to the views and feelings of others, to define and clarify issues, to build mutual trust, and to displace emotional exchanges with rational dialog.

The four-week program is carefully structured while at the same time being remarkaly free of constraint. This is not the inconsistency it may sound to be but is a condition brought about by virtue of the nature of the conflict exercises, which require meticulous planning in order to set the stage properly for a realistic confrontation and to allow both parties in the conflict plenty of elbow room to take and defend a position that they can earnestly feel would best serve their particular interests.

At the outset, participants are divided into four groups, each group as similar to the others as possible with regard to racial mix, proportion of men and women, and occupations of the members. It is considered important that the members within each group get to know one another and develop mutual trust, for intragroup cohesiveness is closely related to intergroup hostility. The planning of the exercise is also evidenced during the first week in the lectures and other presentations that are meant to provide some background on group culture, power structures, the roots of racism, the nature of conflict, and other subject matter relevant to the issues the groups will deal with.

During the second and third weeks of the workshop, the participants involve themselves in group conflict exercises, using issues that reflect authentic societal or community problems. Every exercise begins with each of the four groups being assigned a specific role. One particularly stimulating exercise, for instance, assumes an urban educational situation in which three sticky issues converge— the transfer of a teacher, the replacement of a principal, and community control of a school. One group took the role of a parents' organization, the second played the part of a teachers' association, the third was theoretically composed of principals, and the fourth represented the board of education.

Each group had specific tasks assigned to it—but how it carried out those tasks was up to the members themselves. They were given free rein; they could devise any plan or maneuver that they felt would be effective. The only provision was that a group was required to interact in some fashion with the other groups.

During the exercise, the debate over community control (which lasted for three days) got especially hot: The president of the principals' association threatened to resign; the teachers' union threatened a strike; and black parents along with some white sympathizers threatened to shut down the school regardless of what the other groups did. In response to that last threat, other white parents gave a stiff warning to the board of education: They wanted the school kept open —or else. At a board meeting a coalition of militants from different racial communities caused massive disruptions. All these events transpired spontaneously. Despite day-to-day planning on the part of members of each group on how they would react to the other groups, all of them got caught up in the heat of the battle. Finally, the board of education reached some muddy conclusions which, typically, made nobody happy. End of exercise.

High drama this. One of the participants expressed the general feeling of all. "I never thought I'd become so emotional about an issue. I forgot it was pretend."

But there was much more to the simulation than some exciting role playing that caught up the players. During the two-day "debriefing" session that follows every exercise, participants have a chance to analyze what went right and what went wrong. In this case, the very fact that all the groups were dissatisfied with the board's decisions meant something had gone wrong indeed.

Actually the analysis showed that each group had stumbled into the same pitfalls that often trap groups in real-life situations and cause them to use conflict in a destructive rather than constructive manner. The parents, teachers, and principals had an unrealistic view of what each of their groups could achieve; hence they rejected any possibility of compromise. They should have recognized that they were boxing in the board; they should have offered it some alternatives. It was a classic case of one party in a disagreement not putting itself into the shoes of the other. For its part, the board of education failed to make effective use of its position. It neglected to solicit community proposals in an effort to find ways out of its dilemma. Moreover, it was too conscious of its position of authority, too anxious to maintain it while at the same time being reluctant to offend anyone. The result was almost predictable: The board did not create any alternatives of its own that might have been acceptable to some

236 groups even if they were distasteful to others.

As they hashed over the exercise during the debriefing session, the participants also came upon other revelations of themselves that tie in with their membership in the human family. Power, for instance. Those in the group acting the part of the school board discovered that they really relished their power and even enjoyed it for its own sake. In this same vein, some members of the other groups confessed to an envy of the board's power and believed this feeling to be at least partly to blame for the strain that had developed among and between groups.

In another exercise, certain decisions had to be made with respect to the goals of a school. The teachers' and administrators' groups involved themselves in the decision-making process as a matter of course. Then a group representing the school's paraprofessionals said it wanted also to be involved. As the exercise unfolded, giving forth much heat and little light, most of the teachers stated that the paraprofessionals didn't have enough skill and professionalism to participate in such a decision. Naturally, the paraprofessionals fought back, but in the end they were overcome and shut out of the decisionmaking process, a result that sowed the seeds for future conflict.

In the debriefing session, the teachers came to realize that their narrow view of professionalism had shut them off from communication with another group, the paraprofessionals. Some, in looking back on their classroom experience and recognizing how valuable their own paraprofessionals really were to them, had a feeling of genuine shame and loss. From the ensuing discussions, insights emerged: for instance, the proposition that decisions relating to school goals are a citizenship responsibility rather than the province solely of those with special training. Also made apparent was the strong urge felt by many people to belong to an "in" group that acts to exclude other groups. The exercise demonstrated how strong are the pressures exerted by a group on its own members, even to the point of altering previously held convictions.

Participants often discover, too, that they haven't been as sensitive in their relations with their own group members as they might have been, ignoring or not even eliciting minority opinions. They tend to be much more goal-oriented than process-oriented. In their eagerness to get the task done, they lose sight of the fundamental human-relations aspects that are essential to success in group undertakings.

"The workshop clarifies and brings to the surface the feelings that people have for one another," explains Joseph A. Polka, an assistant professor of sociology at Southern Connecticut State who works closely with Dr. Levy. Polka makes the point that only when feelings are exposed and examined can change be effected.

Since participants are free to carry out their exercises in any way they choose, some groups elect to organize demonstrations. During last summer's workshop, in an exercise that brought into conflict the pros and cons of abortion, the antiabortion group made up a huge banner that read, "FETUS POWER" and carried it around the campus while chanting their protests. A pregnant student, mistaking the mock demonstration for a real one, cornered one of the antiabortionists and gave him a tongue-lashing. On another occasion, hordes of students joined a demonstration, not knowing it to be part of an exercise, and thereby caused some uneasy moments for the school's security guards.

Sit-ins and other demonstrations, the workshop students learn, serve dual purposes. They are useful at times as a tactic to accomplish a specific goal. And—few realize this— they also serve to increase the cohesiveness and to mark the identity of the group that is demonstrating. "Every group needs something to rally around. It's necessary for its survival," says Levy. Prejudice, he notes, often works in similar ways, building an identity for the in-group through the very antipathy the group holds toward an out-group.

Though exercises vary from year to year (the staff tries to make them as relevant to current issues as possible), the final one is always the same. All the workshop participants are regrouped (this time according to their real-life occupations) and asked to design programs that would enable them to put into practice on their own jobs and with their own colleagues the principles learned in the workshop. In attempting this exercise, two policemen came up with a plan that called for changes in the way their police department related to community groups. A teachers' group developed a plan that had students on an equal level with teachers and administrators in certain decisionmaking areas. The rub is that when workshop participants attempt to implement their plans at home, they usually meet up with a lot of resistance.

Two or three months after each workshop's conclusion the staff tries to meet with those who had taken part in it to find out whether the program has given them any useful and enduring information. Most report that the workshop has had an impact and that it has made a difference; that now they are able to deal much more securely and effectively with group conflict situations.

Some find the principles governing conflict to be making a difference for them even while the workshop is in progress. Constance Middlebrooks, an experienced, supportive inner-city teacher enrolled in the 1972 workshop, told a visitor that she had already learned how easy it was to fall into the trap of making one's own group look good, the other bad. "I'm beginning to realize how destructive that can be," she said last summer, adding that she was even then rethinking some of her views about her own board of education. "In order to get things done there has to be some trust."

Gilbert Rozier, a 30-year-old staff member with the Urban League, said that just two weeks' exposure to the workshop had helped him to identify issues and pinpoint power sources more effectively. "I'm learning to maneuver a group more to my own point of view," he said.

An analysis of test data taken from attitude tests administered to participants at the start and again at the close of the workshop shows the strengths and weaknesses of the program. For example, both white and black participants assume more favorable attitudes toward themselves and others at workshop's end, with indications that the more favorable their own self-attitude, the more favorable will be their attitude toward others. The data shows, however, that this change in attitude does not spill over into the area of race. Specific racial attitudes are changed—that is, improved—only among the white participants. Blacks in workshops in previous years did not seem to acquire a more favorable attitude toward whites. In fact, several blacks commented that what they had observed during the course of the workshop in terms of white behavior only reinforced their views about the prejudice of whites. This

238 may have been due to the workshop's emphasis on white relationships to blacks—to the near exclusion of black relationships to whites. The omission is being remedied.

One of the laws of the physical world would seem to have application to the phenomenon of group conflict: For every action there is an equal and opposite reaction. Push someone and that someone will push back; push someone harder and that someone will push back harder. Like the physicist who strives to use nature by applying her laws creatively, the Intergroup Conflict Workshop staff tries to turn the dynamics of conflict to man's advantage instead of his embarrassment and frustration. Push in the same direction as someone else and there is no telling what mountains you and that someone will be able to move.

——————◆◆——————

QUESTIONS FOR DISCUSSION

1. What elements of the culture of the United States are particularly essential to the survival of representative democracy as a form of government?
2. What values should the school transmit as being representative of our culture?
3. Should the schools be used as agents of planned social change?
4. What provisions, if any, should be made for the schools to transmit the cultural elements of local ethnic subgroups?
5. Which of the many social problems facing the United States do you consider to be the most serious? What role can the school play to help resolve this problem?

SUPPLEMENTARY LEARNING ACTIVITIES

1. Gather and analyze demographic and sociological data in the area of the institution that you attend, looking specifically for cultural diversity.
2. Devise a questionnaire designed to secure societal expectations for schools and use it to interview individuals selected in a random fashion.
3. Invite persons of different cultural backgrounds and different socioeconomic classes to your class to gain their perceptions of American education.
4. Invite authorities from various social service agencies in your area to discuss what they perceive the functions of schools to be in relation to the social problems with which they are concerned.
5. Arrange for interviews with practicing front-line school social workers, both those who work in cities and in rural areas, to gain their perceptions of the role that schools can play in solving social problems.

SELECTED REFERENCES

American Association of School Administrators. *Christopher Jencks in Perspective.* Arlington, Va.: American Association of School Administrators, 1973.

Baltzell, E. Degby. *The Protestant Establishment.* New York: Random House, Inc., 1964.

Bayles, Ernest E., and Bruce L. Hood. *Growth of American Educational Thought and Practice.* New York: Harper & Row, Publishers, 1966.

Brameld, Theodore. *Education for the Emerging Age.* New York: Harper & Row, Publishers, 1965.

————. *The Climactic Decades: Mandate to Education.* New York: Praeger Publishers, Inc., 1970.

Brubacher, John S. *A History of the Problems of Education.* 2nd ed. New York: McGraw-Hill Book Company, 1965.

Butts, R. Freeman, and Laurence Cremin. *A History of Education in American Culture.* New York: Holt, Rinehart and Winston, Inc., 1953.

Clark, Kenneth B. *Dark Ghetto: Dilemma of Social Power.* New York: Anti-Defamation League, 1965.

Corwin, Ronald G. *A Sociology of Education.* New York: Appleton-Century-Crofts, 1965.

Counts, George S. *Education and American Civilization.* New York: Teachers College Press, 1952.

Dropkin, Stan; Harold Full; and Ernest Schwarez, eds. *Contemporary American Education: An Anthology of Issues, Problems, Challenges.* 2nd ed. New York: Macmillan Company, 1970.

Eddy, John. *The Teacher and the Drug Scene.* Bloomington, Ind.: Phi Delta Kappa, 1973.

Goals for Americans: The Report of the President's Commission on National Goals. Englewood Cliffs, N.J.: Prentice-Hall, Inc., 1960.

Goslin, David A. *The School in Contemporary Society.* Chicago: Scott, Foresman and Company, 1965.

Gross, Ronald, and Beatrice Gross, eds. *Radical School Reform.* New York: Simon & Schuster, Inc., 1969.

Hartford, Ellis Ford, *Education in These United States.* New York: Macmillan Company, 1964.

Havighurst, Robert J., and Bernice L. Neugarten. *Society and Education.* 3rd ed. Boston: Allyn & Bacon, Inc., 1967.

Landes, Ruth. *Culture in American Education.* New York: John Wiley & Sons, Inc., 1965.

Linton, Ralph. *Tree of Culture.* New York: Alfred A. Knopf, Inc., 1955.

Myrdal, Gunnar. *An American Dilemma: The Negro Problem and Modern Democracy.* rev. ed. New York: Harper & Row, Publishers, 1944.

National School Public Relations Association. *Drug Crisis: Schools Fight Back with Innovative Programs.* Arlington, Va.: National School Public Relations Association, 1971.

"Perspectives on Inequality." *Harvard Educational Review.* reprint series no. 8, 1973.

Pounds, Ralph L., and James R. Bryner. *The School in American Society.* New York: Macmillan Company, 1967.

Report of the National Advisory Commission on Civil Disorders. New York: Bantam Books, Inc., 1968.

Stent, Madelon D.; William R. Hazard; and Harry N. Rivlin. *Cultural Pluralism in Education: A Mandate for Change.* Appleton-Century-Crofts, 1973.

Strom, Robert D. *The Inner-City Classroom: Teacher Behavior.* Columbus, Ohio: Charles E. Merrill Publishing Company, 1966.

Westby-Gibson, Dorothy. *Social Perspectives on Education.* New York: John Wiley & Sons, Inc., 1965.

chapter 9

Individual Expectations
for Education

goals

● Describes aspirations of the various individuals involved in the educational process.

● Presents the purposes of the Educational Policies Commission in its role as interpreter of educational objectives.

● Discusses objectives of self-realization, human relationship, economic efficiency, and civic responsibility associated with the educated person.

● Lists and questions the relationships of many activities which have been relegated to the schools over the years.

● Concludes by asking questions which necessarily involve the way elements interact in making school decisions.

Greeting his pupils, the master asked:
What would you learn of me?
And the reply came:
How shall we care for our bodies?

How shall we rear our children?
How shall we work together?
How shall we live with our fellowmen?
How shall we play?

242

For what ends shall we live? . . .
And the teacher pondered these words, and
sorrow was in his heart, for his own learning
touched not these things.[1]

Chapman and Counts

Nearly half a century has passed since Chapman and Counts submitted the above dialogue, which illustrates individual learning needs and desires for other than "book larnin' " the academic subject matter. How well have we done in meeting such individual learning needs? Daily newspapers yield indications that these learning needs have not as yet been satisfactorily met. During the decade of the sixties, the criticism of irrelevance was leveled against existing operations of the schools. The first years of the seventies show the American experiment struggling for survival in an era marked by misplaced loyalties in the political realm, by deprivation and material scarcities, by high crime rates, and by a myriad of other urgent human problems. It seems likely that today's pupils would respond to the master's question in much the same way as pupils responded half a century ago.

One challenge for today's teacher in assisting his pupils in finding individual answers to such questions is in keeping abreast of the times. Pupils prefer those teachers who possess current knowledge, who have an outlook on life which goes beyond the knowledge domain, and who demonstrate attitudes which are flexible to the stresses of the times. Consider just one of the pupils' questions—How shall we rear our children? During the last half century the answers to that question have been dealt with primarily within the home. Since the family unit served as the general environ-

ment within which to raise children, the schools were not expected to be deeply involved with the question of rearing children. It has been suggested that recent social changes—including more women in the work force, fewer numbers of relatives living in the household, and greater geographic mobility of families—have combined to make the the family a less effective agent within which to raise children.[2] These changes in the family are directly related to changes in the ways children are raised today. However, many teachers obtained their knowledge and attitudes regarding the rearing of children within the traditional family setting. Therefore, some teachers are still likely to feel that the family should be the agent for providing child-rearing knowledge. But, *if* the family setting today is truly a less effective agent in rearing children than when our teachers were raised, then such teachers are likely to have difficulty accepting contemporary attitudes regarding the basic question—How shall we rear our children?

During the past half century the schools have adjusted in many ways to the shift of many former family responsibilities on the school. Teachers have inherited many of the responsibilities formerly reserved for the home. Today's schools and teachers are very much expected to be involved with various responsibilities related to rearing children. A very significant aspect of the operations of the schools deals with pupil personnel services, including health and dental care, sex education, guidance, discipline, manners, and codes of dress. Increasing emphasis is being placed on early childhood education. Some programs propose parental involvement ex-

---

1. J. Crosby Chapman and George S. Counts, *Principles of Education,* p. ii.

2. James S. Coleman, "Social Change," *Bulletin of National Association of Secondary Principals 49,* pp. 11–18.

tended as far as to prenatal care. At the same time, much attention is being directed toward the adult and continuing education aspect which stresses education as a lifelong process.

Educators are now questioning—Where does all this end? Who decides what the limits are? What are or should be the actual responsibilities of the teacher in this regard? Our schools have made valiant strides in attempting to meet the various student needs which were formerly within the province of the family household. By high school age, many of today's pupils are sophisticated enough to be able to determine their own unique needs and the schools should be flexible enough to meet individual needs regarding things other than subject matter. Perhaps the most relevant questions are those which ask the individual what it is that *he* desires or needs assistance with as related to his health, his sex education, his guidance, or his manners.

Many other persistent needs exist which pupils expect their education to satisfy whatever the societal setting. The task of the teacher becomes that of constantly examining the ways in which individual expectations can be satisfied within the framework of the school system which has been typically group-oriented (giving primary attention to societal needs). The current acceptance of the interaction of societal and individual needs is a recent development which has generated new excitement within the school setting as related to individual needs. The general axiom that new teachers tend to teach as they have been taught needs careful examination in light of increased emphasis on individual expectations with regard to education. Teachers, particularly new teachers, must find the appropriate means for directing knowledge and understanding gained from their own educational experiences toward the individual expecta-

tions their pupils have regarding their education.

Parental and Pupil Expectations

Expectations of education have become American tradition. Both parents and pupils expect the schools to satisfy a wide variety of individual needs. When parents and pupils are asked "What are the most important reasons for going to school?" their responses concur, for the most part, with the major societal expectations of the schools as previously discussed. For example, pupils of all ages are quick to suggest that intellectual development is the highest expectation within their educational experiences. Likewise, individuals expect the schools to provide meaningful school experiences with regard to citizenship, personality, vocational training, recreation, and health. Parents from all segments of society generally influence their children to believe that education is the main ingredient for being a successful person and for being an effective individual within the societal setting.

A major source of information concerning the status and trends of opinion about school questions is the annual poll of public attitudes toward education conducted by George H. Gallup. The fourth annual Gallup poll utilized the following open question to get at the public's ideas of the ultimate goals of education:

> People have different reasons why they want their children to get an education. What are the chief reasons that come to your mind?

After the person interviewed had answered this question, he was asked if he could

244 think of anything else. One further attempt was made to see if he could add to his list.

Here are the responses and the percentage of respondents mentioning each in some form:

- To get better jobs   44%
- To get along better with people at all levels of society   43%
- To make more money—achieve financial success   38%
- To attain self-satisfaction   21%
- To stimulate their minds   15%
- Miscellaneous reasons   11%

These responses show that the public thinks of education largely in a pragmatic way. But this heavy emphasis on material goals, at the expense of those concerned with intellectual and artistic development, should come as no shock. Americans are a practical people who believe firmly that education is the royal road to success in life.[3]

Educational Policies Commission

One of the landmark documents related to the purposes of education was the report of the Educational Policies Commission approved for publication by vote of the commission on April 25, 1938. The commission was appointed jointly by the National Education Association and the American Association of School Administrators. A statement of the purposes of education was considered of such magnitude and importance that the commission worked on the project at each of the seven meetings held during a three-year period prior to publication of the report. Over one thou-

3. George H. Gallup, "Fourth Annual Gallup Poll of Public Attitudes Toward Education," *Phi Delta Kappan*, September 1972, p. 35.

sand educators contributed to the development of these objectives. Four major lists of interrelated objectives which characterize an educated person were identified by the commission and are listed below as presented in the report. It is suggested that the entire publication be read for a more thorough study and interpretation of these objectives.

The Objectives of Self-Realization

The Inquiring Mind. The educated person has an appetite for learning.

Speech. The educated person can speak the mother tongue clearly.

Reading. The educated person reads the mother tongue efficiently.

Writing. The educated person writes the mother tongue effectively.

Number. The educated person solves his problems of counting and calculating.

Sight and Hearing. The educated person is skilled in listening and observing.

Health Knowledge. The educated person understands the basic facts concerning health and disease.

Health Habits. The educated person protects his own health and that of his dependents.

Public Health. The educated person works to improve the health of the community.

Recreation. The educated person is participant and spectator in many sports and other pastimes.

Intellectual Interests. The educated person has mental resources for the use of leisure.

Esthetic Interests. The educated person appreciates beauty.

Character. The educated person gives responsible direction to his own life.

The Objectives of Human Relationship

Respect for Humanity. The educated person puts human relationships first.

Friendships. The educated person enjoys a rich, sincere, and varied social life.

Cooperation. The educated person can work and play with others.

Courtesy. The educated person observes the amenities of social behavior.

Appreciation of the Home. The educated person appreciates the family as a social institution.

Conservation of the Home. The educated person conserves family ideals.

Homemaking. The educated person is skilled in homemaking.

Democracy in the Home. The educated person maintains democratic family relationships.

The Objectives of Economic Efficiency

Work. The educated producer knows the satisfaction of good workmanship.

Occupational Information. The educated producer understands the requirements and opportunities for various jobs.

Occupational Choice. The educated producer has *selected* his occupation.

Occupational Efficiency. The educated producer succeeds in his chosen vocation.

Occupational Adjustment. The educated producer maintains and improves his efficiency.

Occupational Appreciation. The educated producer appreciates the social value of his work.

Personal Economics. The educated consumer plans the economics of his own life.

Consumer Judgment. The educated consumer develops standards for guiding his expenditures.

Efficiency in Buying. The educated consumer is an informed and skillful buyer.

Consumer Protection. The educated consumer takes appropriate measures to safeguard his interests.

Social Justice. The educated citizen is sensitive to the disparities of human circumstance.

Social Activity. The educated citizen acts to correct unsatisfactory conditions.

Social Understanding. The educated citizen seeks to understand social structures and social processes.

Critical Judgment. The educated citizen has defenses against propaganda.

Tolerance. The educated citizen respects honest differences of opinion.

Conservation. The educated citizen has a regard for the nation's resources.

Social Applications of Science. The educated citizen measures scientific advance by its contribution to the general welfare.

World Citizenship. The educated citizen is a cooperating member of the world community.

Law Observance. The educated citizen respects the law.

Economic Literacy. The educated citizen is economically literate.

Political Citizenship. The educated citizen accepts his civic duties.

Devotion to Democracy. The educated citizen acts upon an unswerving loyalty to democratic ideals.[4]

———— • ————

Perhaps the reason that these objectives have stood the test of time is that they were specified in terms of the individual as "the educated person," "the educated producer," "the educated consumer," and "the educated citizen." It has since been suggested that

———— • ————

4. *The Purpose of Education in American Democracy,* Educational Policies Commission, National Education Association and American Association of School Administrators, 1938, pp. 50, 72, 90, 108.

246   these objectives place upon the school an immense, if not impossible, task. Neither the schools nor the pupils have sufficient time or energy to engage in activities that will enable pupils to achieve fully all these goals by the time these pupils graduate from high school. Furthermore, education does not cease when pupils graduate. As a result, the committee expressed the feeling that a guiding principle was needed so that the school would be able to identify its necessary and appropriate contributions to individual development and the needs of society.[5]

As a Citizen

An individual's attitudinal development is considerably influenced by his environment, including the influences of various societal institutions. In turn, an individual's attitudes and values influence his behavior. Each individual is ultimately privately responsible for determining what his citizenship

> *. . . Democracy is always weakened from within. Only its own feebleness or complacency destroys it. We in Europe see more clearly than you that democracy dies from lack of discipline, unwillingness to compromise, group pressure, corruption, usurpation of public power because the public is greedy or indifferent. It dies unless it draws life from every citizen. . . .*
> A statement from Czechoslovakia published in the New York Times, September 25, 1937.

5. Robert W. Richey, *Planning for Teaching*, 5th ed. (New York: McGraw-Hill Book Co., 1973), p. 514.

behavior shall be. He elects to vote or not, to violently protest or not, to accept normative standards or not. Notwithstanding these many influences upon an individual, as a participatory citizen the individual eventually stands alone and practices the act of citizenship in his unique way.

One of the functions ascribed to the public schools has been that of helping students become "good citizens." Parents, board of education members, school administrators, teachers, and legislators have given much attention to citizenship as a dimension of an individual's education. Most states have laws which direct the schools to engage in specific teaching tasks aimed at developing citizenship. For example, an Illinois law states that every public school teacher shall teach the pupils honesty, kindness, justice, and moral courage for the purpose of lessening crime and raising the standard of good citizenship (sections 12–27, School Code of Illinois, 1965). Implied in this law is that honesty, kindness, justice, and moral courage are criteria for lessening crime and, therefore, contribute to the promotion of good citizenship. Terms such as honesty, kindness, justice, and moral courage are not only difficult to define, but are also difficult to teach within the school setting. In spite of such difficulties, schools (that is, teachers) are expected to accept the challenge of providing individual pupils with learning experiences which will help each of them to develop alternatives for solving the moral problems of life. The schools are also expected to help cause youth to understand the desirableness of being kind and just individuals even if some adults they know are unkind and unjust. Individual moral courage, while an admirable attribute of character, and important to citizenship, is difficult to attain in a formalized school setting.

Teaching as related to these aspects of good citizenship draws heavily from an idealistic premise that charges teachers to serve as models in their manner of participation as citizens. Likewise, this idealistic approach draws heavily upon the character analysis of great citizens past and present. The risk of this latter kind of teaching is that the "gospel" becomes Pollyannaish and at times unreal. One aspect of the teaching task is to enlarge upon the dimensions of this idealism and "tell it like it is" so that the students have several alternatives to model, choose from, or modify for their own personal life-style.

Since the early 1930s the American public schools have also been charged with the responsibility for developing other aspects of citizenship. American patriotism, the principles of representative government as enunciated in the American Declaration of Independence, and the Constitution of the United States of America have been emphasized in citizenship training. For many years, teachers have taught that each good citizen should demonstrate his patriotism by serving his country in peace as well as in war, by respecting the United States flag, and by voting in elections. A kind of nationalistic idealism was assumed when good citizenship was taught in this manner. This form of idealism seemingly held true in an era when our society was closer knit, less complex, and agrarian-oriented. Many living Americans coming from this heritage continue to operate from such a basis of idealism, not being cognizant of the conflicts resulting from the impersonal, complex, and multigroup influences of the contemporary, urban, pluralistic, machine-oriented society. Our younger people tend to utilize bold dramatic methods in their desire to be heard whereas older people believe the way to be heard is through more traditional, "good ol' days" procedures. In the reality of today, when an individual pursues the traditional channels of expression he is frequently overwhelmed by the massiveness and complexity of our contemporary society. With all of our technological sophistication, communication problems are still manifest among us. A small voice is practically unheard and a letter to an elected governmental representative is likely to be of minor importance in and of itself. Thus, an increasing number of young people seem to find it necessary to pool their efforts for the purposes of being heard. Consequently, a tense climate has developed between the active, impulsive, "tell it like it is," *now*-oriented young citizens and their dramatic ways of communicating, and the less active, deliberate, "it was good enough for me," traditionally oriented older citizens. All are involved in a kind of trial-and-error reexamination of the dimensions of good individual citizenship. Obviously, each individual must ultimately make his choice as to what kind of citizen he is to be.

Self and Social Identity

Individuals are unique with regard to personality. While it may be that, particularly between siblings, certain characteristics of personalities are similar, no two personalities are exactly alike. One's *personality* is considered to be the habitual patterns and qualities of behavior as expressed by physical and mental activities and attitudes, and also the distinctive individual qualities of a person considered collectively.

Many differing experiences affect the personality development of an individual. Since the experiences of life vary among indi-

248 viduals, it follows that personalities also differ among individuals. Behavioral scientists have observed that, in addition to the influences of heredity, similar personality characteristics in individuals are related to the similarities of life experiences of the individuals. In essence, this line of reasoning assumes that personality characteristics are learned from experience. Thus, particularly with peers, school experiences do in fact contribute to the development of one's personality. An individual's peer group identity and his experiences with the peer group are strong influences on his personality development. Therefore, it appears to be a reasonable expectation of parents that schools should provide experiences that will enhance the personality development of their children. As pupils mature, they become increasingly aware of many dimensions of their own personality and often select activities and courses which they believe will help develop their personality.

Biological qualities such as age, sex, stature, and pigmentation also influence one's personality. Various ethnic and racial groups influence the behavior patterns of their young through the sharing of similar experiences. Characteristics of an individual's personality are in part reflections of the individual's age group, sex group, and racial group. An individual's behavior is partially adjusted to the forces of these biological qualities impinging upon him.

An individual's behavior is affected by the total impact of his life's experiences. Heredity and environment interact to make each individual a distinct and unique person.

Considerable research has been conducted about the adolescent and his world, including findings on what adolescents have

Activities and personality development—Is there a relationship?

expressed regarding their development. The introductory paragraph of a research study by Dr. Herschel D. Thornburg suggests three concerns of primary importance to adolescents:

———◆•◆———

Adolescents have vital concerns about the individuals and situations that affect their development. Of primary importance to each adolescent are (1) his society and his peers, (2) gaining self and social identity, and (3) social maturation. Most behavioral scientists agree that these factors are essential to the successful development of adolescents. They also recognize that these factors are worked

> *And, if we think of it, what does civilization itself rest upon . . . but rich, luxuriant, varied personalism? To that all bends; and it is because toward such result democracy alone, on anything like Nature's scale, breaks up the limitless fallows of humankind, and plants the seed, and gives fair play, that its claims now precede the rest. The literature, songs, esthetics, etc., of a country are of importance principally because they furnish the materials and suggestions of personality for the women and men of that country, and enforce them in a thousand effective ways.*
>
> *The purpose of democracy . . . is, through many transmigrations, and amid endless ridicules, arguments and ostensible failures, to illustrate, at all hazards, this doctrine or theory that man, properly trained in sanest, highest freedom, may and must become a law, and series of laws, unto himself . . . .*
>
> Walt Whitman

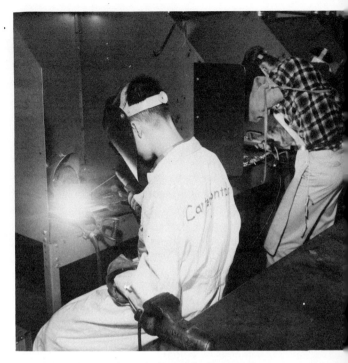

A salable skill such as being able to operate welding machinery is a common expectation for schools.

out mostly within one's own world—among one's peers.[6]

———◆•◆———

> *All youth need to develop salable skills and those understandings and attitudes that make the worker an intelligent and productive participant in economic life.*
>
> Education Policies Commission
> *Education for all American Youth*
> (Washington, D.C.: National
> Education Association, 1944), p. 26.

6. Hershel D. Thornburg, "Peers: Three Distinct Groups," *Adolescence*, September 1971, p. 59.

250　**Vocational Education**

"While general education may be defined as those curricular experiences designed for all citizens in a democratic society, vocational education is concerned with those curricular experiences necessary for proficiency in a specific vocation. Obviously, general education is the foundation for any vocation."[7] As an individual progresses through school he needs assistance in deciding how much general education is required to provide himself with an adequate foundation for a selected vocation. A part of such decision making is the universal expectation of education which suggests that the more education you have, the better job you can obtain. Since this is a generalized expectation, it says very little about the question—"What kind of education is needed to assure one of a better job?"

As is suggested in the next chapter, the schools of colonial America were generally not expected to deal with vocational subjects. The reading and writing expectations were not considered as the general education bases upon which to build for vocational education, but rather were considered as the bases for spiritual salvation.

As the societal and individual expectations of the schools increased, vocational education slowly came into the curriculum. The so-called comprehensive high school is unique to America and has gained considerable reputation as an excellent secondary educational prototype. The term "comprehensive" implies that both general education and vocational education be provided in order to meet the *individual* needs of the pupils. With both the general education and vocational education curricula provided, high school students are

The demand for technicians continues to rise.

able to pursue a common general curriculum, plus vocational subjects and a wide range of school activities to satisfy their own individual interests and vocational plans.

Typing is a very valuable skill.

7. Daniel Tanner, *Schools for Youth*, p. 353.

Vocational education as a concerted public movement did not gain momentum in the United States until after World War I. It is true that there were several federal acts, such as the Morrill Act of 1862, which provided for certain aspects of vocational education prior to the close of World War I. During World War I, the nation's need for technically trained manpower was the primary thrust for the passage of the Smith-Hughes Act of 1917. From that time to the present there has been an increasing amount of federal and state legislation providing funds for vocational education. Since vocational education is more expensive than the traditional academic subjects, and since most of our schools continue to give most attention to the academic subjects, additional funds must continue to be provided to operate effective vocational programs. The curriculum of the comprehensive high school can be expected to contain programs of vocational education which have essentials as follows:

Girls and drafting?? Why not?

1. The program is directly related to employment opportunities, determined by school officials in cooperation with occupationally concerned and competent individuals and groups.
2. The content of courses is confirmed or changed by periodic analyses of the occupations for which the training is being given.
3. The courses for a specific occupation are set up and maintained with the advice and cooperation of the various occupational groups concerned.
4. The facilities and equipment used in instruction are comparable to those found in the particular occupation.
5. The conditions under which instruction is given duplicate as nearly as possible desirable conditions in the occupation itself and at the same time provide effective learning situations.
6. The length of teaching periods and total hours of instruction are determined by the requirements of the occupation and the needs of the students.
7. Training in a particular occupation is carried to the point of developing marketable skills, abilities, understandings, attitudes, work habits, and appreciations sufficient to enable the trainee to get and hold a job in that occupation.
8. Day and evening classes are scheduled at hours and during seasons convenient to enrollees.
9. Instruction is offered only to persons who need, desire, and can profit from it occupationally.
10. The teachers are competent in the occupation for which they are giving instruc-

252

tion and possess adequate professional qualifications for teaching.

11. Vocational guidance, including effective follow-up of all students who finish or drop out of a course, is an integral and continuing part of the program.

12. Continuous research is an integral part of the program.[8]

———◆—◆———

For an individual to eventually become a productive member of our society, he must be prepared to engage in a specific vocation. Therefore, at some point in one's educational development, even for the college-bound student, exposure to and involvement with some aspect of a vocational education program is a desirable prerequisite to entering the world of work. One of the contributing factors to the unemployable status of many of our youth is that large numbers of them leave school without having acquired a salable vocational skill. Pupils (and parents) are often so convinced of the panacea notion ascribed to education that many pupils who ought to be acquiring a salable vocational skill pursue college-bound curricula instead. A challenge to the schools and to teachers in meeting individual expectations is to increase the vocational education opportunities and communicate the nature of such opportunities to the students prior to their leaving school. When this is accomplished, fewer of our students will be entering the world of work poorly prepared.

Recreation

As an educational concept, *recreation* is particularly concerned with the after-work-

8. U.S. Office of Education, *Public Vocational Education Programs* (Washington, D.C.: U.S. Government Printing Office, 1960), pp. 2–3.

School dances are a part of the social recreation program of the school.

hours activities. Such recreational pursuits should be enjoyable as well as constructive for the individual. Recreational activities are primarily those engaged in during one's leisure time. The historic traces of mankind indicate that individuals within the various civilizations throughout our world have always participated in music, games, sports, painting, and other recreational activities. During the last century in the United States there has been a steady progression of park site purchases, developments of state and national parks and lakes, formations of camping clubs, gun clubs, fishing clubs, as well as immense growth in the manufacturing of recreational materials. Recreation continues to grow as a means of satisfying certain basic human needs.

Various statistics cite the recreation need. For example, the average life span is continually increasing. The average length of life in 1885 was 40 years; in 1950 it was 70 years; the prediction for 2000 is 75 years.

Individual learning activities are an important part of the school program, and can be influential in determining future recreational activities.

While man's average life span is being extended due to the impact of advanced technology and research in the field of medicine, the percentage of man's total lifetime spent in leisure time activities is increasing due to the impact of advanced technology and research in the field of work. Man is living longer, working less, and has more leisure time, with the prognosis that this pattern will continue well into the future of society. In addition, American incomes have been rising and are predicted to continue rising, barring an economic depression. Americans with increased leisure time, along with increased income, seek more and more recreational pursuits.

In order to satisfy the growing recreation need among individuals, adequate recreation programs must continue to be developed and sponsored by the several agencies of local, state, and federal governments. In addition, volunteer and private organizations such as the Boy Scouts, Girl Scouts, YMCA, YWCA and industry sponsor recreational programs. In many communities the schools cooperate with local governments in providing recreational activities. Recreation programs which effectively satisfy such objectives will do much to satisfy the recreation need for individuals in our American Society.

What can individuals expect of the schools in terms of recreation? Throughout

254

Hot lunch programs enhance good health.

the history of education in the United States there have been conflicting philosophies regarding the curricular offerings of the school. Some proponents of general education restrict the role of the school to the academic subject disciplines, and argue that our schools should erase the so-called frills, including recreation programs. A comprehensive curricular approach suggests that the recreation program should be an integral part of the overall school program. Presently, most of the schools in the United States are actively engaged in recreation. Also, school buildings are being used and school personnel are contributing more and more to community recreation programs. The elements of school recreation programs are drawn from many departments within the school. While the physical education department plays a vital role with various activities involving sports and games, it is a misconception to believe that the physical education departments can provide all that is needed in an all-inclusive recreation program. In addition to sports and games activities, other activities in the school recre-

ation program include music activities, dance, arts and crafts, dramatics, outdoor activities, and hobby clubs. In again stressing the worth of the program to the individual pupil, it follows that recreational programs consisting solely of group activities are less than satisfactory. It is highly probable that the recreational offerings of the school may be the only opportunities many students will have to learn to satisfy their own personal recreational needs.

Health

In 1918 the Commission on Reorganization of Secondary Education set forth the Seven Cardinal Principles of Education. The first principle listed was *health*. Since that time other committees, commissions, and groups have reiterated the health objective as a function of the schools. Outcomes expected from the school health program include development of desirable health attitudes, a development of health knowledge, the development of desirable health practices, and development of health and safety skills.[9]

Since health education is really everybody's business, and since every state has compulsory school attendance laws, it seems reasonable to expect that the schools educate for health. The public health agencies are also charged with the responsibility for health education and services within cities, states, and the nation. Initially the public health agencies, under the supervision of medical personnel, appeared to be the more competent agency for meeting public health needs. With increasing expectations of the schools to provide for all of one's education, health educa-

9. Charles A. Bucher, *Foundations of Physical Education,* pp. 238–39.

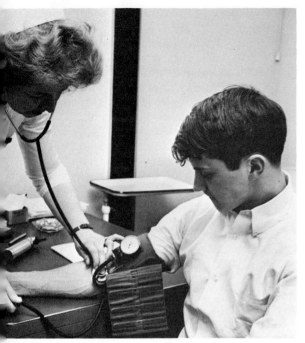 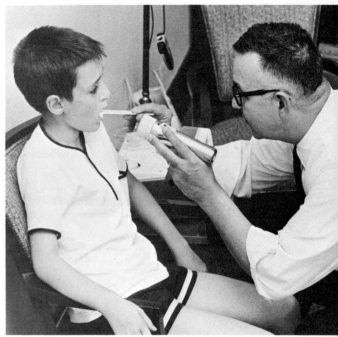

Health is also the business of the school.

tion in the schools has greatly expanded. At the present time, some schools have very adequate health programs including facilities and well-qualified personnel. Other schools provide only minimal, if any, health services.

California has been one of the leaders in providing for health instruction in the public schools. The California State Department of Education publication *Framework for Health Instruction in California Public Schools* has been developed to assist school district personnel in planning their own sequential program of health instruction, kindergarten through grade twelve. *Framework* suggests that in preparing programs of health instruction, educators should give consideration to the following points of view:

1. Health is a state of physical, mental, and moral well-being and is dependent upon the interaction of these dimensions.
2. Health is dynamic in that it is ever-changing.
3. Health is influenced by the interaction of many hereditary and environmental factors and conditions over which the individual may exercise varying amounts of control. Some aspects of everyone's health can be improved.
4. Health is necessary for a person to function optimally as a productive individual, as a worthy family member, and as a contributing member of society.[10]

10. *Framework for Health Instruction in California Public Schools,* 1970 ed. (Sacramento: California State Department of Education, 1972), p. 1.

256   Illinois has also been identified as a leading state in providing for health instruction in the public schools. The Critical Health Problems and Comprehensive Health Education Act was passed by the Seventy-seventh Illinois General Assembly and was signed into law on August 31, 1971. Authority and responsibility for implementing the legislation at the local district level rest with the local board of education and the school administration. Because of the scope and magnitude of the legislation, a carefully developed, long-range plan of program development will be required to implement it fully. Guidelines for implementing the act have been prepared by the office of the Superintendent of Public Instruction for the State of Illinois. The guidelines list the following basic requirements of the comprehensive health education program.

———— • ————

1. Health education should be a planned, sequential program, K–12. Crash programs, emphasizing special health topics only, should be avoided.
2. Individualized instruction is particularly relevant to health education. Class size should be maintained at a level which will provide adequate opportunities for interaction among students and between students and teachers.
3. Typical classrooms should be provided which facilitate the use of modern teaching and learning resources. The environmental setting should provide adequate heat, light, ventilation, and appropriate furniture to enhance learning.
4. Students should receive a grade for a health education course and one-half Carnegie unit of credit or equivalent for successfully completing the program at the high school level. *Health Education must be required for high school graduation.*

5. It is desirable that classes be coeducational.
6. School districts should employ teachers with specific academic preparation in health education.
7. Sufficient funds should be allocated to provide up-to-date and adequate instructional resources for teachers and students.
8. Each school district should appoint a qualified person to assume responsibility for the development, coordination, and implementation of the health education program. A qualified person could be any person with academic preparation and interest in health education. Ideally, the person should have a graduate degree in health education.[11]

———— • ————

Modern schools and teachers are somewhat responsive to the individual needs and expectations of pupils. They must become *more* responsive. Various formal and informal school activities and programs are felt to contribute to the development of desirable citizenship behaviors and personality traits. Vocational education programs help foster the development of salable skills. Dimensions of social poise and physical development are both enhanced through recreation programs. Basic health needs are checked and administered through the expanding health programs of our schools.

Point of View

The advent of the seventies brought to the profession of teaching considerable

11. *Guidelines for Implementing the "Critical Health Problems and Comprehensive Health Education Act,"* Office of the Superintendent of Public Instruction, Springfield, Illinois, 1971, pp. 4–5.

clamor for increased attention to the programs of health education. Health educators have been actively defining the aspects of a complete school health program to include all services provided by physicians, nurses, dentists, social workers, and health educators which contribute to appraising, protecting, and promoting the health of the students and school personnel. This new emphasis on school health education, as with most new educational programs, must also deal with problems associated with definition, purpose, and instructional procedures.

Coupled with the various problems of operationalizing newer modes of health education, all educational programs now face a general clamor for accountability. Taxpayer groups and legislators particularly began to ask for verifiable evidence of accomplishments. Questions posed to the outcomes of teaching as related to per pupil cost have become rather common. From these kinds of pressures, most of the states have passed legislative acts which prescribe procedures and plans for specifying the objectives of education, including health education, in measurable terms. In some cases legislative mandates necessitate the involvement of the community in the formulation of the school goals and objectives.

This recent attention to educational objectives has aroused considerable excitement within the various school settings. Some educators view such thrust as threatening to their profession and personal security. Others welcome this as a challenge long needed for the purpose of clarifying their roles and responsibilities. Somewhat lost in the excitement is our considerable history dealing with the specification of educational objectives. Consequently, many educators are unduly absorbed in "reinventing the wheel" as related to specifying educational objectives. Of considerable importance to the authors is the need for maintaining strong considerations related to individual expectations for education. It would seem regressive to generate substantial and fixed organizational objectives with which the individual could not relate. Hopefully, our schools would continue to strive toward meeting the individual expectations of all pupils while carefully examining educational objectives deemed important by accrediting agencies and community groups.

The notion of health education as a part of the school curriculum bears with it the potential of arousing nonsupportive public sentiment when, for example, discussions of communicable diseases relate to those diseases associated with sexual activity. A significant segment of most school communities seems to continue to prefer that all matters of health education be considered private, that is, a responsibility of the home rather than the school. Dr. Jerald D. Floyd of Northern Illinois University takes the point of view that —"Like it or not, health education is going on in your school." From this assumption he discusses school health education as related to the needs for the implementation of a new definition and a new instructional model.

——————◆•◆——————

School Health Education: Implementation of a New Definition and a New Instructional Model

Jerald D. Floyd

Written for *American Education: The Task and the Teacher* by Dr. Jerald D. Floyd, professor of physical education, Northern Illinois University, DeKalb, Illinois.

258   Introduction

Like it or not, health education is going on in your school. The educational process involves an individual's acquiring experiences that contribute to his understanding himself, to his identifying the factors that influence him, and to his acquiring techniques that will allow him to control the factors that he perceives as influences on his life. A child arrives at school with perceptions about who he is, about what it is that influences him, and about what he can and cannot control in regard to significant events in his life. Regardless of the stage of the process when the child enters school and because the child spends a tremendous amount of time in school, this critical learning process will continue for better or for worse. But, like it or not, all experiences—planned or unplanned, verbal or non-verbal, implicit or explicit—make up what must be broadly conceived as the child's health education.

Consequently, the central issue in this process, is to define what *health* is. Individual and community definitions have traditionally viewed good health as a state in which the individual is free of any illness or disease and poor health as just the opposite. There are also widely accepted teaching methods concerning the achievement of "good" health. These methods that were based upon the assumption that a student who memorized all the signs and symptoms of the various illnesses and diseases would be healthy. For example, a student who had all the "facts" about cancer would not smoke cigarettes, a student who knew the anatomy and physiology of the systems of the human body would take better care of himself, and so on. Further, practitioners of this approach believed that some problems were best ignored lest the children's curiosity result in experimentation with the "problematic behavior." They expected that, informed students would be able to make intelligent decisions regarding drug use, sexual practices, health products and services, mental health practices, and numerous other health affecting areas.

Such expectations have not worked very well. This view of health and health education is too narrow. It eliminates too many areas critical to human behavior and it excludes too many individuals who have health problems over which they have no initial control (e.g., diabetes, club foot, and other congenital defects). Too often using this information giving system, we tell young people what to think instead of helping them discover how to think; we ask them to make intelligent decisions but we have never helped them learn how; or we do nothing at all, leaving the student to the questionable influences of his peer group and the mass media.

A new view of health education is needed. We now require a new set of expectations regarding what health is, what process is necessary to attain a positive health status, and what roles various components of a community will play in achieving this new view of health. Initially we need a perspective of health that is positive and that focuses on a "quality of life," not on morbidity and mortality statistics; one that focuses on individuals and their uniqueness, not on unquestioned standards for a healthy life; one that is dedicated to assisting individuals in becoming independent and self reliant, not one oriented toward dependence upon isolated information sources. Adapting these postures with regard to health and health education, we can (must) facilitate the necessary changes in individual and community expectations.

Orientation

The focus of this overview is on health instruction, but we must understand the organizational structure of the entire school health education program. A comprehensive school health program includes a healthful school environment, health services, and health instruction, according to terms and definitions developed in the 1972–73 Report of the Joint Committee on Health Education Terminology.

School Health Service is that portion of the school health program provided by physicians, nurses, dentists, health educators, social workers and the like to appraise, protect, and promote the health of students and school personnel. These services are designed:

to appraise and council the school community for the purpose of helping pupils obtain health care;

to prevent and control communicable diseases;

to provide emergency care for emergency or sudden illness;

to promote and provide optimum sanitary conditions and safe facilities;

to protect and promote health of school personnel;

and to provide concurrent learning opportunities that are conducive to the maintenance and promotion of individual and community health.

The second component of the school health program is healthful school environment. This aspect of the program has responsibilities for the promotion, maintenance, and utilization and planning of learning experiences to favorably influence emotional, social, physical, value-spiritual, and intellectual health.

Health Instruction, the third component of the school health program, is the process of providing a sequence of planned and spontaneously originated learning opportunities comprising the organized aspects of health education in the school. Of the three components this aspect has had the most varied and most often conflicting expectations from all segments of the community. Federal, state, and local legislation has developed rather rigorous standards to deal with both the environmental and service aspects of school health. Expectations are adequately stated and adhered to by the people involved, both in terms of program standards and personnel certification. For example, it is extremely unlikely that a school would be allowed to operate where fire hazards exist, where sanitation procedures are lacking, or where safety codes are being violated. Such operational difficulty, unfortunately, is not encountered in the health instruction area. Whether the experiences are planned for the classroom or any other area, violations of learning theory, of curricular and administrative processes, and of humanistic conditions are often ignored by health instruction in schools.

The following ideas and suggestions regarding the health instruction phase of the school health program are meant to give perspective, not in-depth information, to clarify pertinent issues, not to be exhaustive. They are intended to be provocative, not definitive. We need to do three things: to redefine health, to develop an instructional model consistent with the "new" definition, and to consider some of the critical issues for implementing such an instructional model.

Health Redefined

First, we must deal with the central issue of what health is. The persistence of those traditional expectations described earlier

260 caused us many difficulties. In general, they have caused us to focus on negative issues, to believe that there was a single set of answers for achieving good health, and to develop in students a helplessly dependent attitude toward ways to exercise control over their own lives. It would be more beneficial to define health in a broader sense, better to work with a definition that would include the reality of good and bad experiences as a part of one's health. A definition that would allow all individuals into the system and give him or her some hope regardless of current status. A definition would allow for the uniqueness of individuals and the divergences of human capacities. I propose the following such definition: "health is the status of the individual that reflects the optimum degree of success he or she has had in fulfilling his or her various capacities."

Accepting such a definition has many worthwhile results. It will allow us to focus on positive aspects of health rather than on disease and illness. As a matter of fact, it will allow into the system individuals who have a disease or illness and enable them to deal with their diminished capacity, whether it be temporary or permanent, in a personally acceptable frame of reference. Each would identify with the idea: "My capacities are uniquely mine and all I really have to be concerned about is *how well I've done with what I've got.*" Consider a man with a broken arm and a woman with diabetes. The man with the broken arm can deal with his health problem as a temporarily diminished physical capacity that will also affect his other capacities (social, mental-emotional, etc.) to deal with life. He will have a different expectation of his abilities than before his arm was broken. He will evaluate his *degree of success* against a different standard in order to determine how

well he does with his disability in continuing to fulfill his total capacity to its optimum level. The woman with diabetes, however, will interpret her diminished capacity somewhat differently than the man with the broken arm, but will identify with the same basic concept: "It is how well I do with what I have that is important." Her perspective now will be that she has a permanent, or at least a long term condition that will diminish her capacities. In this situation a realistic appraisal indicates the need for a review of her capacities and what she will be able to do with the potential she now has. Although it could occur for her, a lowered health status is *not* required. If the woman brings the diabetes under control (with medical supervision) and makes the necessary mental-emotional, intellectual, social, and other physical adjustments, her *degree* of success can be as high or higher than it was before the onset of diabetes. The new definition simply does not ask an individual to achieve something that is beyond his or her capacity. It does not demand or set specific barometers for health success for everyone. Nor does it define anyone as unhealthy when he acquires a temporary, long term, or permanent health problem. It simply asks that we do the best possible with the capacities we have.

What must a school do to utilize such a concept of health in the instructional phase of its school health program? First of all, it must spend time "selling" the new concept of health and must make a commitment that will establish an atmosphere to allow students to attain the desired goals. The long range goals are for the students to understand themselves, to identify the factors that influence their health, and to develop techniques and methods of controlling those factors. In addition, these goals must be focused on as part of an individual's basic need system and viewed as the motivation for all student behavior. In turn, the goal, and/or the reason for the actions, feelings, and decisions for each student will be the desire to understand himself in one situation or another, to identify factors (physical, social, emotional, spiritual, intellectual) that influence his health, or to develop techniques to control the factors that influence his health.

Instructional Model

The preceding is an extremely broad and abstract concept; it offers nonetheless a system into which individuals can associate isolated learning experiences. It is a concept of health that will not have to be reorganized to accommodate new and changing elements in society. Contrast this to the "answer-man" approach that left us feeling helpless when the answers did not apply any longer.

The instructional phase will be designed to provide experiences that will enable each student to develop knowledge, attitudes, skills, and behavioral patterns that will contribute to his self understanding. It emphasizes the uniqueness of each student, his uniqueness in terms of past, present, and future needs and their role in achieving a "quality of Life." The premise of the program will be that all individuals have physical, emotional, social, intellectual, and spiritual needs that must be satisfied. The instruction will unify experiences by illustrating that all individuals, regardless of their unique need satisfying activities within each dimension, meet their needs by a universal process involving three important factors: (1) the constant demands upon them for decision making, (2) their continual interactions with external and internal environments, and (3) their varying stages of growth and develop-

ment through each of the five dimensions of man.

The aim of the instructional phase is the development of individuals who can function independently, rather than dependently and who are not bound to teachers and isolated sources of information. The process seeks to involve the student as an active participant in his own health education. With this in mind, we will not base our program merely on present needs and interests, but also on experiences that will be a preparation for identification and satisfaction of the ongoing needs arising in the future.

To facilitate such a program, learning will be based on the acquisition of health concepts rather than isolated sets of facts. Such conceptual learning allows the student to construct a framework in which future experiences can be meaningfully related, and it enables him to incorporate new, and at times contradictory, information into his life-style without complete reorganization or disregard for previous learning. This system presents opportunities for students to incorporate their unique needs and develop effective techniques and methods of satisfying them. The same basic concepts will be utilized at all grade levels. As progress is made, different and more complex experiences are used to illustrate the concepts' usefulness and applicability. Instruction then will focus on the question, "HOW CAN *I* USE WHAT *I* HAVE LEARNED?"

The learning experience will be individual-oriented rather than program-oriented. Programs are molded to the learners' needs rather than vice versa. Its frame of reference is people, not facts or programs. Its content is determined by the unique interests and needs of the students involved and is reflected in the methods and materials chosen for in-

262 struction. It creates situations that offer the individual constant opportunities to confront his "self" in the face of others who differ in varying degrees. Its product is a defensible self image for each individual. Evaluation in such a program will serve primarily as a tool to inform students that they have accomplished a specific objective. It is a technique of letting students know they got where they wanted to go. In addition, evaluation is used for teacher and program improvement. Through an understanding of the factors that influence the development of a useful self image and the methods that can be used to control those influencing factors, students will have a sound basis for meeting their ongoing needs. Its ultimate aim, then, is a self-reliant individual who can make rational decisions regarding the pursuit of "quality of Life."

Issues for Implementation

Two central and related issues must be resolved before instructional programs in health education can be effective. Both of these pertinent issues are focused on how to accomplish the program's goals most efficiently and effectively. Typically, we have expected teachers to present a set of guidelines to follow, a group of answers to learn, and a sort of "you should be like me" orientation. Because of the problems this orientation presents, particularly its disregard for the uniqueness of individuals, it creates an untenable position for the learner. It is particularly weak if we accept the possibility of numerous appropriate positions with regard to almost every critical health issue. In contrast to the orientation just presented, which has been described as "selfing," there is another stance—"othering." This position holds that if I want people to do what I want them to do,

I should become more like them. If I want to influence students I should grow my hair longer, forsake my tie and sport coat for patched blue jeans and a faded work shirt. Then, because I'm more like them, they are more apt to do what I want. The problem here is that what I stand for is not dictated by how I look or what I wear. My credibility as a teacher cannot be established and maintained by appearances.

The alternative to "selfing" and "othering" is mutualism. Mutualism holds that we all have contributions to make in attaining the goals of a health course. It is basic that we accept students as credible! They have important insights, feelings, and information that can be shared and applied for the mutual benefit of the group. This sharing process, in fact, increases the chance that each student will be able to draw from as many alternative sources as possible the information that best meets his particular health needs. What's more, he still recognizes many other alternatives to such problems and realizes that should his health needs change he will be able to select a more appropriate alternative for his new situation. In short, students have confidence in themselves because they have been allowed opportunities to actively participate in the decision-making process, opportunities to examine and define their value and attitudinal positions, and opportunities to give and receive through meaningful interaction alternatives to their health problems.

The second issue is the power versus authority dilemma. Schools in general have been run on the power principle. That is, they have focused on the consequences of certain types of behavior and displayed a power source to insure compliance. They told individuals what to think and demonstrated what the consequences would be if they did not follow those dictates. Specifically, the health instructional program has used the power concept to indoctrinate students to believe there are simple rules for solving their health problems. All that is required is that they learn the signs and symptoms of illnesses and disease. The major power source was the threat of bad grades, although the other ever present power source was the hint that if students did not learn and follow the rules something terrible was bound to happen. For instance, it is necessary to learn all the harmful effects of alcohol and tobacco; but most of us learned, and most of us smoke and drink anyway. The problem with the power-orientation is that once a source of power is removed the individual returns to doing what he wants or needs to do in the first place. Once the grade was received, the course passed, or graduation occurred, this major source of the power was removed.

The authority-orientation, by contrast, relies upon a process that assists the individual in making appropriate decisions because he sees that it is in his best interest to do so. The goal of this new definition and model for health instruction is to create in the student a self-generated power source. This process requires establishing the credibility of both the teacher and student. The power-orientation had to deny the credibility of the student in order to maintain its power. This creditability required in the authority-orientation also requires the program to deal with reality. It cannot maintain a position that alcohol is the worst thing on earth when the student's world is full of significant individuals who drink and appear to be happier because of it. This orientation does not have to accept alcohol, but it must allow the student to examine the alternative and make a choice for himself that he considers to be in his best interest in light of

the alternatives he has discovered. The final, and perhaps the most important, advantage in the authority-orientation is that it develops alternatives from which the student can select the one that is most appropriate for him. It also allows him to examine the viability of alternative positions chosen by others. In this way he can keep these in his repertoire of alternatives, and, should his life situation change, he will possess alternative courses of action he might select.

———————•◆•———————

QUESTIONS FOR DISCUSSION

1. How have the schools you have attended helped you to meet the objectives of civic responsibility developed by the Educational Policies Commission? Can you think of better ways the school might accomplish these objectives? Identify them.

2. What are some ways in which personalities are developed? State some ways in which the schools influence personality development.

3. What are the advantages and disadvantages of the specialized high school compared to the comprehensive high school?

4. In what ways are the goals of the interscholastic athletic programs incompatible with the goals of the recreation programs? What should be the relationship of these goals?

5. What do you consider the objectives of college education to be? How have these objectives changed in the last few years?

SUPPLEMENTARY LEARNING ACTIVITIES

1. Poll some public school teachers regarding the kinds of competencies teachers must have to assist students in meeting the needs

264   suggested in this chapter. Formulate a list of these competencies in collaboration with your classmates.

2. Invite a school psychologist to class to discuss personality development. Give attention to the role of the school.

3. Conduct a telephone survey of various employers to determine their views regarding the school's role in vocational education.

4. Survey the total community recreation program. In what ways could the schools and the local government cooperate to improve the community program?

5. Obtain copies of available documents on health education from your state department of education. Analyze and critically appraise one or more of these documents.

SELECTED REFERENCES

Archambault, Reginald, ed. *Dewey on Education*. New York: Random House, Inc., 1966.

Brown, Raloy E. "Can Public Education Survive?" *National Elementary Principal* 52(October 1972):72–75.

Bucher, Charles A. *Foundations of Physical Education*. St. Louis: The C. V. Mosby Company, 1968.

Chapman, J. Crosby, and George S. Counts. *Principles of Education*. Boston: Houghton Mifflin Company, 1924.

Coleman, James S. "Social Change: Impact on the Adolescent." *Bulletin of the National Association of Secondary Principals* 49(1965):11–18.

Cremin, Lawrence A. *The Genius of American Education*. Pittsburgh: University of Pittsburgh Press, 1965.

Denzin, Norman K. *Children and Their Caretakers*. New Brunswick, N.J.: E. P. Dutton & Co., Inc., Transaction Books, 1973.

Dewey, John. *Democracy and Education*. New York: Macmillan Company, 1916.

Edwards, Newton, and H. G. Richey. *The School in the American Social Order*. Boston: Houghton Mifflin Company, 1963.

Erickson, Erik H., ed. *Youth: Change and Challenge*. New York: Basic Books, Inc., Publishers, 1963.

Goodman, Paul. *Compulsory Mis-Education and the Community of Scholars*. New York: Random House, Inc., 1964.

Holt, John. *How Children Fail*. New York: Pitman Publishing Corporation, 1964.

Lee, Gordon C. *Education and Democratic Ideals*. New York: Harcourt, Brace & World, Inc., 1965.

LaNoue, George R. *The Politics of School Decentralization*. Lexington, Mass.: D. C. Heath & Company, Lexington Books, 1973.

Morris, Van Cleve, et al. *Becoming an Educator*. Boston: Houghton Mifflin Company, 1963.

Passow, A. Harry. *Urban Education in the 1970's: Reflections and a Look Ahead*. New York: Teachers College Press, 1971.

Pendergast, Sister M. Richard. "On Inkwells, Hickory Sticks, and Other Memories." *School and Community* 59(January 1973):19–20.

Silberman, Melvin L. *The Experience of Schooling*. New York: Holt, Rinehart and Winston, Inc., 1971.

Simmons, Daniel J. "Beware! The Three R's

Cometh." *Phi Delta Kappan* 54(March 1973):492–95.

Tanner, Daniel. *Schools for Youth.* New York: Macmillan Company, 1965.

Thayer, V. T. *Formative Ideas in American Education.* New York: Dodd, Mead & Company, 1965.

Weiss, Gerald H. "Educating for the Future." *School and Community* 59(May 1973): 19–21.

chapter 10

Our Educational Past in Perspective

goals

- Provides a chronicle of the historical achievements of our educational system.

- Points out the various periods in the development of the American educational system.

- Conceptualizes the historical support that Americans have provided for education.

- Emphasizes the concept that education has played a key role in the growth of our American society.

- Traces the evolution of the elementary and secondary school.

- Highlights the historical development of our teacher-training programs.

- Accentuates the dependency of a democratic society on its educational system to produce an informed citizenry.

268 Many changes have taken place in American education since the first schools were established in this country. In this chapter, we shall take a brief look at some of these changes.

History permits us to climb to a high place and look back over the road that we have traveled. Once we can see this road clearly, we can avoid some of the mistakes that we have made before. By the same token, we can capitalize upon the successes in our educational past. Then too, a knowledge of the history of education permits a teacher to appreciate the proud heritage that American educators possess. Let us proceed then with a brief look at the history of American education—the task and the teacher.

Educational Expectations in Colonial America

When the colonists arrived at Jamestown in 1607, they brought their ideas concerning education with them. Earlier in this book, it was pointed out that Americans today have various expectations of the public schools. Just as contemporary Americans have certain expectations of the present-day educational systems, so were there certain educational expectations in colonial America. Colonial America was divided roughly into three geographical areas—the northern colonies in the New England area, the middle colonies centered in New York, and the southern colonies located in the Virginia area. The colonists in each of these three areas had somewhat different expectations of the schools that existed in their respective areas. A New England Puritan, expressing his expectations in contemporary language, might have said:

I expect two things from our schools here in the northern colonies. First, my children must learn to read so they can understand the Bible. Secondly, the schools must teach my boys Latin and Greek so that if they wish to go on to college they will be qualified to do so.

> *Religion, morality, and knowledge being necessary to good government and the happiness of mankind, schools and the means of education shall forever be encouraged.*
>
> Northwest Ordinance of 1787

A colonial battledore, a variation of the hornbook printed on heavy paper and folded like an envelope.

The earliest known illustration of a secondary school in America. This is the Boston Latin Grammar School founded in 1635. This illustration comes from an old pictorial map of Boston made about 1748, just before this school building was torn down. This was probably not the original building which housed the Boston Latin Grammar School.

This interest in education in the northern colonies coupled with the fact that most of the colonists in that area were of similar religious convictions led to the early establishment of public schools in that area. In fact, by 1635, only fifteen years after Boston had been settled, a Latin Grammar School was established in that area. Grammar schools had existed in Europe for many years prior to their appearance in colonial America. As their name implies, the Latin Grammar Schools included instruction in the classical languages of Latin and Greek. Such instruction was considered to be absolutely essential for the very few colonial boys who went on to a university. The schoolboys—for only boys were admitted—who attended the Latin Grammar School spent most of their time memorizing and then reciting what they had learned to the schoolmaster. Recalling his experiences as a Latin Grammar School student, one graduate recalled:

A colonial hornbook from which children learned the ABCs. It consisted of a heavy sheet of paper tacked to a piece of wood and covered with a thin sheet of cow's horn.

270

At ten years of age I committed to memory many rules of syntax, the meaning of which I had no notion of, although I could apply them in a mechanical way. The rule for the ablative absolute, for instance—"A noun and a participle are put in the ablative, called absolute, to denote the time, cause or concomitant of an action, or the condition on which it depends"—I could rattle off whenever I encountered a sample of that construction, but it was several years after I learnt the rule that I arrived at even the faintest conception of what it meant. The learning by heart of the grammar then preceded rather than accompanied as now exercises in translation and composition.

———•———

The educational expectations of a typical colonist from the middle colonies can be illustrated by the following statement that could have been made by a parent living in that area at that time:

———•———

Since there are many different religions represented here in the middle colonies, I want my children to attend a parochial school where they will not only learn to read and write, but also where they will receive instruction in my particular religion.

———•———

These middle colonies are sometimes referred to as the "colonial melting pot" because they were settled by people of many different nationalities and religions. These divergent backgrounds made it difficult for the middle colonists to agree upon the curriculum for a public school system, and therefore each religious group established its own parochial school system. It is interesting to note that many of these same educational problems that were found in colonial America still exist today. For instance, there are still many divergent groups in the American society, so that we may still be considered a melting pot (or if you prefer to use more recent popular terminology, a vegetable stew).

Yet another example of an educational problem that has persisted since colonial times is that dealing with parochial education. Just as the middle colonists did, a number of religious groups still feel the need to maintain their own parochial school systems.

The southern colonies consisted of large plantations and relatively few towns. This meant that two rather distinct classes of people—a few wealthy plantation owners, and a mass of poor black slaves and white indentured servants who worked on the plantations—lived in the southern colonies. This also meant that people lived far apart in the southern colonies. If we could turn back the clock to colonial days, we would probably hear a southern plantation owner explain his educational expectations something like this:

———•———

Let me say first of all that we don't really need a public school system here in the southern colonies because, in the first place, the plantation workers do not need any education at all, and in the second place, the children of us plantation owners live so far apart that it would be impractical to have a central public school for all of them to attend. For these reasons, we do not have and do not need a public school system. I hire a tutor to live here on my plantation and teach my children. When my boys get old enough I'll send them back to Europe to attend a university.

The only education available to the poorer people in the southern colonies was that provided by individual parents for their children and that provided by certain missionary groups interested in teaching young people to read the Bible. A boy from a poor family who wished to learn a trade would receive his practical education by serving an apprenticeship with a master craftsman who was already in that line of work.

Early School Laws

The first law passed in colonial America dealing with education was passed in Massachusetts in 1642. This law, requiring parents to educate their children, reads as follows:

This Court, taking into consideration the great neglect of many parents and masters in training up their children in learning, and labor, and other implyments which may be proffitable to the common wealth, do hereupon order and decree, that in every towne ye chosen men appointed for managing prudentiall affaires of the same shall henceforth stand charged with the care of the redresse of this evil, so as they shalbee sufficiently punished by fines for the neglect thereof, upon presentment of the grand jury, or other infor-

mation on complaint in any Court within this jurisdiction. And for this end they, or the greater number of them, shall have power to take account from time to time of all parents and masters, and of their children, concerning their calling and implyment of their children, especially of their ability to read and understand the principles of religion and the capitall lawes of this country, and to impose fines upon such as shall refuse to render such account to them when they shall be required; and they shall have power, with consent of any Court or the magistrate, to put forth apprentices the children of such as they shall [find] not to be able and fitt to imploy and bring them up.

In 1647, yet another law dealing with education was passed in Massachusetts. This law, which has come to be known as the "Old Deluder Act," required towns of certain size to establish schools. This law stated:

It being one chiefe project of that old deluder, Satan, to keepe men from the knowledge of the Scriptures, as in former times by keeping them in an unknown tongue, so in these latter times by persuading from the use of tongues, that so at least the true sence and meaning of the originall might be clouded by false glosses of saint seeming deceivers, that learning may not be buried in the grave of our fathers in church and commonwealth, the Lord assisting our endeavors,—

It is therefore ordered that every township in this jurisdiction, after the Lord hath increased their number to 50 householders, shall then forthwith appoint one within their towne to teach all such children as shall resort to him to write and reade, whose wages shall be paid either by the parents or masters of such children, or by the inhabitants in general, . . . and it is further ordered that where

A photograph of the title page and board back of the oldest known edition (1727) of the New England Primer. It was the most widely used textbook in colonial America.

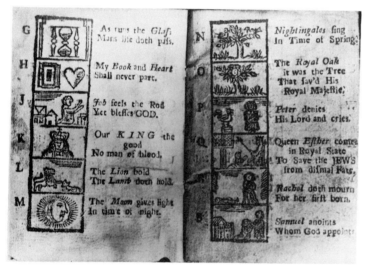

The contents of the New England Primer reflected the religious emphasis of education in colonial America.

The seal of the Society for the Propagation of the Gospel in Foreign Parts. This society, which was the missionary society of the Church of England, was responsible for the support of most of the charity schools in the English colonies during the eighteenth century. The society also furnished books for churches and school libraries.

A popular Government, without popular information, or the means of acquiring it, is but a Prologue to a Farce or a Tragedy; or, perhaps both. Knowledge will forever govern ignorance: And a people who mean to be their own Governors, must arm themselves with the power which knowledge gives.

President James Madison

any towne shall increase to the number of 100 families or householders they shall set up a grammar schoole, the Master thereof being able to instruct youth so farr as they shall be fitted for the University, provided that if any town neglect the performance hereof above one year, that every such town shall pay five pounds to the next school till they shall perform this order.

———•———

In addition to the passage of these laws, further proof of the colonists' early interest in education can be found in the following agreement signed by a number of the citizens living in Roxbury in 1645:

———•———

Whereas, the Inhabitantes of Roxburie, in consideration of their relligeous care of posteritie, have taken into consideration how necessarie the education of theire children in Literature will be to fitt them for public service, both in Churche and Commonwealth, in succeeding ages. They therefore unanimously have consented and agreed to erect a free schoole in the said town of Roxburie, and to allow twenty pounds per annum to the schoolemaster, to bee raised out of the messuages and part of the lands of the severall donors (Inhabitantes of said Towne) in severall proportions as hereafter followeth under their hands. And for the well ordering

thereof they have chosen and elected some Feoffees who shall have power to putt in or remove the Schoolemaster, to see to the well ordering of the schoole and schollars, to receive and pay the said twenty pounds per annum to the Schoolemaster and to dispose of any other gifte or giftes which hereafter may or shall be given for the advancement of learning and education of children. . . .

———•———

Our First Colleges

In 1636, only sixteen years after the settlement of Boston, the first college was established in colonial America. This school was named Harvard College after the man who helped to finance the school's humble beginning. The conditions surrounding the establishment of Harvard, and the school's philosophy and curriculum, are explained in the following document, written in 1643 and entitled *New England's First Fruits,* which is partially reproduced here:

———•———

In Respect of the Colledge, and the Proceedings of "Learning" Therein: 1. After God had carried us safe to New England, and wee had builded our houses, provided necessaries for our livelihood, rear'd convenient places for God's worship, and setled the Civill Government: One of the next things we longed for, and looked after was to advance Learning and perpetuate it to Posterity; dreading to leave an illiterate Ministery to the Churches, when our present Ministers shall lie in the Dust. And as wee were thinking and consulting how to effect this great Work; it pleased God to stir up the heart of one Mr. Harvard (a godly Gentleman, and a lover of Learning, there living amongst us) to give the onehalfe of his Estate (it being in all about 1700.l.) towards

Harvard College buildings constructed in 1675, 1699, and 1720. These buildings were dormitories. Most of the instruction took place in the homes or offices of the president and tutors.

the erecting of a Colledge: and all his Library: after him another gave 300.l. others after them cast in more, and the publique hand of the State added the rest: the Colledge was, by common consent, appointed to be at Cambridge, (a place very pleasant and accommodate) and is called (according to the name of the first founder) Harvard Colledge.

The Edifice is very faire and comely within and without, having in it a spacious Hall; (where they daily meet at Commons, Lectures and Exercises), and a large Library with some Bookes to it, the gifts of diverse of our friends, their Chambers and studies also fitted for, and possessed by the Students, and all other roomes of Office necessary and convenient, with all needfull Offices thereto belonging: And by the side of the Colledge a faire Grammer Schoole, for the training up of young Schollars, and fitting them for Aca-

demicall Learning, that still as they are judged ripe, they may be received into the Colledge of this Schoole: Master Corlet is the Mr., who hath very well approved himselfe for his abilities, dexterity and painfulness in teaching and education of the youth under him.

Over the Colledge is master Dunster placed, as President, a learned conscionable and industrious man, who hath so trained up his Pupils in the tongues and Arts, and so seasoned them with the principles of Divinity and Christianity, that we have to our great comfort, (and in truth) beyond our hopes, beheld this progresse in Learning and godliness also; the former of these hath appeared in their publique declamations in Latine and Greeke, and Disputations Logicall and Philosophicall, which they have wonted (besides their ordinary Exercises in the Colledge-Hall) in the audience of the Magistrates, Ministers, and other Schollars, for the probation of their growth in Learning, upon set dayes, constantly once every moneth to make and uphold: The latter hath been manifested in sundry of them, by the savoury breathings of their Spirits in their godly conversation. Insomuch that we are confident, if these early blossomes may be cherished and warmed with the influence of the friends of Learning, and lovers of this pious worke, they will by the help of God, come to happy maturity in a short time.

Over the Colledge are twelve Overseers chosen by the generall Court, six of them are of the Magistrates, the other six of the Ministers, who are to promote the best good of it and (having a power of influence into all persons in it) are to see that every one be diligent and proficient in his proper place.

———— • • ————

Further insight into the nature of Harvard College may be found in the following entrance requirements published in 1642:

———— • • ————

When any scholar is able to read Tully, or such like classical Latine author *extempore,* and make and speak true Latin in Verse and Prose, and decline perfectly the paradigms of nounes and verbs in the Greek tongue, then may he be admitted into the college, nor shall any claim admission before such qualifications.

* ◆ *

Harvard was the only colonial college for nearly sixty years until William and Mary was established in 1693. Other colleges which were established early in our history included Yale (1701), Princeton (1746), King's College (1754), College of Philadelphia (1755), Brown (1764), Dartmouth (1769), and Queen's College (1770).

Latin Grammar Schools

The Latin Grammar School was the only form of secondary school found in the colonies until the early 1700s, at which time a few private secondary schools were established. These schools were established out of a need for a more practical form of secondary education than the existing Latin Grammar Schools provided. Insight into the nature of these early private secondary schools can be gained from the following newspaper ad, which was published in the October-November 1723 edition of the *American Weekly Mercury* of Philadelphia:

* ◆ *

There is a school in New York, in the Broad Street, near the Exchange where Mr. John Walton, late of Yale-Colledge, teacheth Reading, Writing, Arethmatick, whole Numbers and Fractions, Vulgar and Decimal, the Mariners Art, Plain and Mercators Way; also

Geometry, Surveying, the Latin tongue, and Greek and Hebrew Grammers, Ethicks, Rhetorick, Logick, Natural Philosophy and Metaphysicks, all or any of them for a Reasonable Price. The School from the first of October till the first of March will be tended in the Evening. If any Gentleman in the Country are disposed to send their sons to the said School, if they apply themselves to the Master he will immediately procure suitable Entertainment for them, very cheap. Also if any Young Gentleman of the City will Please to come in the evening and make some Tryal of the Liberal Arts, they may have opportunity of Learning the same things which are commonly taught in Colledges.

* ◆ *

The Academy

In 1751 Benjamin Franklin opened a secondary school in Philadelphia which he called an academy. The curriculum in Franklin's Academy included practical training in areas such as surveying, navigation, and printing, as well as courses in English, geography, history, logic, rhetoric, Latin, and Greek.

Franklin's Academy served a real need as the colonies developed a greater need for technically trained citizens. Other academies were quickly established and this type of school flourished for approximately one hundred years. These academies were private schools and many of them admitted girls as well as boys.

The New Nation and Its Educational Needs

One of the great problems facing the United States, after winning her indepen-

276

A picture of the academy and charitable school of Philadelphia founded by Benjamin Franklin in 1751. It is the first institution in America, so far as present records show, to bear the title of academy. Later on it developed into the University of Pennsylvania.

dence from England, was that of welding her people, who had come from many diverse political and religious convictions, into a nation of informed voters. This meant that all citizens should be able to read so that they could keep informed on the issues the country faced. This interest in education found in the new nation was manifested in a number of different ways; for instance, groups of citizens created petitions for better schools. An example of such a petition is the following, which was submitted in 1799 to the General Assembly of Rhode Island:

A PETITION FOR FREE SCHOOL. *To the Honorable General Assembly of the State of Rhode Island and Providence Plantations, to be holden at Greenwich, on the last Monday of February,* A.D. *1799:*

The Memorial and Petition of the Providence Association of Mechanics and Manufacturers respectfully presents—

That the means of education which are enjoyed in this state are very inadequate to a purpose so highly important . . . we at the same time solicit this Honorable Assembly to make legal provision for the establishment of free schools sufficient to educate all the children in the several towns throughout the state. . . .

Another indication of the new national need for, and interest in, education is the following comment made by Thomas Jefferson in 1816:

If a nation expects to be ignorant and free in a state of civilization, it expects what never was and never will be . . . There is no safe deposit but with the people themselves; nor can they be safe with them without information.

Despite this new interest in education, the school of the early 1800s was very humble and inadequate. An excellent description of an 1810 New England school is contained in the following reflection of a teacher who taught in this school.

> *What indeed is the good teacher if not a well-informed lover? . . . To teach is to love. And in the final analysis we learn only from those whom we love . . . the most important of all qualities in the world . . . . This is because the most important of all desires of a human being is the desire to be loved, and at the same time to love others.*
> Ashley Montagu

(A) The school building: The school house stood near the center of the district, at the junction of four roads, so near the usual track of carriages that a large stone was set up at the end of the building to defend it from injury. Except in the dry season the ground was wet, and the soil by no means firm. The spot was particularly exposed to the bleak winds of winter; nor were there any shade trees to shelter the children from the scorching rays of the summer's sun, as they were cut down many years ago. Neither was there any such thing as an outhouse of any kind, not even a wooden shed.

The size of the building was 22 x 20 feet. From the floor to the ceiling it was 7 feet. The chimney and entry took up about four feet at one end, leaving the schoolroom itself 18 x 20 feet. Around these sides of the room were connected desks, arranged so that when the pupils were sitting at them their faces were towards the instructor and their backs toward the wall. Attached to the sides of the desks nearest to the instructor were benches for small pupils. The instructor's desk and chair occupied the center. On this desk were stationed a rod, or ferule; sometimes both. These, with books, writings, inkstands, rules, and plummets, with a fire shovel, and a pair of tongs (often broken), were the principal furniture.

The windows were five in number, of twelve panes each. They were situated so low in the walls as to give full opportunity to the pupils to see every traveller as he passed, and to be easily seen. The places of the broken panes were usually supplied with hats, during school hours. A depression in the chimney, on one side of the entry, furnished a place of deposit for about half of the hats, and the spare clothes of the boys; the rest were left on the floor, often to be trampled upon. The girls generally carried their bonnets, etc., into the schoolroom. The floor and ceiling were level, and the walls were plastered.

The room was warmed by a large and deep fire place. So large was it, and so efficacious in warming the room otherwise, that I have seen about one-eighth of a cord of good wood burning in it at a time. In severe weather it was estimated that the amount usually consumed was not far from a cord a week. . . .

> *Experience keeps a dear school, but fools will learn in no other.*
> Benjamin Franklin

The school was not infrequently broken up for a day or two for want of wood. The instructor or pupils were sometimes, however, compelled to cut or saw it to prevent the closing of the school. The wood was left in the road near the house, so that it often was buried in the snow, or wet with rain. At the best, it was usually burnt green. The fires were to be kindled about half an hour before the time of beginning the school. Often, the scholar, whose lot it was, neglected to build it. In consequence of this, the house was frequently cold and uncomfortable about half of the forenoon, when, the fire being very large, the excess of heat became equally distressing. Frequently, too, we were annoyed by smoke. The greatest amount of suffering, however, arose from excessive heat, particularly at the close of the day. The pupils being in a free perspiration when they left, were very liable to take cold.

The ventilation of the schoolroom was as much neglected as its temperature; and its cleanliness, more perhaps than either. There were no arrangements for cleaning feet at the door, or for washing floors, windows, etc. In the summer the floor was washed, perhaps once in two or three weeks.

(B) The Instructors: The winter school usually opened about the first week of De-

The town and church schools of the early colonial period were supplemented by the dame school. In fact, it was a common requirement for that period that children know how to read before entering a town school. Hence, the necessity of these dame schools, which taught the children the alphabet, and possibly the catechism and the rudiments of reading.

cember, and continued from twelve to sixteen weeks. The summer term commenced about the first of May. Formerly this was also continued about three or four months, but within ten years the term has been lengthened usually to twenty weeks. Males have been uniformly employed in winter, and females in summer.

The instructors have usually been changed every season, but sometimes they have been continued two successive summers or winters. A strong prejudice has always existed against employing the same instructor more than once or twice in the same district. This prejudice has yielded in one instance, so far that an instructor who had taught two successive winters, twenty-five years before,

was employed another season. I have not been able to ascertain the number of instructors who have been engaged in the school during the last thirty years, but I can distinctly recollect thirty-seven. Many of them, both males and females, were from sixteen to eighteen years of age, and a few, over twenty-one.

Good moral character, and a thorough knowledge of the common branches, formerly were considered as indispensable qualifications in an instructor. The instructors were chiefly selected from the most respectable families in town. But for fifteen or twenty years, these things have not been so much regarded. They have indeed been deemed desirable; but the most common method now seems to be to ascertain, as near as possible, the dividend for that season from the public treasury, and then fix upon a teacher who will take charge of the school, three or four months, for this money. He must indeed be able to obtain a license from the Board of Visitors; but this has become nearly a matter of course, provided he can spell, read, and write. In general, the candidate is some favorite or relative of the District Committee. It gives me great pleasure, however, to say that the moral character of almost every instructor, so far as I know, has been unexceptional.

Instructors have usually boarded in the families of the pupils. Their compensation has varied from seven to eleven dollars a month for males; and from sixty-two and a half cents to one dollar a week for females. Within the past ten years, however, the price of instruction has rarely been less than nine dollars in the former case, and seventy-five cents in the latter. In the few instances in which instructors have furnished their own board the compensation has been about the same, it being assumed that they could work at some employment of their own enough to pay their board, especially the females.

Plan of the University of Virginia drawn by Thomas Jefferson in the early nineteenth century. The University was opened in 1825. This plan represents a radical modification of the semimonastic conception of college life held by the earlier colonial colleges. The building facing in the main court is for lectures and recitations; those flanking it are professors' houses; the smaller buildings are dormitories.

(C) The Instruction: Two of the Board of Visitors usually visit the winter schools twice during the term. In the summer, their visits are often omitted. These visits usually occupy from one hour to an hour and a half. They are spent merely in hearing a few hurried lessons, and in making some remarks, generally in their character. Formerly, it was customary to examine the pupils in some approved Catechism, but this practice has been omitted for twenty years.

The parents seldom visit the school, except by special invitation. The greater number pay very little attention to it at all. There are, however, a few who are gradually awakening to the importance of good instruction; but there are also a few who oppose everything which is suggested as, at the least, useless, and are scarcely willing their children should be governed in the school.

The school books have been about the same for thirty years. Webster's Spelling Book, the American Preceptor, and the New Testament, have been the principal books used. Before the appearance of the American Preceptor, Dwight's Geography was used as a reading book. A few of the Introduction to the American Orator were introduced about

twelve years since, and, more recently, Jack Halyard.

Until within a few years, no studies have been permitted in the day school but spelling, reading, and writing. Arithmetic was taught by a few instructors, one or two evenings in a week, but, in spite of the most determined opposition, arithmetic is now permitted in the day school, and a few pupils study geography.

The Development of the Common School

The national interest in education during the late eighteenth and early nineteenth centuries culminated in a movement to establish free public schools—or common schools, as they were then called—for all children. The man who led this fight for common schools was Horace Mann (1796–1859). Horace Mann became the first secretary (a position we now call the state superintendent of schools) of the Massachusetts state board of education in 1837. In that position, Mann was

280

A portrait of Horace Mann—the father of the common school.

able to do a good deal to promote the common school cause. Each year, Mann wrote an annual report of his work as the secretary of the state board of education. His twelfth annual report included the following statement about the importance of the common school:

Without undervaluing any other human agency, it may be safely affirmed that the common school, improved and energized as it can easily be, may become the most effective and benignant of all the forces of civilization. Two reasons sustain this position. In the first place, there is a universality in its operation, which can be affirmed of no other institution whatever. If administered in the spirit of justice and conciliation, all the rising generation may be brought within the circle of its reformatory and elevating influences. And, in the second place, the materials upon which

it operates are so pliant and ductile as to be susceptible of assuming a greater variety of forms than any other earthly work of the Creator. The inflexibility and ruggedness of the oak, when compared with the lithe sapling or the tender germ, are but feeble emblems to typify the docility of childhood when contrasted with the obduracy and intractableness of man. It is these inherent advantages of the common school, which, in our own state, have produced results so striking, from a system so imperfect, and an administration so feeble. In teaching the blind and the deaf and dumb, in kindling the latent spark of intelligence that lurks in an idiot's mind, and in the more holy work of reforming abandoned and outcast children, education has proved what it can do by glorious experiments. These wonders it has done in its infancy, and with the lights of a limited experience; but when its faculties shall be fully developed, when it shall be trained to wield its mighty energies for the protection of society against the giant vices which now invade and torment it—against intemperance, avarice, war, slavery, bigotry, the woes of want, and the wickedness of waste,—then there will not be a height to which these enemies of the race can escape which it will not scale.

Through his work as secretary to the Massachusetts state board of education, his speaking, and his writing—including his annual reports such as the one just quoted—Horace Mann deserves much of the credit for helping to establish the common school system in the United States. So much so, in fact, that he is now remembered as the "father of the common school."

Another of the many men who did much to help promote education in the United States during the mid-nineteenth century was Henry Barnard (1811–1900). Barnard served as the secretary of the state board of education in Connecticut and then in Rhode Island. Barnard was a prolific writer and his writings were very influential in helping to sell the need for better education. He edited and published the *American Journal of Education* which represented a gigantic compilation of information about education. In 1867 Henry Barnard became the first United States Commissioner of Education.

The work of Horace Mann, Henry Barnard, and many other men of foresight who saw the value—indeed, the essentialness—of a common education for all citizens was firmly established in the United States during the last half of the nineteenth century. Massachusetts, the state that led the way in many facets of education, passed the first compulsory school attendance law in 1852. Other states eventually passed similar laws so that by 1900, thirty-two states required compulsory school attendance.

The Development of the Public High Schools

It was mentioned earlier in this chapter that the Latin Grammar School was the first form of secondary school that existed in this country. The academy eventually replaced the Latin Grammar School as the dominant secondary school in the United States.

In 1821, a new form of secondary school, one unique to the United States, was established at Boston, Massachusetts. This new secondary school was called the "English Classical School" but three years later its name was changed to the "English High School."

The curriculum of this new English High School emphasized mathematics, social

281

> *Laws for the liberal education of youth, especially of the lower class of people, are so extremely wise and useful, that, to a humane and generous mind, no expense for this purpose would be thought extravagant.*
>
> President John Adams

studies, science, and English. The first high schools were for boys between the ages of twelve and fifteen, but later on girls were also admitted.

About 1900, the high school replaced the academy as the dominant type of secondary school in this country, and, needless to say, remains so today. Figure 10.1 shows, in graphic form, the historical development of secondary schools in the United States.

Teacher Education

As the United States developed a need for better schools and better education, it was inevitable that the subject of better-trained teachers should also receive attention. Citizens of the United States were slow to realize that good education required good teachers. Up until the mid-1800s teachers had, for the most part, been very poorly prepared for their work. A teacher's job was not considered very important and commanded very little prestige. In fact, advertisements which appeared in a Philadelphia newspaper during colonial times (one of which is reproduced on page 282) show that even indentured servants were sold as schoolteachers.

Since education had a strong religious motive in the colonies, the schools were often conducted in the church by the minister. When the job got too big for the minister to

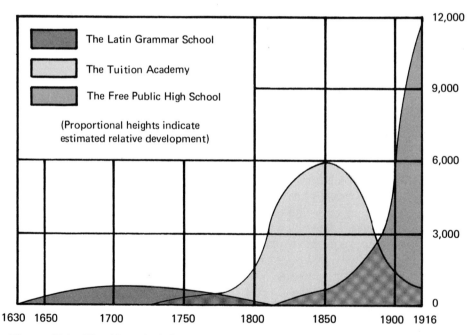

An advertisement in a 1735 issue of the Pennsylvania Gazette showing an indentured servant for sale as a schoolmaster. The lower two ads show Negro slaves for sale.

Figure 10.1 The Historical Development of Secondary Schools in the United States.

Source: E. P. Cubberley, *The History of Education* (Boston: Houghton Mifflin Company, 1920), p. 699. Copyright Board of Trustees of Leland Stanford Junior University, Stanford. Used by permission.

handle by himself, a layman would be hired to teach the school. Oftentimes, in addition to teaching the school, the teacher would be required "to act as court messenger, to serve summonses, to conduct certain ceremonial services at the church, to lead the Sunday choir, to ring the bell for public worship, to dig the graves, and to perform other occasional duties."

Some boys became teachers by serving as an apprentice to a schoolmaster. This method of learning the art of teaching was quite logical since the apprenticeship was a well-established way of learning trades in that day. The following record of such an apprenticeship agreement was recorded in the courts of New York City in 1772:

———•———

This Indenture witnesseth that John Campbel Son of Robert Campbel of the City of New York with the Consent of his father and mother hath put himself and by these presents doth Voluntarily put and bind himself Apprentice to George Brownell of the Same City Schoolmaster to learn the Art Trade or Mystery—for and during the term of ten years . . . And the said George Brownell Doth hereby Covenent and Promise to teach and Instruct or Cause the said Apprentice to be taught and Instructed in the Art Trade or Calling of a Schoolmaster by the best way or means he or his wife may or can.

———•———

Benjamin Franklin, in proposing the establishment of his academy, claimed that

———•———

a number of the poorer sort [of academy graduates] will be hereby qualified to act as School masters in the Country, to teach children Reading, Writing, Arithmetic, and the

Grammar of their Mother Tongue, and being of good morals and known character, may be recommended from the Academy to Country Schools for that purpose; the Country suffering at present very much for want of good Schoolmasters, and obliged frequently to employ in their Schools, vicious imported Servants, or concealed Papists, who by their bad Examples and Instructions often deprave the Morals and corrupt the Principles of the children under their Care.

———•———

It is interesting to note that Franklin suggested that the "poorer" graduates of his academy would make good teachers. This wording indicates again the low esteem of teachers at that time.

The first formal teacher-training institution in the United States was a private normal school established in 1823 at Concord, Vermont. This school was established by the Rev. Samuel Hall and was called the Columbian School. Some insight into the nature of Hall's school can be obtained from the following advertisement which appeared in the May 20, 1823 edition of the North Star newspaper:

———•———

COLUMBIAN SCHOOL, CONCORD, VT.

The second term will commence on the third Tuesday (17th day) of June next. The School will be under the direction, and will be principally instructed by the Rev. Mr. Hall.
Books used in the school must be uniform. Hence, arrangements are made so that they may be obtained at either of the stores in town. Branches taught, if required, are the following: Reading, Spelling, Defining, Geography (ancient and modern), History, Grammar, Rhetoric, Composition, Arithmetic, Construction of Maps, Theoretical Surveying,

284 Astronomy, Natural Philosophy, Chemistry (without experiments), Logic, Moral Philosophy, Mental Philosophy, and General Criticism.

It is wished to have the languages excluded. This will not, however, be strictly adhered to.

TERMS: For Common School studies, $2. per term of 12 weeks. Other branches from $2.50 to $4.

> *To be a schoolmaster is next to being a king. Do you count it a mean employment to imbue the minds of your fellow citizens in their earnest years with the best literature and with the love of Christ, and to return them to their country honest and virtuous men? In the opinion of fools, it is a humble task, but in fact it is the noblest of occupations. Even among the heathen it was always a noble thing to deserve well of the state, and no one serves it better than the molders of raw boys.*
>
> Erasmus

It is intended to have instruction particularly thorough, and hence an additional instructor will be employed, when the School amounts to more than 20. Board obtained near the School room, on reasonable terms.

Application may be made to Mr. Lyman F. Dewey, Mr. John Barnet, or Mr. Hall.

Concord, Vt. May 14, 1823.

———•—•———

This ad points out that the curriculum in Hall's normal school included "Mental Philosophy," which was the forerunner of educational psychology, and "General Criticism" (presumably of the student's practice teaching).

The first high school in the United States, established in 1821 at Boston. This was the counterpart of the Latin Grammar School. The term high school was not applied to it until the school had existed for several years. It was first called an English Classical School.

The first public tax-supported teacher-training school in this country was the Lexington Normal School located in Lexington, Massachusetts. This school was opened in 1839. Horace Mann, as secretary of the state board of education, was very influential in the establishment of this state normal school. The curriculum in the Lexington Normal School, and other similar state normal schools which were quickly established, was patterned after similar schools that had existed in Europe since the late 1600s. These early normal schools offered a two-year program designed to prepare their students, many of whom had not attended a secondary school, to teach elementary school. The normal schools eventually developed four-year programs and, during the 1920s, changed their names to "state teachers' colleges." Then later, during the 1950s, many of these institutions expanded their curricula to include liberal arts and changed their names to "state colleges." During the last decade, many of these same institutions that started as two-year normal schools have begun offering graduate work, including doctoral programs, and have changed their names to "state universities."

It was not until about 1900 that states began passing teacher certification laws which regulated the amount and type of training that a person must have to become a teacher. Prior to the passage of these laws, anyone could legally teach school.

In summary, this chapter has pointed out a number of important concepts concerning the history of education in the United States. These concepts include the following:

- The educational program in colonial America was largely transplanted from Europe.
- The colonists attempted to make educational provisions almost as soon as they set foot on the new world.
- The motive for providing education in colonial America was almost entirely religious in nature.
- Education has played an important role in the development of the United States, from 1607 when the first colonists settled at Jamestown to the present.
- Many of the educational problems of colonial America have persisted to the present time.
- The role of education in the United States has increased in importance down through

time, so that today education has a larger and more important role to play in our country than ever before.

As is pointed out elsewhere in this book, total society and individuals within our society have come to expect a great deal from our contemporary school system. Our educational system has become extremely large and complex in its effort to meet these societal and individual expectations. In the next chapter of this book we will explore a number of different basic views which underpin this enormous, complex educational system.

Point of View

This chapter has attempted to highlight the historical development of the American educational system. Within this general framework, the concept that education has played a key role, perhaps even *the* key role, in the development of America has been articulated. The well-accepted notion that a democratic society such as ours is totally dependent upon its schools' ability to produce an informed electorate has been developed. The idea that Americans have historically insisted upon an adequate educational system is yet another theme woven throughout this chapter.

Though Americans in general, and specifically teachers, can indeed be proud of their educational heritage, and even though there is today a generally high level of support for quality education in our society—there is much debate concerning how much of our national resources should be expended on education. Controversy also exists about what the major purpose and general goals of our public school system should be. The follow-

286 ing "point of view" represents one opinion regarding the basic purpose of American schools.

Dr. R. Freeman Butts is recognized as one of the leading educational historians in the United States. He is the William F. Russell Professor in the Foundations of Education at Teachers' College, Columbia University. This article, entitled "Assaults on a Great Idea," analyzes the historical and contemporary national faith in our educational system. It is a thought-provoking treatment of a very important topic—one which should be of primary concern to all educators.

———————◆•◆———————

Assaults on a Great Idea

R. Freeman Butts

Of all the unsettling results of the malaise of the 1960s the most ominous may be the erosion of America's faith in public education as a cultural and social element in building a sense of national community. This weakening of commitment to public education stems partly from a resurgence of older separatist and centrifugal tendencies of American society, and partly from the thrashing about for ways to loosen up what is described as a rigid and inhumane system. It reflects a general loss of respect for authority in government, school, university, church and community arising from the war in Vietnam, the youth counter-culture, demands for cultural separatism and the militant search for racial or ethnic identity.

R. Freeman Butts, "Assaults on a Great Idea," *The Nation,* April 30, 1973, pp. 553–60. Used by permission.

The general quest for "alternatives" to the existing system is in part deliberately designed to weaken public education, in part unaware that it may have that effect. It is the convergence and mutual reinforcement of so many forces—political, social, economic, racial, religious and intellectual—that makes the search for "alternatives" so beguiling. But if the American people should become disenchanted with the idea of the public school and turn in significant numbers to other means of education, they will weaken, perhaps beyond repair, a basic component of democratic American society.

The clamor for "alternatives" undermines the basic meaning of the public school, which was hammered out in the considerable consensus achieved during nearly two centuries of American history. That there was a consensus may be seen in the fact that by 1900 about 92 percent of elementary and secondary schoolchildren were in public schools. Thereafter, major efforts by religious groups doubled the proportion of children in nonpublic schools by the 1960s (to 14 or 15 percent), but this enrollment has since declined to around 10 percent. The fact that 90 percent of American children are today in public schools does not necessarily mean that all the aspects of public education discussed below are universally accepted, but they are identifiable elements of the public school idea. In the consensus, public schools have been characterized primarily as having a public purpose, public control, public support, public access and public commitment to civic unity.

Purpose

A public school serves a public purpose rather than a private one. It is not maintained for the personal advantage or private gain of the teacher, the proprietor or the board of managers; nor does it exist simply for the enjoyment, happiness or advancement of the individual student or his parents. It may, indeed it should, enhance the vocational competence, or upward social mobility, or personal development of individuals, but if that were all a school attempted, the job could be done as well by a private school catering to particular jobs, or careers or leisure-time enjoyment.

Rather, the prime purpose of the public school is to serve the general welfare of a democratic society, by assuring that the knowledge and understanding necessary to exercise the responsibilities of citizenship are not only made available but actively inculcated. "If," said Thomas Jefferson, "a nation expects to be ignorant and free, in a state of civilization, it expects what never was and never will be."

Achieving a sense of community is the essential purpose of public education. This work cannot be left to the vagaries of individual parents, or small groups of like-minded parents, or particular interest groups, or religious sects, or private enterprisers or cultural specialties. Thus, when the population became ever more heterogeneous after the mid-19th century, the need for compulsory education became increasingly apparent to the lawmakers of the states and of the Union.

Today, however, this basic point is almost entirely overlooked in the furor over the studies of inequality in schools, stemming from the Coleman report of 1966 and expanded upon since by the studies at Harvard of Daniel Patrick Moynihan, Christopher Jencks and others. Their generalizations that public schools have not overcome economic inequality among races or social classes have led to a general impression that public schools

do not make much difference and that the compensatory education advocated by reformers since the mid-1960s has generally failed. Economy-minded politicians pick up this theme with glee and racial minorities are discouraged that just as they are finally making some headway toward equal opportunity in the schools, the word comes down from the scholars, "Don't bother; the public schools don't really matter that much."

To make matters worse, Ivan Illich, Everett Reimer and other radical critics preach that the schools are really instruments of oppression whereby the ruling class maintains itself in power and instills in the other classes attitudes of subservience designed to support the *status quo.* Illich and Reimer argue that, to effect genuine social change, the society must be "deschooled" and all kinds of informal and nonformal means of community education fostered instead. Compulsory attendance must be abolished, so that children, youth and adults of the oppressed classes may be free to develop their distinctive talents and not be forced into a mold by a monolithic and oppressive public school system.

So the discussion has focused on the *economic* inequalities among classes and races and the inability of public schools to remedy what the entire society has wrought. However, there is still enormous disagreement about these generalizations. The historic and comparative evidence is overwhelming that American public schools have been one major factor in producing a higher per capita economic level in America than in any other country, but that is not the critical point here. Even if Jencks should turn out to be right, that compensatory education for the disadvantaged in our society is unable to reduce the economic gap between the rich and the poor, the *economic* argument is not and never has

288 been the fundamental reason for compensatory education. That reason is the public purpose of *justice.* Our conception of a just society based upon principles of liberty and equality requires a public education available to all.

John Rawls, professor of philosophy at Harvard, sees this point more clearly than do his colleagues in the social sciences and education. In order to provide genuine equality of opportunity a just society must give special attention to those born into less favorable social positions. "The value of education should not be assessed only in terms of economic efficiency and social welfare. Equally if not more important is the role of education in enabling a person to enjoy the culture of his society and *to take part in its affairs,* and in this way to provide for each individual a *secure sense of his own worth.*" (*A Theory of Justice,* Harvard University Press.)

If public schools also enable the disadvantaged to improve their economic position, as I believe in the long run they undoubtedly do, that is a social dividend, but the original purpose of public education in the early 19th century was not to provide vocational education or prepare people for jobs. That addendum came along in response to the industrialization and technological specialization of the economy in the later 19th and early 20th centuries. To make the achievement of equal economic condition appear to be the *prime* purpose of public schools and to dismiss rather casually the school system as a "marginal institution" because it does not produce that equality (as Jencks does) is to ignore the fundamental *political* purpose of public education. In the words of Justice Frankfurter, "The school should be the training ground for habits of community." *That* is the ground on which the public schools should be criticized

for failure, and where effort should be exerted for improvement. And that is the area in which there really is no genuine alternative to the public schools.

Control

A public school is one that is under the control of public authorities who own and manage the schools and who are responsible to the people either directly by election or indirectly through publicly designated officers of the civil government. It is significant that Americans speak of "public" schools rather than of "state" or "government" schools, as is the custom in many countries. The term signifies an institution that is directly responsible to the people rather than to one of the legislative, executive or judicial branches of government. Indeed, the distinctive form of school government (the elected lay board of education) was intended to keep the public school responsive to local community interests, yet somewhat free of the narrow partisan politics or bureaucratic controls of the other branches of local government.

In the 19th century it was hoped that a balance would be struck between a central and common authority lodged in the state constitutions, state legislatures and state departments of education, and a flexible operation and management lodged in the local boards of education. However, in the 20th century the matter of control became more complicated when the federal courts increasingly acknowledged their responsibility to interpret the principles of freedom and equality as defined in the Bill of Rights and applied them to all public schools in the states. Although Americans habitually say that public education is a state and not a federal matter, the most difficult and sensitive problems in the past two decades have arisen over federal constitutional issues in the areas of religion and racial segregation.

And in this process the public schools have become a battleground for control by special group interests, some feeling justified because they believe they have not had a fair share in the control of "their" public schools, and others because they have feared the intrusion of "outsiders" into "their" neighborhood schools. The demand of blacks in the urban centers for "community control" or for decentralization is one example of the asserted need to shape local schools to the desires of local groups rather than that such groups be forced to accept teachers or budgets or curricula handed down from some unsympathetic and remote bureaucracy. On the other hand, local white "communities" have declared the right to keep their neighborhood schools white, on the principle of local control and in defiance of desegregation orders by federal courts or central educational authorities.

But the struggles over control are complicated far beyond the question of desegregation. A resurgence of hostility to bureaucratic formalism has led to demands for greater free enterprise in the domain of education. This discontent ranges from demands for "free" or "open" schools to outcries against curriculum or professional requirements that particular groups have felt were irrelevant to their special interests. This attitude fits with the clamor for parents' "freedom of choice" to determine the kind of education they want for their children—whether segregated education for whites or blacks only, or religious education for Catholics or Protestants or Jews only, or political education for radicals or conservatives only. And as the clamor has grown it has seemed easy to argue that such goals could be

better achieved by "alternative" schools. So a Southern reaction to desegregation orders was to seek ways to abolish the free public schools and set up free private schools (with public funds, of course). Some advocates of private enterprise saw this as an opening to get public support for proprietary schools of many kinds. Others saw it as an opportunity to claim that private companies could do a better educational job in the public schools than could the teaching profession, and "performance contracts" were signed with some boards of education to deliver the educational goods for a price and with an efficiency that would outmode the traditional faculty. So far, the evidence in favor of "performance contracting" is dubious, to say the least.

Demands for "accountability" and "management efficiency" and "competency based teacher education" added heat to the arguments over who should control what in the public schools. Meanwhile, the organized teaching profession has launched collective bargaining struggles in most major cities over matters of salary, appointment, tenure and benefits. This has brought teachers and administrators into confrontation not only with the elected boards of education but also with "community demands" that teachers be black or white or religious or ethnic in conformity with the majorities in given neighborhoods. There is no doubt that militancy improves the conditions of professional employment, but it also raises uneasy questions about the control of public schools.

In many of the struggles for control the interests of special groups have taken precedence over the search for rational allocations of authority among local, state and national requirements. The *constitutional* commands of the First Amendment for liberty and the Fourteenth Amendment for equality are in

290 danger of being lost in the uproar, as they have been lost in other aspects of the political process.

The tendency has been to assume that the public school systems are bureaucratically rigid and must be bent to serve the interests of disparate groups. And if the public schools are harmed in the process, too bad; they weren't all that good anyway. The need, rather, is to devise ways of reconciling diverse individual and group freedoms with the common and general freedom. Somehow, as Rawls puts it, in a just society each person is to have an equal right to the most extensive total system of equal basic liberties compatible with a similar system of liberty for all; and any social or economic inequalities are to be so arranged that they adhere to the greatest benefit of the least advantaged. Control of the public schools should be sought in these terms, not simply as means to serve majority or minority or group interests locked in combat.

Support

A public school is primarily supported by public funds raised by taxation at the local, state and federal levels. It does not rely heavily on direct financial charges upon the student or his parents in the form of fees or tuition. Support of education through general taxation was achieved only after a long and bitter fight. It had to overcome the belief that education depended on parental ability to pay and that private tuition was a perfectly natural way to obtain education along with other social goods. But the appeal to the public good gradually won a consensus that general taxation was the only means by which education could be made available to all comers no matter what their economic status.

From the beginning, however, it was clear that local school districts would differ widely in their ability to support public schools or indeed in their willingness to tax themselves for the purpose. The states have thus gone through long and complicated procedures to *require* local districts to tax themselves and to try to equalize the provision of schooling by all sorts of financial formulas for state aid. In recent years it is even being argued (in the *Serrano* case in California) that the local property tax system is essentially so unequal in its ability to provide educational facilities that it violates the Fourteenth Amendment's command for equal protection of the laws; states may thus have to turn from local property taxes for the purpose and adopt statewide taxation.

While the U.S. Supreme Court by 5 to 4 denied this line of argument in a Texas case during March, the New Jersey Supreme Court ruled in April that the New Jersey constitutional requirement for equal educational opportunity outlaws the local property tax as the prime means of support for public schools. Furthermore, the rapidly increased use of federal funds represented by the Elementary and Secondary School Act of 1965 recognized, at least implicitly, that inequality of resources among the states would necessitate a *federal* basis for public school support.

But just when it began to look as though federal support of public schools would finally begin to make a difference, some 200 years after the first federal land grants were made under the ordinances of the 1780s, the clamor for public support of private and religious schools was renewed, this time aided by the President himself. During the 19th and most of the 20th centuries Catholic opposition to federal aid (unless it included Catholic schools in the aid) had prevented the allocation of general federal funds for public schools. Finally, a compromise was reached in 1965 after a quiescent period of ecumenicism in the early 1960s, and thereafter the drive for public funds for private schools gained momentum as the costs of schooling rose and enrollments in private schools dropped.

Whereas in the 1940s and 1950s the claims for public aid for parochial schools had been for auxiliary services such as bus transportation, textbooks, health services and the like, now the campaign is for direct support, and gains have been made in many states for one form or another of public assistance: aid to private schools for buildings or for reimbursement of the costs of testing and record keeping required by the state (a New York State law of 1970 was struck down by a federal court in 1972); payment of salaries for teaching secular subjects (Pennsylvania and Rhode Island laws were struck down by the Supreme Court in June 1971); grants for tuition to low-income parents (Pennsylvania and New York laws were struck down by federal courts in 1972); and tax credits or rebates on income tax payments. Several of these cases are now before the Supreme Court, and a landmark decision is expected by June. Just a few weeks ago a federal court stopped payment of New Jersey state funds to private and parochial schools.

Again, these matters hinge upon the constitutional ban on the allocation of state funds to religious schools. But religious and other private groups have persistently argued that parents and churches have prior rights over the state in the realm of education. They insist that the public pool of tax moneys raised for public education should be divided among parents and churches to support schools of their choice.

And now comes along a plan whereby parents are given vouchers representing public funds, with which they can shop around among various "alternatives." Even the federal government through the Office of Economic Opportunity has promoted a trial of such schemes. In some cases the vouchers are good only within the public school system, but the principle can easily be extended by Roman Catholics to include their schools, or by private entrepreneurs to include theirs, or by white or black separatists to include theirs. A wholesale application of the idea would further undermine the public schools, whose budgets in recent years have encountered ever tougher resistance in local elections.

It is odd that President Nixon and Governor Rockefeller can plead on one hand the shortage of funds for public schools and at the same time promise Catholic voters that they will do all they can to assign tax funds to nonpublic schools. And revenue-sharing will increase pressure at the local level to use the federal funds thus shared for nonpublic schools. Since social science investigators now claim that more money does not really improve the quality of education, it is curious that private schools still seem to think that more money would improve the quality of *their* schools. And still more curious is the outrage expressed against bussing to achieve desegregation in the public schools, when it is juxtaposed with the enthusiastic campaign to use public funds to *assist* bussing of children to parochial schools. In any case, the support of public schools from public funds is weakened whenever dissident groups press for their solutions rather than a public school solution.

292 Access

Public schools are intended to provide access freely and openly to all persons, irrespective of class, religion, race, ethnic or national origin, or sex. Ideally, a public school is thus a school common to all in the society and does not discriminate among pupils on grounds other than educational achievement and age. As everyone knows, however, it was not until 1954 that the principle of equal access was defined unequivocally by the Supreme Court. Before that, the United States had long condoned a dual system of schools for blacks and whites, *de jure* in the South and *de facto* in many parts of the North and West; and with somewhat analogous conditions for American Indians on reservations, and for Spanish-speakers in the Southwest. But in the *Brown* decision the Supreme Court said, "We conclude that in the field of public education the doctrine of 'separate but equal' has no place. Separate educational facilities are inherently unequal." After nearly 150 years the racially disjunctive system of schools in the South began painfully and slowly to coalesce.

Then, as desegregation finally began to be accepted in the South after a decade of confrontations between state and federal authorities and violence in the schools and universities, the action shifted from the legal segregation in the South to the *de facto* segregation in the cities and suburbs of the North. And so the bussing issue came to the fore, as the courts agreed that, when all else failed, bussing had to be tried. Somehow, the Supreme Court said in April 1971, the dual school system *had* to be dismantled in conformity with the requirement of "equal protection of the laws" of the Fourteenth Amendment. Yet, while the proportion of blacks in

majority white schools of the South had grown to some 40 percent, it remained at around 27 percent in the North and West, and in the large Northern cities it was actually decreasing.

So not only did bussing become an explosive political issue by 1972 but also black nationalists themselves began to argue for separatism and seemed to retreat to resegregation in order to gain more control over their own community schools. In September 1970 the Congress of Racial Equality apparently rejected the goal of integration and officially adopted a public school plan in Mobile that would produce "desegregation without integration," a view scarcely distinguishable from the Plessy doctrine of "separate but equal."

At that point, the President and most political leaders were not only not trying to save the public school idea of open access in the face of the bussing clamor but were actually casting a fog over the once widely held faith in the value of common schools to be used by all segments of the community. This could be taken only as an official blessing to the white flight to the suburbs that had accelerated during the decade when the federal courts were defining the goals of integration and of equality demanded by the Constitution. Only a few voices were arguing that integrated public schools *could* be a powerful antidote for the racist attitudes that infected the country, North and South, East and West.

Too little thought was being given to the findings that black pupils did better in integrated schools, or that even if they did not do better academically, they were spared the damage to personality and self-respect endemic in the dual system. It had become clear to the peoples of the world that the most virulent residue of the colonial empires was the resentment against the psychological degradation of being treated as inferiors by colonial masters. What white Americans could not seem to understand was that a similar resentment among blacks was a bitter residue of the dual school system and of continuing humiliation in schools where legal desegregation had been achieved but genuine integration had not even been tried. What was forgotten was that a major task of a public school system was to achieve a truly integrative social and cultural atmosphere wherein students could learn the meaning of mutual dignity, acceptance and self-respect across social and ethnic lines. But that is a task which the public schools cannot adequately undertake while beset by drives to resegregation or separatism, whether in the city ghettos or in the suburban gardens. And if the Nixon Supreme Court should reverse or substantially weaken the constitutional decisions of two decades, the cause would become immeasurably more difficult.

Civic Unity

Finally, public schools have a commitment to elevate the civic goal of unity above the particularist goals of special and self-serving interests in the society. This is one of the most sensitive and complicated of all the tasks of public education, for it is extremely difficult to draw the line between the values of diversity (which a democratic society prizes) and of divisiveness (which may threaten the very society itself). Most modern school systems in the world are torn by two conflicting drives: on the one hand, to help build national unity out of diverse racial, cultural, ethnic, religious and linguistic groups, and, on the other, to honor the drive of particularist groups that demand their own schools for the teaching of different languages, religious beliefs, ethnic customs or regional aspirations. The modernizing world abounds in examples. In 1947 India and Pakistan had to divide along such lines before each could start to build a nation. Since then, India has struggled with the surging forces of more than a dozen major languages, while irreconcilable Bangladesh has split off from Pakistan. Nigeria averted a spinoff of a major ethnic group in its civil war. And a score of nations keep searching for ways to reconcile the separatist drives with the nation-building drive. Division among groups leads to demand for separate schools; separate schools in turn strengthen and perpetuate the group divisions.

The United States evaded the worst of the divisive cultural conflicts in the 18th and 19th centuries, mainly by forbidding the state to intrude in religious matters except to guarantee religious freedom for all. This separation of church and state did not come about easily; but with the adoption of the First Amendment in 1791 and with similar enactments in state constitutions, the worst of the religious violence and antagonisms that wracked Germany, France, the Netherlands, Italy and Spain in the Reformation wars (and Northern Ireland to this day) were avoided here. To be sure, not all has been sweetness and light, but in general the trend has been to reduce the religious and especially the sectarian characteristics of public schools over a period of 150 years. Sometimes this has been done on a principle of religious freedom and separation of church and state; sometimes on a purely pragmatic basis that diverse religious groups could not agree on the specifics of religious instruction, or doctrine, or creed, or devotional exercises that should be required of all children in a common school.

No matter what the reason, the ideal of the public school as a "symbol of our secular

The Gap Between Rich and Poor Schools

State by State Ratio of Assessed Property Valuation per Pupil in School District with the Largest Figure to That in District with Smallest Figure, 1968-69.

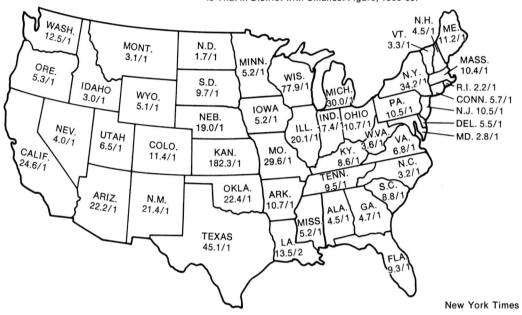

New York Times

society" was nowhere better stated than by Mr. Justice Frankfurter in the *McCollum* case in 1948:

Designed to serve as perhaps the most powerful agency for promoting cohesion among a heterogeneous democratic people, the public school must keep scrupulously free from entanglement in the strife of sects. . . . The public school is at once the symbol of our democracy and the most pervasive means for promoting our common destiny. In no activity of the State is it more vital to keep out divisive forces than in its schools, to avoid confusing, not to say fusing, what the Constitution sought to keep strictly apart. "The great American principle of eternal separation"—Elihu Root's phrase bears repetition —is one of the vital reliances of our Constitutional system for assuring unities among our

people stronger than our diversities. It is the Court's duty to enforce this principle in its full integrity.

But a short twenty-five years after this ringing declaration of faith in the public school, what do we find? Public education is being described by some of our radical revisionist historians of education as no more than illusion or legend or myth. Such radical critics know exactly what they are doing. They see the public school system as standing in the way of revolutionary social change, as do the other institutions of representative government, economy and religion. But their arguments are only part of the story and probably not the most important part. The undermining of the idea of public education by conservative, liberals and the politically neutral or naive is probably even more significant. For now, all five aspects of the meaning of public schools are being eroded in both direct and subtle ways, and when the entire picture is put together it is probably not too extreme to say that a basic reversal of one of our fundamental institutions may be looming for the first time in nearly 200 years. Wouldn't it be ironically tragic if in 1976 we were to "celebrate" the Bicentennial anniversary of the American Revolution by abolishing the public school?

Lest this should happen, I believe that there must be a mobilization to insist that the public schools concentrate as they never have before on the task of building a sense of civic cohesion among all the people of the country. This should become the chief priority for educational planning, curriculum development, organization, research and experimentation. I am not calling for a new patriotism of law and order, nor for loyalty oaths, nor a nationally imposed curriculum in "civics," nor flag salutes, nor recitation of prayers or pledges of allegiance. But I do believe that we require the renewal of a civic commitment that seeks to reverse and overcome the trend to segmented and disjunctive "alternatives" serving narrow or parochial or racist interests.

Our people are badly divided and dispirited, if not demoralized, by trials they underwent in the late 1960s and early 1970s. They badly need a spark to rekindle the sense of community. That is what the French meant when they coined the term *civisme* to denote the principles of good citizenship, the attitudes, virtues and disposition devoted to the cause of the French Revolution of 1789. It was from a similar urgency that the founders of this country argued that a new republic needed an appropriately republican education to assure the stability and success of a democratic government and democratic society. The nation and the world are drastically different nearly 200 years later, but that is only the more reason to concentrate on what the new civism should be and what the public education system should do.

I believe the chief end of American public education is the promotion of a new civism appropriate to the principles of a just society in the United States and a just world community. We have forgotten or simply mouthed these goals; now we must advance them in full seriousness as the first order of business for the future.

Whatever else the general guidelines of the new civism should be, they will be found by renewing the principles of justice, liberty and equality summarized in the Bill of Rights of the Constitution and applied to the states by the Fourteenth Amendment. So far, the federal courts have seen this fact more clearly than have the legislatures or the politicians or the organized teaching profession itself. They have been more faithful to the basic meaning of public education than have the profession, the critics, the reformers or the local or state boards of education.

We must take the judicial doctrines seriously. While the social scientists argue and wrangle over their empirical data, the people of America must preserve their public school system by concerted political action so that there will be something to improve. We can no more dismantle our public schools, or let them be eroded, than we can dismantle our representative government, or our courts or our free press. This is not to say that important changes are not necessary; it *is* to say that undermining free public education is tantamount to undermining the free society itself. In this respect the radicals are correct: the question is whether the government and

296 the society are worth saving. It is my opinion that they are. Therefore I believe that public education must be rejuvenated.

It is a task worth the best efforts of all concerned citizens—professional organizations, political parties, voluntary groups, Common Cause, and all other good-government organizations. If we mean to maintain and improve a cohesive and just society based upon liberty, equality and fraternal civism, there *is* no alternative to the public schools.

———————•◆•———————

QUESTIONS FOR DISCUSSION

1. Briefly trace the history of elementary education in the United States, mentioning only the highlights.
2. What were the basic differences in the early educational programs that developed in the northern colonies, middle colonies, and southern colonies?
3. Briefly describe the function and curriculum of the Latin Grammar School.
4. Trace the historical development of secondary education in the United States.
5. What basic changes have taken place in teacher education in the history of the United States?

SUPPLEMENTARY LEARNING ACTIVITIES

1. Develop a creative project centered around some aspect of the history of American education. (Examples: as one-act drama, a history of education game, or a multimedia presentation.)
2. Write a paper on the contributions to education of Horace Mann, Henry Barnard, or Samuel Hall.
3. Seek out and interview an elderly retired teacher about the nature of his teacher training, and also about his first teaching position. You may wish to tape-record the interview.
4. Attempt to locate some artifact related to the history of education (an old textbook, slate, teaching aid, or school records) and, using library references, write a paper about the artifact.
5. Invite an elderly person to your class to informally discuss "education in the good old days."

SELECTED REFERENCES

Aiken, W. M. *The Story of the Eight Year Study.* New York: Harper and Brothers, 1942.

Bailyn, Bernard. *Education in the Forming of American Society.* Chapel Hill, N.C.: University of North Carolina Press, 1960 (pp. 3–47).

Boorstin, Daniel. *The Americans: The Colonial Experience.* New York: Random House, Inc., 1958 (chapters 24–26).

Brubacher, John S. *A History of the Problems of Education.* New York: McGraw-Hill Book Company, 1947.

Butts, R. F. *Cultural History of Western Education.* New York: McGraw-Hill Book Company, 1947.

Butts, R. F., and Lawrence A. Cremin. *A History of Education in American Culture.* New York: Holt, Rinehart and Winston, Inc., 1953 (chapters 1–2).

Cole, Luella. *Education from Socrates to Montessori.* New York: Rinehart and Co., 1950.

Counts, George S. *Dare the Schools Build a New Social Order?* New York: Intext Publishers Group, The John Day Co., 1932.

Cremin, Lawrence A. *The Transformation of the School.* New York: Alfred A. Knopf, Inc., 1961 (chapter 2).

Curtis, S. J., and M. E. A. Boultwood. *Short History of Educational Ideas.* London: University Tutorial Press, Ltd., 1951.

Dewey, John. *Democracy and Education.* New York: Macmillan Company, 1916 (chapters XI, XII).

————. *Experience and Education.* New York: Macmillan Company, 1938 (chapters I-III, VII).

Drake, William E. *The American School in Transition.* Englewood Cliffs, N.J.: Prentice-Hall, Inc., 1955 (chapters III, IV).

Good, H. G. *History of Western Education.* New York: Macmillan Company, 1947.

Gross, Carl H., and Charles C. Chandler. *The History of American Education through Readings.* Boston: D. C. Heath & Company, 1964 (Part II).

Meyer, Adolph E. *The Development of Education in the Twentieth Century.* 2nd ed. New York: Prentice-Hall, Inc., 1949.

Parrington, Vernon Louis. *Main Currents in American Thought.* vol. I. *The Colonial Mind.* New York: Harcourt, Brace & Co., 1927 (chapters I–IV).

Spencer, Herbert. *Essays on Education.* New York: E. P. Dutton & Co., Inc., 1910 (chapter I).

Thayer, V. T. *The Role of the School in American Society.* New York: Dodd, Mead & Company, 1960 (chapters I–V).

Thut, I. N. *The Story of Education.* New York: McGraw-Hill Book Company, 1957.

mat cat bat

chapter 11
Beliefs About Education

goals

● Compares the current discord regarding the education of our young to similar historical traces of educational confusion.

● Presents a short discussion of a common sense approach to the educational problems of today.

● Lists characteristics of the traditional view of education from the perspective of the student, the teacher, the curriculum, and the method of teaching.

● Lists characteristics of the progressive view of education from the perspective of the student, the teacher, the curriculum, and the method of teaching.

● Outlines a curriculum continuum which contrasts aspects of the subject curriculum notion and the experience curriculum.

Regardless of race, color, or creed, the importance of education to freedom, patriotism, and national security has been the theme of writers, orators, and legislators from the foundation of the republic. If we possessed an infallible means of knowing the way of gov-

> *The principles of American political freedom embody a liberal and dynamic educational philosophy.*
>
> E. Edgar Fuller

ernment and the way of our social life for the years ahead we would be able to look to the contents, objectives, and values stressed in our present-day schools for the purpose of meaningful evaluation. Those things which would be deemed worthwhile in the future life of a person and of a nation would be taught in the schools. Even though we do not have the infallible means for predicting the future, it has been generally approved as a fundamental principle in public education throughout the world that schools should provide worthwhile knowledges, feelings, and skills deemed important for the student's future life. Lingering questions among legislators, parents, students, and teachers are— What knowledges, feelings, and skills are worthwhile to possess? What is the best way to teach those things? What should the school provide? What should other agencies, including home and church, provide? In response to such questions as these, the many and varied beliefs about education surface. Such beliefs vary by race, ethnic character, nationality, economic status, geographical area, and a host of other criteria. It is practically impossible to positively anchor the root cause(s) of one's own educational beliefs. But, each of us as student, parent, or teacher does indeed have convictions about the method and substance of education. One of the main purposes identified with the study of philosophy of education is to provide the prospective teacher with a foundation for analyzing and specifying his or her particular philosophy of education.

Confusion About Education

Present day educators are definitely not in accord regarding the education of our young. When one views the magnitude of the business enterprise of compulsory education the confusion regarding the process of teaching (educating) appears distressing. History reminds us, however, that confusion about education is not unusual. In the time of the famous early Greeks, Aristotle (and his contemporaries) could not agree upon the method of educating the young because social conditions were in a state of rapid change. The political institutions were undergoing change, the economy of Greece was burgeoning, there were international conflicts, problems with foreign trade, and problems resulting from times of war. In the field of education the fundamental question arose whether or not the traditional educational stereotype would any longer fit the new world into which the Greeks were moving or whether new times demanded a revision of their educational ideal.[1]

Seemingly, the problems regarding education in the twentieth century have similar tones. One of the most noticeable effects of the advance of contemporary science and technology is the constant doubling and redoubling of the knowledge domain. The notion that a person may be possessed of almost all knowledge has long been vanquished. Today, the matter of choice boils down to one of deciding upon which small area to specialize in. Given that specialization decision, subsequent decisions must be made regarding method of study and choice of schools. Through the high school years the

1. John S. Brubacher, *Modern Philosophies of Education* (New York: McGraw-Hill Book Company, 1962), pp. 1–2.

choice of schools is limited, but even that dimension is undergoing change. Beyond high school, the school choice is often very much related to methodology and curriculum approach. It is small wonder that "people today, as twenty-five hundred years ago, are raising the age-old questions about how to educate their children for the dynamic social conditions in which they live. If their answers are confused and faltering, there should be no occasion for surprise. . . ."[2] Faced with this continuing conflict regarding educational practice, beginning teachers are likely to find themselves inconsistent with their classroom tactics and mentally anguished by the lack of direction among their experienced colleagues. Typically, and oftentimes slowly, teachers tend to settle their thinking toward the "traditional" approach, on the one hand, or toward the "progressive" approach, on the other hand. Beliefs regarding educating from the traditional stance to meet the demands of changing times focus on a program of studies selected for their enduring value. Literature, history, mathematics, sciences, languages, logic, and doctrine provide the basis of subject matter content. The more progressive view stresses content which aims at the reconstruction of experience. Subject matter of social experiences are emphasized through social studies, projects, and problem-solving exercises. The major point of this brief chapter is to call the attention of prospective teachers to this traditional-progressive schism in pedagogical practice. The matter of fashionable advocacy of one approach over the other is of little importance. One often hears that most of our teacher-preparation programs are too progressive-oriented. Whether that be the case or not, beginning teachers,

2. Ibid., p. 2.

once in the classroom, are just as inclined to traditional as to progressive pedagogy. Since it is almost always difficult to believe one way and practice another way, prospective teachers would do well to begin to think about, to examine, and to pull together their particular beliefs about education. Surely, the pedagogical practice of any one teacher which is consistent with known and verified beliefs about the education of young minds will be the most effective practice that that teacher can provide.

Common Sense

School administrators and parents often identify good teachers as those who use common sense as a guide. One of our reputable contemporary philosophers of education is Dr. John S. Brubacher. He discusses the common sense aspect of educational philosophy as follows:

——— • • ———

Perhaps the philosophical quest for principle will be simpler to understand if we start with a common-sense approach to the sort of educational problems just mentioned. Ask the average layman or teacher untrained in educational philosophy what action to take in meeting any of these problems and he will, in all probability, have a ready answer for you. Where did he get the resources for such an answer? From common sense, we say, from the common allowance of wits which everyone has to understand practical affairs. But it is more than that; it is also a capacity of wit armed with a mass of accumulated convictions which he shares with his fellows and which social convention endorses. Thus common-sense decisions on educational matters are the individual expression of a kind of underlying public opinion. Or, stated differ-

302   ently, common sense is the theoretical group premise or bias by which everyone undergirds his decisions and conducts his practical affairs.

It is often remarked that every teacher has a philosophy of education whether he is aware of it or not. This is probably true if what is meant is that every teacher has a common-sense outlook on education. Doubtless, common sense as a homespun philosophy of education is often adequate to make immediate resolutions of conflicting demands on the teacher's attention, but it easily breaks down if the severe strain is placed on it of formulating long-range educational policies. Properly speaking, the philosophical outlook results from much more rigorous thinking—from giving thinking much greater scope and also from making it much more logical. Although this is true, it would be a mistake to conclude that the difference between philosophy and common sense is so abrupt or sharp as to amount to a difference in kind. The difference is rather one of degree. Yet even here we must exercise caution in the use of our terminology. While on occasion we may be justified in using the term philosophy to cover a common-sense viewpoint, we should beware of using it to describe every sort of educational viewpoint from mere fancy to severe logical reasoning.

Yet, however ready or in vogue common-sense decisions on education may be, they have their shortcomings. When we stop to do the uncommon-sense thing of asking common sense for its credentials, we perceive at once how unsatisfactory is their authenticity. A critical examination of the past of common sense alone quickly reveals its fickleness. It has vacillated from time to time and place to place. While yesterday it may have been common sense to make a dull child wear a dunce cap, today this practice would not make sense to the community at all. And while it may have been common sense in ancient Greece to practice educational eu-

genics by exposing deformed infants to death, in modern America this custom would seem monstrous to current standards of common sense. Consequently as good a point of departure as common sense may be for the solution of educational controversies, it can hardly be a satisfactory court of final appeal.

Obviously the earnest professional student of education must go beyond the common sense of the lay community if he is to form educational policies which are to have any scope and stability. The way for him to do this is to subject common sense to careful refinement, that is, to bring in further data so that his judgment can reach conclusions which will be valid for more people in more times and more places.[3]

---◆·◆---

Traditional View

Two American educational philosophies form the foundation for what is here considered as the traditional view. William C. Bagley defined Essentialism as a clearly delineated educational philosophy in 1938. Essentialism suggests that emphasis on subject matter provides the essential components of education. The learner is expected to master facts in order to learn through observation and nature. Discipline, required reading, memorization, repetition, and examinations are considered important to learning.

Perennialism, sometimes suggested as the parent philosophy of Essentialism, is a significant part of the traditional view. The early work of Thomas Aquinas is recognized as the cornerstone of Perennialism. Thomism placed much emphasis on the discipline of the mind. In this respect, the study of subject matter is

3. Ibid., pp. 3–4.

considered important for disciplining the mind. Attention to Perennialism in America has been associated with the works of Robert M. Hutchins and Mortimer Adler. Hutchins and Adler advocate study of the great books as a desired means to education. The processes of both Essentialism and Perennialism are strongly subject-centered and authoritarian in that subjects of study are prescribed. Advocates argue that the educated person must be firmly drilled in content in order to possess the tools required for rational thinking. The traditional view toward education is probably still the most common approach throughout the international scene. The progressive view is practiced more in America.

Figure 11.1 outlines a few considerations of the student, the teacher, the curriculum, and the method of education as associated with the traditional view of education.

Traditional View	
Student	Reasoning is learned through mental exercise. Student can learn through conditioning. Mind is capable of integrating pieces of learning. Mental calisthenics are important to develop the mind.
Teacher	Model of study, scholarliness, expert stance. Demonstration of content and knowledge. Mental disciplinarian, spiritual leader. Curator of knowledge and tradition.
Curriculum	Literature and history as subjects of symbol. Mathematics and science as physical world subjects. Languages and logic as subjects of the intellect. Great books and doctrine as subject matter of spirit.
Method	Mastering facts and information. Stress on rote and memorization. Assigned reading and homework. Study as a means of intellectual discipline.

Figure 11.1 Traditional View of Education

Progressive View

As previously indicated, Progressivism as an educational view is uniquely American, established in the 1920s. The early pragmatism of Charles S. Pierce and William James serves as the origin of Progressivism. The writings of John Dewey provide the principles of Progressivism as an educational philosophy. Dewey opposed the thesis that schools should be exclusively concerned with the development of mind. His pragmatic antithesis held that schools should provide for the growth of the whole child.[4] Subject matter may be considered as fruitful experience which may further new experiences. Subject matter of social experience is deemed highly important. The experimental method is held to be one of the best methods of achieving the continuity of unity of subject matter and method.

Another dimension of the progressive view about education stems from the influence of Existentialism as a newer mode of thought. Existentialism is not considered as a single school of philosophy since it encompasses many variations and opposing views. It is accepted as a movement which touches upon the field of philosophy and human thought with implications for educational practice. With Existentialism most considerations begin with the individual person. The act of personal existence makes possible freedom and choice. Other significant concepts which can be identified as existentially oriented relate to human personality as a foundation for education and the goals of education expressed in terms of awareness, acceptance, commitment, and affirmation. With today's

4. Bob Burton Brown, *The Experimental Mind in Education* (New York: Harper & Row, Publishers, 1968), p. 65.

	Progressive View
Student	Learner is an experiencing person. Learner has freedom of choice. Student awareness and acceptance highly esteemed. Human experiences important as related to change. Learning through experiences.
Teacher	Research project director. Teacher serves as guide for learner activities. Teacher is never obstrusive, always respecting rights of all. Motivator.
Curriculum	Content should not be compartmentalized. Interest of pupils may demand what is to be studied. Group learning and field trips are valuable. Subject matter of social experience.
Method	Maximum of self-expression and choice. Formal instruction minimized in favor of areas of learning which appeal to the student. Problem solving. Teach how to manage change.

Figure 11.2 Progressive View of Education

emphasis on individualization of instruction Existentialism seemingly is gaining in prominence as an influence on education.

Figure 11.2 outlines a few considerations of the student, the teacher, the curriculum, and the method of education as associated with the progressive view of education.

Curriculum Continuum

Another way of examining the polarity of the traditional and progressive views of education is by the so-called curriculum continuum. It should be kept in mind that the pitting of subject matter against method in an "either . . . or" dichotomy is somewhat shortsighted in that both the traditional and progressive views of education cherish the importance of content. Perhaps it is the differences in method which are of primary significance. At any rate, the subject curriculum and the experience curriculum represent the two extremities of the curriculum continuum.

Thomas Hopkins contrasts the two extreme positions as shown in chart on page 305.

Hopefully, in the short space of this chapter some consideration for the importance of identifying and pulling together one's specific view of educational practice has been highlighted for prospective teachers. The resulting task would be to seek out that specific course of study which could provide the basic examination of the underlying philosophical tenets. The study of philosophy is rigorous and demanding—almost of the traditional vein so far as the subject matter content is concerned. Whatever the method of philosophical study, successful teachers appear to be the ones who have refined their beliefs about education upon which they base their classroom practice.

Point of View

As illustrated in several of the chapter discussions in this and other education books,

Subject Curriculum	*Experience Curriculum*	**305**

Subject Curriculum	*Experience Curriculum*
1. Centered in subjects.	1. Centered in <u>learners</u>.
2. Emphasis upon teaching subject matter.	2. Emphasis upon promoting the all-around growth of the learners.
3. Subject matter selected and organized <u>before</u> the teaching situation.	3. Subject matter selected and organized cooperatively by all learners <u>during</u> the learning situation.
4. Controlled by the teacher or someone representing authority external to the learning situation.	4. Controlled and directed cooperatively by learners (pupils, teachers, parents, supervisors, principals, and others) in the learning situation.
5. Emphasis upon teaching facts, imparting information requiring knowledge for its own sake or for possible future use.	5. Emphasis upon meanings which will function immediately in improving living.
6. Emphasis upon teaching specific habits and skills as separate and isolated aspects of learning.	6. Emphasis upon building habits and skills as integral parts of larger experiences.
7. Emphasis upon improving methods of teaching subject matter of specific subjects.	7. Emphasis upon understanding and improving through use of the process of learning.
8. Emphasis upon uniformity of exposures to learning situations and, insofar as possible, uniformity of learning results.	8. Emphasis upon variability in exposures to learning situations and variability in the results expected and achieved.
9. Education as conforming to the patterns set by the curriculum and its various associated instruments.	9. Education as aiding each child to build a socially creative individuality.
10. Education considered as schooling.	10. Education considered as a continuous intelligent process of growth.[5]

the problems facing our schools are considerable, to say the least. The woes of educational finance seem never-ending. Teacher militancy and administrative rigidity work at times to be divisive forces within the educational community. One of the problems which faced our schools during the sixties but is now subsiding is the lack of classroom space. As enrollments pass peak positions and begin to subside, instructional space quickly approaches adequacy. Likewise, as enrollments drop and

5. L. Thomas Hopkins, *Interaction: A Democratic Process* (Boston: D. C. Heath & Company, 1941), p. 20.

306 monies are less available, an oversupply of excellent teachers begins to develop. When instructional space and abundant teacher supply become realities, many educators and parents tend to begin thinking that the time is approaching when children can be educated as they "ought to be." Interestingly, consideration of the "ought to be" is a philosophical one and is fraught with many difficult problems.

Whatever the means for examining the beliefs about education, whether within the educator segment or within the community segment, lines are usually drawn along the traditional versus progressive views. While there have been all sorts of programs which strive to minimize this polarity within educational philosophy, the traditional-progressive dichotomy appears as vivid as ever. One of the current movements which arises from traditional-progressive dichotomy is the alternative education approach. One of the early proposers of alternative education was Mario Fantini. In the Fantini discussion which follows, he outlines the need for transferring to the schools the notion of informed citizen decision making. There are many discussions and definitions of alternative education. Fantini suggests that the appropriate options for students, parents, and teachers can best be obtained through public schools of choice. In this fashion an entire school district would not be committed to either the traditionally oriented approach or to the progressively oriented approach. Obviously, this does not resolve what has been a long-standing schism within education generally. However, this approach does permit equally good educational programs to exist within the same school system regardless of the divergent beliefs among alternative programs.

———— •◆• ————

Options for Students, Parents, and Teachers: Public Schools of Choice

Mario Fantini

The art of governance in a free society rests with citizen decision making. The more informed the citizen, the more capable he is of making decisions. The more options he has, the more chance he has of making a selection which is self-satisfying.

Transferring this notion to schools, the citizen as consumer should be able to decide on the kind of school his child should attend or the kind of educational environment he would like his children to have. This type of decision making would be school governance in its purest form. Making every parent the decision maker for his family's education is a significant stage beyond electing representatives to decide what kind of education makes the most sense for the majority in the locality. This is what we now have through our representative form of school governance, that is, through electing local school boards. In any majority-rule approach, significant numbers of citizens must accept majority rule in the kind of education their children receive. Therefore, diversity in education is severely restricted. Public schools then become social institutions which foster uniformity rather than diversity. Citizens who want other options must turn to private schools, if they can afford them. The private-school option is not available to many low-income citizens.

The trick is to get the *public schools* to respond to both diversity and individual

Mario Fantini, "Options for Students, Parents, and Teachers: Public Schools of Choice," *Phi Delta Kappan,* May 1971, pp. 541–43. Used by permission.

rights in school decision making. However, in addition to governance, both *substance* and *personnel* are essential pillars which must be altered if genuine reform is to take place in American education. We therefore need to examine the implications of these two areas in a pattern which maximizes choice for the consumer.

A system of choice maximizes variation in both the substance and personnel of education. For example, consumers who select a school program based on a Montessori model will have important substantive differences from those who select a classical school. Choice does legitimize new programs, each of which carries with it new curriculum and new personnel.

Certainly, professionals who are attracted to a Summerhill-like school are different from those who prefer a classical school environment.

The point is that a public school system that maximizes consumer choice legitimizes new as well as old educational approaches to common objectives. The new educational approach will be made operational by public consent. Moreover, *educators* will also be able to choose from among these educational alternatives, possibly enhancing their sense of professional satisfaction.

This choice model, therefore, tends to minimize conflict among interest groups because *each* individual is making *direct* decisions in educational affairs. Furthermore, as a supply and demand model, the choice system has a self-revitalizing capability. As the options prove successful, they will increase in popularity, thereby increasing the flow of successful programs into the public schools and generating a renewal process for public education.

Under the present system, new programs

are introduced into the public schools largely through professional channels, with parents, students, and teachers having little say. However, parents, students, and teachers can actually veto any new program. Some programs, such as sex education, become controversial, especially if they are superimposed by the administration.

School systems are currently structured to present only one model or pattern of education to a student and his parents. If economic factors or religious beliefs preclude nonpublic schools as an alternative, the parent and student have no choice but to submit to the kind and quality of public education in their community. With the exception that one or two schools may be viewed as "better" or "worse" by parents and students (generally because of "better teachers" or because "more" graduates go to college or because the school is in a "good neighborhood"), the way materials are presented and "school work" is done is essentially the same in all schools on the same level. It should be possible to develop within one school or cluster of schools within a neighborhood, district, or system several different models that would offer real choices to all those involved in the educative process.

A school district might offer seven different options in its elementary schools:

Option one: The concept and programs of the school are traditional. The school is graded and emphasizes the learning of basic skills—reading, writing, numbers, etc.—by cognition. The basic learning unit is the classroom, which functions with one or two teachers instructing and directing students at their various learning tasks. Students are encouraged to adjust to the school and its operational style rather than vice versa. Students with recognized learning problems are re-

308 ferred to a variety of remedial and school-support programs. The educational and fiscal policy for this school is determined entirely by the central board of education.

Option two: This school is nontraditional and nongraded. In many ways it is very much like the British primary schools and the Leicestershire system. There are many constructional and manipulative materials in each area where students work and learn. The teacher acts as a facilitator—one who assists and guides rather than directs or instructs. Most student activity is in the form of different specialized learning projects done individually and in small groups rather than in the traditional form where all students do the same thing at the same time. Many of the learning experiences and activities take place outside of the school building.

Option three: This school emphasizes learning by the vocational processes—doing and experiencing. The school defines its role as diagnostic and prescriptive. When the learner's talents are identified, the school prescribes whatever experiences are necessary to develop and enhance them. This school encourages many styles of learning and teaching. Students may achieve through demonstration and manipulation of real objects, as well as through verbal, written, or abstractive performances. All activity is specifically related to the work world.

Option four: This school is more technically oriented than the others in the district. It utilizes computers to help diagnose individual needs and abilities. Computer-assisted instruction based on the diagnosis is subsequently provided both individually and in groups. The library is stocked with tape-recording banks and "talking," "listening," and manipulative carrels that students can operate on their own. In addition, there are Nova-type video-retrieval systems in which students and teachers can concentrate on specific problem areas. This school also has closed-circuit television facilities.

Option five: This school is a total community school. It operates on a 12- to 14-hour basis at least six days a week throughout the year. It provides educational and other services for children as well as adults. Late afternoon activities are provided for children from the neighborhood, and evening classes and activities are provided for adults. Services such as health care, legal aid, and employment are available within the school facility. Paraprofessionals or community teachers are used in every phase of the regular school program. This school is governed by a community board which approves or hires the two chief administrators and is in charge of all other activities in the building. The school functions as a center for the educational needs of all people in the neighborhood and community.

Option six: This school is in fact a Montessori school. Students move at their own pace and are largely self-directed. The learning areas are rich with materials and specialized learning instruments from which the students can select and choose as they wish. Although the teacher operates within a specific and defined methodology, he remains very much in the background, guiding students rather than directing them. Special emphasis is placed on the development of the five senses.

Option seven: The seventh is a multicultural school that has four or five ethnic groups equally represented in the student body. Students spend part of each day in racially heterogeneous learning groups. In another part of the day, all students and teachers of the same ethnic background meet together. In these classes they learn their own culture, language, customs, history, and heritage. Several times each week one ethnic group shares with the others some event or aspect of its cultural heritage that is important and educational. This school views diversity as a value. Its curriculum combines the affective and cognitive domains and is humanistically oriented. Much time is spent on questions of identity, connectedness, powerlessness, and interpersonal relationships. The school is run by a policy board made up of equal numbers of parents and teachers and is only tangentially responsible to a central board of education.

Distinctive educational options can exist within any single neighborhood or regional public school. The principle of providing parents, teachers, and students with a choice from among various educational alternatives is feasible at the individual school. In fact, this may be the most realistic and pervasive approach, at first. For example, in early childhood a single school might offer as options: 1) a Montessori program, 2) an established kindergarten program, 3) a British infant school program, and 4) a Bereiter-Engleman program. Again, parents, teachers, and students will have to "understand fully" each program and be free to choose from among them.

Some may ask whether a Nazi school or a school for blacks that advanced the notion that all white people were blonde-haired, blue-eyed devils and pigs could exist within the framework of a public system of choice. Plainly, no. Our concept speaks to openness: it values diversity; it is nonexclusive: it embraces human growth and development and is unswerving in its recognition of individual worth. Within these bounds, however, is an infinite spectrum of alternative possibilities in creating new educational and learning forms.

Although we have suggested several different ways in which schools might be structured under a public schools of choice system, it should be clear that there are many other possibilities. The flexibility of the concept lends itself to a whole range of options without forcing people to accept any one option they are not attracted to. The choice educational system starts where the public school system and the clients are and develops from that point. For example, we have described above what could be developed within a school district. The same variety of offerings, teaching styles, and learning environments could be presented within *one* school facility. This would permit the bulk of parents and students in our hypothetical district to continue with educational programs and activities just as they have been, but those who wanted to try different options could do so. There could be six or seven choices in the educational supply of options from which parents and students could choose.

Another application of the public schools of choice system could be implemented on the high school level in a moderate-size city.

Distinctive high school models could be integrated into the public system, providing parents and students with choices about learning style, environment, and orientation that best met the individual needs of the learner and teacher. For example, there could be a standard or traditional high school; a university experimental high school that is a learning center for students, teachers, and those who train teachers; a classical school that emphasizes languages, learning, and rigid disciplines (Boys Latin in Boston is an example); a vocational-technical complex; a high school that emphasizes independent

310 work and personal development, where students and teachers share a joint responsibility for the program; a high school (or student-run high school supplementary program) that in some way addresses itself to the special concerns of particular students—where perhaps black students could work out questions of identity, power, and self-determination on their own terms in their own style; and, finally, a high-school-without-walls concept, such as in Philadelphia, where students utilize the resources and institutions of the city and community as learning environments.

These alternatives, and others, are not unrealistic or significantly beyond the reach of a city school system that is concerned with the quality of its public education. Although many of these ideas have been tried in isolation, they have not been incorporated into a public education system. When they are, we will have entered a new era of public education.

We have learned from our early experience with participation that the mood among the major parties of interest is tense. The lessons from our experiences with reform can be summarized as follows. A good reform proposal:

1) demonstrates adherence to a comprehensive set of educational objectives—not just particular ones. Proposals cannot, for example, emphasize only emotional growth at the expense of intellectual development. The converse is also true. Comprehensive educational objectives deal with careers, citizenship, talent development, intellectual and emotional growth, problem solving, critical thinking, and the like.

2) does not substantially increase the per student expenditure from that of established programs. To advance an idea which doubles or triples the budget will at best place the proposal in the ideal-but-not-practical category. Further, an important factor for reformers to bear in mind is that the new arena will deal with wiser use of *old* money, not the quest for more money.

3) does not advocate any form of exclusivity—racial, religious, or economic. Solutions cannot deny equal access to any particular individual or groups.

4) is not superimposed by a small group which is trying to do something *for* or *to* others.

5) respects the rights of all concerned parties and must apply to everyone—it cannot appear to serve the interests of one group only. Thus, for instance, if decentralization plans of urban school systems are interpreted to serve only minority communities, then the majority community may very well oppose such efforts. Similarly, if plans appear to favor professionals, then the community may be in opposition.

6) does not claim a single, across-the-board, model answer—is not a blanket panacea to the educational problem. Attempts at *uniform* solutions are almost never successful.

7) advocates a process of change which is democratic and maximizes *individual* decision making. Participation by the individual in the decisions which affect his life is basic to comprehensive support.

These seven ground rules should be borne in mind, whatever options we offer, but, above all, we must offer options, through public schools of choice.

———•·•———

QUESTIONS FOR DISCUSSION

1. What are the implications of the progressive education concept for you as a teacher?

2. Which educational view seems most satisfactory for you? Why?
3. Alternative schools are popular notions which offer alternatives to what has been going on in the schools. Why is this notion so popular? How would you defend the education you have received thus far?
4. What differences would exist in the ways in which a traditional teacher and a progressive teacher would direct the classroom? What discipline techniques would be used?
5. What do teachers mean when they refer to "educating the whole child"? What implications does this offer you as a teacher?

SUPPLEMENTARY LEARNING ACTIVITIES

1. Identify a list of modern critics of education. Research their complaints and share with your peers in a class discussion.
2. Arrange a class discussion about the various educational views. Which seems to be the most defensible?
3. Discuss the rationale for the inclusion of athletics, music, drama, and other extracurricular activities as a part of the school offerings.
4. Invite a superintendent of schools to your class to discuss the meaning of philosophy of education to his responsibilities.
5. Invite a teachers' union leader to your class to discuss his philosophy of education as related to his job.

SELECTED REFERENCES

Bagley, William C. "An Essentialist's Platform for the Advancement of American Education." *Educational Administration and Supervision* 24(April 1938):241–56.

Bassett, T. Robert. "It's the Side Effects of Education that Count." *Phi Delta Kappan* 54(September 1972):16–17.

Billings, Charles E. "Black Activists and the Schools." *High School Journal* 54(November 1970):96–107.

Brameld, Theodore. "Education as Self-Fulfilling Prophecy." *Phi Delta Kappan* 54(September 1972):8–11, 58–61.

———. *Patterns of Educational Philosophy.* New York: Holt, Rinehart and Winston, Inc., 1971.

Brubacher, John S. *Eclectic Philosophy of Education.* Englewood Cliffs, N.J.: Prentice-Hall, Inc., 1962.

Cronin, Joseph M. "Educating the Majority: A Womanpower Policy for the 1970's." *Phi Delta Kappan* 55(October 1973): 138–39.

Dewey, John. *Democracy and Education.* New York: Macmillan Company, 1916.

Ebel, Robert L. "What Are Schools For?" *Phi Delta Kappan* 54(September 1972): 3–7.

Fantini, Mario. "Options for Students, Parents, and Teachers: Public Schools of Choice." *Phi Delta Kappan* 52(May 1971):541–43.

Gagné, Robert M. "Some New Views of Learning and Instruction." *Phi Delta Kappan* 51(May 1970):468–72.

Hechinger, Grace and Fred M. Hechinger. "Are Schools Better in Other Countries?" *American Education* 10(January-February 1974):6–8.

Hutchins, Robert M. "The Schools Must Stay." *The Center Magazine* 6(January-February 1973):12–23.

Illich, Ivan. "The Alternative to Schooling." *Saturday Review,* June 19, 1971, pp.44–48, 59–60.

312   Jackson, Philip W. "Deschooling? No!" *Today's Education* 61 (November 1972): 18–22.

Morris, Van Cleve. *Philosophy and the American School*. Boston: Houghton Mifflin Company, 1961.

Palardy, J. Michael, and James E. Mudrey. "Discipline: Four Approaches." *The Elementary School Journal* 73 (March 1973): 297–305.

Scheffler, Israel. *Philosophy and Education*. Boston: Allyn & Bacon, Inc., 1966.

Weber, Lillian. "Development in Open Corridor Organization." *National Elementary Principal* 52 (November 1972): 58–67.

"We Can't Afford Freedom." *Time,* September 20, 1971, pp. 47–53.

Whitehead, Alfred North. *The Aims of Education*. New York: The New American Library Inc., 1929.

the Learning Process

Section IV is concerned with the learning process and basic to this process is the learner. There are many different kinds of learners; differing, for example, in age, intelligence, background, and purposes. In fact, no two individuals are exactly alike. By the same token it is doubtful that they learn in the same way. Teachers, and others who work in education, find that knowledge about human growth and development, variability, and motivation, is valuable knowledge to have.

A second important part of the learning process is the curriculum. In most basic terminology the curriculum consists of "what is taught, or perhaps, what is learned." While experts might disagree on the technical definitions of curriculum, for purposes of this book it is defined as consisting of three parts: (1) *goals,* or what students should learn, (2) *methodology,* or how they are going to learn it, and (3) *evaluation,* or how well students have learned. The teacher as a front-line person interacting daily with students can be a valuable resource person in developing curriculum.

In the past decade tremendous strides have been made in the area of instructional re-

314 sources. Chapter fourteen is devoted to this pertinent and important topic. Multimedia resources, while frequently used by one teacher or one learner, are also often used with paraprofessional help. Many of the resources are helpful in individualizing instruction.

The learning process is both fascinating and frustrating. When learning occurs, teaching can be a most gratifying profession. When learning does not occur, teaching can be challenging and frustrating. Teachers exist to facilitate the learning process.

chapter 12
The Nature of Learners

goals

- Reviews the individual elements of the learning process.

- Magnifies the vastness of individual resources into a clear and descriptive image related to learning.

- Analyzes the differences of people and implies the need for differences in educational objectives.

- Devotes attention to the collection of data about and definition of child growth and development terminology.

- Distinguishes motivation as being a complex rather than simple phenomenon.

I Taught Them All

I have taught in high school for ten years. During that time I have given assignments, among others, to a murderer, an evangelist, a pugilist, a thief, and an imbecile.

The murderer was a quiet little boy who sat on the front seat and regarded me with pale blue eyes; the evangelist, easily the most popular boy in the school, had the lead in the junior play; the pugilist lounged by the window and let loose at intervals a raucous laugh

316

that startled even the geraniums; the thief was a gay-hearted Lothario with a song on his lips; and the imbecile, a soft-eyed little animal seeking the shadows.

The murderer awaits death in the state penitentiary; the evangelist has lain a year now in the village churchyard; the pugilist lost an eye in a brawl in Hong Kong; the thief, by standing on tiptoe, can see the windows of my room from the county jail; and the once gentle-eyed little moron beats his head against a padded wall in the state asylum.

All of these pupils once sat in my room, sat and looked at me gravely across worn brown desks. I must have been a great help to those pupils—I taught them the rhyming scheme of the Elizabethan sonnet and how to diagram a complex sentence.[1]

The brief quote above suggests that the function of teaching may be so subject-centered as not to be meaningful or relevant for individual learners within the classroom setting. For most of our educational history, schools have brought students together in groups with a teacher for the purpose of studying (learning) various selected and elected subjects. This so-called traditional arrangement has recently been the subject of considerable criticism. Some of the common complaints about American education have been suggested as:

1. The impersonal nature of it all, the restricted opportunities for teachers and pupils to interact in a personal way.
2. The mass production, assembly line, compartmentalized character of much teaching and learning.
3. The lack of "relevance" of what is taught, meaningless memorization.
4. Extrinsic motivation, over-emphasis on tests and grades.
5. Authoritarian teachers who don't allow for response or individuality.[2]

From these kinds of criticism considerable support has grown for a greater degree of individualization of instruction. Further extension of this thinking suggests that in a freer approach to education the learners will seek that which they need to know when they desire to do so. Implied is the notion that the student's motives for learning will be intrinsic with a greater degree of persistence associated with what is learned.

While most educators are quick to express the need for greater attention to the individual needs of the learner, most do not sanction undirected chaos in the learning environment. Most students seem to desire direction and consider initiating structure to be important. Likewise, students seem to need some means of knowing that they have accomplished something. The task for the beginning teacher is to experiment with the various techniques of meeting the needs of individuals within the framework of the school system where employed. More often than not, it takes rare ability to function as a teacher who eliminates such rote dimensions as memorization, all forms of extrinsic motivation, and all tests and grades. On the other hand, traditional dependence on such procedures to the exclusion of the unique needs of each learner is a rather common fault in pedagogical practice which requires remediation.

1. N.J.W., "I Taught Them All," *The Clearing House,* November 1937.

2. Robert F. Biehler, *Psychology Applied to Teaching,* p. 577.

Teachers sometimes tend to minimize the fact that learning is natural. Children do not have to be forced to learn; they have to be forcibly restrained to prevent them from learning something. But this does not mean that they will learn what we want them to learn. Teaching may be generally defined as the process by which one person helps others achieve new skills, knowledge, and attitudes. While teaching involves both the teacher and the learner, learning is an activity of the learner. Guidance for the learner is provided by good teachers who help create conditions which direct learning toward that which the teachers want to be learned.

Teachers at all levels need mastery of their subject matter specialization. However, mastery of subject matter areas is not enough.

> *Education is the leading of human souls to what is best, and making what is best out of them; and these two objects are always attainable together, and by the same means; the training which makes men happiest in themselves also makes them most serviceable to others.*
>
> John Ruskin

In most states, before the teaching certificate is issued prospective teachers are required to include in their study professional education courses which include educational psychology. A basic intent of educational psychology is to assist teachers in using the principles of psychology (behavior) to help students learn.

Psychology is the science that studies human and animal behavior. Psychologists are interested in understanding the needs and motives of people, their thought processes, their feelings and emotions, and how people learn. Psychology is usually classed with biology, sociology, and anthropology as one of the behavioral sciences. The modern psychologist is concerned with behavior rather than skills, knowledge, and attitudes. Therefore, psychologists generally agree that learning refers to change in performance (behavior) arising from experience.

Individual Differences

There is a wide range of differences among individuals. At the approximate age of puberty individual differences in physical size among youngsters are particularly evident, including such differences as size, physical fitness, and motor coordination. As children grow and mature, sex differences become pronounced with regard to size and strength, aptitude and motivation. Age differences, socioeconomic differences, and intellectual and academic differences also exist. These many differences among individuals play a great part in the patterns of adjustment pupils make with regard to the typical school setting. A study of children's behavior systems and their relationship to school adjustment involving over eight hundred third grade pupils revealed that twenty percent were well adjusted to school, fifty-two percent had no significant problems, twenty percent were subclinically disturbed, and eight percent were disturbed.[3] It would not be surprising to find similar degrees of adjustment for any age pupils to any level of education, or for that matter, similar degrees of adjustment for adults to such a

3. I. N. Mensh, M. B. Kontor, H. R. Domke, M. C. Gildea, and J. C. Gledwell, "Children's Behavior Systems and Their Relationship to School Adjustment, Sex, and Social Class," *Journal of Social Issues,* 1959, pp. 8–15.

Our schools must be sensitive to the fact that each child is a unique individual and needs to be treated uniquely.

setting as their job environment. The point of mention here is that school personnel must constantly be reminded that the school setting does not adequately deal with the wide range of differences among individual pupils.

Schools have responded in one way to individual differences by providing programs centered around ability groups, ranging from gifted children to retarded children to many others. Generally, such attempts by our schools for dealing with individual differences have not been glowingly successful. Classroom teachers are, and have been, somewhat adept at providing for individual differences within our schools. This aspect of the teaching task is becoming increasingly more difficult, since increasing numbers of children of varied abilities and backgrounds are in attendance. The contemporary teacher comes into daily contact with much larger numbers of pupils than ever before. Further, the impact of science and technology on teaching can be accompanied by a strong tendency for having teaching become more and more impersonal. Yet teachers are constantly and continually called upon to be skilled at providing for individual differences. In the future, teachers who will be the most competent at providing for individual differences will be those who continue to learn about learners. This will enable them to know how to better provide for human variability and learning within the group framework of our American public schools.

Human Variability and Learning

Any discussion regarding human variability and learning, however long or brief, brings together several theoretical assumptions which are fraught with controversy.

Hardly a statement can be made regarding human variability and learning which some psychologist or educational psychologist will not take exception to as being over-simplified, incomplete, or irrelevant. George W. Denemark cited six areas of human variability and their implications for learning which he deemed especially salient, such as: differences in perceptions, variations in types of intelligence, differences in rate of maturation, variations in societal demands, and differences in objectives.[4]

Differences in Perception

Perhaps the most important perception of all is self-perception. Who does the individual perceive himself to be? Teachers often find that some of their pupils associate with themselves prospects of failure rather than ambitious self-expectations for success. Whether or not such expectations evolved from previous school experiences which involved both their parents and teachers, the self-perception of mediocrity is a major determinant in subsequent behavior of the learner in new classroom settings. If the pupil holds low expectations for himself it is unlikely that he will perform beyond those low expectations.

Another dimension of differences in perception as related to learning, which teachers often overlook, is the fact that people usually behave in accordance with what *they* perceive to be the related conditions rather than what others might wish them to believe the conditions to be. Most of us can quickly recall certain teachers and their "pet" subjects which

4. Walter B. Waetjen, *Human Variability and Learning*, pp. 1–13.

320   they would assist us in coming to love. One music teacher was sure that each of her pupils would demonstrate appreciation of the musical classics by recognizing various music themes for the rest of their lives, whether the selection was heard in total or as part of a popular tune, or whatever. The outcomes, in terms of the students' feelings, may be far different from the objectives. In the case of at least one pupil, some musical themes have indeed been recalled (from memory). But in this instance there is no pleasure, love, or appreciative feeling associated with such recall. Rather, what is recalled is the painful experience of being hit with a ruler across the knuckles for talking during music appreciation class, or of being shouted at, or of the intense dissatisfaction which accompanied compulsory attendance for that activity. In these kinds of instances, the teacher has a set of perceptions about the teaching-learning experience while the student may have a very different perception of the same experience. Indeed, in terms of the students' feelings, it could be readily envisioned that some of the learners would come to very much dislike classical music as an outcome.

Variations in Intelligence (Abilities)

Intelligence and ability have many varying dimensions among children. It should be obvious to educators that the school population represents cross sections of many kinds of ability and many levels of intelligence. Some argue about the causes of these kinds of differences. Others hold that the schools cannot provide totally adequate learning environments needed to rule out such differences among pupils. Some suggest that the curriculum provisions must be formulated from the premise that "all learners are equal" with equal potential for learning. The adult population provides information which suggests that differences are obvious and continuous. Many adults do not read well or compute well and probably never will read or compute well. For most of those adults there may never be a need for improved proficiency in those areas. From this, our conception of excellence must embrace many kinds of achievements (and performances) at many levels. If the assumption is valid that each learner has equal potential for learning, motivational factors are absolutely necessary to overcome certain limited learning rates among pupils for effective learning to occur.

Differences in Maturity Levels

Most educational psychology textbooks devote considerable attention to age level characteristics among pupils. Discussion usually deals with differences such as attention span, muscle coordination, capacity for dealing with self-direction, and many other variations associated with maturation. Robert Biehler, in his excellent book *Psychology Applied to Teaching,* discusses age level characteristics according to kindergarten (five to six years), primary grades (first, second, third: six to nine years), elementary grades (fourth, fifth, sixth: nine to twelve years), junior high grades (seventh, eighth, ninth: twelve to fifteen years), and senior high grades (tenth, eleventh, twelfth: fifteen to eighteen years). Consideration is given to physical characteristics, social characteristics, emotional characteristics, and mental characteristics. For example, kindergarteners are extremely active physically; socially quarrelsome, frequently, though quick to forget; tend to express emotions openly; and are skillful with language, liking to talk. Primary grade children are prone to the common illnesses of childhood; tend to become more selective in choosing friends; are sensitive to criticism and need frequent recognition; and have more facility in speech than in writing. Elementary grades mark the time when a physical growth spurt occurs in most girls; the peer group begins to serve as the standard for behavior; pupils are emotionally torn between the group code and adult rules; and pupils often set unrealistically high standards for themselves. For junior high students, secondary sex characteristics become increasingly apparent; best friends may replace parents as confidants; intolerance and opinionated behavior arise; and comprehension of abstract concepts increases. By the senior high grades, most students reach physical maturity; girls remain more mature socially than boys; anguish and revolt are reflected in changeover from childhood to adulthood; and students have a high degree of intellectual efficiency.[5]

Hopefully, these thumbnail sketches serve to illustrate the strong need for prospective teachers to have considerable knowledge about differences in maturity levels of children in order to best recognize and serve the unique needs of each pupil. Too often, however, teacher preparation programs permit sketchy information to serve in meeting this very strong need. Very much is known about the physical, social, emotional, and mental characteristics of children at each age level of development. Likewise, much evidence related to successful teaching illustrates that the best teachers possess such knowledge about their pupils.

5. Biehler, *Psychology Applied to Teaching,* pp. 90–144.

We have just been considering some implications for learning of different maturity levels. It is also important to recognize that among individuals within the same general age group there are wide variations in rate of maturation and development.

Our failure to recognize variations in the rate of development among children, to recognize the importance of the concept of readiness, can cause us to devote tremendous energy to and be terribly wasteful in the educational enterprise, trying to accomplish objectives that are simply not appropriate to a child at that point. The same goals may be reached quickly and easily when the organism has developed the kinds of physical and mental maturity necessary for them. Trying to achieve such objectives too early may not only be wasteful of the school's efforts but may leave the children with initial negative experiences in such areas—experiences that will be difficult to overcome later.[6]

One of the frequent criticisms of teachers is that they do not keep themselves informed of changes which have occurred relative to the differences in rate of maturation. Ruth Weinstock's report *The Greening of the High School* listed the following selected illustrations as representative of the fact that "the young aren't as young as they used to be."

———————

Biological growth. The average age of menarche (the first appearance of the menses in girls) now begins at least two years and as many as five years earlier than in the past.

Voice change. In the 18th century, in Bach's boys choir, the boys stopped singing

6. Waetjen, *Human Variability and Learning,* p. 9.

soprano because of voice change at an average age of 18. The average age of voice change today is just over 13 years.

Early maturity. Not only does the growth spurt come earlier in life, but growing stops earlier. At the turn of the century, men stopped growing at about 26 years of age. Now, there is little if any growth after the age of 17 or 18.

Sex. Among unmarried girls, more than one-fourth are not virgins by the time they are of an age to graduate from high school.

Motherhood. There are some 200,000 pregnancies per year among high-school-age girls. The rate of illegitimate births in this age group has more than doubled since 1940.

Marriage. Over one-fourth of high school age girls are married.[7]

———•———

Variations in Societal Demands

The problems and issues with which the schools are confronted represent kinds of societal expectations associated with the function of the schools. When the public is asked to state opinions about the schools, problem lists are generally formulated (see chapter six). Such problem lists reflect those aspects of operations which the public view suggests need remediation. In some cases, segments of society often take up the clamor for solving school problems by bringing direct pressure upon school boards, school administrators, and teachers. The scope of societal demands upon the schools and school personnel is as

7. Ruth Weinstock, *The Greening of the High School* (report), Conference cosponsored by Educational Facilities Laboratories and Institute for Development of Educational Activities, Inc., March, 1973, p. 19. Used by permission.

varied as society itself, ranging over such dimensions as patterns of school organization, curriculum, facilities, teacher-pupil relationships, race relationships, interscholastic and intrascholastic programs, custodial services, food and health services, and parent involvement in decision-making processes within the schools. While the institutions of society are typically characterized as being slow to adjust to changes in society, nonetheless, societal demands are ultimately reflected within the total school program.

Much has been said of the rapidly changing nature of the world around us. The pace of change continues to accelerate, bringing with it an increased desire on the part of society for the schools to accelerate the ways in which adjustments to change are being made. Teachers moving into the profession will encounter societal pressures directly and indirectly. The role teachers play in responding to societal concerns can be of vital importance. It is crucial that the underlying causes and sources of all sorts of school concerns be known by teachers. It is also important that teachers carefully assess the validity of all the demands placed upon them and offer their professional expertise when pressures or criticisms are seemingly unwarranted.

Assorted problems associated with the general welfare of the local, state, and federal community often serve as the basis for new, or renewed, societal demands upon the schools. Governmental crises such as Watergate, Secretary of State Paul Powell's illegal money scandal in Illinois, and criminal activities by local officials in various communities prompt suggestions that the nation's schools are poorly educating so far as morality, ethics, and honesty are concerned. Economic slowdowns bring about either unemployment or a tightened job market, or both. The impact

324 upon the schools is subsequently represented in demands for more and better retraining opportunities, career and vocational education, and needs assessments to determine new programs to assist students in entering the economic marketplace. Court decisions dealing with religious concerns, individual rights and privileges, segregation matters, academic freedom and academic choice, and sex bias, often alter the processes of school management. Many of these kinds of societal pressures for change in the schools become emotion-laden when transferred to the local community. Much attention is given to localities having difficulty accomplishing local racial integration in the schools, for example, when forces at the local level muster against racial integration. Most of these situations arise when a demand from the national society does not square with the local societal expectation. At the same time, rare attention is given to localities which have little, if any, difficulty accomplishing local racial integration in their schools. Prospective teachers need to be aware of the emotion-laden view they personally possess as related to the multitude of societal demands upon the schools. How will you serve the school organization as well as the school constituents? What are the principles against which you intend to check your emotions prior to reacting? When, if ever, will the demands of society take precedence over your personal beliefs? It appears relatively simple to assume that modern education must be sensitive to the changing demands today's world places upon our children and their schools. The task is, however, to guarantee that educators actually do more than merely tolerate the fact that changes are necessary to meet the demands of society and the educational needs of children attending school.

Differences in Objectives

As previously suggested in chapter nine, one of the most significant statements of educational objectives was formulated in 1938 by the Educational Policies Commission of the National Education Association. In that study, a large group of educators collaborated in the development of objectives under the list headings "objectives of self-realization," "objectives of human relationships," "objectives of economic efficiency," and "objectives of civic responsibility." Throughout the years since that report, those lists of educational objectives have served as a basis for much of the curriculum thrust within the schools of America. To be sure, many other study groups, as well as individual educators, have extended, modified, or more definitely specified additional lists of educational objectives. Examinations of various publications reveal objectives by organizational structure to be commonplace. Guidelines, objectives, organizational suggestions, and the like have been detailed from nursery school to kindergarten, to elementary school, to secondary school, to junior college, to higher education, to the realm of continuing or adult education. Considerable attention has also been given to the objectives of career, vocational, and technical education within the school structure.

A vital component in programs for the preparation of future teachers is a comprehensive study of educational objectives with particular emphasis on the level which the student aspires to teach. Further, the study of and work with educational objectives is a continuing dimension of the work of teachers. Classroom teachers must constantly strive to develop and refine appropriate instructional objectives which relate directly to the more general objectives of the total educational program. While it is the professional task of the teacher to formulate instructional objectives, their students sometimes feel that preset objectives are not important for satisfying their learning needs. Some teachers, particularly at the upper grade level, involve their students in the formulation of the most appropriate learning objectives for the particular class activity. Obviously, there are many variations concerning the specification of meaningful learning objectives. Some of these variations include: (a) the objectives of general education versus specialized education; (b) the objectives linked to the development of a reasonable level of literacy over a broad range of fundamentals, contrasted with the conception of developing considerable depth in one field; and (c) objectives associated with social class or other group factors. Failure to recognize that the purposes of schooling may be quite different for different individuals may cause us to draw many unwarranted conclusions about the appropriateness of certain content or teaching procedures. The sensitive teacher cannot assume that all come to school with the same objectives, or that those with purposes and interests different from those of the teacher must be remade in his image.

Psychology provides vast additional information which ought to be included in any discussion of human variability and learning. A continuing task of the contemporary educational psychologist is to draw from available information that which has greatest significance for the professional educators. Teacher-preparation institutions are charged with the responsibility of providing relevant and meaningful experiences for prospective teachers enrolled in their programs. Certified teachers are assumed to be knowledgeable regarding the determinants of human behavior, includ-

ing the concept of needs and satisfaction of needs, motives and theories of motivation, and the effects of child-rearing practices on motivation. Teachers should be competent in understanding learners as persons, with special consideration for their self-concepts.

Child Growth and Development

Growth and development are inclusive terms, each influenced by the contributions of the factors of both heredity and environment. Whether heredity or environment contributes most to one's level of development is open to speculation and disagreement. Of special interest to teachers is knowing the extent to which the behavior of pupils is the result of their inherited potential and/or the result of the influences of their environment.

At times like this during the school day, teachers become most aware of the variations among children regarding growth and development.

326 The influence of inherited factors upon behavior is not under the control of the teacher. The influence of environmental factors is at least partially under the control of the teacher. Teachers most effective in bringing out the potential of their pupils are those who are capable of coordinating the maturational processes with the environmental influences of their classrooms.

In their study of child growth and development, prospective teachers explore specific aspects such as physical and motor development, emotional development, social development, and individual differences.

Physical and Motor Development

Wide variations exist among children of any given age group with regard to physical growth and motor coordination. As a group, girls mature earlier than boys. During the years of approximately eleven through fourteen, girls are superior to boys in height, weight, and motor coordination. One's sense of physical adequacy enhances one's self-concept. Motor proficiency is important in the satisfaction of various needs. Problems associated with physical and motor development, the formation of the self-concept, and the advent of sexual maturity may be relatively serious for both the early-maturing child and the late-maturing child. Schools should provide a variety of motor skill activities to satisfy the needs of children at all levels of development.

Emotional Development

Human behavior encompasses nearly unlimited varieties of emotions. Emotions vary from a state of mild pleasure to intense states of anger and panic. Many body changes occur during intense emotions. Consequently, one's nervous system and endocrine glands work to regulate intense emotions. Emotions are not readily differentiated in a child at birth; emotional differentiation is associated with maturity. Familiarity with the kinds of emotions identified by the age level of the learners, along with knowledge about what constitutes emotion-producing situations, is of great significance for classroom teachers.

The school "commons" area contributes to the socialization process of the school.

Social Development

Social development involves the ability to get along with others. It is important for an individual to achieve social adequacy while attaining his individuality. Schools can make special contributions to the social development of children. Factors influencing one's social development are peer groups, sex drives, friendships, and sense of security. The importance of group activities upon the social development of group members is great. Manifestations of various kinds of behavior can be viewed as part of the process of attaining social adequacy.

Motivation and Learning

Learning takes place best when the learner is motivated. Thus, an important aspect of the teachers' job is to help provide their pupils with motives to learn what is being taught. In addition to a desire to learn all that can be learned about learners, teachers should also desire to learn more and more about motivation and learning.

It may be said that individuals are never without motivation. Each of us continually endeavors to maintain and enhance personal adequacy. We tend to remain motivated toward those activities which provide success rather than failure. It follows that a pupil who does well and likes school will be more likely to respond to school-related activities than a pupil who does poorly in school. As a consequence of this specific aspect of motivation considerable speculation and debate exists among educators as to the grading practice in schools, particularly since most grade systems include a failing grade. Some argue that if we wish learners to be continually motivated

Motivation is a complex phenomenon. In side-by-side situations some students are motivated, some are not.

toward school activities learning experiences should not permit failure. However, if success consists of reaching a goal, somewhere along the way the determination of whether the goal has been reached must be made by the teacher. The learner must be made aware of his progress toward goals. Hopefully, teachers can provide learning situations in which realistic goals are set for each learner at his threshold of achievement and motivation encourages each to persist until these goals are successfully reached.

Motivation is a complex phenomenon. Factors influencing motivation and learning, in addition to firsthand experiences, in-

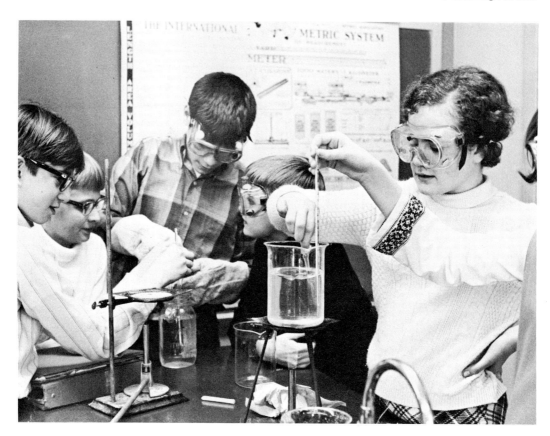

Active involvement is often a motivation key.

clude the learner's perception of these experiences, values ascribed to the experiences, and the self-concepts of the learners. Teacher and student variables, such as personality, and teacher and learner styles, are related to motivation and learning.

Self-concept. Increasing evidence indicates close relationships between self-concept and learning. Inadequate perceptions of the self may bring about misguided motivation and student failures in school subjects. Many students who do poorly in school have learned to consider themselves in-

capable of being successful in academic work. Students with such low academic self-concepts also perceive others as having little faith in them and in their ability to do well in schoolwork. A student's motivation and learning may also be closely related to his perceptions of others' expectations for him.

Teacher and learner styles. The *best* teacher style or the *best* learner style cannot be generalized. Caution must be taken to avoid the trap of judging a teaching style or a learning style as wrong just because it doesn't match one's own style or one's own belief about a learning style. There is considerable overlap between the personal characteristics of teachers and teaching styles, and between the personal characteristics of learners and learner styles. A summary of research evidence reported by Don E. Hamachek states that when it comes to classroom behavior, interaction patterns, and teaching styles, teachers who are superior in encouraging motivation and learning in students seem to exhibit more of the following characteristics:

1. Willingness to be flexible, to be direct or indirect, as the situation demands.
2. Capacity to perceive the world from the student's point of view.
3. Ability to "personalize" their teaching.
4. Willingness to experiment, to try out new things.
5. Skill in asking questions (as opposed to seeing self as a kind of answering service).
6. Knowledge of subject matter and related areas.
7. Skill in establishing definite examination procedures.
8. Willingness to provide definite study helps.
9. Capacity to reflect an appreciative attitude (evidenced by nods, comments, smiles, etc.).
10. Conversational manner in teaching— informal, easy style.[8]

In addition to individual differences in personality factors, assessment of motiva-

tion must give consideration to student reactions to praise and blame, student reactions to success and failure, and student differences in learning style. In the interests of effective motivation, it is important to identify each student's learning style as quickly as possible. Hamachek's summary statement regarding student variables related to motivation and learning states:

What is important for one student is not important to another; this is one reason why cookbook formulas for good teaching are of so little value and why teaching is inevitably something of an art when it comes to motivating students and helping them learn. The choice of instructional methods makes a big difference for certain kinds of pupils, and a search for the "best" way to motivate can succeed only when student variables such as intellectual and personality differences are taken into account.[9]

Point of View

For the last few years publishing houses have been searching for new manuscripts which deal with the processes of learning within the classroom setting. Much knowledge has been generated by the research of psychologists as related to learning. The task for the contemporary teacher is relating this kind of knowledge to pedagogy. What goes on in the classroom to deter learning? To motivate learning? What must the teacher know about learning to adequately meet the day-to-day demands placed upon the teacher? Is teaching an art or a science which can be demon-

8. Don E. Hamachek, *Motivation in Teaching and Learning,* 1968, p. 15. Association of Classroom Teachers, NEA Publications Division. Used by permission.

9. Ibid., p. 21.

330 strated? Can teacher effectiveness be enhanced through careful application of the principles of educational psychology? Research continues to strive for better answers to such questions. At the same time, considerable research in educational psychology is presently available for use by the classroom teacher.

Some of the important elements of the learning process have been reviewed. One of the most important elements recently considered to a significant degree by educators is the simple fact that a wide range of differences among learners must be accommodated by the schools. Teachers have long provided "lip service" to this concern and have practiced their style of pedagogy by plunging along the least common middle ground of the course content being taught. More than that is now expected of teachers. Teachers are expected not only to recognize the individual differences among their students, but to know how to meet those needs through their teaching. Many other considerations must be understood and dealt with by the modern classroom teacher. In addition, human growth and development factors must be studied for knowledge's sake and for incorporation into the teaching style. Differences in perception, variations in intelligence, differences in maturity levels, and differences in rate of maturation are some of the kinds of human variability which teachers must deal with. Other considerations such as various societal demands and differences in objectives are also important considerations for examining the whole of the learning environment.

Manifestations of the recognition of individual differences are shown in special programs for minority students. An important concern in the domain of minority programs is that of self-esteem. The Chicano student in the Edgewood Independent School District in San Antonio, Texas may find his desire to be bright-eyed, bilingual, brown, and beautiful more easily fulfilled because the leadership

of that school district had the courage to make attempts to correct the inferior educational programs provided Chicanos. Blandina and Jose Cárdenas discuss the development of the theory of incompatibilities in the following statement.

———————•◆•———————

Chicano—Bright-eyed, Bilingual, Brown, and Beautiful

Blandina Cárdenas and Jose A. Cárdenas

Seven-year-old Carolina Perez is bright-eyed, bilingual, brown, and beautiful. She is intimidated by no one. If the important-looking men and women who frequently come to her school give her an inkling that she's at the center of an educational revolution, it doesn't seem to faze her in the least.

Carolina is a second grader in the Edgewood Independent School District in San Antonio, Texas, site of the landmark Rodriguez school finance case. Since she was three, Carolina has been part of a program based on the rationale that she is beautiful just the way she is and that the school must change to respond to the cultural, linguistic, socioeconomic, and perceptual characteristics of its pupils.

Until recently, self-confident seven-year-olds like Carolina were the exception rather than the rule throughout the Southwest. For most Chicano children, entry into the public schools was a negative experience. If poverty, discrimination, and institutional neglect had

Blandina Cárdenas, and Jose A. Cárdenas, "Chicano —Bright-Eyed, Bilingual, Brown, and Beautiful," *Today's Education, NEA Journal,* February 1973, pp. 49–51. Used by permission.

not already broken their self-concept, a culturally alienating first grade could be counted upon to do so. The first grades in the Edgewood School District were no exception.

Then, a nonviolent, if stormy, revolution began: The Edgewood community announced to the world, by filing the Rodriguez case and by instituting a series of political and administrative changes, that it would no longer accept the inferior educational programs heretofore received by the children.

In past years, this district experienced a distressing 80 percent retention rate for the first grade. Another disturbing statistic was the dropout rate prevalent throughout the 12 years of school. Estimates on the percentage of the school population withdrawing from the public schools before high school graduation ranged from 50 to 80 percent.

Still another problem was revealed by poor achievement test results: At the end of the third grade, the typical student performed one full year below national norms; at the end of the sixth grade, he performed one and one-half years below the national norms; at the end of the seventh grade, he performed two full years below national norms.

Attempts to explain the inadequate performance of the children in this school district led to the development of the Cárdenas-Cárdenas Theory of Incompatibilities.

Mexican Americans and blacks have not enjoyed the same success in school as that of the typical, middle-class American child. The Cárdenas-Cárdenas Theory of Incompatibilities states that this lack of success can be attributed to the incompatibilities between the typical instructional program of American schools and the characteristics of the deprived, minority-group population.

An instructional program developed for a white, Anglo-Saxon, English-speaking,

332 middle-class school population is not adequate for a nonwhite, non-Anglo-Saxon, non-English-speaking, non-middle-class school population like that of the Edgewood District. To reverse the pattern of failure of the pupils in this school district, an instructional program had to be developed that eliminated incompatibilities between the traditional instructional program and the characteristics of the learner.

To develop such an instructional program, it was necessary to identify characteristics of the school population which produce incompatibility with the instructional program. In a preliminary study made with the assistance of Egon Guba and John Horvat from Indiana University and Daniel Stufflebeam from Ohio State University, we were able to identify over 40 such incompatibilities. Subsequently, we grouped these incompatibilities into the following five major categories: poverty, culture, language, mobility, and societal perceptions, each of which we will briefly discuss.

Over half the pupils in the Edgewood District come from homes with an annual family income of less than $2,600. Much has been written about the effects of poverty on the development of the individual. Nevertheless, the typical American instructional program fails to take into account the effect of large families living in crowded surroundings, the absence of typical adults in a family, the dissipation of adult energies in meeting the basic necessities of life, and the relative absence of communications media and academic-oriented tradition in the home. It also fails to take into account the absence of success models and intellect-developing toys as well as activities, and the deprivational effects of inadequate housing, malnutrition, and poor health.

Ninety percent of the population of the Edgewood School District is Mexican American. An additional 6 percent is black. The traditional instructional programs utilized in the Edgewood District lacked cultural relevance. The typical stories and pictures in basal readers developed for typical middle-class Americans are meaningless to Mexican American and black children.

We are of the opinion that cultural incompatibilities between disadvantaged minority group children and the traditional school can be summarized in these generalizations:

1. Most school personnel don't know the cultural characteristics of the minority school population.

2. The few school personnel who are aware of the cultural characteristics of minority groups seldom do anything about them. And, on those rare occasions when the school does attempt to do something concerning cultural characteristics of minority groups, it is almost sure to do the wrong thing.

The school is responsible for differentiating between the "culture of poverty" and "cultural poverty." Responsiveness to the characteristic of poverty is a prerequisite to providing equal access to the full benefits of the educational program to minority-group children. It is incumbent upon the school district to remove the constraints which poverty places on the educational success of children and to compensate for deprivations that are correlated with poverty.

There is a fine distinction, however, between the effects of poverty and the effects of culture. While it is the school district's responsibility to eradicate the effect of poverty, it is not the school's prerogative to reverse the effects of culture. Mexican American and black children are culturally different children who are deprived because they are poor; cultural difference becomes cultural deprivation only after culturally biased institutions succeed in damaging the fabric of culture through consistent attack.

Language is an element of culture so significant in its role as an impediment to learning that it must be listed as a separate incompatibility even though it is part of culture.

Over 80 percent of the Mexican American children in the Southwest enrolling in school for the first time are more fluent in Spanish than in English.

It's apparent that an incompatibility exists when a Spanish-speaking child is placed in an English-language instructional program. Past attempts to eliminate this incompatibility through English-as-a-second-language (ESL) programs have resulted in academic retardation. The ESL approach has required the child to master both a new language system and the first grade content material at the same time.

To a large extent, the instructional program for typical children is one designed for a stable population. Such a program is unsuitable for the Edgewood District because the school population is characterized by high mobility. At least 10 percent of the school-age population are children of migrant agricultural laborers who must move from community to community in search of work opportunities. The urban population in the district is no less mobile.

The education of these mobile children suffers from program discontinuity. The sequence and continuity of the instructional program, which is frequently determined at the local school district level, may not be present for a mobile child.

The incompatibility resulting from negative societal perceptions blights a child's educational progress. Research has shown that teachers' low expectations for disadvantaged minority-group children tend to become self-fulfilling prophecies. Teacher attitudes and resultant teacher behavior may substantially alienate the child from the instructional program and intensify the negative feelings about self that many disadvantaged minority-group children bring to school.

The five categories of incompatibility listed do not operate independently of each other. On the contrary, they are interrelated, and each one reinforces the others.

For example, mobility in itself is not necessarily disabling, as witness the frequent success of the offspring of mobile military personnel or chain store executives. However, mobility coupled with poverty, cultural, language, or perceptual characteristics—or combinations of two, three, or even four of the incompatibilities—produces the disastrous educational results so characteristic of Mexican American children.

Language and cultural incompatibilities, even in tandem, are not necessarily disabling. Educators in the Southwestern states immediately adjacent to Mexico have long been acquainted with the temporary problems of immigrating Mexican children. Though such children frequently enter American schools unable to speak any English, they can in a matter of weeks overcome their incompatibilities and subsequently outperform U.S.-born Mexican American children in the same classrooms. (Further research into this phenomenon would probably reveal marked differences in the school's perceptions and the self-perceptions operative in relation to immigrant children and U.S.-born minority children.)

Evidence suggests that a programmatic

334 effort aimed at reducing or eliminating only one of the five incompatibilities will probably have little, if any, effect on the improvement of educational performance of Mexican American children.

The incompatibilities between the characteristics of the learner and the characteristics of the instructional program have long been known to exist. Unfortunately, past efforts to reduce the incompatibilities have generally led to attempts to change the child rather than the program.

Traditionally, disadvantaged Mexican American and black children have been expected to exhibit American middle-class values, traditions, and orientations when participating in an instructional activity. The instructional program was a constant; the characteristics of the learner, a variable.

Such an approach can no longer be justified for the following reasons:

1. It has been a failure. There is no way to change a nonwhite into a white or to change a Mexican American boy or girl into a child of northern European descent. Mass efforts in welfare legislation have barely made a dent in the incidence and extent of poverty. Past legislation in the state of Texas prohibiting the use of any language other than English for instructional activities in Texas schools did little to reduce, let alone eliminate, the speaking of Spanish among Mexican Americans in Texas.

2. The melting pot myth is rapidly being replaced by concepts of cultural pluralism. Before attempts to change the characteristics of the learner are implemented, it is necessary to raise the question: Is it desirable to do so?

3. Changing the individual in order to produce compatibility between the instructional program and the learner is futile unless the changed individual is also accepted into the larger society. Social, political, military, and economic discrimination against Mexican Americans in this country will continue to constrain any ethnic disposition to change for the sole purpose of participating in the educational program.

4. The process of change is destructive when it calls on Mexican Americans to reject themselves in order to assume a new identity.

Edgewood's educational revolution does not stop at the development of the Theory of Incompatibilities or at the filing of the Rodriguez case. The theory is being applied in massive innovation projects including the Experimental Schools Project, one of five in the nation funded by the U.S. Office of Education.

Regardless of the Supreme Court ruling on the Rodriquez case, the country is at least addressing itself to the matter of school finance reform. The success of these efforts may well result in a whole generation of bright-eyed, bilingual, brown, and beautiful children who are intimidated by no one.

———◆•◆———

QUESTIONS FOR DISCUSSION

1. Do you feel that the various aspects of human differences can be adequately considered in planning for class instruction?

2. What is your opinion regarding the respective influences of the factors of heredity and the factors of environment upon maturation of children?

3. Do you think that the objectives of education in our American system specifically differ from those in a totalitarian system? How?

4. Much recent attention has been directed toward the importance of developing positive self-concepts among learners. Some

suggest this is much more important than the content being studied. What should be the relation between self-concept of the learner and what is being studied (taught)?

5. How important is the knowledge of subject matter to a teacher? In what areas should a teacher be most knowledgeable?

SUPPLEMENTARY LEARNING ACTIVITIES

1. Engage the members of your class in a discussion for the purpose of identifying and listing the competencies for teaching which the content of this chapter suggests.
2. Assign a panel discussion of the factors of personality as related to learning.
3. Read and report on the findings of a research study related to self-concept and learning.
4. Visit a special education class. List the techniques used by the teacher to motivate her pupils. Discuss the effects of those techniques.
5. Invite a school psychologist to address the class about the nature of his job. Conduct a question and answer session following the presentation.

SELECTED REFERENCES

Allport, Gordon W. *Pattern and Growth in Personality.* New York: Holt, Rinehart and Winston, Inc., 1961.

Baker, Eva L., and James W. Popham. *Expanding Dimensions of Instructional Objectives.* Englewood Cliffs, N.J.: Prentice-Hall, Inc., 1973.

Biehler, Robert F. *Psychology Applied to Teaching.* Boston: Houghton Mifflin Company, 1971.

Bruner, Jerome S. "The Process of Education Revisited." *Phi Delta Kappan* 53(September 1971):18–21.

Cofer, C. N., and M. H. Appley. *Motivation: Theory and Research.* New York: John Wiley & Sons, Inc., 1964.

Coleman, James E. *Personality Dynamics and Effective Behavior.* Chicago: Scott, Foresman and Company, 1960.

Combs, Arthur W., and Donald Snygg. *Individual Behavior: A Perceptual Approach to Behavior.* rev. ed. New York: Harper & Row, Publishers, 1959.

Dinkmeyer, D., and R. Dreikurs. *Encouraging Children to Learn: The Encouragement Process.* Englewood Cliffs, N.J.: Prentice-Hall, Inc., 1963.

Eyesenck, H. J., ed. *Experiments in Motivation.* New York: Macmillan Company, 1964.

Gagné, Robert M. *The Conditions of Learning.* 2nd ed. Holt, Rinehart and Winston, Inc., 1970.

Gale, Raymond F. *Developmental Behavior.* New York: Macmillan Company, 1969.

Gronlund, Norman E. *Stating Behavioral Objectives for Classroom Instructions.* New York: Macmillan Company, 1970.

Haber, R. N., ed. *Current Research in Motivation.* New York: Holt, Rinehart and Winston, Inc., 1966.

Hamachek, Don E. *Motivation in Teaching and Learning.* Association of Classroom Teachers of the National Education Association. Washington, D.C.: National Education Association Publications, 1968.

Johnston, Bernard, ed. *The Literature of Learning (A Teacher's Anthology).* Holt, Rinehart and Winston, Inc., 1971.

336

Lindgren, H. C. *The Psychology of Personal and Social Adjustment.* New York: John Wiley & Sons, Inc., 1962.

Logan, F. A., and A. R. Wagner. *Reward and Punishment.* Boston: Allyn & Bacon, Inc., 1965.

Madsen, K. B. *Theories of Motivation.* Cleveland: Howard Allen, Inc., 1964.

Maslow, A. H. *Motivation and Personality.* New York: Harper & Row, Publishers, 1954.

Prescott, Daniel. *The Child in the Educative Process.* New York: McGraw-Hill Book Company, 1957.

Richey, Robert W. *Planning for Teaching.* 5th ed. McGraw-Hill Book Company, 1973.

Severin, F. T. *Humanistic Viewpoints in Psychology.* New York: McGraw-Hill Book Company, 1965.

Silberman, Charles E. *Crisis in Education: The Remaking of American Education.* New York: Random House, Inc., 1970.

"Skinner's Utopia: Panacea, or Path to Hell." *Time,* September 20, 1971.

Teevan, R. C., and R. C. Birney, eds. *Theories of Motivation in Learning.* Princeton, N.J.: D. Van Nostrand Company, Inc., 1964.

Travers, Robert M. W. *Educational Psychology.* New York: Macmillan Company, 1973.

Waetjen, Walter B., ed. *Human Variability and Learning.* Association for Supervision and Curriculum Development. Washington, D.C.: National Education Association Publications, 1961.

Weinstock, Ruth. *The Greening of the High School.* report to conference cosponsored by Educational Facilities Laboratories (EFL) and Institute for Development of Educational Activities, Inc. New York: EFL, 1973.

Wilson, John A. R.; Mildred C. Robeck; and William B. Michael. *Psychological Foundations of Learning and Teaching.* New York: McGraw-Hill Book Company, 1969.

chapter 13
The Nature of Curriculum

goals

- Identifies the sources of curriculum.

- Presents the interrelationships of goals and objectives, instructional strategies, and evaluation as they represent the curriculum.

- Stresses the important role of teachers in curriculum development.

- Analyzes and appraises innovative techniques in respect to their contribution to improved effectiveness of education.

- Explains the difficulties in conducting definitive research on curriculum.

Earlier in this book the societal expectations for schools were discussed. These expectations in a sense are representative of society, its problems, and its ideals. They represent society as seen by its members, seen as it is and as its members want it to become. These expectations serve as one basic source of the curricula of our schools. A second basic source is the body of organized knowledge that man has accumulated over the centuries. This vast reservoir is selectively tapped to provide the elements of knowledge deemed necessary as basic material for general education. A third source resides within the needs

338 and desires of the learners—learners that in our formal system range from the preelementary school child to the mature adult. From these three sources school curricula are evolved.

There have been many definitions of curriculum over the years. These various definitions have reflected both the thinking of the times and sources of curriculum as discussed previously. Historically the curriculum was thought of as the list of subjects taught in school. This definition reflects the body of knowledge or subject-centered approach. While more recent definitions tend to be broader, content is still an important part of curriculum. Foshay has concluded that the subject-centered emphasis dominated the educational philosophy of the 1890–1930s period.[1] Since the 1930s, the idea of

> *Subject matter is the medium through which the adult mind of the teacher and the immature mind of the learner find communion.*
>
> Earl C. Kelley

experience as proposed by John Dewey has steadily gained impetus. In terms of experience Ragan has defined curriculum "to include all of the experiences of children for which the school accepts responsibility."[2] Smith, Stanley, and Shores have stated that the curriculum is "a sequence of potential experiences set up in the school for the purpose of disciplining children and youth in group ways of thinking and acting."[3] These definitions are relatively broad with the word "experience" implying an active involvement of the learner rather than a passive receptivity. In addition to reflecting the concept of the needs of learners as serving as a source for curriculum, they also relate to the importance of learning theory as presented in chapter twelve. Beauchamp has defined curriculum as "the design of a social group for the educational experiences of their children in school."[4] This definition and that of Smith, Stanley, and Shores stress the importance of society as a source of curriculum.

Goals and Objectives

School curricula, in order to be functional, must eventually be expressed in terms of specific goals and objectives. In chapter fifteen, broad goals as expressed by various national committees and authorities are discussed, particularly as they relate to the conventional graded levels of school organization. For purposes of illustration, let us examine three broad statements of objectives as they might appear in a curriculum guide for a local school system. The following three objectives of American education are from a 1955 White House Conference on Educational Problems:

1. The fundamental skills of communication —reading, writing, spelling, as well as other elements of effective oral and written expression; the arithmetical and

1. George Beauchamp, *Curriculum Theory*, p. 36.
2. William B. Ragan, *Modern Elementary Curriculum*, rev. ed. (New York: Holt, Rinehart and Winston, Inc., Dryden Press, 1960), p. 3.
3. B. Othanel Smith, William O. Stanley, and J. Harlan Shores, *Fundamentals of Curriculum Development*, rev. ed. p. 3.
4. Beauchamp, *Curriculum Theory*, p. 34.

mathematical skills, including problem solving.

2. Civic rights and responsibilities and knowledge of American institutions.
3. Physical and mental health.

Specific behavioral objectives that might be developed from the above for a first grade class might include:

1a. Count aloud from 1 to 100.
2a. Tell other members of the class two ways in which policemen are important.
3a. Wash hands before eating.

At the secondary level, the same broad objectives might yield the following specific behavioral objectives:

1b. Derive the correct algebraic equation to solve a word problem dealing with time, rate, and distance.
2b. List the steps necessary for a bill to become a law in the United States.
3b. After proper medical clearance, run one quarter mile in two minutes.

It should be noted that in this illustration the objectives are written in performance terms; that is, in terms of behavior that can be observed in the learner. The writing of objectives in this fashion facilitates evaluation.

In many states in recent years local school districts have been required by the states to develop overall broad goal statements for their schools. Frequently it was mandated that there be community involvement in goal generation, definition, and development. Such mandates clearly recognize the local community prerogative in determining curricula. The goals so developed must then be translated into general objectives and more

specific performance objectives to provide a basis for evaluation. Broad goals and general objectives cannot ordinarily be measured directly. Their attainment is supported by logical inference by the achievement of the performance objectives. The development of general objectives and performance objectives is most often a professional prerogative; that is, the prerogative and responsibility of the teaching, administrative, and supervisory staff. The instructional strategies and teaching methodologies are also considered the prerogative of the professional staff.

The previously identified objectives also illustrate different domains of learning. Bloom has identified three domains of objectives—cognitive, affective, and psychomotor.[5] Cognitive objectives are those that are concerned with remembering, recognizing knowledge, and the development of intellectual abilities and skills. Objectives *1a* and *1b* are clearly in this category. Affective objectives are those which are concerned with interests, attitudes, opinions, appreciations, values, and emotional sets. Objective *2a,* since it may elicit opinions or values, is in the affective domain. Objective *3b* is most clearly psychomotor, involving large muscles.

Thus the broad objectives of American education can be specifically transformed into specific objectives for children in classrooms.

Methodology

Objectives are only one part of the curriculum. They represent the desired goals or outcomes. After a teacher has decided upon

5. Benjamin S. Bloom, ed., *Taxonomy of Educational Objectives* (New York: Longman, Green and Co., Inc., 1956), pp. 6–8.

340

> *Education is life, not subject matter.*
> John Dewey

the objectives, it then becomes necessary to decide upon a method or means of achieving them. Thus methodology, since it provides the "experiences," is often included in the concept of curriculum. Some authorities, however, consider methodology as instruction. It is most important at this point in planning that the methodology be appropriate to the attainment of the objective. For example, if an objective for the student is to moderate a small group discussion of four people causing them to arrive at a plan for action on a current social problem, then the teaching method would most certainly include practice discussion sessions. It would probably also include an explanation by the teacher as to how discussions are led. Using other information from learning theory is also important in determining methodology. For example, in the previous illustration involving discussion leadership, the notion of having the students actually lead and participate in discussions rather than merely listen to an instructor tell them how discussions should be led reflects the principle that active participation results in more learning than passive receptivity. Further, if one were to consider motivation as a factor, the topic for discussion would be very important. Since the objective in this case is not specifically aimed at a precise body of content, the topic of discussion could and should be one in which students are interested. Since methodology, in fact, determines the experiences that students have in achieving objectives, it is an important part of the curriculum.

Evaluation

A third essential part of curriculum is a scheme of evaluation. Teachers, parents, school authorities, and many others need to know what progress students are making. So, in addition to decisions as to what it is students are to learn (objectives), and how they are going to learn (methodology), a curriculum must include a measure of how well students have learned (evaluation). Carefully formulated objectives assist immensely in this task, for it is practically impossible to determine students' achievement if it is not clear what objectives the students are to have achieved. As teachers develop curricula for their students, plans for evaluation which are appropriate for the objective should be included.

The Teacher and Curriculum

While national commissions and community groups write goals, academic specialists analyze content, and other experts theorize about curriculum, it is the teacher on the front line who actually makes the curriculum. Each day as teachers interact with students they produce and present curriculum. Even without advance planning, as has been advocated, a teacher in doing whatever he or she does with students is in a sense implementing a curriculum.

The role of teachers in formally planning curricula is becoming increasingly important. Teachers today are asking for greater participation in educational decision making. Perhaps the most important role they can play in decision making is in cooperatively building curricula. Teachers are experts in providing particular information about curricula from their experiences in working with students. They are also very often academic specialists. They should participate actively in determining objectives, methodology, and evaluation techniques. Once these facets of curriculum have been decided for a school system or a school, the teacher must then put his talents into action in implementing the curriculum. Resourceful teachers at this point develop their own style of teaching as they bring their own uniqueness to the task of teaching.

It is not unusual for professional educators or laymen to debate whether teaching is an art or a science. It is both, and both are essential for superior instruction to occur. Planning—that is, setting objectives, developing instructional strategies, and evaluating performance—is predominately a scientific activity. The act of teaching, however, which involves the orchestration of the plan as teachers interact with students projecting their personalities and using their style, approaches an art.

Trends

Recent activity in the area of curriculum can be classified into three areas: (1) efforts that have to do with reorganizing or restructuring academic content, (2) efforts that have to do with reorganizing the ways in which teachers and other instructional personnel work with students, and (3) the application of advanced technology to teaching and learning (technology is considered as a part of instructional resources in chapter fourteen).

Interest and involvement increase motivation for learning.

Concepts in Content

It has been mentioned earlier in this text that one of the problems of selecting the content to be taught in our schools is that of deciding what shall be selected out of the tremendous amount of content available. The knowledge explosion of the last few years has caused this problem to be more

342 complex. Scholars in the academic areas have begun to address themselves to this problem. At the risk of understating or oversimplifying their work, it can be said that academic scholars have attempted to select general concepts from their disciplines that should be taught, rather than specific factual materials. Their emphasis also tends toward process, that is, an emphasis on the methods of inquiry and discovery, rather than on the content. In practice one finds that content, concept, and process are inseparable, but the relative emphasis can be altered.

For example, the emphasis in mathematics as developed by the School Mathematics Study Group and the University of Illinois Committee on School Mathematics tends more toward problem solving than it does toward basic operations. Other programs developed in mathematics include the University of Maryland Mathematics Project piloted in the school systems of Montgomery County, Maryland and Arlington, Virginia, designed for the junior high grades and focused upon deductive reasoning, number theory, and logic; and the Greater Cleveland Mathematics Project developed and first implemented in the schools of Cleveland, Ohio and later revised and programmed by Science Research Associates. In programs such as those developed by the Biological Science Curriculum Study Group, Physical Sciences Study Committee, and the Chemical Education Materials Study Group, the emphasis is also placed on basic theoretical concepts rather than on facts, and on discovery through experimentation rather than presentation or perusal of textbooks. Similar activity by scholars has occurred in foreign languages, English, and social studies. Much of the monies needed to finance these curriculum efforts have come from private foundations such as Carnegie,

Danforth, Ford, Kellogg, Kettering, Rockefeller, and Sloan. The federal government has also participated through grants under the National Defense Education Act, and more recently under the Elementary and Secondary Education Act of 1965. The National Education Association, through its Project on Instruction, was also active in inspiring and presenting innovative practices. While many of these projects have been deemed successful, their evaluation has been difficult. As they were implemented they were frequently altered making a sophisticated research design type of evaluation nearly impossible. Educators have been plagued by inadequate evaluation of their efforts toward improvement. John Goodlad, noted curriculum expert, observed that

Researchers know little about what happens in the classroom: how those carefully developed materials are used if they are used at all; how conflicts between the ideological curriculum of teachers are reconciled; what reaches and attracts the student and what does not, and on and on . . . .[6]

Curriculum evaluation will not be effective until designers clearly specify goals, objectives, and methodologies as baseline data for evaluation. Further, assurances must be made that the program has been implemented as planned.

Organizing Students for Individualized Learning

One problem of instruction that has been mentioned in a number of places in this text

6. John Goodlad, "Curriculum: State of the Field," *Review of Educational Research* 39, p. 369.

Intense individual participation.

is that of finding ways to individualize instruction. We know that students are different—they differ in intellectual capacity, interests, rate of achievement, and many other ways. This knowledge indicates that students should be treated and taught as individuals as much as is possible. At the same time, the United States is committed to universal education, and to accomplish this goal we have tended to group students. In chapter fifteen it is pointed out that historically the most common grouping pattern has been grouping by chronological age. We have also usually assumed that one teacher can instruct thirty youngsters that are within defined limits of normality. Under these circumstances, try as a teacher may, it is extremely difficult to teach

343

Active group participation in learning.

344 individuals. In a general way it can be said that teachers tend to teach to what they perceive to be a composite average. Of course, there is no such individual as the "average." The problem of individualizing instruction in mass education within the limits of the public's willingness to pay still plagues our educational system.

Homogeneous Grouping

A number of ways have been attempted to bring about the individualization of instruction. One of the initial methods was that of homogeneous grouping—that is, grouping students by some predetermined criteria such as intelligence, reading achievement, or any number of other criteria. This does reduce the range of differences with which the teacher must work; however, it does not individualize instruction. Recently homogeneous grouping has come under attack as being discriminatory. Judge J. Skelly Wright of the U.S. Court of Appeals for the District of Columbia, sitting as a district judge, stated in his opinion in *Hobson* v. *Hansen* that the track system, a form of homogeneous grouping, should be eliminated. The track system was portrayed by Judge Wright as being a rigid one in which students were grouped by ability on the basis of standardized test scores, and in which it was extremely difficult to move from one track to another. While the major thrust of the *Hobson* v. *Hansen* case was directed toward eliminating racial segregation, Judge Wright apparently saw fit to make additional comments on the track system. There are many arguments that can be presented for and against the many ways of homogeneous grouping; yet, the available research on the topic does not indicate that a teacher can consistently achieve better re-

sults with homogeneous groups.[7] Grouping is far from the complete answer to individualizing instruction.

Team Teaching and Flexible Scheduling

Team teaching and flexible scheduling are two closely related organizational schemes designed in part to enhance individualizing instruction. Both of these organizational concepts provide opportunities for independent study which is essential for individualization. In team teaching a number of staff members cooperatively plan and carry out instruction for students. Basically, these types of instructional groupings are employed: large group (100–150 students), small group (8–15 students), and independent study. The team usually consists not only of members of the teaching staff with their specialized competencies, but also other staff members such as teacher aides, intern teachers, media specialists, and clerks. The grouping used for instruction is designed to be appropriate for the expected learnings. Most often special facilities such as resource material centers, learning centers, laboratories, and libraries are made available with capable personnel on hand to guide independent study. It is the independent study phase of the team teaching plan that facilitates individualized instruction.

The object of teaching a child is to enable him to get along without his teacher.

Elbert Hubbard

7. Miriam L. Goldberg, A. Harry Passow, and Joseph Justman, *The Effects of Ability Grouping,* p. 150.

A modern elementary school building, PS219, Flushing, New York.

The time allotted to independent study varies; however, it is generally recommended that independent study consist of thirty percent of the student's time. Flexible scheduling, which is particularly pertinent to departmentalization, is based upon organizing the school day with shorter time periods. Typically school periods are forty-five to sixty minutes; in flexible scheduling the day is composed of twenty to thirty minute modules. The shorter modular type of programming permits greater flexibility. Student's programs could consist of some sessions being as short as twenty minutes and other sessions of various additive combinations of twenty minutes, dependent upon the learning activity. Flexible scheduling enhances the potential of team teaching. Used together with a combination of special resources available for independent study, team teaching and flexible scheduling have possibilities for individualizing instruction. In and of themselves, however, they do not guarantee individualization. They only create opportunities which staff members need to capitalize on. At the very least, through encouraging independent study, they encourage the development of students toward accepting greater responsibility for their own progress.

Minicourses

Minicourses are courses of short duration—that is, three, six, or nine weeks. Nine-week courses dovetail into the traditional Carnegie unit by allowing one quarter of Carnegie credit for each course that is successfully completed. They add considerable flexibility to educational programs because of the large numbers of them that can be offered. For example, the traditional American History course *could* be divided into four minicourses retaining much of the same content. On the other hand, a large number of non-

346　sequential courses could be developed in the general field of American History. Examples could be History of American Wars, The Depression, The American Labor Movement, Famous Black Americans, The Presidents of the United States Washington to Lincoln, American Statesmen, Immigration and Settlers, and The Constitution. Schools utilizing the extended school year or year-round schools have made extensive use of minicourses.

The advantages of the minicourse program are seen as:

———•———

1. It provides the opportunity for increased numbers of course offerings which may be elected by the student.
2. If a student fails a minicourse, he is not forced to repeat that short learning experience but may elect to participate in another course to meet his required Carnegie credit.
3. During any one school year, teachers may teach a greater variety of course offerings and provide some specialization as it relates to their particular areas of competence.
4. During their school program, students may come in contact with a greater number and variety of teachers.
5. Students may be grouped by grade level or not grouped by grade level if the school district so desires.[8]

———•———

Nongraded Programs

Two techniques that seem to have particular merit for individualizing instruction

8. James A. Johnson, et al., *Foundations of American Education,* pp. 444–45.

are nongraded programs and individually prescribed instruction. Both require determining the threshold of achievement of individual learning, and as with most other innovative techniques they require a definite change in the teacher behavior. Teachers must devote more of their energies to guiding individual learners and acting as resource persons.

The nongraded school operates under the assumption that each child should progress through school at his own unique rate of development. The nongraded school when functioning as it should is a form of continuous progress education. The pupils are organized within the school to facilitate their individual development. For example, in an elementary school operating under the nongraded plan, what were originally the kindergarten, grades one, two, three, and four are likely to be called the primary school, while grades five, six, seven, and eight are likely to be called the middle school. This arrangement, however, in and of itself does not make a nongraded school. The distinctiveness of the nongraded school lies in the fact that youngsters progress on the basis of achieving specified learning skills, whether or not those skills are typically thought of as being affixed to a particular grade. In a sense, instead of grouping children by chronological age, they are grouped by their achievement of a specific skill. The skills are arranged sequentially in order of difficulty. Ideally, there is much flexibility among this grouping. For example, a child who learns the elementary skills of reading is moved into another group appropriate to his reading development, or perhaps given more independent study time. It is also possible that a youngster could be placed at an advanced level in his attainment of reading skills and at the same time be placed at a lower level in arithmetic reasoning. Nongraded schools, when functioning ideally, permit flexibility. There should be less failure in the traditional sense because grade level standards have been removed. Further, the child who learns rapidly should have greater opportunity to do so because specific arrangements are made for him to progress as rapidly as he can. He is not locked into a graded grouping in which it is likely that instruction will be aimed at the "average" child. The nongraded plan attempts through grouping by developmental achievement skills, along with flexibility and the opportunity for movement between groups, to provide greater avenues for individualization. It has potential to accomplish this task. Much of its potential, however, resides in skills of teachers and administrators to assure that it does in fact promote individual development. There is a persistent danger that nongraded schools based on developmental achievement grouping can become just as rigid as the traditional graded organization. While most nongraded schools are at the elementary school level, the plan is also used at the high school level.

Criticisms of the nongraded school center around the lack of research evidence indicating that it is more effective than the graded plan. McLoughlin, after an extensive review of research, concluded:

———— • ————

Research then, finds little to impel or impede practitioners interested in nongrading. Under either organization children's adjustment and achievement appear to remain remarkably constant. For those to whom the nongraded school is a magnificent obsession, these findings must come as a numbing disappointment. Taken at face value, current research on the nongraded school seems to say that its con-

tribution to the academic, social, and emotional development of children is marginal.[9]

———— • ————

McLoughlin seriously questioned the findings of the research he reviewed. It is possible that what was researched as a nongraded school was, in fact, nongraded only in name —not in operation. Again it must be recognized that valid research findings are needed for wise decision making.

Individually Prescribed Instruction (IPI)

Individually prescribed instruction represents a most direct and specific effort to meet the individual needs of students. The basic materials for students consist of a sequentially ordered listing of performance objectives. To date, the greatest effort in preparing objectives has been in mathematics and reading. An illustrative objective in mathematics might be to count to one hundred by tens. The objectives are organized by area and by level of difficulty. Among the areas in mathematics are: numeration, place value, addition, subtraction, multiplication, combinations of processes, fractions, money, time, systems of measurement, and geometry. Some reading areas are: visual discrimination, auditory discrimination, literal comprehension, oral reading, library skills, and phonetic analysis.

The first step in implementing individually prescribed instruction is to determine each student's threshold of achievement in each area by diagnostic testing. This information then serves as a basis for prescribing the student's activities. Most often the stu-

9. William P. McLoughlin, "The Phantom Nongraded School," *Phi Delta Kappan* 69, p. 249.

348   dent's activities will be in a programmed booklet, but they may involve the use of various manipulative activities. Ideally the student receives immediate feedback on his success in accomplishing the prescribed instructional objectives. The system in order to be effective requires the help of teacher aides to relieve the teachers of clerical tasks. Aides assist students in filling prescriptions and scoring their work to assure immediacy of feedback.

IPI then requires (1) determining the achievement status of a child on specific objectives, (2) prescribing future objectives and activities to achieve the objectives, and (3) posttesting to assess progress. The process is then recycled.

Open Education

Open education is a concept difficult to define with brevity. Robert H. Anderson has written that schooling may be open in at least five ways: (1) open with respect to the internal environment, (2) open with respect to the surrounding physical environment, (3) open with respect to the organization and administration of the school, (4) open with respect to the curriculum, and (5) open with respect to a humane and child-centered approach.[10] The open internal environment refers to flexibility—or, the ability to create large spaces and small places so that a variety of ways are possible in utilizing human and material resources. Open to the surrounding environment implies that school can be conducted in places other than the conventional classroom. Pupils can be "edu-

cated" in other places. These places include the greater community with its many resources, banks, museums, stores, factories, parks, libraries, offices, and many other places. Open organization and administration predicates greater flexibility in the ways in which pupils and teachers interact with one another than is customary in self-contained classrooms or the conventional graded school. An open curriculum implies greater choices and more options. Children can decide what they will study, how long they will be involved in it, how they will go about it, and what they expect to achieve. Basic skills are not neglected; however, they are more likely to be learned as a part of a project in which a student is interested. There is structure, but it differs from the structure in traditional classrooms; prime ingredients of open structure are choice and self-direction. Anderson's fifth mode of open education implies that the child's happiness and well-being are central concerns.[11]

Advocates of open education argue that learning—

- is a personal matter that varies for different children, and proceeds at many different rates
- develops best when children are actively engaged in their own learning
- takes place in a variety of settings in and out of school
- gains intensity in an environment where children—and childhood—are taken seriously[12]

Open education has historical roots. The progressive education movement in the early

10. Robert H. Anderson, *Opting for Openness,* pp. 10–12.

11. Ibid.
12. Vito Perrone, *Open Education: Promise and Problems,* p. 8.

1900s was similar in conceptualization to today's open education. The writings of scholars such as Rousseau, Pestalozzi, Montessori, Froebel, Dewey, and Piaget are supportive of the concept. In more recent years authors such as Jerome Bruner, John Holt, Herb Kohl, and James Herndon have been supportive.

Open education is consistent with other practices mentioned earlier in this chapter, namely, nongradedness, team teaching, flexible scheduling, and individualization. In chapter fifteen alternative schools are discussed. Many alternative schools are "open" schools. While open education is utilized more at the elementary level, alternative schools such as the Metro High School in Chicago, and the Philadelphia Parkway High School have many of the characteristics of open education.

Open education has much promise. There is little doubt that it can be accomplished and that it can be effective. Its greatest weakness probably lies in misuse, which could cause it to degenerate into careless permissiveness by teachers who do not understand it or do not have the skills to function in the manner that it requires. Hopefully open education is being researched in terms of its effectiveness in meeting its purposes.

National Assessment of Progress

The importance of each teacher assessing the progress of his students toward achieving specified objectives has been stressed. In addition to this, it is important to know how our educational system is functioning on a broader level. In a decentralized system such as ours this is difficult to accomplish. It must, however, be done. At the suggestion

A concern for each child is basic to a child-centered approach.

of Francis Keppel, U.S. Commissioner of Education from 1962 until January 1966, the Carnegie Corporation began to explore this problem. They created a committee headed by Ralph Tyler of the Center for Advanced Study in the Behavioral Sciences to study and set forth the purposes of such a program. In terms of purposes the committee said:

First, it would give the nation as a whole a better understanding of the strengths and weaknesses of the American educational system. Thus, it might contribute a more accurate guide than we currently possess for allocation of public and private funds, where they are needed, what they achieve, and decisions affecting education.

Second, assessment results, especially if coupled with auxiliary information on charac-

350 teristics of the various regions, and would provide data necessary for research on educational problems and processes which cannot now be undertaken.

Third, when sampling and testing procedures are adequately developed, international comparisons might be possible.[13]

Their purposes seem reasonable, though many objections were raised to national assessment. Most of these objections centered about the undesirability of comparing school districts and states. Finally a program was worked out to the satisfaction of most authorities and the national assessment became a reality. The Committee on Assessing the Progress of Education (CAPE) was incorporated in 1964 as a nonprofit corporation of the regents of the state of New York. Funds to operate came from the Carnegie Corporation, Ford Foundation, and the U.S. Office of Education. On July 1, 1969 the assessment project was turned over to the Education Commission of the States.

A more recent statement of the purpose of the National Assessment of Educational Progress pinpoints more accurately the focus of their activity:

. . . National Assessment has the purpose of providing dependable information describing what young Americans (9, 13, 17-year olds and young adults 26–35) know and can do. More specifically the assessment is designed (1) to obtain, at regular, periodic intervals, census-like data on the knowledge, skills, understandings, and attitudes possessed by various subpopulations in the United States,

and (2) to measure the growth or decline in educational attainment that takes place over time in learning areas of educational concern.[14]

The areas to be surveyed included: science, writing, citizenship, reading, literature, music, social studies, math, career and occupational development, and art. By the end of the academic year 1972–73 eight of the ten learning areas were to have been surveyed, the two remaining being career and occupational development and art. In 1972–73, science data were gathered for the second time.

Educational objectives were developed for each area and then exercises were developed to measure the attainment of the objectives. For example, the objectives in reading were:

—Comprehend what is read
—Analyze what is read
—Use what is read
—Reason logically from what is read
—Make judgments concerning what is read
—Have attitudes about and an interest in reading[15]

The data gathered are reported in terms of the percent who have responded correctly to each exercise. These percentages are known for each of the selected characteristics, that is, sex, color, city size, region, and parental education. The percentages provide baseline data which can be used to make comparisons after test recycling.

13. American Association of School Administrators, *National Education Assessment: Pro and Con.* p. 6.

14. Selma Mushkin and Stephen Stageberg, *National Assessment and Social Indicators*, p. 11.
15. Ibid., p. 44.

Flexible spaces for learning activities, PS219, Flushing, New York.

352   General findings from the data available show:

—Reading scores are higher than experts expected.
—The edge in success of adults over 17 year olds in science appears mostly in exercises drawing on personal experience; the edge for 17 year olds is marked where formal learning is being tested.
—Writing skills are generally deficient. The median score at age 9 is 33.0 percent for those in the Northeast, and 10 percentage points lower in the Southeast.
—Overlapping exercises, those given to more than one age group, indicate gains between age 9 and age 13 in science vary between exercises, but are substantial enough in percentage points to suggest progress in learning. Similar gains are not as marked in the older ages.[16]

The data gathered by national assessment have provided indicators of educational achievements. Questions are now being asked and methodologies being explored as to the use of the data as indicators of the general aspects of social life. For example, "Can we get some insight into health habits, attitudes toward public order and safety, equality of opportunity for women and blacks?" Attempts are being made to use the data from the science and citizenship exercises to gain insight into their efficacy as social indicators.[17]

The major contributions of national assessment to education may be to help gain more learning by new practices. For example,

—Identification of gaps in knowledge for use in teacher training, curriculum development, textbook and other educational materials development.
—Creation of new test instruments that go beyond pad and pencil tests, but also include some innovative pad-pencil testing methods.
—Formulation of objectives and subobjectives in sufficient detail to give new direction to teacher training, curriculum development, and textbook preparation.
—Suggestions for new teaching methods that come out of the new test instrumentation.[18]

The assessment project was not designed and is not being conducted to report test results from individual students, schools, or teachers. It was designed to report on regional and nationwide educational levels. As a nation we need such information. The American people expect much of education—they deserve to know what is being accomplished.

Point of View

One aspect of chapter thirteen was the description of curricular innovations, their rationale, evaluation, success, and failure. Many critics of education in America feel that the innovative efforts of the public schools in the past decades have failed. Prominent critics such as Ivan Illich, John Holt, and the late Paul Goodman argue that improving what we have will be an inadequate remedy. In essence, they convey the message that today's schools have outgrown their usefulness and education must proceed in a

16. Ibid., p. 13.
17. Ibid., pp. 1–10.

18. Ibid., p. 15.

totally new way. Illich has said, "In short, we can disestablish schools or we can deschool culture."[19]

In Illich's article "The Alternative to Schooling"[20] he discusses, analyzes, and evaluates proposals for new educational institutions. He also presents points of view related to why our schools as they now exist are inappropriate for the present society and will be inappropriate and ineffective in the future.

Illich challenges most of the common practices in education, among them the professional status of teaching. "Deschooling society means above all the denial of professional status for the second-oldest profession, namely teaching."[21] Students of education will find this article thought provoking as they examine teaching as a career and the role of education in the American society.

————————◆◆————————

The Alternative to Schooling

Ivan Illich

For generations we have tried to make the world a better place by providing more and more schooling, but so far the endeavor has failed. What we have learned instead is that forcing all children to climb an open-ended education ladder cannot enhance equality but must favor the individual who

19. Ivan Illich, "The Alternative to Schooling," *Saturday Review,* June 19, 1971, p. 45.
20. Ibid.
21. Ibid., p. 48.
Ivan Illich, "The Alternative to Schooling," *Saturday Review,* June 19, 1971, pp. 44–48, 59–60. Used by permission.

starts out earlier, healthier, or better prepared; that enforced instruction deadens for most people the will for independent learning; and that knowledge treated as a commodity delivered in packages, and accepted as private property once it is acquired, must always be scarce.

In response, critics of the educational system are now proposing strong and unorthodox remedies that range from the voucher plan, which would enable each person to buy the education of his choice on an open market, to shifting the responsibility for education from the school to the media and to apprenticeship on the job. Some individuals foresee that the school will have to be disestablished just as the church was disestablished all over the world during the last two centuries. Other reformers propose to replace the universal school with various new systems that would, they claim, better prepare everybody for life in modern society. These proposals for new educational institutions fall into three broad categories: the reformation of the classroom within the school system; the dispersal of free schools throughout society; and the transformation of all society into one huge classroom. But these three approaches —the reformed classroom, the free school, and the worldwide classroom—represent three stages in a proposed escalation of education in which each step threatens more subtle and more pervasive social control than the one it replaces.

I believe that the disestablishment of the school has become inevitable and that this end of an illusion should fill us with hope. But I also believe that the end of the "age of schooling" could usher in the epoch of the global schoolhouse that would be distinguishable only in name from a global madhouse or

354 global prison in which education, correction, and adjustment become synonymous. I therefore believe that the breakdown of the school forces us to look beyond its imminent demise and to face fundamental alternatives in education. Either we can work for fearsome and potent new educational devices that teach about a world which progressively becomes more opaque and forbidding for man, or we can set the conditions for a new era in which technology would be used to make society more simple and transparent, so that all men can once again know the facts and use the tools that shape their lives. In short, we can disestablish schools or we can deschool culture.

In order to see clearly the alternatives we face, we must first distinguish education from schooling, which means separating the humanistic intent of the teacher from the impact of the invariant structure of the school. This hidden structure constitutes a course of instruction that stays forever beyond the control of the teacher or of his school board. It conveys indelibly the message that only through schooling can an individual prepare himself for adulthood in society, that what is not taught in school is of little value, and that what is learned outside of school is not worth knowing. I call it the hidden curriculum of schooling, because it constitutes the unalterable framework of the system, within which all changes in the curriculum are made.

The hidden curriculum is always the same regardless of school or place. It requires all children of a certain age to assemble in groups of about thirty, under the authority of a certified teacher, for some 500 to 1,000 or more hours each year. It doesn't matter whether the curriculum is designed to teach the principles of fascism, liberalism, Catholicism, or socialism; or whether the purpose of the school is to produce Soviet or United States citizens, mechanics, or doctors. It makes no difference whether the teacher is authoritarian or permissive, whether he imposes his own creed or teaches students to think for themselves. What is important is that students learn that education is valuable when it is acquired in the school through a graded process of consumption; that the degree of success the individual will enjoy in society depends on the amount of learning he consumes; and that learning *about* the world is more valuable than learning *from* the world.

It must be clearly understood that the hidden curriculum translates learning from an activity into a commodity—for which the school monopolizes the market. In all countries knowledge is regarded as the first necessity for survival, but also as a form of currency more liquid than rubles or dollars. We have become accustomed, through Karl Marx's writings, to speak about the alienation of the worker from his work in a class society. We must now recognize the estrangement of man from his learning when it becomes the product of a service profession and he becomes the consumer.

The more learning an individual consumes, the more "knowledge stock" he acquires. The hidden curriculum therefore defines a new class structure for society within which the large consumers of knowledge—those who have acquired large quantities of knowledge stock—enjoy special privileges, high income, and access to the more powerful tools of production. This kind of knowledge-capitalism has been accepted in all industrialized societies and establishes a rationale for the distribution of jobs and income. (This point is especially important in the light of the lack of correspondence between schooling and occupational competence established in studies such as Ivar Berg's *Education and Jobs: The Great Training Robbery*.)

The endeavor to put all men through successive stages of enlightenment is rooted deeply in alchemy, the Great Art of the waning Middle Ages. John Amos Comenius, a Moravian bishop, self-styled Pansophist, and pedagogue, is rightly considered one of the founders of the modern schools. He was among the first to propose seven or twelve grades of compulsory learning. In his *Magna Didactica,* he described schools as devices to "teach everybody everything" and outlined a blueprint for the assembly-line production of knowledge, which according to his method would make education cheaper and better and make growth into full humanity possible for all. But Comenius was not only an early efficiency expert, he was an alchemist who adopted the technical language of his craft to describe the art of rearing children. The alchemist sought to refine base elements by leading their distilled spirits through twelve stages of successive enlightenment, so that for their own and all the world's benefit they might be transmuted into gold. Of course, alchemists failed no matter how often they tried, but each time their "science" yielded new reasons for their failure, and they tried again.

Pedagogy opened a new chapter in the history of Ars Magna. Education became the search for an alchemic process that would bring forth a new type of man, who would fit into an environment created by scientific magic. But, no matter how much each generation spent on its schools, it always turned out that the majority of people were unfit for enlightenment by this process and had to be discarded as unprepared for life in a man-made world.

Educational reformers who accept the idea that schools have failed fall into three groups. The most respectable are certainly the great masters of alchemy who promise better schools. The most seductive are popular magicians, who promise to make every kitchen into an alchemic lab. The most sinister are the new Masons of the Universe, who want to transform the entire world into one huge temple of learning. Notable among today's masters of alchemy are certain research directors employed or sponsored by the large foundations who believe that schools, if they could somehow be improved, could also become economically more feasible than those that are now in trouble, and simultaneously could sell a larger package of services. Those who are concerned primarily with the curriculum claim that it is outdated or irrelevant. So the curriculum is filled with new packaged courses on African Culture, North American Imperialism, Women's Lib, Pollution, or the Consumer Society. Passive learning is wrong—it is indeed—so we graciously allow students to decide what and how they want to be taught. Schools are prison houses. Therefore, principals are authorized to approve teach-outs, moving the school desks to a roped-off Harlem street. Sensitivity training becomes fashionable. So, we import group therapy into the classroom. School, which was supposed to teach everybody everything, now becomes all things to all children.

Other critics emphasize that schools make inefficient use of modern science. Some would administer drugs to make it easier for the instructor to change the child's behavior. Others would transform school into a stadium for educational gaming. Still others would electrify the classroom. If they are simplistic disciples of McLuhan, they replace black-

356 boards and textbooks with multimedia happenings; if they follow Skinner, they claim to be able to modify behavior more efficiently than old-fashioned classroom practitioners can.

Most of these changes have, of course, some good effects. The experimental schools have fewer truants. Parents do have a greater feeling of participation in a decentralized district. Pupils, assigned by their teacher to an apprenticeship, do often turn out more competent than those who stay in the classroom. Some children do improve their knowledge of Spanish in the language lab because they prefer playing with the knobs of a tape recorder to conversations with their Puerto Rican peers. Yet all these improvements operate within predictably narrow limits, since they leave the hidden curriculum of school intact.

Some reformers would like to shake loose from the hidden curriculum, but they rarely succeed. Free schools that lead to further free schools produce a mirage of freedom, even though the chain of attendance is frequently interrupted by long stretches of loafing. Attendance through seduction inculcates the need for educational treatment more persuasively than the reluctant attendance enforced by a truant officer. Permissive teachers in a padded classroom can easily render their pupils impotent to survive once they leave.

Learning in these schools often remains nothing more than the acquisition of socially valued skills defined, in this instance, by the consensus of a commune rather than by the decree of a school board. New presbyter is but old priest writ large.

Free schools, to be truly free, must meet two conditions: First, they must be run in a way to prevent the reintroduction of the hidden curriculum of graded attendance and certified students studying at the feet of certified teachers. And, more importantly, they must provide a framework in which all participants—staff and pupils—can free themselves from the hidden foundations of a schooled society. The first condition is frequently incorporated in the stated aims of a free school. The second condition is only rarely recognized, and is difficult to state as the goal of a free school.

It is useful to distinguish between the hidden curriculum, which I have described, and the occult foundations of schooling. The hidden curriculum is a ritual that can be considered the official initiation into modern society, institutionally established through the school. It is the purpose of this ritual to hide from its participants the contradictions between the myth of an egalitarian society and the class-conscious reality it certifies. Once they are recognized as such, rituals lose their power, and this is what is now beginning to happen to schooling. But there are certain fundamental assumptions about growing up —the occult foundations—which now find their expression in the ceremonial of schooling, and which could easily be reinforced by what free schools do.

Among these assumptions is what Peter Schrag calls the "immigration syndrome," which impels us to treat all people as if they were newcomers who must go through a naturalization process. Only certified consumers of knowledge are admitted to citizenship. Men are not born equal, but are made equal through gestation by Alma Mater.

The rhetoric of all schools states that they form a man for the future, but they do not release him for his task before he has developed a high level of tolerance to the ways of his elders: education *for* life rather than *in* everyday life. Few free schools can avoid doing precisely this. Nevertheless they are among the most important centers from which a new life-style radiates, not because of the effect their graduates will have but, rather, because elders who choose to bring up their children without the benefit of properly ordained teachers frequently belong to a radical minority and because their preoccupation with the rearing of their children sustains them in their new style.

The most dangerous category of educational reformer is one who argues that knowledge can be produced and sold much more effectively on an open market than on one controlled by school. These people argue that most skills can be easily acquired from skill-models if the learner is truly interested in their acquisition; that individual entitlements can provide a more equal purchasing power for education. They demand a careful separation of the process by which knowledge is acquired from the process by which it is measured and certified. These seem to me obvious statements. But it would be a fallacy to believe that the establishment of a free market for knowledge would constitute a radical alternative in education.

The establishment of a free market would indeed abolish what I have previously called the hidden curriculum of present schooling—its age-specific attendance at a graded curriculum. Equally, a free market would at first give the appearance of counteracting what I have called the occult foundations of a schooled society: the "immigration syndrome," the institutional monopoly of teaching, and the ritual of linear initiation. But at the same time a free market in education would provide the alchemist with innumerable hidden hands to fit each man into the multiple, tight little niches a more complex technocracy can provide.

Many decades of reliance on schooling has turned knowledge into a commodity, a marketable staple of a special kind. Knowledge is now regarded simultaneously as a first necessity and also as society's most precious currency. (The transformation of knowledge into a commodity is reflected in a corresponding transformation of language. Words that formerly functioned as verbs are becoming nouns that designate possessions. Until recently dwelling and learning and even healing designated activities. They are now usually conceived as commodities or services to be delivered. We talk about the manufacture of housing or the delivery of medical care. Men are no longer regarded fit to house or heal themselves. In such a society people come to believe that professional services are more valuable than personal care. Instead of learning how to nurse grandmother, the teenager learns to picket the hospital that does not admit her.) This attitude could easily survive the disestablishment of school, just as affiliation with a church remained a condition for office long after the adoption of the First Amendment. It is even more evident that test batteries measuring complex knowledge-packages could easily survive the disestablishment of school—and with this would go the compulsion to obligate everybody to acquire a minimum package in the knowledge stock. The scientific measurement of each man's worth and the alchemic dream of each man's "educability to his full humanity" would finally coincide. Under the appearance of a "free" market, the global village would turn into an environmental womb where pedagogic therapists control the complex navel by which each man is nourished.

At present schools limit the teacher's competence to the classroom. They prevent him from claiming man's whole life as his domain. The demise of school will remove

358 this restriction and give a semblance of legitimacy to the life-long pedagogical invasion of everybody's privacy. It will open the way for a scramble for "knowledge" on a free market, which would lead us toward the paradox of a vulgar, albeit seemingly egalitarian, meritocracy. Unless the concept of knowledge is transformed, the disestablishment of school will lead to a wedding between a growing meritocratic system that separates learning from certification and a society committed to provide therapy for each man until he is ripe for the gilded age.

For those who subscribe to the technocratic ethos, whatever is technically possible must be made available at least to a few whether they want it or not. Neither the privation nor the frustration of the majority counts. If cobalt treatment is possible, then the city of Tegucigalpa needs one apparatus in each of its two major hospitals, at a cost that would free an important part of the population of Honduras from parasites. If supersonic speeds are possible, then it must speed the travel of some. If the flight to Mars can be conceived, then a rationale must be found to make it appear a necessity. In the technocratic ethos poverty is modernized: Not only are old alternatives closed off by new monopolies, but the lack of necessities is also compounded by a growing spread between those services that are technologically feasible and those that are in fact available to the majority.

A teacher turns "educator" when he adopts this technocratic ethos. He then acts as if education were a technological enterprise designed to make man fit into whatever environment the "progress" of science creates. He seems blind to the evidence that constant obsolescence of all commodities comes at a high price: the mounting cost of training people to know about them. He seems to for-

get that the rising cost of tools is purchased at a high price in education: They decrease the labor intensity of the economy, make learning on the job impossible or, at best, a privilege for a few. All over the world the cost of educating men for society rises faster than the productivity of the entire economy, and fewer people have a sense of intelligent participation in the commonweal.

A revolution against those forms of privilege and power, which are based on claims to professional knowledge, must start with a transformation of consciousness about the nature of learning. This means, above all, a shift of responsibility for teaching and learning. Knowledge can be defined as a commodity only as long as it is viewed as the result of institutional enterprise or as the fulfillment of institutional objectives. Only when a man recovers the sense of personal responsibility for what he learns and teaches can this spell be broken and the alienation of learning from living be overcome.

The recovery of the power to learn or to teach means that the teacher who takes the risk of interfering in somebody else's private affairs also assumes responsibility for the results. Similarly, the student who exposes himself to the influence of a teacher must take responsibility for his own education. For such purposes educational institutions—if they are at all needed—ideally take the form of facility centers where one can get a roof of the right size over his head, access to a piano or a kiln, and to records, books, or slides. Schools, TV stations, theaters, and the like are designed primarily for use by professionals. Deschooling society means above all the denial of professional status for the second-oldest profession, namely teaching. The certification of teachers now constitutes an undue restriction of the right to free speech: the corporate structure and professional pretensions of journalism an undue restriction on the right to free press. Compulsory attendance rules interfere with free assembly. The deschooling of society is nothing less than a cultural mutation by which a people recovers the effective use of its Constitutional freedoms: learning and teaching by men who know that they are born free rather than treated to freedom. Most people learn most of the time when they do whatever they enjoy; most people are curious and want to give meaning to whatever they come in contact with; and most people are capable of personal intimate intercourse with others unless they are stupefied by inhuman work or turned off by schooling.

The fact that people in rich countries do not learn much on their own constitutes no proof to the contrary. Rather it is a consequence of life in an environment from which, paradoxically, they cannot learn much, precisely because it is so highly programed. They are constantly frustrated by the structure of contemporary society in which the facts on which decisions can be made have become elusive. They live in an environment in which tools that can be used for creative purposes have become luxuries, an environment in which channels of communication serve a few to talk to many.

A modern myth would make us believe that the sense of impotence with which most men live today is a consequence of technology that cannot but create huge systems. But it is not technology that makes systems huge, tools immensely powerful, channels of communication one-directional. Quite the contrary: Properly controlled, technology could provide each man with the ability to understand his environment better, to shape it powerfully with his own hands, and to permit him full intercommunication to a degree never before possible. Such an alternative use of technology constitutes the central alternative in education.

If a person is to grow up he needs, first of all, access to things, to places and to processes, to events and to records. He needs to see, to touch, to tinker with, to grasp whatever there is in a meaningful setting. This access is now largely denied. When knowledge became a commodity, it acquired the protections of private property, and thus a principle designed to guard personal intimacy became a rationale for declaring facts off limits for people without the proper credentials. In schools teachers keep knowledge to themselves unless it fits into the day's program. The media inform, but exclude those things they regard as unfit to print. Information is locked into special languages, and specialized teachers live off its retranslation. Patents are protected by corporations, secrets are guarded by bureaucracies, and the power to keep others out of private preserves—be they cockpits, law offices, junkyards, or clinics—is jealously guarded by professions, institutions, and nations. Neither the political nor the professional structure of our societies, East and West, could withstand the elimination of the power to keep entire classes of people from facts that could serve them. The access to facts that I advocate goes far beyond truth in labeling. Access must be built into reality, while all we ask from advertising is a guarantee that it does not mislead. Access to reality constitutes a fundamental alternative in education to a system that only purports to teach *about* it.

Abolishing the right to corporate secrecy —even when professional opinion holds that this secrecy serves the common good—is, as shall presently appear, a much more radical political goal than the traditional demand for

360 public ownership or control of the tools of production. The socialization of tools without the effective socialization of know-how in their use tends to put the knowledge-capitalist into the position formerly held by the financier. The technocrat's only claim to power is the stock he holds in some class of scarce and secret knowledge, and the best means to protect its value is a large and capital-intensive organization that renders access to know-how formidable and forbidding.

It does not take much time for the interested learner to acquire almost any skill that he wants to use. We tend to forget this in a society where professional teachers monopolize entrance into all fields, and thereby stamp teaching by uncertified individuals as quackery. There are few mechanical skills used in industry or research that are as demanding, complex, and dangerous as driving cars, a skill that most people quickly acquire from a peer. Not all people are suited for advanced logic, yet those who are make rapid progress if they are challenged to play mathematical games at an early age. One out of twenty kids in Cuernavaca can beat me at Wiff 'n' Proof after a couple of weeks' training. In four months all but a small percentage of motivated adults at our CIDOC center learn Spanish well enough to conduct academic business in the new language.

A first step toward opening up access to skills would be to provide various incentives for skilled individuals to share their knowledge. Inevitably, this would run counter to the interest of guilds and professions and unions. Yet, multiple apprenticeship is attractive: It provides everybody with an opportunity to learn something about almost anything. There is no reason why a person should not combine the ability to drive a car, repair telephones and toilets, act as a midwife, and

function as an architectural draftsman. Special-interest groups and their disciplined consumers would, of course, claim that the public needs the protection of a professional guarantee. But this argument is now steadily being challenged by consumer protection associations. We have to take much more seriously the objection that economists raise to the radical socialization of skills: that "progress" will be impeded if knowledge—patents, skills, and all the rest—is democratized. Their argument can be faced only if we demonstrate to them the growth rate of futile diseconomies generated by any existing educational system.

Access to people willing to share their skills is no guarantee of learning. Such access is restricted not only by the monopoly of educational programs over learning and of unions over licensing but also by a technology of scarcity. The skills that count today are know-how in the use of highly specialized tools that were designed to be scarce. These tools produce goods or render services that everybody wants but only a few can enjoy, and which only a limited number of people know how to use. Only a few privileged individuals out of the total number of people who have a given disease ever benefit from the results of sophisticated medical technology, and even fewer doctors develop the skill to use it.

The same results of medical research have, however, also been employed to create a basic medical tool kit that permits Army and Navy medics, with only a few months of training, to obtain results, under battlefield conditions, that would have been beyond the expectations of full-fledged doctors during World War II. On an even simpler level any peasant girl could learn how to diagnose and treat most infections if medical scientists prepared dosages and instructions specifically for a given geographic area.

All these examples illustrate the fact that educational considerations alone suffice to demand a radical reduction of the professional structure that now impedes the mutual relationship between the scientist and the majority of people who want access to science. If this demand were heeded, all men could learn to use yesterday's tools, rendered more effective and durable by modern science, to create tomorrow's world.

Unfortunately, precisely the contrary trend prevails at present. I know a coastal area in South America where most people support themselves by fishing from small boats. The outboard motor is certainly the tool that has changed most dramatically the lives of these coastal fishermen. But in the area I have surveyed, half of all outboard motors that were purchased between 1945 and 1950 are still kept running by constant tinkering, while half the motors purchased in 1965 no longer run because they were not built to be repaired. Technological progress provides the majority of people with gadgets they cannot afford and deprives them of the simpler tools they need.

Metals, plastics, and ferro cement used in building have greatly improved since the 1940s and ought to provide more people the opportunity to create their own homes. But while in the United States, in 1948, more than 30 per cent of all one-family homes were owner-built, by the end of the 1960s the percentage of those who acted as their own contractors had dropped to less than 20 per cent.

The lowering of the skill level through so-called economic development becomes even more visible in Latin America. Here most people still build their own homes from floor to roof. Often they use mud, in the form of adobe, and thatchwork of unsurpassed utility in the moist, hot, and windy climate.

In other places they make their dwellings out of cardboard, oil-drums, and other industrial refuse. Instead of providing people with simple tools and highly standardized, durable, and easily repaired components, all governments have gone in for the mass production of low-cost buildings. It is clear that not one single country can afford to provide satisfactory modern dwelling units for the majority of its people. Yet, everywhere this policy makes it progressively more difficult for the majority to acquire the knowledge and skills they need to build better houses for themselves.

Educational considerations permit us to formulate a second fundamental characteristic that any post-industrial society must possess: a basic tool kit that by its very nature counteracts technocratic control. For educational reasons we must work toward a society in which scientific knowledge is incorporated in tools and components that can be used meaningfully in units small enough to be within the reach of all. Only such tools can socialize access to skills. Only such tools favor temporary associations among those who want to use them for a specific occasion. Only such tools allow specific goals to emerge in the process of their use, as any tinkerer knows. Only the combination of guaranteed access to facts and of limited power in most tools renders it possible to envisage a subsistence economy capable of incorporating the fruits of modern science.

The development of such a scientific subsistence economy is unquestionably to the advantage of the overwhelming majority of all people in poor countries. It is also the only alternative to progressive pollution, exploitation, and opaqueness in rich countries. But, as we have seen, the dethroning of the GNP cannot be achieved without simultaneously subverting GNE (Gross National Education

362 —usually conceived as manpower capitalization). An egalitarian economy cannot exist in a society in which the right to produce is conferred by schools.

The feasibility of a modern subsistence economy does not depend on new scientific inventions. It depends primarily on the ability of a society to agree on fundamental, self-chosen anti-bureaucratic and anti-technocratic restraints.

These restraints can take many forms, but they will not work unless they touch the basic dimensions of life. (The decision of Congress against development of the supersonic transport plane is one of the most encouraging steps in the right direction.) The substance of these voluntary social restraints would be very simple matters that can be fully understood and judged by any prudent man. The issues at stake in the SST controversy provide a good example. All such restraints would be chosen to promote stable and equal enjoyment of scientific know-how. The French say that it takes a thousand years to educate a peasant to deal with a cow. It would not take two generations to help all people in Latin America or Africa to use and repair outboard motors, simple cars, pumps, medicine kits, and ferro cement machines if their design does not change every few years. And since a joyful life is one of constant meaningful intercourse with others in a meaningful environment, equal enjoyment does translate into equal education.

At present a consensus on austerity is difficult to imagine. The reason usually given for the impotence of the majority is stated in terms of political or economic class. What is not usually understood is that the new class structure of a schooled society is even more powerfully controlled by vested interests. No doubt an imperialist and capitalist organiza-tion of society provides the social structure within which a minority can have disproportionate influence over the effective opinion of the majority. But in a technocratic society the power of a minority of knowledge capitalists can prevent the formation of true public opinion through control of scientific know-how and the media of communication. Constitutional guarantees of free speech, free press, and free assembly were meant to ensure government by the people. Modern electronics, photo-offset presses, time-sharing computers, and telephones have in principle provided the hardware that could give an entirely new meaning to these freedoms. Unfortunately, these things are used in modern media to increase the power of knowledge-bankers to funnel their program-packages through international chains to more people, instead of being used to increase true networks that provide equal opportunity for encounter among the members of the majority.

Deschooling the culture and social structure requires the use of technology to make participatory politics possible. Only on the basis of a majority coalition can limits to secrecy and growing power be determined without dictatorship. We need a new environment in which growing up can be classless, or we will get a brave new world in which Big Brother educates us all.

———◆•◆———

QUESTIONS FOR DISCUSSION

1. What has been the major source of curricula in American education? Will this same source serve effectively for the future? Why?

2. How should national objectives or goals for education be developed? What individuals or groups should be involved? Why?

3. What should be the role of the teacher in developing curricula?
4. Why has it been so difficult to achieve individualization of instruction in American schools?
5. Is national assessment a legitimate and necessary procedure? Why?

SUPPLEMENTARY LEARNING ACTIVITIES

1. Invite a curriculum coordinator to your class to explain his role.
2. Prepare a list of performance objectives for a group of your own definition. Include objectives from the cognitive, affective, and psychomotor domains.
3. Visit a nearby school to observe their techniques for individualizing instruction.
4. Interview lay citizens and teachers to gain their impressions of what a school curriculum should be like. Report your findings to the class.
5. Interview students to ascertain their perceptions of the objectives of their instruction.

SELECTED REFERENCES

American Association of School Administrators. *National Education Assessment: Pro and Con.* Washington, D.C.: National Education Association Publications, 1966.

Anderson, Robert H. *Opting for Openness.* Arlington, Va.: National Association of Elementary School Principals, 1973.

Association for Supervision and Curriculum Development. *Curriculum Decisions: Social Realities.* Washington, D.C.: Association for Supervision and Curriculum Development, 1968.

————. *New Curriculum Developments.* Washington, D.C.: Association for Supervision and Curriculum Development, 1965.

Beauchamp, George. *Curriculum Theory.* Wilmette, Ill.: The Kagg Press, 1961.

Clark, Leonard H.; Raymond L. Klein; and John B. Burks. *The American Secondary School Curriculum.* New York: Macmillan Company, 1965.

Conant, James Bryant. *The American High School Today.* New York: McGraw-Hill Book Company, 1959.

Frost, Joe L., and Rowland G. Thomas. *Curricula for the Seventies.* Boston: Houghton Mifflin Company, 1969.

Goldberg, Miriam L.; A. Harry Passow; and Joseph Justman. *The Effects of Ability Grouping.* New York: Teachers College Press, 1966.

Goodlad, John I. "Curriculum: State of the Field." *Review of Educational Research* 39, no. 3, June 1969.

————. *The Future of Learning and Teaching.* Washington, D.C.: National Education Association Publications, 1968.

Gwynn, J. Minor, and John B. Chase. *Curriculum Principles and Social Trends.* New York: Macmillan Company, 1969.

Hertzberg, Alvin, and Edward Stone. *Schools Are for Children: An American Approach to the Open Classroom.* New York: Schocken Books Inc., 1971.

Holt, John. *How Children Fail.* New York: Pitman Publishing Corporation, 1964.

Hopkins, L. Thomas. *Interaction: The Democratic Process.* Boston: D. C. Heath & Company, 1941.

Inlow, Gail M. *The Emergent in Curriculum.*

364   New York: John Wiley & Sons, Inc., 1966.

Johnson, James A., et al. *Foundations of American Education.* 2nd ed. Boston: Allyn & Bacon, Inc., 1973.

Keith, Lowell; Paul Blake; and Sidney Tiedt. *Contemporary Curriculum in the Elementary School.* New York: Harper & Row, Publishers, 1968.

Kohl, Herbert. *The Open Classroom.* New York: Random House, Inc., Vintage Books, 1970.

Krathwohl, David R.; Benjamin S. Bloom; and Bertram B. Masia. *Taxonomy of Educational Objectives.* New York: David McKay Company, Inc., 1964.

McLoughlin, William P. "The Phantom Nongraded School." *Phi Delta Kappan* 69(1968):248–50.

Miller, Richard I. *The Nongraded School: Analysis and Study.* New York: Harper & Row, Publishers, 1967.

Mushkin, Selma, and Stephen Stageberg. *National Assessment and Social Indicators. January 1973.* Washington, D.C.: U. S. Government Printing Office, 1973.

National Education Association Project on the Instructional Program of the Public Schools. *Education in a Changing Society.* Washington, D.C.: National Education Association Publications, 1964.

Perronne, Vito. *Open Education: Promise and Problems.* Bloomington, Ind.: Phi Delta Kappa, 1972.

Rathbone, Charles, ed. *Open Education: The Informal Classroom.* New York: Scholastic Book Services, Citation Press, 1971.

Shaplin, Judson T., and Henry F. Olds, Jr., eds. *Team Teaching.* New York: Harper & Row, Publishers, 1964.

Smith, B. Othanel; William O. Stanley; and J. Harlan Shores. *Fundamentals of Curriculum Development.* rev. ed. New York: Harcourt, Brace & World, Inc., 1957.

Trump, J. Lloyd, and Delmas F. Miller. *Secondary School Curriculum Improvement.* 2nd ed. Boston: Allyn & Bacon, Inc., 1972.

chapter 14
Instructional Resources

goals

● Describes the many areas of resources available for instructional purposes.

● Explains aspects of the technology involved in producing the final product of many materials used in the classroom.

● Illustrates the various types of media and their utilization by teachers.

● Diagrams and discusses selected educational facilities in relation to instruction and technology.

● Presents brief statements regarding the use of community resources and outdoor resources as parts of the total learning environments.

Historically, the teacher's primary role has been that of presenting information to students in a demonstration or lecture discussion manner. Various kinds of devices, including books, have always been used by teachers as instructional resources for assist-ing them in reaching their pupils. Johannes Gutenberg invented the type mold during the mid-1400s, making printing from movable metallic type practical for the first time. Educational historians record this breakthrough in printing as greatly significant in that teachers have since had books and other printed materials more readily available as resources. In addition to printed materials, teachers have used such things as wax tablets, slate boards, blackboards and chalk, hornbooks, microscopes, animal cadavers, works of art, architecture, music and musical instruments, and the theatre to facilitate learning.

> *In the invention of the motion picture, I intended it—conceived it—as a contribution to education. I am disappointed that it has been turned into an entertainment toy.*
>
> Thomas Edison

> *A fully vigorous personal, intellectual, and social education can be created only if the teacher and the student, as they work together, have many options available to them—options which enable students to engage in a large variety of instructional activities and which assist teachers to perform a corresponding diversity of instructional roles. They need a rich laboratory of books, audiovisual media, and other technological resources. . . .*
>
> National Commission on Teacher Education and Professional Standards

As long ago as 1923 the importance of the general field of instructional resources was formalized by the founding of the Association for Educational Communication and Technology (AECT). At the half-century mark since the founding of AECT, the idea of instructional technology has solid acceptance.

With a relatively stable society prior to the end of World War II changes in the institutions of society were few. Thus, the development of instructional resources was slow, moving with little more than bare essential expenditures allocated from school budgets.

Schools have undergone a great deal of change since the end of World War II. Extensive building programs and experiments with modular scheduling, team teaching, and educational television were brought about by the increasing numbers of students during the 1950s. The suddenly changing world of education was spurred by the launching of the Russian satellite Sputnik in 1957. Following Sputnik, the American public demanded improvements in school curricula. The federal government enacted the National Defense Education Act of 1958 which expanded federal financial aid to education for programs to improve instruction. This act also provided funds to develop audiovisual media services and facilities. Modifications to this act culminated in several federal programs being enacted by the Eighty-ninth Congress. Federal research funds were granted for educational media research and for library research. Big businesses jumped into the competition for this new source of federal money for education and the pace quickened in the development of many kinds of instructional resources.

The growth of knowledge during the post–World War II years has provided not only an additional stimulus to the growth of educational media, but also provided one of the greatest challenges to teaching. Teachers have come more and more to understand that learning is an active rather than passive process. Information-giving pedagogy, assigning facts to be studied and memorized, is considered out of vogue in many schools

Many kinds of printed materials are often produced within the school.

today. A contemporary view of the teacher's primary task is that of facilitator, planner, and director of varied active learning experiences. The teacher also serves as a diagnostician who must demonstrate his competencies for organizing instructional material and techniques geared to the achievement of teaching-learning objectives.

As often happens when sudden attention is showered upon a new dimension within the educational setting, the development of instructional technology has at times seemed haphazard and loosely structured. However, the federal establishment continues to increase efforts toward the application of technological solutions to educational problems.

Recent reorganization of the Office of Education resulted in the formation of a National Center for Educational Technology under an Associate Commissioner for Educational Technology. This center now focuses attention on educational technology concepts and programs and administers funds to support them.

Continued legislative effort is expected to aid the development of educational technology for the United States. While minimal attention was given to the bill, Congress has been asked to pass the Educational Technology Act. Hearings were held in conjunction with a bill designed to establish a Council on Educational Technology. The various in-

368 terests of the instructional technology groups and individuals will continue to press for the reintroduction and passing of such legislation by the Congress.

Mediaware

Educational media are the tools of the professional teacher. Educational media in-clude printed, audio, visual, and real materials. Certainly, texts, graphs, pictures, newspapers, magazines, encyclopedias, and comics are educational media. Other important media include films, filmstrips, film loops, slides, overhead and opaque projectors, commercial and educational television, records, audiotapes, cassette television tapes, and the radio. Other things such as animal pets, insects, models of real things such as skele-

Paperbacks have reduced the cost of many great books.

tons and machinery, simulation devices such as driver trainers and communication kits, as well as computers, desktop calculators, and other electronic devices are also important pieces of ware. The media list is ever-increasing as it must be, to accompany the ever-increasing knowledge growth. Future teachers will be more and more media-minded as they assume their teaching tasks.

Software

Software products are those generally associated with the teacher which have been used for years. Software media include textbooks, paper and pencil learning materials, workbooks, encyclopedias, newspapers, magazines, graphs, charts, posters, maps, globes, and, most recently, various kinds of programmed materials. The kinds of materials found in typical school libraries are generally considered as software. Many software products have been manufactured specifically for sale to the homes, such as encyclopedias, book-of-the-month publications, and school-oriented papers and magazines. Software materials are very important to the teaching-learning process and continue to undergo changes in form and patterns of use.

Hardware

Only recently have we begun to make applications of technology and the products of technology to improve education. Such hardware products of technology include all kinds of mechanical and electronic devices which aid or supplement the software products. In many schools, movie projectors, filmstrip and slide projectors, record players, tape recorders, opaque projectors, overhead projectors, reading machines, and other devices of an audiovisual nature are stored in a central location so that use of the equipment may be coordinated for the entire faculty. While much equipment usage takes place in learning centers in some schools, the classroom teacher most frequently uses the normal classroom as the laboratory where instructional hardware is used. Many schools employ a director of audiovisual education who is responsible for the maintenance of equipment and for the coordination of teacher utilization of equipment. The concept of audiovisual (AV) programs to enhance instruction is considered the forerunner for the contemporary thrust in the applications of technology to education.

Large sums of money have been invested by private business and by federal acts during the past few years for modifying, adapting, and producing hardware for specific classroom use. The effect of this emphasis has been the expanding and upgrading of the audiovisual program concept. The impact of software and hardware development has brought to focus the systems approach to instruction. An instructional system includes careful planning of instructional objectives and consideration of methods, facilities, and people in performing various instructional activities, in addition to the valid selection of media. In effect, the systems approach to instruction brings together the audiovisual program, the school library, and school personnel. Later in this chapter attention is given to the changing view with regard to future school libraries.

Title II of the Elementary and Secondary Education Act of 1965 provided to the states $100 million to improve educational quality through grants for the acquisition of school

Wall charts and maps are important aids for learning.

Audiotapes are available for several kinds and types of machines.

Elementary students use tapes to help develop listening skills.

Instructional Resources

Tapes and texts may be coordinated for specific learning activities.

Only a small space is required for several students to use a single tape.

The Education Digest, February 1974, p. 53.

Taped programmed laboratory instruction can be supplemented by visuals.

A teacher prepares to change transparencies on an overhead projector during a class presentation.

Maps project brightly on blackboards in normally lighted rooms—one of the advantages derived from using overhead projectors.

A junior high school student uses a machine to help her accelerate her reading speed.

Two young teachers preview a filmstrip before presentation in class.

Movie cameras are easy to use for filming class activities.

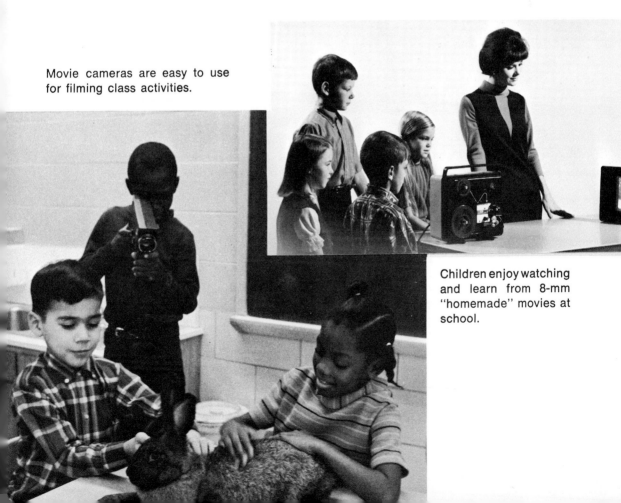

Children enjoy watching and learn from 8-mm "homemade" movies at school.

A teacher records a story for her class.

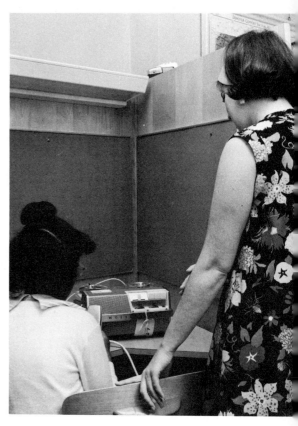

In Shaker Heights, Ohio a volunteer mother assists a child to record a poem.

library resources. The three categories of materials eligible for acquisition under Title II included software and hardware of various kinds. The categories were school library resources (includes audiovisual materials), textbooks, and other printed and published instructional materials. Most states allocated all or most of their Title II funds for school library resources, or for a combination of school library resources and other instructional materials. The expenditure of the original Title II appropriations firmed up the trend among schools to capitalize upon the availability of new software and hardware in instruction.

The continued availability of federal, state, and local dollars for instructional technology materials and equipment has also been the boon for the introduction of various "fly-by-night" businesses peddling poorly developed goods. Likewise, reputable established businesses have brought into or joined in the production of instructional technology materials and equipment. Some after-the-fact evaluative efforts reveal that some very expensive technologically refined instructional systems have not produced results originally hoped for. In some cases large sums of money have been invested in equipment which is now considered obsolete. For example, some of the first videotape equipment was not only unwieldy in size but also very expensive. The newer electronic equipment is much easier to use and less expensive. In this area, the video cassette tapes appear to offer excellent potential.

From all this rapid activity, there now is apparent a clamor for carefully evaluating the many materials and assorted equipment for the purpose of providing sharper tools for better learning. The National Association for Secondary School Principals directed attention to these concerns through their Committee on Educational Technology. Part of a monograph developed by this committee responded as follows to the question—Why sharper tools?

Students at San Rafael, California learn to read from sound tapes.

Taped instructions permit an individual student to conduct a biology experiment.

A biology class conducts experiments to taped instructions.

Classroom laboratory experiments can be videotaped for replay many times.

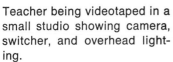

Special education students being videotaped in physical education class.

Teacher being videotaped in a small studio showing camera, switcher, and overhead lighting.

Two elementary students watch themselves on videotape playback.

Students in a parochial school watching program received from an instructional television system.

Taping Meet: A member of the University of Washington gymnastics team performs a routine on a sidehorse at the Seattle campus. His routine is picked up by a television camera and recorded on a videotape recorder as part of a meet with the University of Illinois. Each team competed on its own campus, with an impartial panel of judges viewing the videotapes of both teams to render its decision. It was the first such meet ever held. Illinois was the winner, 180.65–173.10.

Instant Replay: Coach and performer review the athlete's routine seconds after its completion. The two are watching a sidehorse routine taped at the University of Washington.

Schools today are demanding better and sharper educational tools—tools that will be more effective than traditional ones in meeting the needs of individualized student learning, greater teacher accountability, and additions to the curriculum.

We are now only beginning to realize that independent learning materials, oriented to the individual, differ in many ways from the teacher-dependent materials, oriented to the class, which still predominate in schools. We are gradually discovering that the inadequacies of traditional materials cannot be compensated for by adding new and different materials merely because they are new and different.

We are also very slowly coming to the realization that, in the interest not only of education but also of economy, materials must demonstrate the degree of their effectiveness before we buy them, not after a somewhat haphazard on-the-job trial in our schools.[1]

Learning Resource Centers

Existing public school libraries have been criticized severely by various study groups. In 1961, the National Committee for Support of the Public Schools reported that (a) more than 10 million children go to public schools with no school libraries, and (b) more than half of all public schools have no library. Such criticism has generated renewed interest in the directions school libraries ought to be taking in order to meet the needs of today's pupils. "Beyond question, the traditional concept of a public school library, with its stiff overtones of hardback chairs and rectangular tables, is now obsolete; it has matured into a concept of a total learning resource center, which like a candy store displays what it has to offer in the most appealing way possible."[2] The trend of the future with regard to the school library concept is to arrange the various software and hardware media in a common setting which provides space specifically allocated for individual and small group usage. Individual study carrels will have individual lighting controls and electrical outlets. Small groups will have access to specific resource centers such as math and science centers. Comfortable furniture, small study desks, and carpeting will replace obsolete furnishings. The learning resource center concept demands a high level of utilization necessitating flexible schedule arrangements to permit students time to use the center.

> *But whatever they call it, and wherever they put it, public schools everywhere are going to have to find space for reducing, retaining, reproducing and displaying the incredible mountain of information that new technology now makes available. Sooner than we think, a public school without such facilities will be about as educationally effective as a log without Mark Hopkins there on the end.*
>
> Aaron Cohodes

The creation of a learning resource center is not an attempt to do away with the school library. Instead, it attempts to utilize

1. *Sharper Tools for Better Learning* (Reston, Va.: National Association of Secondary School Principals, 1973), p. 1.

2. Aaron Cohodes, "Put It in the Middle and Call It a Learning Center," *Nation's Schools* 77(March 1966):85.

380 the typical verbal materials of the library and supplement them with additional software and hardware instructional media now available to the teacher. As children become involved in the learning process at different rates of growth they have a need to pursue learning on an individual basis and also in small group activities. The teacher may now free the learner to go to a center where materials are provided for individual and small group learning. The center is equipped with books, programmed materials, television, tape banks with headsets, and a variety of other materials which will provide auditory, visual, and audiovisual learning.

This type of learning center has been more readily adopted at the elementary level but more recently has begun to move into the newer junior and senior high schools. Some of the types of materials that may be found in a learning center follow. This list is by no means all-inclusive, but only representative.

1. *Controlled Readers*. This is a mechanical pacing device. A moving slot travels across the screen covering and uncovering reading material as it goes. Speeds of these machines range from 60 to 1000 words per minute.
2. *Tapes for Speech Patterns*. These tapes attempt to teach the child to make correctly a particular sound with his lips and teeth and teach him to become aware of the sound when he hears it.
3. *Listening Laboratories*. Listening laboratories will accommodate from one to eight students. They may be used with records or audio tapes. Currently there are some laboratories which have audiovisual facilities. These laboratories are not as fully developed as they will be in the future.
4. *Library and Reading Kits*. Multi-level

reading laboratories have short stories and excerpts from great works in literature. They cover areas of poetry, history, fiction and nonfiction. A student uses these on an individual basis and it helps supplement the multi-level reading program of the school.

5. *Controlled Reader for Mathematics*. This is a mechanical device with filmstrips and headsets. Emphasis is on comprehension of basic number facts and problem-solving techniques.
6. *Elementary Science Units*. These kits include microviewers with filmstrip slides. Information is given in reading form and then strips are used to demonstrate points made in the printed discussion.
7. *Video Tapes*. These tapes are prepared as teaching aids for the teacher and do not replace whole units of instruction. Students may obtain general information individually or in groups and later interact with other students and teachers in a seminar setting. The tapes are of particular value for such difficult and costly things as laboratory presentations and for specialists who otherwise could not be introduced to the learners. With the addition of color tapes this supplemental source will become even more stimulating to the learner.
8. *Computer Assisted Instruction Laboratory*. Although it is rather costly because of the hardware involved, the techniques of linear and branch programing can be utilized in a variety of ways to accommodate individual or small group (2–5) learning sessions. This type of laboratory is still in the experimental stage, but holds promise for individualizing instruction.[3]

3. James Johnson, et al., *Introduction to the Foundations of American Education*, pp. 412–14. Copyright Allyn and Bacon, Inc., 1969. Used with permission.

From this type of descriptive listing it appears that the teaching task has been greatly simplified. On the contrary, the teacher must now come face to face with issues in the curriculum that have usually been reserved for administrators, supervisors, and the like. The learning resource center is little more than an administratively planned learning area and as such is not different in purpose than the classroom. Although it holds promise for the future in its potential for individualized learning, it must for the greater part be planned and developed by teachers. It should be supplied with materials that teachers have selected and developed through their experiences with children.

Recently, the nation has witnessed vast mergers of publishing companies, research bureaus, and manufacturers. Seeing a growing need for all kinds of educational software and hardware, plus an economy that promises to allocate increasing funds for education, it appears that these corporations have struck a bonanza. The American businessman has traditionally operated on a profit motive and now his market research has shown a lucrative economic quest in education. Capitalizing on a national concern for increased educational output, these corporations now have the capacity to hypothesize, research, develop, produce, and market an endless variety of educational software and hardware which may be used in the learning process. The knowledge explosion, increasing rates of mobility, the quest for more knowledge in a shorter time, the complex pressures of providing individualized educational opportunity for all citizens, and the educational establishment's seeming inability to direct educational change effectively have all contributed to the birth of these corporations.

This type of industrial movement has placed an ever greater responsibility on the teacher working in curriculum. Among the many splendid products on the market today there also may be found hastily developed and poorly researched materials which purport to provide the teacher with "the answer" to learning problems. As a result the teacher has the special task of discarding these inferior or worthless programs and adapting those which are useful to his particular situation. Of a highly more critical nature, the teacher should, in addition to the culling of manufactured materials which may be used for the learning process, continue to develop his own new materials in light of his experience with the learner.

Westinghouse Learning Corporation (WLC)

An example of a largely industrial company which has entered into activity in the field of education is the Westinghouse Learning Corporation. WLC was founded in February 1967 as a subsidiary of the Westinghouse Electric Company. The primary activity of the Westinghouse Learning Corporation has been in the development of PLAN (Program for Learning in Accordance with Needs). PLAN was initiated in September 1967 through cooperative efforts of the Westinghouse Learning Corporation, the American Institutes for Research, and several school districts. The system utilizes the computer as an aid to the teacher in providing each student with an individual program of study, designed to meet his needs, abilities, and interests.

Initially, in September 1967, grades one, five, and nine were involved. For the second year of operation, grades two, six, and ten

382 were added. In four years, PLAN will encompass all levels one through twelve in selected schools within the twelve school research and development districts. It is operating at levels one and two in five extension districts. Mathematics, language arts (English, reading, etc.), science, and social studies are presently involved in PLAN. Other subject areas are to be added as soon as the modules are completed.

School Building in the City

Some of the special problems encountered when building in the city are illustrated in Figure 14.1. As indicated, the urban school is best when integrated with the total urban environment including other cultural and educational agencies. Where land is very expensive it can be expected that schools may come to share multiuse structures with other agencies. A concept for creating territory for learning in the secondary school level is illustrated in Figure 14.2. When planning for the secondary schools in the city the multischool concept suggests several one thousand student schools would surround and be attached to a specialized facilities and services hub. The areas immediately adjacent to the school would deliberately include other cultural, educational, commercial, and residential components. Another consideration in the multischool concept relates to the expensive costs of city land. Figure 14.3 suggests that space along and above expressways be utilized for school-building purposes. The expensive city land costs also suggest that the components of the multischool could be stacked to create a high-rise multischool. In a high-rise multischool design, the foyer and surrounding land-level areas could provide for parking, outdoor recreational facilities, and other agencies such as theatre and music facilities. The multischool hub would be at a lower level (second floor) with the schools stacked above on a floor-by-floor basis. Lockers, pools, gyms, and multipurpose play areas would be above the schools. The remainder of the high-rise structure would be used to house offices and apartments in the top floor levels.

What Tomorrow's Library Will Look Like

A special report from the Bureau of School Planning, State of California Department of Education, has suggested that tomorrow's library will have decentralized study areas, extensive disposable media, and electronic retrieval equipment tapping audio and video material stored at regional knowledge centers. Clair L. Eatough, supervising architectural advisor to the California Bureau of School Planning, wrote the following article for *Nation's Schools* based on suggestions made at a seminar on school libraries.

———•—•———

The school library of the near future will be a single canopy under which all media, present and future, can be coordinated. It will have decentralized study centers, extensive paperback collections, and—most importantly—electronic retrieval systems that by the touch of a button or dial will bring televised texts, lectures, filmstrips and movies from distant knowledge centers.

The library of tomorrow will be a knowledge Resource Center. To understand the KRC concept, school districts must think of library materials as three types of media.

Media A—Traditional material: books, films, records and so forth.

NOTE SOME OF THE SPECIAL PROBLEMS ENCOUNTERED WHEN BUILDING IN THE CITY

. . . NEW FORMS FOR URBAN SCHOOLS ARE NEEDED.

SITES ARE SMALL . . . LAND IS EXPENSIVE . . .
URBAN BUILDING FORMS (COMPACT, MULTILEVEL)
ARE MOST APPROPRIATE . . .

THE URBAN SCHOOL (STRONGLY INFLUENCED BY NEIGHBORS)
IS BEST WHEN INTEGRATED WITH THE TOTAL URBAN
ENVIRONMENT, WITH OTHER CULTURAL & EDUCATIONAL
AGENCIES . . .

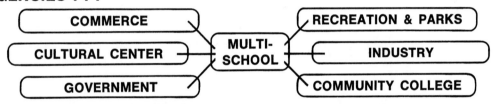

COMMERCE

RECREATION & PARKS

CULTURAL CENTER

MULTI-SCHOOL

INDUSTRY

GOVERNMENT

COMMUNITY COLLEGE

AIR RIGHTS DEVELOPMENT IS NOW AN OPPORTUNITY
FOR PRIME LOCATION, GOOD ACCESS, SPACE, DRAMA . . .

EXPRESSWAY →

WHERE LAND IS VERY EXPENSIVE
THE HIGH-RISE SCHOOL MAY BE APPROPRIATE . . .

NEXT—SCHOOLS WILL SHARE
MULTIUSE STRUCTURES WITH OTHER TENANTS!

Figure 14.1 City Building Problems

Source: *Nation's Schools* 81 (March 1968). By permission.

384
IN THE CITY, PLAN THE MULTISCHOOL WITH OTHER EDUCATIONAL, CULTURAL, AND COMMUNITY FACILITIES

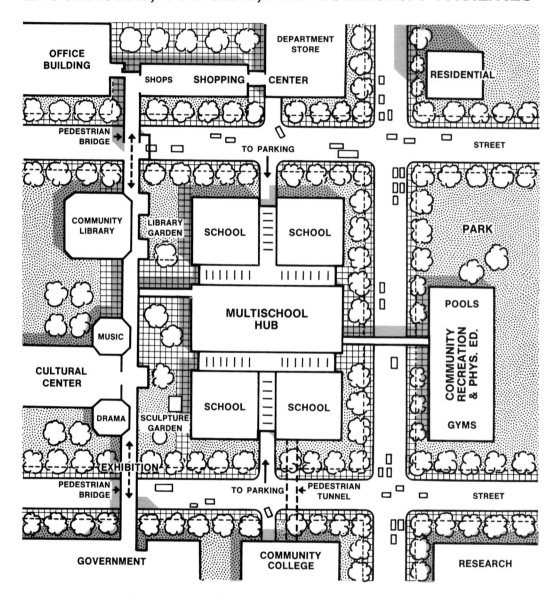

Figure 14.2 City Planning for the Schools

Source: *Nation's Schools* 81 (March 1968). By permission.

HIGHWAY AND CITY PLANNERS NOW ENCOURAGE DEVELOPMENT OF SPACE ALONG & ABOVE EXPRESSWAYS.
WHY NOT USE IT?

A BRIDGE-LIKE MULTISCHOOL CAN SPAN THE EXPRESSWAY . . . TYING THE AREA BACK TOGETHER.

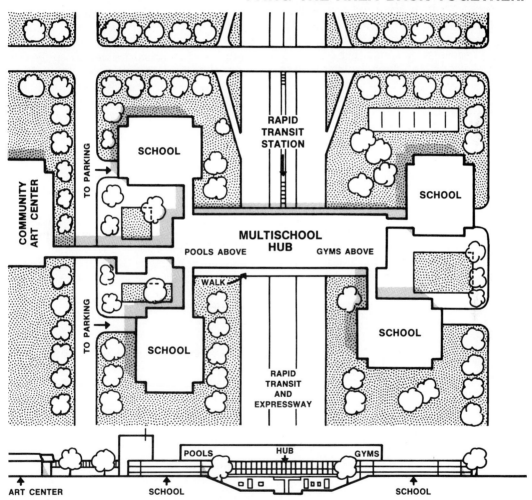

Figure 14.3 Suggested Use of Expressway Space

Source: *Nation's Schools* 81 (March 1968). By Permission.

386   Media B—Disposable material: paperbacks, mimeographs, and so forth.

Media C—Audiovisual material: transmitted electronically.

Media A

This is the material that every librarian and every school teacher is using now. It includes: hard cover books; 35-mm, 16-mm, and 8-mm movie tapes; filmstrips; sound tapes; phonograph records; periodicals. It requires hand delivery from supplier to user, and schools consider it valuable and therefore catalog, file or store it and set up a staff for its control and use.

Type A media is the justification for our present library concepts. It is likely that most of this media eventually will phase out because of expense and inefficiency. Its value will be almost exclusively for specialized research. School libraries below university levels normally do not have funds to acquire and maintain sufficient quantities of esoteric material or enough advanced students to make the concept productive. Most schools have little to gain by the archival approach to media.

Media B

This media in whatever form is *disposable.* Proper use of this material can achieve some dramatic developments. But this depends on the recognition by educators that there is a great body of printed material that can be purchased at a price that permits it to be discarded after limited use yet still achieve a high educational return on the investment.

The paperback book; reproduction by such processes as dry photocopying; the mimeographed sheet; the blue print or ozalid are examples of common disposable material.

We are assuming that in tomorrow's library the school will make available means for reproduction of Type B media to every student as well as staff.

It is a mistake to think that because disposable material in many forms is in use now it will have no more impact on tomorrow's schools than it has on today's. The *extent* of use will be new. If the school were to make full use of paperbacks, purchasing mostly books of this type, it would not need to bother with cataloging, filing, storing. Only initial dispersal to various study centers would be important. Shelves could be open, and students could be given totally free access. We could at last free ourselves of the ancient phobia that the books, rather than the knowledge they contain, are valuable and must be restricted in use.

Ideally, librarians and instructors would evaluate this material and key the selection to the curriculum as carefully as is now done with expensive, more permanent material. Basic reference texts and encyclopedias would have to be purchased in quantity and distributed to each study center. These items must be given extensive exposure to obtain extensive use. They too should be replaced often, perhaps every year, not only because of ill treatment or loss, but because the information they contain becomes rapidly obsolete.

Disposable books and related materials permit the development of elements of a Parisian "left bank" by locating book stalls next to outdoor reading areas. These can be enhanced by snack bars and art displays.

Media C

This media is the heart of KRC. It includes any material that can be transmitted electronically to the user in audio or visual form or both. Normally the media is a car-

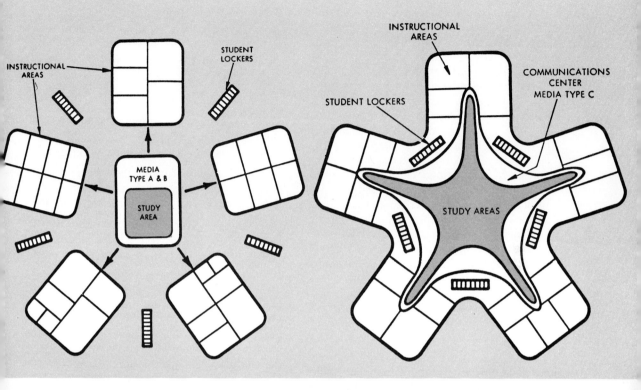

Figure 14.4 The Library of Today and of Tomorrow. Today's library, often central in location, may separate students from materials and teachers from study areas. Tomorrow's KRC may serve 5 to 6 teaching stations, 100 to 200 students and integrate study, materials, and instruction.

tridge loaded magnetic tape which stores both sound and picture.

Electronic retrieval systems require a centralized facility for the production and storage of programed material, and decentralized study areas. They are coupled with a network of communication channels. The receiving stations (where the students are) have instant access to the available programed material by pushing buttons or twirling a telephone dial to audio and video channels which can tap live or stored presentations.

The communication center is a great storehouse for magnetic tapes containing programed material which includes almost all texts, lectures, filmstrips and movies in all fields of knowledge. Duplication and exchange of tapes is coordinated with all other communication centers throughout the country. All indexing, filing and retrieval are computerized. The facility includes production studios and a complete staff organization for its operation. A vast electronic network links it to all schools and study centers within the geographic region which it serves. A student can then dial a number and through a telephone or television receiver listen to a lecture,

388 view a film, read a research article from a professional journal, or take a lesson in a foreign language. When combined with independent study materials a student or teacher has all available resources at his finger tips. Catalogs are similar to telephone directories. They are designed to cover subject areas at various levels of education. School curriculum planners create and distribute special directories which are available to students. This is coordinated with the teacher's planned sequence of instruction. Thus, a sixth grade English student has the titles and numbers to dial the entire selected resource material which his teacher wishes to make available. Students working independently have more extensive directories available at major study centers. Suggested material is recommended for study by teachers and counselors so that the student is guided to available material based on his curriculum goals, state of readiness, interest and skills. This permits students to work on an individualized schedule to a degree not possible in traditional patterns.

Not only are materials containing audio-visual sequences capable of being presented to a student almost any place where desired on a campus, but eventually this service will expand beyond the confines of the school and permit a student to dial a lesson from his home in the evening. It will be possible for the student in the one-room school to have equal access and exposure to available information as the student in the large urban school. It can encompass all ages. It can serve the learner from the beginning reader in elementary school through high school and college and on through a useful adult lifetime.

KRC assumes that the student and his study centers will be dispersed throughout the campus, and eventually throughout the community. *Bringing the resources to the student rather than the student to the material* is the essence of the KRC. This requires a reappraisal of student study centers.

Students Want Study Centers

There has been much recent concern about how and where students prefer to study. The Community College Planning Center at Stanford University sent questionnaires to students. Their responses show:

—Students prefer small as against large study areas; they considered moderately sized study rooms superior to small study areas.

—Students prefer to study where there is easy access to special equipment (e.g. drafting equipment, art equipment, and so forth).

—Students expressed a strong desire to study where there is easy access to instructors.

The conclusion of the published report was, "Clearly, students generally want contact with their instructors and prefer to study in the familiar surroundings of their 'home base' classrooms, labs, practice rooms, and so forth. There seems to be a clear implication that study space should not be concentrated entirely in the library but should be available throughout the campus."

KRC study centers can be as varied as the places where people desire to study. However, a typical study center should have certain essential elements such as:

1. It is located adjacent to and perhaps as part of the instructional area of the school. (It might be a core area of a cluster type building supported directly by four or five teaching stations.)

2. It resembles an informal lounge area utilizing comfortable furniture and carpeted floors.

3. Its standards for lighting, acoustics and the thermal environment are as high as any area in the school.

4. It typically provides space and equipment for 25 to 50 students. Study areas are duplicated and distributed as required throughout the campus or building.

5. Each study center is so located that it becomes the home base for 100 to 200 students, depending on the schedule. The students' lockers (silenced by use of plastic, fibrous glass or other nonmetallic material) are located either in or immediately adjacent to his study center.

6. Each study center is equipped to supply and to use disposable media. This includes reference books, encyclopedias, dictionaries, but especially large quantities of paperbacks and other types of disposable material.

7. The study centers have a number of stations where the students dial for and receive by television monitors media from a central communications center. Directories listing the programed material are available.

8. Adjacent to most study centers are rooms or alcoves for copying machines, duplicators, silent typewriters, and so forth— all available for student and teacher use.

9. Teacher-student counseling areas and work areas are adjacent to and part of these study centers.

Many schools now in existence could be adapted to introduce some of these elements. Schools now being planned should give serious consideration to decentralizing study areas.

KRC needs a broad base for its support. Any school can implement a few of its features at little cost or effort. No single school and few school districts can create all of it by themselves. Eventually if it is to fulfill its potential of bringing available knowledge to everyone upon demand, it will require a statewide or regional organization for its operation.

The size of the central communication center would be determined by financial considerations and it is likely that one center would need a great many students to operate efficiently. California, for example, might require 5 or 10 of these centers located geographically throughout the state, probably at major colleges or universities since it could then utilize the resources from these library archives.

California is currently installing a state-wide network of computerized indexing and cataloging which will link together all state college and university libraries and the state library in Sacramento so that any item at any library can be located and transferred to the seeker. KRC could be working for these combined institutions if equipment were installed for electronic transfer of the material.

At present there are several obstacles to overcome before dial-access systems can gain wide usage. Most critical is the limited material presently available in programed form. Also lacking are trained personnel to prepare and present the material for use. Existing retrieval equipment is already more sophisticated than the staff in most schools.[4]

Community Resources

More than three-fourths of our population now live in either the central city areas or their suburbs. Improved transportation facilities have expanded the availability of community resources for school use. Students now have increased opportunities to learn about many things in their own communities. Many school boards, school administrators, and creative teachers are finding different ways in which to utilize community resources to supplement the learning activities of the schools.

Considerable educational planning is a prerequisite to the proper utilization of

4. Clair L. Eatough, "What Tomorrow's Library Will Look Like," *Nation's Schools* 77(1966):107–9. Reprinted with permission from *Nation's Schools,* March 1966. Copyright McGraw-Hill, Inc., 1966. All rights reserved.

A museum is a typical example of a community resource which has great educational value.

Outdoor educational opportunities provide valuable learning experiences for these young boys.

Outdoor educational opportunities provide valuable learning experiences for these young boys.

A student teacher enjoys working with her students in an outdoor teaching experience.

community resources. Educators ought to carefully develop community resource guides for the purpose of identifying and describing available educational resources, including community resource persons. Proper utilization of community resources for educational field trips requires subsequent planning which considers certain educational criteria for field trips. Finding and using resource persons, either at their place of work or in the classroom, also requires careful planning for coordinating the contributions of the resource person with the sequence of work students are doing in the classroom.

Obviously, the scope of available community resources is prescribed to a large measure by the nature of the community. However, every school community, large or small, has community resources at its disposal.

Outdoor Education

The concept of outdoor education has gained considerable acceptance during the last few years. Programs of outdoor education are increasing in popularity at all levels of the school organization. The simple essence of the outdoor education concept deals with activity and study in an outdoor setting. In some areas the community resources of agencies such as Boy Scouts and Girl Scouts, YMCA and YWCA, churches, private clubs, and service organizations are utilized in providing outdoor facilities for educational programs sponsored by the local schools. With continued acceptance of the concept the trend has been toward the development of especially designed and planned outdoor education facilities which are maintained as cooperative ventures among several school districts. In this fashion, the cooperating districts would have at their disposal the services of professionally trained outdoor education personnel hired on a full-time basis. Classroom teachers involved in outdoor education programs would then typically accompany their students on the overnight expeditions to the outdoor education facility.

Many teacher-preparation programs have built into their programs professional laboratory experiences with children in an outdoor setting. For example, the Lorado Taft Campus in Oregon, Illinois is the outdoor education extension of Northern Illinois University which is located in DeKalb, Illinois approximately forty miles away. The elementary teacher-preparation program of the university requires periods of several days to be spent at the outdoor education facility by both junior and senior students. Other teacher education programs which require senior year experiences at the outdoor education facility are programs in special education, women's physical education, and industry and technology. The university also offers a master's degree program in Outdoor Education which leads to the supervision and administration endorsements required by Illinois state law for directors of outdoor education facilities.

Another significant aspect of outdoor education acceptance is the considerable emphasis growing in nations throughout the world. The international influence of outdoor education is evidenced in the field study centers of Great Britain, the country schools in Germany, and the schools of the snow in the French Alps. Australia and Japan are leaders in the outdoor education movement in their part of the world. One of the noticeable program trends, especially on the international scene, is the rapid development of so-called outward bound schools. Such schools usually pit the physical prowess of the participants against the elements of nature. Thus, emphasis on physical survival and adventure experiences are basic to these programs.

In summary, the laboratory concept as associated with today's schools requires the availability of many kinds of materials, equipment, and facilities to assist the teacher in his work with students. The range of such needs includes the software and hardware; library resource centers or learning centers where multimedia systems may be assembled and operationalized; and utilization of available community resources, including the use of outdoor education facilities. All of these things add to the excitement of teaching and greatly assist the teacher in meeting his daily tasks.

Point of View

It seems natural to assume that large numbers of pupils in the schools of today have learned much of what they know from television, movies, and magazines in their homes and in other outside-of-school settings. It seems reasonable to further assume from

394 this that students in school should also learn through a wide use of media in the schools. Thus, the range of materials and devices available for classroom instruction continues to increase. With the increase in quantity have come significant increases in quality. Electronic research has proven vital in the refinement of media technology and the improvement of equipment.

Teachers must consider the total educational setting in order to appreciate the utilization of media in the teaching-learning process. Such consideration of the total educational setting is important to assure that the use of media does not become incidental or superficial. Media must be chosen carefully and must perform a particular function in the learning process. Such selection of media requires a wide knowledge of what is available for instructional use. It has been the purpose of this chapter to survey the media resources available, to explain selected aspects of technology, and to illustrate various uses of media by teachers.

A specific example of a program planned around the utilization of media is described in the following article by Leslie Rich. The program, called Remote Training of Early Childhood Educators, involved teachers of disadvantaged children of ages three, four, and five. Through a system which used a portable TV camera and recorder the teacher's performance was recorded, reviewed, and returned to the teacher along with a critique of the teacher's performance. In this manner the techniques of teaching were conveyed to locations throughout the United States. One of the implications of this program to teacher-training programs generally is that the use of media for the training of teachers also has considerable merit.

————●•●————

Learning by Seeing

Leslie Rich

To Bill Borthick, the simplest way to explain the program called Remote Training of Early Childhood Educators is to use what he calls the Betty Crocker analogy, which runs this way: Suppose Ms. Crocker incarnate were to walk into your kitchen with the purpose of teaching you the very best way to bake a cake. What would she do?

"In my opinion," says Borthick, "she'd bring along a 66-pound assembly of portable TV camera, recorder, and monitor. She'd set it up, turn it on, and have you bake a cake the best way you know how. Then she'd play the videotape and, with frequent stops, show you where you goofed up with the mixture or at the spice cabinet. Then she'd have you repeat the process until you were more efficient at producing palatable pastries."

That's pretty much what took place in the training program, of which Borthick was assistant director, except that the people being taped were not bakers but teachers of disadvantaged children of ages three, four, and five. The trainees sent their tapes through the mails to the John F. Kennedy Child Development Center, an affiliated interdisciplinary training program at the University of Colorado Medical Center in Denver, where they were reviewed and returned to the teacher along with a critique of the teacher's performance.

Thus the techniques of teaching were conveyed from Denver to locations scattered all over the map—predominately black schools in cities like Dallas, Little Rock, or

Leslie Rich, "Learning by Seeing," *American Education,* January-February 1974, pp. 13–17.

Auburn, Alabama; Indian schools at Wind River Reservation, Wyoming, or Fort Peck, Montana; Eskimo schools in Ketchikan and Kotzebue, Alaska; and a school for handicapped children in Honolulu. At its height the program served 15 sites and, as a matter of fact, some of that teaching technique transference is still going on. The program's grants initially under the National Defense Education Act and later the Education Professions Development Act have run their course, but some ten sites are in process of buying their own equipment in order to continue the instruction in some form.

The instructional package for the remote training—recently revised and amounting to more than 900 looseleaf pages—is known formally as the System for Open Learning (SOL). But since the author and director of the program, John H. Meier, is a broad-shouldered third-generation Coloradan, he tends to use a term that carries the cooking comparison a step further.

"Call it mountain stew," says Meier. "That's what you have when you're out camping and everyone pours his can of soup into the pot, whether it's Gesell, Piaget, Deneberg, or even Freud. We've tried to be eclectic, using only substantive ingredients which are essentially compatible and which lend themselves to a wide variety of combinations to suit local tastes. But the heart of our system is videotaping the teacher at work in the classroom as she goes through certain SOL learning episodes of five to seven minutes, then providing a critique of the tape and also having the teacher look at herself to see what she's doing ineffectively and what she's doing well. The three-volume series of SOL Facilitator Handbooks serves as the cookbook: It contains the rationale for SOL, several hundred tried and tested learning episodes, and

guides for developing the skills of early childhood educators.

All this educational gourmet cookery started in the mid-1960s when Meier served as associate director and research psychologist for the New Nursery School, a Greeley, Colorado, program for environmentally deprived children, mostly Chicanos. Located in a frame house on the edge of the Spanish-speaking neighborhood, the school attempted to entice children in "self directed" learning in which they would work on such things as puzzles and stacks of building rings much on their own.

Instead of routinely gathering children together for a story, teachers would tend to wait for each child to *ask* for a story. "The teacher responds to the child, rather than the children responding to her," was the explanation given by Glen Nimnicht, director of the school. Progress was slow. Most pupils knew little English and some had never before held crayons or scissors. But results were favorable enough for Meier to build on the "teacher response" concept while he was co-director of an experimental program at the University of Northern Colorado (Colorado State College) in Greeley.

Charged with more effectively disseminating this model for early childhood education, Meier helped set up an exemplary training center for Head Start teachers who would come to Greeley for an eight-week session. Again there was some progress, but from Meier's point of view there were several things wrong.

First there was the problem of bringing trainees in from Indian reservations and small rural Spanish communities located all over this part of the West and from Eskimo communities in Alaska. Because of the expense and inconvenience, they would straggle across

396

the prairies and the mountains and end up jammed together in whatever motel accommodations they could find.

"An overriding thought," says Meier, "was that the training was somewhat irrelevant. When they came to us, they would be trained in a model center, using beautiful toys in an exemplary academic setting. Then they'd go back to the reservation and everything would be different. Many did profit from the training. But they were subject to a lot of emotional turmoil, being away from their families, their familiar customs and foods."

How could these teachers from the outlands get more realistic training? In pondering that problem, Meier looked at it from a point of view considerably at variance from that of the average psychologist—because he was not an average psychologist. Still in his 30s, he had explored several careers. He was a baseball pitcher signed by the Yankees but prevented from attending spring training because of a ski accident. He was a prospective clergyman entering a seminary before deciding to pursue a Ph.D. in educational and developmental psychology. His earliest fascination, however, was electronics. As a kid in Denver he had built his own TV set before there were even any broadcasts. And it was this hobby that made him intensely aware of the emergence of videotape, that marvelous stuff that made possible the "instant replays" on television.

It occurred to Meier that videotape was the perfect way to teach the teachers by long distance. He secured funding for a small experiment, bought some equipment, and visited several Indian reservations where, using short learning episodes, he taped teachers during classroom sessions. He used a process called "micro-teaching," with "micro" referring not only to a scaling down in lesson and class size but also to an analysis in great detail of a teacher's performance—as if under a microscope—made possible by repeated replays of the film.

Again he ran into a roadblock: the primitiveness of the equipment. The first generation of videotape machinery was heavy, expensive, complicated, and unreliable. But improved equipment began to appear on the market, and finally the package of camera, recorder, and monitor was reduced in weight to just 66 pounds—fine for luggage or even hand-carrying on a plane. What's more, it worked properly even when packed over a back road through clouds of dust at temperatures of over 100 or less than 20 degrees. Evidently technology had arrived at that point which, in Meier's view, "would make it possible to bring sophisticated teaching concepts to places they wouldn't get to otherwise."

The program of Remote Training of Early Childhood Educators started at the University of Northern Colorado and moved with Meier when he became director of Denver's JFK Child Development Center. Advertised in education journals, it annually drew a long list of trainee applicants from preschool organizations all over the country. Trainees were chosen on the basis of need and also on the basis of the likelihood of their being able to be of significant benefit to indigent children. From its base in the Indian country, the project spread to southern blacks and Alaskan Eskimos. Participants' educational backgrounds ran the gamut from GED's (high school equivalency) to Ph.Ds. Some of the latter took the training to apply the process in other programs.

Usually, the trainee's first direct contact with the trainers came at one of the two week-long workshops held annually at headquarters in Denver. One teacher and one aide would be invited from each site to become immersed in techniques and subject matter which they would later pass along to their colleagues at home. First they would be introduced to the equipment, later working with it, taking turns playing the role of children in the classroom. Then they would work with actual children from the JFK Center. Finally they would return home taking along the equipment as luggage—a considerable savings in shipping costs.

Beyond the names of the trainees and a general description of their schools, Meier and his staff knew little about the people coming in for training. So they were prepared to make the training more or less complicated as the situation indicated. One thing they noticed about all groups, however, was that their first reaction on seeing themselves on videotape was one of cosmetology. Almost everyone seemed to require time to be aghast at his or her own appearance. After being "desensitized" to their own images, the trainees would begin to notice reactions of the children to what they, the trainees, did and how they did it.

What, exactly, was being taped? Meier's SOL curriculum, as it emerged, consisted of games and exercises organized progressively from sections on the five senses to sections on gross motor development to fine motor development to language, music, dance, and miscellaneous activities such as ethnic cooking and celebrations appropriate to holidays in the various cultures. More than 150 "learning episodes" were ultimately included. Here are a few chosen at random:

Senses: Hearing. A series of containers such as cans, boxes, or Montessori sound cylinders are filled with salt, nails, beans, and the like, so that two of them make the same sound when shaken. Students are to find the two that match acoustically.

Senses: Touching. Paper cut-outs of capital letters are placed on a metal board or chalkboard. Students are given plastic letters with magnets in them and asked to place the right plastic letter over the right paper one. As they progress, they do the same with lower-case letters and with numerals.

Language: Receptive-Expressive Development. A guinea pig is brought to class. Students observe it and are encouraged to verbalize on how the fur feels, how big it is, what color it is, and so forth. As they talk, the teacher writes down some of the things said, resulting in an "experienced-dictated story." Example: "Joe said, 'Mr. G., the guinea pig, looks like a floppy dustmop.' Maria said, 'Mr. G runs around in his cage and gets cedar chips all over the place.' Michael said. 'Mr. G makes a funny chirping noise. Why?"

Number Relationships. A small cardboard box is covered with material, and felt dots are glued on the sides—one dot on two sides, two dots on two sides, and three dots on two sides. By a nearby flannel board are piles of similar felt dots, along with numerals 1, 2, and 3. After a period of exploring the material, students roll the box, learn to count the dots on the side that falls up, then count out the same number of dots from the pile. Finally they identify the correct numeral—1, 2, or 3—and place it on the board.

Creativity: Art Activities. To further self-expression, students make "thing" paintings, using such articles as twigs, paperclips, and string along with tempera paints. They also make "potato prints," in which slices of potato are dipped in paint and pressed onto paper, and "soap flake paintings," done with whipped soap flakes and water for a "wonderfully free sensory experience."

398

By putting this sort of thing on tape, having the teacher see her own actions, then discussing the episode with her, Meier planned to get each teacher to develop a better understanding of herself and of her role in helping children learn. Why do children do certain things at certain times? Why do I get angry about it? These were the kinds of questions asked during the workshops and later when staff members of the project visited the teachers in their home locations.

At the end of the workshop, the teachers took home with them the equipment (rented under the grant), the SOL Facilitators' Handbooks of learning episodes, and a wealth of tips on how to put the two together. One piece of literature, for instance, reviewed the "Five R's of Micro-Training"—recording, reviewing the tapes (privately, at least the first time), responding, refining, and redoing. When teachers who attended the workshop returned home, they trained other teachers at their sites, making tapes to be sent back to Denver along with the new trainees' own fairly complex self-evaluations. The trainees could check off from a list of various descriptions of behavior those they felt applied to their own performance—"stimulates creative thinking," "tells learners what to do," "is warm and friendly," "shows disgust and disapproval," among others.

At first, all tapes made by all the trainees at the sites were sent to Denver. Despite the heroic efforts of a quickly formed staff, this proved impractical. A better method was for the leader who had attended the workshop to review the tapes of other trainees and send only selected ones to Denver. Of course, there was never any intention that each trainee would plow through all the dozens of segments in the SOL. They used the ones they

wanted and needed—and also at times made up some of their own.

In Denver, Meier's staff reviewed the tapes and returned them with their own appraisals in narrative form—almost invariably starting with praise for what was done effectively.

Despite their orientation, quite a few trainees had some difficulty using the equipment. There were broken tapes, incidents of tape being consumed by rotating recording heads, to mention the commoner troubles. One trainee accidentally plugged the 110-volt camera power cord into the 12-volt battery input of the monitor, then watched in horror as the monitor flashed and went up in smoke. And the Denver staff got accustomed to calls for help from mobile radiophones in isolated places where regular telephone service wasn't available. A trainee wanting to know how to get the videocorder going would take instructions over the car telephone and relay them vocally to an assistant who would make repairs. In some cases, portable generators were used to power the equipment.

After he became director of the university-affiliated JFK center—which is a training, service, and research program concerned with children who have developmental disabilities of all kinds—Meier has less time to devote to the Remote Training project. Much of the responsibility was transferred to four staffers who worked closely with Meier: Bill Borthick, a young speech pathologist who had previously been in commercial TV production in Tulsa, Oklahoma; Ron Nichols, his assistant; and curriculum writers Rita Stewart and Pat Spitzmiller.

This group, together or separately, logged a great deal of travel time. They visited most sites at least twice a year, usually staying for several days of training sessions. No two places were alike.

One Indian group in Billings, Montana, held its workshop in a downtown hotel. In contrast, on the Sioux reservation at Wolf Point, also in Montana, the visitors found the workshop site to be two mobile homes in an open field, and joined together by a one-room frame building. At another site on the same reservation was a toy playhouse, with scaled-down furniture, laboriously built by parents and personnel of the school which was located in the basement of a church.

At the Wind River Indian Reservation in Wyoming, Borthick spent considerable time working with the somewhat rival Apaches and Shoshones. He met the grandson of Chief Washakie and went on a pilgrimage to the hillside grave of Sacajawea, the Indian maiden who guided Lewis and Clark.

In cities like Dallas, team members found themselves in relatively modern schoolrooms within the black ghettos. In Artesia, New Mexico, they came upon a tense situation involving racial rivalries which greatly complicated the training sessions. "Also Artesia was one of the places where we had to hold our training sessions on Saturday and Sunday," says Borthick. "The people worked from 7 a.m. to 7 p.m. and were usually too tired for training after that."

Ketchikan, Alaska, was much like Artesia in having long working days. Flying in on an antiquated seaplane to this island community of fishing and pulp mills, Borthick found the teachers gallantly facing the problem of having to keep their children indoors almost all the time (besides the cold, Ketchikan has an average rainfall of 180 inches). Illumination in the schoolroom—again in a church basement—depended on

bare 25- and 60-watt bulbs. Borthick considers one of his real accomplishments was to install 200-watt bulbs—"which was more like sunlight than what they usually see, and seemed to turn the children on."

But Borthick also found that the teachers there had made considerable progress since he had met them at the workshop in Denver. There they had been painfully shy, unable to understand "big words," and generally unsophisticated.

"Now, not just our workshop people but also those they helped train were getting to be accomplished teachers, self-confident and professional," Borthick says. "I was told that when the cameras were first introduced up there, all the teachers took one look at themselves and came back the next day with makeup, false eyelashes, and hair falls. But like all the others, they got over the cosmetology hangups. They have learned, for example, to use their own environment for the SOL learning episodes. Instead of using materials we had suggested in one learning episode to show children that one thing was bigger than another, they used miniature replicas of their traditional totem poles."

In many cases, trainee teachers dreamed up entirely new learning episodes, quite a few of which found their way into the SOL handbooks as curriculum writers discover them on their field trips. In Ketchikan, for instance, teacher Miriam Kotlarov and aide Francine Jim invented something called "Make a Face Game." Using a ten-inch outline of a face, teacher and students would put in cut-outs of eyes, ears, hair, and other features, discussing and commenting on each one. Racial characteristics of the Eskimo children would be noted favorably, leading to a more positive self-image.

400

In La Junta, Colorado, a game called "Bunny Black Ears" was devised by teacher Virginia Burr and aide Hiastolia Sanchez. Built around a Spanish folk tale, it had to do with coordinating motor movements of the body with words spoken by the teacher. At one point in the game, students move in unison with a puppet manipulated by the teacher.

In Fort Peck, Montana, teacher Marilee Johnson and aide Mary Jackson developed the "Make Believe Man," later amended to read "Make Believe Man and/or Woman." The teacher would tell a story and simultaneously the children would draw the leading character of the story, using a chalkboard to make corrections as their conceptions changed.

At the Variety Club Preschool in Honolulu, Hawaii, Rose Lee and her staff broke the SOL Curriculum into many smaller units and reorganized the materials to meet the needs of the children with many different handicaps who attended the school. Their suggestions for making the SOL handbooks more useful to programs with developmentally disabled children were extremely helpful in preparing the final version of the SOL materials.

Contributions like these were, of course, welcome at Denver. At one of the last workshops held in the program, all the participants were encouraged to make up a learning episode for possible inclusion in the SOL handbooks. Not everyone succeeded, but at least they all tried.

For his part, John Meier believes that the technique of micro-training by videotape has extremely wide implications. Already there has been some fall-out from it.

"A fellow in Durango has been using the technique to coach his ski team," he says.

"That's not exactly what we had in mind, but it's not a bad idea.

"More serious use of the technique is being made right here at the JFK Center whenever we respond to requests for diagnosis of handicapped children from clinics all over this region. Often it's inconvenient for the children to be transported here. So, under a small Federal grant from the Social Rehabilitation Service, we were able to bring in the heads of participating clinics and show them how to work up a mini-exam on TV for our purposes. Now, back in their clinics, they can tape these exams and send them to us to be studied by eight or ten experts from various disciplines. Sometimes the child still has to come in, but often the evaluation by tape is sufficient. It saves a lot of painful, expensive trips through the snow for the child and family, while at the same time it serves to train the staff at the participating clinic in the latest techniques and knowledge available at the JFK Center."

As for Remote Training of Early Childhood Educators, right now Meier, Borthick, and their associates are evaluating quite a few tapes at no cost. This is a service to early childhood programs in various places that have managed to scrape up the $2,000 for the TV equipment, plus the tape which costs about $35 for an hour reel. A number of early childhood educators who had been in the program for two or three years have moved up to more responsible and better-paying jobs on the basis of their new skills.

Odetta Russeau, now with the Jeanetta Foundation in Dallas, is one of them. "What did the program mean to me? It made me a much better teacher for, I hope, all time," says Mrs. Russeau. "It also gave me the chance to meet a lot of really neat people who showed me fine points of teaching that I probably never would have discovered for myself."

———◆◆———

QUESTIONS FOR DISCUSSION

1. In what ways will the recent formation of the National Center for Educational Technology (within the Office of Education) be of importance to teachers?
2. How could uses of new educational media aid in solving some of the school problems arising from increased enrollments and greater range of abilities and more varied backgrounds among students?
3. What features make the overhead projector a particularly useful teaching tool?
4. How would you use educational television and commercial television as teaching resources?
5. Do you believe that school districts should spend additional monies to send students outside the school building for outdoor education experiences? If outdoor education trips require overnight lodging, is it reasonable to require classroom teachers to accompany their classes?

SUPPLEMENTARY LEARNING ACTIVITIES

1. Interview the personnel of the instructional technology staff of your school. Obtain information about the kinds of services offered and the extent of their use in the classes.
2. Visit a local travel agency to obtain various materials advertising foreign countries. Arrange these materials in a display for use in classroom instruction.
3. Obtain information about cassette television equipment. Discuss the uses of cas-

Various business agencies have elaborate equipment which may be made available to the community for educational purposes.

sette television for classroom instruction.
4. Construct a device to aid in teaching an important concept in your teaching field. Demonstrate and discuss the teaching aid which you constructed.
5. Select a desirable field trip for your teaching field in your community. Visit the location selected and develop the plans needed for the class visit.

SELECTED REFERENCES

American Association of Elementary-Kindergarten-Nursery Educators. *Elementary School Media Programs: An Approach to Individualizing Instruction*. Washington, D.C.: National Education Association Publications, 1970.

402 Bright, R. Louis. "The Place of Technology in Educational Change." *Audiovisual Instruction* 12(1967):340–43.

Bruner, Jerome, ed. *Learning about Learning.* U.S. Office of Education. Washington, D.C.: U.S. Government Printing Office, 1966.

Campion, Lee. "A Department Promotes Media." *Educational Screen and Audiovisual Guide* 49(1966):32–33.

Chu, Gordon C., and Wilbur Schramm. *Learning from Television: What the Research Says.* Stanford, Calif.: Institute for Communications Research, Stanford University, 1967.

Goodlad, John I. "Directions of Curriculum Change." *NEA Journal* 55(1966):33–37.

Greenhill, L. P., et al. *Research in Instructional Television and Film.* Bureau of Research, U.S. Office of Education. Washington, D.C.: U.S. Government Printing Office, 1967.

Johnson, James, et al. *Introduction to the Foundations of American Education.* Boston: Allyn & Bacon, Inc., 1969.

Joyce, Bruce R. *Man, Media, and Machines.* Teacher Education and Professional Standards, National Education Association. Washington, D.C.: National Education Association Publications, 1967.

Klasek, Charles B. *Instructional Media in the Modern School.* Lincoln, Neb.: Professional Educators Publications, 1972.

Lange, Phil C. "Technology, Learning, and Instruction." *Audiovisual Instruction* 13(1968):226–31.

Mitzel, Harold E. "The Impending Instruction Revolution." *Phi Delta Kappan* 51(April 1970):434–39.

Moss, James W. "Resource Centers for Teachers of Handicapped Children." *Journal of Special Education.* Winter-Spring 1971, pp. 67–71.

Passantino, Richard J. *Found Spaces and Equipment for Children's Centers: A Report from Educational Facilities Laboratories.* New York: Educational Facilities Laboratory, 1972.

Reid, J. Christopher, and Donald W. MacLennan. *Research in Instructional Television and Film.* U.S. Department of Health, Education, and Welfare, Office of Education, Bureau of Research. Washington, D.C.: U.S. Government Printing Office, 1967.

Schneider, Donald O. "Guidelines for Selecting Media." *Social Education* 36(November 1972):799–802.

Tesconi, Charles A., and Morris Van Cleve. *The Anti-Man Culture; Bureautechnocracy and the Schools.* Urbana, Ill.: University of Illinois Press, 1971.

Tobrin, Warner E. "A Principal Looks at Evaluation." *National Elementary Principal* 52(February 1973):92–95.

Torkelson, Gerald M., issue ed. "Instructional Materials: Educational Media and Technology." *Review of Educational Research* 37(April 1968):111–96.

Travers, Robert M. W., ed. *Research and Theory Related to Audiovisual Information Transmission.* Kalamazoo: Western Michigan University, Publications Dept., 1967.

Wyman, Raymond. "The Instructional Materials Center: Whose Empire?" *Audiovisual Instruction* 12(1967):114–15.

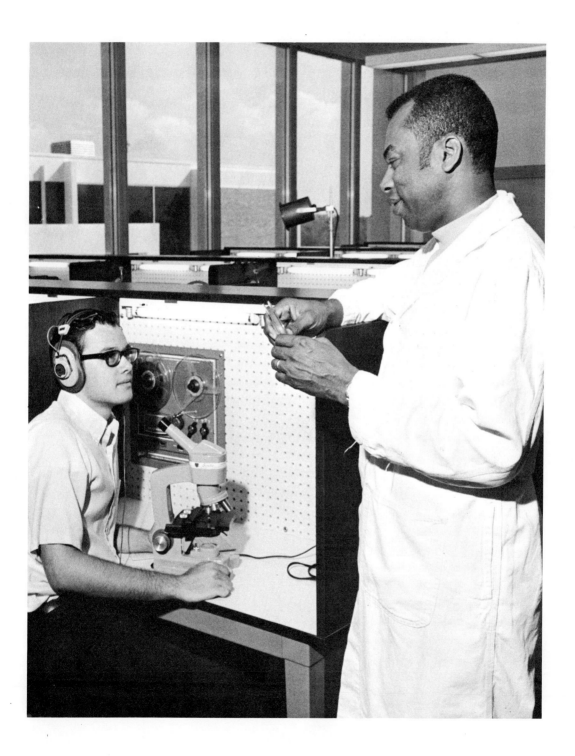

the Organization and Administration of Public Education in the United States

This section of the book is devoted to the ways that schools in the United States are organized, controlled, and financed. Each of these functions of the educational enterprise has evolved as the nation has developed. Patterns of organization, control, and finance reflect rather directly the needs and expectations of society.

The patterns of organization for public education in the early days of the nation were not complicated. Our society was basically an agrarian one with a widely scattered population. Men were concerned with conquering the frontier. One-room schools for grades one through eight were built in the rural areas, while the multigraded common school developed in towns and cities. Private universities were also established in the very early days. As the frontier was developed, and as the nation began to change to an industrial and urban way of life, the needs of the nation

406 changed and so did its patterns for the organization of education. Today we have public education from the nursery school level through the university along with many other forms of adult education. Each of these levels has purposes and programs which have their roots in the needs of society and the expectations of people.

The control of education in the United States is both unique and complicated. It is unique because of its decentralization. Local people have more to say about education in the United States than in most other nations of the world. It is complicated because it involves at least three and sometimes four levels of government. The legal responsibility for education in the United States rests with state government; however, the actual operation of schools is delegated to local government. At the same time the federal government is interested in the enterprise. Again, as our society has changed from agrarian to industrial and as our population has become increasingly mobile, the patterns of control of education have changed. The trend has been toward greater direct control of education at the state level, and a greater interest shown in education by the federal government, particularly in the areas of civil rights, poverty, and other national problems. New patterns of control are emerging.

The financing of education has changed from an almost complete local effort to where, in most states, the local contribution is currently about fifty percent. The state and federal government make up the remainder of the costs. The property tax provides most of the revenue at the local level, sales and income taxes at the state level, and the income tax at the federal level. State contributions to school financing have tended to equalize the amount of money spent per pupil in a state. Federal monies have been directed toward specific projects at specific times in our history.

As society changes, the methods of organizing, controlling, and financing education are also likely to change. Frequently the institutions of society lag in making the necessary accommodations to society. It should be remembered that institutions are created to serve society, and therefore should be changed by society when necessary.

chapter 15
Structural Organization
for Learning

goals

- Relates the purposes and goals of the various levels of education to the structure provided at each level.

- Evaluates the rationales for the increased emphasis on early childhood and adult education.

- Appraises the success of secondary schools in meeting their expressed purposes.

- Analyzes the alternative school movement.

As was indicated in chapter eight, formal programs of education evolve from the needs and expectations of societies and individuals. As our colonial settlements grew and developed, the colonists recognized that some of their desires for the education of their children could be better met by organizing children in groups and assigning specific adults from the communities to serve as teachers. Thus began the formal organizational patterns for education in the United States. They began with a basic idea of efficiency; it was felt that one adult could teach a group of children, and in so doing permit other adults to pursue other important duties. As the population began to grow and people began to cluster in communities, other principles of organization emerged—for example, the grouping of chil-

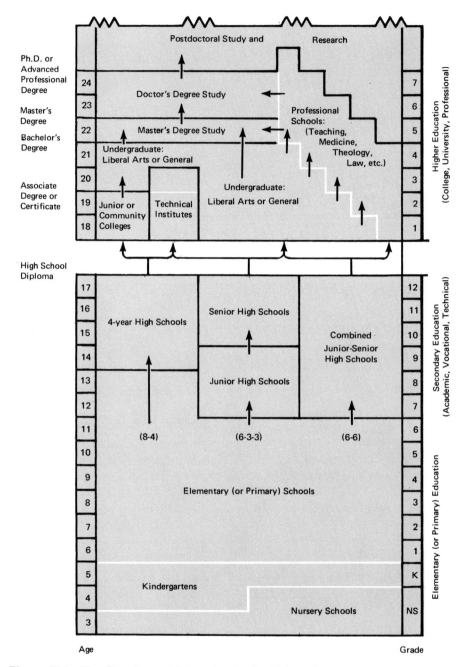

Figure 15.1 The Structure of Education in the United States.

Source: Kenneth A. Simon and W. Vance Grant, *Digest of Educational Statistics, 1972,* U.S. Office of Education (Washington, D.C.: U.S. Government Printing Office, 1973), p. 4.

dren by age so that one teacher could concentrate his efforts in teaching specific content in the most appropriate way to a particular age group. Later the principalship and superintendency emerged as specialties needed to effectively conduct the educational program in an organized fashion. While there is still disagreement regarding the *best* organization for learning, particularly for the individual child, it is nevertheless quite clear that American education was organized on at least two basic principles: (1) division of labor—that is, let some adults teach while others engage in other productive work; and (2) classification of students by age or common developmental levels. Organization for learning in the United States, while it has become increasingly refined, still reflects these two basic principles.

Purposes and Programs

Today four general divisions of vertical progression in educational organization are clearly recognized: preelementary, elementary, secondary, and higher education. Within these levels many subdivisions exist. Figure 15.1 illustrates the overall status of educational organization as it exists today.

At each of the levels certain goals and purposes are expected to be accomplished. A sequential program is envisioned based primarily on developing maturity and content complexity. One pertinent general observation that can be made about content is that as the vertical progression proceeds from preelementary to higher education the overall educational programs contain less general education and become increasingly specialized. Figure 15.2 illustrates this idea. General education is that portion which concerns itself

> *No other people ever demanded so much of education as have the Americans. None other was ever served so well by its schools and educators.*
> Henry Steele Commager

with the development of basic skills and common understandings. These include:

---

1. Communication arts: speech, language usage, reading, writing, listening, discussing, and spelling.
2. Computational skills and quantitative thinking: arithmetic, reasoning, and problem solving.
3. Social and group living: history, geography, government, community living, human relations, citizenship, value building, character building and sensitivity to problems of group living.
4. Science: understanding of scientific phenomena and natural law, the use of methods of science in problem solving, understanding the world.
5. Aesthetic development: music, art and handicrafts.
6. Health: knowledge of the body, nutrition and health habits.
7. Recreation: play, physical education and handicrafts.[1]

Specialized education represents that part of the program, generally elective, wherein an individual student pursues a specialty. For example, Johnny Jones and his parents may decide at the end of the eighth

1. Galen J. Saylor and William M. Alexander, *Curriculum Planning* (New York: Holt, Rinehart and Winston, Inc., 1954), p. 356. Used by permission.

410

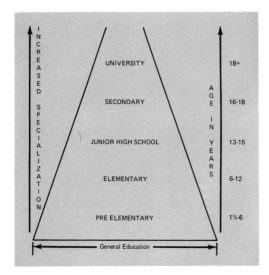

Figure 15.2. The Decrease in Time Allotted to General Education as Related to Vertical Progression.

grade that the only general education that Johnny will take in the future is that which is required by law, and that his program in secondary education will be vocational with his eventual goal that of becoming an automotive mechanic. At the same time, Ray Noble and his parents may decide that Ray will continue to higher education and therefore take a specific college preparatory curriculum in high school. Ray may eventually decide to become a lawyer and then will specialize further at the university level. Ann Smith may decide to pursue the college preparatory curriculum in secondary school and if she so desires and is financially able, could pursue liberal arts in higher education, and in so doing specialize almost completely in general education. It is significant to note that the choice of specialization in the United States is that of the individual student and his parents,

and not that of the government or society. To be sure, various state laws do prescribe general education requirements and societal and economic conditions often limit the available occupational choices, but basically the choice is the individual's, limited only by his particular talents, ambitions, and financial circumstances. In general today, elementary and secondary education is assured for all regardless of their individual financial resources. Higher education in the form of tax-supported community colleges has increased its availability to all. The trend in the United States today is toward making more and more education available for academically able students at lowered costs to the individual.

The remainder of this chapter presents brief descriptions of the organization and purposes of each of the major levels of education. Community colleges and adult education programs are discussed separately because of their increasing popularity in the contemporary American scene.

Preelementary

Basically, preelementary education consists of two divisions: nursery school and kindergarten. Nursery schools generally include children from the ages of eighteen months to four years, whereas kindergartens generally accept children between the ages of four to six years.

The first nursery school in the United States was opened in 1826, in the model community established by Robert Owen in New Harmony, Indiana; however it was not until 1919 that the first public nursery school was established. The concept of nursery school education has gained only slow acceptance. Public nursery schools seem to have gained their greatest impetus in the depression era. Recently, through the war on poverty, nursery school education was again stimulated. Operation Head Start, operating under the Office of Economic Opportunity, was illustrative of this trend. The number of day-care centers is also increasing, resulting in part from the increased numbers of working mothers. While many day-care centers admittedly do not represent the epitome of nursery schools, they do in fact represent a form of early childhood education which is carried on outside of the home and family. A recent article by Harold Shane succinctly points out the major reasons for increased interest in early childhood education.

———— • • ————

A major contemporary development in education—one which seems certain to influence public schools in the 1970's—is the widespread reawakening of interest in the very young child. It is important at this juncture for educational leadership to be aware of some of the factors and events which have led to this new concern for early childhood. In particular, thought needs to be given to the practices and policies which will be introduced, studied, and evaluated as a downward extension of the public schools occurs in the coming decade.

A Long History

For centuries great educators such as Comenius, Pestalozzi, Froebel, Basedow, and Montessori intuitively sensed the importance of children's experiences before the age of six. Also, during the past 40 years, nursery and pre-school specialists have made a strong case for the guidance of boys' and girls' early learning. Rose Alschuler, James Hymes, and Laura Zirbes are representative

of the many contemporary figures who, beginning in the 1920's, made important contributions to pre-school practice.

Sometimes this was accomplished through research, but more often through reasoned conjectures based upon empirical study and personal insight.

In years past, children were, of course, also made the object of quite careful medical and psychological research. For example, the writings of Arnold Gesell and Frances Ilg provided useful longitudinal child-growth data. Willard Olson and Robert Havighurst,

> *. . . If our schools are to serve as positive agencies for the maintenance of a "free" society, they must be concerned today with "society" as well as with the "child," with "subject matter" as well as with "method" with "product" as well as with human "freedom," and with social and moral "ends" as well as with classroom "procedures" and educational "means" . . .*
>
> John L. Childs

respectively, made "organismic age" and "developmental tasks" standard pedagogical phrases, while Jean Piaget for a quarter century has been respected for his developmental-cognitive studies.

But despite enthusiastic supporters and a substantial literature before 1960, no priority and frequently little heed was given by the public schools or the general community to the development of programs for children in the four-year span beginning at two and extending through age five. True, the Lanham Act expediently provided money for the care of children of working mothers during World War II, and some districts began to offer kindergarten programs for two or three hours a

411

412   day. But for the most part, the importance of early childhood was honored more by words than by actions in the schools. Even today in many states considerable parental pressures (or tuition) is required before kindergarten programs are launched for four-year-olds. In wide areas there are no kindergartens at all.

Let us now look at the confluence of events and circumstances that have led to the present renaissance of interest, which holds promise for the long delayed provision for education of two-to-five-year-olds.

Factors in Renaissance

The renaissance of interest in the very young has been stimulated by many things. An inventory of some of these elements and events follows.

Political decisions. To be both blunt and succinct, it seems rather obvious that policies and "politics" at the federal level have had a distinct bearing on the funding of educational programs begun prior to the kindergarten level. By the earlier Sixties it was becoming clear that there was much social dynamite in the ghettos of the city and in Appalachia-type rural slums. One of a number of ways of postponing or precluding explosions was providing educational programs for the children of the poor.

Current social commentaries. Recent attention-capturing books that focus on the complex challenges and appalling conditions of ghetto education have helped to convince many citizens of the importance of an early, problem-preventive approach to educating our children of poverty. Although they vary appreciably in quality and insight, this genre of book includes such titles as *Education and Ecstacy, Our Children Are Dying, Death at an Early Age, How Children Fail,* and *The Way It 'Spozed To Be.*

The great national concern which has

developed for the problems of rural areas and the inner city has quickened interest in the young child and lent support to providing for education of the culturally different.[2] Educators have begun to point out that it is short-sighted and wasteful to have so-called compensatory education in elementary and secondary schools to repair damage done to boys and girls before they enter kindergarten or the primary school.

Head Start. Operation Head Start, as part of the war on poverty, is both a result of the new recognition for the importance of children's early experiences and a cause of the current awareness of these early years.[3]

Environmental mediation. One important influence in developing programs for very young children is the concept of environmental mediation—the idea that during the child's early life wholesome forms of intervention in his milieu can help him become more effective in his transactions and interactions with others. While a sentimental interest in improving the environment of children has existed for centuries, the concept of a deliberate, planned intervention is, for practical purposes, a phenomenon of the Sixties.

Creating intelligence. Closely related to the point above is the accumulating evidence suggesting that the young child's intelligence is modifiable, that we can in effect "create" what we measure as an I.Q. The old "ages and stages" concept simply does not correspond with new information about childhood, the ways in which children learn, and the ways in which they develop. Benjamin Bloom, Ira

2. The January, 1969, *Kappan* contains a number of provocative and relevant articles on the inner city and segregation. Also cf. Edward T. Hall's article [*Phi Delta Kappan* 50(1969): 379–80].

3. For a succinct assessment see Keith Osborn, "Project Head Start," *Educational Leadership,* November, 1965.

Gordon,[4] and J. McVicker Hunt[5] are among writers who stress the significance of a facilitating environment for the optimal development of children and emphasize the importance of children's early years. Research done by David Krech[6] with infrahuman subjects strongly suggests that glia (memory) cells, brain size, and the blood supplied to the cerebral hemispheres actually can be increased by intervening in the milieu to create stimulating surroundings. His article is especially provocative in that it implies that we may have been losing out on the best years of the learner's life by postponing his in-school education—until the ripe old age of six.

Psychoneurobiochemeducation. The rapidly developing field which Krech has called "psychoneurobiochemeducation" has implications for early contacts with children. Specialists in certain disciplines such as biochemistry have conducted experiments with both subhuman and human subjects that are beginning to demonstrate the use of drugs (such as pipradol, or magnesium pemoline) in influencing mind, mood, and memory. While pharmacies and surgical suites operated by boards of education seem unlikely to dominate our schools, there is reason to believe that very early school contacts for children having personality and learning prob-

lems may permit chemical therapy to reclaim **413** these boys and girls who would otherwise become liabilities to society.

Experiments in early learning. Experiments in early learning, although not unique to the present decade, have fueled discussions and provided relevant—and sometimes disputed—data to the process of creating education policies which will govern school practices in the 1970's.[7] O. K. Moore's[8] inquiries into responsive environments, Dolores Durkin's[9] exploration of pre-school reading instruction, and Bereiter and Engelmann's[10] controversial work on early academic learning through predominantly oral methods at the University of Illinois as they attempted early cognitive training are illustrative of contemporary projects.

Improved understanding of subcultures and group membership. Cultural anthropologists such as Edward T. Hall[11] have begun to point out the implications of membership in a given U.S. subculture. Accumulating evidence suggests that it is during the first four or five years of life that many personal behaviors—in language, attitude, values, even ways of learning—begin to take on the form they will retain for a lifetime. We now spend billions for remedial work, for penal and mental institutions, and for belated com-

4. Cf. Ira Gordon's article [*Phi Delta Kappan* 50 (1969):375–78].

5. The following references are helpful: Benjamin S. Bloom, *Stability and Change in Human Characteristics.* (New York: John Wiley & Sons, Inc., 1964); Ira J. Gordon, "New Conceptions of Children's Learning and Development," in *Learning and Mental Health in the School.* (Washington, D.C.: Association for Supervision and Curriculum, 1966, pp. 49–73); and J. McVicker Hunt, *Intelligence and Experience.* (New York: The Ronald Press, 1961).

6. David Krech, "The Chemistry of Learning," *Saturday Review,* January 20, 1968, p. 48–50. Also cf. Krech's article [*Phi Delta Kappan* 50(1969): 370–74].

7. Cf. Bernard Spodek's article [*Phi Delta Kappan* 50(1969): 394–96].

8. O. K. Moore, "Autolectic Responsive Environments for Learning," in *The Revolution in the Schools,* edited by Ronald Gross and Judith Murphy, pp. 184–219. (New York: Harcourt, Brace and World, 1964).

9. Dolores Durkin, *Children Who Read Early.* (New York: Teachers College Press, Teachers College, Columbia University, 1966).

10. Carl Bereiter and Siegfried Englemann, *Teaching Disadvantaged Children in the Preschool.* (Englewood Cliffs, N.J.: Prentice-Hall, Inc., 1966).

11. Cf. Edward T. Hall, *The Silent Language* (1959) and *The Hidden Dimension* (1966), both published by Doubleday & Co., Inc., New York.

414   pensatory or supportive education necessitated, in a number of instances, because schools have not had early contacts with the children who will become their clientele.

The early influences of social class. Research by Jerome Kagan[12] has begun to suggest that social class membership—closely related to subculture group membership—begins permanently to influence personality, for better or worse, by the age of five or before.

Ethnicity as a mediating factor. Gerald Lesser[13] and his associates convincingly state, as a result of several replicated studies, that ethnicity (i.e., ethnic, subculture group membership) apparently causes children to learn in different ways.

Language development. For years now, Basil Bernstein's[14] work, which demonstrates that social class and one's linguistic characteristics are intimately related, has been widely accepted. The research cited, as well as analogous studies, which space precludes listing, are beginning to form a mosaic of data suggesting that these years of early childhood are more critical than any other stage of human development. In other words, if society, through its educational planning, does not vigorously begin to foster facilitating environments for very young children, it may be too late or immensely expensive to remove the psychological scar tissue that has long since formed on the personalities of certain young children before they enter school at the age of six.

Educational technology. A number of other elements have made educators more acutely interested in the initial years of childhood.[15] Improved technology has produced "talking" typewriters, "talking" books, and other teaching aids that can be used by boys and girls of three and four if they are in a school setting where they are available. Also, the progress made in developing Stage III computers promises to provide equipment that can be used in four- and five-year-old kindergartens.

Mass media: the phantom curriculum. The "phantom curriculum" to which mass media daily expose the child also has a bearing on early childhood education. By the time the child is enrolled in kindergarten or the primary school, he has an ill-assorted but important array of information.[16] There are those who not only contend that the massive sensory input of mass media is making children educable sooner, they also contend that the schools have a responsibility to help children at an early age acquire more coherent input. The problems here have been widely recognized, although much remains to be done in coping with them.

The rediscovery of Montessori, Piaget, and Vygotsky. While it is difficult to determine whether it is a cause or a result of the renaissance in early childhood education, the rediscovery of the work of Montessori, Piaget, and Vygotsky certainly has helped to enliven the instructional scene. These distinguished persons focused their work on aspects of methods, cognition, human development, and language growth at age five or below.

A decline in the elementary school population. Finally, a small group of prescient educational leaders, persons who are of a pragmatic turn of mind, are casting a speculative eye on the two- to five-year-old group

12. Jerome Kagan, "The Many Faces of Response," *Psychology Today,* January, 1968, pp. 60–65.

13. Cf. the article by Fort, Watts, and Lesser [*Phi Delta Kappan* 50(1969): 386–388]. Also cf. Susan S. Stodolsky and Gerald Lesser, "Learning Patterns in the Disadvantaged," *Harvard Educational Review,* Fall, 1967, pp. 546–93.

14. Basil Bernstein, "Language and Social Class," *British Journal of Sociology,* November, 1960, pp. 271–76.

15. Cf. article by Meierhenry and Stepp [*Phi Delta Kappan* 50(1969): 409–411].

16. John McCulkin, "A Schoolman's Guide to Marshall McLuhan," *Saturday Review,* March 18, 1967.

because of the widespread use of the "pill." In view of the drop in the U.S. birth rate in the last few years, there will be an inevitable decline in the gross elementary school population by 1975. One way of utilizing the staff and the space that are likely to become available will be to extend the school's responsibility downward . . . .[17]

———•·•———

Nursery schools can be categorized by their form of financial support: public or governmental, private, and parochial. Nursery schools that serve as a downward extension of the local public elementary schools and are supported by local district tax monies are very rare. However, the impetus being provided by the federal government to develop preschool programs for children of poverty, accompanied by research findings which indicate the significance of early childhood experiences to later intellectual development, may very well cause more local school systems to extend their public school education to include the nursery school group. While Head Start did not have the dramatic effect that was anticipated, it did have an effect, and perhaps the experience served to point out that greater effectiveness could have been achieved with children younger than four years of age. While public schools hesitate for a variety of reasons—primarily financial, coupled with public reluctance—to embrace the nursery school children into their system, private and parochial nursery schools will continue to function, fulfilling the needs of those who want this service and can afford to pay for it or who happen to be fortunate

enough to have philanthropic facilities available.

Kindergartens have received greater public acceptance than nursery schools. The first permanent public school kindergarten in the United States was established as a part of the St. Louis, Missouri public school system in 1873. Since then public school kindergartens have grown slowly but steadily. In 1940 approximately 661,000 pupils were enrolled in kindergarten; by 1969 kindergarten enrollment had climbed to 2,821,000. Ninety-seven percent of all five-year-olds enrolled in primary programs were enrolled in kindergarten. Three- and four-year-olds were enrolled predominantly in nonpublic schools. Eighty-three percent of the kindergarten enrollees were in public kindergartens.[18]

Kindergartens and nursery schools have similar goals. Major efforts are made to (1) develop body skills, (2) develop skills in interpersonal relationships, (3) enhance the development of a positive self-concept, (4) develop both oral and written language skills, and (5) enhance intellectual concept development.[19] In addition to these developmental tasks, which incidentally are applicable at all levels of education, the preelementary curriculum content includes mathematics, science, social science, humanities, health, and physical education. The uniqueness of preelementary education resides in the selection of appropriate content and materials, and the use of appropriate methodology for very

17. Harold G. Shane, "The Renaissance of Early Childhood Education," *Phi Delta Kappan* vol. L, no., 7, 1969): 369, 412–13. Used by permission.

18. Kenneth A. Simon and W. Vance Grant, *Digest of Educational Statistics, 1972.* p. 40.

19. Richard M. Brandt, "Readiness for Kindergarten," *Kindergarten Education,* Department of Elementary-Kindergarten-Nursery Education, National Education Association (Washington, D.C.: National Education Association Publications, 1968), pp. 14–21.

Developing body skills is an important goal in early childhood education.

young children. Preelementary programs are extremely flexible; the key principle is to learn by doing—that is, to gain enriching experiences without the encumbrance of accomplishing specific content, and in so "doing" learn to work and play effectively with others.

Elementary

The elementary schools have been the backbone of American education. Historically they are referred to as common schools, and traditionally under the graded organization they contained grades one through eight. As was indicated in chapter ten, elementary schools were organized in the colonies, and the "Old Deluder Act" passed in Massachusetts required towns to establish and maintain

schools. While Massachusetts had the first compulsory school attendance law in 1852, Pennsylvania, in 1834, became the first state to provide a program of free public schools. The phrase "public schools" as used in the early days of the nation is practically synonymous with the term "elementary schools" today. Horace Mann, known as the "father of the common schools," was most influential in spreading the concept of the importance of a common school education for all citizens of a democracy. An elementary school education was at one time considered to be the terminus in formal education in America. Now it is more truly only the end of one of our most basic steps.

The traditional elementary school organization contained grades one through eight. Frequently these grades were envisioned within the structure as consisting of three levels: (1) *primary,* containing grades one through three, (2) *intermediate,* containing grades four through six, and (3) *upper,* containing grades seven and eight. After the completion of the traditional eight grades in the elementary school the student entered a four-year high school. This traditional plan (8–4) dominated the organizational scene up and through the early twentieth century. In fact, in 1920, ninety-four percent of the public secondary schools were four-year high schools.

Modifications have been made in this plan. In 1910, the first junior high schools were established. They included the upper grades of the elementary schools, and in some instances, if legal district organization permitted, they included the first year of the four-year high school. This was the beginning of the 6–3–3 plan. By 1958 only twenty-five percent of the public secondary schools were of the traditional four-year high school variety. Twenty percent of the schools were two-

Elementary children pursue reading skills.

or three-year junior high schools. By 1966 thirty-one percent of the schools were traditional four-year schools, while thirty percent were of the two- or three-year junior high school variety. The trend seems to be returning to a four-year high school, with a two- or three-year feeder school. There is a decided decline in the high schools made up of five or six years. Under the 6–3–3 plan elementary education is thought of as including only the first six grades.

Another modification of a more recent vintage is the grouping of grades five through eight and referring to that grouping as a middle school. With this arrangement the ninth grade is considered as a part of a four-year senior high school. A school system using the middle school organization is referred to as having the 4–4–4 plan. In addition to the 8–4, 6–3–3, and 4–4–4, other plans are used including 6–6, 7–2–3, and 8–2–2. There are a number of reasons for these various plans, some of the reasons directly related to the

goals of instruction, others being only tangential. Let us examine briefly the goals of elementary education as they relate to the organizational patterns.

The goals of the elementary schools, particularly through grade six, are the goals of general education stated earlier in this chapter. Many of these goals are subject matter content-oriented and can be sequentially developed. In arithmetic, for example, the child counts before he adds, and adds before he multiplies. This reasoning is sound and the graded organization is in part based on this rationale. However, other goals of general education such as those dealing with interpersonal relationships, group living, and socialization are more closely related to the personal-social needs of learners. It is from these personal-social needs of learners, resulting from their developing maturity, that different organizational patterns have emerged. It reflects an effort again to group students, and again by age, but based on developmental personal-social needs of the members of an age group other than the purely academic content-oriented function of the school.

The junior high school student, for example, is a young adolescent. Thirteen-year-old seventh or eighth graders in terms of personal and social development have been recognized as having significantly different needs than those of the preadolescent ten- or eleven-year-olds. This recognition suggests a separate organization for these youngsters with somewhat different goals and procedures. A unique feature of most junior high schools recognizing these differences is that of exploratory education. The student is introduced to a variety of specialized educational areas. He may be given the opportunity to explore course work in business, agricul-

Many modern elementary schools have gymnasiums.

ture, home economics, and various trades, plus being given counseling regarding his interests and abilities for further academic pursuits. The junior high school is looked upon organizationally as including the group of youngsters between childhood or preadolescence and the recognized adolescent of the senior high school. Tangentially, many junior high schools came into existence to facilitate school building housing problems. In very practical terms, many junior high schools are converted senior high school buildings. As such, new high schools could be constructed, the old high school put to good use, and pupil housing pressures reduced at the elementary school level. Unfortunately, sometimes this type of growth has admittedly produced a distinct junior high building and a distinct organizational structure, but *not* a distinct or unique educational program for young adolescents.

The middle school represents a recent effort to bridge the gap between childhood and adolescence. The junior high school, while designed for this purpose, has tended to become high school-oriented. Perhaps the knowledge explosion and the concomitant increased knowledge expectations for younger children, along with increasing social maturity at a lower chronological age, have in part precipitated this development. Nevertheless, many educators feel that today a fifth or sixth through eighth grade grouping can more suitably meet the needs of the ten- to fourteen-year-old population than can either the elementary or junior high school grouping.

Maurice McGlasson in a recent pamphlet, "The Middle School: Whence? What?

Whither?" wrote specifically to the rationales of middle schools.

———— • • ————

The late 1950s and the decade of the 1960s saw mounting criticism of the junior high school: it housed the wrong students, had lost sight of its transitional nature and purpose, and was too subject-matter oriented. In short, it was merely an imitation of the senior high school. In suggesting another realignment of grade levels, the proponents of the new "Middle School" cited the growth and development of today's youth that seemed to indicate they are maturing earlier, both physically and socially, than they were fifty years ago. Thus the sixth graders of today are equivalent to the seventh graders of a half century ago. At the same time (following Sputnik) Middle School proponents, in what seemed to be an inconsistent rationale in light of the junior high school imitation criticism, cited the need for a more rigorous academic program for ninth graders, implying that the rigorous program would more likely be developed in the senior high school than in the junior high school. Thus the Middle School would contain grades six to eight or five to eight.

At any rate, following these basic tenets the Middle School movement met with almost spectacular success during the 1960s, both with local problems first and subsequently with the educational case for the Middle School, which was woven into the fabric of local sociology, economics, and government. Thus the Middle School has served as a partial solution to problems other than educational problems, and within the educational program it has served as a partial solution to administrative problems rather than curricular problems. Expediency has been the key word, but it has not necessarily been a negative one.

In New York city and Philadelphia, for example, the Middle School has been used as a vehicle moving toward earlier racial integration. In the 6–3–3 pattern formerly characteristic of both cities, the student moved from his neighborhood elementary school to a junior high school, drawing from a larger geographic district and thus a more varied population at the beginning of the seventh grade. In a 4–4–4 pattern this same move occurs two years earlier, when racial and cultural integration can be brought about in a less forced manner.

Physical facilities have also been a major factor in many school systems, particularly in smaller ones in which changes in organizational pattern are easier to effect than in large systems. School boards have had to take a critical look at the local situation in an attempt to answer the question: "How can we utilize the physical facilities presently available and reasonably available in the near future to provide the best possible program of education for boys and girls?" Current enrollments, projected enrollments, birth rates, and local economic factors all combine to provide bases for reasonable guesses in some cases. In some school districts introducing public kindergartens for the first time, 1–6 elementary schools become K–5 schools, 7–9 junior high schools become 6–8 middle schools, and 10–12 senior high schools become 9–12 senior high schools.

School district legalities have also affected grade level organization in some instances. In parts of Illinois, for example, a dual district pattern exists, an elementary school district and a secondary school district, each with its own school board and administration, covering the same geographic area. Thus it is much easier locally to operate a 6–8 middle school, all of whose grades fall within the elementary district, than a 7–9 junior high school, whose grades are divided between the elementary and secondary districts. In larger cities which have traditionally

420 followed an 8–4 pattern, it is usually simpler to change to the Middle School and a 5–3–4 pattern, leaving the senior high schools intact.[20]

————•—•————

Figure 15.3 points out what educators expect the middle school to do as well as what

20. Maurice McGlasson, *The Middle School: Whence? What? Whither?* pp. 12–13. Bloomington, Indiana: Phi Delta Kappa Educational Foundation, 1973. Used by permission.

many educators perceive that the junior high school is doing.

It should be noted that the differences pointed up in Figure 15.3 are matters of emphasis. Further, they are presented as ends of a continuum. In reality, probably very few schools could be clearly designated as functionary at either end. It is possible that a middle school in operation could emphasize the characteristics attributed to a junior high school and a junior high school could have

---

A middle school program is designed to recognize the uniqueness of the growth stage spanning the transition from childhood to adolescence.

The junior high has evolved into exactly what the name implies—*junior* high school.

MIDDLE SCHOOL EMPHASIZES—	JUNIOR HIGH SCHOOL EMPHASIZES—
.. a child-centered program	.. a subject-centered program
.. learning how to learn	.. learning a body of information
.. creative exploration	.. mastery of concepts and skills
.. belief in oneself	.. competition with others
.. student self-direction, under expert guidance	.. adherence to the teacher-made lesson plan
.. student responsibility for learning	.. teacher responsibility for student learning
.. student independence	.. teacher control
.. flexible scheduling	.. the six-period day
.. student planning in scheduling	.. the principal-made schedule
.. variable group sizes	.. standard classrooms
.. team teaching	.. one teacher for a class
.. a self-pacing approach, with students learning at different rates	.. a textbook approach, with all students on the same page at the same time.

A middle school program is designed to foster the intellectual, social, and emotional growth of children without snatching their childhood from them.

Figure 15.3 Differences Between Middle Schools and Junior High Schools.

Source: Educational Research Service Circular, *Middle Schools In Action*, Washington, D.C.: American Association of School Administrators, 1969, p. 17. Used with permission.

the characteristics emphasized for a middle school. It seems true, however, that many junior high schools have drifted away from the unique rationale which brought about their creation. The middle school represents yet another effort to create educational experiences most appropriate for the preadolescent age grouping. Educationally, if it functions as it should, the middle school provides a gradual transition from teacher-directed study to responsible independence, and greater flexibility and opportunity for various instructional methodologies. It also encourages the development of programs designed specifically for preadolescents. Socially and physically it groups youngsters of similar levels of maturity together. Administratively it permits a four-year sequence in high schools, can relieve enrollment bulges, may fit into an overall building pattern, and may facilitate plans for integration. A combination of these factors brought about the middle school. The middle school has potential, yet it does not seem to be a panacea for the education of preadolescents. The middle school concept is still too new to assess either its effectiveness or acceptance as an organizational pattern.

It is important to point out again that organizational patterns are related to goals, but they are also related to physical facilities and in the case of the middle school to social problems. It is further pertinent to note that in order to achieve efficiency in educating masses, the American system of education has attempted to group pupils by age and by developmental characteristics. While these efforts have resulted in admirable accomplishments, the public schools still have not resolved organizationally the nagging persistent problem of individualizing instruction. Each student is a unique individual who de-

velops and learns at his own rate. Can a program of universal education designed to serve the masses of elementary school children be organized to suit each and every individual? Can each student be made to feel important? Can his individual expectations be met? These are some of the challenges facing educators today, not only at the elementary school level, but at all levels.

Secondary

Secondary education began in the early colonies with the establishment of the first Latin Grammar School in Boston in 1635. Its purposes were reflective of the expectations of the people. It was to prepare students for college—colleges in those days were predominantly concerned with preparing clergymen, and clergymen could in turn help the people achieve their goal of salvation. The Latin Grammar School was eventually replaced by the tuition academy, the first of which was established by Ben Franklin in Philadelphia. Franklin is accredited with broadening the base of secondary education. His academy included students who did not intend to go on to college as well as those who did. He recognized that our developing nation needed men trained in commerce and surveying, for example, as well as theology and the classics. The concept of the academy grew and flourished, reaching its greatest heights in the middle of the nineteenth century. It met in part the societal needs of a developing nation. It was semipublic in nature and supported chiefly by tuition and donations. The academies were gradually replaced by the free public high school, the first of which was established in Boston in 1821. This high school, called the English

421

422 Classical High School, was for boys only—a high school for girls was established in Boston in 1826. The first coeducational high school was established in Chicago in 1856. Perhaps the biggest boost to free public secondary education, however, was the decision of the Supreme Court of Michigan in 1872 which established the legality of communities to tax themselves for the support of public high schools. The American secondary school over a span of three centuries has developed from a privately supported college preparatory institution for a few elite to a publicly supported comprehensive institution available to most American youth. The Bureau of Census reported that in 1971 93.7 percent of the youths ages fourteen to seventeen were enrolled in school either public or private. The U.S. Office of Education has reported that the graduating classes in 1970–71 constituted 75.9 percent of the population of persons seventeen years of age.

No other nation in the world can match this record. While the record is admirable, American secondary education still does not live up to the ideal expectations held for it. There is still a high school dropout rate of about 25 percent.

In a report prepared for the Association for Supervision and Curriculum Development, Wiles and Patterson identified the following American democratic commitments for the education of adolescents.

1. Universal education should be provided for all youth through the high school years.
2. The educational system should enable youth to secure the type of experiences which develop the personal, social, and vocational competencies needed in our society.
3. Various community agencies should be available to serve the educational needs of youth.

A student commons area, Winona Senior High School, Winona, Minnesota.

4. A suitable program should be provided by the secondary school for all youth through the legal authority of the community.
5. Each youth should be free to select his vocational goals and pursue an educational program leading to these goals.[21]

———•—•———

Have we met these commitments? Can they be met? Universality, a commitment of no small magnitude, has almost been achieved. In regard to the other four however, serious questions can be raised. Wiles and Patterson pose these questions:

———•—•———

Do boys and girls gain mental health, the clarity of purpose, the self-reliance, the values and the problem solving skills that are needed for them to be effective individuals? Do they achieve the social insight, the empathy, the cooperative attitude, the democratic commitments that will help them live with others in our society? Do they come to possess the skills and knowledge that will enable them to support themselves and contribute to the economic development of the nation?[22]

———•—•———

The answers to the questions will vary dependent upon the experience and perspective of the respondent; however, it would be an unusual individual who could respond strongly and affirmatively to all these queries.

The organization of secondary education in the United States today is related to the previously stated commitments. Secondary education includes the broad spectrum in

21. Kimball Wiles and Franklin Patterson, *The High School We Need,* pp. 2–4, 23. Washington, D.C.: Assn. for Supervision and Curriculum Development, National Education Assn., 1959. Used with permission.
22. Ibid., p. 3.

the graded classification of grades 7–14. The lower portion of the spectrum includes the junior high while the higher portion is represented by community colleges. The middle portion including either grades 9–12 or grades 10–12 describes the senior high school. Let us consider briefly the senior high school.

The ideal senior high school is a comprehensive school. By comprehensive it is meant that (1) its curricular offerings present a balance of general and specialized education along with sufficient guidance services and elective courses so that a student may pursue a program of his choice, and (2) its pupil population is diverse, representing different cultures and socioeconomic groups. If its program is functioning effectively, students should become increasingly different in their achievement; that is, higher ability students should become increasingly superior in their attainments as compared to the less able students. This principle should be equally applicable in the college preparatory, vocational, and general curricula students. The comprehensive high school should also permit a student to elect courses of his choice in any of the curricula. In other words, a college preparatory student would not be restricted from taking a beginning course in typewriting. While ideally students should become increasingly different in their pursuits of specialized education, the comprehensive high school also should cause them to become increasingly alike in such things as their social insight, their attitudinal commitments toward democratic principles, and their empathy for others. Are our high schools accomplishing these goals? Can we have comprehensive high schools in this country when demographically, for example, the poor live with the poor, the rich with rich, and the black with black?

Can students learn to live with others when they only interact with their own kind in schools? Is the comprehensive high school a realistically attainable organizational goal? Can a high school in a rural area with a total pupil population of less than four hundred pupils be comprehensive? The answers to these questions are being sought—they constitute part of the task of secondary education in America.

Community Colleges

The junior college or community college has emerged on the American scene in the last seventy years. The Joliet Junior College established in Joliet, Illinois in 1901, has the distinction of being the oldest extant public junior college; that is, of the public junior colleges founded in the late 1800s and early 1900s the Joliet Junior College survived and

Vocational education in Quincy Vocational-Technical School, Quincy, Massachusetts.

Quincy Vocational-Technical School, Quincy, Massachusetts.

continues to operate as a junior college today. It is interesting to note that it was originally conceived as an extension of the high school and therefore considered as a part of secondary education and not higher education.[23] The organizational chart presented earlier in this chapter illustrates the junior college as being a part of higher education. Therein lies part of the dilemma of this sector of the American educational organization.

> *Colleges aren't strictly for geniuses. We can't afford to slam the door of opportunity in the faces of C-level high school seniors, who will help make our country's future. We must fight for our average students.*
>
> Arthur S. Fleming

Model of proposed community college buildings, Joliet Community College.

Perhaps it is most accurate to state that for some students the community college is truly an extension of secondary school; for others it is truly higher education, as they transfer to four-year colleges or universities and graduate; for others it is terminal in specialized education and not an extension of high school, for they pursue goals not related to their previous secondary school experience. The confusion of classification in the educational hierarchy is normal for emerging institutions such as the community college. The community colleges as they are now organized and operated do have characteristics in common with both high schools and universities. This is as it should be, particularly if community colleges are truly going to become unique educational organizations dedicated to their purposes.

Thornton's research has identified six purposes:

- Occupational education of post-high school level
- General education for all categories of its students
- Transfer or preprofessional education
- Part-time education
- Community service
- The counseling and guidance of students.[24]

In the light of the avowed purposes, it is easy to understand why it is difficult to classify the community college unequivocally as either secondary or higher education.

The community college in meeting its purposes, which reflect both individual and societal needs, has emerged as a unique and

23. James Thornton, Jr., *The Community Junior College* (New York: John Wiley and Sons, 1966), p. 47.

24. Ibid., p. 59.

426　growing segment of American education. From meager beginnings in the early twentieth century the number of junior colleges has grown to 934 institutions in 1971 which enrolled 2,485,911 students.[25] Further growth is predicted.

The community college provides for "at home" post-high school education. Students who cannot financially afford to pursue higher education elsewhere can start in the community college. Others can acquire necessary occupational skills. If an institution is truly a community college, it is responsive to the needs of the members of the community. It provides services for the people of the community. As such it fulfills the expectations of the people for education, expectations that either cannot or may not have been met by other institutions. Therein may reside the reason for its uniqueness and success.

Higher Education

Higher education, the capstone of American education, began in the early colonies with the establishment of Harvard College in 1636. It is significant to note that higher education began as a private endeavor. Today, approximately 63 percent of the 2,200 institutions of higher education are still under private control. Nevertheless, almost two-thirds of the students in higher education are enrolled in public institutions. The Morrill Act signed into law by President Lincoln was a tremendous boost to public higher education. This Act provided 30,000 acres to each state for each representative and senator then in Congress, or when a state was admitted, for

the "endowment, maintenance and support of at least one college where the leading object shall be, without excluding other scientific and classical studies and including military tactics, to teach such branches of learning as are related to agriculture and mechanic arts."

Higher education is specialized education. Its purposes as delineated by the Educational Policies Commission are:

———— · ————

1. To provide opportunity for individual development of able people.
2. To transmit the cultural heritage.
3. To add to existing knowledge through research and creative activity.
4. To help translate learning into equipment for living and social advance.
5. To serve the public interest directly.[26]

———— · ————

The organization of higher education is such that it facilitates the accomplishment of the purposes. Great responsibilities are placed upon the independent judgment of the students as they pursue their elected course of study; freedoms are provided for professors as they conduct their research; and both philanthropic and public monies are provided to sponsor research in the public interest.

The diversity of institutions both in kind and control contributes to meeting the purposes of higher education. The kinds of institutions include community colleges, technical colleges, liberal arts colleges, municipal colleges and universities, universities, land grant colleges and universities, and graduate and professional schools. Control

25. Simon and Grant, *Digest of Educational Statistics, 1972*, p. 93.

26. Educational Policies Commission, *Higher Education in a Decade of Decision* (Washington, D.C.: National Education Association Publications, 1957), pp. 6–10.

differences include local, state, federal, sectarian, and nonsectarian private. This diversity permits a wide offering of specialized courses befitting the needs of individuals and society, and at the same time assures academic freedom and responsibility through an almost automatic system of checks and balances.

Adult Education

Adult education in its broadest sense includes any learning activity engaged in by an adult to promote his better living. In a more restricted sense it refers to programs of education formally organized for people beyond the compulsory school age. These programs are offered by colleges and universities, employers and unions, private specialty schools, armed forces and other governmental agencies, and public elementary and secondary schools. They may be oriented toward a degree or a certificate, or toward specific occupational or life skills. A recent report by the Carnegie Commission on Higher Education has proposed the following definitions which clarify adult education beyond high school.

———— • ————

Postsecondary education as all education beyond high school.

Higher education as oriented toward academic degrees or broad educational certificates. It takes place on college or university campuses or through campus-substitute institutions such as the "open university" with its "external degrees."

Further education as oriented toward more specific occupational or life skills rather than academic degrees. It takes place in many non-campus environments—industry, trade

unions, the military, proprietary vocational schools, among others.[27]

———— • ————

Adult education, of course, does include persons who have not completed high school. There are many purposes for adult education. Among them are attaining literacy and basic education skills for adults whose schooling for one reason or another was incomplete, and for persons who have immigrated to the United States who do not speak English; updating occupational and vocational skills in order to keep pace with industrial and technological changes; gaining better understanding of increasingly complex social, economic, and political institutions; finding ways of utilizing increased leisure time; and adjusting to problems of aging and retirement. One need only read the advertisements in newspapers and magazines, or examine the offerings of the many community colleges, to recognize some of the specific purposes of adult education.

In 1969 there were approximately 13 million participants in adult education. They were almost evenly divided by sex and by age with thirty-five years of age as the dividing line. Over 12 million were white as opposed to 980 thousand of the Negro race.[28] From a survey conducted in 1972 under the sponsorship of the Commission on Non-Traditional Study, it was estimated that 32.1 million out of approximately 104 million persons ages eighteen to sixty had received instruction within the preceding twelve months in activities such as evening classes, exten-

27. Carnegie Commission on Higher Education, *Toward a Learning Society*, p. 15. Copyright McGraw-Hill Book Co., 1973. Used by permission.
28. Simon and Grant, *Digest of Educational Statistics, 1972*, p. 10.

428 sion courses, correspondence courses, on-the-job training, private lessons, independent study, and TV courses. The data excluded subjects taken as full-time students. These data would indicate that approximately 30.9 percent of those adults ages eighteen to sixty would have been involved in some form of adult education.[29] Adult education has grown and will continue to grow in the future.

Of the students engaged in postsecondary education, 62.4 percent were in higher education, with 11.2 percent of these being part-time and nondegree credit students. Of those engaged in further education, 15.6 percent received their education from employers and unions, 8.2 percent from private specialty schools, 6.9 percent from the armed forces, 3.6 percent from elementary and secondary schools and other public postsecondary programs, and 3.3 percent from other sources.[30]

The Commission on Non-Traditional Study also provided information on the areas studied by adult learners. Thirty-five percent of the students had taken courses in vocational subjects other than agriculture, 41.8 percent had enrolled in courses dealing with hobbies and recreation, 25.2 percent in general education, 13.3 percent in home and family life education, 11.4 percent in personal development, 6.4 percent in public affairs, 13.8 percent in religious studies, and 3.4 percent in agriculture. The total percentages exceed 100 because persons were engaged in more than one area of learning.[31]

While a number of general and specific recommendations were made in the Carnegie report *Toward a Learning Society,* the central messages of the report were:

- That postsecondary education should be concerned comparatively less with the welfare of a minority of the young and more with that of a majority of all ages.
- That more and better channels for all of youth should be created into life and work and service; for the one-half that do not now go to college, as well as for the one-half that do go.
- That age should be welcomed along with youth into the facilities for education; that continuing education, like libraries and museums, should be open to all ages; that the educational barriers separating the age groups should be removed.
- That education should help create an easier flow of life for all persons from one endeavor to another; that it be a more universal tool of leverage on the processes of life; that in particular, the walls between work and education and leisure be torn down.
- That postsecondary education take more forms; but that academic programs remain at the center of attention with the highest prestige and the greatest support.
- That higher education concentrate on academic programs, leaving the quasi- and nonacademic programs largely to others; that it continue as the great source of scholarship and the preeminent leader in terms of high standards of effort.
- That new policies reflecting these goals be developed on financing, accreditation, and coordination.
- That the "learning society" can be a better society.[32]

---

29. Commission on Non-Traditional Study, *Diversity by Design,* p. 18.

30. Carnegie Commission on Higher Education, *Toward a Learning Society,* p. 2.

31. Commission on Non-Traditional Study, *Diversity by Design,* p. 17.

32. Carnegie Commission on Higher Education, *Toward a Learning Society,* p. 15.

The recommendations are powerful ones. They reflect the concept of continuing education, that is, learning throughout life. The adult education now underway is only a beginning toward continuing education. Continuing education has been defined as "a way of life—namely that of a single, vital, genetic, developmental continuity."[33] It embraces the notion that education is qualitative as well as quantitative—that it can lead to a quality of life for all, that education is more than increasing one's storehouse of knowledge.

The age groups in our population that are showing the greatest increases are those of young adults (ages twenty to thirty-four) and older adults (sixty-five and over). Between 1970 and 1980 they will increase by 36 percent and 18 percent respectively. By the same token, children and teenagers (through age nineteen) will increase by only 4 percent, young middle-age adults (thirty-five to forty-nine) by 3 percent, and older middle-age adults (fifty to sixty-four) by 9 percent.[34] These population tendencies along with the economic and social factors previously mentioned emphasize the compelling need for adult education. Societal conditions seem right for the implementation of the concept of continuous education—developmental in nature, for all who desire more education with freedom and easy access. "Drop-ins" should be welcome.

While adult education occurred in many forms early in our history, the beginning of the modern era of the organized movement occurred in 1926 with the formation of the American Association for Adult Education.

This organization later merged with the Department of Adult Education of the National Education Association to form the Adult Education Association of the U.S.A. Much of the inspiration and support to organize adult education came from the Carnegie Corporation and its president, Frederick P. Keppel.

Alternative Education

Alternative education has been available for many years in this nation through the vehicle of private or parochial education. Parents who were dissatisfied in one way or another with public schools organized private schools. Frequently they were formed because of religious reasons. Today there is renewed thrust for alternative education. This thrust has also been inspired somewhat by dissatisfaction with public schools. As such, many alternative schools start with a negative ideology, that is, the initiators "know what they do not like about traditional schools—bigness, regimentation, tracking, passive learning and student powerlessness."[35] At the same time, since the dissatisfaction is multifaceted, they start with either too many goals, unclear goals, or in some cases no goals. Their founders frequently ". . . emphasize process, believing that things will work out naturally when everybody 'gets it together,' believing that, in the absence of the restrictions of traditional schooling, students and staff alike will immediately embrace or create new patterns of interaction and become the new man, the new woman."[36]

Alternative schools are seen by some as

33. Maxwell H. Goldberg, "Continuous Education as a Way of Life," *Adult Education* 16(Autumn 1965):6.
34. U.S. Department of Commerce, Bureau of the Census.

35. Robert C. Riordan, *Alternative Schools in Action*, p. 39.
36. Ibid.

430 a way to solve societal problems. The school system as it is currently structured, according to Fantini, cannot hope to begin to attack such problems as poverty, drug addiction, alienation, delinquency, and racism. Furthermore, he has asserted that the real cause of the present malaise in education is the outdated nature of the institution we call the school. Alternative schools can best serve the plurality of publics, that is the many types of students, with their own types of learning styles, values, and backgrounds.[37]

Gross has conceptualized alternative education as the third step in the movement of change in American education. Prior to alternative education, the change movement went through the innovative period of the mid-fifties, followed by the radical reform efforts of the late sixties and early seventies.[38] Writers such as John Holt, Paul Goodman, George Leonard, Peter Marin, and Edgar Friedenberg have all castigated the existing public school system in a variety of ways. Gross has synthesized the principles that he feels radical reformers would adhere to in reconstituting education.

———•—•———

1. Students, not teachers, must be at the center of education.
2. Teaching and learning should start and stay with the students' real concerns, rather than with artificial disciplines, bureaucratic requirements, or adult's rigid ideas about what children need to learn.
3. The paraphernalia of standard classroom practice should be abolished: mechanical order, silence, tests, grades, lesson plans, hierarchical supervision and administration, homework, and compulsory attendance.
4. Most existing textbooks should be thrown out.
5. Schools should be much smaller and much more responsive to diverse educational needs of parents and children.
6. Certification requirements for teachers should be abolished.
7. All compulsory testing and grading, including intelligence testing and entrance examinations should be abolished.
8. In all educational institutions supported by tax money or enjoying tax exempt status, entrance examinations should be abolished.
9. Legal requirements which impede the formation of new schools by groups of parents—such as health and safety requirements should be abolished.
10. The school's monopoly on education should be broken. The best way to finance education might be to give every consumer a voucher for him to spend on his education as he chooses, instead of increasing allocations to the school authorities.[39]

———•—•———

Alternative schools have begun based on some of these principles. They have been organized both within and outside of the public school system. The trend today seems to be toward alternative schools within the existing school structure. Illustrations of alternative schools within public school systems include Cambridge Pilot School, Cambridge, Massachusetts; Hanover High School, Hanover, New Hampshire; Philadelphia Parkway School; and Chicago's Metro High. Seattle

37. Mario D. Fantini, "Public Schools of Choice and the Plurality of Publics," *Educational Leadership,* March 1971, pp. 585–86.

38. Ronald Gross, "From Innovations to Alternatives: A Decade of Change in Education," *Phi Delta Kappan,* September 1971, pp. 22–24. Used by permission.

39. Ibid., p. 23.

public schools have a number of alternative options. Philadelphia's Parkway and Chicago's Metro High are representative of "schools without walls." The human and physical resources of the cities are the environment for education. Students "study" in businesses, museums, universities, social agencies, and with a number of community groups and individuals. They may have some classes at "headquarters." Counseling is an integral part of the programs. These programs and others are described in detail in educational periodicals and popular magazines.

Recently an organization has been formed which acts as a clearinghouse of information on alternative schools within public schools. The organization, known as the National Consortium on Options in Public Education, is located in Bloomington, Indiana and is affiliated with Phi Delta Kappa.

The alternative school movement is underway. How successful it will be remains to be seen.

Reflections

The American pattern of educational organization has been relatively effective in providing mass education. Grouping individuals by developmental maturity, presenting content in sequential order, and recognizing the increasing independence of the student to make his own specialized choices as he progresses through the hierarchy, seem to be sound principles. The challenge today, however, is to develop methods of individualizing instruction within the group plan.

The role of private education in America was and still is an important role. We had private nursery schools, kindergartens, elementary schools, secondary schools, and colleges before any of them were accepted in the public domain. In a sense the expectations of a few people were met through private means, before they became the expectations of many and gained public acceptance. In this sense, private schools provide a seed bed for innovative activity.

The alternative school movement represents an effort to provide options within the public schools for those who want different programs. Successful developments will probably find their way into the mainstream.

As the organizational patterns of the past evolved from the needs and expectations of individuals and society, we can expect that the patterns of the future will arise from these same sources. Educators and citizens must be perceptive to recognize and delineate their goals, and then effective in designing patterns of organization to meet those goals. Teachers should not only expect change; they should be agents of change.

Point of View

Alternative schools have been developed by individuals and groups that have been dissatisfied with traditional education. Some alternative schools have been developed merely as alternatives to the existing situation. They function with negative ideology. Others seem to have been developed with clear purposes and goals. They have ranked their goals in order of priority, recognized constraints and limitations. The latter model seems more likely to succeed. Riordan has noted that "Alternative schools must realize that structure and discipline, far from being antithetical to their principles, are the prerequisites to building a viable alternative setting." In addition he has stated that they need to develop

432 procedures for systematic supportive evaluation and feedback.[40]

Many educators have questioned the rationale for alternative schools. Professor Harry S. Broudy, an eminent educational philosopher, has raised questions about alternative schools. In his article "Educational Alternatives—Why Not? Why Not" he addresses himself to the rationale and claims of alternative education. Professor Broudy asks: Do alternatives promote freedom? Do they promote better choice? Do they provide for differences? Do they promote creativity? His analysis of alternative education as he answers the questions is insightful and provocative. The reader, as he reflects on Professor Broudy's comments, must provide some of his own answers.

--------◆◆◆--------

Educational Alternatives—Why Not? Why Not

Harry S. Broudy

The dual title of this paper reflects the current ambivalence toward the demand for alternatives in education. "Why not?" says that since we cannot think of good reasons against alternatives, let's have them. Or, more cynically, since nothing we do in education seems to make much difference, what have we to lose by trying something—anything—else?

"Why *not*" implies there may be good reasons for not trying this or that alternative, and that good and bad alternatives can be

40. Robert C. Riordan, *Alternative Schools in Action,* pp. 42–43.
Harry S. Broudy, "Educational Alternatives—Why Not? Why Not," *Phi Delta Kappan,* March 1973, pp. 438–40. Used by permission.

distinguished. In defending the second interpretation of the title one does not reject alternatives to the current school organization. However, one is not compelled to admit that alternatives are *necessarily* productive of freedom, intelligent choice, the satisfaction of individual differences, creativity, and zestful involvement.

The claims for alternatives can be defended (or attacked) on logical grounds or empirical evidence, or both. On logical grounds it may be argued that a multiplicity of alternatives would be more likely to meet a wider variety of individual needs than a single system. Or one might appeal to the principle that cultural pluralism is a self-evident good and that therefore educational pluralism is also good. Such arguments can be attacked only by challenging the interpretation of the concepts and principles and the conclusions drawn from them.

However, the claim for alternatives is sometimes defended empirically by pointing to experiments that claim to have achieved the benefits expected of them. According to Albert Shanker (*New York Times,* April 23, 1972), such claims are being made for the results achieved by such alternative schools as the Parkway project in Philadelphia and Harlem Prep in New York. Shanker notes that even if the claimed results or improvements did accrue, the comparison with traditional schools is faulty. He cites the small size, the availability of funds from special grants, and pupil selectivity as characteristics that could not be duplicated throughout the public schools. Conceivably, however, there could be enough decentralized alternative schools to enable *all* pupils to attend small, selective, tailor-made schools. Aside from the extreme unlikelihood that the funds would be available, what about the principle that each parent is entitled to choose the type and amount of schooling that he judges his children need, and that to implement this principle a large number of alternative schools must be available at public cost?

The principle is false if the state supports schools because education is a *public* good and not *merely a private one*. The same distinction is invoked to justify taxing people for roads that they may or may not use or the fluoridation of the water supply of which they may or may not approve. Those who argue for alternatives on the ground that choice of schooling is an individual right are thinking only of individual benefits, or they are asserting that the public good can be satisfied by whatever educational alternatives parents choose. The first argument simply misunderstands the nature of social institutions; the second overlooks the historical evidence to the contrary.

I shall not try to assess the success of alternative schools, because "success" is about as firm a criterion as a water bed floating on a pool of mercury, and we all know about the no-fail characteristics of educational experiments. Nor can I subscribe to the notion that one can ignore the possibly irreversible adverse effects of educational experiments, because I do not believe that nothing we do in education makes any difference. Instead, I propose to analyze the concepts underlying the claims of the alternatives advocates to produce greater freedom and creativity, promote more intelligent and responsible choice, and provide for individual differences in educational decision making.

Do Alternatives Promote Freedom?

The literature in favor of alternative schools abounds with references to freedom.

Sometimes the freedom is from rules governing the personal lives of pupils, e.g., hair styles, class attendance, deportment, etc. Sometimes the freedom wanted is from the control of schools by the Establishment bureaucracies; sometimes it is freedom to do one's own thing whenever and wherever the person is moved to do it. Sometimes it is freedom from the established curriculum. Presumably the advocates of free schools are not in agreement as to the sort of freedom that is crucial or that alternative schools are attaining it.*

At any rate, alternative schools are supposed to enhance freedom for the pupil from diverse kinds of educational constraints. Are there, however, some educational constraints over which we have no control? Two sorts of constraint cannot be evaded if we are to have *formal* schooling. One kind is the constraint implied in the formal schooling as a process; the other kind is the constraints imposed by the demands of the culture in which one intends to participate fully or, at the least, adequately.

As to the first kind of constraint, what one learns in school does not come naturally. If it did we would not bother with schools. Schools are deliberate interventions in uncultivated modes of human experience, i.e., in what comes "naturally." Uncoerced or painless schooling is to the schoolmaster what the Holy Grail was to Sir Galahad, something to be forever sought and rarely found.

Furthermore, if schooling involves induction of the young into the intellectual resources of the culture, then the logical structure of those resources (the disciplines) as well as their results become constraints. To

* A special issue of the *Harvard Educational Review* on alternative schools, August, 1972, catalogs the confusion.

434 free the pupil from these constraints, as some counterculture reformers urge, is to free him from knowledge itself. Are alternatives that promise this kind of freedom good alternatives?

As to the second sort of constraint, one must ask what the culture demands as conditions for coping with it. At least three kinds of demand are imposed on all of us: occupational adequacy, civic adequacy, and personal adequacy. The first is needed to earn a living, the second to plan one's role in a social order, and the third to live as a fully developed, authentic human individual.

It is unrealistic and mischievous for a school system to ignore these constraints, however much one may wish to reform the way in which they operate. It is mischievous deliberately to maladapt the young to the culture, for those who are so maladapted cannot survive in it, let alone reform it. In this sense alternative schools in which the "standard" English dialect is denigrated in favor of ethnic minority dialects are mischievous, because the important transactions of society are carried on in the standard dialect. That is all that "standard" means, and those who do not master it cannot participate fully in the society. It is one thing to urge multilingualism as a means to learning the "standard" communication medium; it is another to use it as a means of evading the need to master it.

In short, alternatives are good if they increase the freedom of the pupil to achieve the three kinds of adequacy mentioned above; they are not good if they simply free the pupil from the task of achieving them.

Do They Promote Better Choices?

What about the claim that the more alternatives the greater the opportunity for intelligent and responsible choice? An intelligent choice presupposes that one knows the end and can evaluate a diversity of means purporting to reach that end. The child, especially the young child, qualifies on neither count. Parents and educators may make a stronger claim as far as ends are concerned, and the educator is supposed to be more knowledgeable than parents about means.

As to ends, aside from very specific vocational training, there is neither consensus nor clarity. Educational goals can be formulated in terms as general and abstract as the good life here or in the hereafter or as particular and concrete as learning to do subtraction in arithmetic; and it is difficult to keep controversialists on the same level of objective* for more than a minute at a time. About the nearest we get to agreement on objectives is the objective of moving from one step in the educational ladder to the next. This works pretty well if there is agreement about the desirability of making the journey up the ladder; when alternatives to going up the ladder are proposed, even this agreement vanishes. As to means, aside from well-developed vocational curricula, there is no more consensus than on ends. To make the situation comical, the educators who have claimed authority over the schools on the ground of superior expertise now proclaim that their expertise lies in finding out what their clients would like to have them do. And the parents, at a loss as to how to advise the experts and reluctant to have sullen children around the house, half-heartedly embrace the doctrine that the most reliable guide to educational choice is the interest of the pupil at any given moment.

---

* I have tried to map this morass in "The Philosophical Foundations of Educational Objectives," *Educational Theory,* winter, 1970, pp. 3–21.

It is also argued that if choice is free and the alternatives plentiful, decisions will be not only more intelligent but also more responsible. Responsible choice means 1) that relative merits of alternatives are taken into account or 2) that the chooser is worried about making the right choice or 3) that he has the means and will to remedy the consequences of the wrong choice. How difficult it is to make a responsible choice in the first sense has already been pointed out; being anxious to choose correctly is a morally admirable trait, but it is relevant only if there is a way of distinguishing right from wrong alternatives, and finally, making good on the wrong educational choices is virtually impossible.

I am sure that many advocates of alternatives do believe that they can choose among them intelligently and want to do so. They usually can justify their choices by some theory of education that in turn is justified by some fairly coherent view about the good society and the qualities of the good life. The advocates of progressive schools, the Montessori schools, and the open classrooms are not irresponsible. I am far less sure about those advocates of alternatives who base their case on " failure" of the public schools to achieve this or that political or social objective, or who justify their advocacy on the general ground that all institutions are oppressive, or that all formal schooling is a fraud perpetrated by the bourgeoisie on the proletariat.

I believe we have reached this stage of cynicism with respect to public schooling and to some extent higher education as well. In time even the most solid ramparts of common sense and intuition are breached by books, articles, and researches that "prove" that there is no positive relationship between school and economic success, civic competence, and personal adequacy. Propelled by the massive impact of the mass media, these messages come through faster and faster, so that to shake confidence takes less time—especially when funds for schools impose heavy tax burdens.

I shall not assay the validity of this literature. I have tried to do so elsewhere (*The Real World of the Public Schools,* 1972), and the tide may turn more quickly than one might anticipate by virtue of the rapidity with which education doctrines change. Nevertheless, at the moment many of the pressures for alternatives can be construed as a flight from responsibility for and commitment to formal schooling.

Do They Provide for Differences?

Perhaps the most persuasive argument for alternatives is that individuals vary in interests, needs, and competence so much that only a multiplicity of alternatives will save them from the rigidity of a uniform public school system. However, the amount of uniformity in the American public schools is highly overrated. If anything, the diversity in schools is so great that it is only by extreme courtesy that one can speak of a public school system.

Furthermore, not all individual differences require differentiated schooling. For example, we do not believe, in principle at least, that differences in skin color constitute a basis for school differentiation.

Finally, important individual differences such as in learning readiness, talents and aptitudes, and previous achievement often can be met without necessarily setting up alternative schools. Indeed, one important way of meeting individual differences is to allow the individual to make his unique ap-

436 propriation of a uniform set of studies. He will do it anyway.

So alternatives as such do not of themselves guarantee the satisfaction of the demands of individuality, and certainly not with respect to general education. The case with vocational training, of course, is quite different. Since there are many vocational tracks and since not all pupils will or can follow the same one, alternatives are the rule. But I take it that alternative tracks in vocational education are not in controversy.

Do Alternatives Promote Creativity?

Not the least attractive argument for alternatives in schooling is that they provide much-needed novelty and freshness in school life. A single system of formal schooling makes for uniformity and boredom; anything that relieves boredom is welcome.

But as with the other claims for alternatives, one must make distinctions. For example, teachers use a thousand tricks to vary the monotony of drill or to relieve the lassitude of the afternoon school hours. Pupils appreciate sprightly variations in speech and clothing on the part of teachers, and indeed any departures from routine. Such novelties are not in controversy. We are talking about "imaginative breakthroughs" such as life curricula, ecstatic expansions of consciousness, free schools, schools-without-walls, storefront schools, and the like. Are these creative variations or not? Is there a criterion for judging, or are we to rely on the intrinsic values of pluralism as such?

Although no definition of creativity will satisfy everybody, we do recognize that there is a difference between trivial and important novelties. If education had a body of highly organized and widely accepted theory and a considerable range of problems for which there were standard solutions, we would know when an innovation was really important. But education has no such consensus, so that all innovation is equally important; unfortunately, more often than not it is sporadic, episodic, short-lived, and faddish. The operative criterion is likely to be the amount of grant money and publicity a project attracts.

Accordingly, the most frequent defense of alternatives in schooling is that ours is a pluralistic society, and that just as a plurality of cultures is desirable, so is a plurality of school designs. But is the matter so simple? William James argued that this may be a pluralistic universe in which entities are related loosely, as beads on a string, and not as premises and conclusions in a monolithic syllogism. Nevertheless, society is never merely the sum of individual beads on a geographical string. For there to be a plurality of cultures, each culture must have some kind of unity by which it can be distinguished from the others, and there must be some unity among the cultures that makes it possible for us to speak of a pluralistic *society* rather than of a collection of discrete societies. The rationale for a public school system is that, interesting as the diversity of subcultures is, cultural unit is never zero. This constitutes the limit of pluralism in culture and schooling.

Celebrants of alternatives sagely remark that there are many paths to the same mountain top, but tend to forget that when one opts for pluralism for its own sake, there is no *one* mountain top to which all are climbing and by which we can judge whether the goal is being reached or not.

In the absence of consensus on such a goal, indeed if it is denied that it is even desirable to have one goal, then the search for alternatives can be justified either by asserting complete independence of diverse cultural entities or by the need for relief from sameness. The first justification does not make sense so long as we continue to talk about one nation or about one human race; as to the second, inventing and marketing educational novelties can be a stimulating and profitable pastime. Unfortunately, the need for excitement and novelty is insatiable, and the attempt to provide a supply of alternatives to keep up with the demand is a task too exhausting even to contemplate.

Creative diversity is not random pluralism, but rather imaginative variations on a theme. If we can be clear about the role of the school in a genuine society in which basic features of the good life are shared by all the members, then there can be creative diversity within the public school and outside of it, and these variations will be neither random nor mutually destructive.

———————•◆•———————

QUESTIONS FOR DISCUSSION

1. How are the developmental tasks specified as kindergarten goals applicable to other levels in the organizational hierarchy?
2. Is individualized instruction possible in mass education as it exists in the United States today?
3. How can the organizational patterns of American education be utilized to aid in resolving some of America's social problems?
4. Can the personal-social needs of students be met in a graded organization?
5. In your judgment what is the most commonly used rationale for grouping students for learning in contemporary America? Is it sound?

SUPPLEMENTARY LEARNING ACTIVITIES

1. Visit a nursery school or kindergarten to specifically observe how the developmental goals are being accomplished.
2. Visit a middle school and a junior high school, looking for differences related to their purpose.
3. Invite a community college official to your class to discuss the relationship of the community college to the community.
4. Conduct a survey to determine the adult education opportunities available in your immediate area.
5. Visit an alternative school, seeking to determine how its purposes differ from traditional schools.

SELECTED REFERENCES

Adult Education Association of the U.S.A. *Handbook of Adult Education in the United States.* New York: Macmillan Company, 1970.

Barker, Roger G., and Paul V. Gump. *Big School, Small School.* Stanford, Calif.: Stanford University Press, 1964.

Bossing, Nelson L., and Roscoe V. Cramer. *The Junior High School.* Boston: Houghton Mifflin Company, 1965.

Brown, Frank B. *The Nongraded High School.* Englewood Cliffs, N.J.: Prentice-Hall, Inc., 1963.

Carnegie Commission on Higher Education. *Toward a Learning Society.* Hightstown, N.J.: McGraw-Hill Book Company, 1973.

Commission on Non-Traditional Study. *Diversity by Design.* San Francisco: Jossey-Bass, Inc., Publishers, 1973.

Conant, James B. *The American High School*

438   *Today.* New York: McGraw-Hill Book Company, 1959.

———. *Slums and Suburbs.* New York: McGraw-Hill Book Company, 1961.

Fields, Ralph R. *The Community College Movement.* New York: McGraw-Hill Book Company, 1962.

Frazier, Alexander, ed. *The New Elementary School.* Association for Supervision and Curriculum Development, Department of Elementary School Principals, National Education Association. Washington, D.C.: National Education Association Publications, 1968.

Goodlad, J. I. "Individual Differences and Vertical Organization of the School." In *Sixty-first Yearbook. National Society for the Study of Education.* Chicago: University of Chicago Press, 1962.

Knowles, Malcolm S. *The Adult Education Movement in the United States.* New York: Holt, Rinehart and Winston, Inc., 1962.

Logan, Lillian M. *Teaching the Young Child.* Boston: Houghton Mifflin Company, 1960.

McConnell, T. R. *A General Pattern for American Public Higher Education.* New York: McGraw-Hill Book Company, 1962.

McGlasson, Maurice. *The Middle School: Whence? What? Whither?* Bloomington, Ind.: Phi Delta Kappa, 1973.

Miller, Richard I. *Education in a Changing Society.* Washington, D.C.: National Education Association Publications, 1963.

Moore, Elnora H. *Fives at School.* New York: G. P. Putnam's Sons, 1959.

Popper, Samuel H. *The American Middle School: An Organizational Analysis.* Waltham, Mass.: Ginn and Company, Blaisdell Publishing Co., 1967.

Riordan, Robert C. *Alternative Schools in Action.* Bloomington, Ind.: Phi Delta Kappa, 1972.

Simon, Kenneth A., and W. Vance Grant. *Digest of Educational Statistics, 1972.* U.S. Office of Education. Washington, D.C.: U. S. Government Printing Office, 1973.

Thornton, James, Jr. *The Community Junior College.* New York: John Wiley & Sons, Inc., 1966.

U.S. Office of Education. *A Lifetime of Learning.* Washington, D.C.: U. S. Government Printing Office, 1969.

Wiles, Kimball. *The Changing Curriculum of the American High School.* Englewood Cliffs, N.J.: Prentice-Hall, Inc., 1965.

Wiles, Kimball, and Franklin Patterson. *The High School We Need.* Association for Supervision and Curriculum Development, National Education Association. Washington, D.C.: National Education Association Publications, 1959.

chapter 16

The Control of American Education

goals

● Presents the roles and interrelationships of federal, state, and local governments in American education.

● Explains the federal role in education particularly as it relates to the protection of individual rights under the United States Constitution, and in using federal aid under the general welfare clause to utilize education as a vehicle in resolving domestic and foreign issues.

● Points out that education is a function of the state, and identifies the roles of the various state controlling bodies.

● Evaluates the operation of education by local school districts in terms of both strengths and weaknesses.

The educational system of the United States is unique among the nations of the world. In terms of control, its most distinctive feature is decentralization. In other words, local governments have wide decision-making powers in terms of operating local school systems. Education in the United States is a legal function of state government; however, much of the authority of the separate states has been delegated to local government—more specifically, to local boards of education. The federal government also plays a role which can

440 perhaps best be described as one of an interested party. As the educational system in the United States has developed, the roles of the different levels of government have changed. While education still remains basically a local

> *"The powers not delegated to the United States by the Constitution, nor prohibited by it to the States, are reserved to the States respectively, or to the people."*
>
> Tenth Amendment
> United States Constitution

operation, the participation of state and federal governments has increased. The remainder of this chapter examines the current roles of the various levels of government as they relate to the control and operation of education today in the United States.

Federal Government

The federal government has become involved in education in four different, yet related, ways: (1) the application of the United States Constitution, (2) the function and operation of the United States Office of Education & NIE, (3) the direct operation of educational programs by various agencies of the federal government, and (4) the provision of federal aid in its various forms.

United States Constitution

The United States Constitution is the basic law of the land, and as such has had its effects on education. While no specific mention of education is made in the Constitution, the Tenth Amendment has been interpreted

as implying that education is a function of the respective states. This interpretation in a sense resulted in the development of fifty different state systems of education. Further, it reinforced the type of educational decentralization that had begun to develop in colonial America. While the fifty states are markedly similar in their patterns of education, differences do exist. Examples of differences that exist include: (1) requirements for teacher certification, (2) provisions for financial aid, (3) regulations for compulsory attendance, and (4) provisions for teacher pension plans.

The First and Fourteenth Amendments have also had a definite impact on the administration of education in the United States. The First Amendment insures freedom of

> *"Congress shall make no law respecting an establishment of religion or prohibiting the free exercises thereof; or abridge the freedom of speech or of the press; or the right of the people peaceably to assemble and to petition the government for redress of grievances."*
>
> First Amendment
> United States Constitution

speech, religion, the press, and the right of petition. The Fourteenth Amendment provides for the protection of specified privileges of citizens. Based upon these amendments, the Supreme Court of the United States has made many decisions that have influenced the course of education in the United States.

Court Decisions

Court decisions based upon the First Amendment have been particularly influential in clarifying the relationship between religion and education. There have been a number of these decisions, and basically they can be classified into three groups: (1) those having to do with the rights of parents to educate their children in private schools, (2) those having to do with the use of public funds to support private education, and (3) those having to do with the teaching or practice of religion in the public schools.

An important case influential in determining the rights of parents to provide education for their children was the Oregon case. Briefly, in 1922 the legislature of Oregon passed a law requiring all children to attend public schools. The Supreme Court of the United States ruled that the law was unconstitutional (*Pierce* v. *Society of Sisters,* 1925). The reasoning of the Court was that such a law denied to parents the right to control the education of their children. This decision of

> *"No State shall make or enforce any law which shall abrogate the privileges or immunities of citizens of the United States; nor shall any state deprive any person of life, liberty, or property without due process of law; nor deny to any person within its jurisdiction the equal protection of the laws."*
>
> Fourteenth Amendment
> United States Constitution

the Supreme Court in addition to establishing that private schools have a right to exist, and that pupils may meet the requirements of compulsory education by attending private schools, also established that a state may regulate all schools, public and private, and require the teaching of specific subjects. The Oregon decision reinforced a historical tradi-

tion of private and sectarian education in the United States and gave further impetus to the development of private schools. Thus, two systems of education, public and private, developed in the United States.

Cases having to do with the use of public funds to support private education are numerous. Prominent among them are the *Cochran* and the *Everson* cases. In *Cochran* v. *Louisiana State Board of Education,* 1930, the United States Supreme Court held that a Louisiana textbook statute that provided for furnishing textbooks purchased with tax-raised funds to private school pupils was valid. The ruling was technically based on the Fourteenth Amendment.

More recently the United States Supreme Court supported a New York law providing for the free loan of public school books to students in private schools (*Board of Education of Central School District No. 1, Towns of Greenbush et al.* v. *Allen*). The majority opinion stated "The law merely makes available to all children the benefits of a general program to lend school books free of charge. Books are furnished at the request of the pupil and ownership remains, at least technically, in the state. Thus no funds or books are furnished to parochial schools, and the financial benefit is to parents and children, not to schools." In *Everson* v. *Board of Education,* 1947, the United States Supreme Court held that tax-raised funds in a New Jersey school district could be used to reimburse parents for bus fares expended to transport their children to church schools. The decision of the Court in the *Everson* case was based on a five-to-four vote. These decisions permitting the use of public funds to provide transportation and textbooks for students attending private schools were based in the main on *child benefit theory,* the rationale

442 being that the aid benefited the children and not the school or religion. Child benefit theory, while seemingly becoming an established phenomenon at the federal level, has not been unanimously accepted by the states. Decisions by the highest courts in a number of states, among them Alaska, Wisconsin, Oklahoma, Delaware, and Oregon, have struck down enactments authorizing either transportation or textbooks for children attending denominational schools.

The matter of the use of public funds for private education is far from settled. Rising costs have made it increasingly difficult for nonpublic schools to survive. As nonpublic schools close, and their pupils enroll in public schools, the financial effort for public schools must be increased.

Since 1968 many states have introduced legislation providing for a variety of forms of direct aid to nonpublic schools. Legislation originating in Pennsylvania and Rhode Island eventually was ruled upon by the United States Supreme Court. The Court ruled in both the Pennsylvania case (*Lemon* v. *Kurtzman,* 1971) and the Rhode Island case (*DiCenso* v. *Robinson,* 1971) that the respective laws were unconstitutional. The majority opinion stated: "We conclude that the cumulative impact of the entire relationships arising under the statutes in each State involves excessive entanglements between government and religion." Entanglements were anticipated in accomplishing the necessary state supervision to ensure that state aid would support only secular education in nonpublic schools.

The matter of the practice of sectarian religion in public schools has been treated by the United States Supreme Court as recently as 1963. In that instance they ruled that the reading of the Bible and the recitation of the Lord's Prayer are religious ceremonies, and if done in public schools are in violation of the First and Fourteenth Amendments of the Constitution. The decision resulted from the appeals of two lower court decisions, one from Pennsylvania, *Schempp* v. *School District of Abington Township,* and the other from Maryland, *Murray* v. *Curlett.* These earlier decisions had held that reading the Bible and saying the Lord's Prayer were not illegal. In *People of the State of Illinois ex rel. McCollum* v. *Board of Education of School District No. 71, Champaign, Illinois,* 1948, the Supreme Court ruled that release time for religious instruction, with voluntary pupil participation, but conducted on public school property, was a violation of the separation of church and state. In 1952 in *Zorach* v. *Clausen,* the Court upheld a New York statute which provided for release time for religious instruction off the school premises.

The rights assured under the First Amendment have been tested in their relationships to education in areas other than religion. A landmark decision in the area of student rights was made by the United States Supreme Court in 1969 (*Tinker* v. *Des Moines Independent Community School District*). The *Tinker* case centered around a school board's prevention of the wearing of black armbands by students protesting the hostilities in Vietnam. The Court in its majority opinion stated:

———•———

. . . the wearing of armbands in the circumstances of this case was entirely divorced from actually or potentially disruptive conduct by those participating in it. It was closely akin to "pure speech" which, we have repeatedly held, is entitled to comprehensive protection under the First Amendment . . . .

It can hardly be argued that either students or teachers shed their constitutional rights to freedom at the schoolhouse gate.

———◆—◆———

The *Tinker* case has and will undoubtedly affect the age-old doctrine of in loco parentis. The in loco parentis doctrine functioned under the traditional notion that schools and teachers could exercise total control over students because they acted as parent substitutes and out of concern for student welfare. Undoubtedly the Court's opinion in the *Tinker* case will have an effect on the operation of schools in the United States.

A most pertinent illustration of the use of the Fourteenth Amendment was the United States Supreme Court decision in *Brown* v. *Board of Education of Topeka,* 1954. The impact of this landmark decision repudiating the separate but equal doctrine is still being felt and reacted to. The judicial pronouncement in this case had legislative power added to it by the Civil Rights Act of 1964.

A number of cases directly related to the *Brown* decision have arisen. Most notable in recent years are those dealing with desegregation where segregation has been attributed to housing patterns (de facto) (Denver), and those dealing with metropolitan desegregation (Richmond, Virginia and Detroit). The U.S. Supreme Court ruled in the *Denver* case in June 1973. The decision determined that de jure segregation in one part of a school system is material to the legal determination of whether or not the remainder of the school system also is de jure segregated. The case was remanded back to the trial court for further proceedings with detailed specific procedures for taking further evidence. The *Denver* case could have a profound impact on school districts outside the South who have regarded themselves as having only de facto segregation. The metropolitan desegregation case arising in Richmond was heard by the United States Supreme Court in 1973. With a 4–4 tie vote, with Justice Powell disqualifying himself, the Court upheld a Fourth U.S. Circuit Court of Appeals reversal of the metropolitan plan. In general, the metropolitan plan would have called for the consolidation of the Richmond, Virginia schools with the suburban Henries and Chesterfield County school systems. The consolidation was ordered by U.S. District Court Judge Robert Merhige. Richmond schools were approximately seventy percent black, while the suburban schools were approximately ninety percent white. A similar case has arisen in Detroit and will be heard by the U. S. Supreme Court.

In addition to the First, Tenth, and Fourteenth Amendments to the United States Constitution, the Preamble to the Constitution has also had its effect on the development of education in the United States. The phase "promote the general welfare," known as the *general welfare clause,* has been the basis for much of the federal support of education. The general welfare clause permits the infusion of federal monies into education as seen fit by the Congress.

In summary, the United States Constitution, while it has been interpreted as delegating the function of education to the states, does contain within it protection for the rights of individuals which must not be violated in the operation of education by states and local districts.

Federal Offices and Agencies Involved in Education

The United States Office of Education represents a formalized federal effort in ed-

"We the people of the United States in order to form a more perfect Union, establish justice, insure domestic tranquility, provide for the common defense, promote the general welfare, and secure the blessings of liberty to ourselves and our posterity, do ordain and establish the Constitution for the United States of America.

Preamble
United States Constitution

ucation. It was originally established in 1867 as the Federal Department of Education. In 1953, after several changes of names, its title officially became the United States Office of Education, and it became part of the Department of Health, Education, and Welfare with a secretary in the President's cabinet. The Commissioner of Education is appointed by the president with the advice and consent of the Senate. The Office collects and publishes information about all phases of education in the United States, engages in conducting and disseminating educational research, provides leadership, and administers much of the federal funding for education. From a meager and mild beginning, the Office of Education, particularly in the last few years, has grown to become a powerful and influential agency. It has even been suggested that a Secretary of Education in the president's cabinet is now needed and justified. The increasing strength of the United States Office of Education is viewed by some as a distinct trend away from the traditional pattern of decentralizing of educational authority in our nation. Other authorities are quick to point out that while its influence has grown, an examination of the record would reveal that federal control has

not been increased. Nevertheless, it must be recognized that the Office of Education has become a more powerful agency than it once was, and it must further be recognized that forces within our society (social, economic, and demographic) are such that in fact the resultant and concomitant problems cannot be resolved by local or state efforts. Thus, the role of the Office of Education has changed a great deal, and undoubtedly will continue to change.

In July 1972 a new federal agency dealing with education was established—the National Institute of Education (NIE). Its goal is to solve education's problems through research. NIE has taken over some responsibilities formerly associated with the Office of Education. Included among these are: Educational Resources Information Clearinghouses (ERIC), experimental "extension agent" projects, career education model development, and experimental schools.

Federally Operated Schools

The federal government has accepted responsibility for and directly operates some educational institutions. The Congress provides funds for the operation of the school system of the District of Columbia. The Department of the Interior is responsible for the education of children of National Park Employees, and for outlying possessions (Samoa) and trust territories (Caroline and Marshall Islands). The Bureau of Indian Affairs finances and manages schools on Indian reservations. The Department of Defense is responsible for the four military academies and also operates a school system for children of military personnel wherever they may be located. Further, the education given in the various training programs of the military services has made a tremendous contribution to the overall educational effort in our nation.

Federal Financial Support

Federal funding represents a fourth way in which the federal government has become involved in education. Figure 16.1 lists some selected illustrative federal acts which either directly or indirectly have provided support for education.

The list of federal acts presented in Figure 16.1, while by no means exhaustive, is

1785	Ordinance of 1785
1787	Northwest Ordinance
1862	Morrill Land Grant Act
1887	Hatch Act
1914	Smith-Lever Agriculture Extension Act
1917	Smith-Hughes Vocational Act
1930	Civilian Conservation Corps
1933	Public Works Administration
1935	National Youth Administration
1935	Works Program Administration
1940	Vocational Education for National Defense Act
1941	Lanham Act
1944	G.I. Bill of Rights
1946	National School Lunch Act
1950	National Science Foundation
1954	Cooperative Research Program
1958	National Defense Education Act
1963	Manpower Development and Training Act
1964	Economic Opportunity Act
1965	Elementary and Secondary Education Act

Figure 16.1 Selected Federal Acts That Have Provided Funds for Education.

illustrative. Some general observations can be made from an examination of the list. It is apparent that federal funding for education is not a new phenomenon. The 1785 and 1787 Northwest Ordinance Acts encouraged the establishment of education in the Northwest Territory. The Ordinance of 1785 required the reservation of the sixteenth section of each township for the maintenance of schools. Federal funding since this early beginning has increased steadily. It is also apparent that the funding has been categorical —that is, for a specific purpose. Each of the acts listed had or has a purpose. Let it suffice for purposes of illustration to point out that (1) the Morrill Acts and the Hatch Act encouraged expanded agricultural, mechanical, and scientific education in institutions of higher education; (2) the Smith-Lever and Smith-Hughes Acts encouraged vocational education in secondary schools; (3) the CCC, PWA, NYA, and WPA, while in the main designed to alleviate the economic depression of the 1930s, provided incidental aid to education and youth; (4) the NDEA Act specifically affirmed the feelings of Congress toward the importance of education for national defense; and (5) the ESEA provided many thrusts, including efforts to meet the needs of children of poverty and to encourage research. The ESEA was somewhat unique in federal funding legislation in that it came as close to general aid as any federal legislation ever has, and it further provided the means whereby federal tax funds could be made available to private and church-related schools. In a sense it represented an infusion of the judicial child benefit theory attitudes into legislation. ESEA has been regularly extended with amendments since 1965.

A fourth observation that can be made is that federal funding originates and is ad-

446

> *"Religion, morality, and knowledge being necessary to good government and happiness of mankind, schools and the means of education shall forever be encouraged."*
>
> Northwest Ordinance, 1787

ministered through a number of federal agencies. For example, in addition to the Department of Health, Education, and Welfare, funds are administered through the Departments of Agriculture, Defense, Housing and Urban Development, Labor, and Interior; and through agencies such as the Office of Economic Opportunity, Veteran's Administration, and the Peace Corps.

Federal Influence: Direct and Subtle

In summary, the federal government is an influential agent in American education. Its influence has been felt directly in terms of protecting individual rights as provided in the Constitution, attaining equality of opportunity for all, promoting general welfare in terms of domestic social and economic problems and national defense, and operating specific educational agencies. Its subtle effect is most strongly exerted through the financial incentives offered to stimulate specific programs.

State Government

Public education in the United States is a state function. States have recognized this function in their respective constitutions and have established laws directing the way in which it shall be conducted. Most states, the exception being Wisconsin, have established state boards of education. The executive duties of administering education at the state level are primarily the responsibility of a state department or office of public instruction. These departments in the various states are headed by a chief executive officer, frequently called the state superintendent of public instruction or the chief state school officer. Let us examine briefly how each of these segments of control and operation at the state level influence education.

State Constitutions

The constitutional provisions of the states for education, while differing slightly in their precise wording, are markedly similar in their intent. An illustrative example is a statement in Section 2, Article VIII of the Constitution of the State of Michigan. It reads, "The Legislature shall maintain and support a system of free public elementary and secondary schools as defined by law. Each school district shall provide for the education of its pupils without discrimination as to religion, creed, race, color, or national origin." The various state constitutions are interpreted by state courts and legal counsel as conflicts arise. The decisions of state courts may be appealed to the United States Supreme Court. The United States Supreme Court will usually hear the case if in their judgment it is in the domain of the United States Constitution or federal law.

State Legislatures

The enabling legislation to conduct the educational enterprise is prepared by state legislatures. This legislation is usually classified and bound in a volume referred to as the *school code*. Legislation is both mandatory and permissive, therefore directing and guiding local school boards in their task of operating schools. The greater the tendency to enact permissive legislation, the greater amount of control is delegated to the local boards of education. State legislation is concerned with many aspects of education—for example, district organizational patterns, teacher certification and tenure regulations, financing of schools, attendance laws.

State legislatures, because of their important and vital position in education, are the subject of much lobbying. In the realm of education the laws that they formulate deal with children and money, both of which are precious to most citizens. Influential lobbying groups may include: taxpayers' federations; patriotic groups; labor, business, and professional organizations; humane societies; and the various organizations concerned directly with education, such as state teachers' associations, school administrator associations, and school board associations.

State Boards of Education

State boards of education concerned with elementary and secondary education are now in operation in forty-nine of the fifty states, Wisconsin being the exception; however, Wisconsin does have a state board for vocational education since this is a federal requirement in order to be eligible to receive funds for these activities.

Historically, the prototype of the modern-day style of state boards of education was the board established in Massachusetts in 1837. It was the first state board with an appointed secretary—in the person of Horace Mann. Henry Barnard, another pioneer educator, became the first secretary of the Connecticut State Board of Education, and later, after serving in the same capacity in Rhode Island, became the first United States Commissioner of Education.

The duties of state boards of education vary; however, in general they serve in a policy-making capacity. In 1952 the National Council of Chief State School Officers recommended a specific list of responsibilities for state boards of education. This listing is still appropriate; it is presented in Figure 16.2.

An examination of the recommended responsibilities of state boards of education reveals that in addition to a policy-making function, it is recommended that they serve in both regulatory and advisory capacities. Recommendations 2, 3, 4, and 5 are illustrative of regulatory activities, while 7 and 9 are distinctly advisory. The regulatory function of state school boards is of primary importance in achieving consistent operation of local schools, and the advisory function can be of particular importance to the legislature, especially in the light of lobbying pressures applied to the legislative decision-making process.

Membership on state boards is attained in three ways: election by the people or their representatives, appointment by the governor, or ex officio by virtue of other office held. Figure 16.3 provides this information for each state.

It is interesting to note the differences among states as to their preference in methods of selection. Iowa, New York, and Washington are somewhat unique in their elective procedures. In Iowa, conventions of delegates from areas within the state send

1. Formulate policies and adopt such rules and regulations as are necessary to carry out the responsibilities assigned to it by the constitution and the statutes of the state.

2. Appoint and fix the salaries of the professional staff of the state department of education on the recommendation of the chief state school officer.

3. Establish standards for issuance and revocation of teacher certificates.

4. Establish standards for classifying, approving, and accrediting schools, both public and nonpublic.

5. Prescribe a uniform system for the gathering and reporting of educational data, for the keeping of adequate educational and finance records, and for the better evaluation of educational progress.

6. Submit an annual report to the governor and legislature covering the areas of action of the state board of education and the operations of the state department of education and to support education throughout the state.

7. Consider the educational needs of the state and recommend to the governor and the legislature such additional legislation or changes in existing legislation as it may deem desirable.

8. Interpret its own rules and regulations and upon appeal hear all controversies and disputes arising therefrom.

9. Publish the laws relating to education with notes and comments for the guidance of those charged with the educational responsibility.

10. Provide through the state department of education supervisory and consultative service and issue materials which would be helpful in the development of educational programs.

11. Accept and distribute in accord with law any monies, commodities, goods, and services which may be made available from the state or federal government or from other sources.

12. Designate the extent to which the board is empowered to exercise supervision over public and nonpublic colleges, universities, state institutions and public and nonpublic elementary and secondary schools in accord with the law and sound public policy on education.

Figure 16.2 Suggested Responsibilities for State Boards of Education.

Source: Council of Chief State School Officers, *The State Department of Education* (Washington, D.C.: The Council, 1952), pp. 14–16. Used with permission.

nominations to the governor for his appointment; in New York the Board of Regents is elected by the legislature; and in Washington the state board is elected by members of boards of directors of local school districts. Needless to say, there are advantages and disadvantages of both the elective and appointive procedures in selecting state school board members. The appointive procedure is considered by its proponents to be more efficient in that it is more likely to establish a harmonious relationship with the governor, and that it facilitates the placement of highly qualified persons who would not for various reasons seek election. The proponents of the elective procedures cite the "grass-roots" control feature, and the lesser likelihood of political manipulation. In either case, once members are selected, they usually have staggered terms to avoid a complete change in membership at any one time; they usually serve without pay, but with reimbursement for their expenses. Both of these provisions serve as safeguards from political patronage.

Chief State School Officers

The chief state school officer occupies an important position in the administration of education in his respective state. Usually he is the executive head of the state department of education, and as such through his staff provides leadership and supervisory service in addition to the customary clerical and regulatory functions of state departments of education. He presents his interpretation of educational needs to the governor, state board of education, and legislature. He frequently influences legislation, both directly and indirectly. While the provision for his duties vary from state to state, they are quite specifically delineated for him by a combination of the respective state constitution and school code. He also is likely to receive direction from the state board of education.

Information as to how chief state school officers are selected is presented in Figure 16.3. Currently, twenty-one state officers are elected by the people or their representatives, twenty-five are appointed by state boards of education, and four are appointed by the

governor. The trend has been away from election and toward appointment, specifically appointment by the state board of education. Arguments advanced in favor of appointment include the notion that policy making should be clearly differentiated from policy execution; that educational leadership should not depend so heavily on one elected official; and that a greater likelihood exists of recruiting and retaining qualified career personnel. Opponents to the appointment procedure claim mainly that the official selected under this system would not be responsible to the people. A major objection raised to gubernatorial appointment is the danger of involvement in partisan politics. It is important to note that an elected state school officer is legally a state "official," while an appointed officer is an "employee." As a result of these differences, the working relationship of an elected official with the state board of education is not as likely to be clear and as cleanly defined as it is in instances where the chief state school officer is appointed by the state board of education and therefore is clearly an employee.

State Departments of Education

The state departments of education, under the direction of the chief state school officer, carry out the activities of state government in education. A recent monograph has classified their activities into five categories: operational, regulatory, service, developmental, and public support and cooperation.[1] Until recent years, their activities

1. Roald F. Campbell, Gerald E. Stroufe, and Donald H. Layton, *Strengthening State Departments of Education*, p. 10.

State	Members of State Boards of Education			Chief State School Officers		
	Elected by People or Represent. of People	Appointed by Governor	Ex Officio	Elected by Popular Vote	Appointed by State Board of Education	Appointed by Governor
Alabama		X		X		
Alaska		X			X	
Arizona		X		X		
Arkansas		X			X	
California		X		X		
Colorado	X				X	
Connecticut		X			X	
Delaware		X			X	
Florida			X	X		
Georgia		X		X		
Hawaii	X				X	
Idaho		X		X		
Illinois	(No State Board)			X		
Indiana		X		X		
Iowa	X				X	
Kansas	X				X	
Kentucky		X		X		
Louisiana	X			X		
Maine		X			X	
Maryland		X			X	
Massachusetts		X			X	
Michigan	X				X	
Minnesota		X			X	
Mississippi			X	X		
Missouri		X			X	
Montana		X		X		
Nebraska	X				X	
Nevada	X				X	
New Hampshire		X			X	
New Jersey		X				X
New Mexico	X				X	
New York	X				X	
North Carolina		X		X		
North Dakota		X		X		
Ohio	X				X	
Oklahoma		X		X		
Oregon		X		X		
Pennsylvania		X				X
Rhode Island		X			X	
South Carolina	X			X		
South Dakota		X		X		
Tennessee		X				X
Texas	X				X	
Utah	X				X	
Vermont		X			X	
Virginia		X				X
Washington	X			X		
West Virginia		X			X	
Wisconsin	(No State Board)			X		
Wyoming		X		X		
Total	15	31	2	21	25	4

Figure 16.3 Methods of Selection of State School Board Members and Chief State School Officers.

Sources: Adapted from R. F. Will, *State Educational Structure and Organization,* U.S. Office of Education, O.E.-23038, misc, no. 46 (Washington, D.C.: U.S. Government Printing Office, 1964). By permission.
* Illinois changes to appointment in 1975.

have been largely operational and regulatory. Operational activities are those that have to do with the direct operation of schools such as those for the deaf or blind; regulatory activities center around the enforcement of state regulations for schools, such as making certain that only properly certified teachers are employed, and that buildings are safe. The service function has to do with helping local school districts. It includes the sharing of the knowledge and expertise of the state by providing consultant service, research information, or legal advice. Most states have improved their service activities in the past few years. Developmental activities have to do with planning in order to improve the state departments themselves so that they may further develop their capabilities. Public support and cooperation activities involve communicating effectively with the people of the state, the legislature and governor, and other governmental bodies.[2]

While the traditional roles of state departments have emphasized the operational and regulatory functions, the problems of education today indicate that the state departments of education should play a stronger leadership function. Leadership can be accomplished with or without legislation. The federal government, through the Elementary and Secondary Act of 1965, Title V, provided money to be used by state departments of education for self-study and strengthening.

Local School Districts

The agency of control in education most visible to both citizens and teachers is the local school district. The school district is controlled by a governing board made up of citizens residing in the geographical area that makes up the district.

Local school districts, while similar in their major purpose—educating children—are widely different in their characteristics. In 1971, there were 17,289 districts in the United States having a total enrollment of approximately 46 million students in elementary and secondary schools.[3] These districts differ in many ways: geographical size; enrollment; geographical location (urban, suburban, rural); socioeconomic composition; heterogeneity and homogeneity; wealth; type of organization (K–8, 9–12, K–12); and many other ways. Most of the school districts in the United States are small in terms of enrollment. It has been estimated that forty-eight percent of the districts enroll less than 299 pupils, and that this total enrollment makes up only about one percent of the total national enrollment. Yet, only about seven-tenths of one percent of the districts have enrollments greater than 25,000, but these districts enroll about twenty-nine percent of the total national enrollment.[4] The trend in school district organization has been to reduce the number of districts to obtain a more effective and efficient organization. The number of districts has been reduced from over 100,000 in 1945 to the current 17,289. Such school reorganization is a slow but inevitable process. Along with consolidation the trend has also been to establish more districts that include both elementary and secondary education (K–12).

While the "putting together" or consolidation of smaller districts is being encour-

451

2. Ibid., pp. 10–15.

3. Kenneth A. Simon and W. Vance Grant, *Digest of Educational Statistics,* 1972.
4. Ibid., p. 53.

452 aged, problems have become apparent in very large city systems such as New York, Chicago, and Los Angeles that can be partly attributed to their immense enrollments. Communications in such districts can become distant and distorted. Patrons in such systems often express strong feelings that their districts are not responsive. They are calling for decentralization to enable them to gain some control over their neighborhood schools. Experimental efforts toward decentralization are being made in large urban areas such as New York, Chicago, and Pittsburgh to meet these desires.

Local Control

Local control becomes a reality through the governing boards of local districts. They may make decisions within the power delegated to them by the state. Some of their powers include those to raise monies; obtain sites; build buildings; provide curricula; employ teachers and other personnel; and admit and assign pupils to schools. Local school boards must conform to mandatory statutes, and operate within powers delegated to them. It is within their power to enact local policies for education providing those policies do not violate existing state laws. Board members are local people. Ninety-five percent of them in the United States are elected by popular vote, most frequently in special elections on a nonpartisan basis. The remaining five percent are appointed. Appointed boards occur most often in school districts enrolling over 25,000 pupils.[5]

5. Roald F. Campbell, Luvern L. Cunningham, and Roderick F. McPhee, *The Organization and Control of American Schools,* p. 165.

Local control is a characteristic that can be either advantageous or disadvantageous. The local school district, represented in personages by board members, often provides the closest relationship that many citizens have with a local form of government. This intimacy results not only from physical proximity, but also from the fact that schools deal with an extremely precious possession, the children of the people. Schools also frequently represent the agency which collects the largest amount of local tax monies. Further, education is viewed by more and more citizens as the most practical way to resolve social problems, particularly at the grass roots level. There is little doubt that local control permits citizens to have their say in providing school programs that will be responsive to their local desires and needs. Conversely, local control also permits wide variances in educational opportunity. Local control historically has been conservative and provincial, each district's concern being for their own welfare without a strong regard for state or national problems. It can be argued, for example, that one factor, the mobility of our population, is sufficient reason to support greater centralization. Further, national domestic problems and our national defense require national policies and programs to be implemented in local schools. Social and economic trends in the last few years have resulted in a gradual erosion of local control of schools.

Federal-State-Local Interrelationships

The federal-state-local relationships of the past evolved as our country grew and developed. As our nation changed from basically a sparsely populated and agrarian society to an urban industrialized society, the nature of the federal-state-local relationship changed. While the states have been and still are the major source of legal control, the federal government has increased its influential and legal roles, particularly in efforts to assure constitutional rights and to respond to both foreign and domestic issues. The federal government's response to domestic problems which relate to education, such as poverty and segregation, and their tendency to attack such problems quite directly, rather than channel their efforts through state agencies, has at least in part caused state school officials to organize to have their views heard.[6] The Education Commission of the States was formed and currently has forty-one states and territories as members.[7] The stated purpose of the organization is to further a working relationship among state governors, legislators, and educators for the improvement of education. It is interesting to note that ECS is now playing a major role in national assessment, a project designed to assess educational achievement nationwide.[8] It has been suggested, however, that the Education Commission of the States represents a counterthrust toward more state-local direction of education.[9]

New federal-state-local relationships are emerging. Each level of government tends

to look at the purposes of education from its own perspective: local school districts see their immediate local needs; states, the welfare of the state and its overall constituency; the federal government, its concern with equality, national security, and national domestic problems. While it is difficult to predict what the future relationships will be, it is clear that educational purposes and problems that are not resolved at the local level will likely to taken on by another level of government. The problems that we face seem to be of the magnitude that state and federal involvements are necessary to resolve them. A new federal-state-local educational partnership is necessary and is emerging to forge solutions to problems of and related to education.

Teacher Power

As earlier portions of this chapter have indicated, public school control from a legal point of view is variously vested in federal, state, and local governments. This control, however, does not preclude the power of teachers through their organizations to exert considerable influence on the operations of schools. There was a time in our history when teachers for all practical purposes had little or no influence in determining the conditions of their employment, let alone have enough power to influence educational policies. In recent years, however, teachers have begun to exert their power through their professional organizations. Local teacher groups are affiliated with national organizations, namely the National Education Association with its one million plus membership, or the American Federation of Teachers, with its one hundred thousand

6. Roald F. Campbell and Donald H. Layton, "Thrust and Counterthrust in Education Policy Making," *Phi Delta Kappan* 49(1968):290–94.
7. Education Commission of the States, *Compact,* vol. 3, no. 4, August 1969.
8. Frank Womer, "ECS Takes Reins of National Assessment; Project Will Continue as Planned," *National Assessment of Educational Progress* 2 (1969):1.
9. Campbell and Layton, "Thrust and Counterthrust," *Phi Delta Kappan* 49, pp. 290–94.

454 plus membership located predominantly in urban centers. The topic of professional organizations and their roles in teacher power was considered in greater depth in chapter seven. Let it suffice to say at this point that today teachers do have power.

Teacher power is manifested at the local district level by the use of a local organization to press for negotiations. While the term *negotiations* has been defined in many ways, in terms of power it means a formalization of access procedures to the legally defined school power structure. Physically it results in a written document, called an *agreement,* which most frequently spells out conditions of employment. The question of what is and what is not negotiable has not yet been clearly defined. It ranges from the broad definition of everything that affects a teacher, including curriculum, textbooks, in-service training, student teaching programs, and many other items to a narrow limitation considering just salaries. In some states the state legislature has clearly defined the subject matter for negotiation. In other states the issue is still wide open. Teacher groups have been extremely powerful in lobbying for and against various negotiation bills at the state level.

The power that teachers have gained they have gained through organization. Their ultimate weapon has been a work stoppage or strike, which incidentally is not considered under the traditional judicial view as being legal. Nevertheless, the number of teacher strikes has steadily increased.

The rise of teacher power should be accompanied by a corresponding rise in their responsibilities. Teachers have asked for, and in some cases demanded, a share in educational decision making. In some cases these requests have been formalized, and in

a sense legitimatized as a part of a negotiations agreement. In general teachers have expressed disagreement and resistance to the traditional flow of authority for decision making from the top down. They have been asking to be heard as citizens and as responsible, trained professionals. Their voices are being heard today. As they collectively speak, they should be constantly aware of their responsibilities—responsibilities that they have as citizens and educators for the destinies of children and our society. If their actions and their use of power are perceived by many citizens as being irresponsible, it can be predicted that the power of the general public will be exerted as a counterthrust. The ultimate power for education in a democratic nation resides in the people.

Point of View

The first paragraph of this chapter cites decentralization as a distinctive feature of American education. It is true that at this point in time local boards of education have more control over education in this nation than in any other developed nation of the world. In other nations a much greater national control is exerted. Both national and state control have increased in the United States over the past few years.

How much control do citizens have over education through their local school boards? Information presented earlier in this chapter noted that forty-eight percent of the school districts in the United States enrolled less than 299 pupils. In these small districts, which enroll less than one percent of the pupils in the United States, citizens probably feel that they have as much say in their local schools as the law permits. The "social distance" between school board members and citizens is small. Board members know citizens and citizens know board members. Community control of schools is not a hot issue, except perhaps as it is exerted in opposition to state or federal controls. Further, most of these small districts probably are quite homogeneous in their culture and value systems. At the same time less than one percent of the districts in the nation have enrollments greater than 25,000 pupils. In these districts, which enroll approximately twenty-nine percent of the pupils in the nation, the cry for community control has been loud and clear. Citizens don't feel like they have much say about their schools in New York, Chicago, Los Angeles, Washington, D.C., and many other large cities. Large cities are also heterogeneous and pluralistic. Many cultures and value systems are present. Furthermore, achievement levels of pupils in city schools are lower than they are in other schools in the nation.

Community control has been demanded in many cities and implemented in some in a variety of ways. In some instances it has been traumatic with confrontations between professionals (teachers) and parents. After evaluating decentralization in New York City, one writer noted: "Between the professionals and parents, one may safely conclude, there is no match. To expect decentralization to close the gap between them is perhaps to expect too much."[10] The article "Community Control Can Work" in describing community control in one school in Washington, D.C. presents the other viewpoint.

10. Bernard Bard, "Is Decentralization Working?" *Phi Delta Kappan* 54, pp. 238–43.

Community Control Can Work   455

Susan Jacoby

"Community control" is a phrase that conjures up frightening images for many teachers—vigilante parents intruding on the daily classroom routine, fierce racial and political tensions in the schools, vulnerability to the educational whims of "nonprofessionals." There is also the gut fear that community school boards may pose a direct threat to the hard-won job security of teachers by introducing, or reintroducing, a spoils system in public education.

But in a setting where concern for education prevails over inflated rhetoric, community control has a chance to succeed. The Morgan Community School, located about a mile from the White House in a troubled area of Washington's inner city, offers an example of both the potential successes and limitations of neighborhood control as a tool for improving public education.

Until 1967, Morgan was an indistinguishable cog in the District of Columbia public school system, probably best known for its poor reputation among the neighborhood parents. Today, Morgan is in its seventh year as a community school, run by a locally elected, 15-member board which manages its own affairs under a contract with the city's central board of education.

The school's immediate neighborhood is largely poor and black, although a small

Susan Jacoby, "Community Control Can Work," *Learning,* December 1973, pp. 51–54. Reprinted by special permission of *Learning,* The Magazine for Creative Teaching, December, 1973. Copyright 1973 by Education Today Company, Inc., 530 University Avenue, Palo Alto, Cal. 94301.

456 number of young white families moved into the area about a decade ago and began restoring old houses. The impetus for local control came from black neighborhood leaders angry over the poor education their children were receiving, and from white parents anxious to avoid the usual alternative of affluent liberals, the private school. The two groups successfully presented their case to the District of Columbia board of education, and shortly thereafter, the local board entered into an agreement with Antioch College to provide the professional skills all concerned hoped would help them bring about desired educational change.

No educator could have quarreled with the complaints Morgan parents were then voicing about the school. I recorded some of these comments at a workshop for parents before school opened under the auspices of the community board in the late summer of 1967:

> *Teachers won't let kids take their reading books home because they say the books will get marked up. Do those teachers really want the kids to learn to read? If the kids could read, maybe the teachers couldn't call them dumb anymore. I want to see my kids bringing books home this year.*

> *I have two boys going into fifth grade and they can't read first grade books. That's just not right. . . . all I want is for them to read.*

> *My kids were passed on to the next grade on account of their age. I saw their report cards with D's and E's. It don't seem right to pass them when they don't know nothing.*

In the years since, community control has not fulfilled all of the high hopes and expectations expressed by parents at the outset of the Morgan experiment. But neither has it fulfilled any doomsday prophecy. It is easy to find parents in the neighborhood who say they turned down chances to move to better apartments in another part of the city because they wanted to remain in the Morgan attendance zone. Morgan teachers offer widely differing opinions about the quality of the school, but they are a dedicated group of men and women who arrive early and leave long after the end of the official day. And above all, the children seem to like school. When I visited Morgan in the fall of 1967, its students were predictably suspicious and uncommunicative in the presence of most adults. In 1973, the youngsters communicate pride and enthusiasm; they hug strangers as well as their own teachers, show off whatever they are working on, unself-consciously ask for help with their exercises.

"Honey, when a kid isn't scared to ask for help, that's progress," says Kathryn Briley Lewis, an expansive woman who has worked in the school as a community intern since the project began.

The community board is comprised of seven parents with children attending Morgan, two school staff representatives, three neighborhood residents between the ages of 16 and 23, and three residents over 23. The board has the vital power to establish spending priorities within the school after receiving a lump-sum allotment from the central D.C. board, which in turn gets its appropriation from the U.S. Congress. Like most urban schools, others in Washington have virtually no budgetary discretion; the sums they receive are strictly earmarked. The Morgan board also has substantial control over curriculum planning and extracurricular activities, but naturally can do nothing that violates the legally determined policies of the central board, including the system's contract with the Washington Teachers Union. Teachers applying for jobs at Morgan are interviewed by community board representatives, but they meet the same central licensing standards and receive the same contract guarantees as teachers in any other school.

The teachers' union—in sharp contrast to New York City's United Federation of Teachers—took a positive attitude toward experiments in community control. The union leadership felt—correctly, as it turned out—that teachers who objected to local control could easily transfer to other schools and that Morgan would attract those teachers eager to work with a community board.

In the classroom, community control is reflected more in terms of a general tone than in specific guidelines for teachers.

"It certainly doesn't mean that somebody is looking over your shoulder all the time," says Patricia Pryde, who began teaching at Morgan in 1971. "On the whole, I find less interference with the teacher's judgment here than in other schools where I have taught. And here you get to know more people in the community. Things aren't perfect, but I feel they are a little more possible."

Pat Pryde is a sparkling young woman with a modified Afro hairdo—the kind of teacher a small boy would be inclined to fall in love with and a small girl to imitate. She works with four- and five-year-olds in the school's federally financed Follow Through program. Morgan's other Follow Through teacher is Sister Agnes Kelly, one of the many young nuns who has left convent-run schools for work in the inner city. Sister Agnes and Pryde work as a team, although their separate classrooms are across the hall from each other.

Pryde and Sister Agnes agree that their curriculum should stress both black identity and the development of linguistic skills, two goals which are considered extremely important by the community school board. "Reading is the most important thing," says Sister Agnes. "If we don't give them that by third or fourth grade, it's all over. The parents in this community feel this very urgently. It's not something that comes from the school. We hear this over and over when we talk to the mothers and fathers of our children."

Another direct product of local control is Morgan's effective community intern program. The interns are all neighborhood residents who are paid approximately $5,500 a year each; in combination with the teachers, they enable the school to provide a ratio of three adults to 30 children. The role of the interns varies, depending both on their own competence and the willingness of the teachers to use them. Some interns seem occupied mainly with custodial and secretarial chores, while others are capable of providing high-quality teaching for an individual child or an entire class.

One of the interns who does just that is Kathryn Lewis, who spends most of her time doing the work of a remedial reading specialist. She is not a licensed teacher, although she taught as a substitute many years ago in a segregated school in South Carolina. She is tough, outspoken and totally dedicated to improving the education of the children in her neighborhood.

"I used to feel sick when I'd see 13-year-old kids who couldn't make out the letters of the alphabet," Lewis says. "I'd know they were smart, because out on the street they were the cleverest kids alive, but somehow

458 they were failing to learn the things in school that they would need to survive later on. Morgan hasn't accomplished everything I wanted it to, but I can say with certainty that we've cut down the number of kids who used to leave this school as illiterates."

Lewis can be found most days at a table in the basement, working with children who have special problems in reading or math. She simultaneously lavishes praise and affection on them and demands their total attention.

"Come on now," she tells one girl. "I know you know the difference between vowels and consonants—you got them all right yesterday. You just aren't paying attention to the shapes and sounds of the letters." To a boy: "This is the first time you've gotten all the vowels right without my help. I was talking to your daddy about you in the grocery store the other day—he'll be so proud of you. You tell him first thing when you go home, and I'll tell him when I run into him next week."

Lewis says that "the best thing about Morgan is you reach the kids any way you can. Last year I had a Spanish-speaking boy who just didn't function in English. I wasn't getting anywhere with him until I noticed he liked to draw. So I had him draw pictures and make up stories to go with them. He would draw a picture of a sports car and—surprise, surprise—he knew a lot of heavyweight English words to go with it. Then I would use the words he gave me in his reading lesson. That child was reading English by the end of the year. You use the kids' experiences to teach them skills. If they're pitching horseshoes or shooting dice, you teach them math right along with it."

Morgan's principal, John H. Anthony, shares the philosophy that everyday experiences should be used to help children learn.

In one inspired move, he enlisted the help of a neighborhood crapshooter in a plan to teach addition, subtraction, multiplication and division through the card games that are familiar to Morgan's children from an early age. "Well, you're asking the right man," the neighborhood expert gravely told him.

"Why should I be jealous of 'nonprofessionals' helping me do a good job?" asked one teacher. "Of course, there are plenty of community people who haven't got a brain in their heads and shouldn't be working with kids. There are plenty of brainless teachers, too. That isn't the point. The point is what every good teacher in an urban school knows—we have so much work here, so many kids who need individual help, that there's more than enough to do for everyone with a head and a heart. It doesn't matter who has a license and who doesn't."

Along with its successes, Morgan has the usual array of serious urban school problems. Standardized reading and math test scores showed a slight improvement between 1970 and 1972, but the school thus far has been unable to reverse the familiar pattern of poor black children falling further and further below national norms with each year they spend in school. But Morgan counselor Eddie C. Wright thinks that's only a part of the story and would like to do a long-term study of those children who have attended Morgan throughout their elementary school years. "This would give us an accurate idea of just how much difference it makes for a child to be in this particular school," Wright says. "Many of us teachers feel that the achievement of our kids has improved significantly from year to year. But a standardized score that includes hundreds of students who may be brand new to Morgan doesn't really tell you about the quality of the school."

The Morgan community board members know that if the quality is to be improved still more, staff development must be given top priority. But it is one thing to state the problem and another to solve it. It is difficult to retain teachers when community control at Morgan has always been intertwined with a continuing conflict over the extent to which the school should depart from traditional teaching methods and classroom organization. From the first, many of the black leaders who have been the strongest supporters of community control have also been the staunchest conservatives in regard to discipline and traditional teaching of the three R's. In the face of their intransigence, a number of the young blacks and whites who were active in the early days of the fight for local control and helped work out the original agreement with Antioch College threw up their hands and departed. After one year, so did Antioch; the staff had been badly prepared to cope with the neighborhood educational politics and with the real educational problems of children and teachers in the classroom.

The school's first principal, Kenneth Haskins, is a highly respected black educator who was committed to innovation and change but who also understood the views of those black parents who wanted more traditional classrooms. "Sometimes the parents will walk down the hall and hear noise coming from a roomful of six-year-olds," Haskins told me while he was still at Morgan. "Then they'll come to me and ask how education can be going on when the children are making so much noise. Well, it takes time and patience to get across the idea that noise and education can go together."

Haskins' departure for a Harvard fellowship in the spring of 1969 was a blow to Morgan's innovators. A year later, more than a dozen teachers who felt the community board was too conservative also left. But the situation seems to have stabilized since 1970; although there are still disagreements over educational policy, teacher turnover has been almost nonexistent. Some teachers, like Pat Pryde and Sister Agnes, work as a team and are moving rapidly toward an open classroom; others run traditional self-contained classes. There are good and bad teachers in both categories.

The current community board stands somewhere between the more liberal originators of the Morgan experiment and the old-line traditionalists. One recent day, Mary French, one of the board's founding members, sat and talked about the need for more discipline as she disapprovingly watched teacher Sarah V. Miles Day, who was giving up her own time after school to work with a sixth grade modern dance group. "Now that's one thing that should stop," French asserted stoutly. "Classical ballet would be much better for them; it would really give them a sense of discipline." (The sixth graders are so professional that they have performed before a large audience at Washington's Constitution Hall.) But another conservative board member, sitting nearby, chided her gently. "Now, Mary, I don't agree with you about this. That teacher gives her own time. She even sees that the children get home after the dancing is over. A teacher who is that dedicated is an asset to the school."

One distinctly encouraging fact about Morgan today is that the staff and community board members are at least publicly civil about their disagreements. The contrast between Morgan and the situation in New York City, where furious, unbridled rhetoric has made a fiasco out of community control ef-

460 forts, is startling. There appear to be four basic reasons for that:

1. In Washington, the scale of the problems has been kept manageable. At first, only Morgan was under community control; today, so is nearby Adams School. But the number of students, teachers and parents involved is still very small compared to the hundreds of thousands involved in the New York experiment.

2. In New York, more than half the students in community control schools were black or Puerto Rican—and more than 90 percent of the teachers were white. Racial conflict was thus virtually built into the situation. At Morgan, most of both the students and the teachers are black. "We have proved," says a Morgan community leader, "that blacks can shoot it out with blacks over issues that would turn into a black-white quarrel in other places."

3. The Washington Teachers Union supports community control; the New York union opposes it.

4. At Morgan, most of the important policy battles were fought out inside the local community. No one has tried to use the Morgan experiment as a springboard to political office.

Policy battles undoubtedly will, and should, continue at Morgan. But Robert E. Brown, the 26-year-old chairman of the Morgan board, says he believes there is "general agreement" among parents and teachers on the need for both tighter discipline and a move toward a schoolwide open classroom system. Moreover, he thinks that delicate balancing act can be brought off. "A true open classroom involves great self-discipline on the part of students and teachers," he says. "Staff development is the key to achieving it."

Symbolic of what community control has brought Morgan is the fact that in 1974 the school will be housed in a spanking new $6.3 million building designed for open classrooms and team teaching. The Morgan board had a major say in both the design and the site selection—something, the members all agree, that would have been out of the question before community control came into being in 1967.

So would the sort of campaign for parental involvement in school affairs waged last spring. Community interns from Morgan fanned out through the neighborhood carrying with them a detailed financial report on how the school had spent every last penny of its budget—teacher salaries, field trips for the children, textbooks, whatever. Before they were done, they had reached nearly every family in the school area.

It all adds up to a promising, though far from perfect, experiment in community control. Hilda Mason, a member of the central board of education in Washington and formerly number two administrator at Morgan, puts it this way:

"How do you measure progress in a school? The education at Morgan is unquestionably better than it was before community control. And Morgan is ahead of every other school in the city in terms of local management—which I firmly believe is the key to improving schools. Morgan isn't everything we wanted it to be at the beginning. But progress comes by inches, and you can see it happening there."

———————— ◆•◆ ————————

QUESTIONS FOR DISCUSSION

1. What factors have caused the federal government to increase its participation in the educational enterprise?

2. Can education in the United States continue to be effective by continuing its long-term tradition of local control? Provide a rationale for your answer.
3. What recommendations would you make in designing an organization at the level of state government to most effectively administer education?
4. Should members of local school boards be typically representative of the social composition of their respective communities? Why?
5. What role do you believe teachers should assume in fostering local educational improvements? How can they best use teacher power?

SUPPLEMENTARY LEARNING ACTIVITIES

1. Visit local school board meetings and report your observations to the class.
2. Invite members of the state legislature to your class to seek out their opinions on school legislation.
3. Examine copies of the school code for your state.
4. Invite persons from nonpublic schools to your class to seek out their opinions on the concept of the separation of church and state.
5. Invite officers from a local teachers' association to your class to seek out their opinions on teacher power.

SELECTED REFERENCES

American Association of School Administrators. *School District Organization.* Report of the AASA Commission on School District Reorganization. Washington, D.C.: American Association of School Administrators, 1958.

Bard, Bernard. "Is Decentralization Working?" *Phi Delta Kappan* 54(December 1972):238–43.

Campbell, Roald F., and Donald H. Layton. "Thrust and Counterthrust in Education Policy Making." *Phi Delta Kappan* 49(1968):290–94.

Campbell, Roald F.; Luvern L. Cunningham; and Roderick F. McPhee. *The Organization and Control of American Schools.* Columbus, Ohio: Charles E. Merrill Publishing Company, 1965.

Campbell, Roald F.; Luvern L. Cunningham; Roderick F. McPhee; and Ray Nystrand. *The Organization and Control of American Schools.* 2nd ed. Columbus, Ohio: Charles E. Merrill Publishing Company, 1970.

Campbell, Roald F.; Gerald E. Stroufe; and Donald H. Layton. *Strengthening State Departments of Education.* Chicago: University of Chicago Press, 1967.

Carlton, Patrick W., and Harold I. Goodwin. *The Collective Dilemma: Negotiations in Education.* Worthington, Ohio: Charles A. Jones Publishing Company, 1969.

Carver, Fred D., and Thomas J. Sergiovanni. *Organizations and Human Behavior: Focus on Schools.* New York: McGraw-Hill Book Company, 1969.

Fantini, Mario D., and Milton A. Young. *Designing Education for Tomorrow's Cities.* New York: Holt, Rinehart and Winston, Inc., 1970.

Fellman, David, ed. *The Supreme Court and Education.* New York: Teachers College Press, 1969.

Fuller, Edgar, and Jim B. Pearson. *Education in the States: Nationwide Development*

462

Since 1900. Washington, D.C.: National Education Association Publications, 1969.

Iannaccone, Lawrence, and Frank W. Feltz. *Politics, Power and Policy: The Governing of Local School Districts.* Columbus, Ohio: Charles E. Merrill Publishing Company, 1970.

Knezevich, Stephen J. *Administration of Public Education.* 2nd ed. New York: Harper & Row, Publishers, 1969.

Koerner, James D. *Who Controls American Education?* Boston: Beacon Press, 1968.

Lieberman, Myron. "Teacher Strikes: Acceptable Strategy?" *Phi Delta Kappan* 46(1965):237–40.

Lieberman, Myron, and Michael H. Moskow. *Collective Negotiations for Teachers: An Approach to School Administration.* Chicago: Rand McNally & Company, 1966.

National Council of Chief State School Officers. *The State Department of Educa-tion.* Washington, D.C.: The Council, 1952.

National School Public Relations Association. *Student Rights and Responsibilities.* Arlington, Va.: National School Public Relations Association, 1972.

Ostrander, Raymond H., and Ray C. Dethy. *A Values Approach to Educational Administration.* New York: American Book Company, 1968.

Reller, Theodore L., and Edgar L. Morphet. *Comparative Educational Administration.* Englewood Cliffs, N.J.: Prentice-Hall, Inc., 1962.

Simon, Kenneth A., and W. Vance Grant. *Digest of Educational Statistics,* 1972. U. S. Office of Education. Washington, D.C.: U. S. Government Printing Office, 1973.

Stinnett, T. M.; Jack H. Kleinmann; and Martha L. Ware. *Professional Negotiation in Public Education.* New York: Macmillan Company, 1966.

chapter 17
Financing the Educational Enterprise

goals

- Identifies the magnitude of the educational enterprise in terms of monies spent and people involved.

- Analyzes the concept of education as an investment in individuals, government, social development, and the economy.

- Explains the separate sources of public school revenue, their advantages and disadvantages, and their systematic relationship to one another.

- Presents the basic relationship between school finance and the concept of equality of opportunity.

- Identifies the reasons for the current call for accountability and suggests proposals for responsive action.

Education in the United States is big business. There are over 51 million pupils enrolled in public and private elementary and secondary schools, over 2 million teachers employed to provide instruction for those students, and approximately $42 billion spent for current operating expenditures to conduct the enterprise. It has been estimated that in

464   1981 there will be approximately 50 million pupils, 2.4 million teachers, and the current operating expenditures will exceed $59 billion. Another way to look at the magnitude of the enterprise is to recognize that education today is the major occupation of 62.8 million people in the United States. Included in the 62.8 million are 59.5 million students enrolled in schools and colleges, 3 million teachers, and 300 thousand administrators and supporting instructional staff. In a nation of 209 million people about three out of every ten persons are directly involved in the educational process.[1] It is also pertinent to note that in many communities education is the biggest business in the community.

Education as an Investment

As a nation our investment in education has been a sizable amount. Figure 17.1 illustrates the nation's effort to support education by comparing educational expenditures with gross national product (GNP). Gross national product, calculated by the Bureau of Economic Analysis, U.S. Department of Commerce, represents the total national output of goods and services at market prices. It measures this output in terms of the expenditures by which the goods and services are acquired. The expenditures comprise purchases of goods and services by consumers and government, gross private domestic investment, and net exports of goods and services. GNP provides one measuring stick of our national investment in education. With some fluctuation educational expenditures as a percent-

age of GNP have steadily risen from 3.1 percent in 1929 to 8.0 percent in 1971. The lowest percentages, all below 3.0 percent, occurred during World War II in the period between 1941 and 1945.

Education competes with other governmental needs for the tax dollar. An indication of its priority is demonstrated by the fact that in 1969–70, forty cents out of every dollar spent by local and state governments went for education, as compared to thirteen cents for highways, eleven cents for public welfare, seven cents for hospitals, five cents for police and fire protection, four cents for administration, three cents for interest, and seventeen cents for all other general expenditures.[2] Yet, many authorities and citizens have been severely critical of our *under*spending for education. Others call for greater cost-effectiveness. Still others decry the lack of a solid research base that demonstrates clearly the relationship between the dollars expended for education and its benefits to individuals and society. How much should a nation spend for education?

While it approaches the impossible to estimate what proportion of the wealth of a nation *should* be allocated for education, it does seem clear that we in the United States are limited more by our willingness to pay than by our ability to pay. In other words, our task as a nation seems to be to delineate a hierarchy of values—that is, to clearly spell out and place in rank order what we desire or what "ought to be." Once this is done we must commit monies to convert our words into action.

Education provides substantial eco-

1. Kenneth A. Simon and W. Vance Grant, *Digest of Educational Statistics, 1972;* Kenneth A. Simon and Martin M. Frankel, *Projections of Educational Statistics to 1981–82.*

2. U.S. Department of Commerce, Bureau of the Census, *Government Finances in 1969–70,* series GF70, no. 5 (Washington, D.C.: U.S. Government Printing Office).

Percent

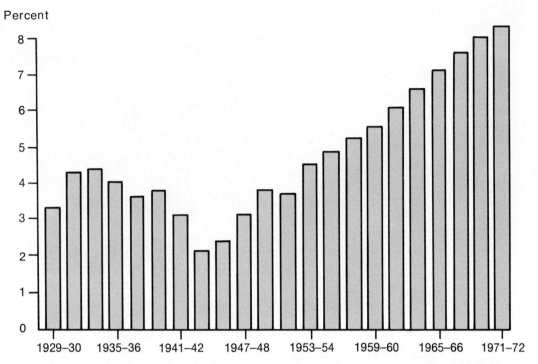

Figure 17.1 Total Expenditures for Education as a Percentage of the Gross National Product: United States, 1929–30 to 1971–72.

Source: Kenneth A. Simon and W. Vance Grant, *Digest of Educational Statistics, 1972,* U.S. Office of Education (Washington, D.C.: U.S. Government Printing Office, 1973).

nomic returns for both society and individuals. At one time economists used a formula containing the elements of land, labor, and capital to estimate economic development. It soon became evident that another variable was exerting a significant influence. There is general agreement among economists that education is that significant variable. Using gross national product as an economic index, it can be shown that there is a positive relationship between gross national product and educational development. While this type of analysis is beset with some difficulties, such as

comparable data indices and the time lag associated with the contribution of education in terms of when the education was acquired and when its effects were realized, nevertheless the evidence does indicate the importance of education to economic development. Investment in education is an investment in the basic human resources of our society. A second benefit accrued to society from education is the training of skilled manpower. As the demand for unskilled labor decreases, and concomitantly the demand for skilled labor increases, education can fulfill the need to

466 train the skilled manpower our society needs. In terms of individual economic returns, let it suffice to say that in our society the average income of families headed by high school graduates is more than twice that of those who did not complete elementary school.

> *Education is an investment, not a cost. It is an investment in free men. It is an investment in social welfare, in better living standards, in better health, in less crime. It is an investment in higher production, increased income, and greater efficiency in agriculture, industry, and government. It is an investment in a bulwark against garbled information, half-truths, and untruths; against ignorance and intolerance. It is an investment in human talent, human relations, democracy, and peace.*
>
> President's Commission on Higher Education

Social development, closely intertwined with economic development, is also related to education. A basic premise undergirding our form of government is that informed citizens are necessary to our national survival. The skills necessary to be an informed citizen (such as literacy) and the skills necessary for problem solving are enhanced through education. The values of society, on the ways of life that we cherish, are transmitted in part through our educational system.

> *There are obviously two educations. One should teach us how to make a living, and the other how to live.*
>
> James Truslow Adams

Investment in education is an investment in society, both economically and socially. Education in a sense is the servant of society. Americans must continue to use education to foster the achievement of their ideals.

> *The whole people must take upon themselves the education of the whole people and must be willing to bear the expense of it.*
>
> John Adams

Sources of School Revenue

The monies used to finance the public educational enterprise today come largely from taxation. It has not always been so. In colonial America monies for schools were often obtained from lotteries and charitable contributions. Churches of the various denominations financed education for some. It was not unusual in the very early days of our nation for the patrons of the schools to provide services such as supplying wood, making building repairs, or boarding teachers in lieu of money.

Public support for education in this nation in terms of taxes was secured only after a long, hard battle. However, the concept that education should be a public responsibility dates back to our early heritage. The Massachusetts laws of 1642, 1647, and 1648 referred to in chapter ten illustrate the New England attitude that at least common school education should be a public rather than a private responsibility. In the early 1800s, the movement for free public schools gained impetus. Pennsylvania in 1834 became the first state to adopt free elementary education. In 1872, the village of Kalamazoo,

Michigan voted to establish a public high school to be supported by taxation. A lawsuit was filed to test the legality of using taxation to provide a high school. The opinion of the State Supreme Court of Michigan was that the action was legal and constitutional. By the end of the nineteenth century, public schools were financed almost completely by local funds derived from local taxation.

Important to the rise of public financial support for education (taxes) was the belief that education benefited the public as well as the individual or his family. Today money to support education comes from a variety of taxes collected by local, state, and federal governments. These governments in turn distribute taxes to local school districts to operate their schools. The three major kinds of taxes used to provide revenue for schools are property taxes, sales or use taxes, and income taxes. In general, local governments use the property tax, state governments rely upon the sales tax—though they are increasingly using the income tax—and the federal government relies heavily upon the income tax.

It is important to note the percentage of support for public elementary and secondary schools contributed by each level of government. In 1920–21, about 83.0 percent of school revenues came from local governmental sources, 16.5 percent from state sources, and about .3 percent from federal sources. Over the years this has changed with a marked increase in state support, and most recently in 1965, a definite increase in federal support. Figure 17.2 illustrates the percent of revenue received from the three sources since 1919.

While Figure 17.2 provides data from an overall national viewpoint, an examination of the data from selected individual states reveals wide variations from the national statistics.

It should be remembered that education is a function of the state and therefore variability is to be expected. Figure 17.3 illustrates the

467

School Year	Federal	State	Local
1919–20	.3%	16.5%	83.2%
1929–30	.4	16.9	82.7
1939–40	1.8	30.3	68.0
1949–50	2.9	39.8	57.3
1955–56	4.6	39.5	55.9
1957–58	4.0	39.4	56.6
1959–60	4.4	39.1	56.5
1961–62	4.3	38.7	56.9
1963–64	4.4	39.3	56.4
1965–66	7.9	39.1	53.0
1967–68	8.0	39.3	52.7
1969–70	8.0	39.9	52.1

Figure 17.2 Percent of Revenue Received from Federal, State, and Local Sources for Public Elementary and Secondary Schools

Source: Simon and Grant, *Digest of Educational Statistics, 1972.*

State	Percent of Revenue		
	Local	State	Federal
New Hampshire ..	89.8	6.1	4.1
Nebraska	75.8	17.4	6.7
Wisconsin	64.5	31.7	3.8
Illinois	55.2	38.6	6.2
Pennsylvania	46.2	47.5	6.3
Florida	35.3	53.9	10.8
Mississippi	24.2	48.9	26.9
New Mexico	18.9	63.0	18.2
Alaska	11.7	72.4	15.9
Hawaii	3.0	89.0	8.0

Figure 17.3 Estimated Percent of Revenue by Governmental Source for Public Elementary and Secondary Schools, 1972–73, for Selected States

Source: National Education Association, Research Division, *Rankings of the States, 1973,* research report 1973–R1 (Washington, D.C.: National Education Association Publications, 1973), pp. 49–51.

468 estimated percent of revenue by governmental source for public elementary and secondary schools in 1972–73 for selected states. The states are arranged in the table in a descending order in terms of local support. The average percentages in the United States for the same period are estimated to be: local 51.2, state 41.0, federal 7.7.

The variation in state financial support illustrated in Figure 17.3 represents primarily a variation in general state aid. That is, state monies are provided to supplement the local education effort and for the most part are not "earmarked" or "tagged" for special purposes or programs. The variation in federal support in the main is a reflection of *categorical aid*—that is, specific aid for a specific purpose or to resolve a unique problem. For example, the Smith-Hughes Act provided a stimulus for vocational education; the National Defense Education Act of 1958 emphasized the enhancement of science, mathematics, foreign languages, and counseling services; the Elementary and Secondary Act of 1965 had as one important feature the provision of monies to assist school districts in providing programs for children of poverty. Other federal aid programs are designed to aid school districts that are affected by federally induced population impaction such as may occur near a military installation or major federal research installation. Both state and federal aid are aimed at enhancing equality of opportunity, which is to be considered later in this chapter.

As was mentioned earlier, the local support for schools comes predominantly from the property tax. The property tax is one of the oldest forms of taxation, based on the premise that a measure of a man's property was a measure of his wealth. Property is most often considered in two categories, real estate and personal. Personal property may include such things as automobiles, furniture, machinery, livestock, jewelry, and less tangible items as stocks and bonds. The property tax was particularly appropriate for an agrarian economy.

The property tax, as with most forms of taxation, has both distinct advantages and disadvantages. Its major advantage is that it provides a regular and stable form of income. While it is perhaps not as sensitive to economic changes as the sales and income taxes, neither is it absolutely rigid. In fact, recent studies have indicated that it is quite elastic and responsive to economic growth.[3] The stability of the property tax will likely cause it to continue to be the mainstay of local public school support.

A major disadvantage of the property tax has to do with establishing equality of assessment. In other words, parcels of property of equal value should be assessed at the same value. This is extremely difficult to accomplish. Wide variations exist within school districts, states, and the nation. Studies have indicated variation in assessment of residential property from 5.9 percent of sale value in one state to 66.2 percent in another. Inequality of assessment causes the property tax to be an unfair tax.

The property tax is most generally thought of as a proportionate tax, that is,

3. John Shannon, "Property Taxation: Toward a More Equitable, Productive Revenue Source," *Trends in Financing Public Education* (Washington, D.C.: National Education Association Publications, 1965), pp. 136–43; U.S. Department of Commerce, Bureau of the Census, *Finances of School Districts,* 1962 Census of Governments, vol. IV, no. 1 (Washington, D.C.: U.S. Government Printing Office, 1963).

one that taxes according to ability to pay. However, inequality of assessment and the trend in an urban economy for wealth to be less related to real estate than it was in an agrarian economy have caused the tax to become somewhat regressive. Regressive taxes are those such as sales and use taxes that have a relatively greater impact on lower income groups.

State support for schools comes mainly from the sales tax and income tax. As of 1971, forty-three states had a personal income tax, forty-four had a corporate income tax, and all had a general sales tax of some form. Sales and income taxes are lucrative sources of state revenue. Both taxes are relatively easy to administer. The sales tax is collected bit by bit by the vendor and he is responsible for record keeping and remitting the tax to the state. The state income tax can be withheld from wages, hence facilitating collections. The sales tax is considered a *regressive tax* because all persons pay the sales tax at the same rate; therefore, persons in low income groups pay nearly as much tax for essentials as do those in high income groups. Income taxes are referred to as *progressive taxes* because they are frequently scaled to the ability of the taxpayer to pay. Both state sales and income taxes are direct and certain, they are responsive to changes in the economy, and they can be regulated by the state legislature which is responsible for raising the money. It is interesting to note that in 1971, nationwide approximately 58 percent of all state revenue came from sales taxes, and 27 percent from income taxes. The remainder came from licenses and miscellaneous taxes.

Federal support for schools comes from monies raised primarily from personal and corporate income taxes. These two taxes account for over eighty percent of all tax collections by the federal government.

School Finance and Equality of Opportunity

The opportunity for equal education is related to the financial ability of specific areas to pay for education. While wealth is not the only factor related to equality of opportunity, as was pointed out by the *Brown* decision, it certainly is an important one.

Children are educated in local school districts, which by and large still produce nationwide about 52 percent of the monies used for education. These monies are raised primarily with the property tax, and therefore are dependent upon the real estate wealth of the district. Wealthy districts, therefore, can provide more monies for education than poor districts with the same tax effort. Suppose, for example, that the total assessed valuation, that is, the value of all the property as determined by a tax assessor of a district, is $100,000,000 and that the district has 2,000 pupils. This hypothetical district would have then an assessed valuation of $50,000 per pupil. A tax rate of $2 per $100 of assessed valuation would produce $1000 per pupil. By the same token if a neighboring district had an assessed evaluation of only $10,000 per pupil the same $2 per $100 rate would produce only $200 per pupil. With the same rate, or the same effort, one of these districts could spend $1000 per pupil while the other could spend only $200. In general, this results in children in wealthy districts being provided greater opportunities for education than children in poor districts.

Great differences can exist in wealth per

pupil from school district to school district. Industrial developments can increase valuations in some districts, while at the same time neighboring districts may be largely residential with little valuation and large numbers of pupils.

Recently a number of court cases have arisen in respect to inequality of education as a function of the wealth of school districts. The *Serrano* case is illustrative. In *Serrano* v. *Priest* the California Supreme Court was called upon to determine whether or not the California public school financing system, with its substantial dependence on local property taxes, violated the Fourteenth Amendment. In a 6–1 decision on August 30, 1971, the Court held that heavy reliance on unequal local property taxes "makes the quality of a child's education a function of the wealth of his parents and neighbors." Furthermore, the Court declared, "Districts with small tax bases simply cannot levy taxes at a rate sufficient to produce the revenue that more affluent districts produce with a minimum effort." The data presented in the *Serrano* case revealed that the Baldwin Park school district spent $577 per pupil, while the Beverly Hills school district spent $1,232. Yet, the tax rate of $5.48 in Baldwin Park was more than double the rate of $2.38 in Beverly Hills. The discrepancies are a result of the difference in wealth between the two districts. Beverly Hills had $50,885 of assessed valuation per child, while Baldwin Park had only $3,706 valuation per child—a ratio of thirteen to one. Suits similar to *Serrano* have been filed in at least twenty-two states.

The United States Supreme Court consented to hear an appeal of the *Rodriguez* case, which originated in Texas and was similar to *Serrano*. In *Rodriguez* the U.S. Supreme Court, in 1973 in a 5–4 decision, reversed the lower court and thus reaffirmed the local property tax as a basis for school financing. Justice Potter Stewart voting with the majority admitted that "the method of financing public schools . . . can be fairly described as chaotic and unjust." He did not, though, find it unconstitutional. The majority opinion written by Justice Lewis F. Powell stated "we cannot say that such disparities are the product of a system that is so irrational as to be invidiously discriminatory." The opinion also noted that: the poor are not necessarily concentrated in the poorest districts; states must initiate fundamental reform in taxation and education; and the extent to which quality of education varies with expenditures is inconclusive. Justice Thurgood Marshall in the dissenting opinion charged that the ruling "is a retreat from our historic commitment to equality of educational opportunity." A number of commissions have made recommendations to improve the financing of schools. States have attempted to alter their methods of financing schools. A brief description of state aid prior to *Rodriguez* provides a basis for understanding the problem today.

State Aid—Historically

States have recognized the disparaging differences in wealth among local districts and through state aid programs have attempted to provide financial equalization for educational purposes. This makes good sense, particularly since the state has the primary responsibility for education.

State aid can be classified by its use as being either general or categorical. General aid may be used by the recipient school district as it desires. Categorical aid is "earmarked" for specific purposes. Examples of categorical aid include monies for speech, driver education, vocational education, or transportation. Categorical aid is sometimes used as an incentive to encourage programs that are perceived as being needed.

General aid usually represents the states' efforts to equalize opportunity. The underlying premise is that each child, regardless of his place of residence or the wealth of the particular school district in which he lives, is entitled to receive essential basic educational opportunities. General aid is usually administered through some type of foundation program. The foundation concept involves the establishment of a per pupil dollar value which represents the desired foundation education in a state. The usual connotation of the word "foundation" is basic or minimum. Therefore, the foundation level is usually less than the actual per pupil expenditures. A state in establishing a foundation level is in effect assuring that the amount of the per pupil foundation level will be expended for education for each pupil in the state. Foundation programs do encourage equality of opportunity from a financial viewpoint; however, *it is important to observe that they assure equalization only to a prescribed level.* Districts can and do vary greatly in their expenditure per pupil.

The actual monies used to achieve the foundation level expenditures come from both state and local sources. Most often a minimum local tax rate is established, and the money this tax rate produces is subtracted from the foundation level with the remainder being paid by the state. The local tax rate will produce more money in a wealthy district than it will in a poor district. This concept is also a part of the equalization principle. Figure 17.4 presents a graphic representation of equalization and

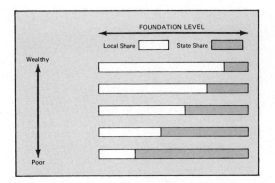

471

Figure 17.4 The Principle of Equalization as Related to the Foundation Level

the foundation principle. *It is important to note, however, that local districts can, and frequently do, spend more than the foundation level.*

Wealth Differences Among States

Differences in wealth exist among states just as they do among school districts within states. Since assessment practices vary from state to state it is difficult to use assessed valuation per pupil as an index to compare the wealth of states. A more accurate index is personal income per child. Figure 17.5 illustrates the variance in wealth among selected states.

Figure 17.5 also illustrates the wide variance in expenditure per pupil in the United States. New York's expenditure of $1,360 per pupil in 1971–72 was the highest, while Mississippi's expenditure of $619 was the lowest. The relationship between expenditure per pupil and personal income per child, while not perfect, does illustrate that high per pupil expenditures are directly as-

State	Expenditures per Pupil	Personal Income per Child
New York	1360	21,153
Connecticut	1108	20,029
California	894	18,926
Maryland	990	17,523
United States	906	16,392
Ohio	795	15,978
Wisconsin	987	14,617
Kentucky	627	12,893
New Mexico	729	11,195
Mississippi	619	9,926

Figure 17.5 Current Expenditures per Pupil 1971–72 and Personal Income per Child of School Age five to seventeen in Selected States, 1972

Source: National Education Association, Research Division, *Ranking of the States, 1973,* research report 1973–R1 (Washington, D.C.: National Education Association Publications, 1973), pp. 36, 64.

sociated with high personal income per child and that low per pupil expenditures are associated with low personal income per child. It is interesting to note that New Mexico and Mississippi, with relatively high state and federal aid (Figure 17.3) are still below the national average per pupil expenditure.

As was indicated previously in this chapter federal aid has increased. However, as was discussed in chapter sixteen, the aid has been categorical. The Elementary and Secondary Act of 1965 with its emphasis toward improving educational opportunities for children of poverty, while categorical, came as close to general aid as any federal aid ever has. Greater federal support is necessary to bolster equality among states.

Recommendations for Equality in Financing Education

The most comprehensive study of school finance ever undertaken was recently completed. Known as the National Educational Finance Project it was directed by R. L. Johns and conducted over a four-year period at a cost of two million dollars. Certain standards were set prior to the study in order to provide benchmarks against which to make measurements. They were:

- The opportunity to receive a good education should be equally available to everyone.
- Education should be seen as helping to break down the barriers of caste and class, providing a path to success for everyone, no matter how humble his birth or circumstances.
- Systems of taxation should be equitable—that people ought to be called upon to support education in proportion to their ability to pay.
- Education is regarded not just as an expenditure, but as an investment in human capital, yielding substantial returns to the individual and society as a whole.

■ Government of the people and for the people cannot succeed with an illiterate, ignorant citizenry.[4]

In volume five of the National Educational Finance Project reports, nineteen plans are presented. In general the report concluded that an optimum model would be one with some small degree of local financing to stimulate innovation and experimentation. There would be heavy reliance on funding from state and federal governments. More specifically the report concluded that the federal government should provide 30 percent of the school revenues, and the local district not more than 10 to 15 percent. The remainder of 55 to 60 percent should come from the state. Funding should be related to program costs, that is, a "weighted pupil" technique should be applied. For example, if a regular elementary pupil is assigned a weight of one (1) and compensatory programs cost twice as much, then a compensatory pupil would be weighted as two (2). The study contended that at least 80 percent of the nation's 18,000 school districts are too small to provide minimal programs economically.

It is interesting to note that in 1972 at least four states had measures on the ballot that would have eliminated the property tax as a source of school revenue or seriously curtailed its use (Colorado, California, Oregon, and Michigan). The issue was defeated in all cases, that is, voters supported the property tax.[5]

The President's Commission on School Finance recommended that the states take over the major responsibility for school costs with the federal government playing only a supplementary role. With the exception of placing a larger burden on the states the report in general concurred with the recommendations of the National Educational Finance Project. The report did, however, question the notion that increased spending produces better schools.[6] At this point in history there appears to be much study, some increase in state and federal aid, but little actual evidence of major reform in the methods of financing public schools. Perhaps the next decade will bring forth changes.

Equality of Opportunity: An Overview

A first step in achieving equality of opportunity in education can be to equalize per pupil expenditures. This equalization must represent a high level of support. Is it possible to equalize expenditures nationally when wide discrepancies exist in local and state wealth, and when at the same time nationally 52 percent of the support for schools comes from local sources, 40.7 percent from state sources, and 7.3 percent from federal sources?

State and federal governments must provide a greater portion of support for schools if equality of opportunity is to be achieved. Both these levels of government can use the progressive income tax, the most fair tax, to gain access to funds. This is not to say that local support is not important. Local interest and initiative, unique to our system, should be expressed. Local financial contributions enhance the opportunity for local initiative. Nevertheless, the social and economic problems that prevail in our nation today, for

473

4. Roe L. Johns et al., "Toward Equity in School Finance," *Financing the Public Schools*, pp. 3–6.
5. *Education USA*, November 13, 1972, p. 61.

6. *Schools, People and Money*, President's Commission on School Finance.

474 which education can be a part of the solution, require more monies than can be raised locally. In a very pragmatic sense, it does not seem possible for local school districts, using only local resources, to resolve state and national problems.

Accountability

Earlier in this book reference was made to the expressed dissatisfaction with the educational accomplishments of the pupils of the public schools. In a sense the educational expectations of individuals and society were not being met. Questions were being raised about the notion that increased spending brings about better education. The term "cost-effectiveness" was being used in respect to education. Citizens seemed to have lost some of their faith in education. The roots of accountability rest in unmet expectations and increased costs as they relate to education. The call for research and data to determine the relationship between dollars expended for education and benefits accrued to individuals and society represents the thrust of accountability.

To be accountable means to be responsible. In schools this requires (1) explicit goal statements that represent outputs or attainments, and (2) the dollar costs of these accomplishments. The end product should be a report of the costs of programs in terms of the accomplishments of the programs.

A danger that lurks in the implementation of an accountability system is the chance that goals that do not lend themselves to objective measurement will be dropped. This must be avoided. A great effort must be made to measure *all* goals as best they can be measured.

Accountability is seen by some as a dehumanizing, growth-stultifying, imposition on children and education. It need not be. In fact, it should and can be the opposite. In the words of Leon Lessinger, one of its strong advocates, accountability calls for a "zero reject system" or "every kid a winner."[7] It is based on the very humane premise that every child can be successful—he or she can learn and his accomplishments can be reported. Each child will be expected to learn, and will learn, beginning at the threshold of his achievement, rather than being marked for failure as he is in many schools today. Accountability will undoubtedly take many forms in its developmental stages. It could very well be the beginning of a promising era in American education. Performance contracting and educational vouchers are forms of the accountability thrusts that students may wish to investigate.

Expectations and Expenses

Early in this chapter it was said that our expenditures for education were limited more by our willingness to pay than our ability to pay. They also seem to be limited by our inability to demonstrate definitively the value of education. Do we have the willingness to support our expectations for education? What are our national priorities? As a nation compared to other nations in the world we are wealthy. We do, however, have pockets of poverty. Parts of our nation are more able than others to support education. If as a *nation* we believe that education is important, and that education can help us achieve our national goals and professed ideals, then we

7. Leon Lessinger, *Every Kid a Winner.*

must muster and utilize our financial resources accordingly.

Point of View

Reference was made in this chapter to
the current call for accountability. Accountability in a sense means responsibility. In education it means being responsible for student
learning and the costs associated with that
learning. Emphasis is placed on output or results—that is, on the knowledge, skills, attitudes, and behaviors that students exhibit
after having learning experiences in school.
In the past, schools have been frequently
judged as to their quality in terms of dollars
spent, facilities provided, or instructional
processes used, all of which are undoubtedly
indirect measures of quality. *Results are direct measures of quality.* Accountability calls
for direct measures of results, and the cost of
the results. It means that goals of education
must be stated and translated into specific,
measurable learner objectives. It further
means that costs must be identified with educational programs.

Leon Lessinger has fostered and nur-
tured the accountability movement. His
article "Accountability for Results: A Basic
Challenge to America's Schools" details the
roots of the accountability movement. He
explains the rationale behind accountability
and advocates its implementation. Many of
his basic ideas have served as an impetus to
others in further developing the concept and
designing means of implementation. Needless
to say his basic ideas have also been attacked,
distorted, and misconstrued. Nevertheless the
movement has had an impact on American
education, and will continue to do so. Anyone
concerned with American education, its purposes and processes, its funding, and its
efforts to provide equality of opportunity will
benefit by reading and reflecting on his
thoughts.

————————•••————————

Accountability for Results: A Basic Challenge to America's Schools

Leon M. Lessinger

Today, too many young Americans leave
school without the tools of learning, an interest in learning, or any idea of the relationship of learning to jobs. It is a mocking
challenge that so many of our children are
not being reached today by the very institution charged with the primary responsibility
for teaching them. A Committee for Economic Development report issued in the
summer of 1968 summarizes the indictment:
Many schools and school districts, handicapped by outmoded organization and a lack
of research and development money, are not
providing "the kind of education that produces rational, responsible, and effective
citizens."

Now, the educational establishment—
right down to the local level—is being asked
ever more insistently to account for the results of its programs. This fast-generating
nationwide demand for accountability promises a major and long overdue redevelopment
of the management of the present educational
system, including an overhaul of its cottage-
industry form of organization. Many believe
this can be accomplished by making use of

Leon Lessinger, "Accountability for Results: A
Basic Challenge to America's Schools," *American
Education* 5(1969):2–4.

476 modern techniques currently employed in business and industry, some of which are already being used in the educational enterprise.

Before America's schools can productively manage the massive amount of money entrusted to them—and the even greater amount they need—they must be armed with better management capability. If education is going to be able to manage its budget properly, it must devise measurable relationships between dollars spent and results obtained. Education, like industry, requires a system of quality assurance. Anything less will shortchange our youth.

Sputniks and satellite cities, computers and confrontation politics, television and the technology of laborsaving devices—all have placed new and overwhelming demands on our educational system. Americans could say with the angel Gabriel of *Green Pastures,* that "everything nailed down is coming loose." How can we provide the kind of education that would assure full participation for all in this new complex technological society? How to prepare people to respond creatively to rapid-fire change all their lives while maintaining a personal identity that would give them and their society purpose and direction? How to do this when the body of knowledge has so exploded that it no longer can be stored in a single mind? How to do this when cybernetics is changing man's function? How to do this when the cost of old-fashioned education soars higher every year with little significant improvement?

In 1965 the passage of the far-reaching Elementary and Secondary Education Act gave the public schools of America a clear new mandate and some of the funds to carry it out. It was a mandate not just for equality of educational opportunity but for equity in results as well. In place of the old screening, sorting, and reject system that put students somewhere on a bell shaped curve stretching from A to F, the schools were asked to bring educational benefits to every young person to prepare him for a productive life. Under the new mandate the schools were expected to give every pupil the basic competence he needed, regardless of his so-called ability, interest, background, home, or income. After all, said a concerned Nation, what's the purpose of grading a basic skill like reading with A, B, C, D, or F when you can't make it at all today if you can't read?

In essence, this meant that education would be expected to develop a "zero reject system" which would guarantee quality in skill acquisition just as a similar system now guarantees the quality of industrial production. Today's diplomas are often meaningless warranties. In the words of one insistent inner-city parent, "Many diplomas aren't worth the ink they're written in." We know, for example, that there are some 30,000 functional illiterates—people with less than fifth grade reading ability—in the country today who hold diplomas. And untold more are uncovered each day as manpower training and job programs bring increasing numbers of hardcore unemployed into the labor market.

Instead of certifying that a student has spent so much time in school or taken so many courses, the schools should be certifying that he is able to perform specific tasks. Just as a warranty certifies the quality performance of a car, a diploma should certify a youngster's performance as a reader, a writer, a driver, and so on.

If, then, the new objective of education

is to have zero rejects through basic competence for all, how can the educational establishment retool to respond to this new challenge? Developing a system of quality assurance can help provide the way.

The first step toward such a system is to draw up an overall educational redevelopment plan. Such a plan must first translate the general goal of competence for all students into a school district's specific objectives. These objectives must be formulated in terms of programs, courses, buildings, curriculums, materials, hardware, personnel, and budgets. The plan must incorporate a timetable of priorities for one year, for five years, 10 years, and perhaps even for 20 years. Such a plan should be based on "market research," that is, an investigation of the needs of the students in each particular school. It should also be based on research and development to facilitate constant updating of specifications to meet these needs. Through the plan the school district would be able to measure its own output against the way its students actually perform. It would be able to see exactly what results flow from the dollars it has invested.

The purpose of the educational redevelopment plan, of course, is to provide a systematic approach for making the changes in educational organization and practice necessitated by the new demands on the education system. To assure that the plan will provide quality, it should use a mix of measurements that are relevant, reliable, objective, easily assessable, and that produce data in a form that can be processed by modern-day technology. As a further guarantee of quality, teams of school administrators, teachers, and modern educational and technical specialists competent to interpret the

results should be available. The plan should also spell out a clear relationship between results and goals, thus providing for accountability.

In reality, this educational plan is only a piece of paper—a set of ideals and a set of step-by-step progressions which schools and districts can approximate. But it does provide a blueprint for the educational managers of the district—the superintendent, teachers, principals, and school boards—who must provide the leadership and the understanding to carry out educational change.

To be effective and to assure that its specifications remain valid, an educational redevelopment plan must set aside dollars for research and development. The Committee for Economic Development in last summer's report revealed that less than one percent of our total national education investment goes into research and development. "No major industry," the report said, "would expect to progress satisfactorily unless it invested many times that amount in research and development." Many private companies plow as much as 15 percent of their own funds back into research and development.

If one percent of the yearly budget for education was set aside for research and development, we would have a national educational research and development fund of roughly $500 million. Such money could attract new services, new energies, new partnerships to education. And they would inspire competition that would spur rapid educational development. This research and development money could be used to buy technical assistance, drawing on the expertise of private industry, the nonprofit organizations, the universities, the professions, and the

478   arts. The administrative functions of a school system—construction, purchasing, disbursement, personnel, payroll—also demand business and management skills.

Why not draw on business for technical assistance or actual management in these areas? Or for that matter, in formulating the educational redevelopment plan itself? The final step in setting up a quality assurance system is providing for accountability of both the educational process and its products, the students. Do pupils meet the overall objectives and the performance specifications that the school considers essential? Can Johnny read, write, figure? Can he also reason? Can he figure out where to find a given piece of information not necessarily stored in his head? Does he understand enough about himself and our society to have pride in his culture, a sureness about his own personal goals and identity, as well as an understanding of his responsibilities to society? Does he have the various cognitive and social skills to enter a wide range of beginning jobs and advance in the job market?

The accountability of process, of classroom practice, is somewhat harder to get at. At the risk of mixing it up with ideas about educational hardware, we might call it the technology of teaching. To find out a little about it, we might start by asking whether things are being done differently today in a particular classroom than they were done in the past.

A host of disenchanted teachers and others—from Bel Kaufman in her *Up the Down Staircase* to Jonathan Kozol in *Death at an Early Age*—have been telling us over the past few years what has up to now been happening in many classrooms in America. In *The Way It Spozed To Be,* James Herndon, a California schoolteacher, describes one kind of advice he got from experienced teachers during his first year in an inner-city school: "This advice was a conglomeration of dodges, tricks, gimmicks to get the kids to do what they were spozed to do. . . . It really involved gerrymandering of the group—promises, favors, warnings, threats . . . A's, plusses, stars. . . . The purpose of all these methods was to get and keep an aspect of order . . . so that 'learning could take place. . . .' "

Today, teachers often try to teach order, responsibility, citizenship, punctuality, while believing that they are in fact teaching reading or French or gym. If Johnny forgets his pencil, for example, he actually may not be permitted to take the French quiz and might get an F—presumably for forgetfulness, certainly not for French, for the grade does not reflect Johnny's competence in French.

In one state's schools, girls' physical education regularly chalks up far more F's than any other course. A study of the reasons indicated that gym teachers actually were attempting to measure citizenship by tallying whether Jane kept a dirty locker or failed to take a shower. The grade hardly reflected her competence in physical education. Requirements such as punctuality, neatness, order, and time served, ought not to be used to reflect school subject mastery.

Despite considerable evidence to the contrary, many schools and teachers are still grouping youngsters as good or bad raw material. What can you do with bad raw material? some teachers ask, much as some doctors once asked about the mentally ill. What we are searching for in place of a "demonology" of teaching is sensitive and sensible classroom practice—a practice that treats every child as a person and uses a variety of pleasurable techniques to improve his performance in anticipated and replicable ways. We are not sure this will result in more learning—though we think it will—but we do know that sensitive and sensible classroom practice is good in itself. As such it will pay off in human ways, even if it doesn't pay off in learning.

As teachers' salaries rise and their demands for rights and benefits are rightfully met by the communities they serve, those communities can expect that teacher responsibility will also grow. In fact, they can insist on it. They can insist that better pay, more rights, and more status bring with them better standard practice in the schools and classrooms. They can insist that teachers become accountable for relating process and procedures to results. And pupil accomplishment, though it may reflect some new hardware and construction, by and large reflects teacher and administrator growth and development. This is the true meaning of a new technology of teaching.

Thus the changes that result when the redevelopment plan has been carried out must be demonstrably apparent in terms of both teacher and pupil progress. In order to measure how these actual results compare to the detailed objectives of the plan, it makes sense to call for an outside educational audit, much like the outside fiscal audit required of every school system today. The school system could request an audit either of its overall program or of specific parts of that program.

This new approach could conceivably lead to the establishment of a new category of certified educational auditors whose principal job would be to visit school districts, on invitation, to help determine the success of local program planning in achieving prestated goals. One expert suggests that an educational audit need take only 10 school days a year for a single school system. His idea is to send a completely equipped and staffed mobile educational audit van to visit about 20 school systems a year.

Educators should also be encouraged to describe and measure the behavior expected of each student upon completion of programs funded from Federal sources. To reinforce accountability for results, contracts for Federal funds might be written as performance agreements. Thus a proposal for funds to back a reading program might stipulate that 90 percent of the participating students would be able to satisfy criteria by demonstrating they had achieved a particular advance in grade level in the time proposed.

Furthermore, special financial incentives based on meeting performance criteria might be specified in these contracts. For example, a certain amount of dollars might be awarded to a school for each student who achieves a high school diploma (defined as a verification that 16 credits have been attained in specific subjects with a credit defined as 72 hours of successful classroom study). Or a school might be given monetary awards for each student who has been employed for a year after leaving the institution.

Lest the idea of performance contracts strike anyone as novel or bordering upon the impossible, it should be pointed out that they have been formulated and applied with great success by both industry and the armed services for years. The fact that many results of education are subjective and not subject to audit should not stop us from dealing precisely with those aspects that do lend themselves to definition and assessment.

Most directors of ESEA projects should have more training in how to manage large sums of money than they have had in the past. Anyone who knows business knows

480 you don't run half-million and million-dollar programs without considerable expertise in management. Obviously, managers of these projects need technical assistance if they are to manage in the best and most modern sense. For example, there should be technical reviews of all successful programs, practices, and materials used in embryo experimental projects. Educational objectives should be translated into a clearer framework for the purposes of reporting, evaluation, and feedback. In most cases, schools would need out-

side technical assistance to carry out either of these tasks.

Greater educational management competence is also needed in an area that might be called "educational logistics." Many projects don't get off the ground because the equipment, personnel, and training they depend upon are not properly coordinated. The notion of staging, for example, to bring together all the elements that are necessary for a project to achieve performance, is very important. Virtually the only time you see

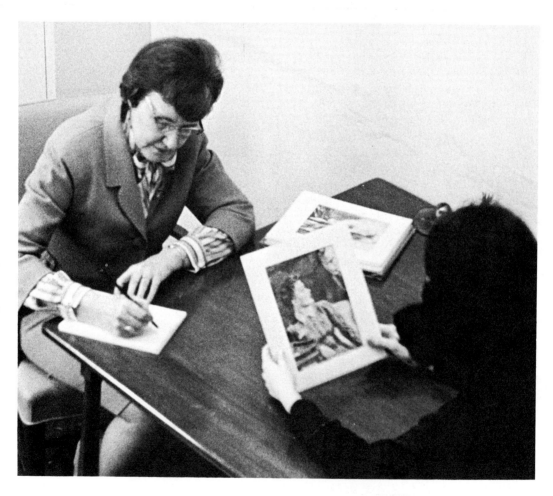

482 this, in education in general as well as in ESEA projects, is in the school drama programs or on the athletic field.

Today formal education is the chief path to full citizenship. School credits and diplomas and licenses are milestones on that path. Schooling is literally the bridge—or the barrier—between a man and his ability to earn his bread. Without it a citizen is condemned to economic obsolescence almost before he begins to work.

If we accept competence for all as one of the major goals of education today, then we must devise a system of accountability that relates education's vast budget to results. It is a paradox that while our technologically oriented society is a masterful producer of the artifacts our civilization needs, it seems incapable of applying that technology to educating our young citizens.

We can change the way our educational system performs so that the desired result —a competently trained young citizenry— becomes the focus of the entire process. In the same way that planning, market studies, research and development, and performance warranties determine industrial production and its worth to consumers, so should we be able to engineer, organize, refine, and manage the educational system to prepare students to contribute to the most complex and exciting country on earth.

QUESTIONS FOR DISCUSSION

1. What are the relationships between education and economic and social developments in a nation?
2. What are the three main kinds of taxes used to produce revenue for schools? Dis-

cuss each of these in terms of their productivity and fairness.
3. What factors in our society have caused the change in the educational support level provided by the three levels of government?
4. What have been some of the noticeable effects of both state and federal categorical aid in the public schools of your area?
5. Do you feel that nationwide equality of opportunity from a financial viewpoint can be achieved under our existing tax structure? Defend your position.

SUPPLEMENTARY LEARNING ACTIVITIES

1. Collect and examine data related to the wealth of school districts in your immediate area or state.
2. Invite a county or township tax assessment official to your class to discuss the assessing process in your area.
3. Study and evaluate the foundation plan of state support for education in your state.
4. Conduct a survey to assess the feelings of citizens about various forms of taxation as they relate to the schools.
5. Interview members of the board of education in your immediate area to determine their opinions about financing of schools.

SELECTED REFERENCES

Advisory Committee on Intergovernmental Relations. *Who Should Pay for Public Schools?* Washington, D.C.: U.S. Government Printing Office, 1971.

American Association of School Administrators. *Christopher Jencks in Perspective.* Arlington, Va.: American Association of School Administrators, 1973.

————. *Education Is Good Business.* Washington, D.C.: American Association of School Administrators, 1966.

Benson, Charles S. *Perspectives on the Economics of Education.* Boston: Houghton Mifflin Company, 1963.

Browder, Lesley, ed. *Emerging Patterns of Administrative Accountability.* Berkeley, Calif.: McCutchan Publishing Corporation, 1971.

Burkhead, Jesse. *Public School Finance: Economics and Politics.* Syracuse, N.Y.: Syracuse University Press, 1964.

Campbell, Roald F.; Luvern L. Cunningham; and Roderick F. McPhee. *The Organization and Control of American Schools.* Columbus, Ohio: Charles E. Merrill Publishing Company, 1965.

Coleman, James S. *Equality of Educational Opportunity.* U.S. Department of Health, Education, and Welfare. Washington, D.C.: U.S. Government Printing Office, 1966.

Conant, James B. *Shaping Educational Policy.* New York: McGraw-Hill Book Company, 1964.

Gauerke, Warren E., and Jack R. Childress, eds. *The Theory and Practice of School Finance.* Skokie, Ill.: Rand McNally & Company, 1967.

Hartley, Harry J. *Educational Planning—Programming—Budgeting: A Systems Approach.* Englewood Cliffs, N.J.: Prentice-Hall, Inc., 1968.

Harvard Educational Review 43 (February, 1973). (Issue devoted to and entitled *Perspectives on Inequality.*)

Hill, Frederick W., and James W. Colmey. *School Business Administration in the Smaller Community.* Minneapolis: T. S. Denison & Co., Inc., 1964.

Innes, Jon T.; Paul B. Jacobson; and Roland J. Pellegrin. *The Economic Returns to Education.* Eugene, Ore.: Center for Advanced Study of Educational Administration, University of Oregon, 1965.

Johns, Roe L. *The Economics and Financing of Education: A Systems Approach.* 2nd ed. Englewood Cliffs, N.J.: Prentice-Hall, Inc., 1969.

————. "Toward Equity in School Finance." *American Education,* 7(November 1971):3–6.

Johns, Roe L., and Alexander Kern. *Alternative Programs for Financing Education.* Gainesville, Fla.: National Educational Finance Project, 1971.

Johns, Roe L., and Edgar L. Morphet. *Financing the Public Schools.* Englewood Cliffs, N.J.: Prentice-Hall, Inc., 1960.

Knezevich, Stephen J. *Administration of Public Education.* 2nd ed. New York: Harper & Row, Publishers, 1969.

Lessinger, Leon. *Every Kid a Winner.* Palo Alto, Calif.: Science Research Associates Inc., 1970.

Lindman, Erick L., ed. *The Federal Government and Public Schools.* Washington, D.C.: American Association of School Administrators, 1965.

Malchlup, Fritz. *Education and Economic Growth.* Lincoln, Neb.: University of Nebraska Press, 1971.

Morphet, Edgar L.; Roe L. Johns; and Theodore L. Reller. *Educational Organization and Administration.* 2nd ed. Englewood Cliffs, N.J.: Prentice-Hall, Inc., 1967.

484   Mort, Paul R.; Walter O. Reusser; and John W. Polley. *Public School Finance.* New York: McGraw-Hill Book Company, 1960.

National Education Association. *Rankings of the States: 1973 Research Report, 1973–R1.* Washington, D.C.: National Education Association Publications, 1973.

————. *What Everyone Should Know about Financing Our Schools.* Washington, D.C.: National Education Association Publications, 1968.

President's Commission on School Finance. *Schools, People and Money.* 1016 16th St. N.W., Washington, D.C.

Schultz, Theodore W. *The Economic Value of Education.* New York: Columbia University Press, 1963.

Simon, Kenneth A., and W. Vance Grant. *Digest of Educational Statistics, 1972.* U.S. Office of Education. Washington, D.C.: U.S. Government Printing Office, 1973.

Simon, Kenneth A., and Martin M. Frankel. *Projections of Educational Statistics to 1981–82.* Washington, D.C.: U. S. Government Printing Office.

Wise, Arthur E. *Rich Schools, Poor Schools: The Promise of Equal Educational Opportunity.* Chicago: University of Chicago Press, 1967.

Synopsis

The tasks of education in our society are many and diverse. This textbook has attempted to depict them in terms of both societal and individual expectations. It has also attempted to briefly depict the educational milieu, the way that it was and the way that it is. The most important persons in education, with the notable exception of the learners, are the teachers.

There is little doubt that teachers are "molders and shapers"; they deal in a way with destinies. It is hoped that this textbook in some small way will help young people decide whether teaching is a career that they wish to pursue.

Index